BLADE OF HEAVEN

VOLUME 3

STORY BY
YONG-SU HWANG

ART BY
KYUNG-IL YANG

D1308130

HAMBURG // LONDON // LOS ANGELES // TOKYO

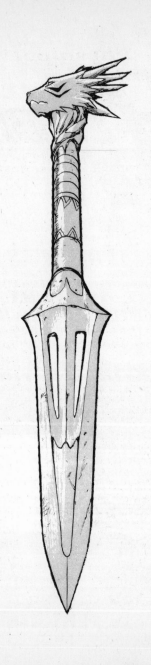

PREVIOUSLY IN

BLADE OF HEAVEN

AS PUNISHMENT FOR STEALING THE BLADE OF HEAVEN, SOMA IS SENTENCED TO ESCORT THE HEAVENLY PRINCESS, AROOMEE AROUND THE MORTAL REALM. GETTING WIND OF THE BLADE'S DISAPPEARRANCE, THE DEMON BARURUGO LAUNCHES AN ATTACK ON HEAVEN. MEANWHILE, EVEN AS MAKUMRANG, THE

DISENCHANTED HEIR TO HELL'S THRONE, JOINS SOMA AND HIS RAG-TAG GROUP, THE KING OF HEAVEN TRAPS BARURUGO AND HIS MARAUDING MINIONS WITHIN THE GATES OF HEAVEN.
BUT WHEN THE PRINCESS COMES TO HER FATHER'S AID, SHE INADVERTENTLY FREES BARURUGO, WHO CAPTURES HER AND GEN. WINTER, PROMPTING SOMA TO CHARGE TO HIS NEWFOUND FRIENDS' RESCUE.

Blade Of Heaven Vol. 3
written by Yong-Su Hwang
illustrated by Kyung-Il Yang

Translation - Lauren Na
English Adaptation - Troy Lewter
Copy Editors - Suzanne Waldman
Retouch and Lettering - Abelardo Bigting
Production Artist - Irene Woori Choi
Cover Design - Al-Insan Lashley

Editor - Bryce P. Coleman
Digital Imaging Manager - Chris Buford
Pre-Press Manager - Antonio DePietro
Production Managers - Jennifer Miller and Mutsumi Miyazaki
Art Director - Matt Alford
Managing Editor - Jill Freshney
VP of Production - Ron Klamert
Editor-in-Chief - Mike Kiley
President and C.O.O. - John Parker
Publisher and C.E.O. - Stuart Levy

A  Manga

TOKYOPOP Inc.
5900 Wilshire Blvd. Suite 2000
Los Angeles, CA 90036

E-mail: info@TOKYOPOP.com
Come visit us online at www.TOKYOPOP.com

ISBN: 978-1-59532-329-3

First TOKYOPOP printing: July 2005
10 9 8 7 6 5 4 3 2
Printed in the USA

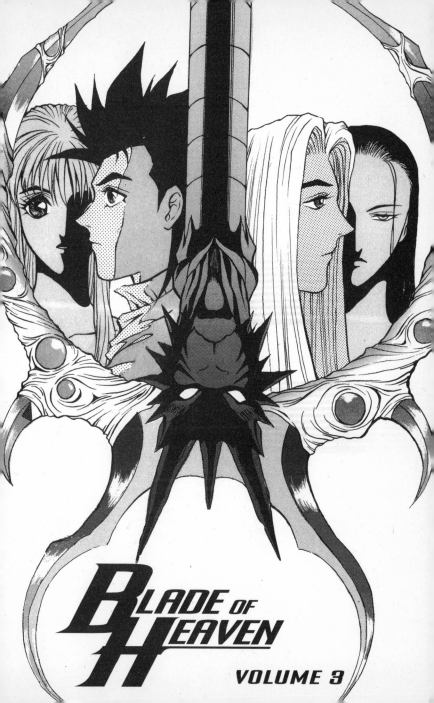

BLADE OF HEAVEN

VOLUME 3

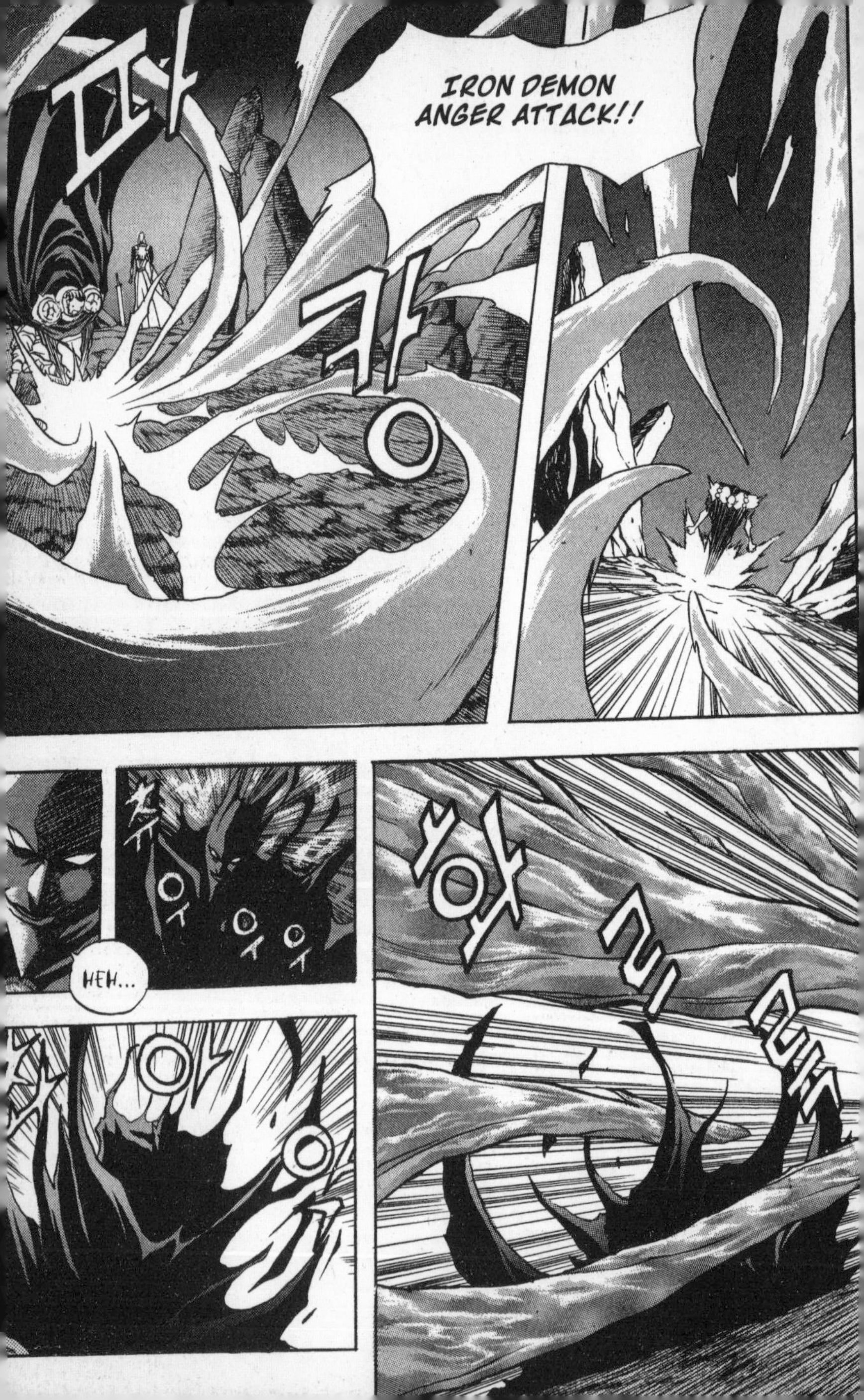
IRON DEMON ANGER ATTACK!!
HEH...

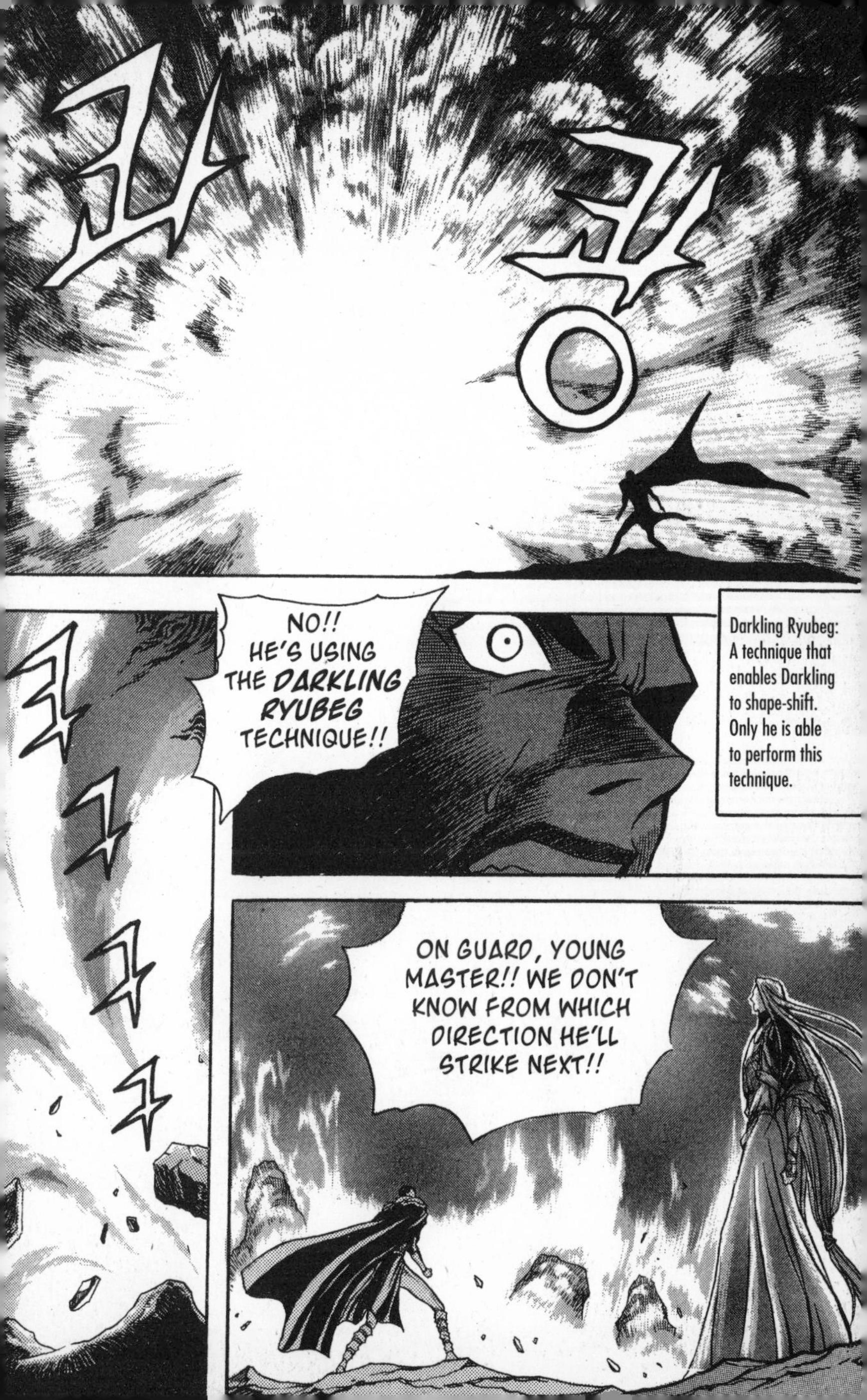
NO!! HE'S USING THE DARKLING RYUBEG TECHNIQUE!!
Darkling Ryubeg: A technique that enables Darkling to shape-shift. Only he is able to perform this technique.
ON GUARD, YOUNG MASTER!! WE DON'T KNOW FROM WHICH DIRECTION HE'LL STRIKE NEXT!!

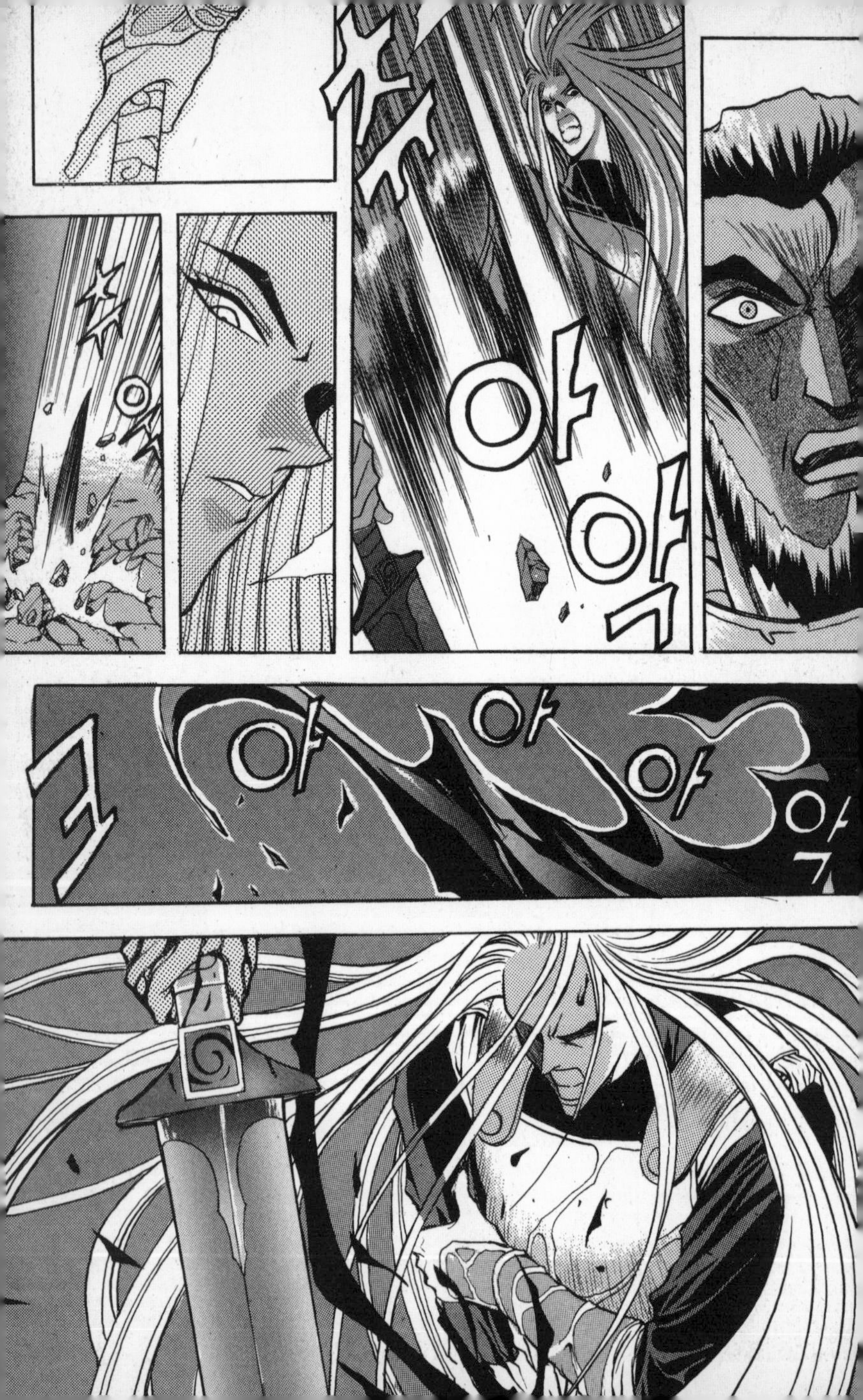

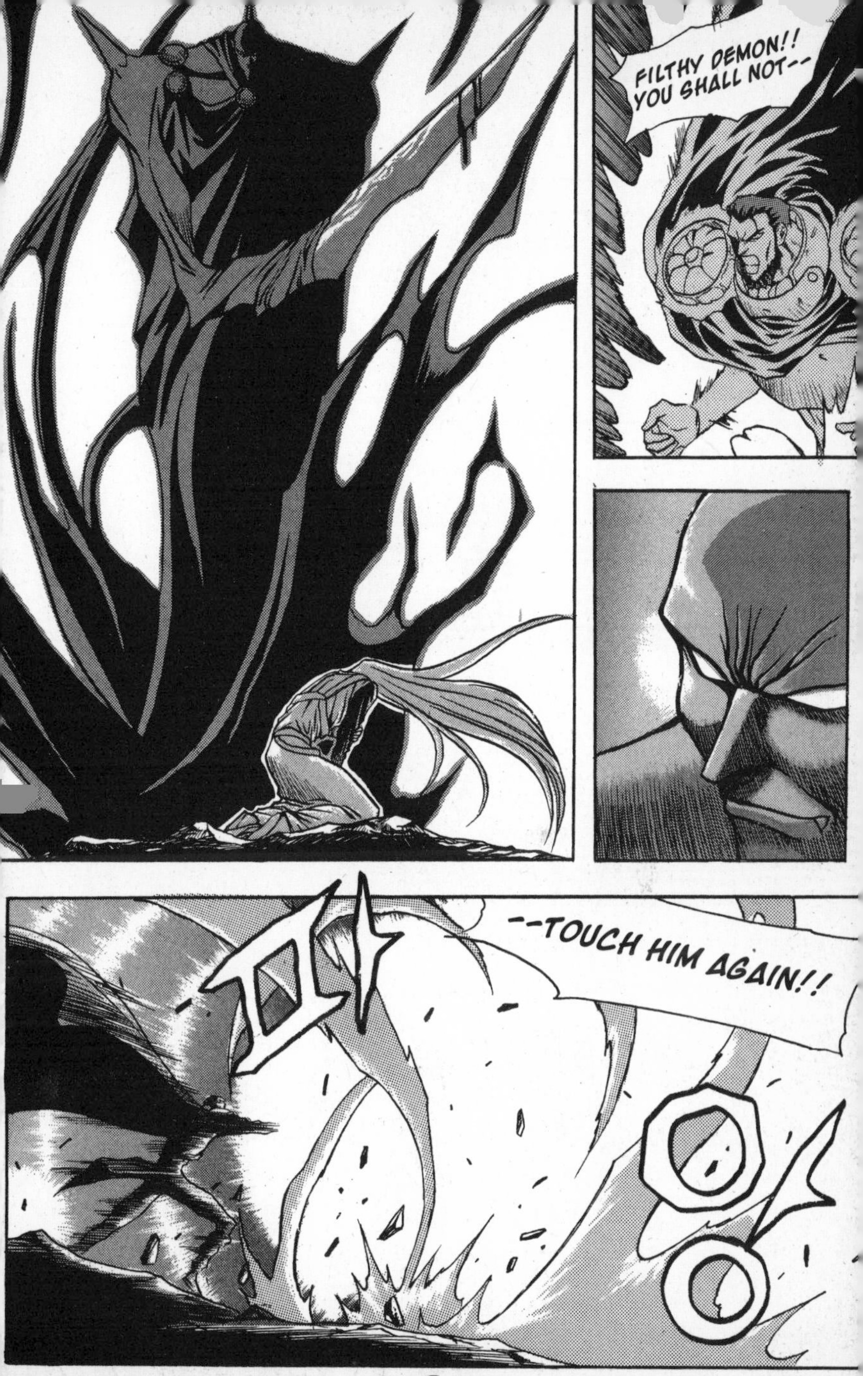
FILTHY DEMON!! YOU SHALL NOT--
--TOUCH HIM AGAIN!!

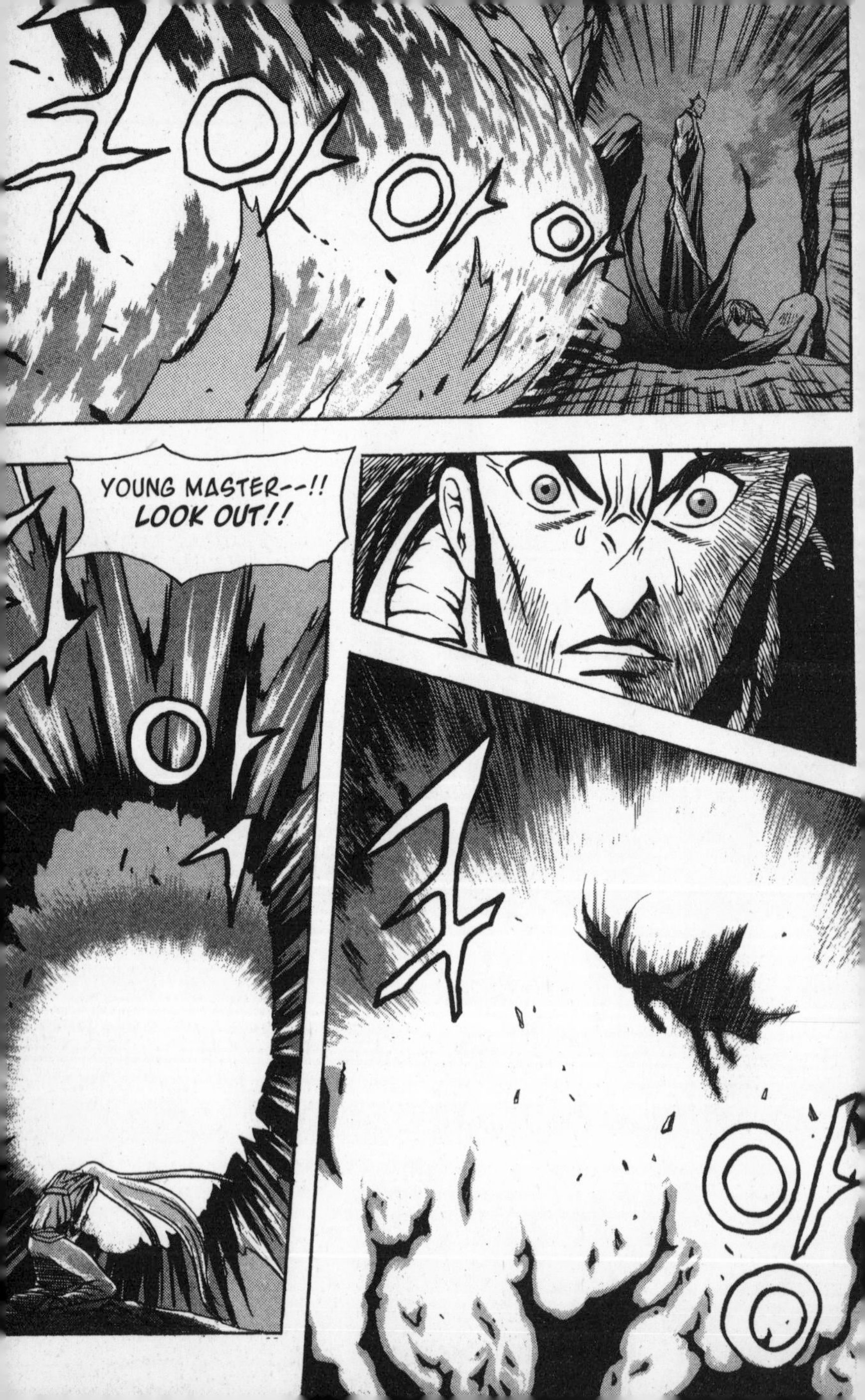
YOUNG MASTER--!! LOOK OUT!!

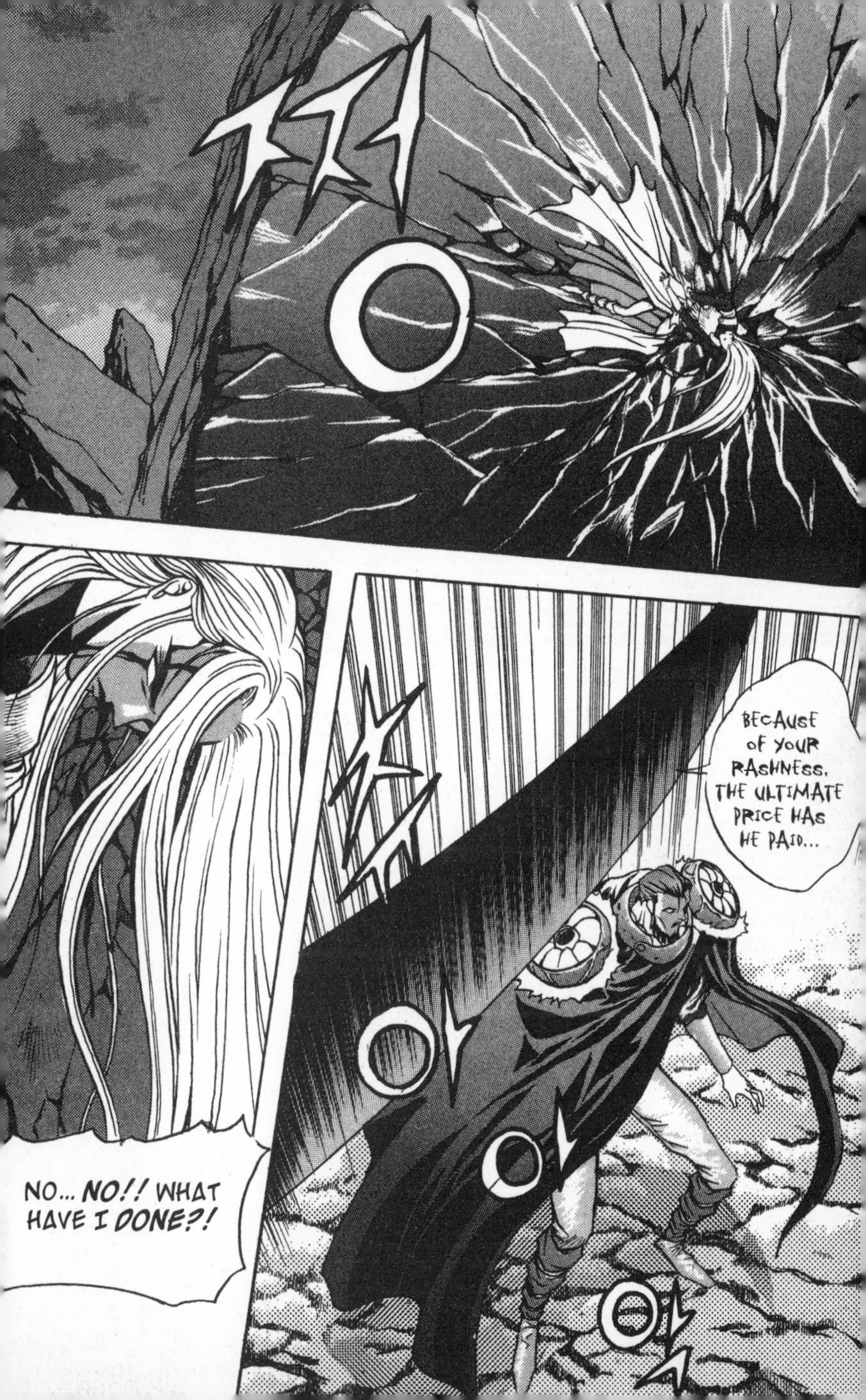
BECAUSE OF YOUR RASHNESS, THE ULTIMATE PRICE HAS HE PAID...
NO... *NO!!* WHAT HAVE I *DONE?!*

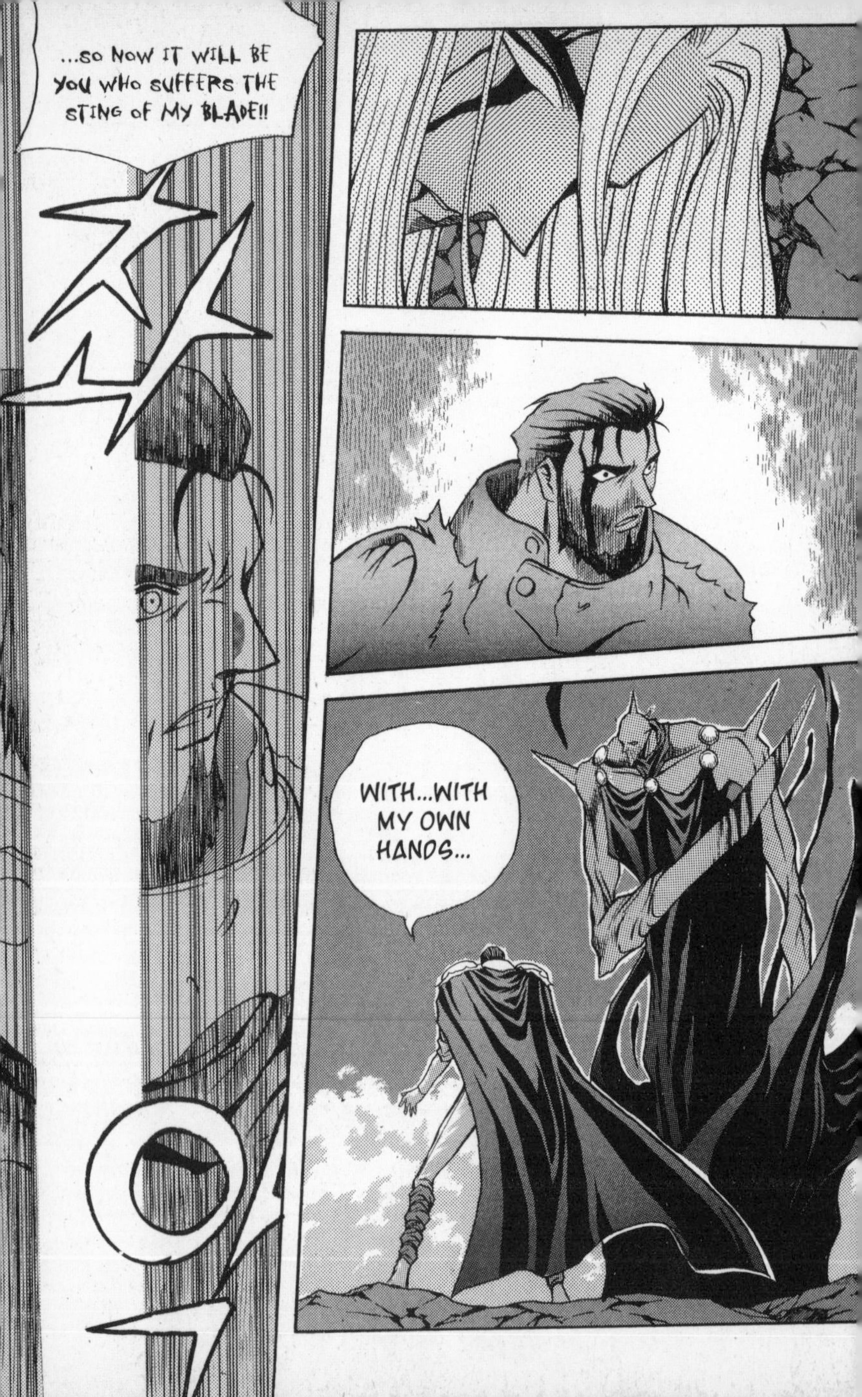
WITH...WITH MY OWN HANDS...
...SO NOW IT WILL BE YOU WHO SUFFERS THE STING OF MY BLADE!!

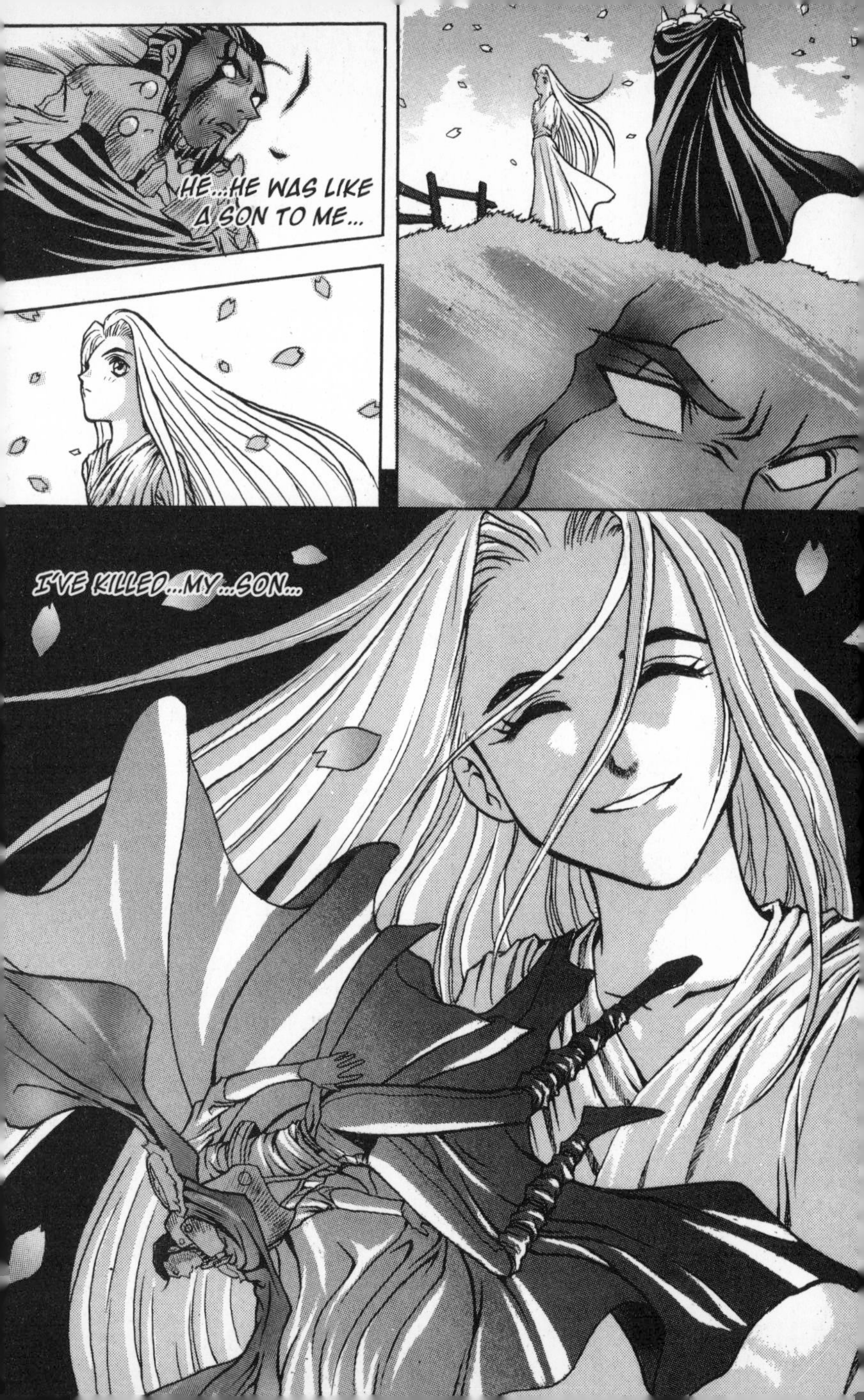
HE...HE WAS LIKE A SON TO ME...
I'VE KILLED...MY...SON...

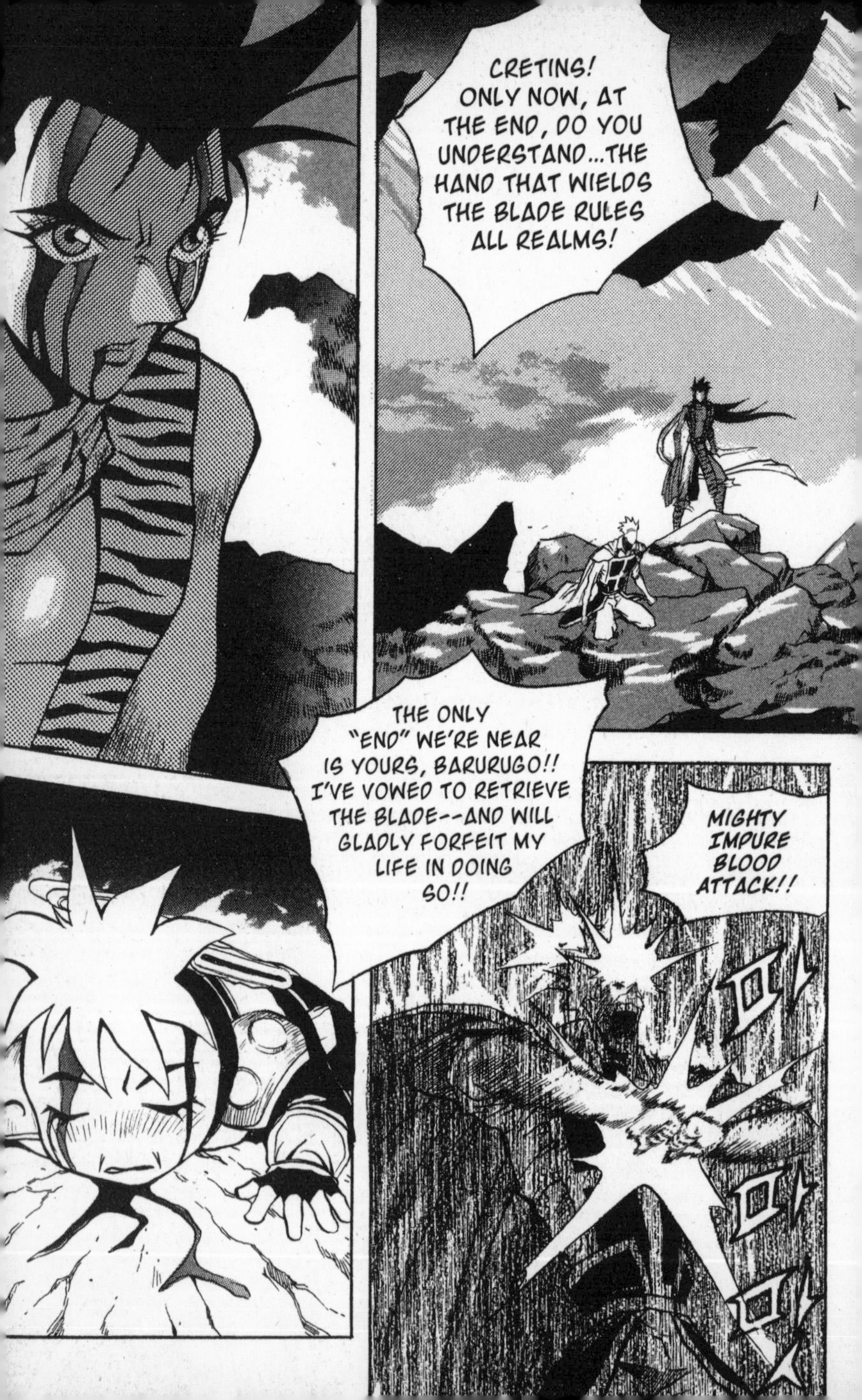
CRETINS! ONLY NOW, AT THE END, DO YOU UNDERSTAND...THE HAND THAT WIELDS THE BLADE RULES ALL REALMS!
THE ONLY "END" WE'RE NEAR IS YOURS, BARURUGO!! I'VE VOWED TO RETRIEVE THE BLADE--AND WILL GLADLY FORFEIT MY LIFE IN DOING SO!!
MIGHTY IMPURE BLOOD ATTACK!!

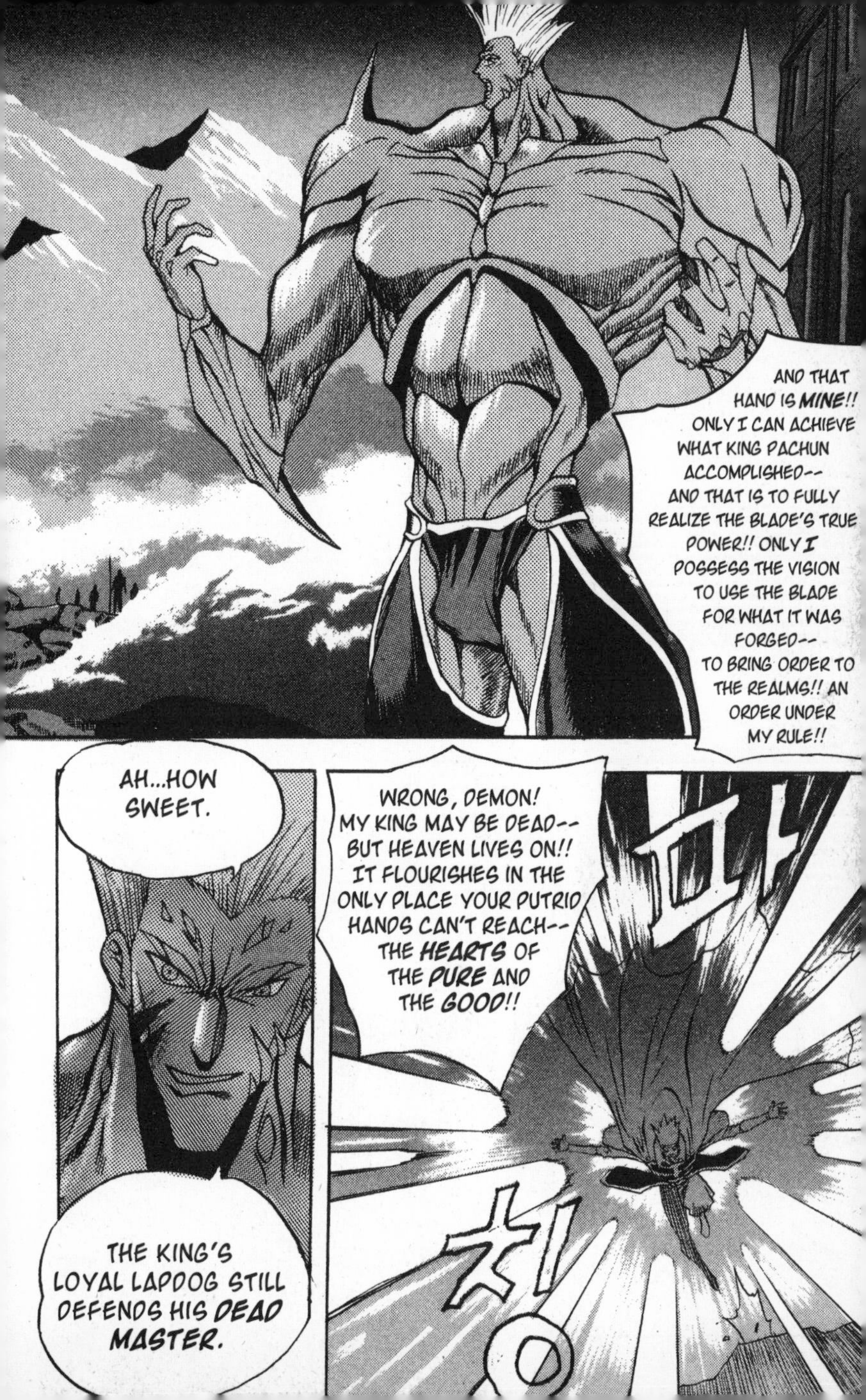
AND THAT HAND IS **MINE**!! ONLY I CAN ACHIEVE WHAT KING PACHUN ACCOMPLISHED-- AND THAT IS TO FULLY REALIZE THE BLADE'S TRUE POWER!! ONLY **I** POSSESS THE VISION TO USE THE BLADE FOR WHAT IT WAS FORGED-- TO BRING ORDER TO THE REALMS!! AN ORDER UNDER MY RULE!!
AH...HOW SWEET.
THE KING'S LOYAL LAPDOG STILL DEFENDS HIS **DEAD MASTER**.
WRONG, DEMON! MY KING MAY BE DEAD-- BUT HEAVEN LIVES ON!! IT FLOURISHES IN THE ONLY PLACE YOUR PUTRID HANDS CAN'T REACH-- THE **HEARTS** OF THE **PURE** AND THE **GOOD**!!

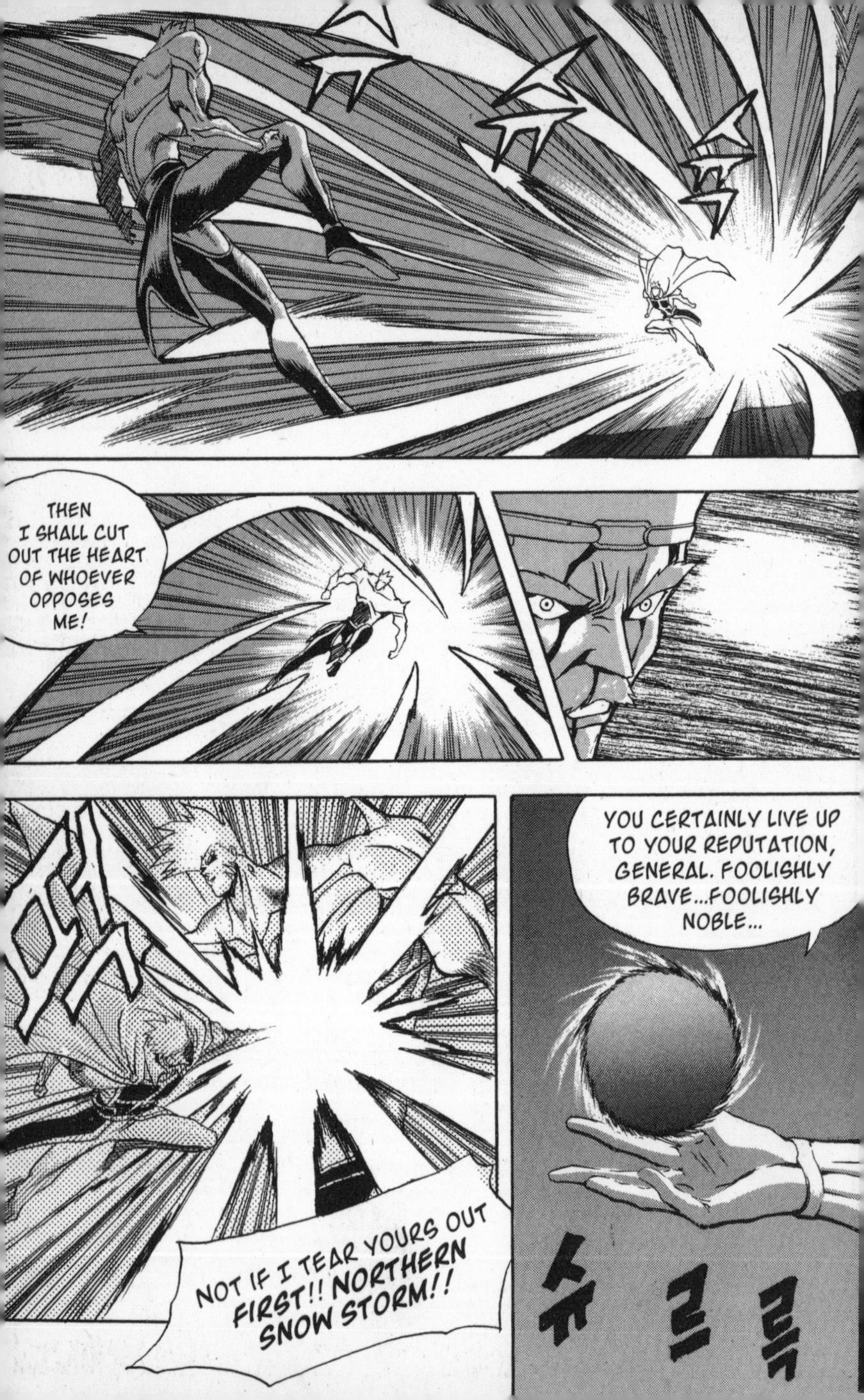
THEN I SHALL CUT OUT THE HEART OF WHOEVER OPPOSES ME!
NOT IF I TEAR YOURS OUT FIRST!! NORTHERN SNOW STORM!!
YOU CERTAINLY LIVE UP TO YOUR REPUTATION, GENERAL. FOOLISHLY BRAVE...FOOLISHLY NOBLE...

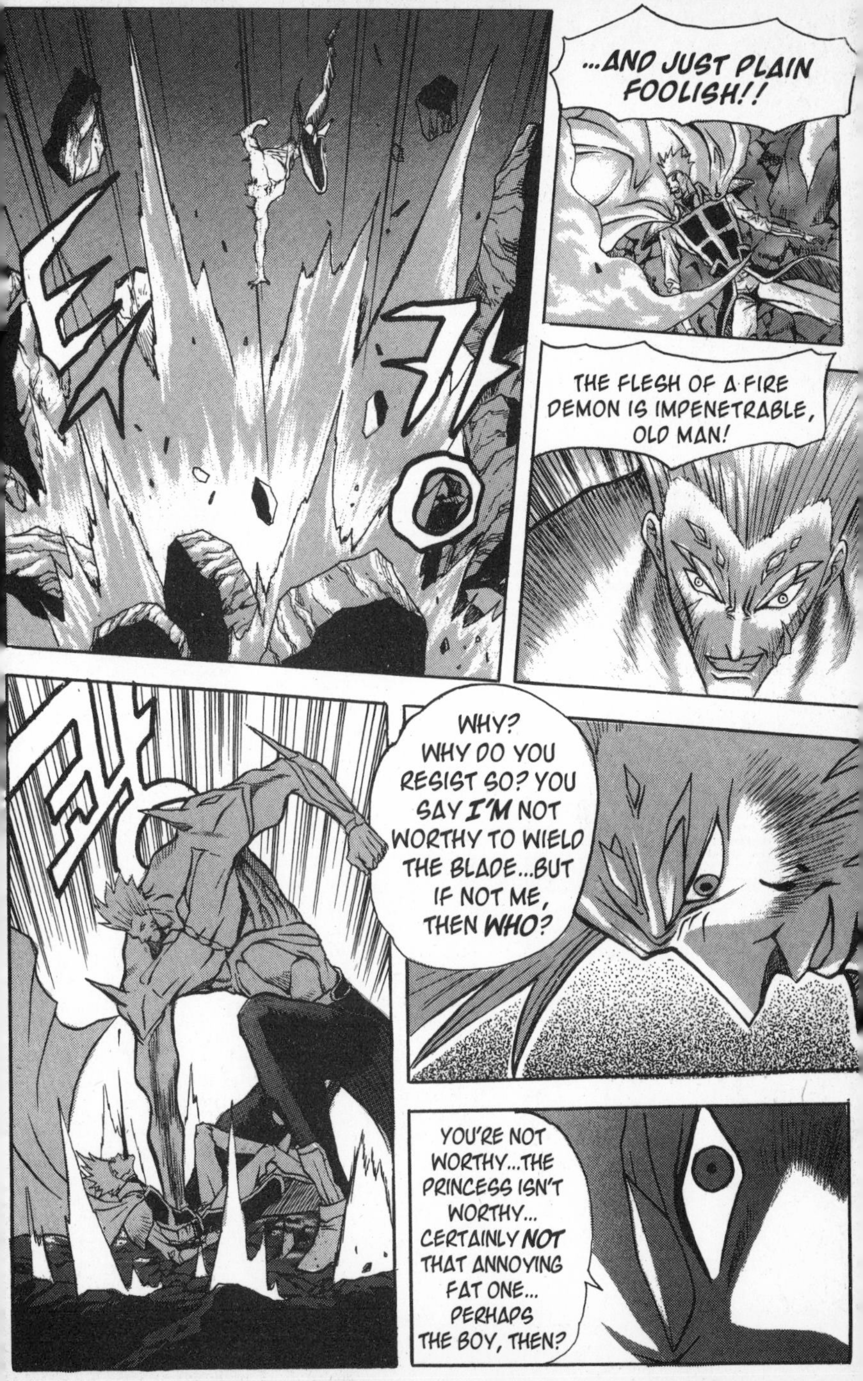
...AND JUST PLAIN FOOLISH!!
THE FLESH OF A FIRE DEMON IS IMPENETRABLE, OLD MAN!
WHY? WHY DO YOU RESIST SO? YOU SAY I'M NOT WORTHY TO WIELD THE BLADE...BUT IF NOT ME, THEN WHO?
YOU'RE NOT WORTHY...THE PRINCESS ISN'T WORTHY... CERTAINLY NOT THAT ANNOYING FAT ONE... PERHAPS THE BOY, THEN?

SOMA!! WHAT ARE YA DOIN'?! GRAB THE PRINCESS AND HIT THA ROAD...!! DON'T LET OUR *DEATHS*...BE IN *VAIN!!*

WAIT... ARE YOU TREMBLING?! DON'T TELL ME YOU'RE...*SCARED?!*

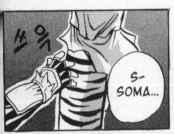

S-SOMA...

THIS...THIS ISN'T... LIKE...YOU... SO...MA...

DAMMIT... YOU'RE GIVIN' THIEVES...A B-BAD...NAME... DON'T LET...THAT BIG LUNKHEAD... INTIMIDATE YA...

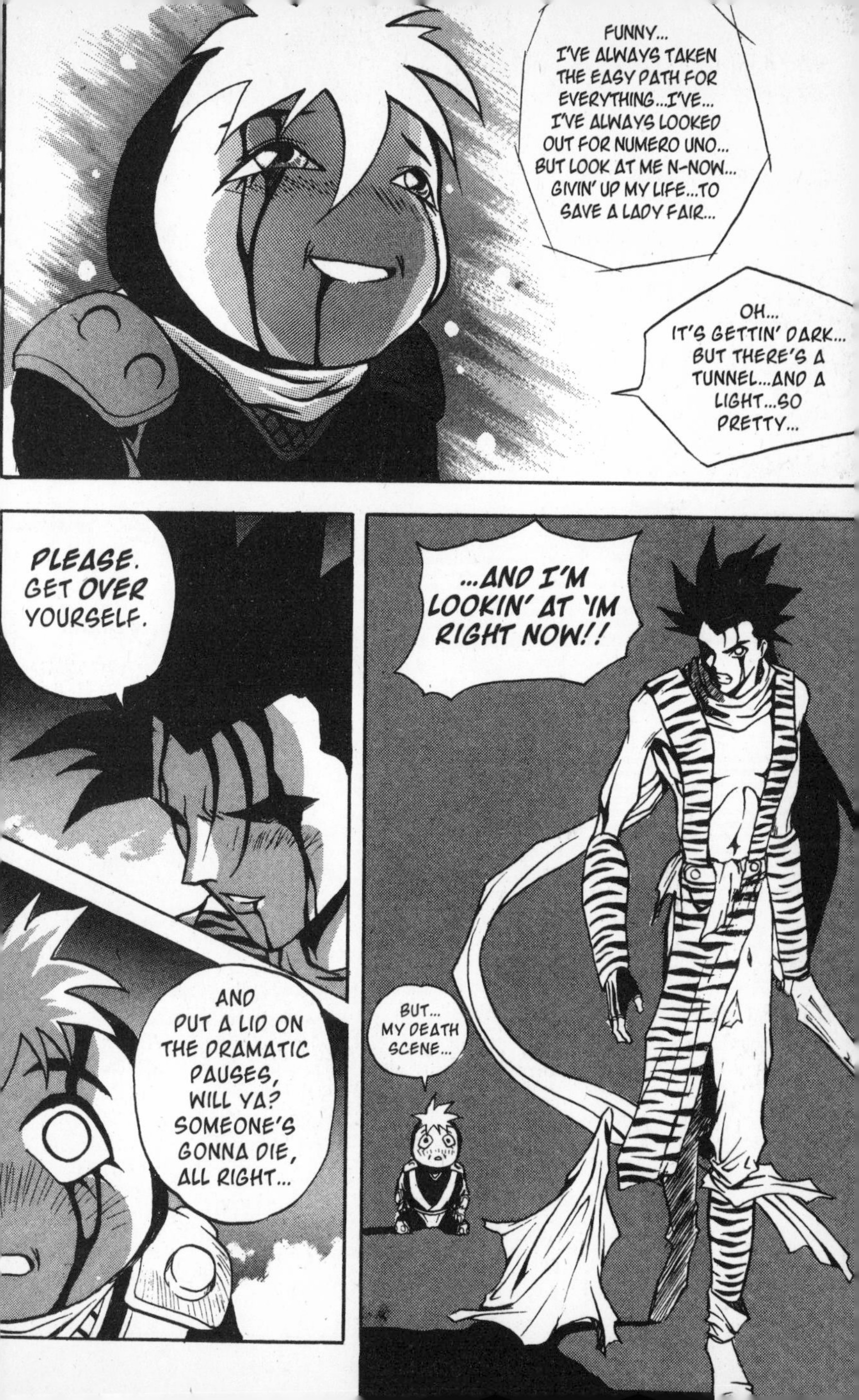
FUNNY... I'VE ALWAYS TAKEN THE EASY PATH FOR EVERYTHING...I'VE... I'VE ALWAYS LOOKED OUT FOR NUMERO UNO... BUT LOOK AT ME N-NOW... GIVIN' UP MY LIFE...TO SAVE A LADY FAIR...
OH... IT'S GETTIN' DARK... BUT THERE'S A TUNNEL...AND A LIGHT...SO PRETTY...
PLEASE. GET OVER YOURSELF.
AND PUT A LID ON THE DRAMATIC PAUSES, WILL YA? SOMEONE'S GONNA DIE, ALL RIGHT...
...AND I'M LOOKIN' AT 'IM RIGHT NOW!!
BUT... MY DEATH SCENE...

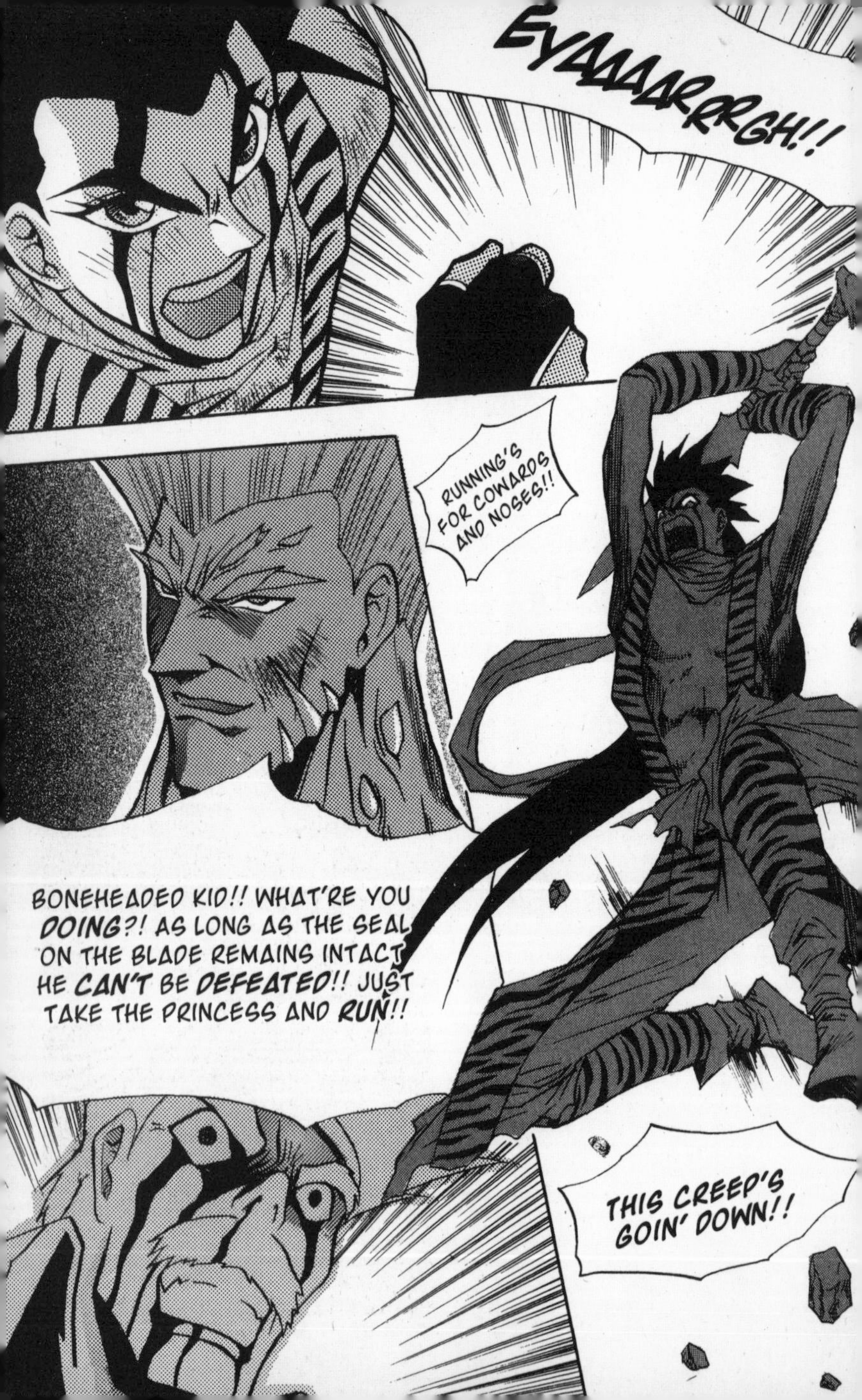
EYAAAARRRGH!!
BONEHEADED KID!! WHAT'RE YOU DOING?! AS LONG AS THE SEAL ON THE BLADE REMAINS INTACT HE CAN'T BE DEFEATED!! JUST TAKE THE PRINCESS AND RUN!!
RUNNING'S FOR COWARDS AND NOSES!!
THIS CREEP'S GOIN' DOWN!!

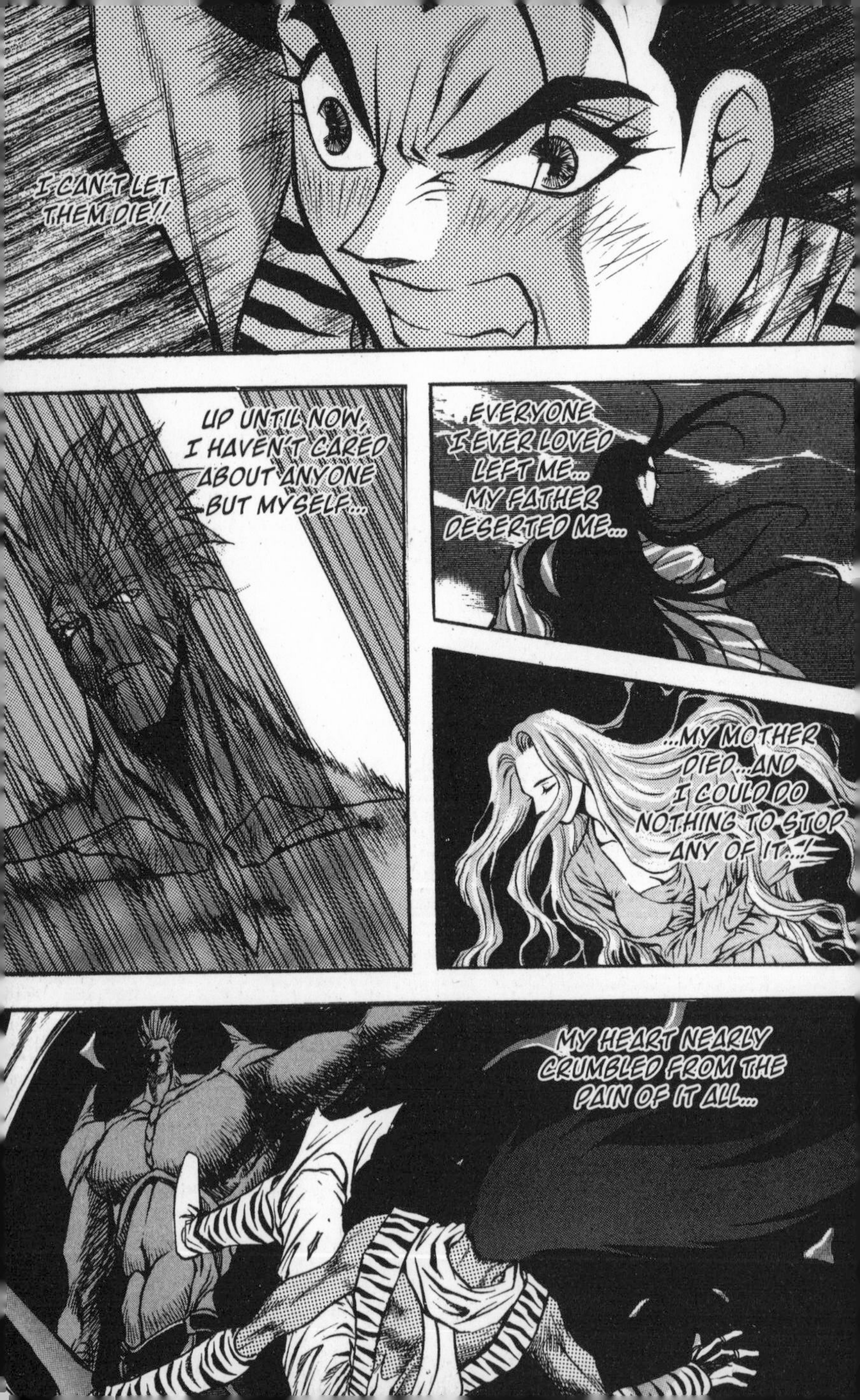
I CAN'T LET THEM DIE!!
EVERYONE I EVER LOVED LEFT ME... MY FATHER DESERTED ME...
UP UNTIL NOW, I HAVEN'T CARED ABOUT ANYONE BUT MYSELF...
...MY MOTHER DIED...AND I COULD DO NOTHING TO STOP ANY OF IT...!
MY HEART NEARLY CRUMBLED FROM THE PAIN OF IT ALL...

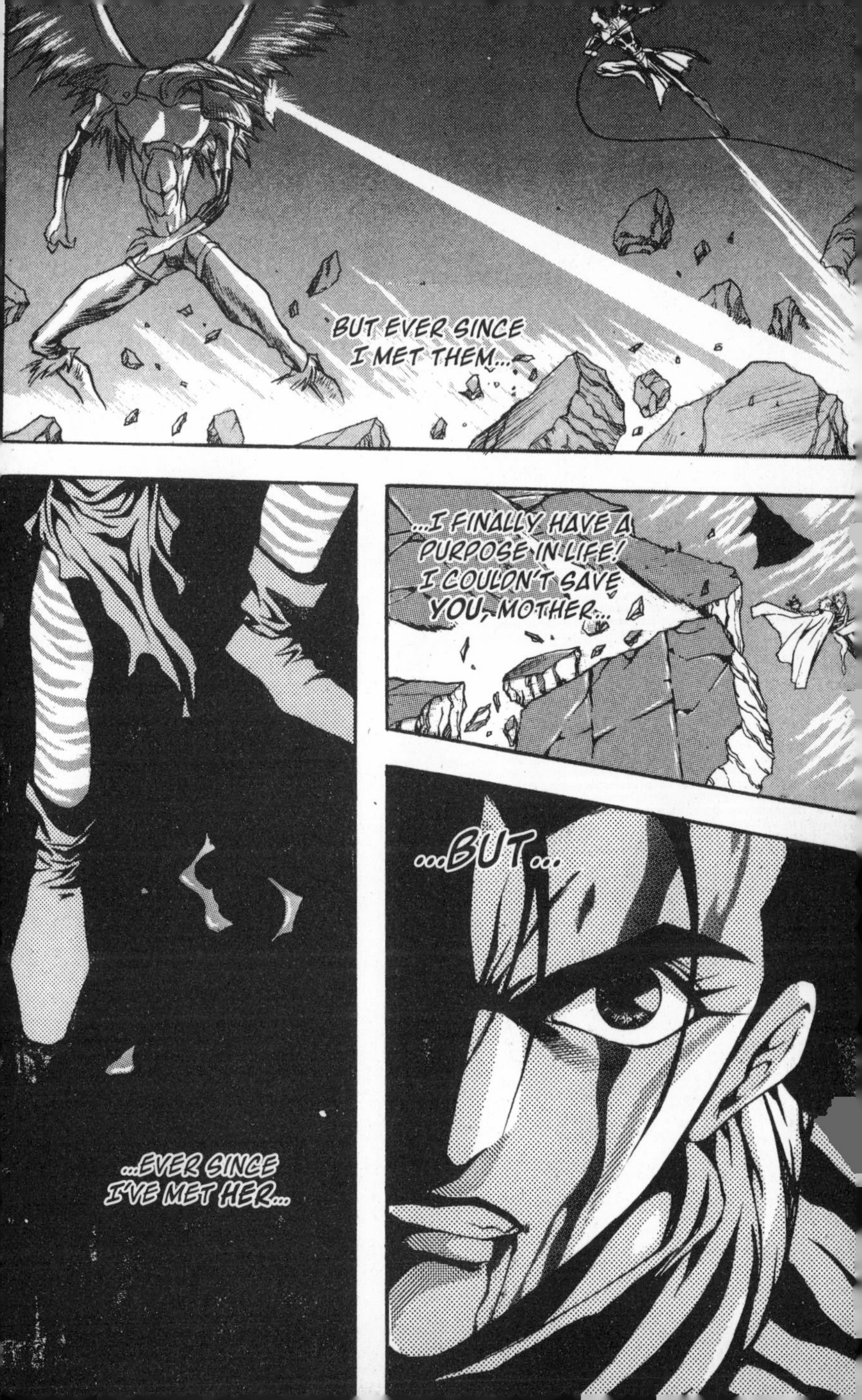
BUT EVER SINCE I MET THEM...
...I FINALLY HAVE A PURPOSE IN LIFE! I COULDN'T SAVE YOU, MOTHER...
...BUT...
...EVER SINCE I'VE MET HER...

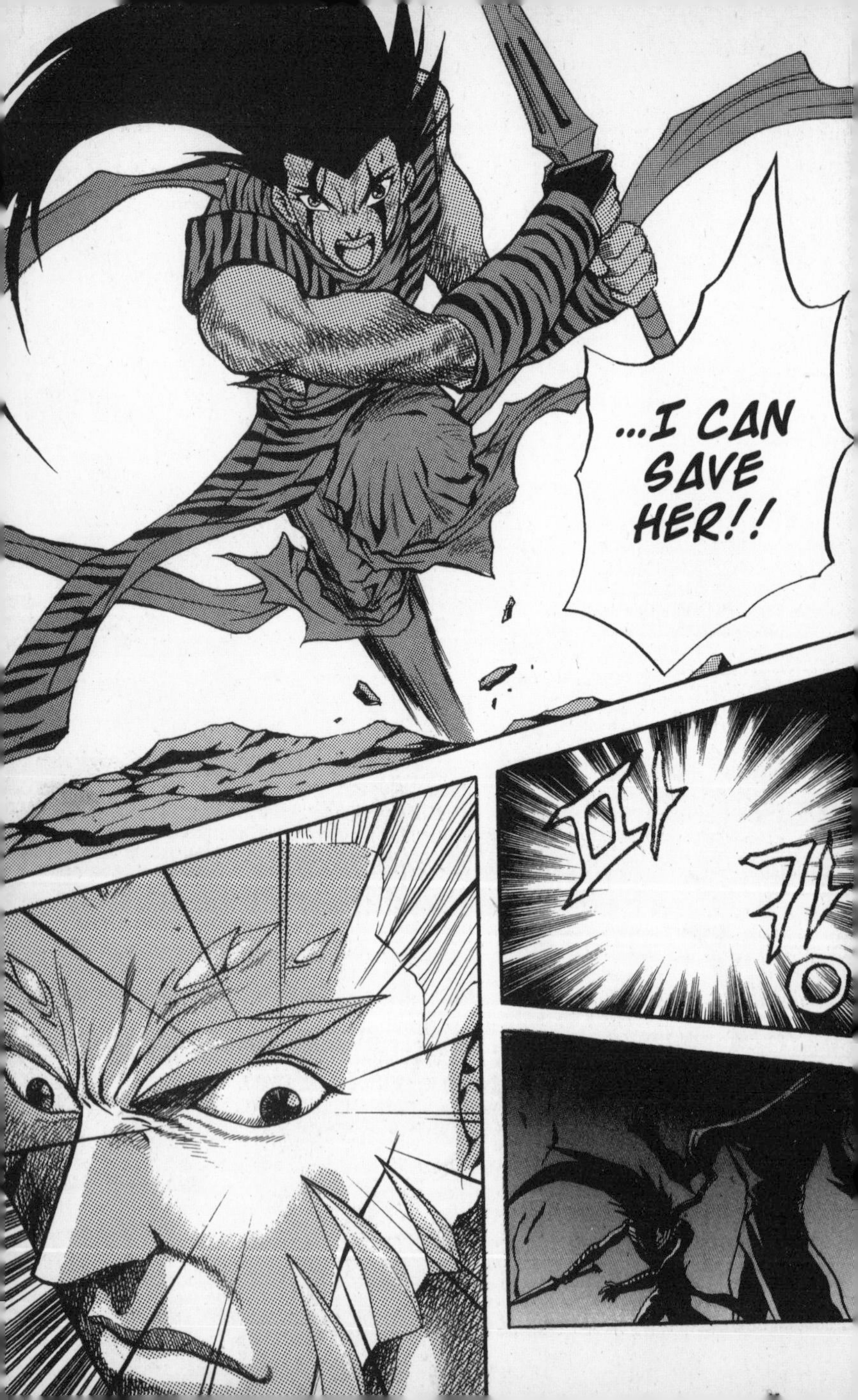
...I CAN SAVE HER!!

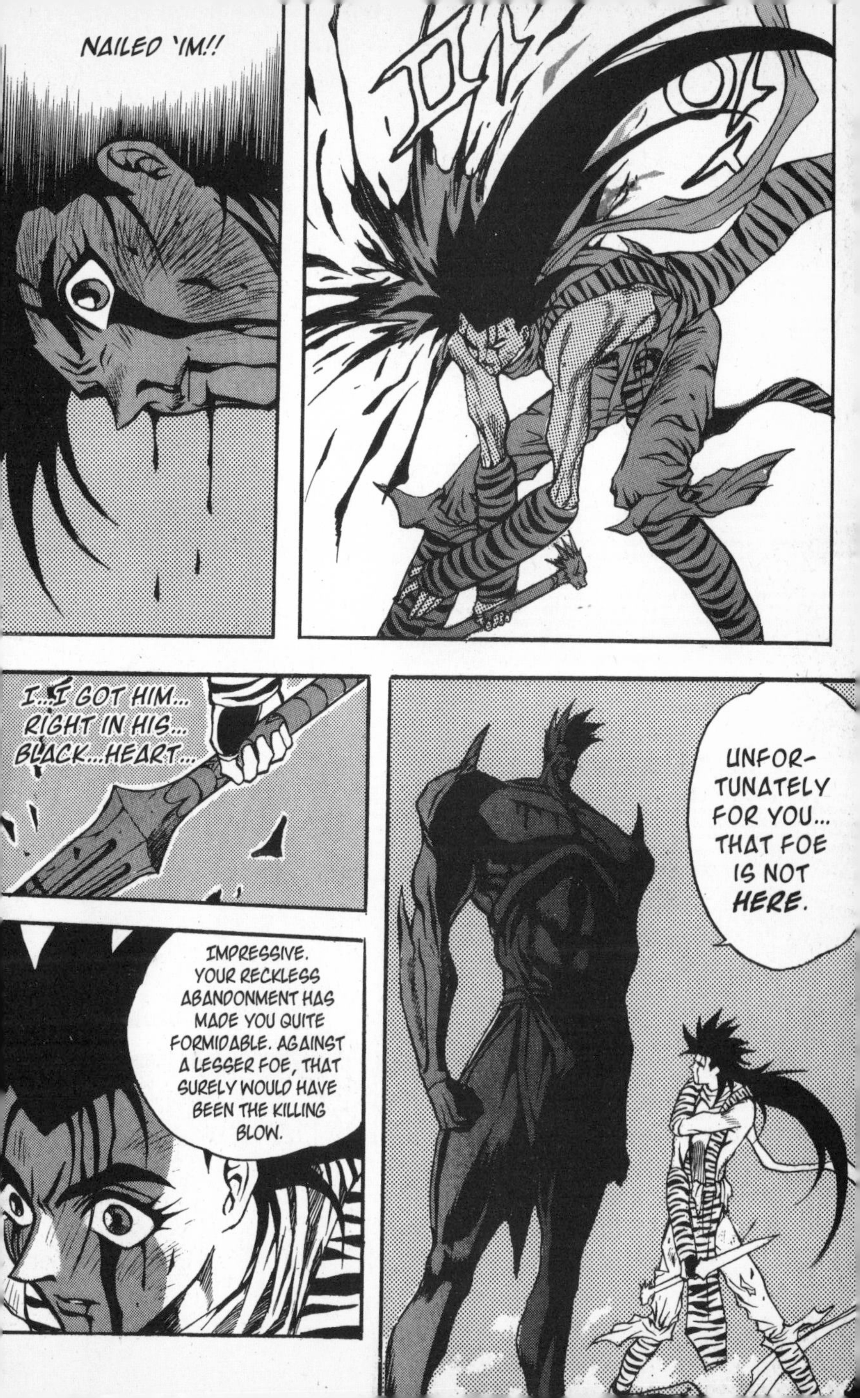
NAILED 'IM!!
I...I GOT HIM... RIGHT IN HIS... BLACK...HEART...
IMPRESSIVE. YOUR RECKLESS ABANDONMENT HAS MADE YOU QUITE FORMIDABLE. AGAINST A LESSER FOE, THAT SURELY WOULD HAVE BEEN THE KILLING BLOW.
UNFOR-TUNATELY FOR YOU... THAT FOE IS NOT **HERE**.

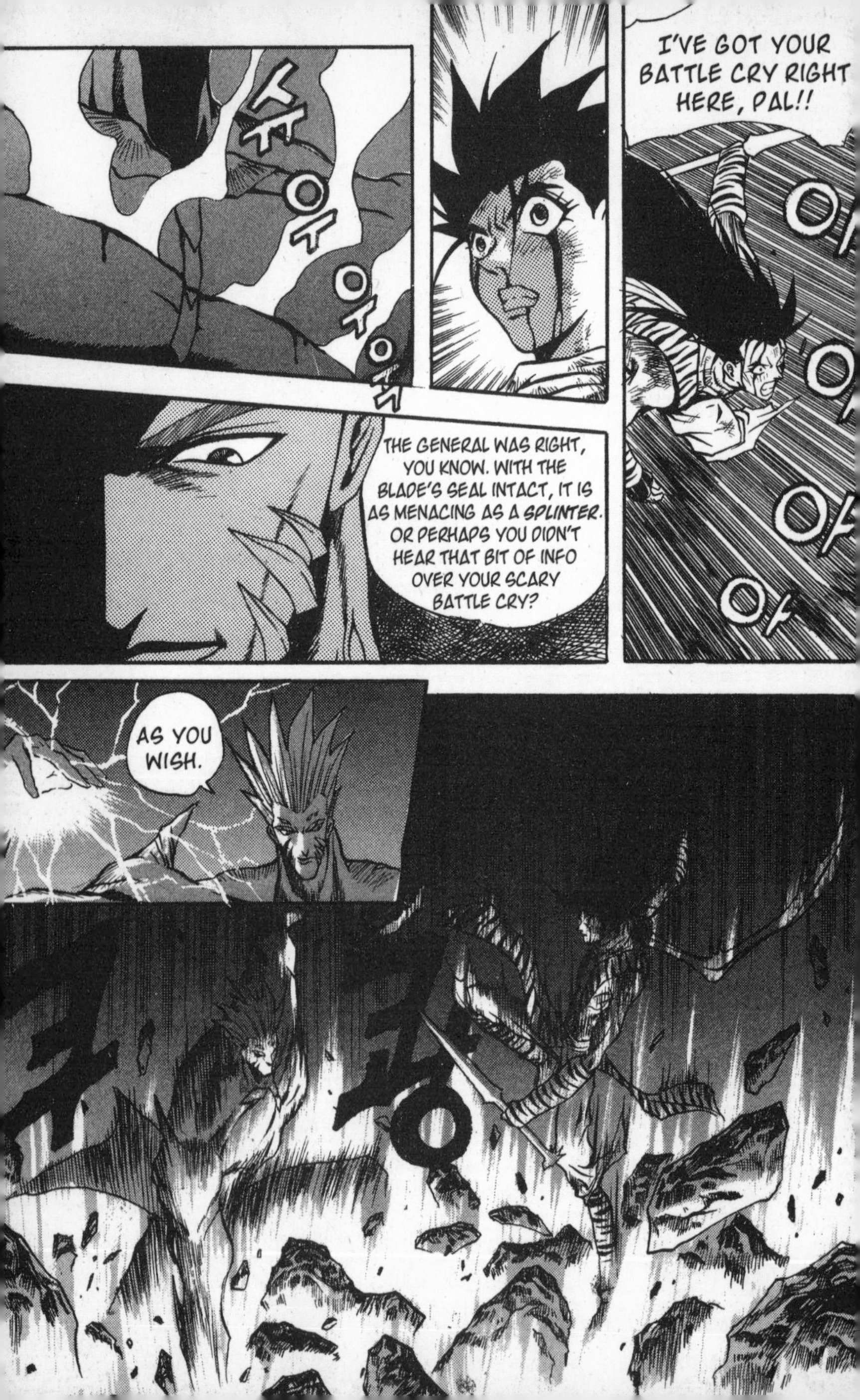
I'VE GOT YOUR BATTLE CRY RIGHT HERE, PAL!!
OHHHHH
THE GENERAL WAS RIGHT, YOU KNOW. WITH THE BLADE'S SEAL INTACT, IT IS AS MENACING AS A SPLINTER. OR PERHAPS YOU DIDN'T HEAR THAT BIT OF INFO OVER YOUR SCARY BATTLE CRY?
AS YOU WISH.

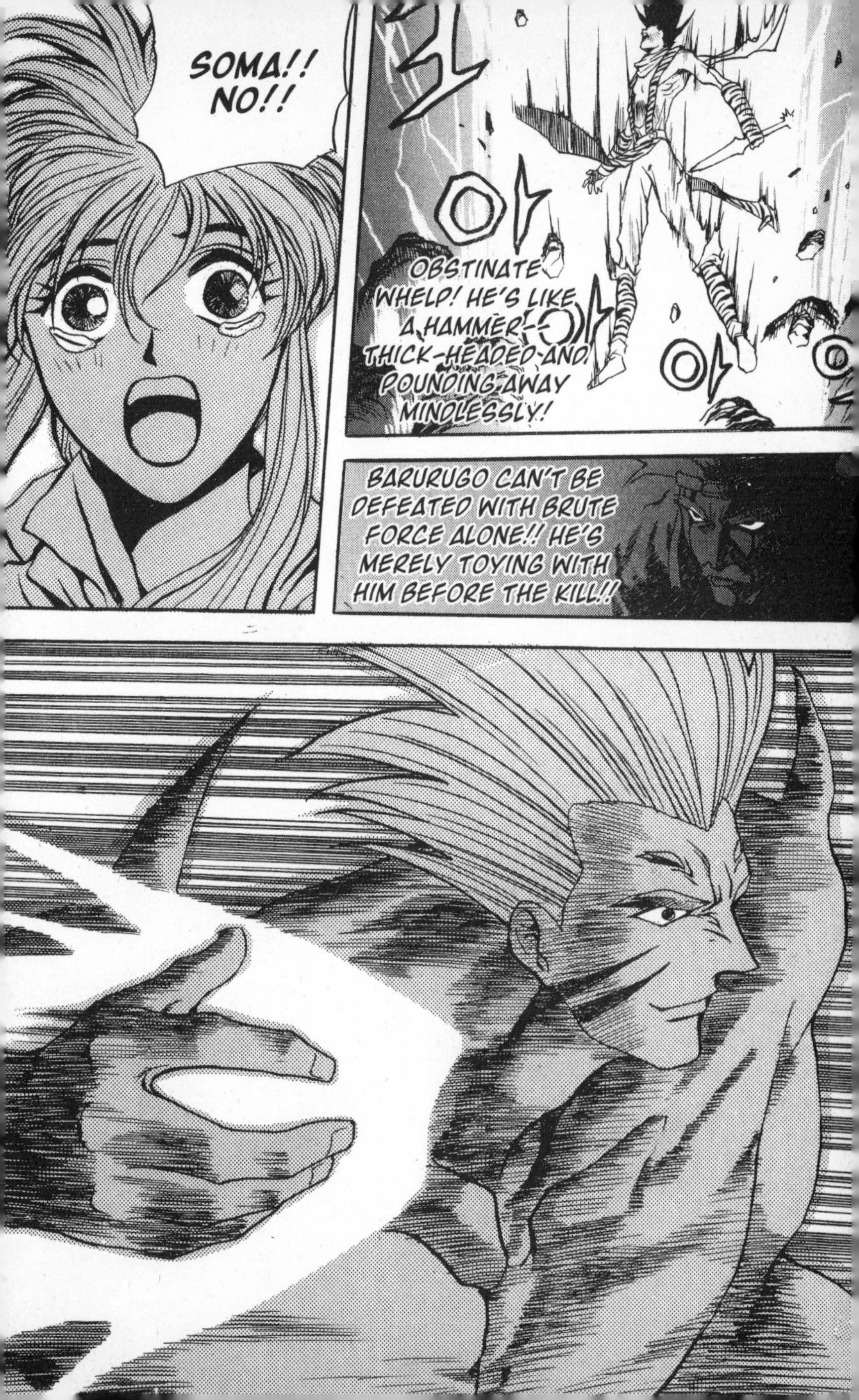
OBSTINATE WHELP! HE'S LIKE A HAMMER-- THICK-HEADED AND POUNDING AWAY MINDLESSLY!
BARURUGO CAN'T BE DEFEATED WITH BRUTE FORCE ALONE!! HE'S MERELY TOYING WITH HIM BEFORE THE KILL!!
SOMA!! NO!!

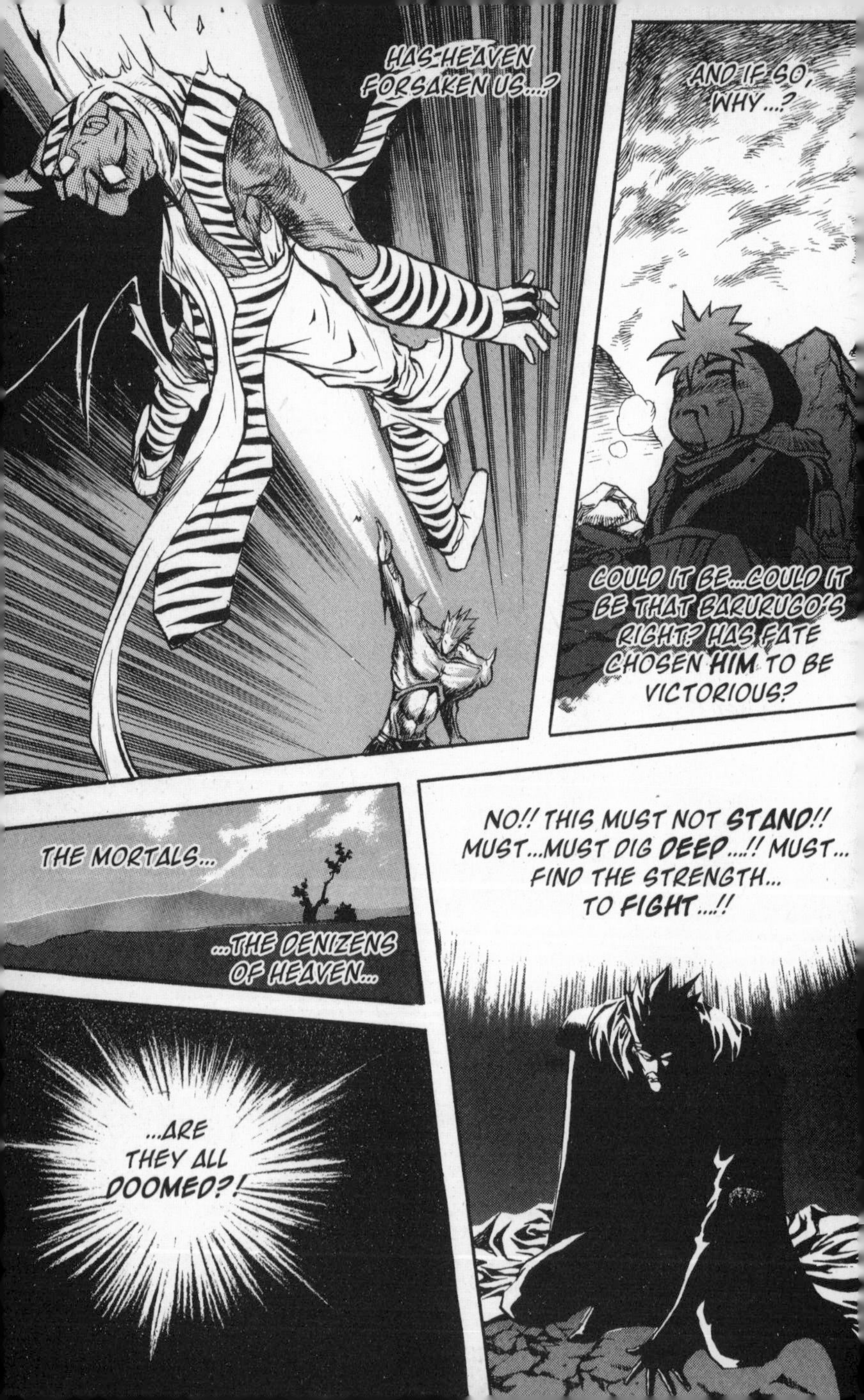

HAS HEAVEN FORSAKEN US...?
AND IF SO, WHY...?
COULD IT BE...COULD IT BE THAT BARURUGO'S RIGHT? HAS FATE CHOSEN HIM TO BE VICTORIOUS?
THE MORTALS...
...THE DENIZENS OF HEAVEN...
...ARE THEY ALL DOOMED?!
NO!! THIS MUST NOT STAND!! MUST...MUST DIG DEEP...!! MUST... FIND THE STRENGTH... TO FIGHT...!!

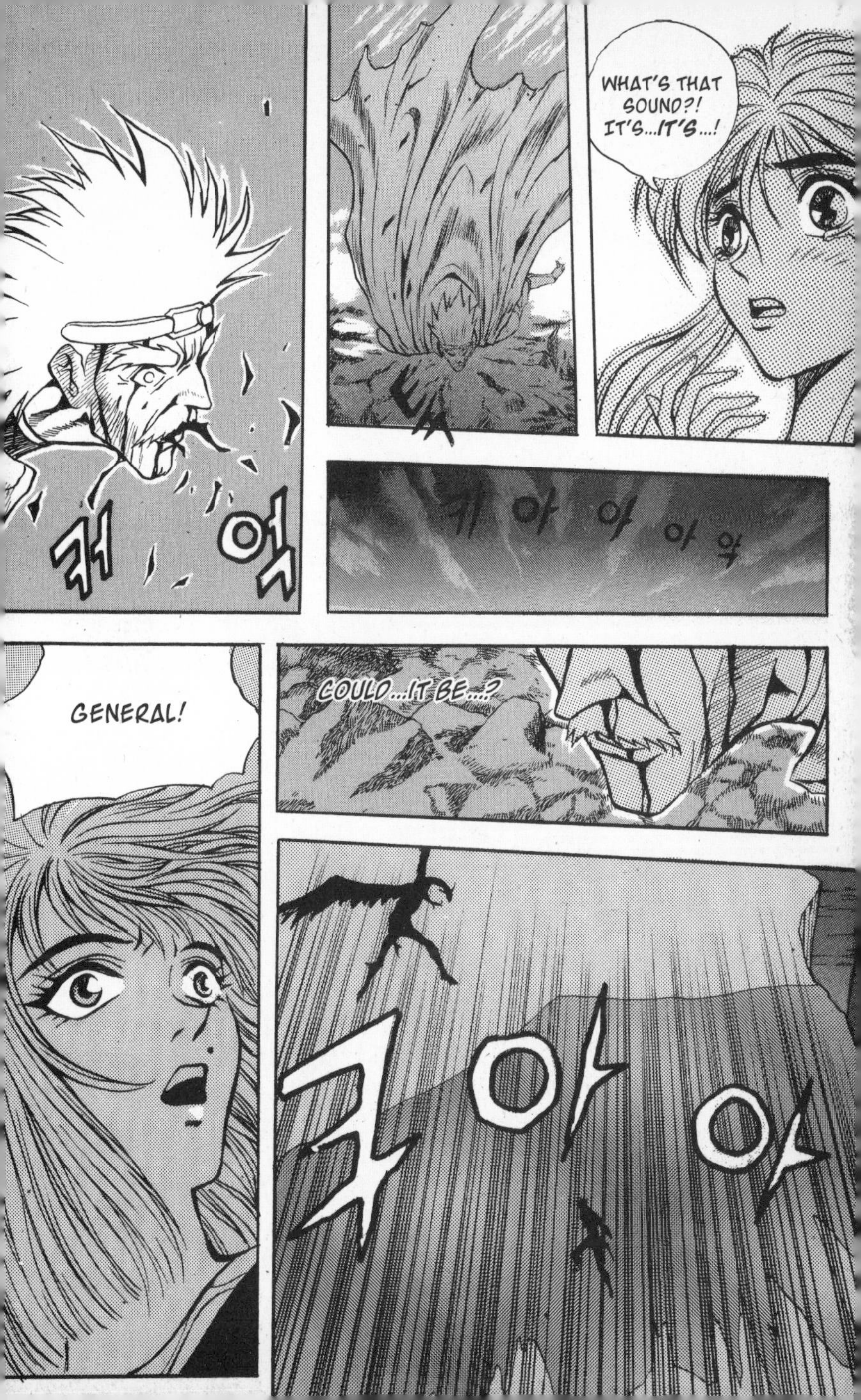
WHAT'S THAT SOUND?! IT'S...IT'S...!
GENERAL!
COULD...IT BE...?

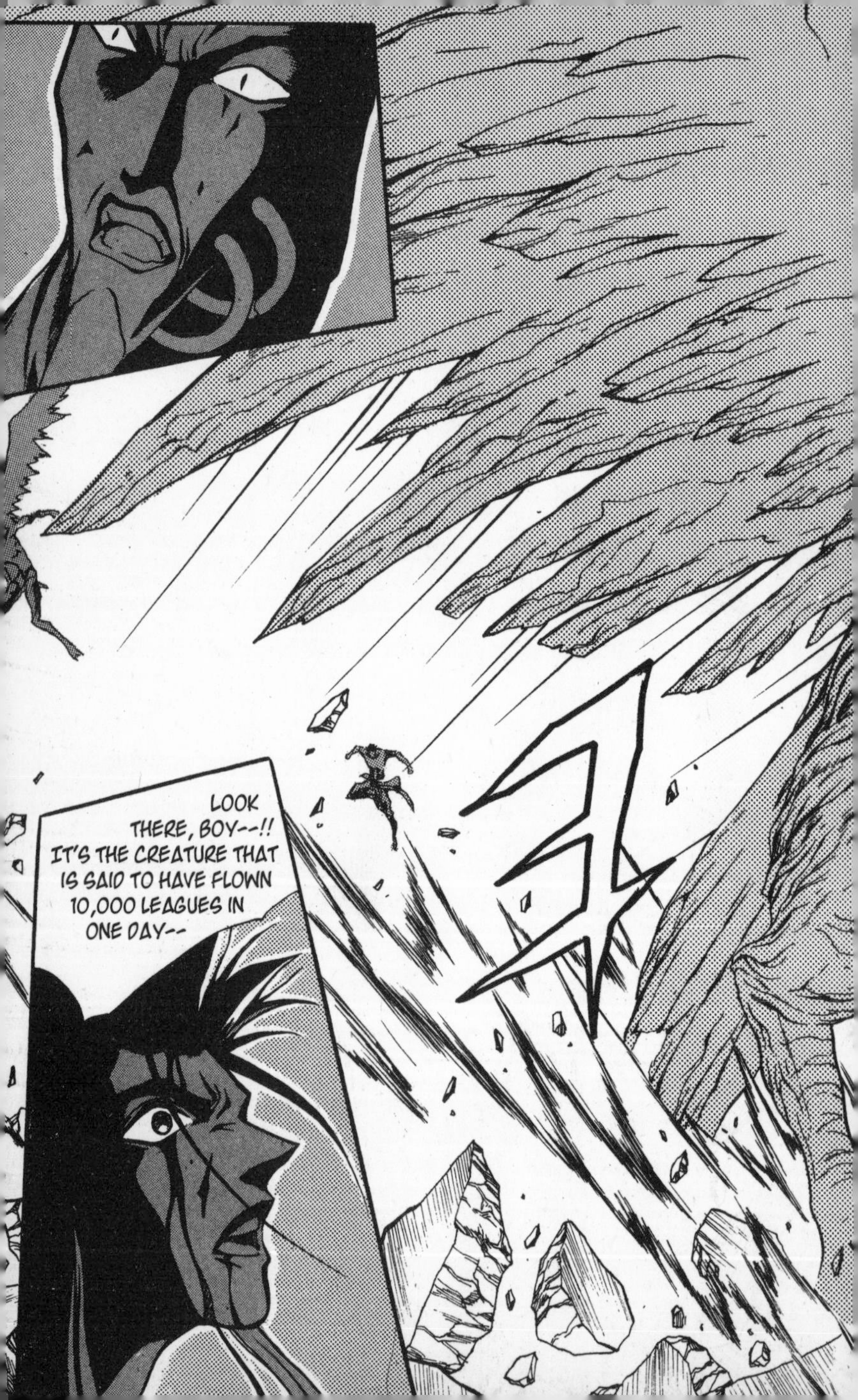
LOOK THERE, BOY--!! IT'S THE CREATURE THAT IS SAID TO HAVE FLOWN 10,000 LEAGUES IN ONE DAY--

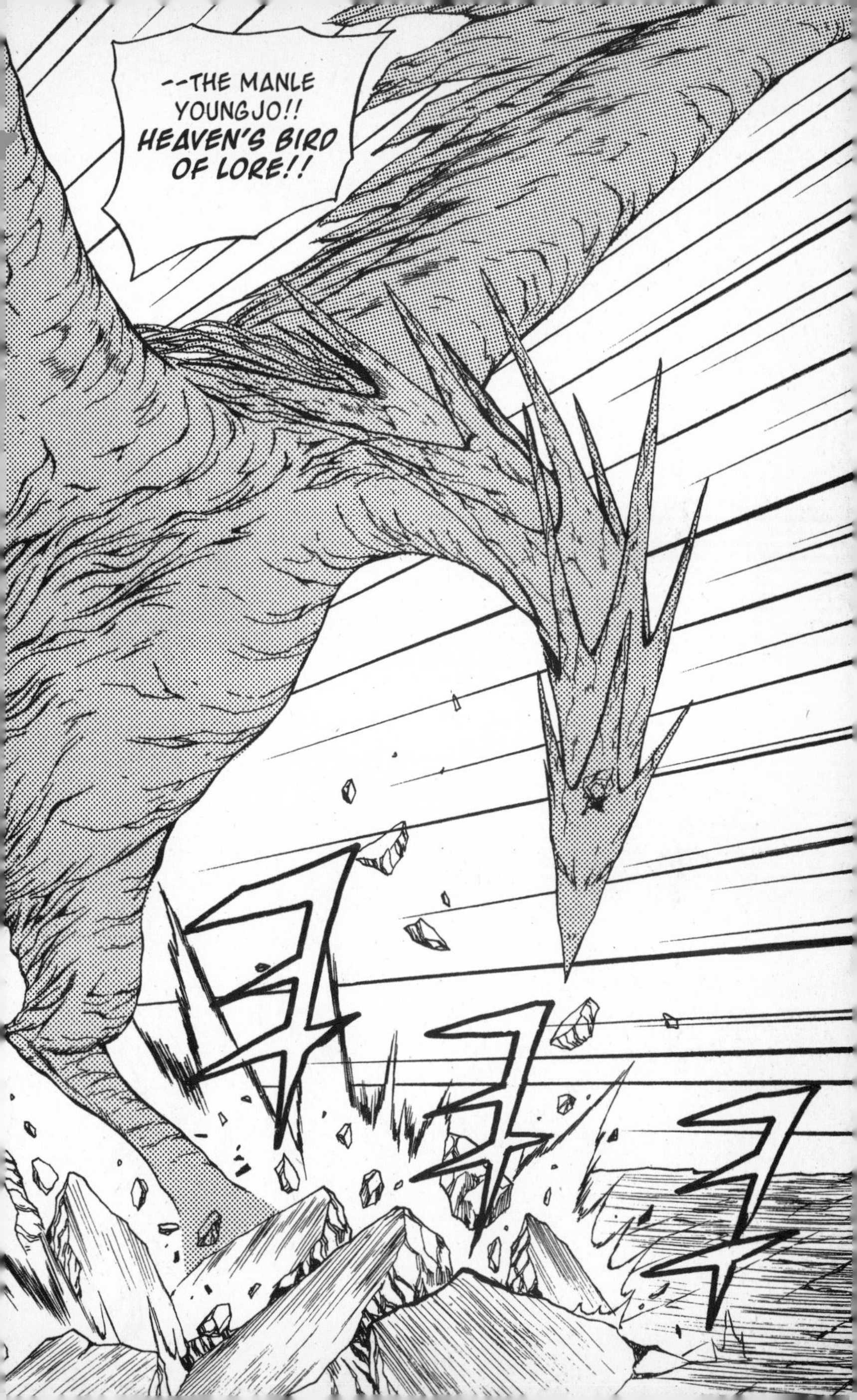
--THE MANLE YOUNGJO!! HEAVEN'S BIRD OF LORE!!

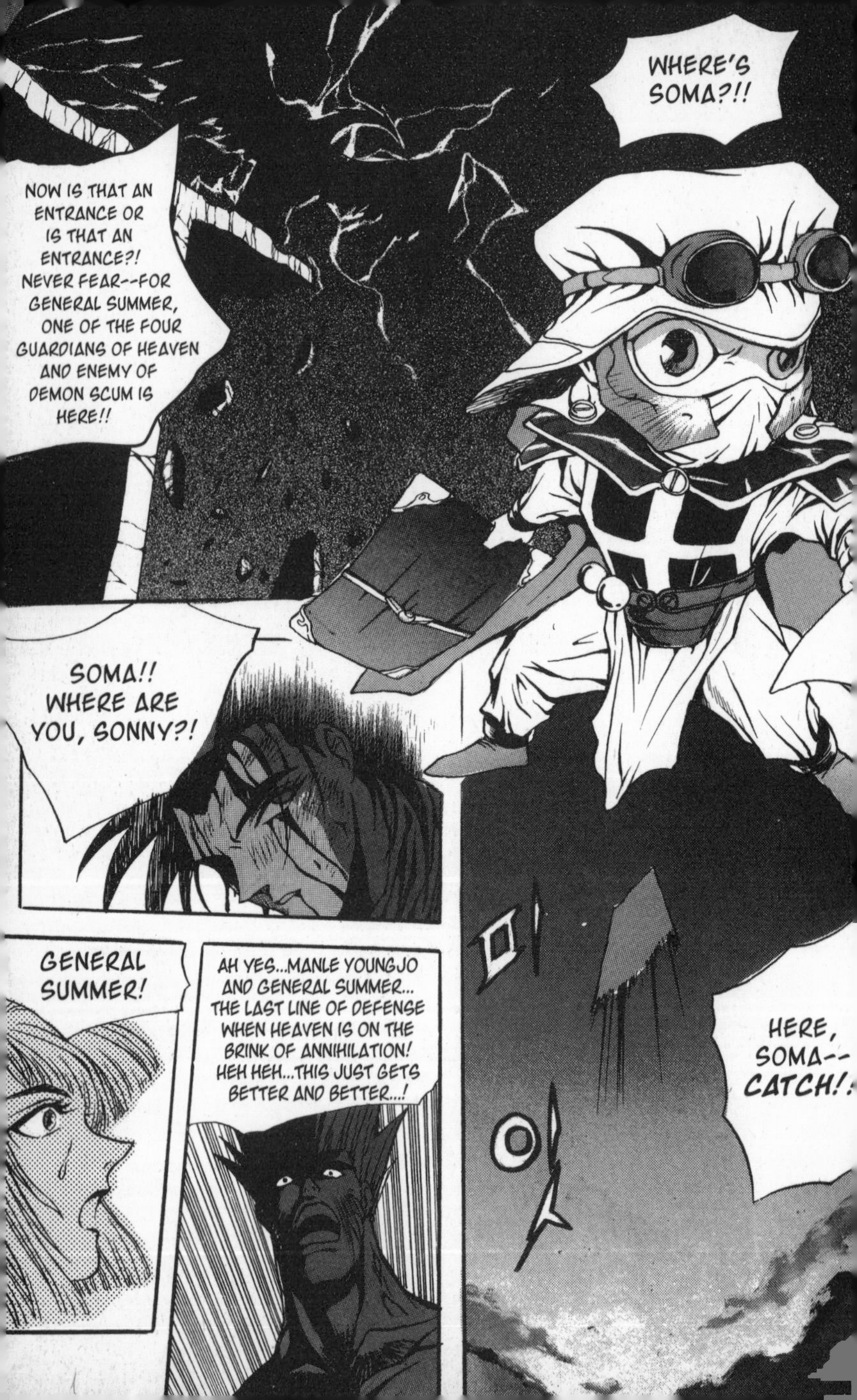
WHERE'S SOMA?!!
NOW IS THAT AN ENTRANCE OR IS THAT AN ENTRANCE?! NEVER FEAR--FOR GENERAL SUMMER, ONE OF THE FOUR GUARDIANS OF HEAVEN AND ENEMY OF DEMON SCUM IS HERE!!
SOMA!! WHERE ARE YOU, SONNY?!
HERE, SOMA-- CATCH!!
AH YES...MANLE YOUNGJO AND GENERAL SUMMER... THE LAST LINE OF DEFENSE WHEN HEAVEN IS ON THE BRINK OF ANNIHILATION! HEH HEH...THIS JUST GETS BETTER AND BETTER...!
GENERAL SUMMER!

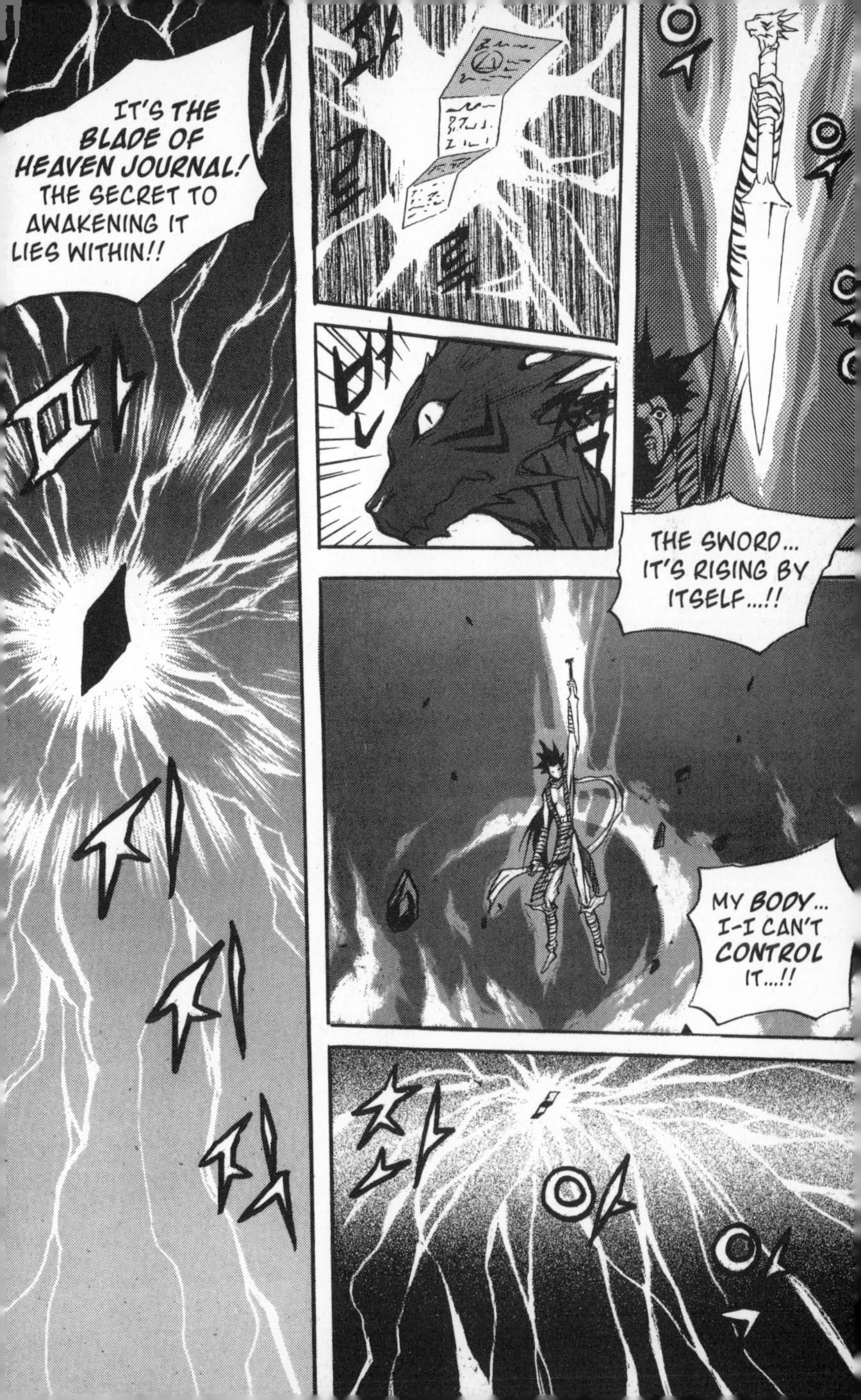
IT'S THE BLADE OF HEAVEN JOURNAL! THE SECRET TO AWAKENING IT LIES WITHIN!!
THE SWORD... IT'S RISING BY ITSELF...!!
MY BODY... I-I CAN'T CONTROL IT...!!

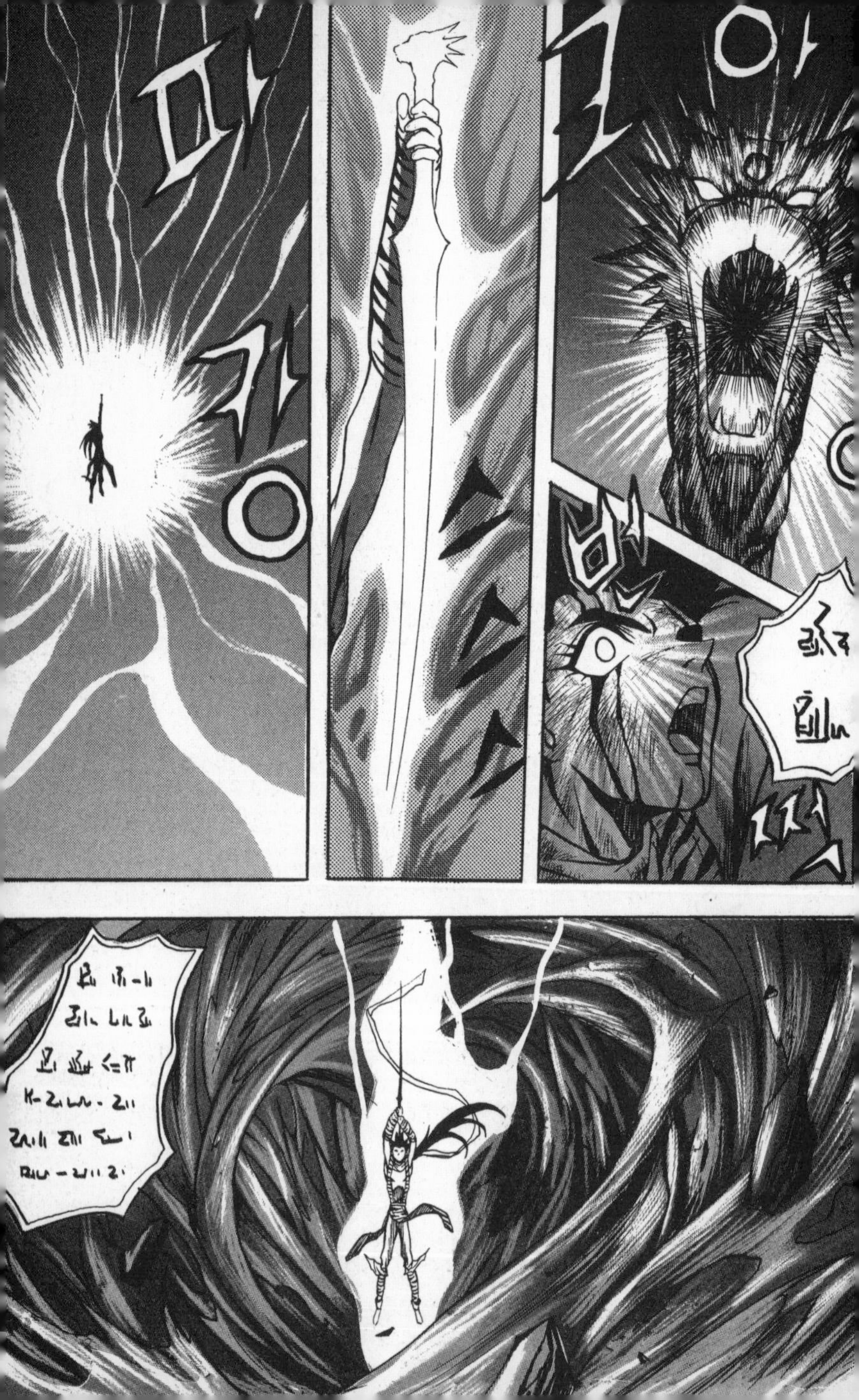

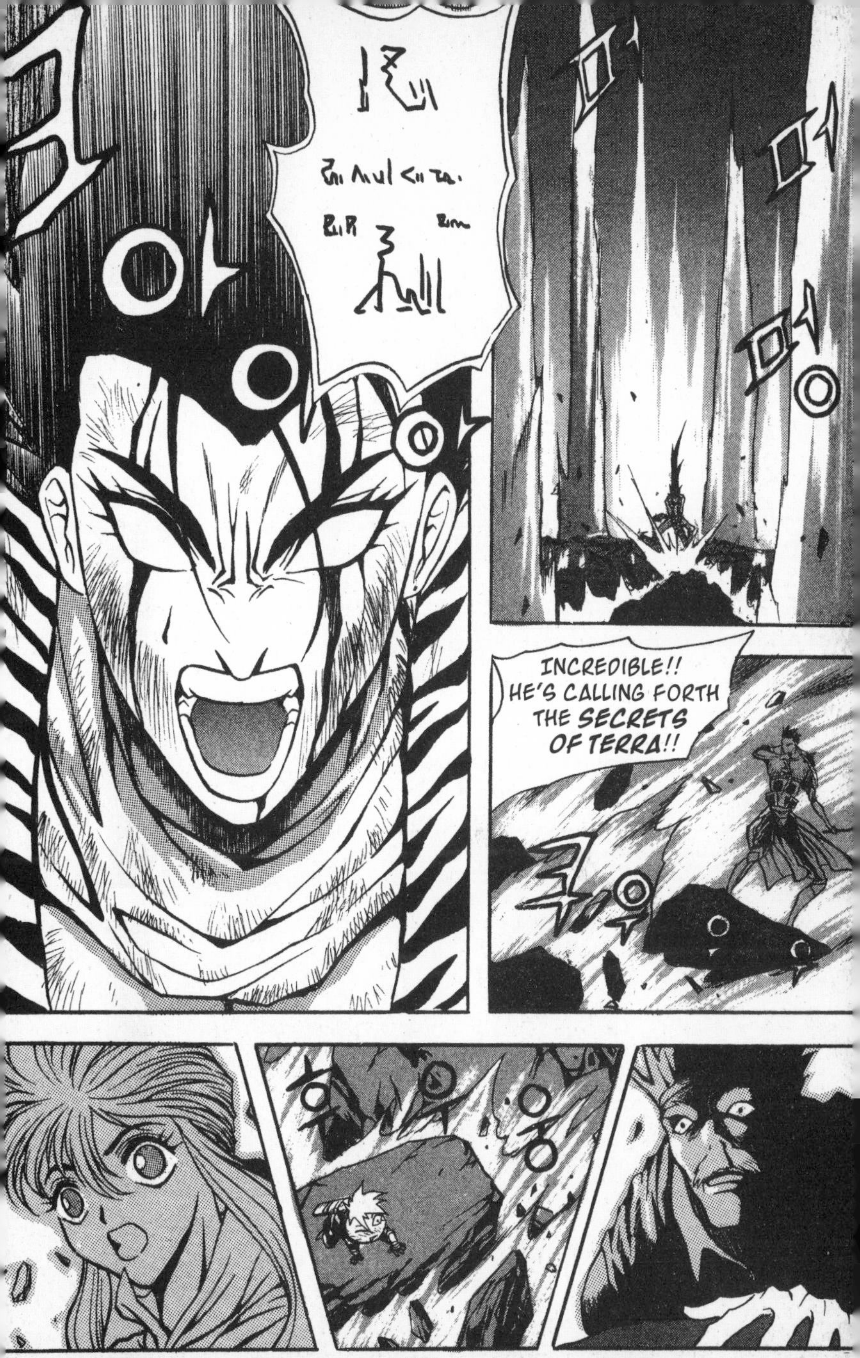
INCREDIBLE!! HE'S CALLING FORTH THE SECRETS OF TERRA!!

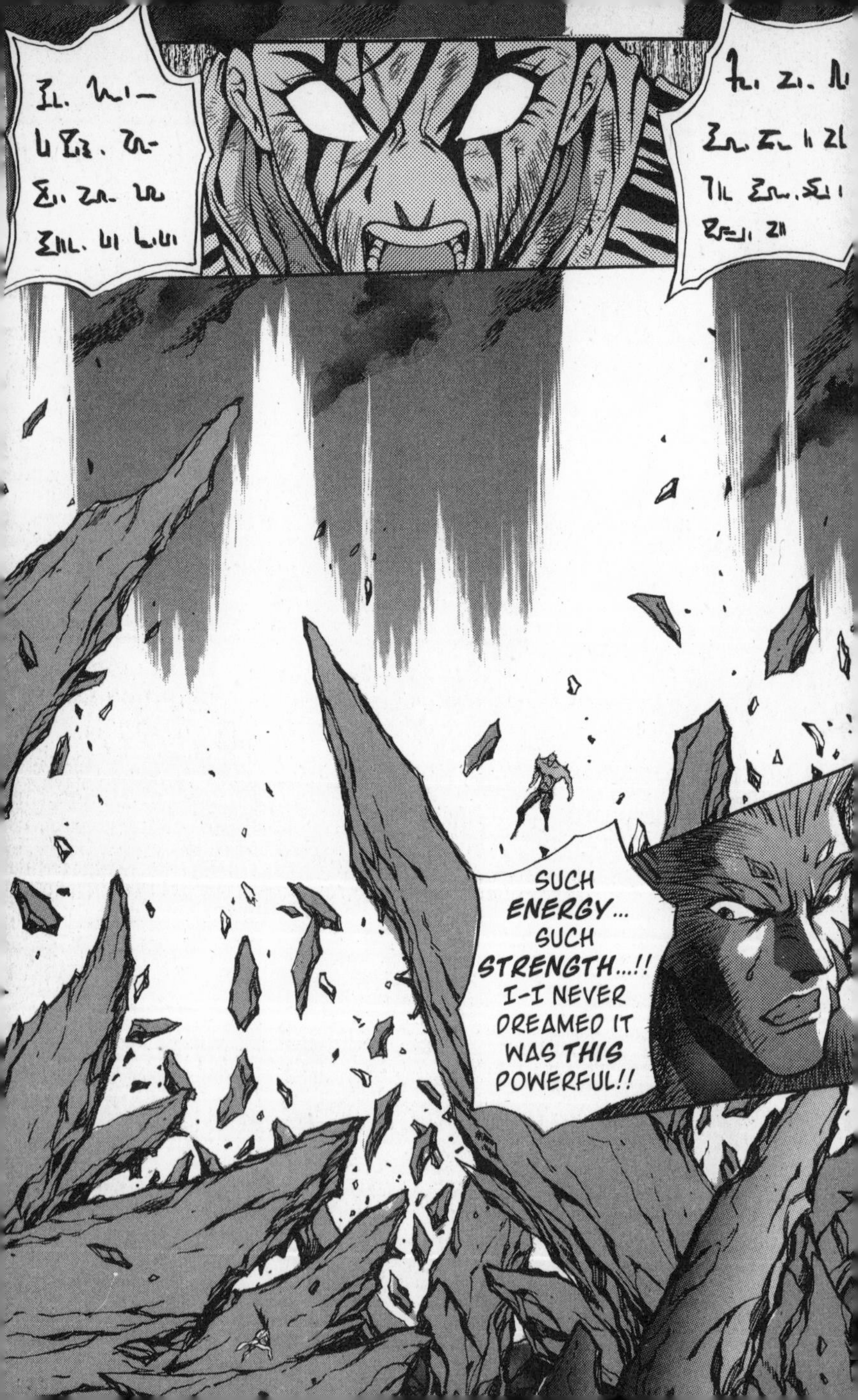
SUCH ENERGY... SUCH STRENGTH...!! I-I NEVER DREAMED IT WAS THIS POWERFUL!!

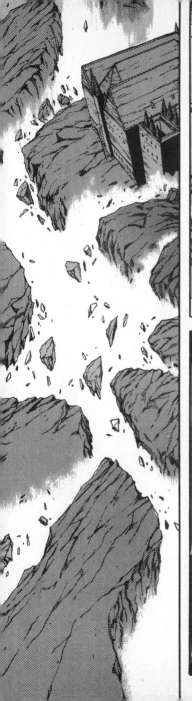

ECHO!!
COME TO
THE AID OF
YOUR
MASTER!!

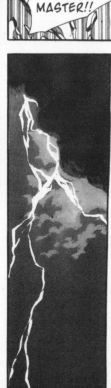

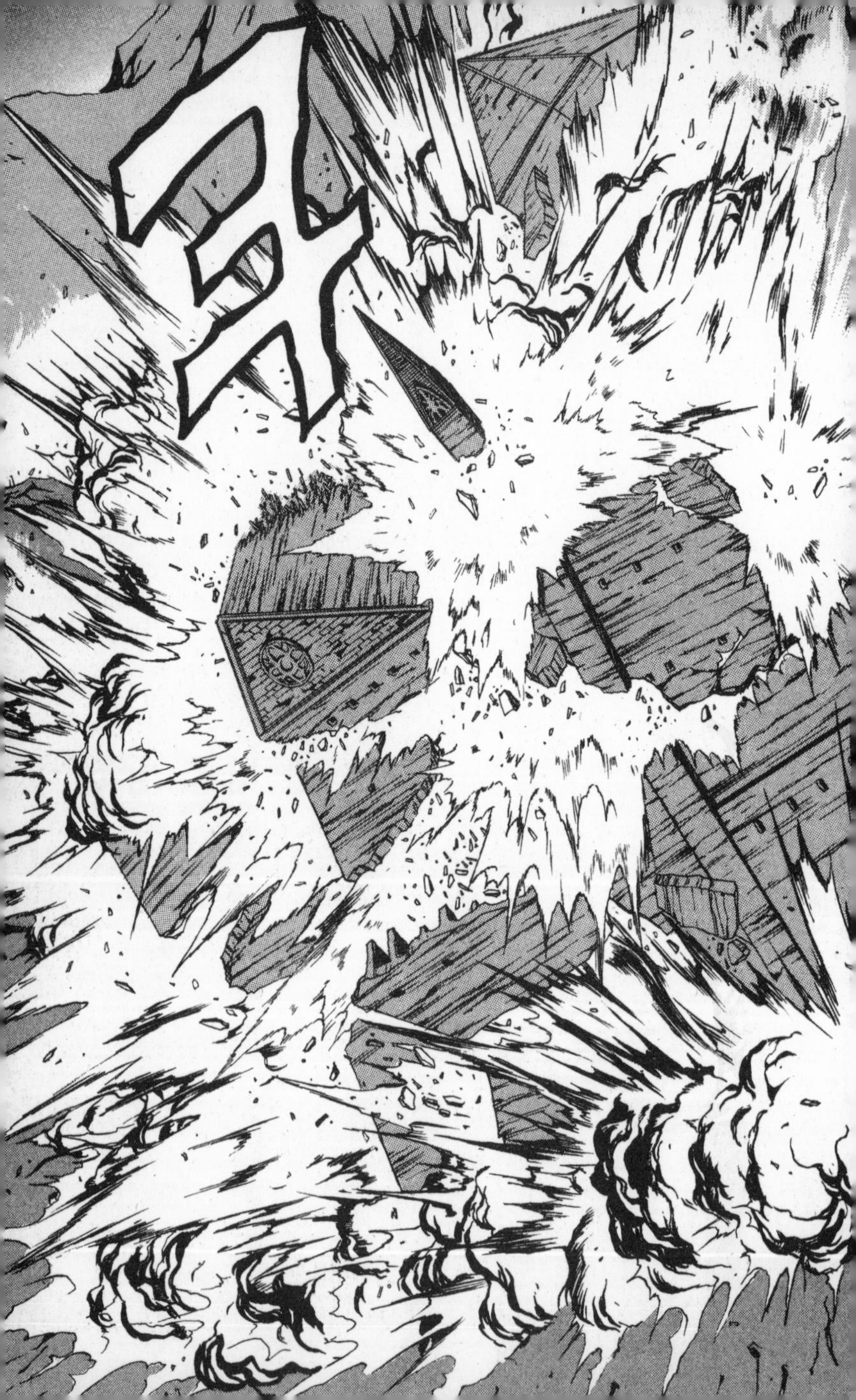

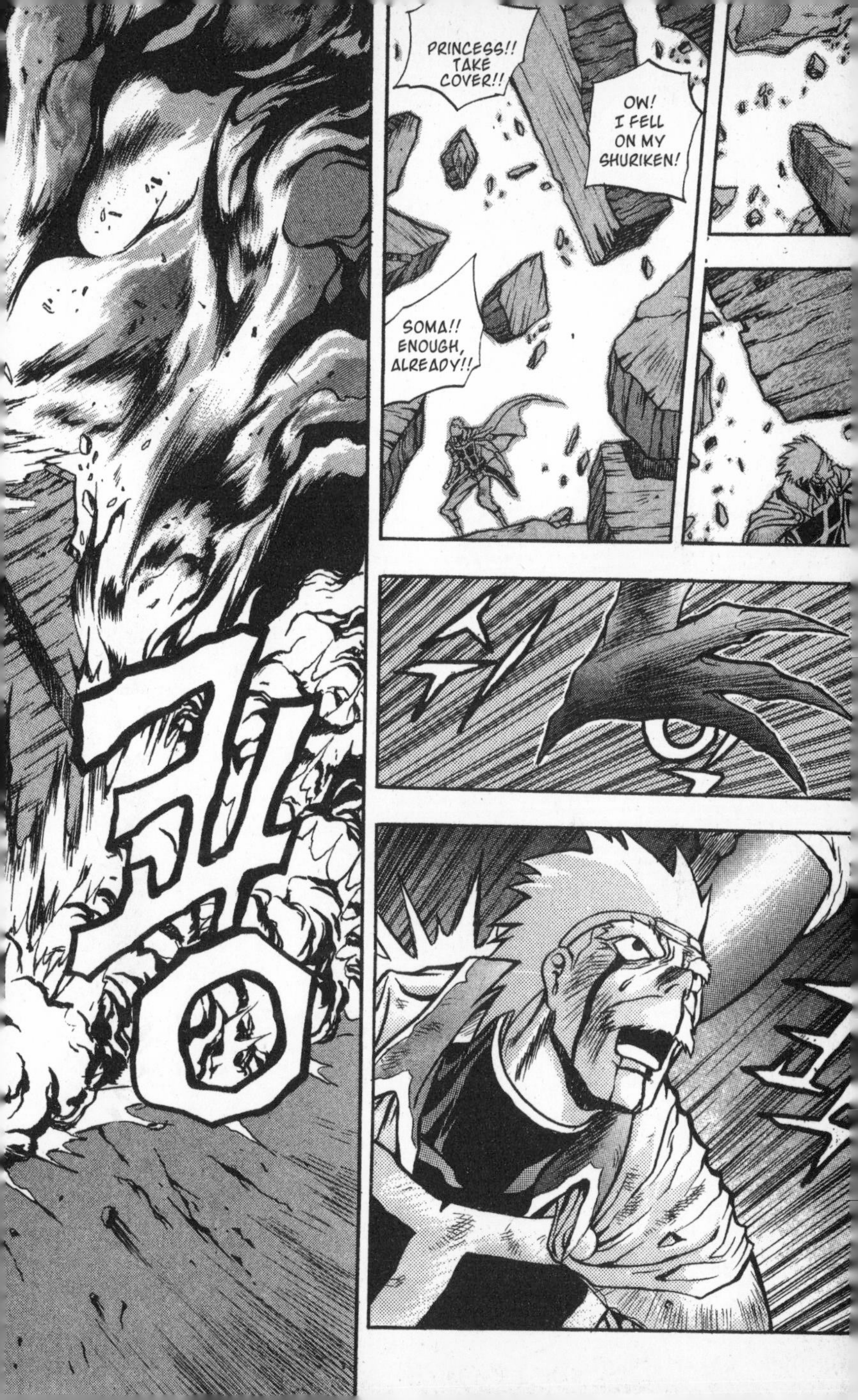
OW! I FELL ON MY SHURIKEN!
PRINCESS!! TAKE COVER!!
SOMA!! ENOUGH, ALREADY!!

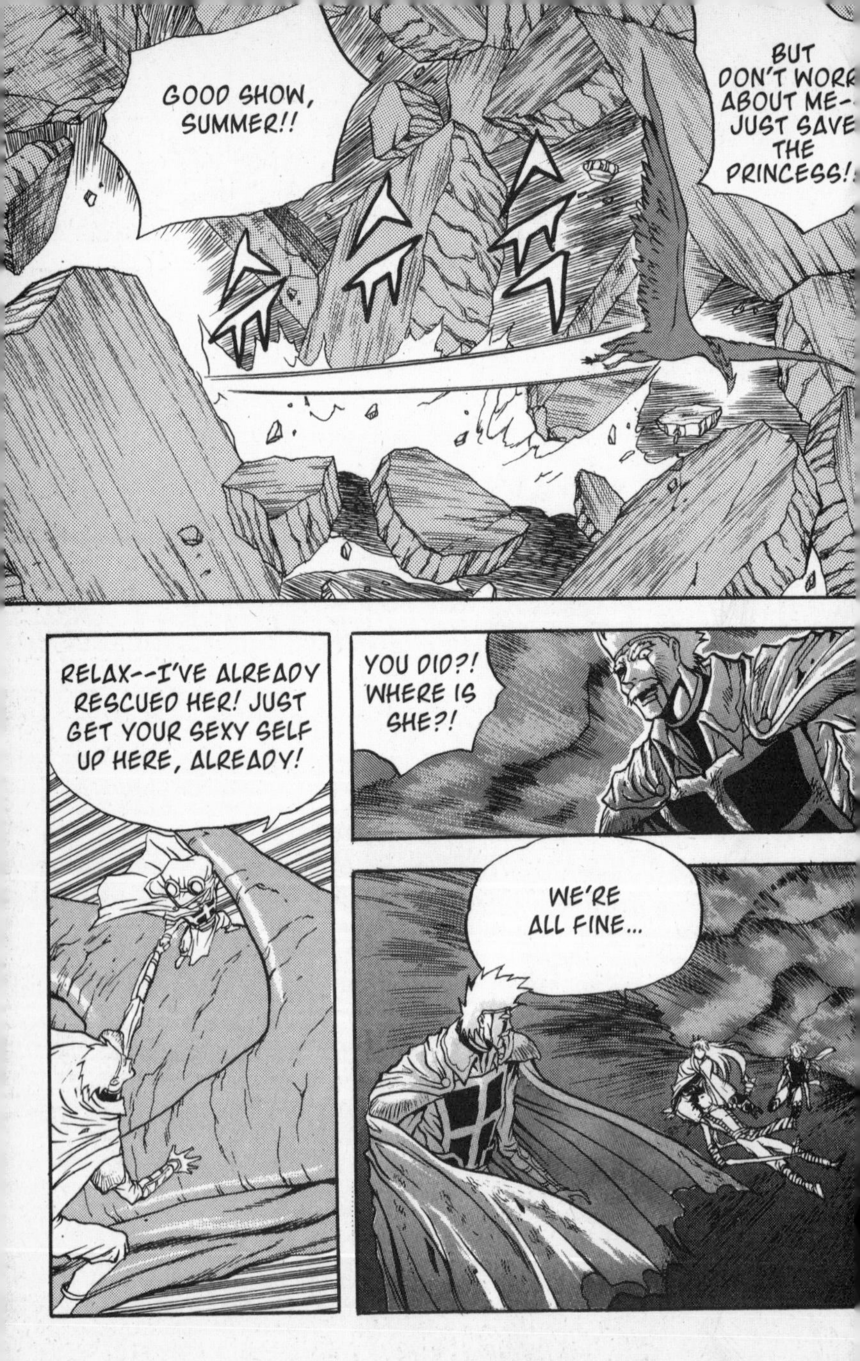
GOOD SHOW, SUMMER!!
BUT DON'T WORR ABOUT ME- JUST SAVE THE PRINCESS!
RELAX--I'VE ALREADY RESCUED HER! JUST GET YOUR SEXY SELF UP HERE, ALREADY!
YOU DID?! WHERE IS SHE?!
WE'RE ALL FINE...

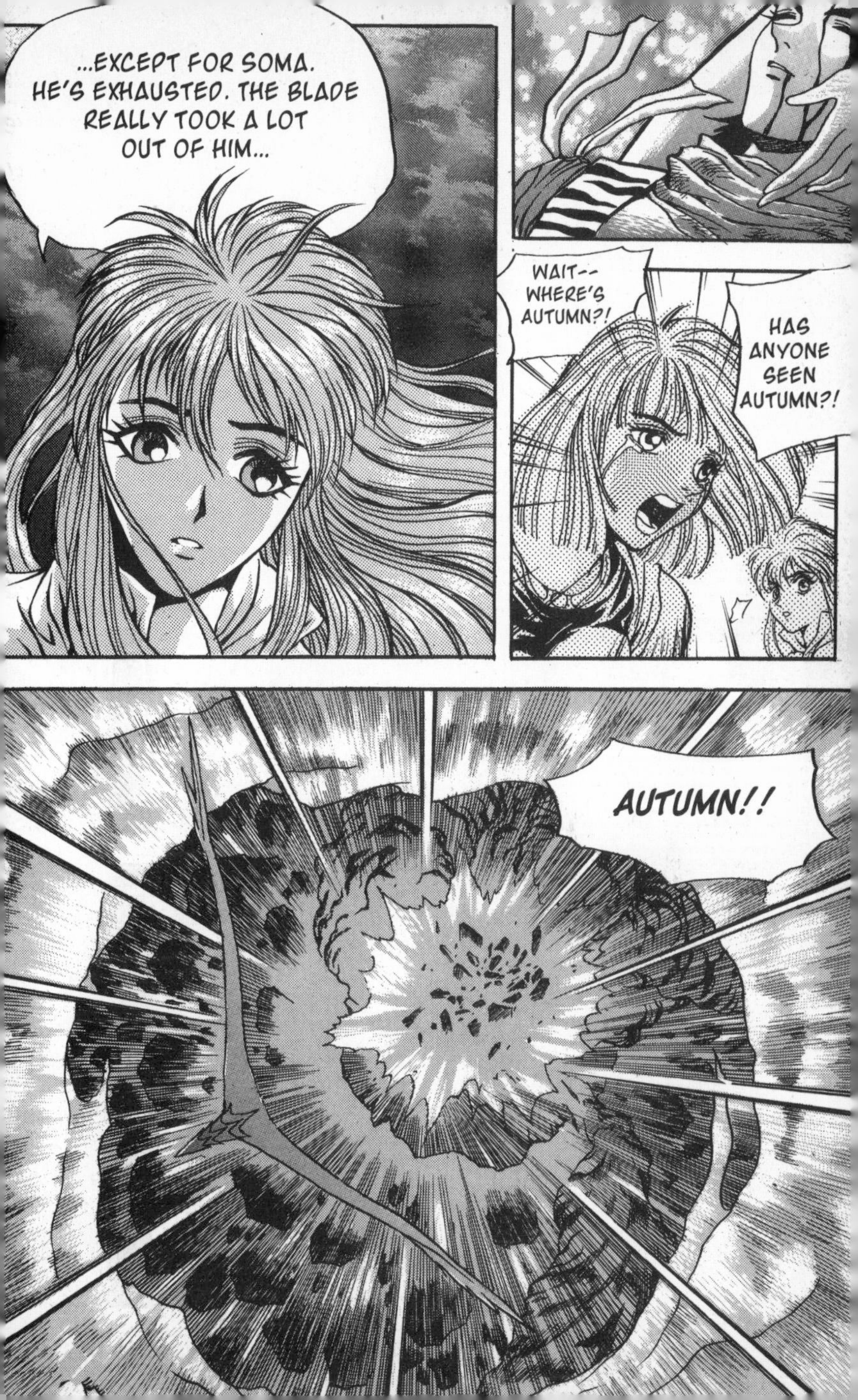
...EXCEPT FOR SOMA. HE'S EXHAUSTED. THE BLADE REALLY TOOK A LOT OUT OF HIM...
WAIT-- WHERE'S AUTUMN?!
HAS ANYONE SEEN AUTUMN?!
AUTUMN!!

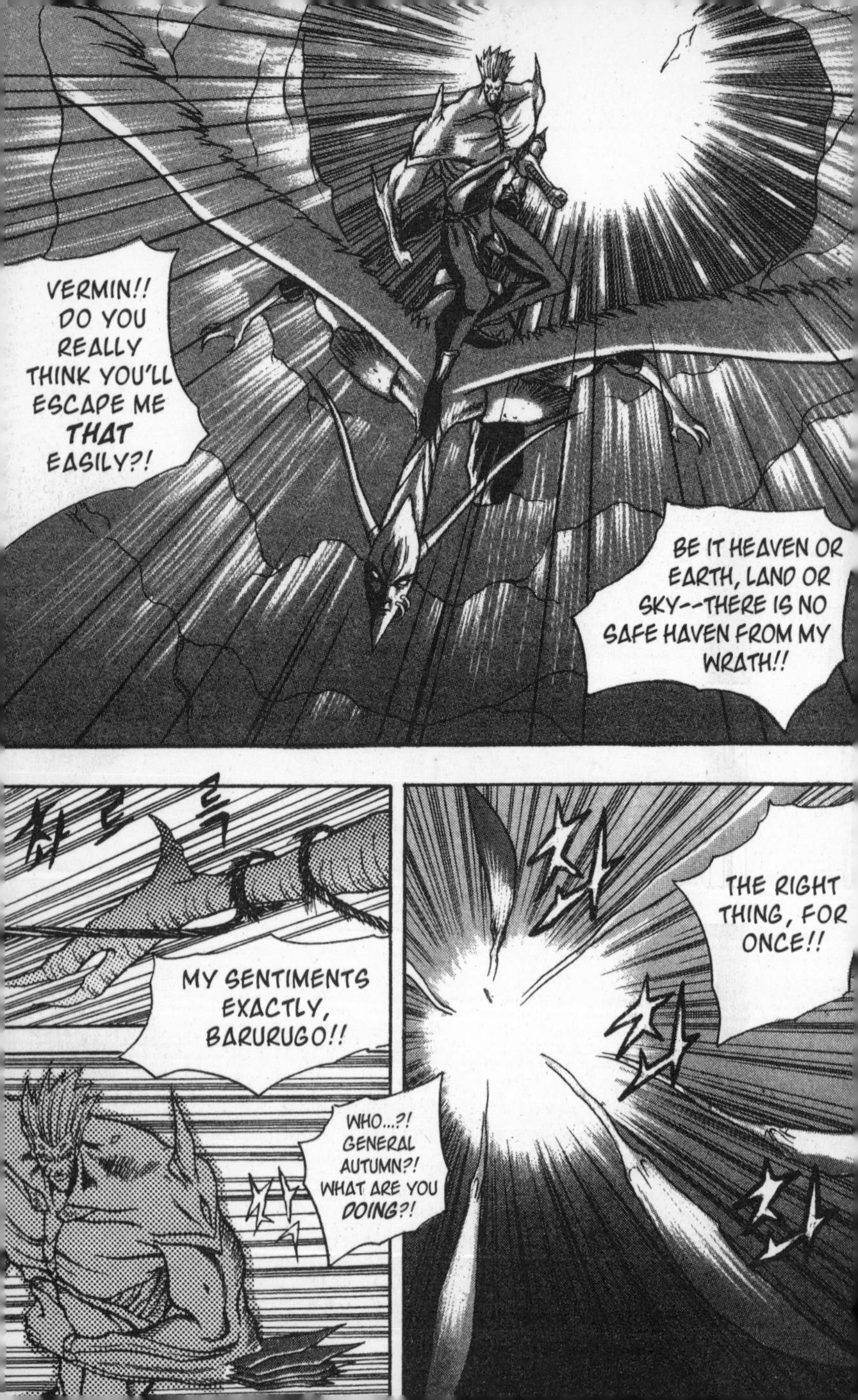
VERMIN!! DO YOU REALLY THINK YOU'LL ESCAPE ME **THAT** EASILY?!
BE IT HEAVEN OR EARTH, LAND OR SKY--THERE IS NO SAFE HAVEN FROM MY WRATH!!
샤르륵
MY SENTIMENTS EXACTLY, BARURUGO!!
WHO...?! GENERAL AUTUMN?! WHAT ARE YOU *DOING*?!
THE RIGHT THING, FOR ONCE!!

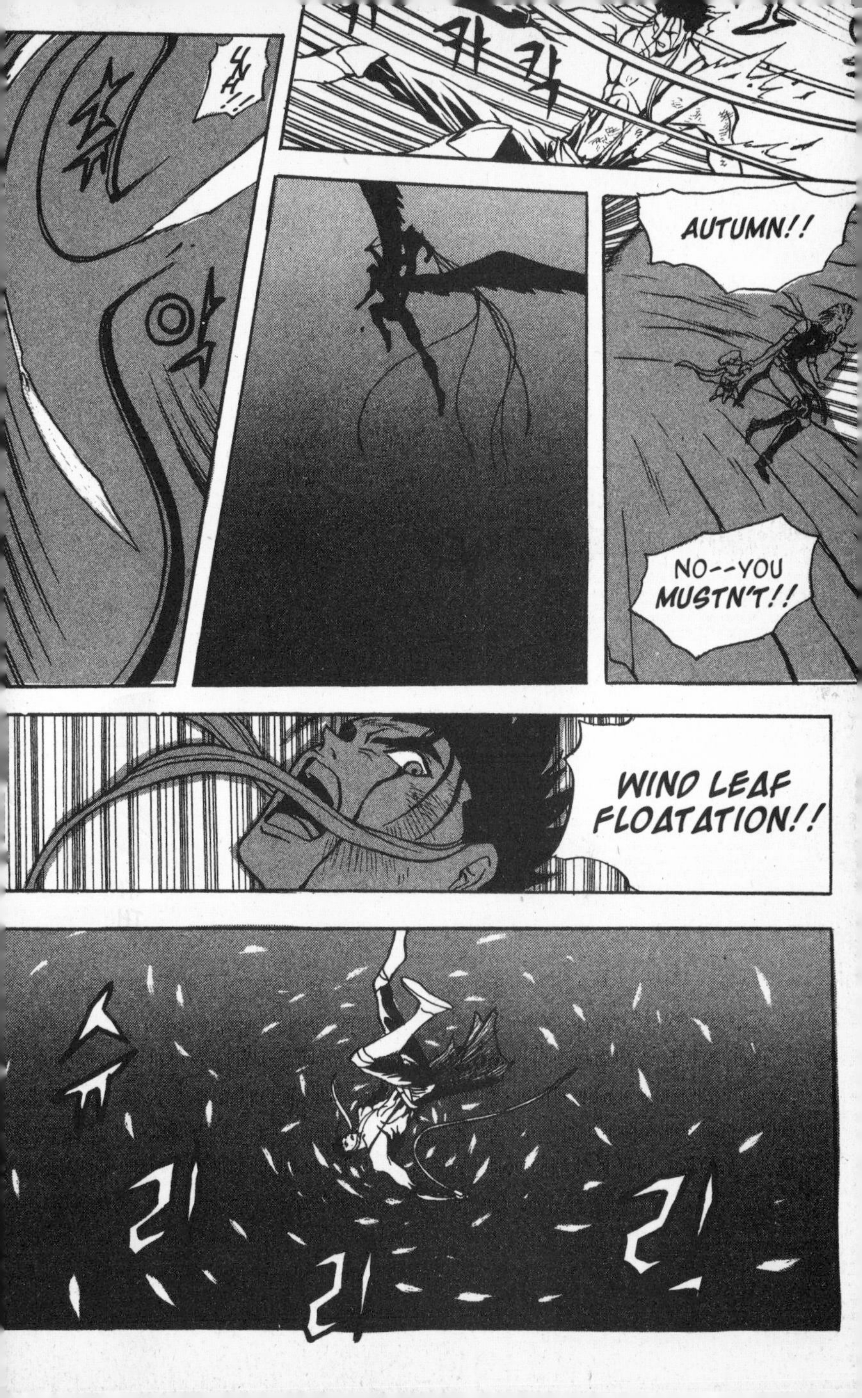
UNH!!
AUTUMN!!
NO--YOU MUSTN'T!!
WIND LEAF FLOATATION!!

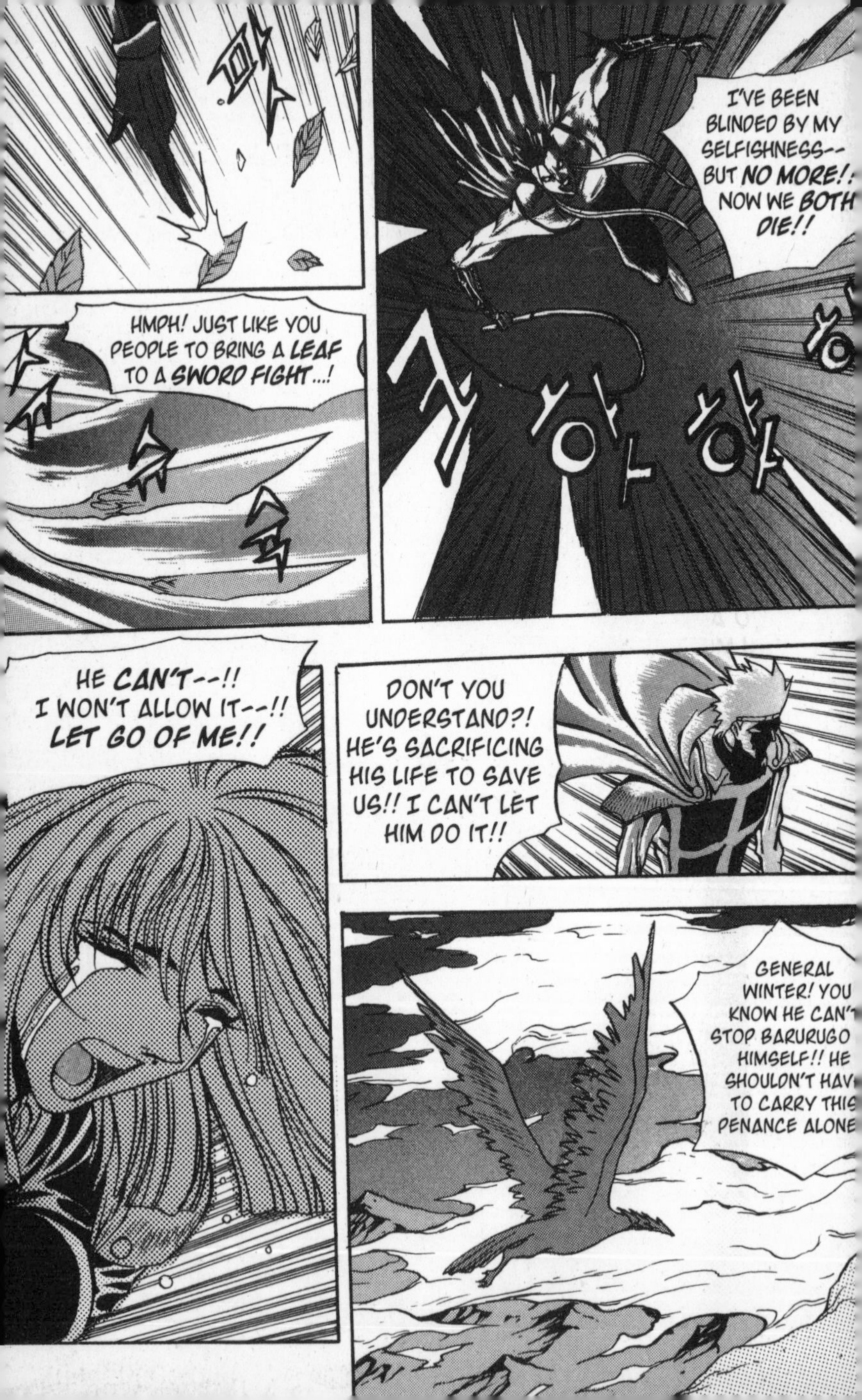
I'VE BEEN BLINDED BY MY SELFISHNESS-- BUT NO MORE!: NOW WE BOTH DIE!!
HMPH! JUST LIKE YOU PEOPLE TO BRING A LEAF TO A SWORD FIGHT...!
DON'T YOU UNDERSTAND?! HE'S SACRIFICING HIS LIFE TO SAVE US!! I CAN'T LET HIM DO IT!!
GENERAL WINTER! YOU KNOW HE CAN' STOP BARURUGO HIMSELF!! HE SHOULDN'T HAV TO CARRY THIS PENANCE ALONE
HE CAN'T--!! I WON'T ALLOW IT--!! LET GO OF ME!!

YES...I, TOO, HAVE BETRAYED HEAVEN...SO IT'S ONLY FAIR THAT I PAY FOR MY SINS AS WELL!

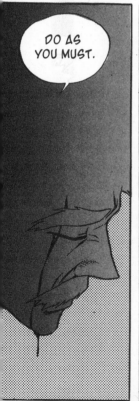

DO AS YOU MUST.

THANK YOU, GENERAL. I PRAY THAT SOMEDAY OUR DEEDS, IF NOT UNDER-STOOD, WILL STILL BE FORGIVEN.

SPRING!! NO!!

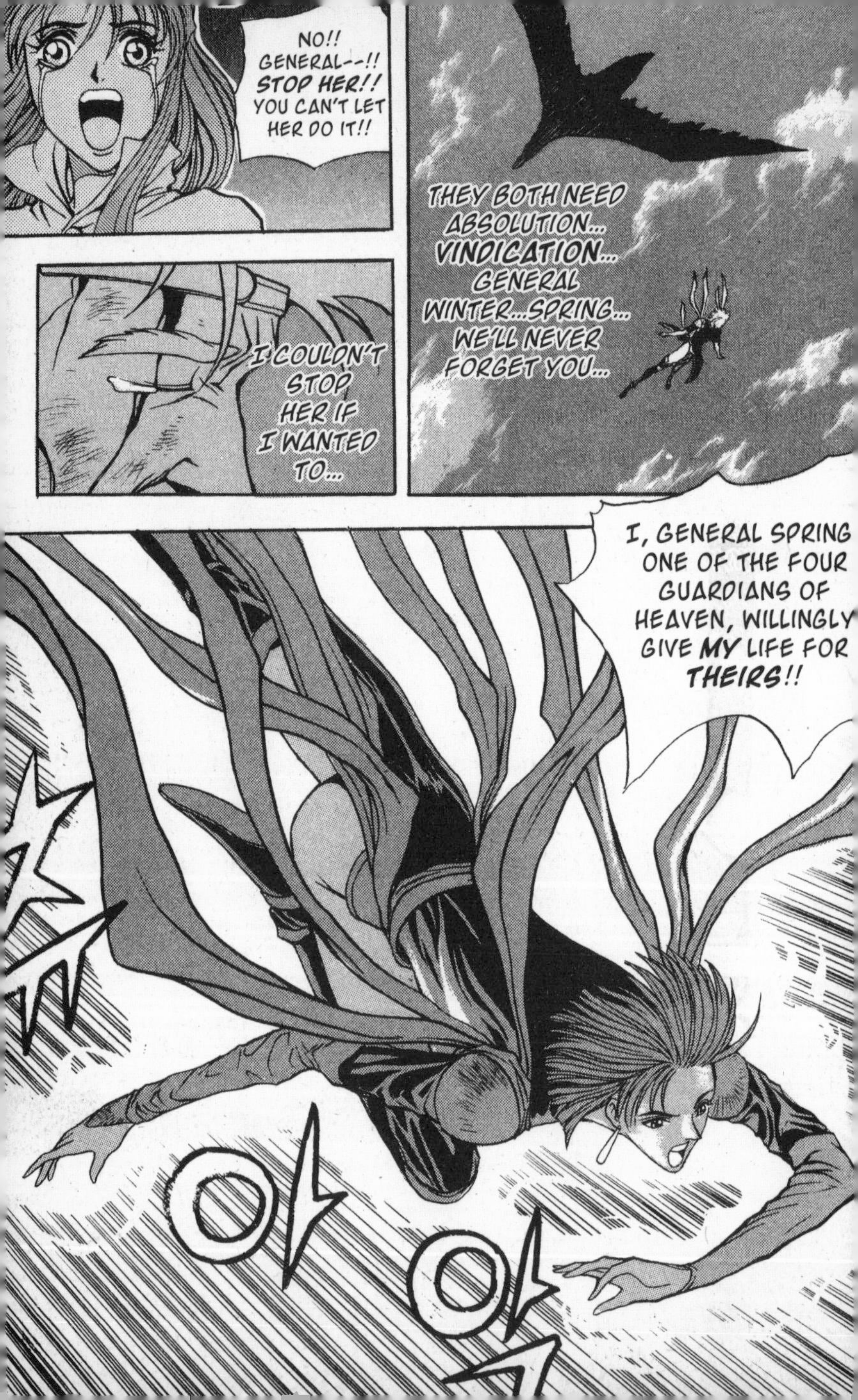
NO!! GENERAL--!! STOP HER!! YOU CAN'T LET HER DO IT!!
I COULDN'T STOP HER IF I WANTED TO...
THEY BOTH NEED ABSOLUTION... VINDICATION... GENERAL WINTER...SPRING... WE'LL NEVER FORGET YOU...
I, GENERAL SPRING ONE OF THE FOUR GUARDIANS OF HEAVEN, WILLINGLY GIVE MY LIFE FOR THEIRS!!

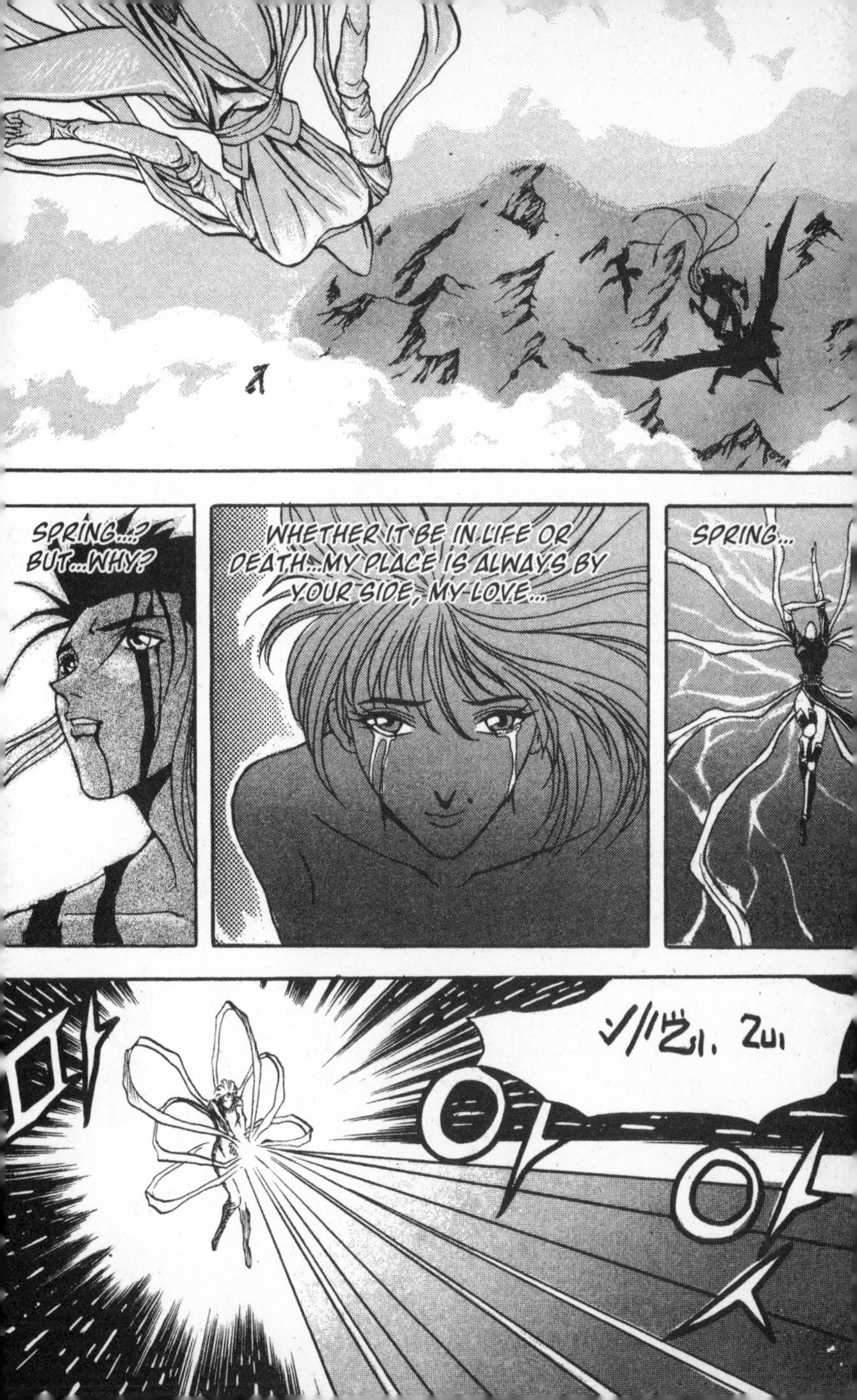
SPRING...
WHETHER IT BE IN LIFE OR DEATH...MY PLACE IS ALWAYS BY YOUR SIDE, MY LOVE...
SPRING...? BUT...WHY?
ZUI

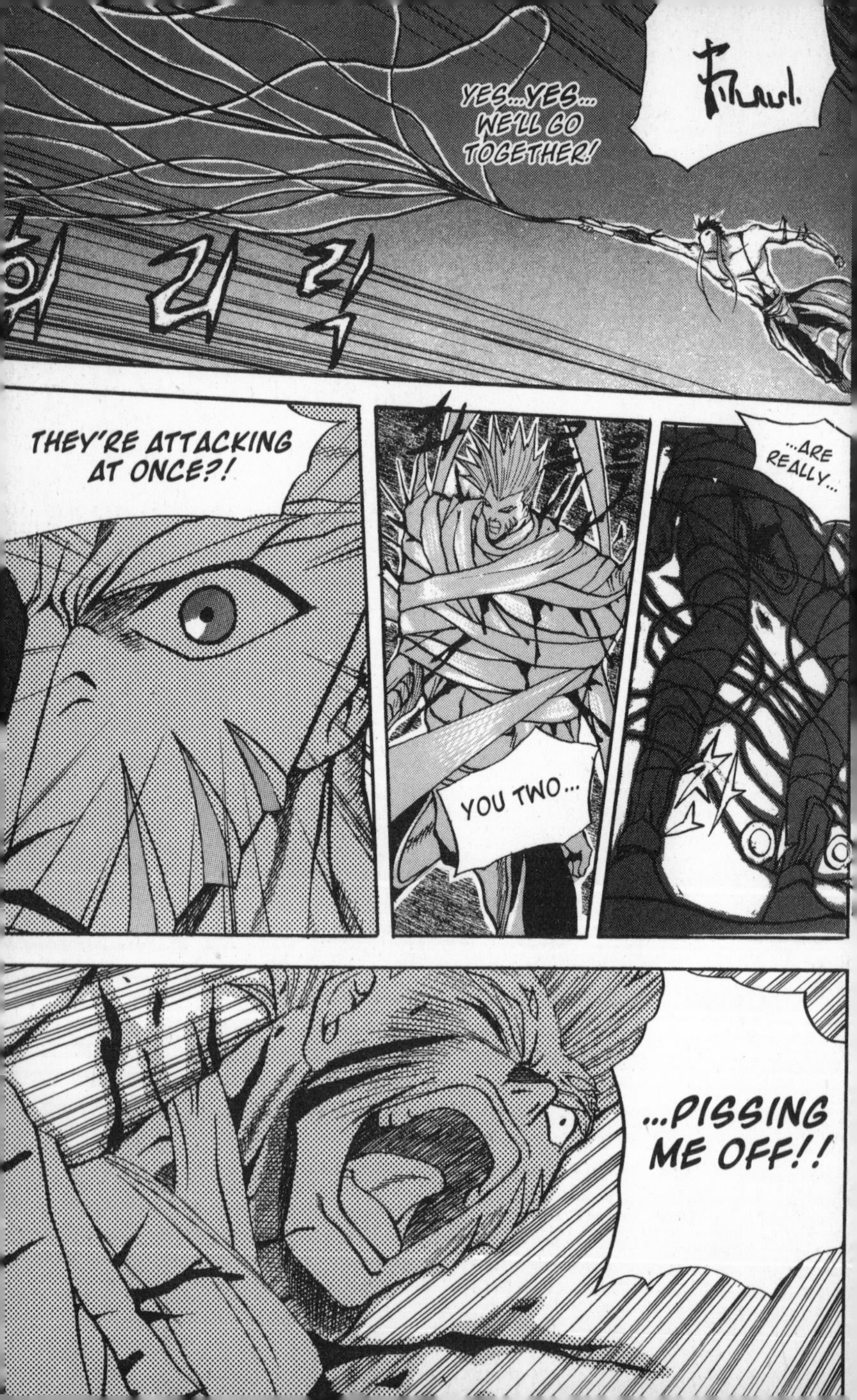
YES...YES... WE'LL GO TOGETHER!
THEY'RE ATTACKING AT ONCE?!
YOU TWO...
...ARE REALLY...
...PISSING ME OFF!!

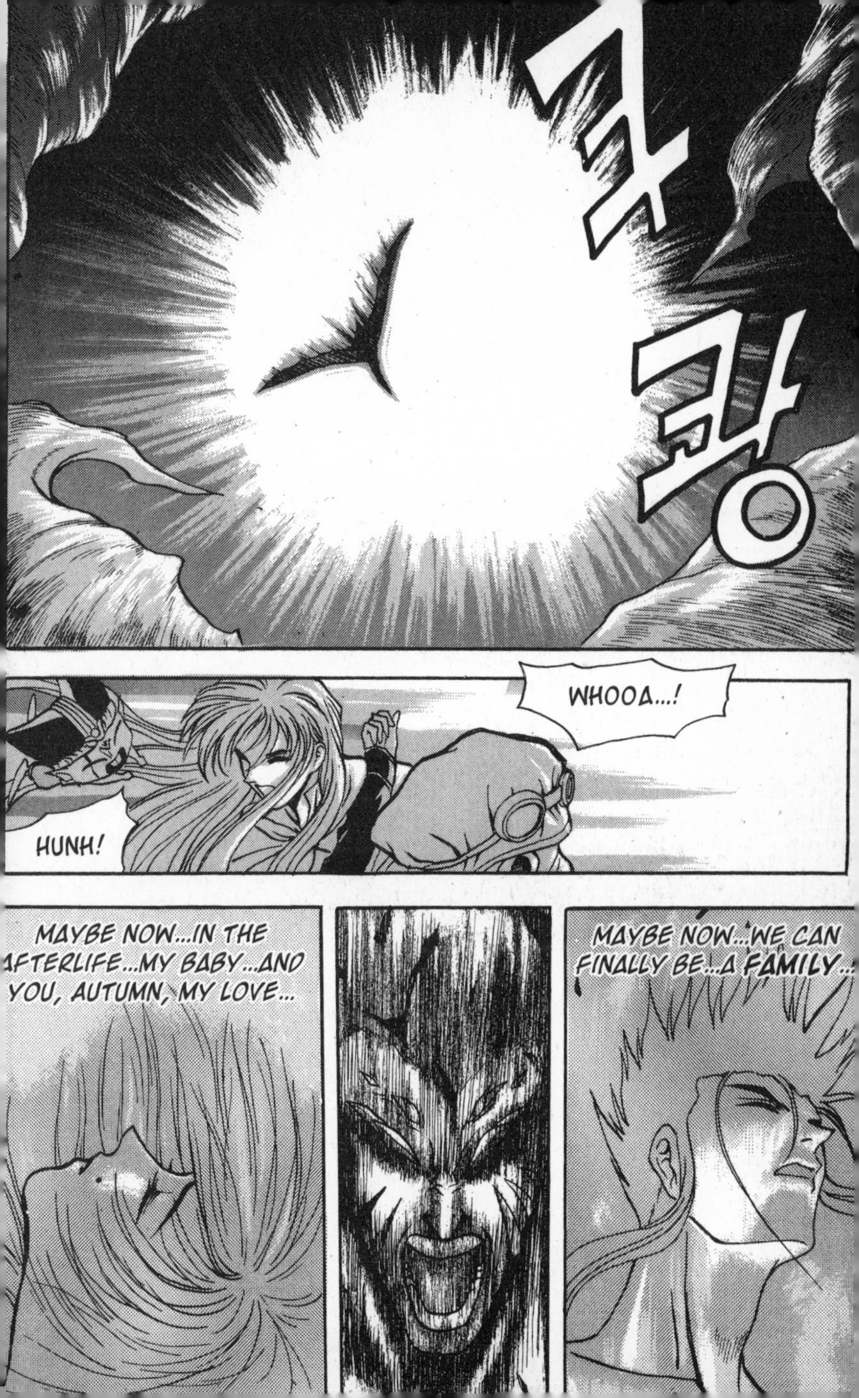
WHOOA...!
HUNH!
MAYBE NOW...IN THE AFTERLIFE...MY BABY...AND YOU, AUTUMN, MY LOVE...
MAYBE NOW...WE CAN FINALLY BE...A **FAMILY**...

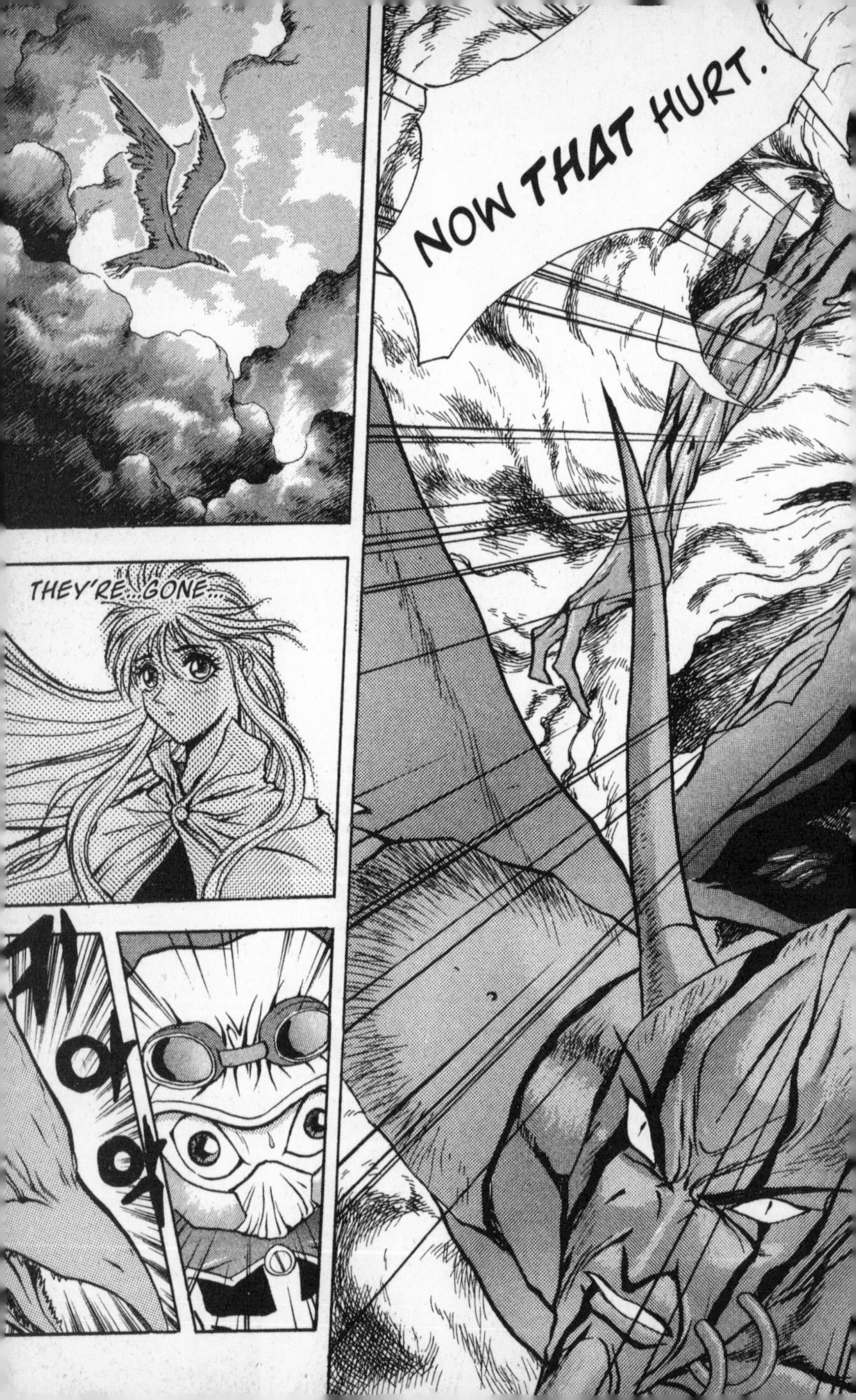
THEY'RE...GONE...
NOW THAT HURT.

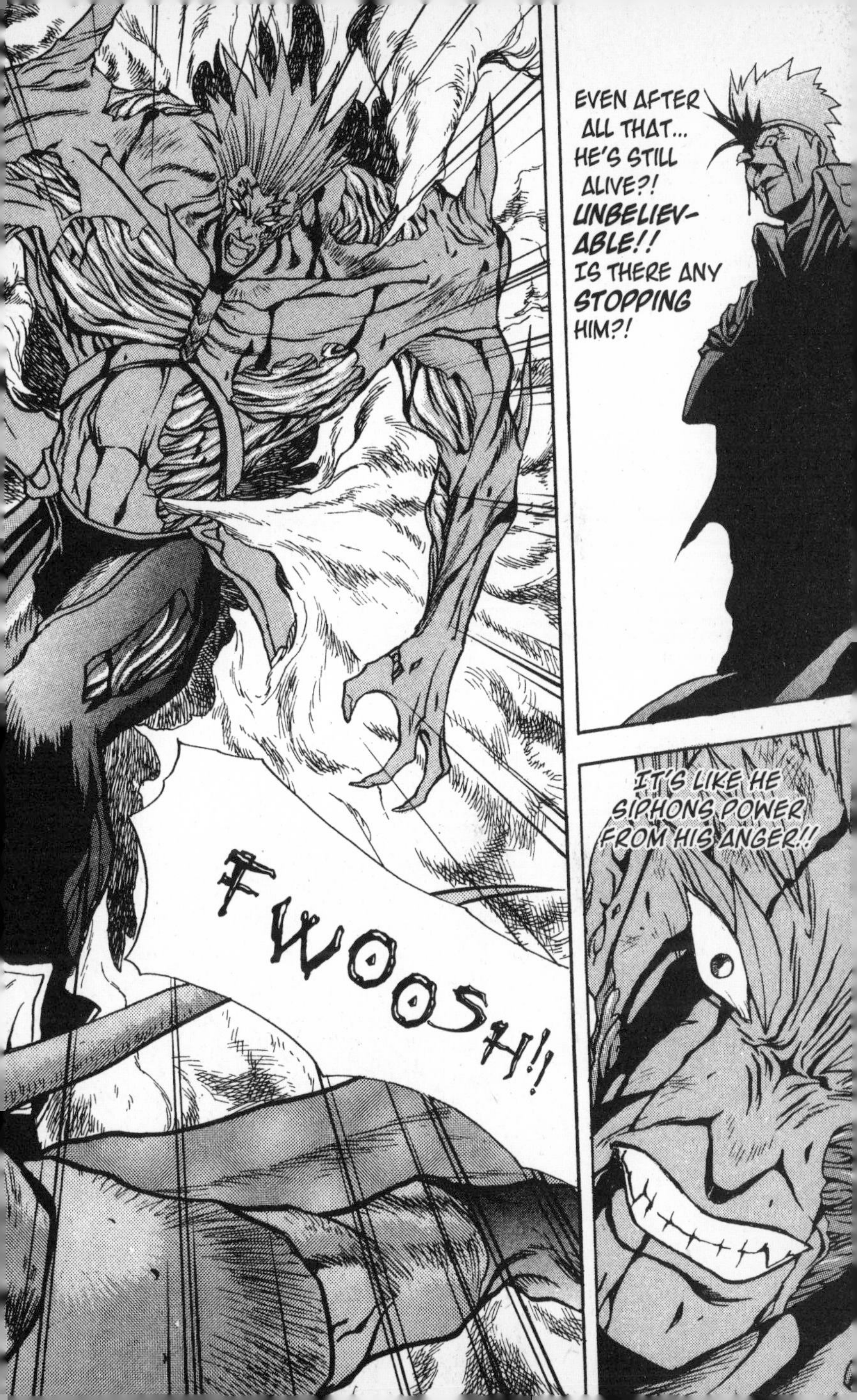
EVEN AFTER ALL THAT... HE'S STILL ALIVE?! UNBELIEVABLE!! IS THERE ANY STOPPING HIM?!
IT'S LIKE HE SIPHONS POWER FROM HIS ANGER!!
FWOOSH!!

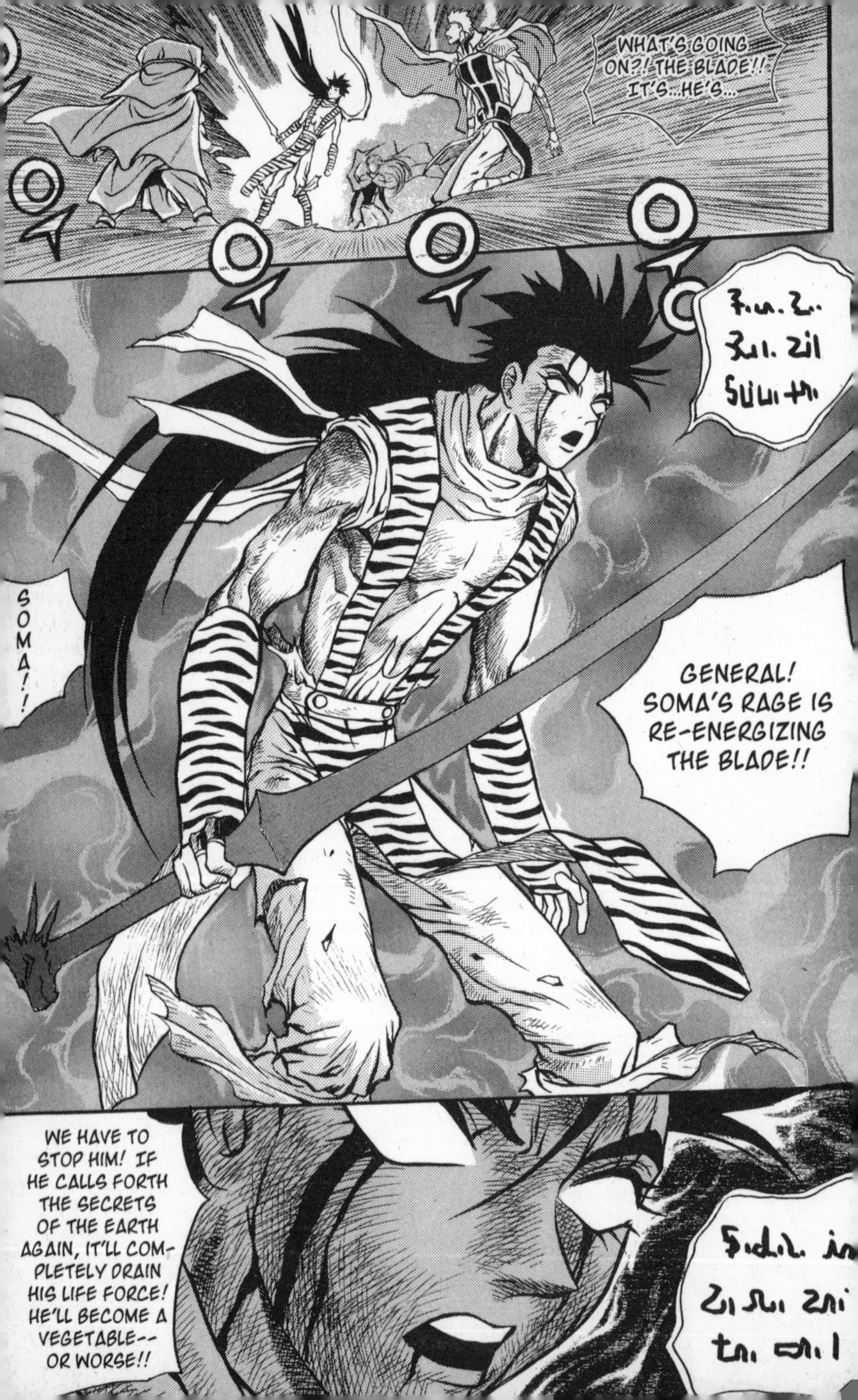
WHAT'S GOING ON?! THE BLADE!! IT'S...HE'S...
GENERAL! SOMA'S RAGE IS RE-ENERGIZING THE BLADE!!
SOMA!!
WE HAVE TO STOP HIM! IF HE CALLS FORTH THE SECRETS OF THE EARTH AGAIN, IT'LL COMPLETELY DRAIN HIS LIFE FORCE! HE'LL BECOME A VEGETABLE--OR WORSE!!

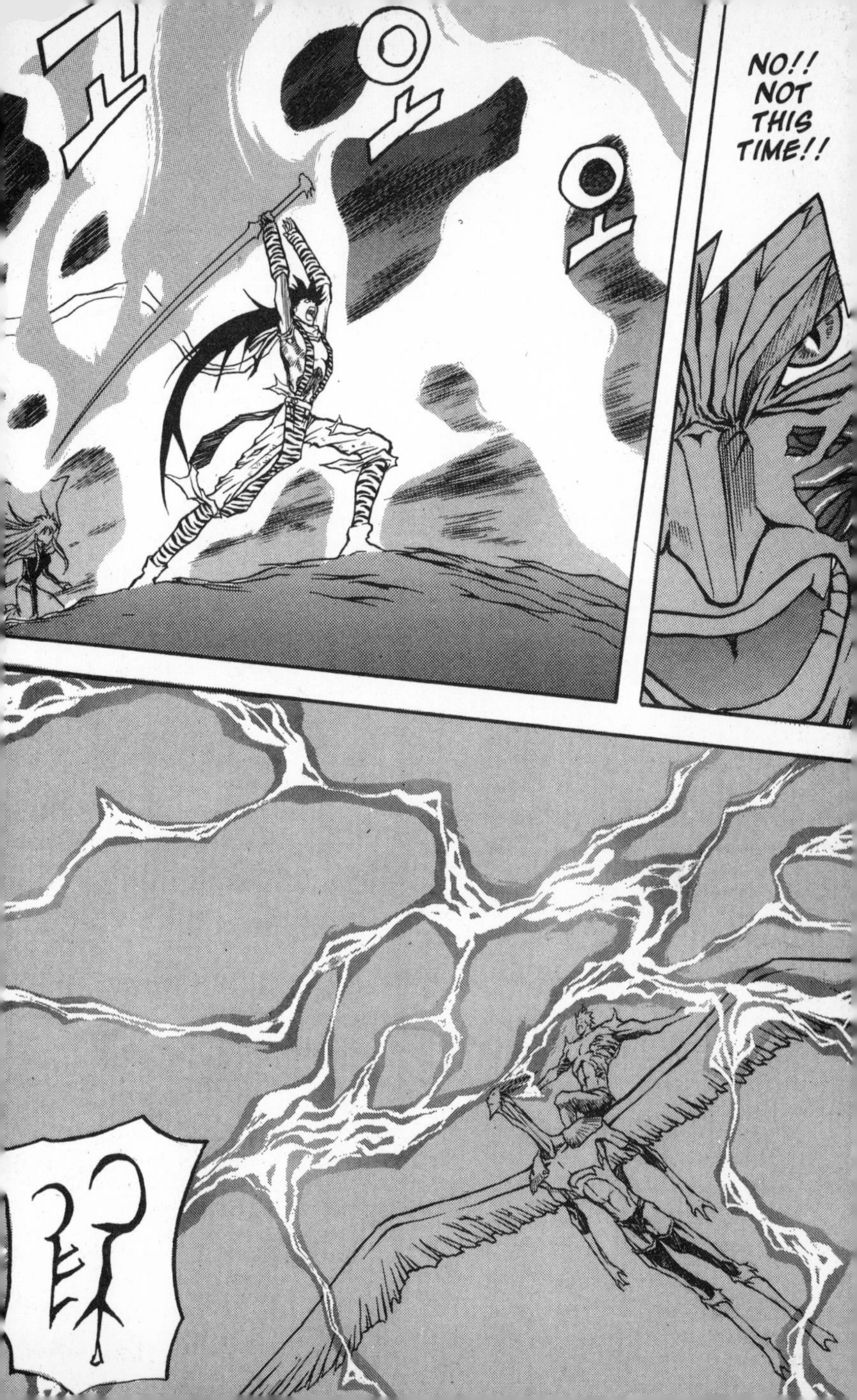
NO!! NOT THIS TIME!!

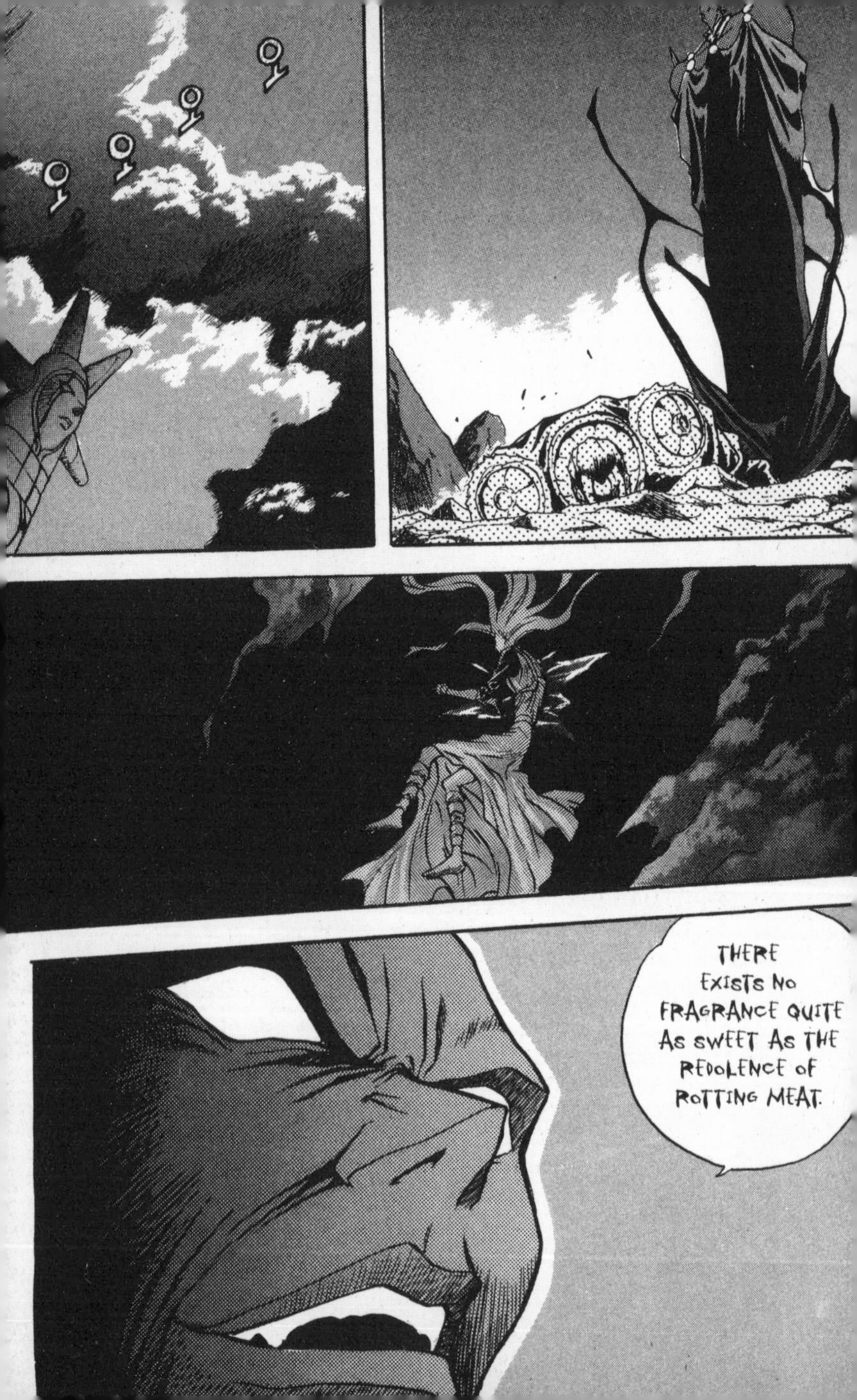
THERE EXISTS NO FRAGRANCE QUITE AS SWEET AS THE REDOLENCE OF ROTTING MEAT.

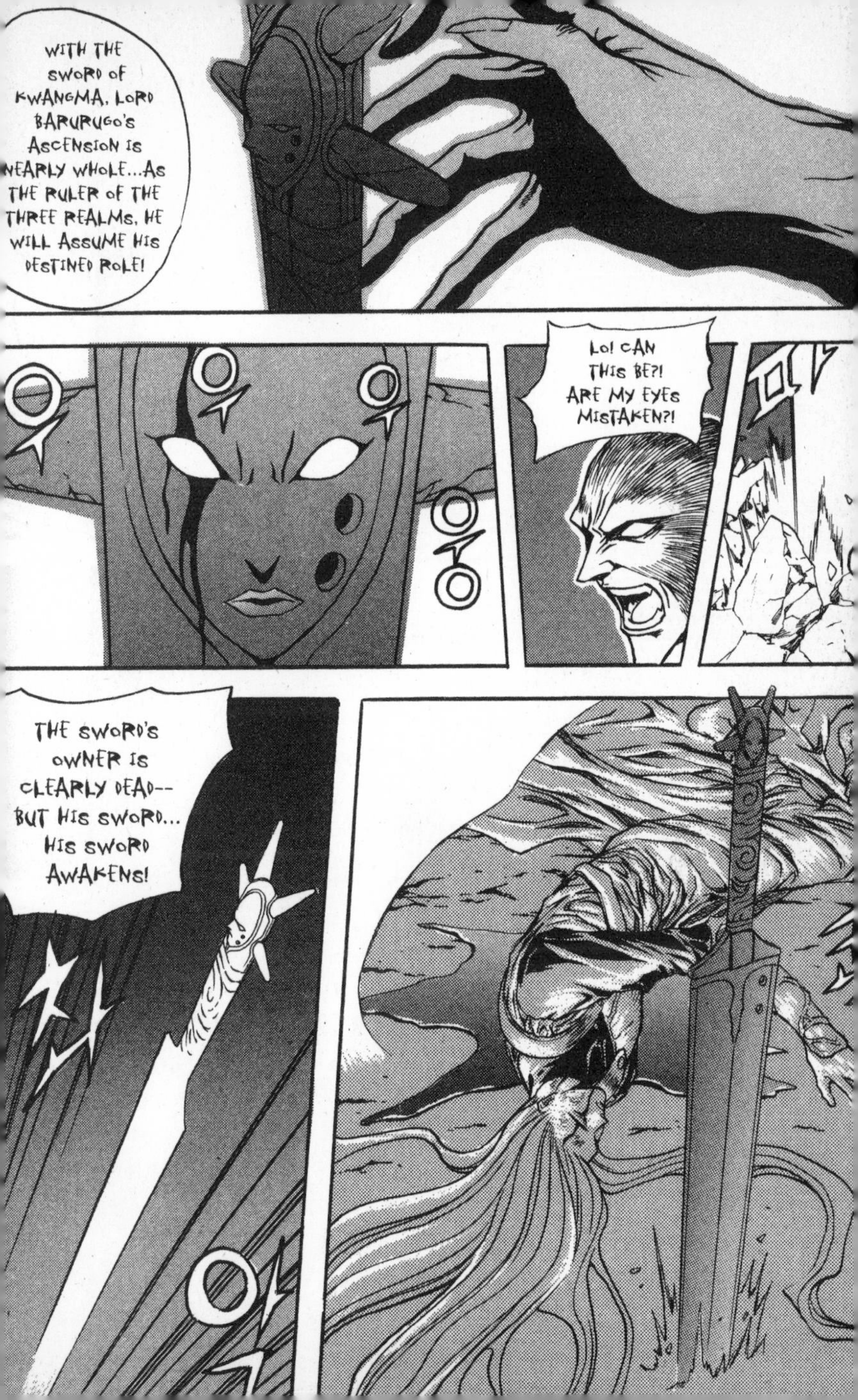
WITH THE SWORD OF KWANGMA, LORD BARURUGO'S ASCENSION IS NEARLY WHOLE...AS THE RULER OF THE THREE REALMS, HE WILL ASSUME HIS DESTINED ROLE!
LO! CAN THIS BE?! ARE MY EYES MISTAKEN?!
THE SWORD'S OWNER IS CLEARLY DEAD-- BUT HIS SWORD... HIS SWORD AWAKENS!

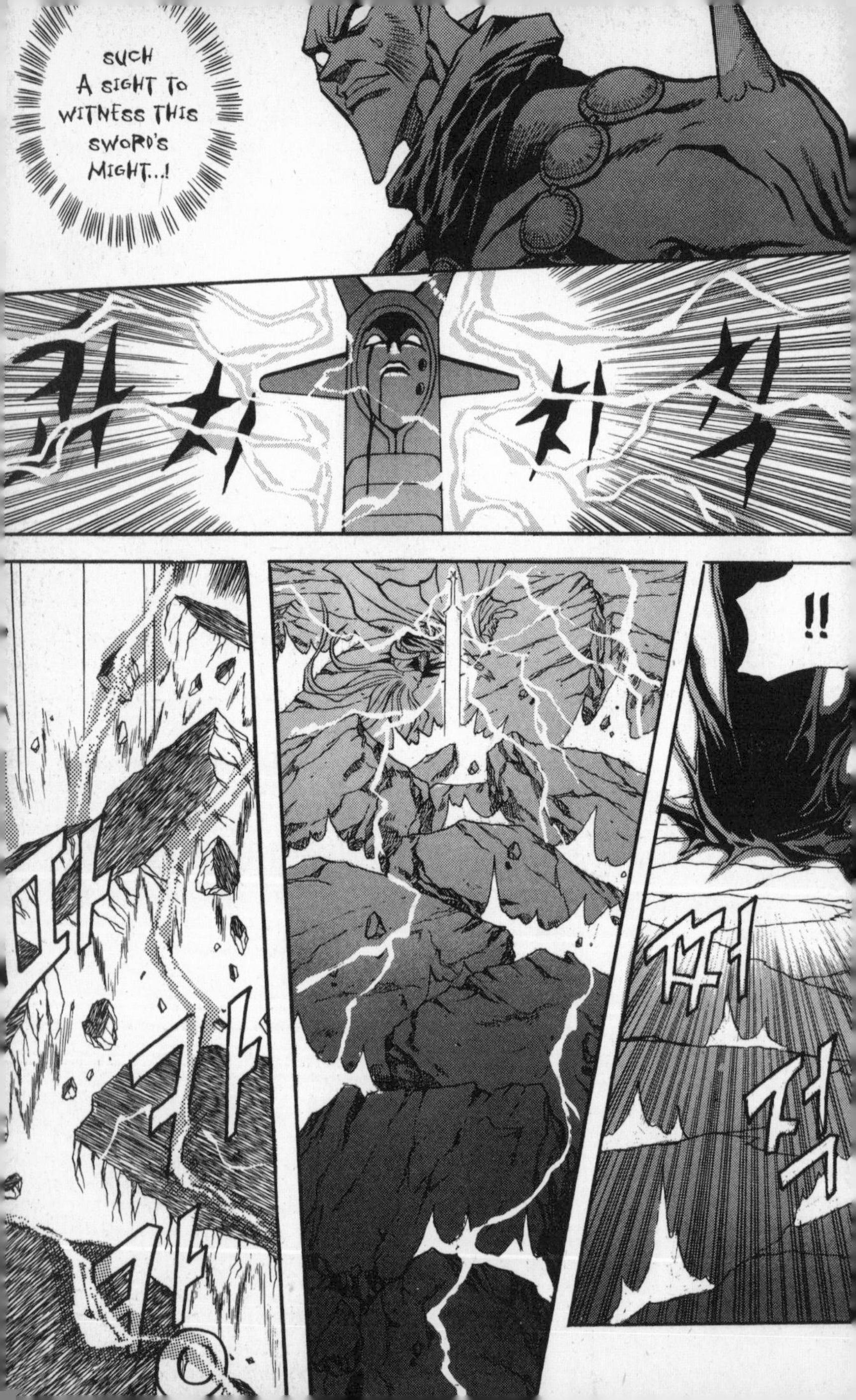
SUCH A SIGHT TO WITNESS THIS SWORD'S MIGHT...!
!!

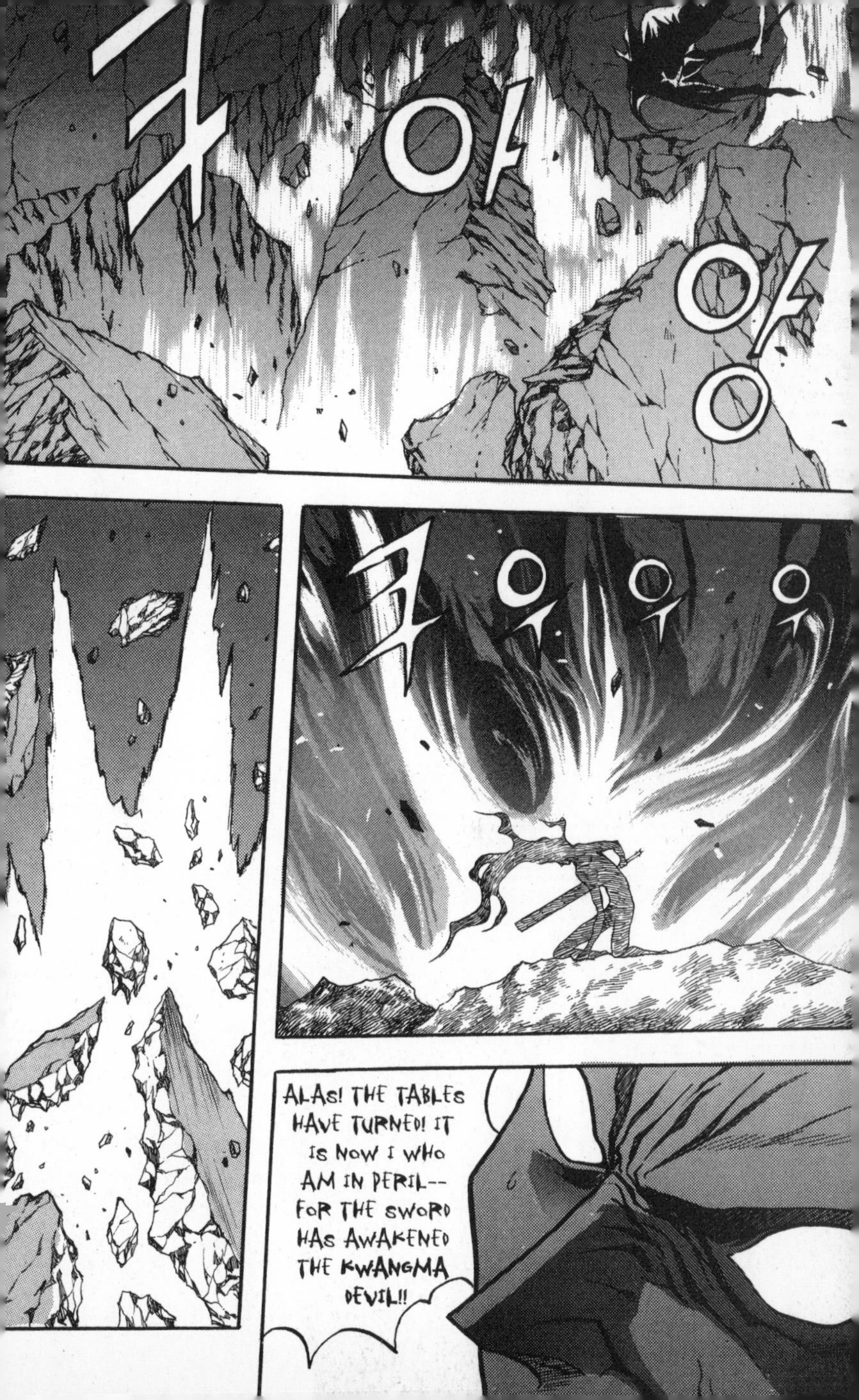
ALAS! THE TABLES HAVE TURNED! IT IS NOW I WHO AM IN PERIL-- FOR THE SWORD HAS AWAKENED THE KWANGMA DEVIL!!

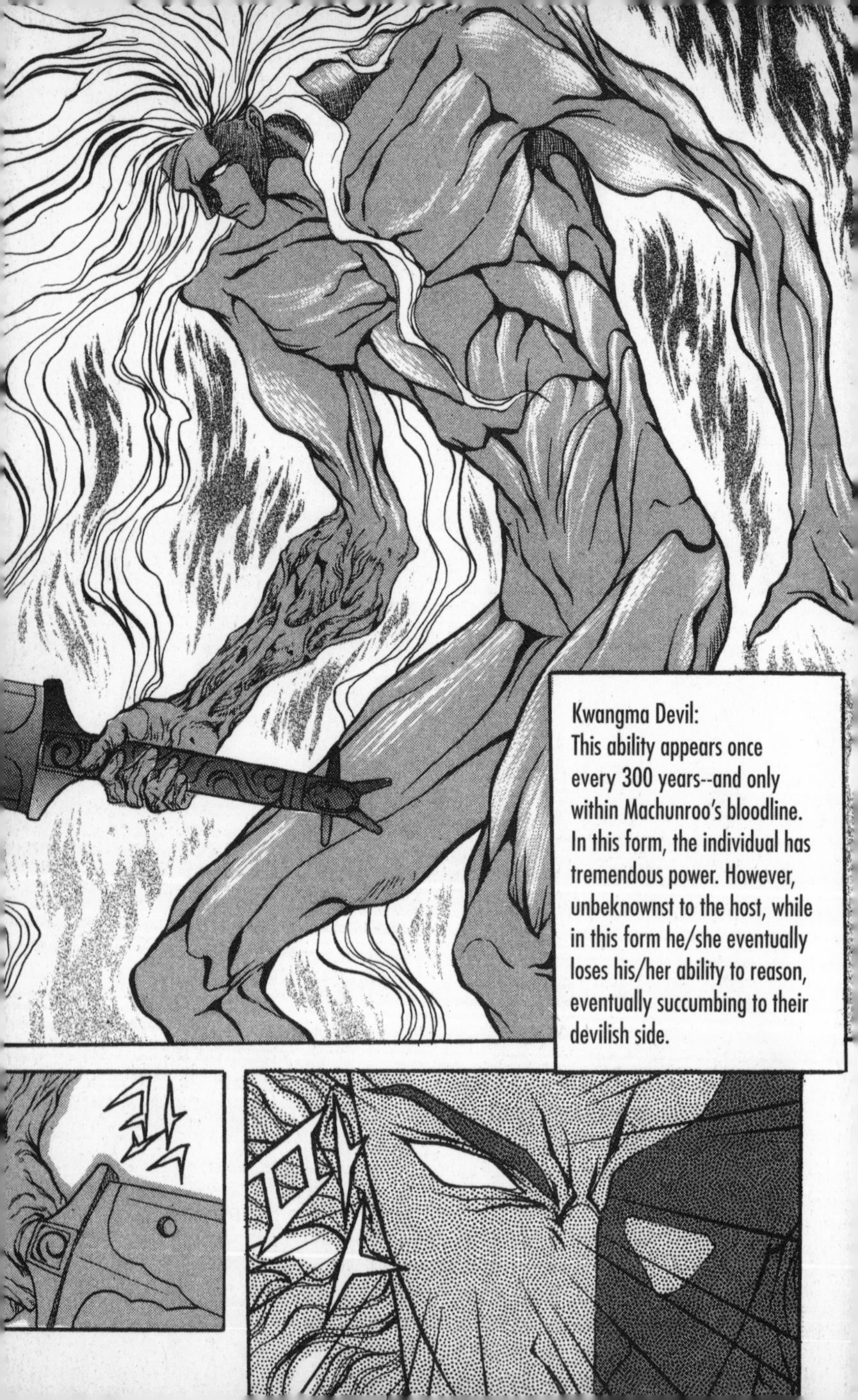
Kwangma Devil:
This ability appears once every 300 years--and only within Machunroo's bloodline. In this form, the individual has tremendous power. However, unbeknownst to the host, while in this form he/she eventually loses his/her ability to reason, eventually succumbing to their devilish side.

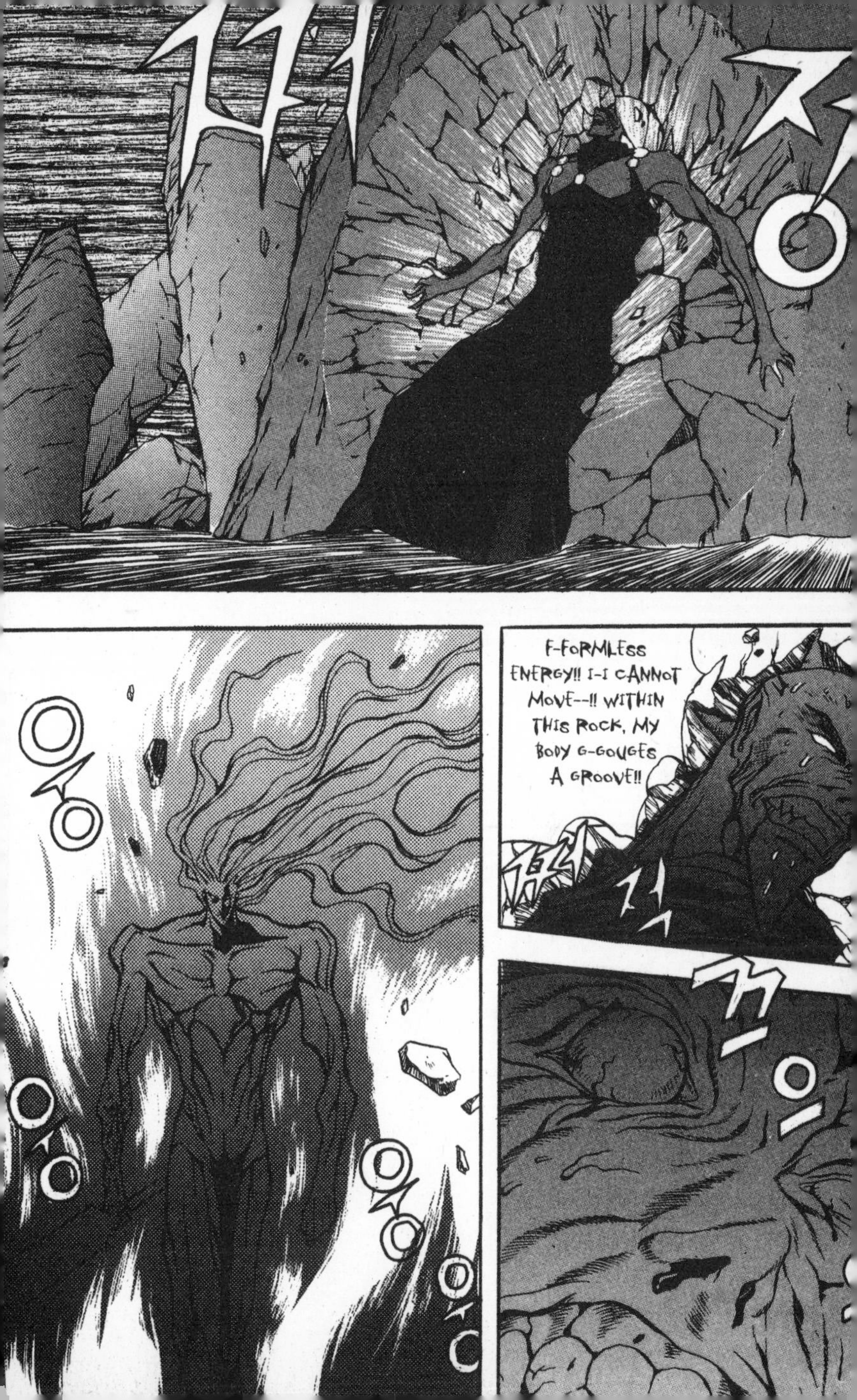
F-FORMLESS ENERGY!! I-I CANNOT MOVE--!! WITHIN THIS ROCK, MY BODY G-GOUGES A GROOVE!!

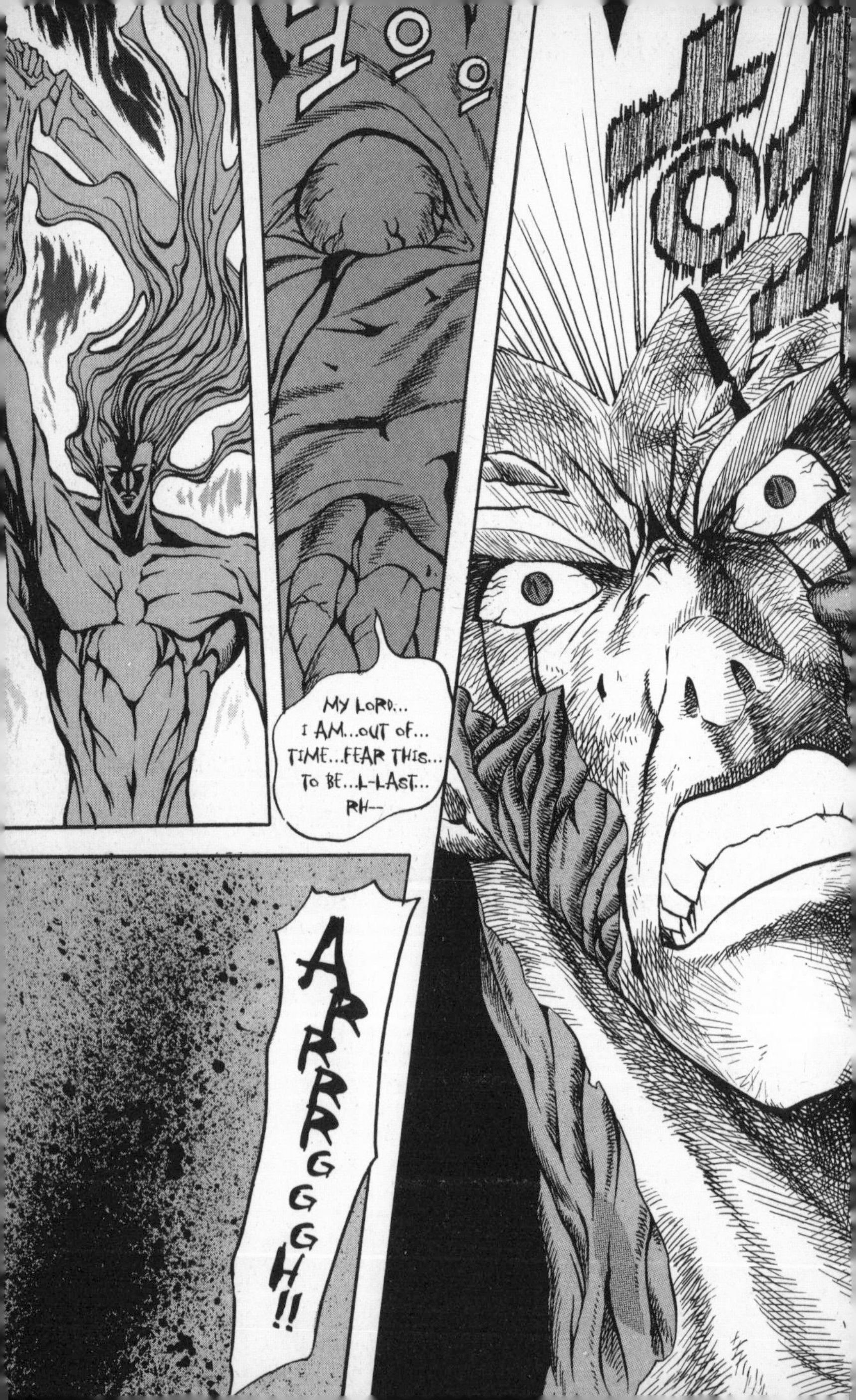
MY LORD... I AM...OUT OF... TIME...FEAR THIS... TO BE...L-LAST... RH--
ARRRRGGGH!!

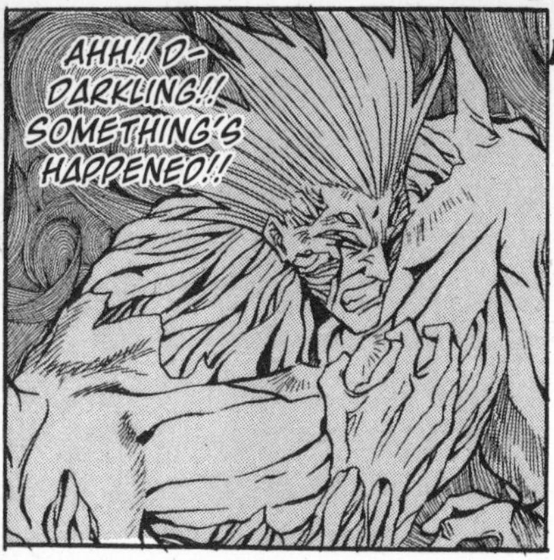
AHH!! D-DARKLING!! SOMETHING'S HAPPENED!!
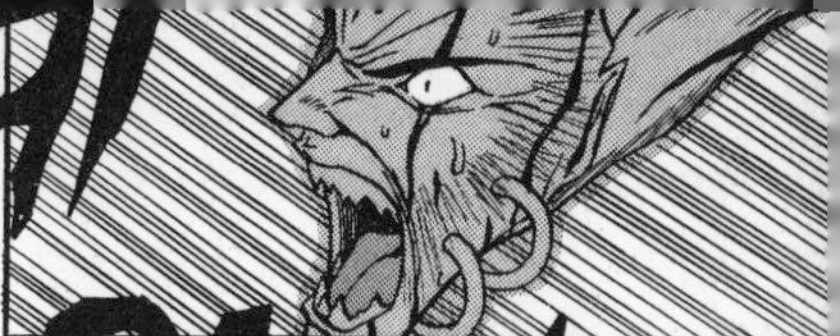
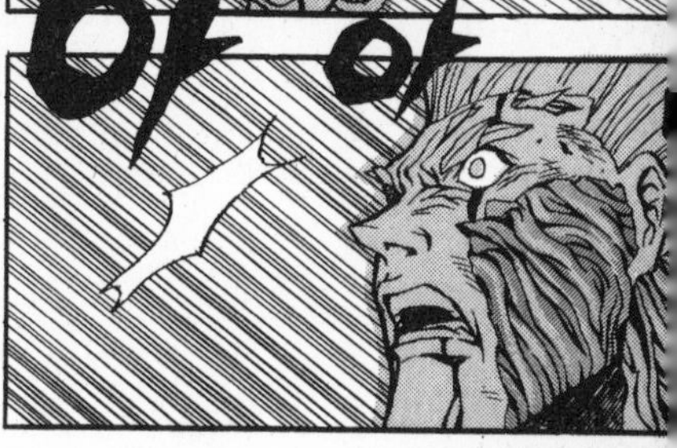
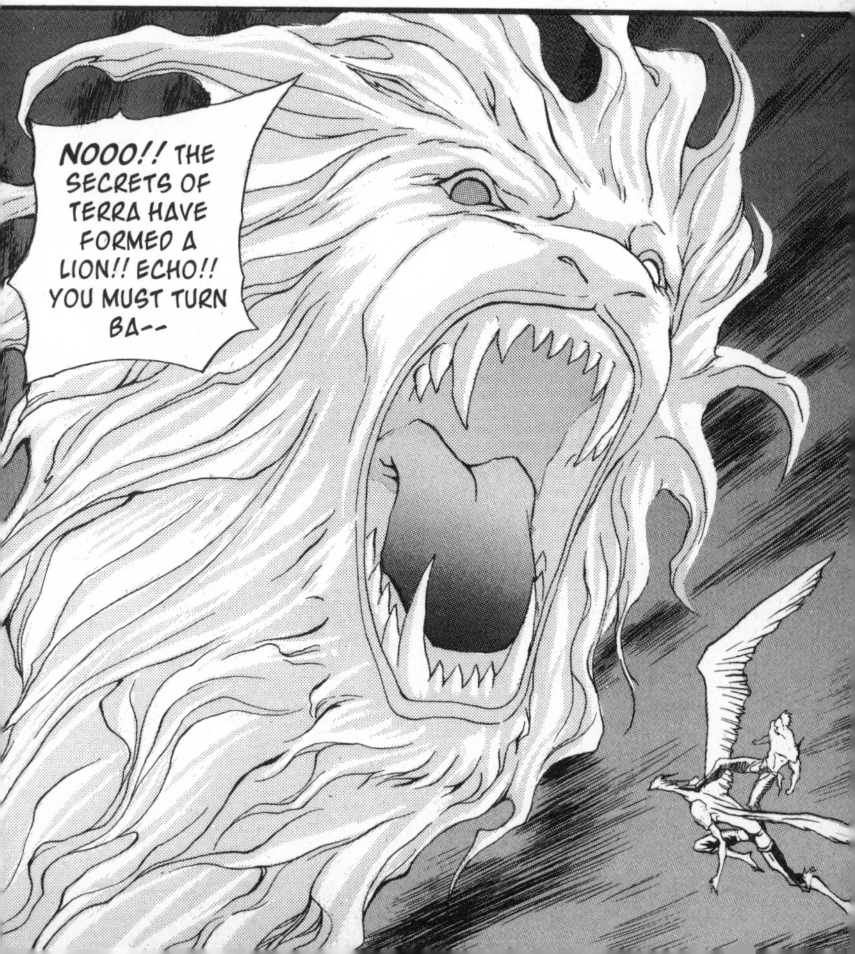
NOOO!! THE SECRETS OF TERRA HAVE FORMED A LION!! ECHO!! YOU MUST TURN BA--

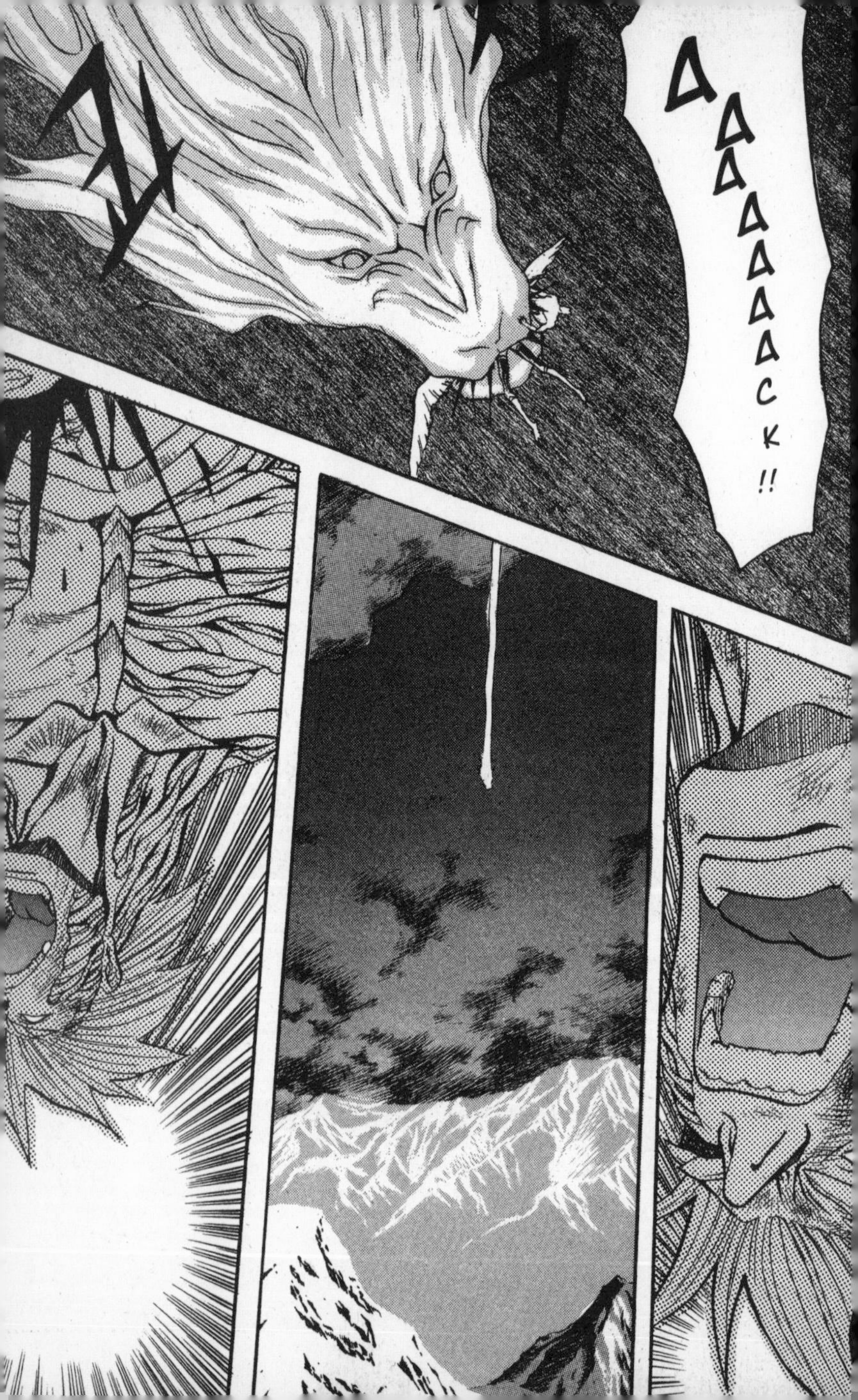
AAAAAAAACK!!

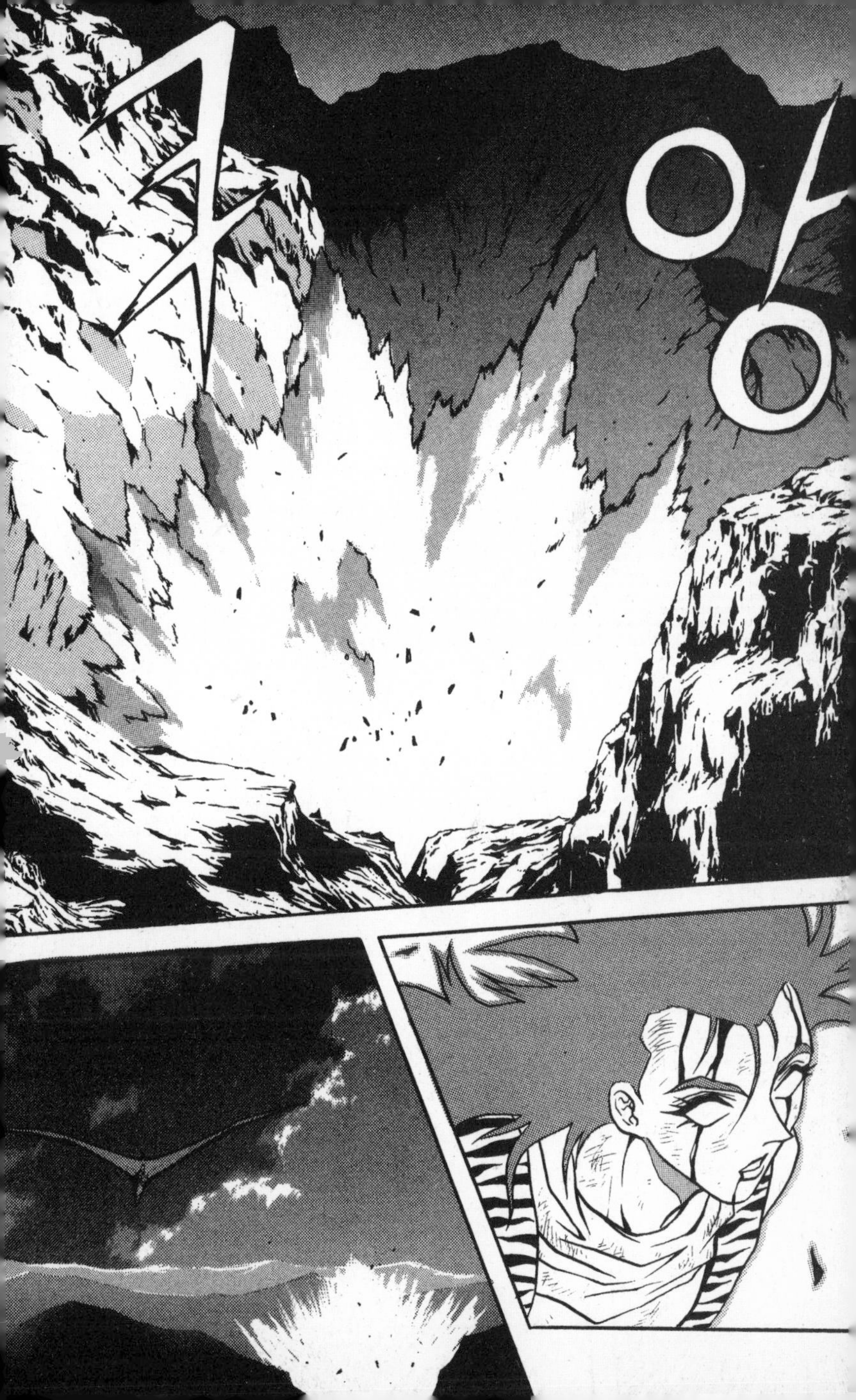

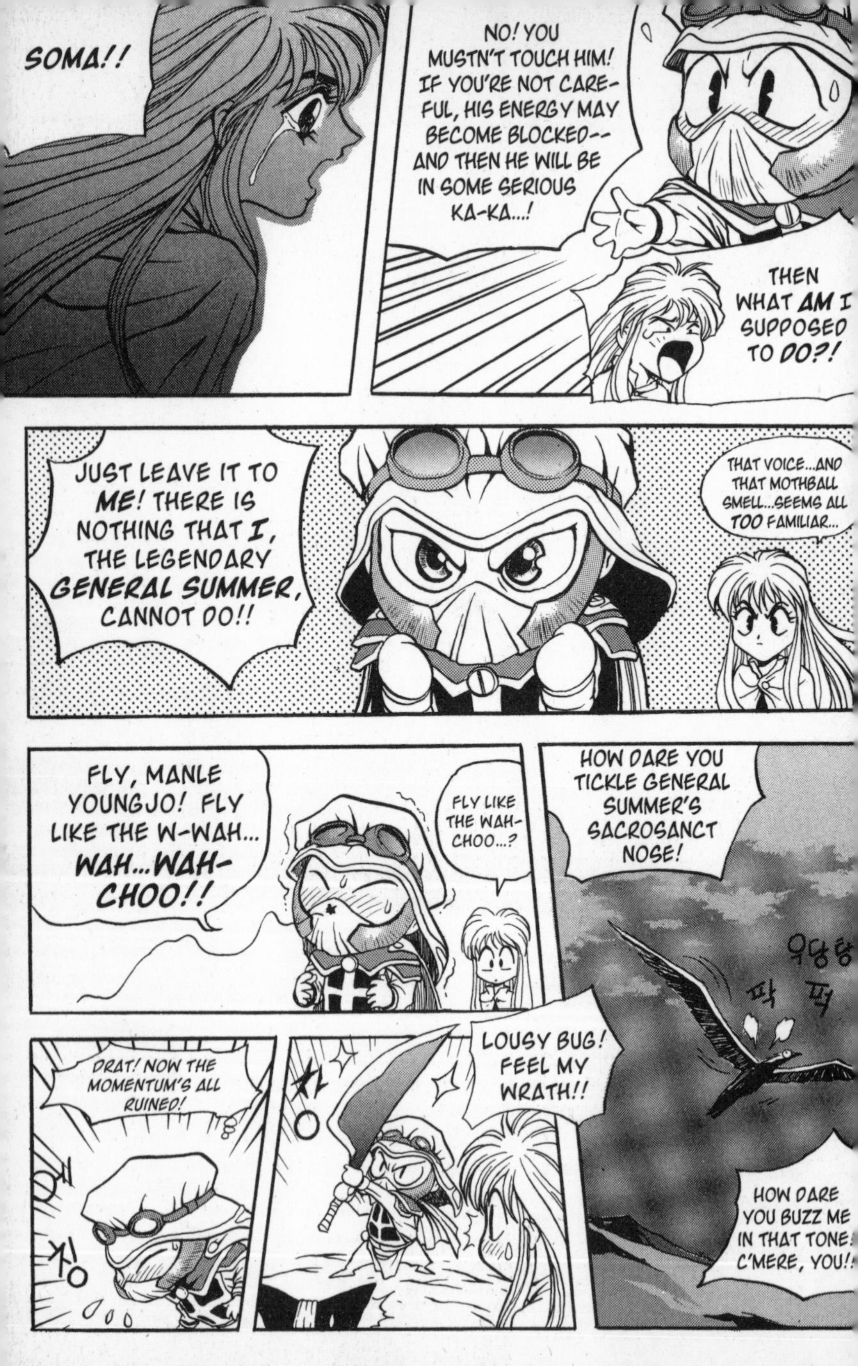
SOMA!!
NO! YOU MUSTN'T TOUCH HIM! IF YOU'RE NOT CARE-FUL, HIS ENERGY MAY BECOME BLOCKED-- AND THEN HE WILL BE IN SOME SERIOUS KA-KA...!
THEN WHAT AM I SUPPOSED TO DO?!
JUST LEAVE IT TO ME! THERE IS NOTHING THAT I, THE LEGENDARY GENERAL SUMMER, CANNOT DO!!
THAT VOICE...AND THAT MOTHBALL SMELL...SEEMS ALL TOO FAMILIAR...
FLY, MANLE YOUNGJO! FLY LIKE THE W-WAH... WAH...WAH-CHOO!!
FLY LIKE THE WAH-CHOO...?
HOW DARE YOU TICKLE GENERAL SUMMER'S SACROSANCT NOSE!
우당탕
팍 팍
DRAT! NOW THE MOMENTUM'S ALL RUINED!
LOUSY BUG! FEEL MY WRATH!!
HOW DARE YOU BUZZ ME IN THAT TONE! C'MERE, YOU!!

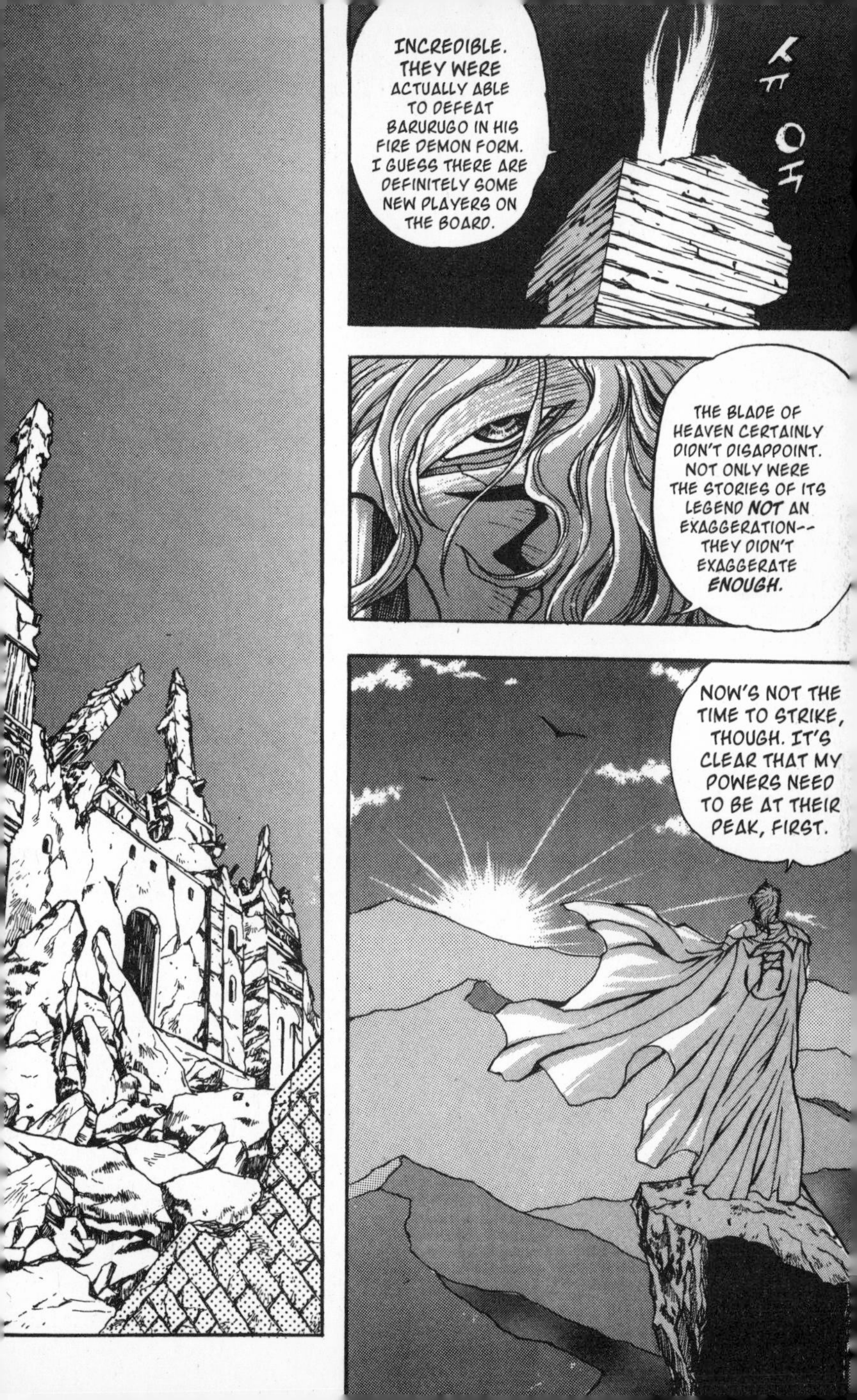
INCREDIBLE. THEY WERE ACTUALLY ABLE TO DEFEAT BARURUGO IN HIS FIRE DEMON FORM. I GUESS THERE ARE DEFINITELY SOME NEW PLAYERS ON THE BOARD.
THE BLADE OF HEAVEN CERTAINLY DIDN'T DISAPPOINT. NOT ONLY WERE THE STORIES OF ITS LEGEND NOT AN EXAGGERATION-- THEY DIDN'T EXAGGERATE ENOUGH.
NOW'S NOT THE TIME TO STRIKE, THOUGH. IT'S CLEAR THAT MY POWERS NEED TO BE AT THEIR PEAK, FIRST.

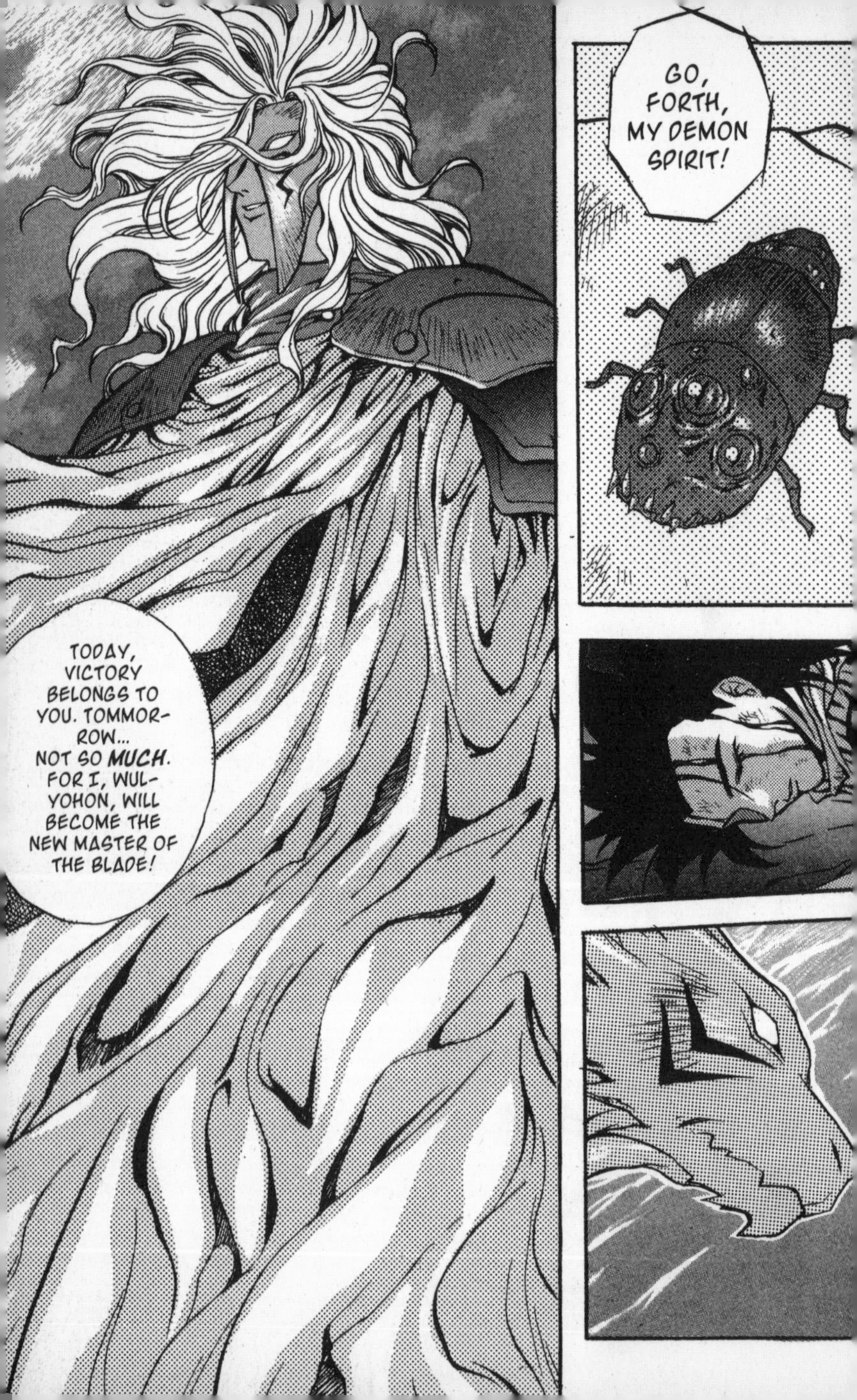
GO, FORTH, MY DEMON SPIRIT!
TODAY, VICTORY BELONGS TO YOU. TOMMOR-ROW... NOT SO *MUCH*. FOR I, WUL-YOHON, WILL BECOME THE NEW MASTER OF THE BLADE!

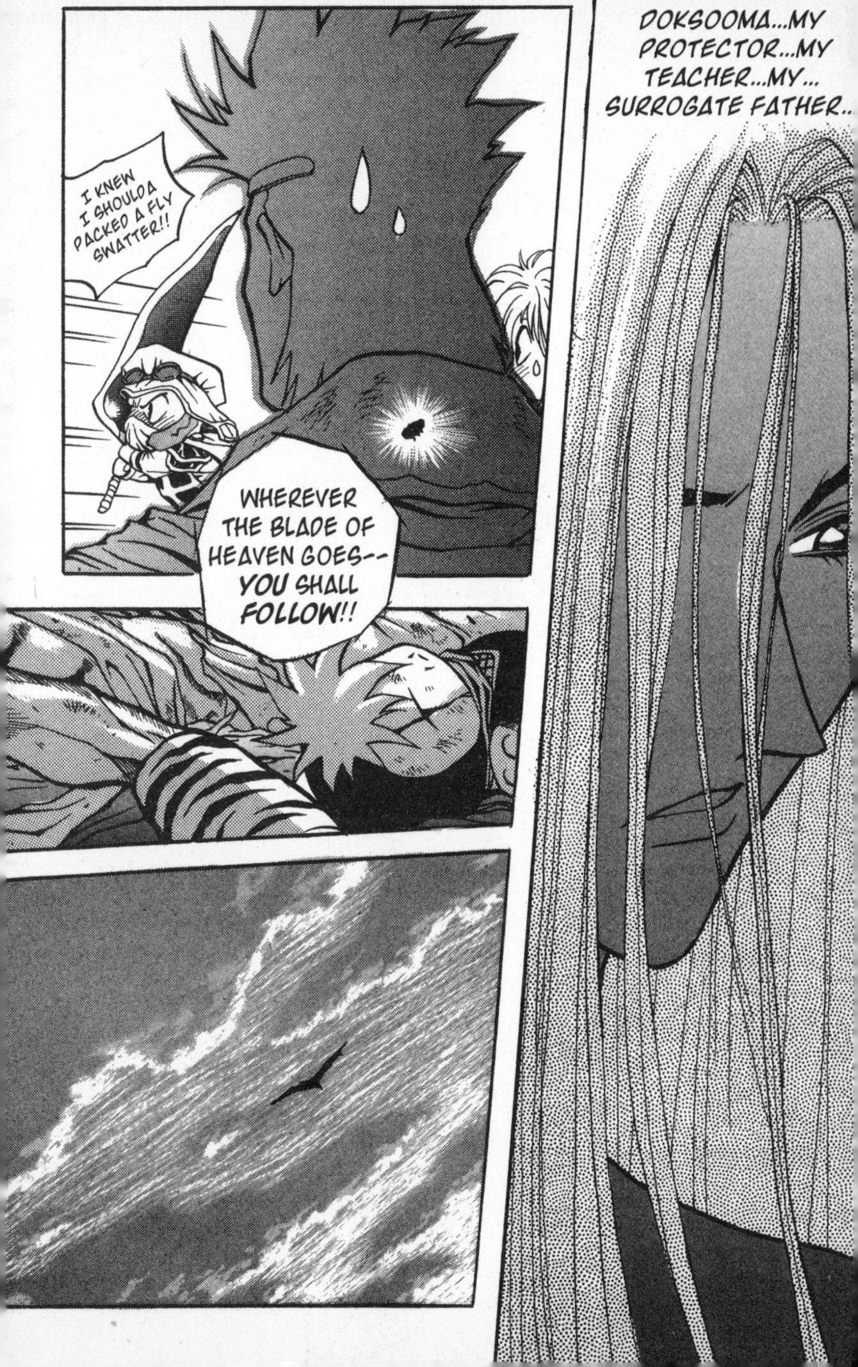
DOKSOOMA...MY PROTECTOR...MY TEACHER...MY... SURROGATE FATHER...
I KNEW I SHOULDA PACKED A FLY SWATTER!!
WHEREVER THE BLADE OF HEAVEN GOES-- YOU SHALL FOLLOW!!

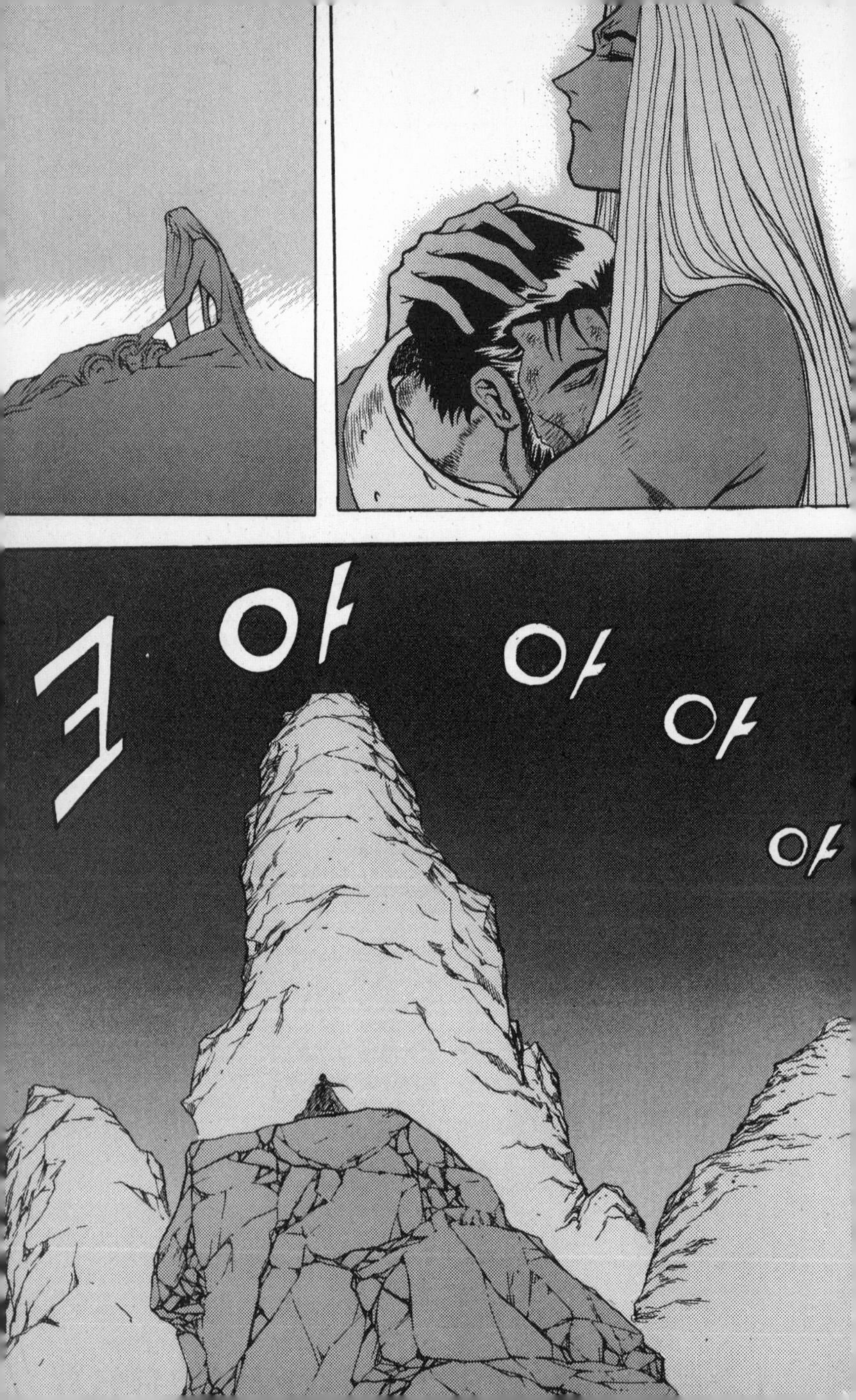
크아아아아

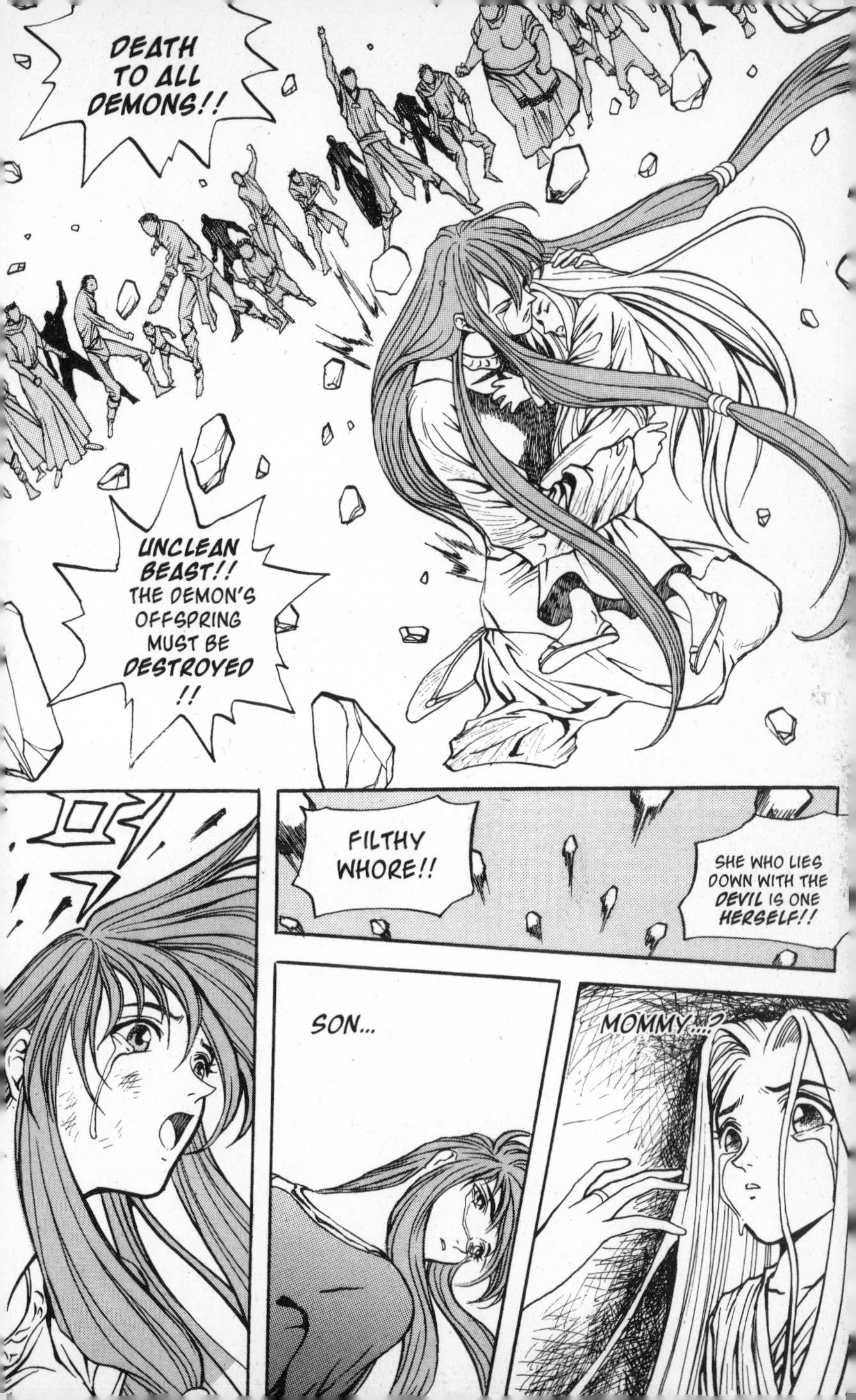
DEATH TO ALL DEMONS!!
UNCLEAN BEAST!! THE DEMON'S OFFSPRING MUST BE DESTROYED!!
SHE WHO LIES DOWN WITH THE DEVIL IS ONE HERSELF!!
FILTHY WHORE!!
MOMMY...?
SON...

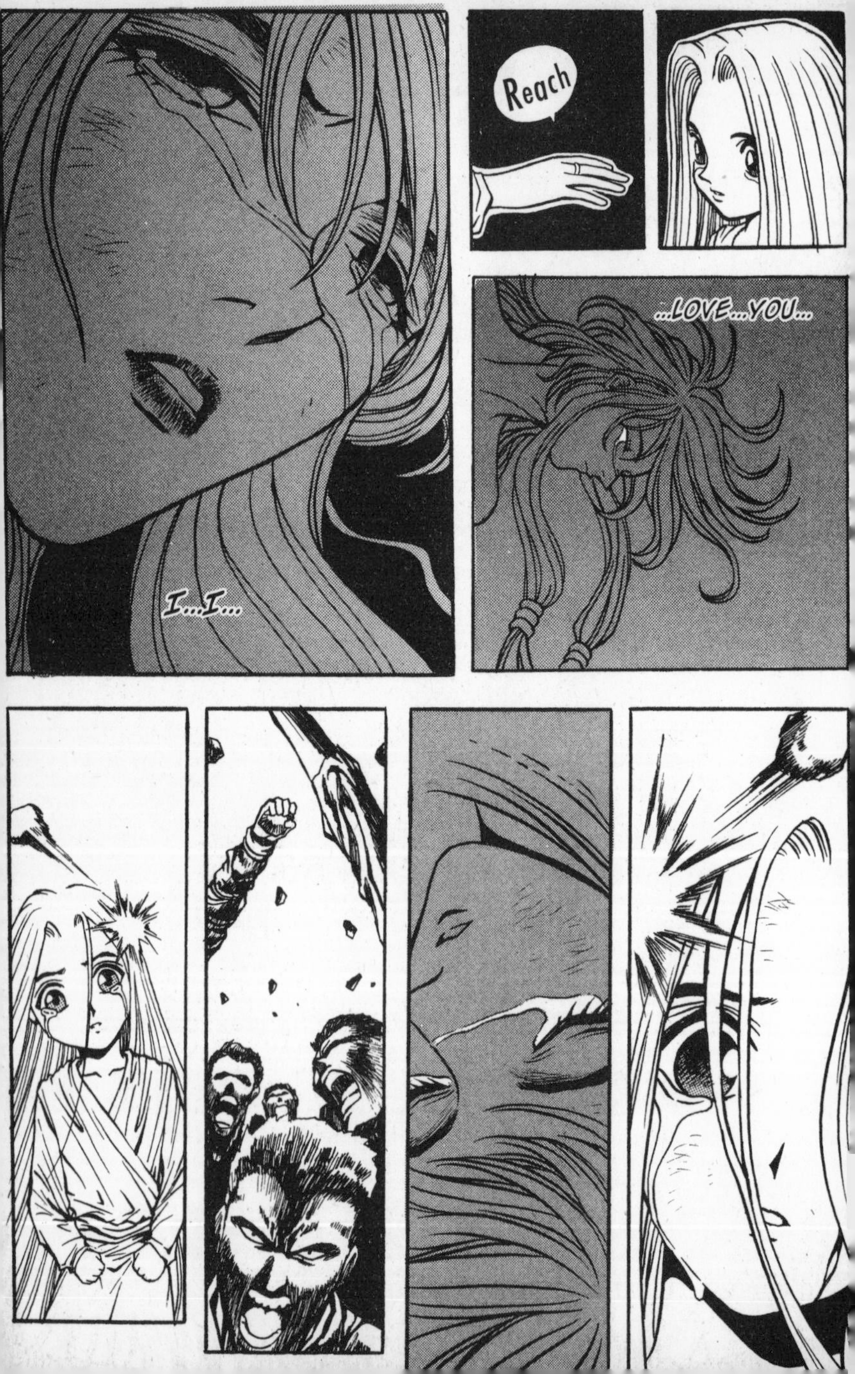
I...I...
Reach
...LOVE...YOU...

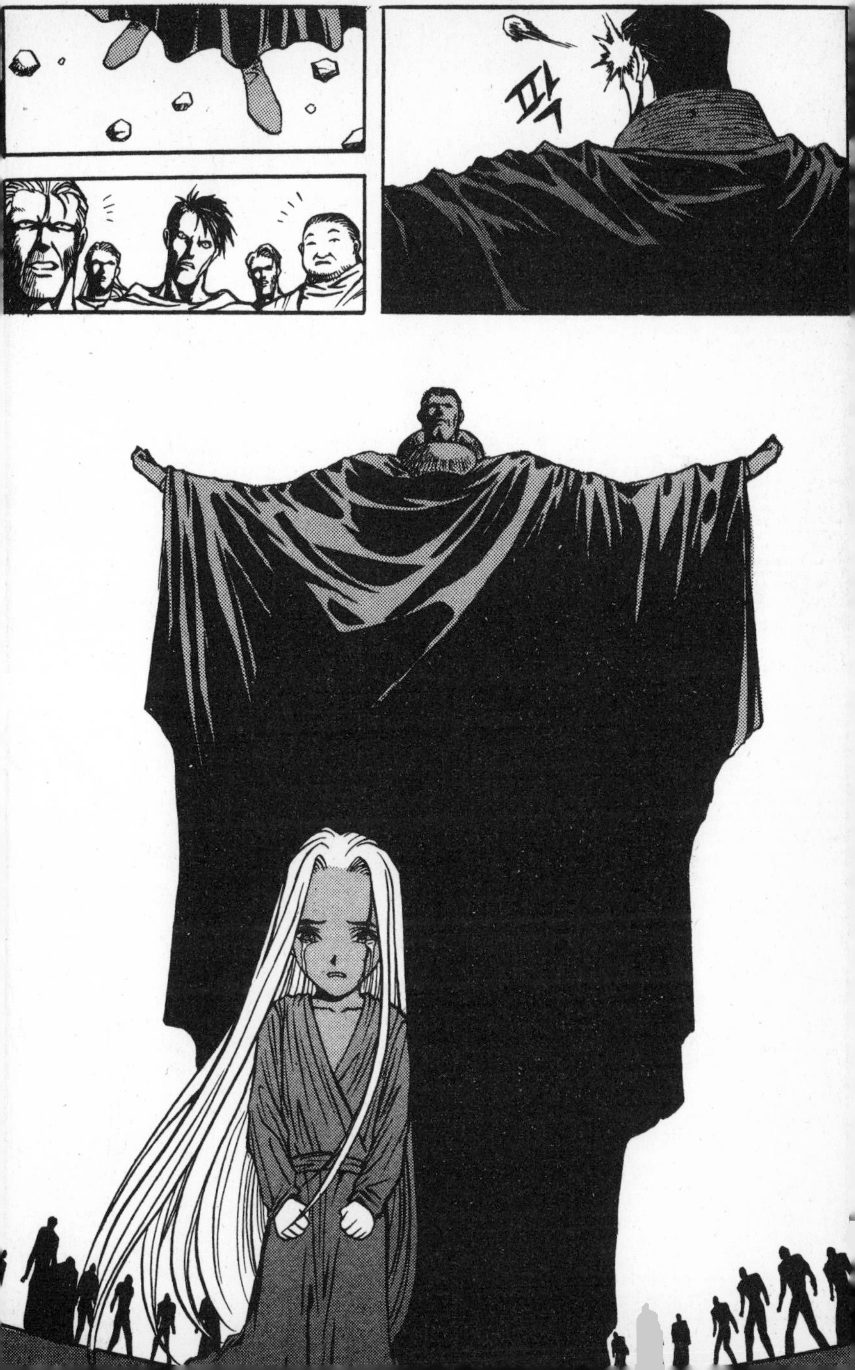
팍

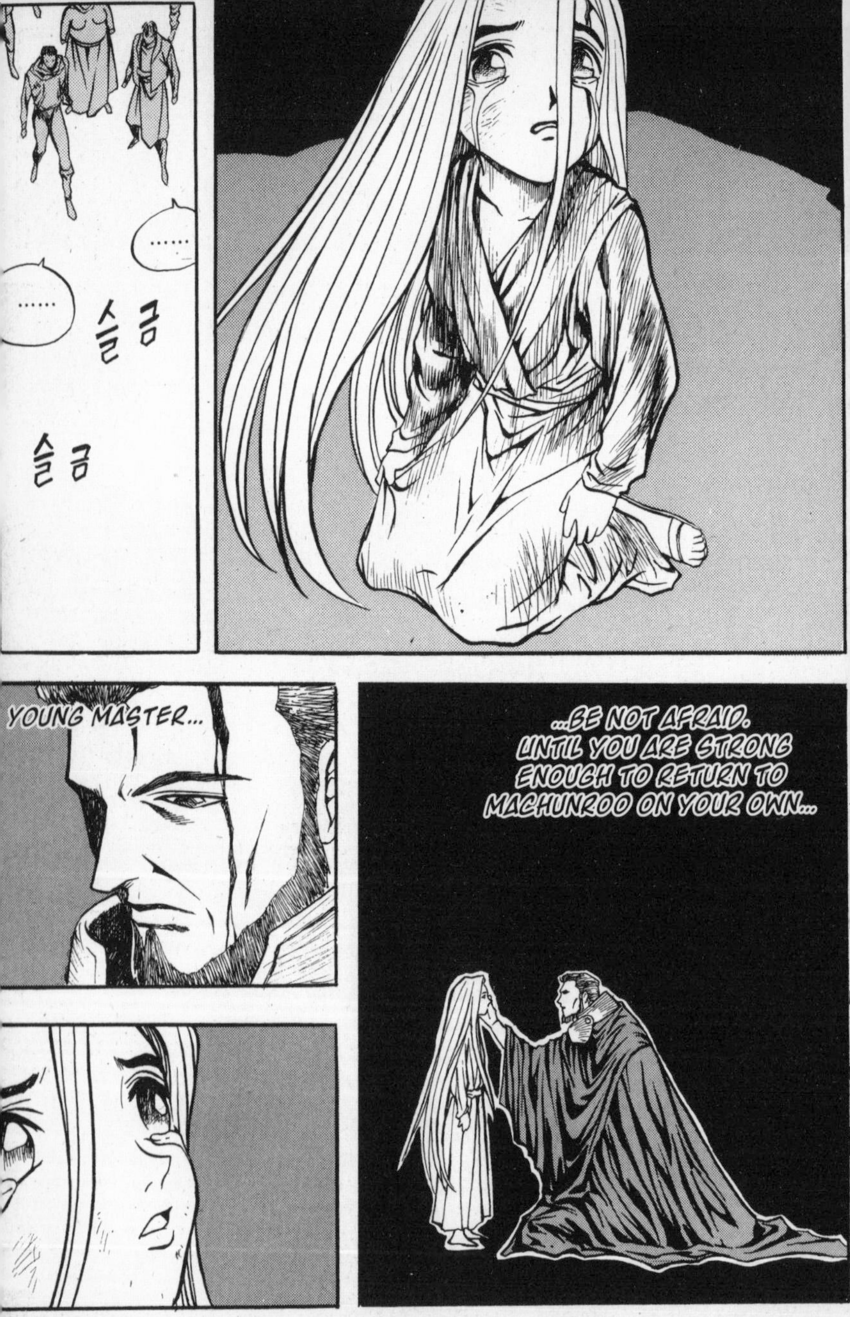
......
......
슬금
슬금
YOUNG MASTER...
...BE NOT AFRAID. UNTIL YOU ARE STRONG ENOUGH TO RETURN TO MACHUNROO ON YOUR OWN...

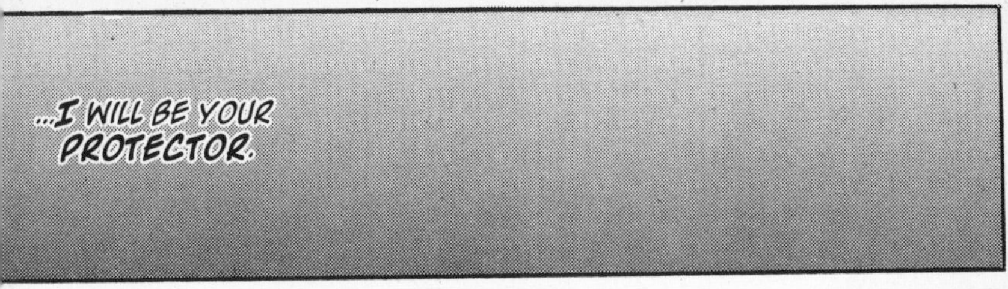
...I WILL BE YOUR PROTECTOR.
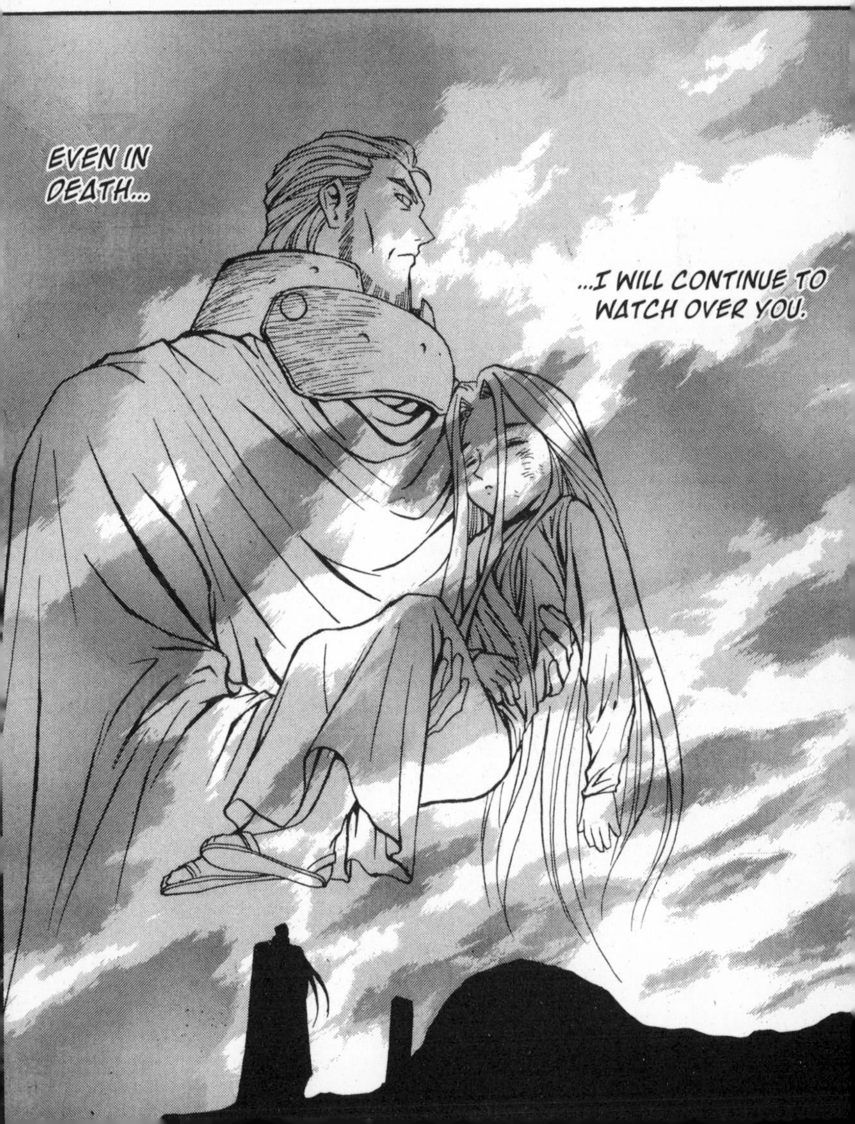
EVEN IN DEATH...
...I WILL CONTINUE TO WATCH OVER YOU.

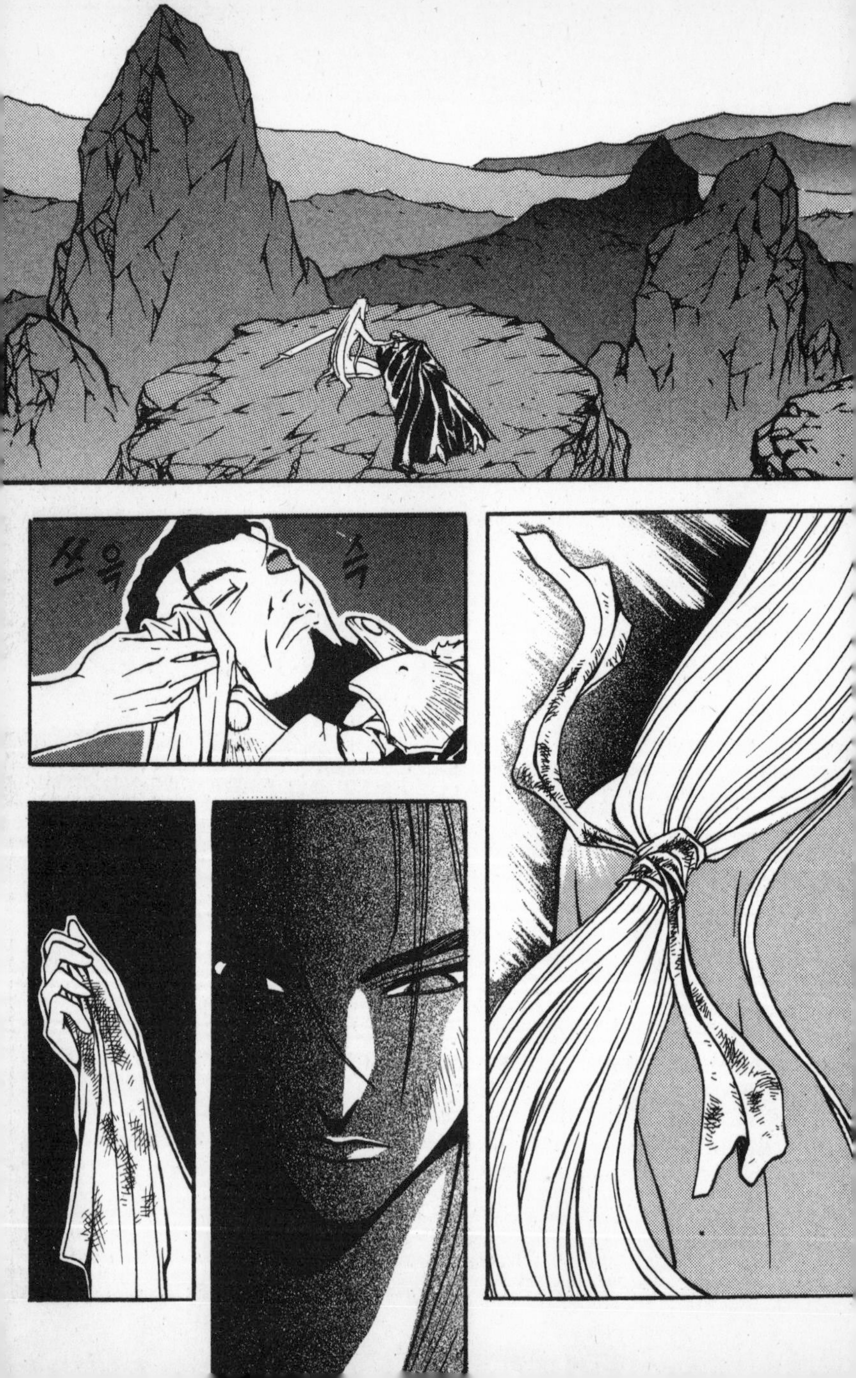
슥
쓰윽

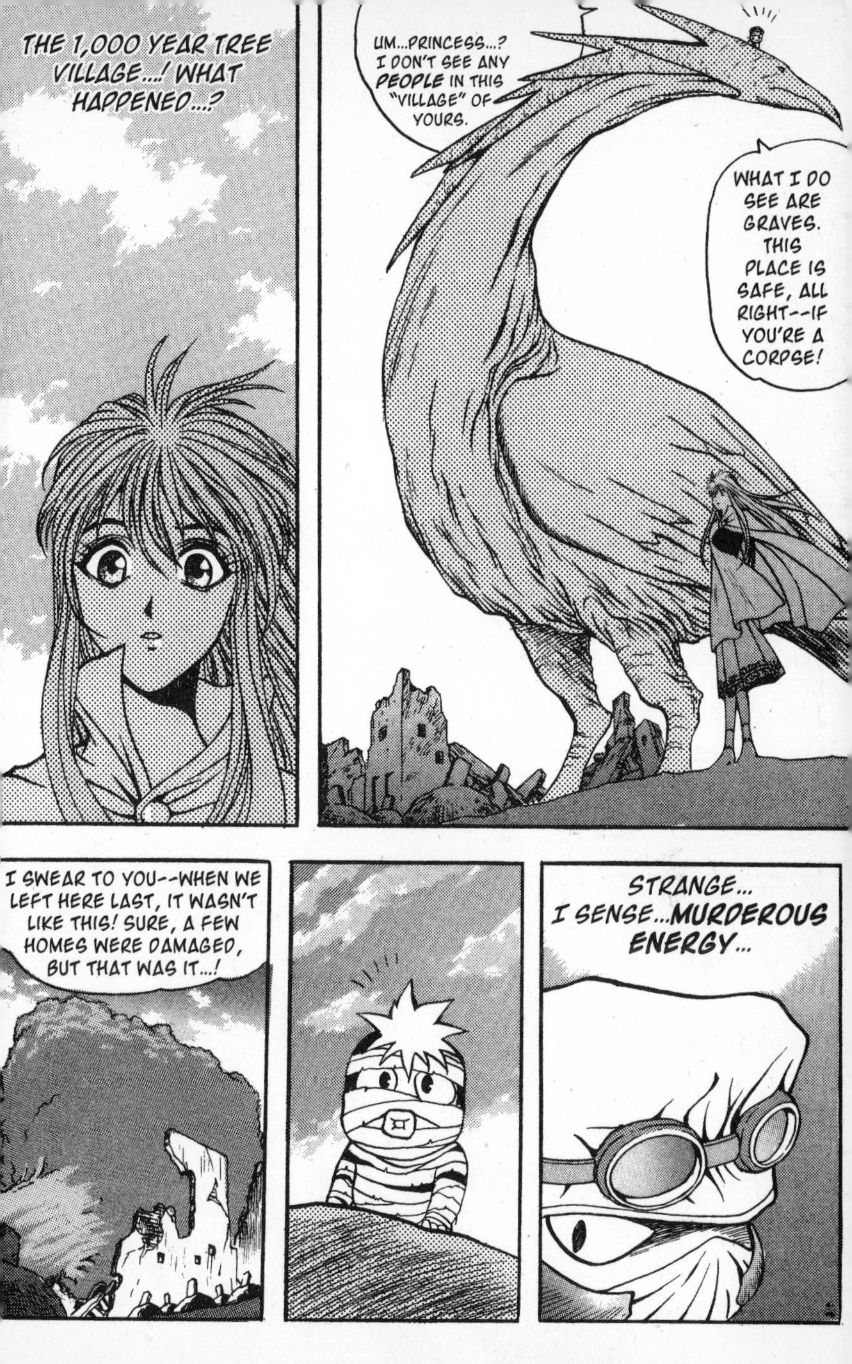
THE 1,000 YEAR TREE VILLAGE...! WHAT HAPPENED...?
UM...PRINCESS...? I DON'T SEE ANY PEOPLE IN THIS "VILLAGE" OF YOURS.
WHAT I DO SEE ARE GRAVES. THIS PLACE IS SAFE, ALL RIGHT--IF YOU'RE A CORPSE!
I SWEAR TO YOU--WHEN WE LEFT HERE LAST, IT WASN'T LIKE THIS! SURE, A FEW HOMES WERE DAMAGED, BUT THAT WAS IT...!
STRANGE... I SENSE...MURDEROUS ENERGY...

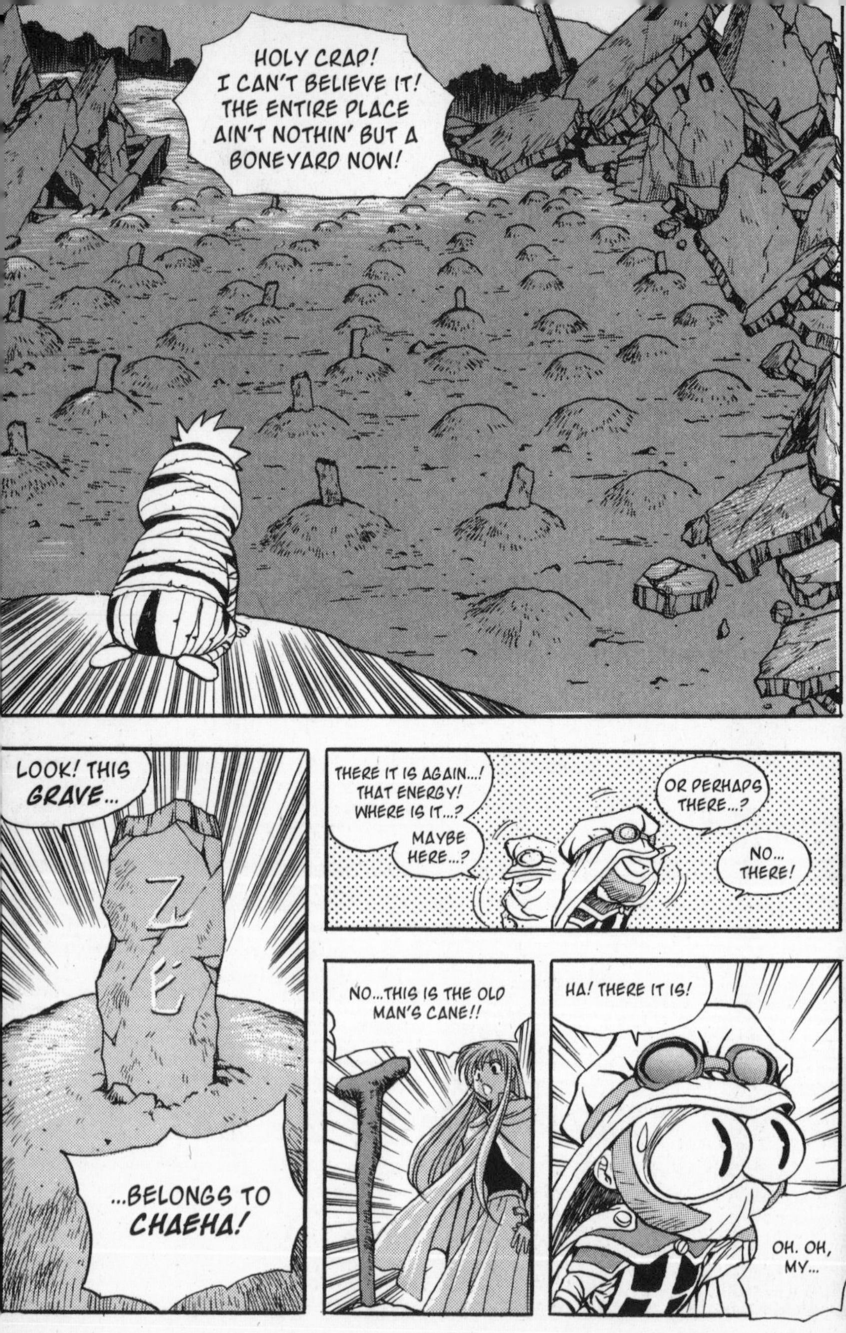
HOLY CRAP! I CAN'T BELIEVE IT! THE ENTIRE PLACE AIN'T NOTHIN' BUT A BONEYARD NOW!
LOOK! THIS GRAVE...
...BELONGS TO CHAEHA!
THERE IT IS AGAIN...! THAT ENERGY! WHERE IS IT...?
MAYBE HERE...?
OR PERHAPS THERE...?
NO... THERE!
NO...THIS IS THE OLD MAN'S CANE!!
HA! THERE IT IS!
OH. OH, MY...

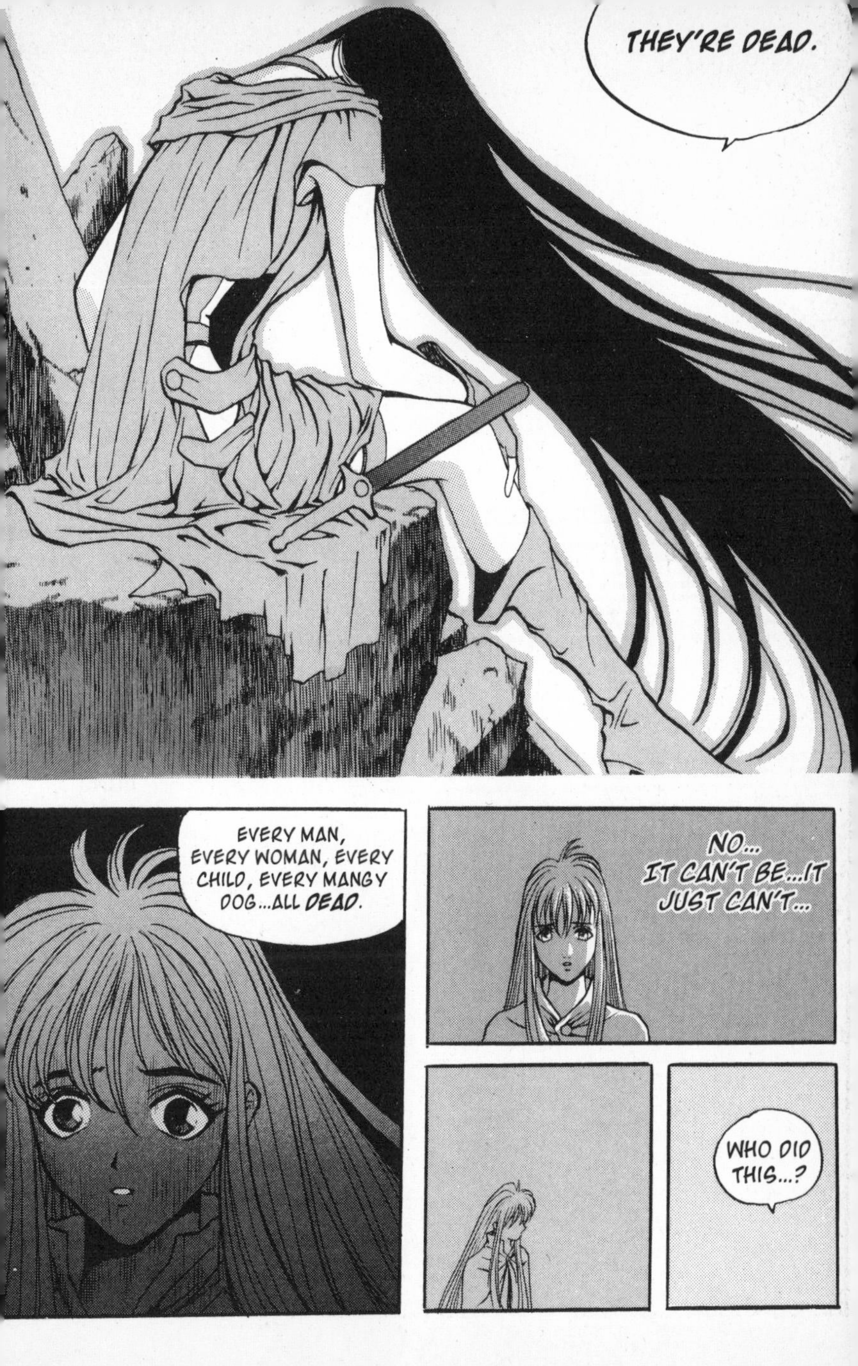
THEY'RE DEAD.
EVERY MAN, EVERY WOMAN, EVERY CHILD, EVERY MANGY DOG...ALL DEAD.
NO... IT CAN'T BE...IT JUST CAN'T...
WHO DID THIS...?

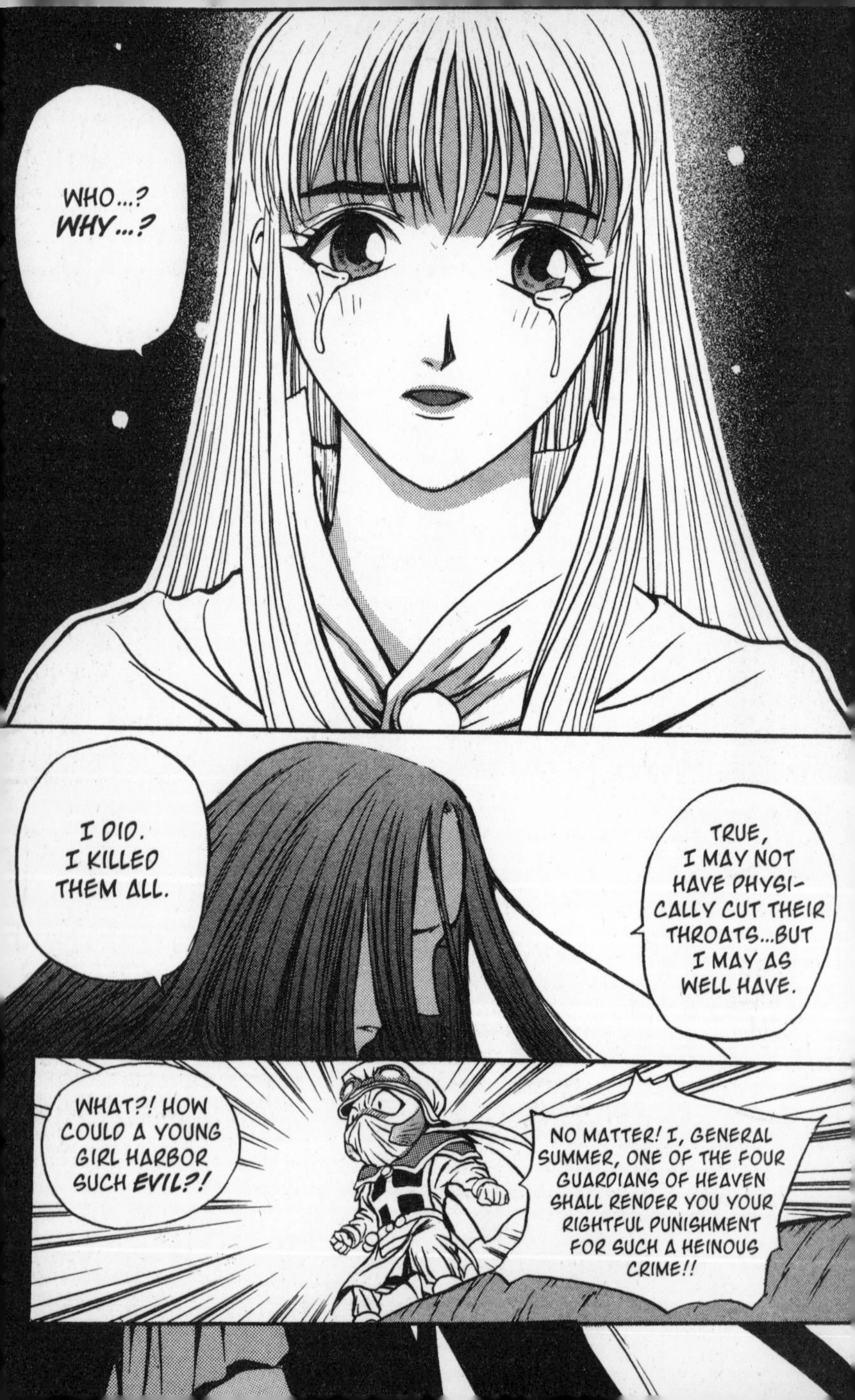
WHO...? WHY...?
I DID. I KILLED THEM ALL.
TRUE, I MAY NOT HAVE PHYSICALLY CUT THEIR THROATS...BUT I MAY AS WELL HAVE.
WHAT?! HOW COULD A YOUNG GIRL HARBOR SUCH EVIL?!
NO MATTER! I, GENERAL SUMMER, ONE OF THE FOUR GUARDIANS OF HEAVEN SHALL RENDER YOU YOUR RIGHTFUL PUNISHMENT FOR SUCH A HEINOUS CRIME!!

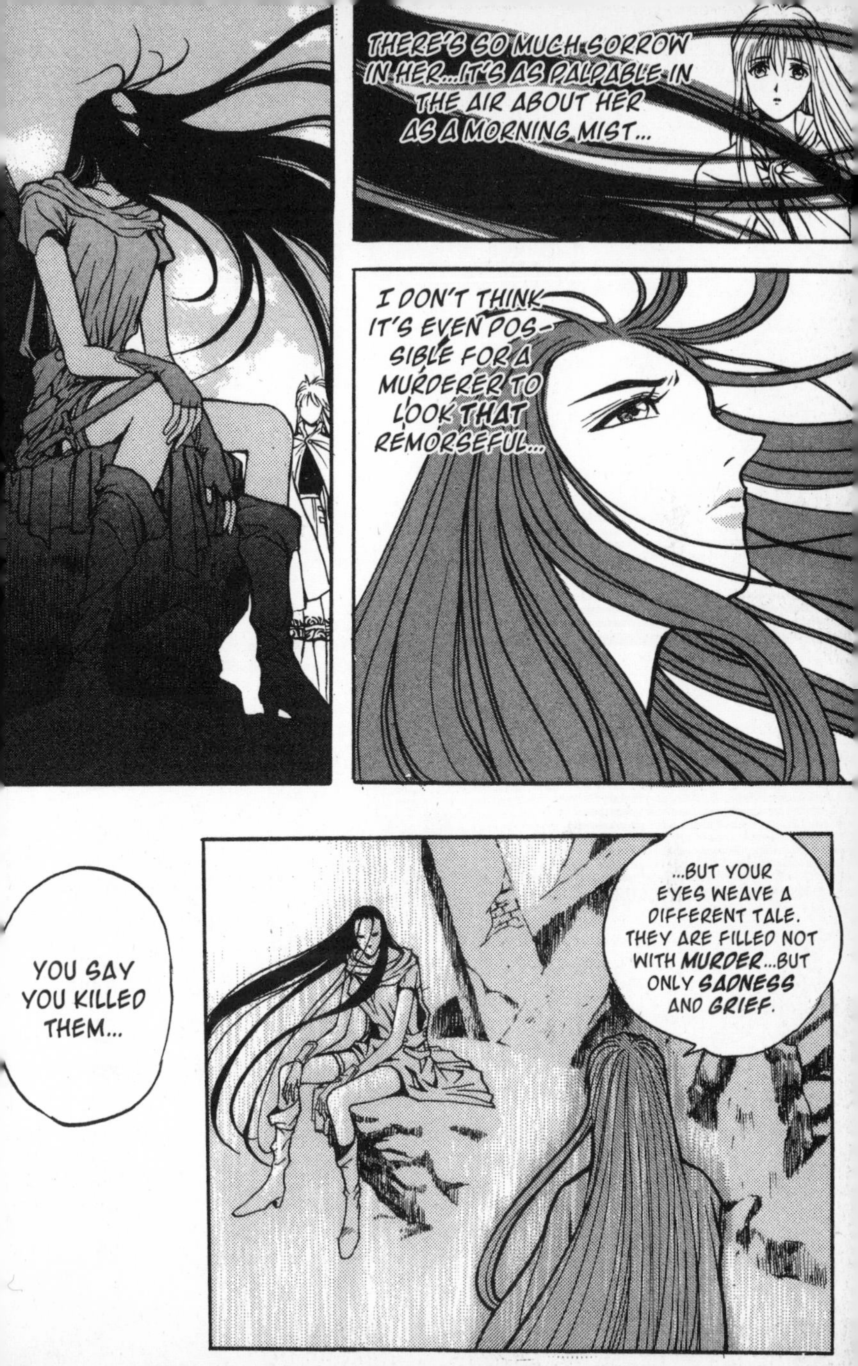
THERE'S SO MUCH SORROW IN HER...IT'S AS PALPABLE IN THE AIR ABOUT HER AS A MORNING MIST...
I DON'T THINK IT'S EVEN POS-SIBLE FOR A MURDERER TO LOOK THAT REMORSEFUL...
YOU SAY YOU KILLED THEM...
...BUT YOUR EYES WEAVE A DIFFERENT TALE. THEY ARE FILLED NOT WITH MURDER...BUT ONLY SADNESS AND GRIEF.

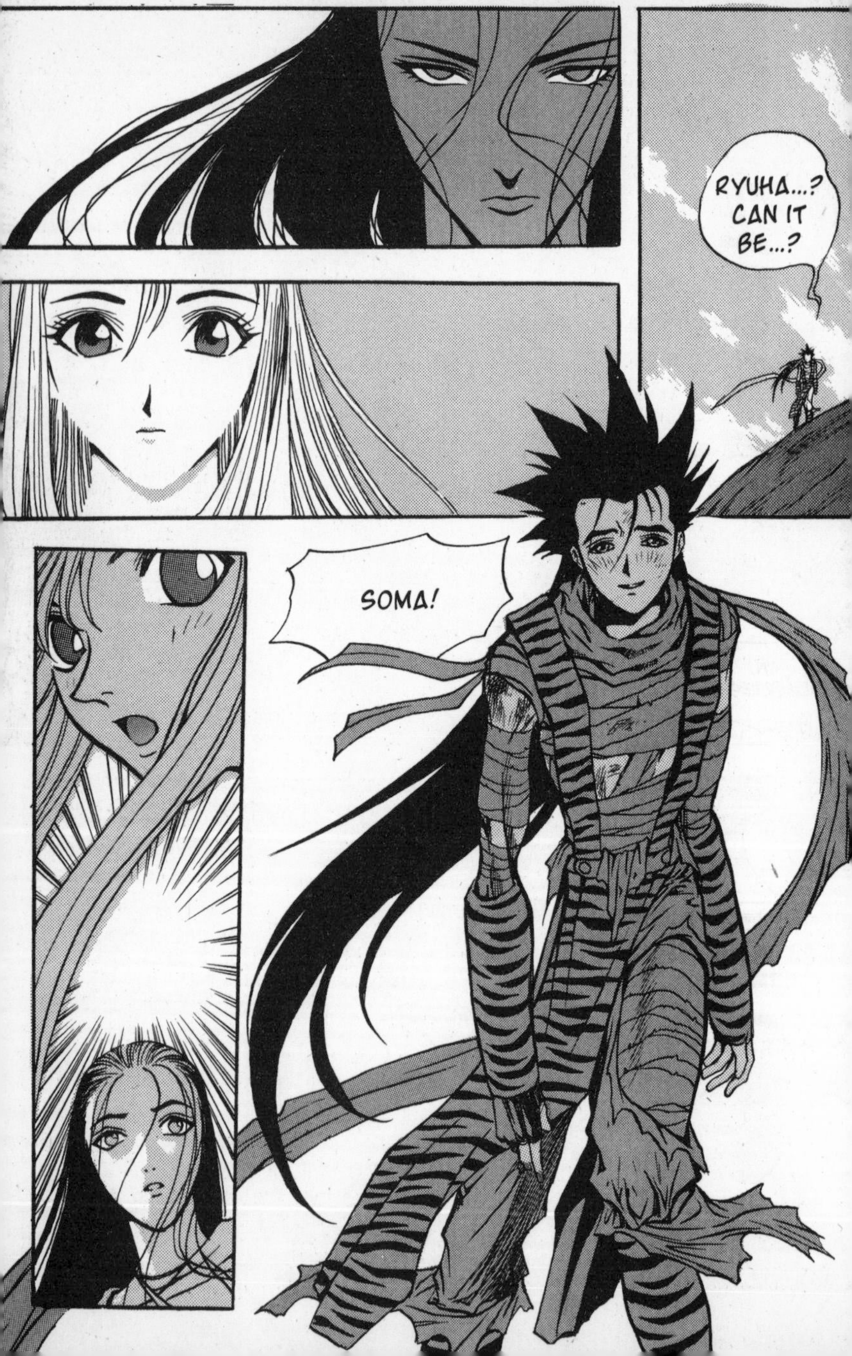
RYUHA...? CAN IT BE...?
SOMA!

RYUHA...
YOU'VE
FINALLY...
RETURNED...

SOMA!!

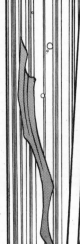

AW,
BLUEBERRIES--!!

?

DON'T YOU WORRY,
SOMA!! I'VE
GOT YOU!!

Grab

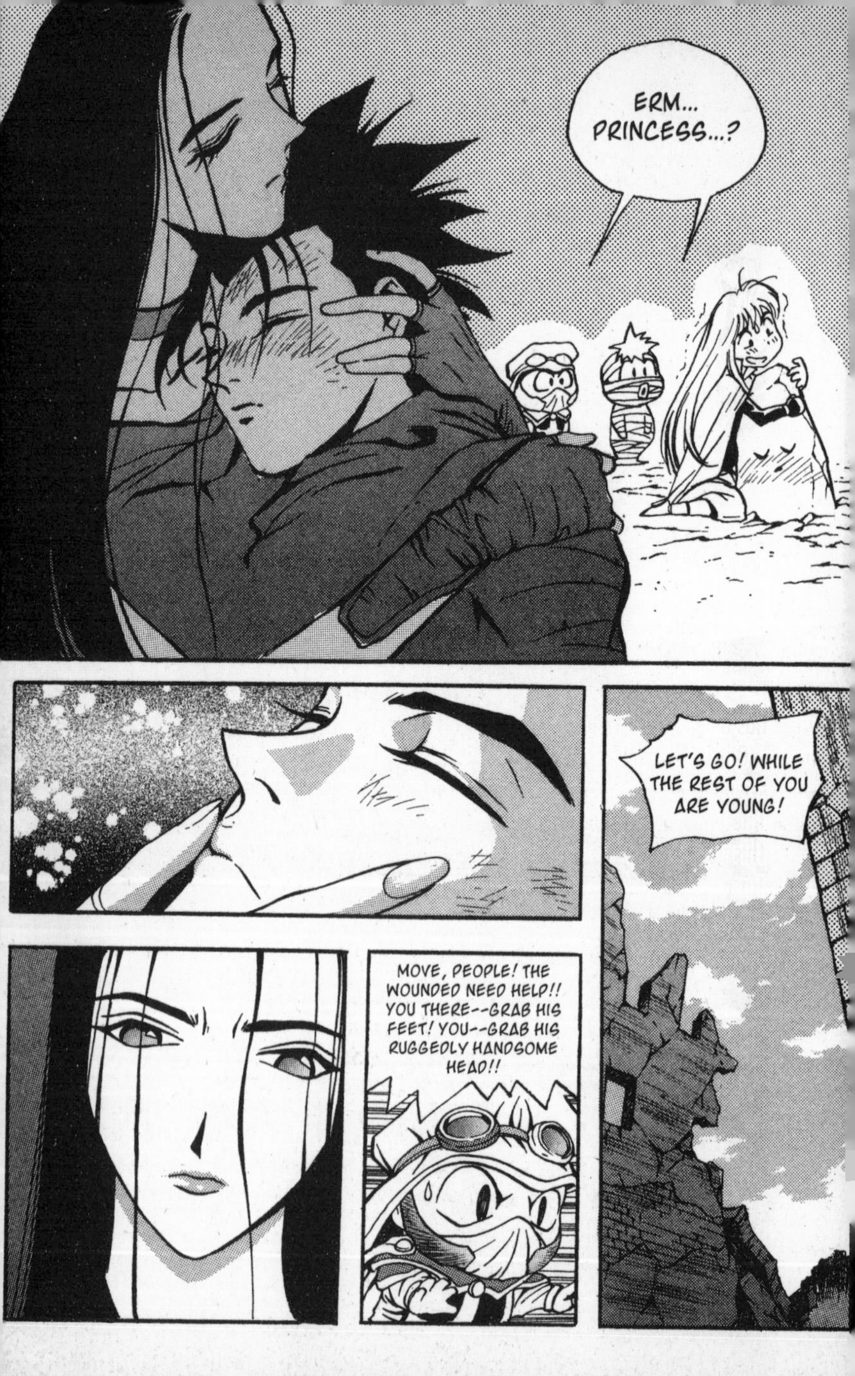
ERM... PRINCESS...?
LET'S GO! WHILE THE REST OF YOU ARE YOUNG!
MOVE, PEOPLE! THE WOUNDED NEED HELP!! YOU THERE--GRAB HIS FEET! YOU--GRAB HIS RUGGEDLY HANDSOME HEAD!!

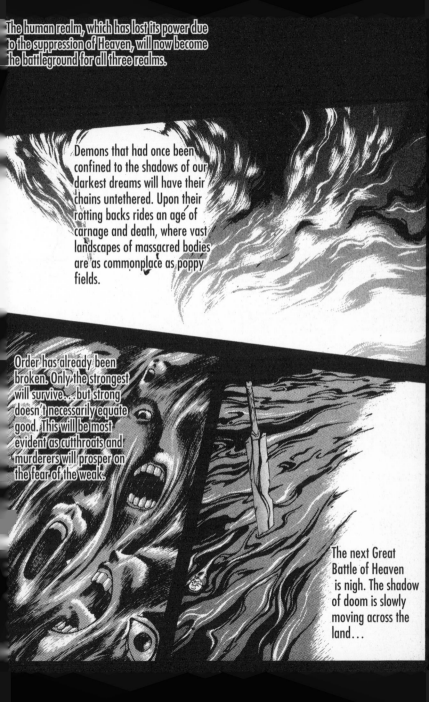

The human realm, which has lost its power due to the suppression of Heaven, will now become the battleground for all three realms.

Demons that had once been confined to the shadows of our darkest dreams will have their chains untethered. Upon their rotting backs rides an age of carnage and death, where vast landscapes of massacred bodies are as commonplace as poppy fields.

Order has already been broken. Only the strongest will survive... but strong doesn't necessarily equate good. This will be most evident as cutthroats and murderers will prosper on the fear of the weak.

The next Great Battle of Heaven is nigh. The shadow of doom is slowly moving across the land...

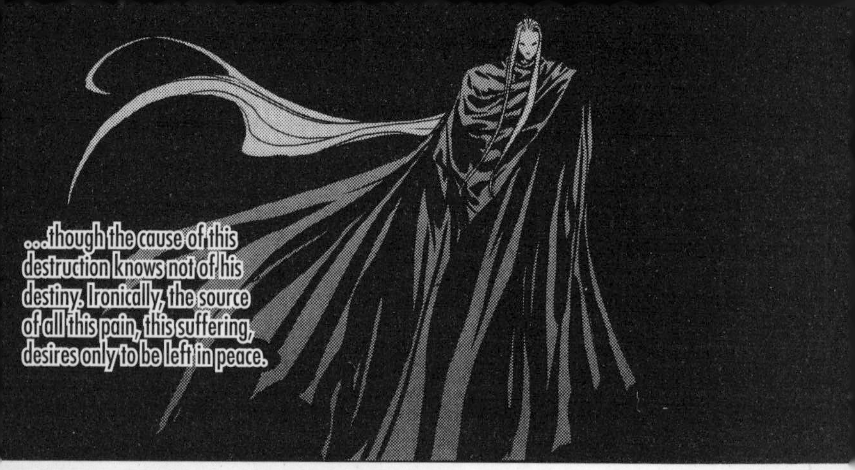
. . .though the cause of this destruction knows not of his destiny. Ironically, the source of all this pain, this suffering, desires only to be left in peace.
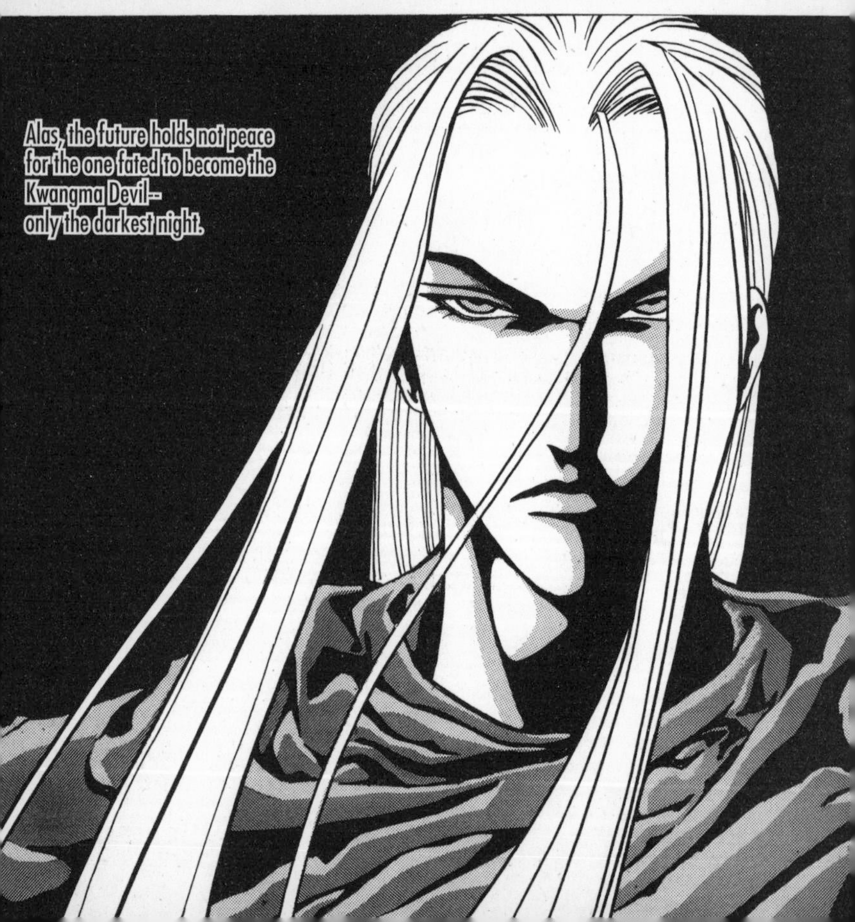
Alas, the future holds not peace for the one fated to become the Kwangma Devil--
only the darkest night.

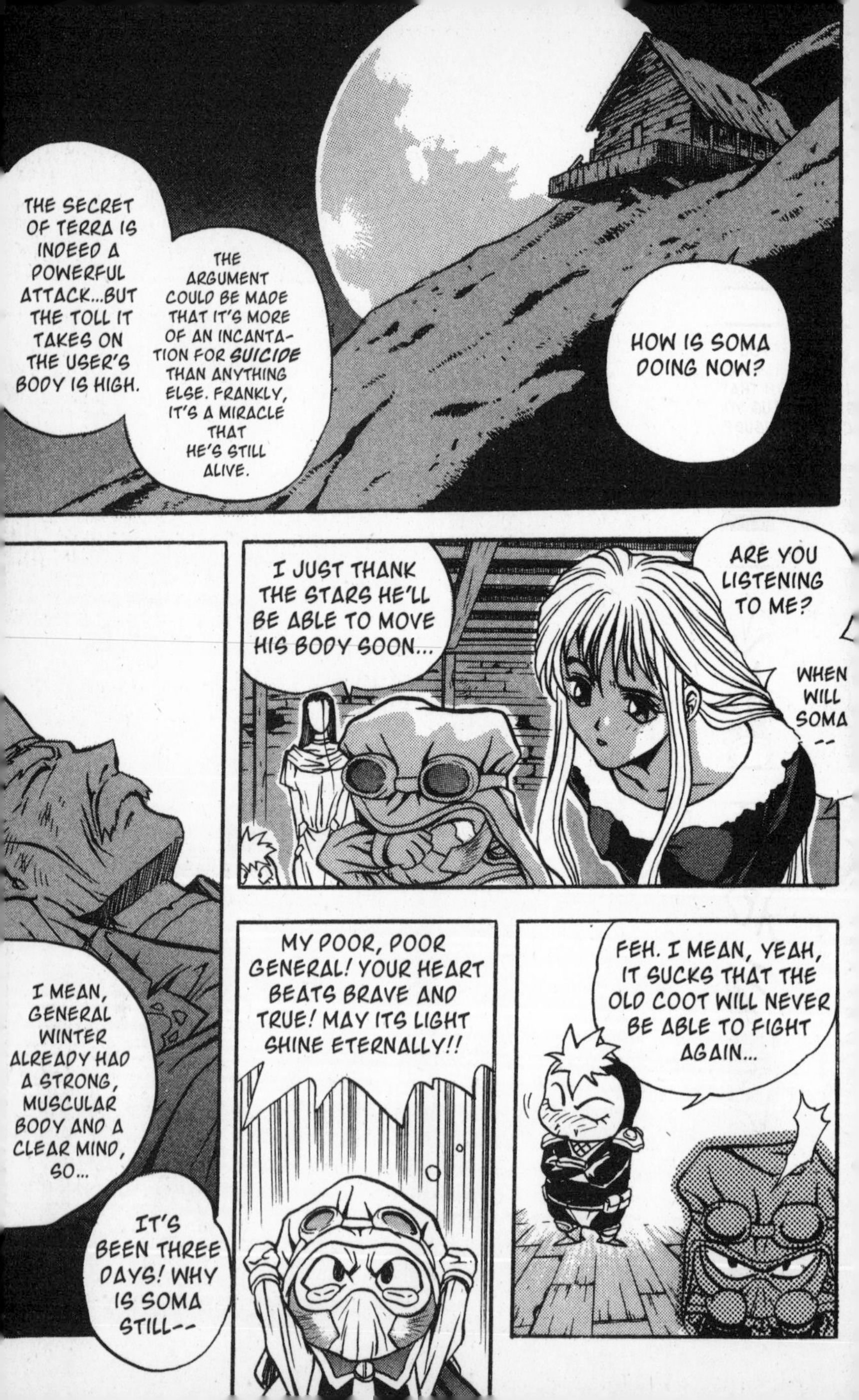
HOW IS SOMA DOING NOW?
THE SECRET OF TERRA IS INDEED A POWERFUL ATTACK...BUT THE TOLL IT TAKES ON THE USER'S BODY IS HIGH.
THE ARGUMENT COULD BE MADE THAT IT'S MORE OF AN INCANTATION FOR SUICIDE THAN ANYTHING ELSE. FRANKLY, IT'S A MIRACLE THAT HE'S STILL ALIVE.
ARE YOU LISTENING TO ME?
WHEN WILL SOMA --
I JUST THANK THE STARS HE'LL BE ABLE TO MOVE HIS BODY SOON...
FEH. I MEAN, YEAH, IT SUCKS THAT THE OLD COOT WILL NEVER BE ABLE TO FIGHT AGAIN...
MY POOR, POOR GENERAL! YOUR HEART BEATS BRAVE AND TRUE! MAY ITS LIGHT SHINE ETERNALLY!!
I MEAN, GENERAL WINTER ALREADY HAD A STRONG, MUSCULAR BODY AND A CLEAR MIND, SO...
IT'S BEEN THREE DAYS! WHY IS SOMA STILL--

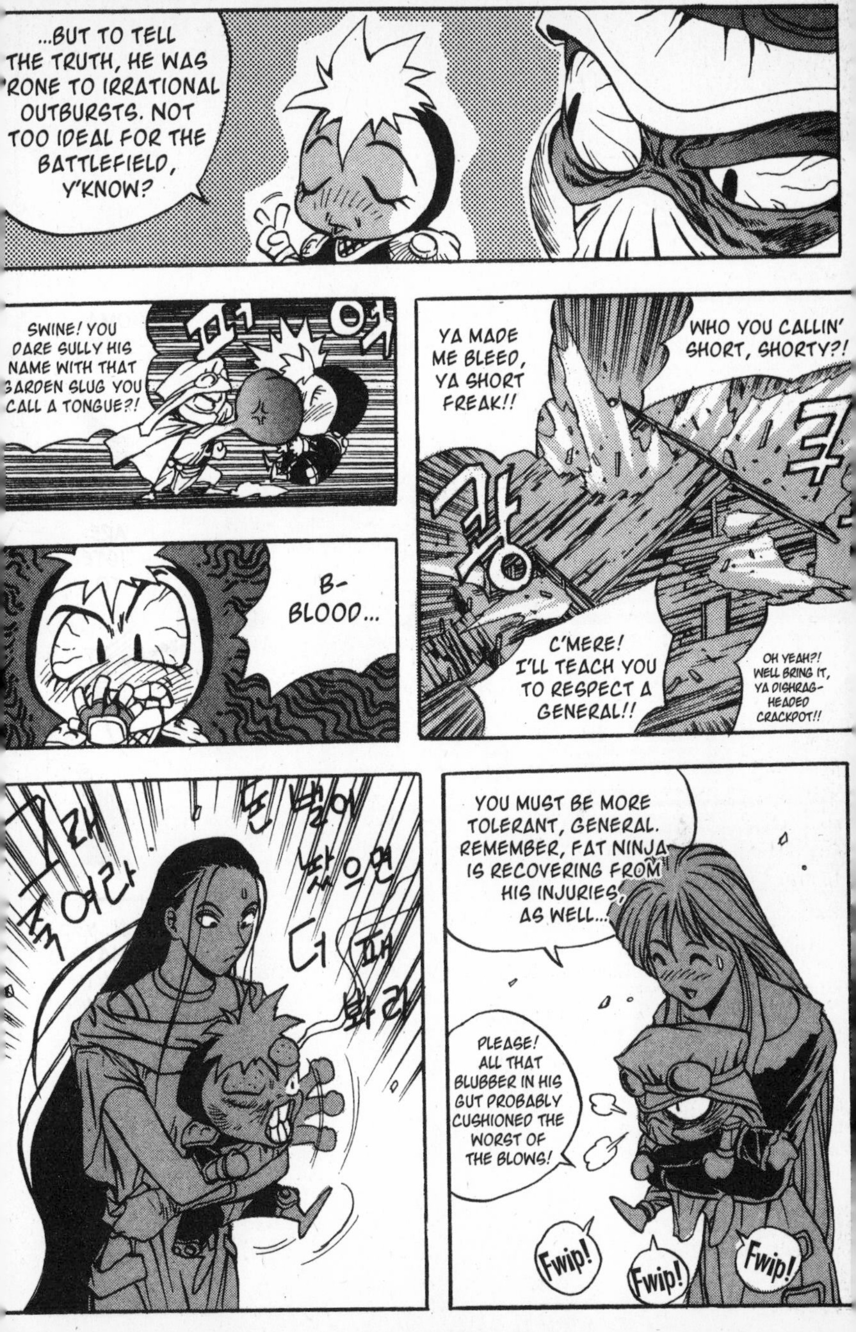
...BUT TO TELL THE TRUTH, HE WAS RONE TO IRRATIONAL OUTBURSTS. NOT TOO IDEAL FOR THE BATTLEFIELD, Y'KNOW?
SWINE! YOU DARE SULLY HIS NAME WITH THAT ARDEN SLUG YOU CALL A TONGUE?!
B- BLOOD...
YA MADE ME BLEED, YA SHORT FREAK!!
WHO YOU CALLIN' SHORT, SHORTY?!
C'MERE! I'LL TEACH YOU TO RESPECT A GENERAL!!
OH YEAH?! WELL BRING IT, YA DISHRAG-HEADED CRACKPOT!!
YOU MUST BE MORE TOLERANT, GENERAL. REMEMBER, FAT NINJA IS RECOVERING FROM HIS INJURIES, AS WELL...
PLEASE! ALL THAT BLUBBER IN HIS GUT PROBABLY CUSHIONED THE WORST OF THE BLOWS!
Fwip!
Fwip!
Fwip!

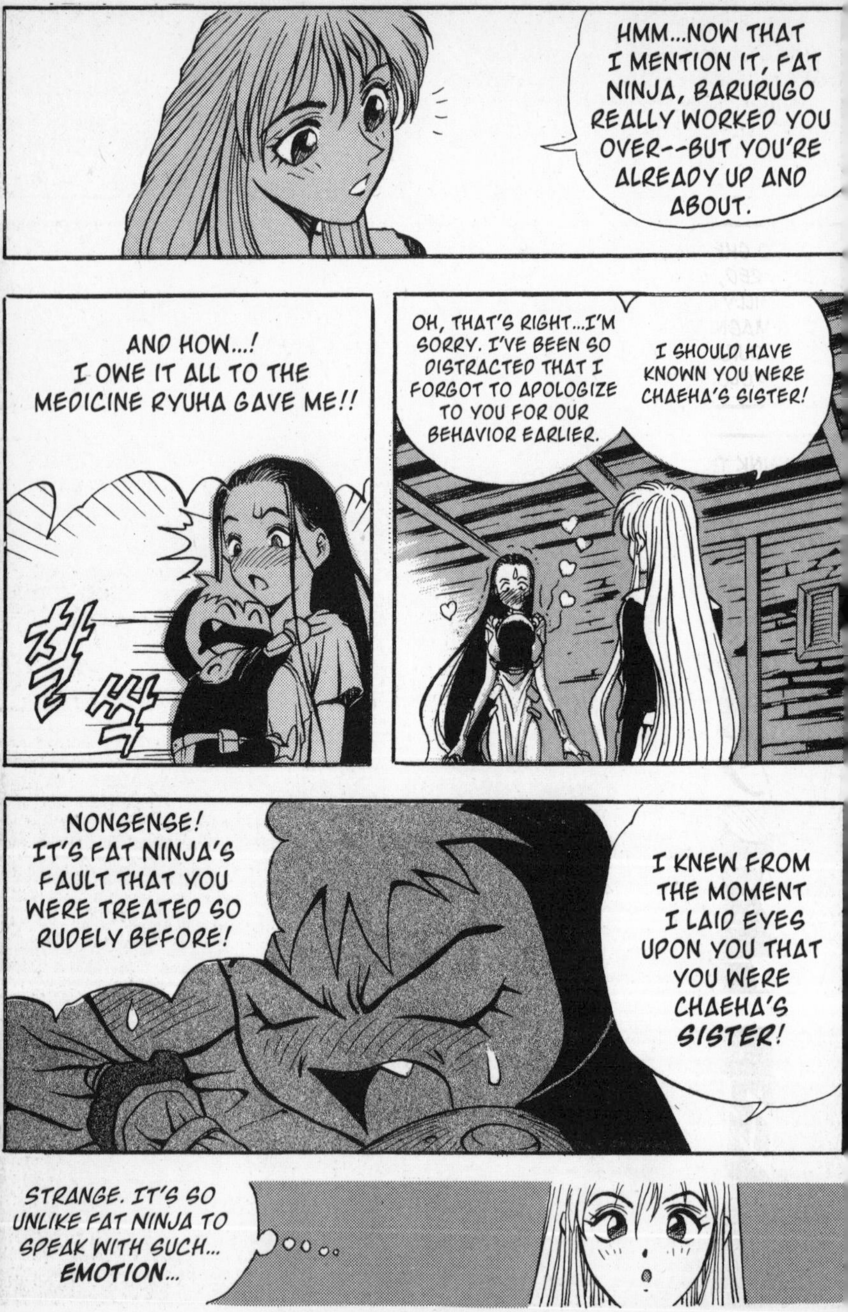
HMM...NOW THAT I MENTION IT, FAT NINJA, BARURUGO REALLY WORKED YOU OVER--BUT YOU'RE ALREADY UP AND ABOUT.
AND HOW...! I OWE IT ALL TO THE MEDICINE RYUHA GAVE ME!!
OH, THAT'S RIGHT...I'M SORRY. I'VE BEEN SO DISTRACTED THAT I FORGOT TO APOLOGIZE TO YOU FOR OUR BEHAVIOR EARLIER.
I SHOULD HAVE KNOWN YOU WERE CHAEHA'S SISTER!
NONSENSE! IT'S FAT NINJA'S FAULT THAT YOU WERE TREATED SO RUDELY BEFORE!
I KNEW FROM THE MOMENT I LAID EYES UPON YOU THAT YOU WERE CHAEHA'S SISTER!
STRANGE. IT'S SO UNLIKE FAT NINJA TO SPEAK WITH SUCH... EMOTION...

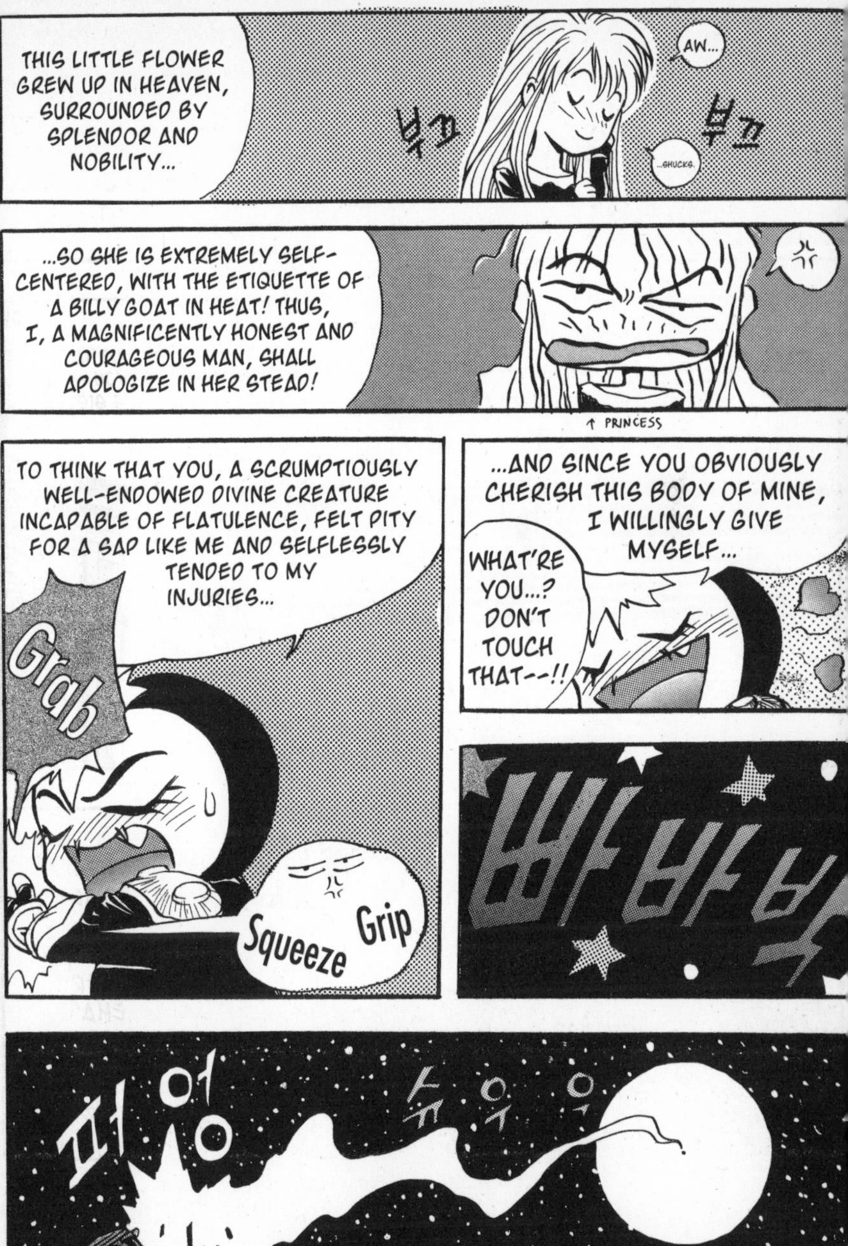
THIS LITTLE FLOWER GREW UP IN HEAVEN, SURROUNDED BY SPLENDOR AND NOBILITY...
부끄
AW...
부끄
...SHUCKS.
...SO SHE IS EXTREMELY SELF-CENTERED, WITH THE ETIQUETTE OF A BILLY GOAT IN HEAT! THUS, I, A MAGNIFICENTLY HONEST AND COURAGEOUS MAN, SHALL APOLOGIZE IN HER STEAD!
↑ PRINCESS
TO THINK THAT YOU, A SCRUMPTIOUSLY WELL-ENDOWED DIVINE CREATURE INCAPABLE OF FLATULENCE, FELT PITY FOR A SAP LIKE ME AND SELFLESSLY TENDED TO MY INJURIES...
Grab
Squeeze
Grip
...AND SINCE YOU OBVIOUSLY CHERISH THIS BODY OF MINE, I WILLINGLY GIVE MYSELF...
WHAT'RE YOU...? DON'T TOUCH THAT--!!

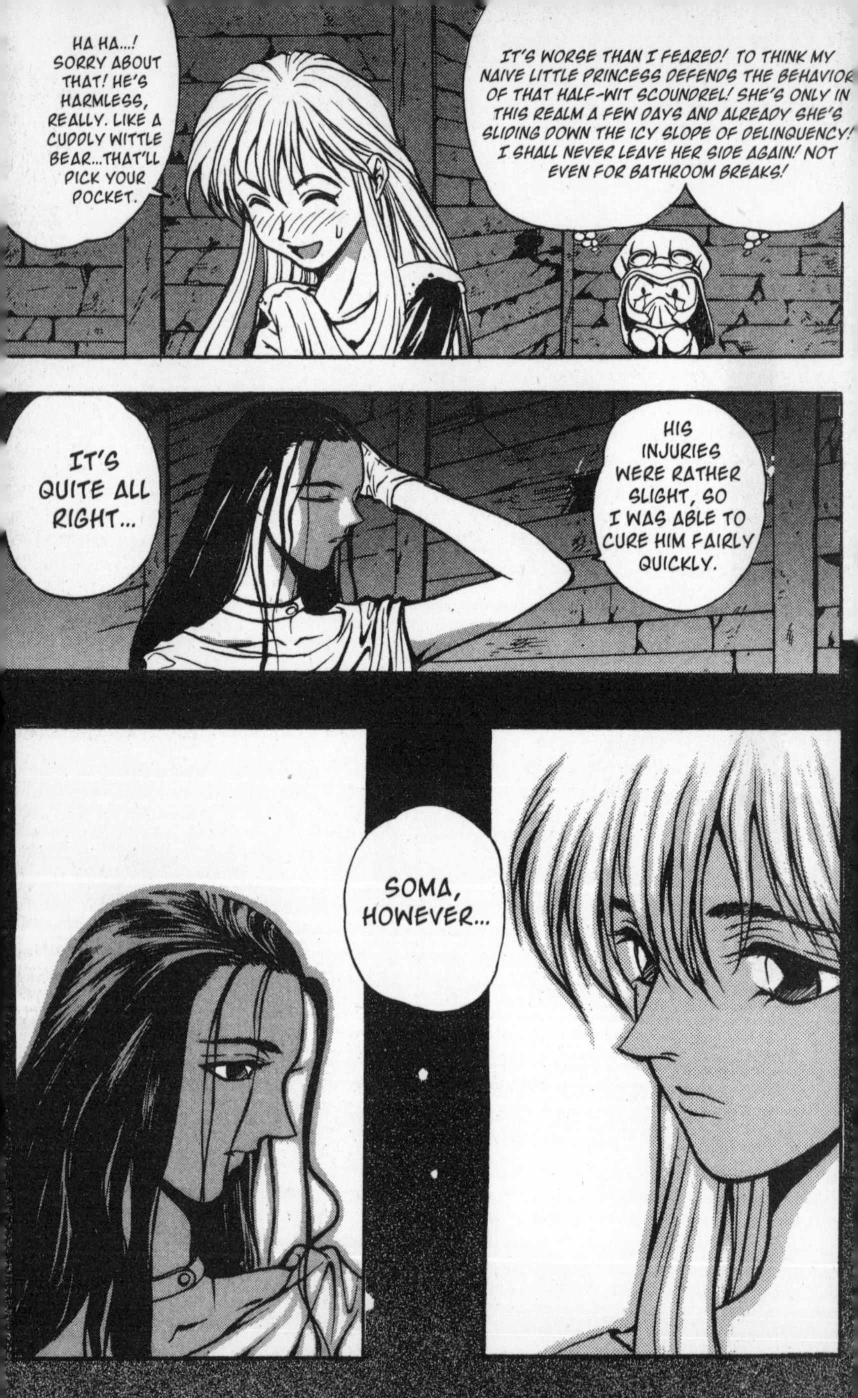
HA HA...! SORRY ABOUT THAT! HE'S HARMLESS, REALLY. LIKE A CUDDLY WITTLE BEAR...THAT'LL PICK YOUR POCKET.
IT'S WORSE THAN I FEARED! TO THINK MY NAIVE LITTLE PRINCESS DEFENDS THE BEHAVIOR OF THAT HALF-WIT SCOUNDREL! SHE'S ONLY IN THIS REALM A FEW DAYS AND ALREADY SHE'S SLIDING DOWN THE ICY SLOPE OF DELINQUENCY! I SHALL NEVER LEAVE HER SIDE AGAIN! NOT EVEN FOR BATHROOM BREAKS!
IT'S QUITE ALL RIGHT...
HIS INJURIES WERE RATHER SLIGHT, SO I WAS ABLE TO CURE HIM FAIRLY QUICKLY.
SOMA, HOWEVER...

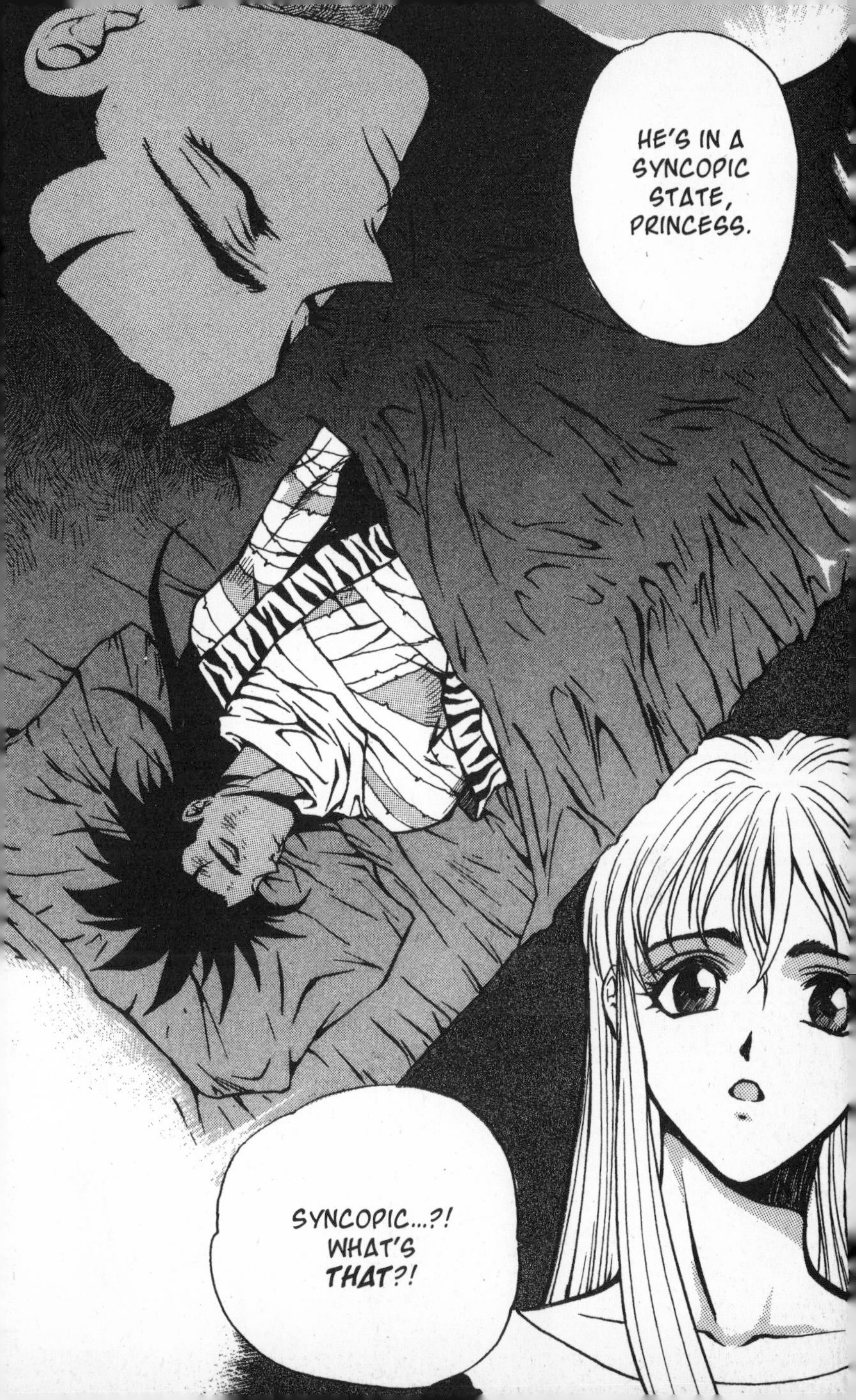
HE'S IN A SYNCOPIC STATE, PRINCESS.
SYNCOPIC...?! WHAT'S **THAT**?!

IT'S JUST A FANCIER WAY TO SAY *COMA*. WHATEVER YOU CALL IT, IT MEANS THE SAME THING--HE'S NEITHER DEAD NOR ALIVE. I MEAN, HIS HEART AND BRAIN ARE FUNCTIONING, SO HE ISN'T DEAD...BUT HE STILL HAS NO SENSE OF HIS SURROUNDINGS.

YOU KNOW, THERE ARE THOSE WHO PURPOSELY PLACE THEMSELVES IN THIS CONDITION...ALSO KNOWN AS "SUSPENDED ANIMATION."

PRACTITIONERS SAY THAT ONLY THOSE OF STRONG BODY AND MIND CAN SURVIVE SYNCOPIC SLUMBER...

...THAT IS, IF THE PERSON CAN RECOVER FROM THE EXTREME SHOCK TO THE BODY AND MIND.

YOU MEAN... THERE'S NO WAY TO CURE HIM?

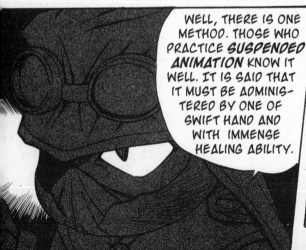

WELL, THERE IS ONE METHOD. THOSE WHO PRACTICE *SUSPENDED ANIMATION* KNOW IT WELL. IT IS SAID THAT IT MUST BE ADMINISTERED BY ONE OF SWIFT HAND AND WITH IMMENSE HEALING ABILITY.

BUT WHERE CAN WE FIND SOMEONE LIKE THAT?

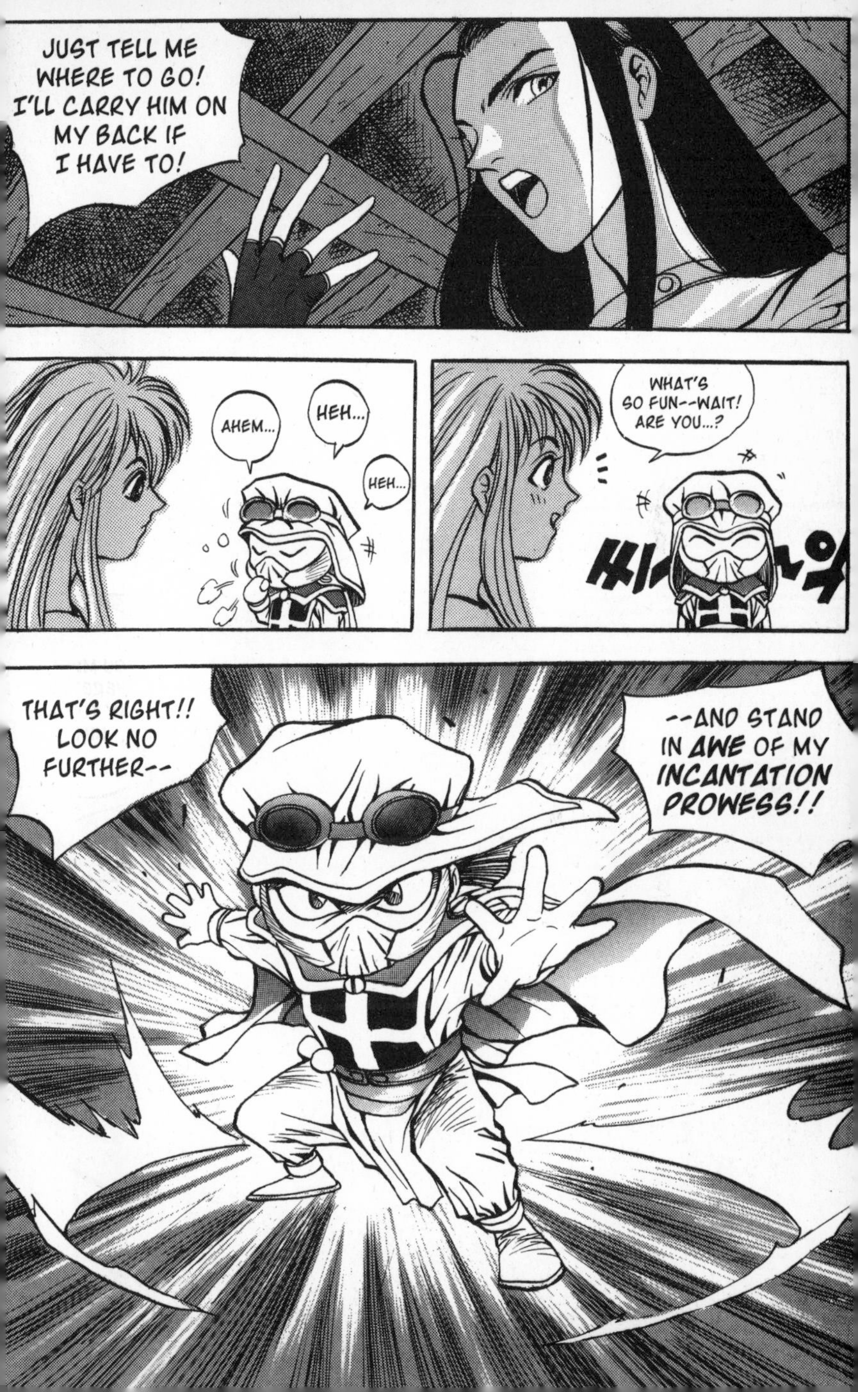
JUST TELL ME WHERE TO GO! I'LL CARRY HIM ON MY BACK IF I HAVE TO!
AHEM...
HEH...
HEH...
WHAT'S SO FUN--WAIT! ARE YOU...?
THAT'S RIGHT!! LOOK NO FURTHER--
--AND STAND IN AWE OF MY INCANTATION PROWESS!!

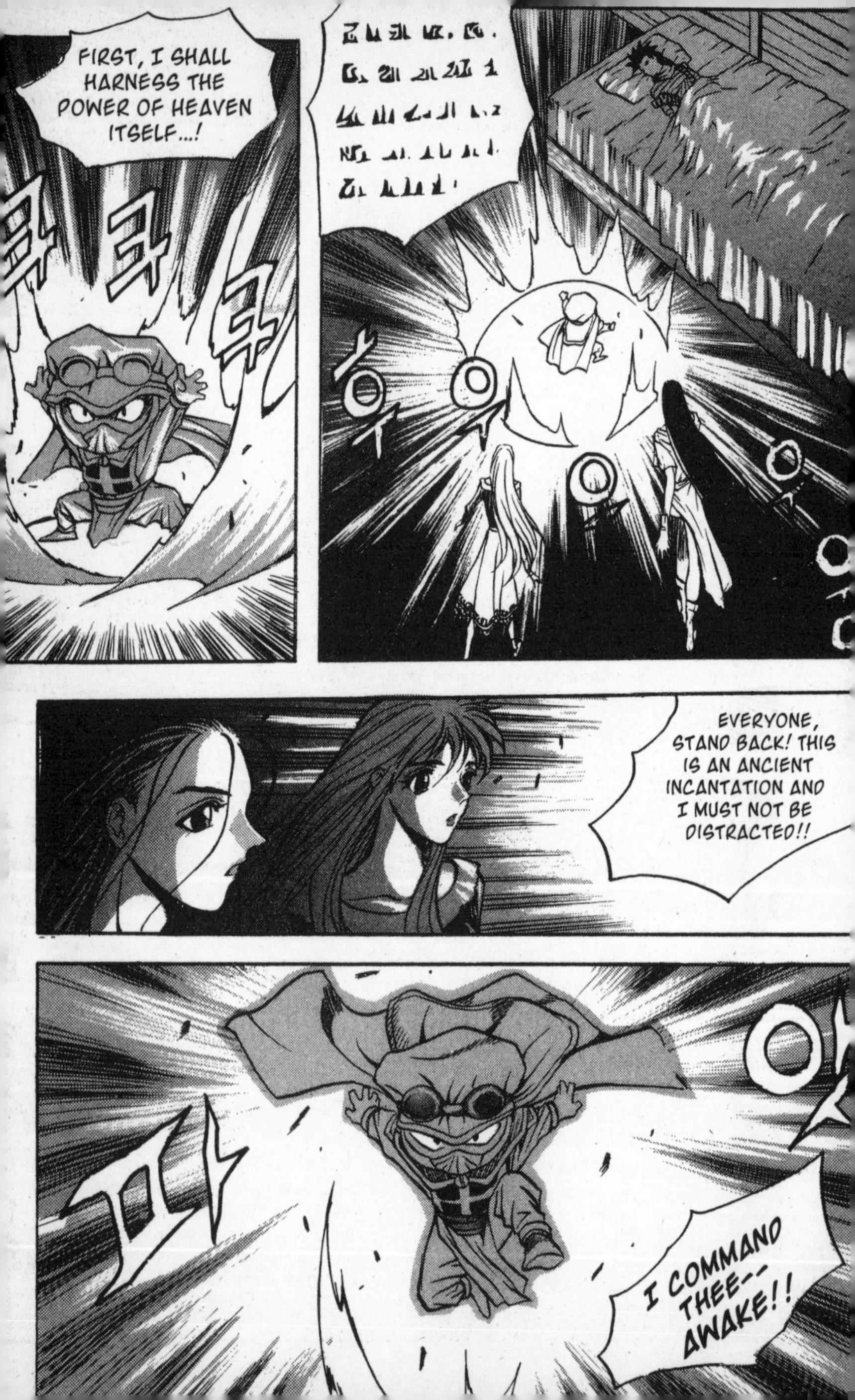
FIRST, I SHALL HARNESS THE POWER OF HEAVEN ITSELF...!
EVERYONE, STAND BACK! THIS IS AN ANCIENT INCANTATION AND I MUST NOT BE DISTRACTED!!
I COMMAND THEE-- AWAKE!!

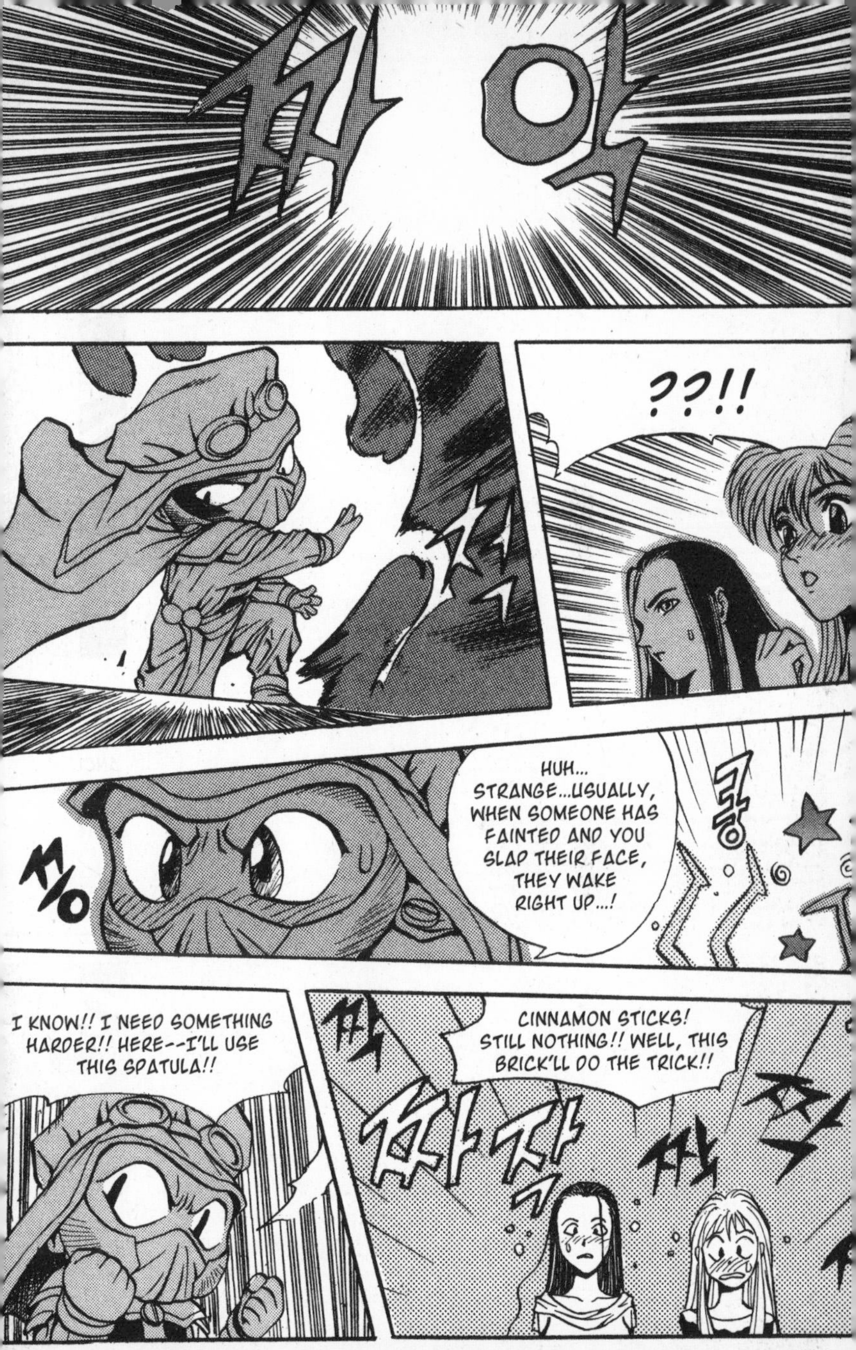
??!!
HUH...
STRANGE...USUALLY,
WHEN SOMEONE HAS
FAINTED AND YOU
SLAP THEIR FACE,
THEY WAKE
RIGHT UP...!
I KNOW!! I NEED SOMETHING
HARDER!! HERE--I'LL USE
THIS SPATULA!!
CINNAMON STICKS!
STILL NOTHING!! WELL, THIS
BRICK'LL DO THE TRICK!!

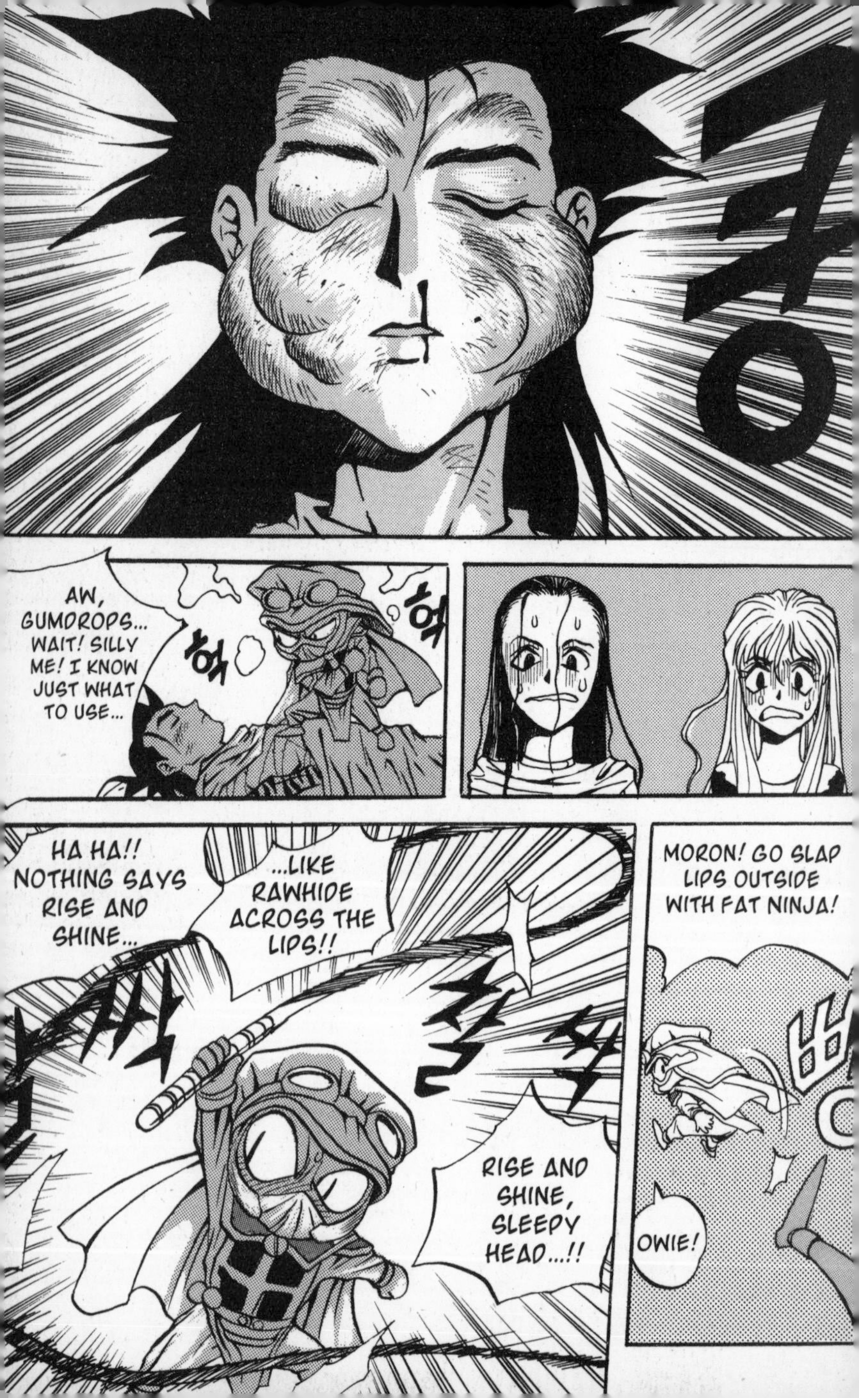
AW, GUMDROPS... WAIT! SILLY ME! I KNOW JUST WHAT TO USE...
HA HA!! NOTHING SAYS RISE AND SHINE...
...LIKE RAWHIDE ACROSS THE LIPS!!
RISE AND SHINE, SLEEPY HEAD...!!
MORON! GO SLAP LIPS OUTSIDE WITH FAT NINJA!
OWIE!

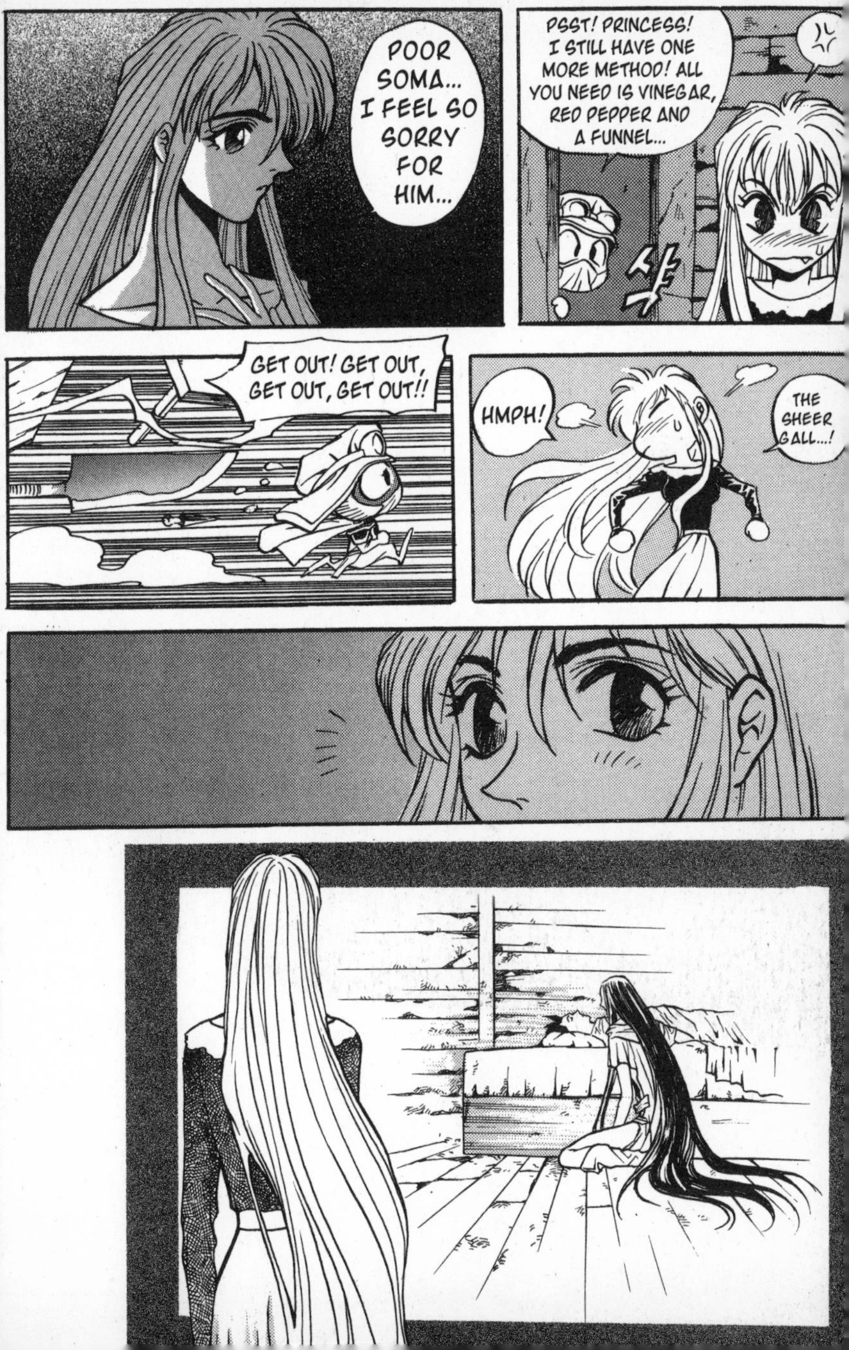
POOR SOMA... I FEEL SO SORRY FOR HIM...
PSST! PRINCESS! I STILL HAVE ONE MORE METHOD! ALL YOU NEED IS VINEGAR, RED PEPPER AND A FUNNEL...
GET OUT! GET OUT, GET OUT, GET OUT!!
HMPH!
THE SHEER GALL...!

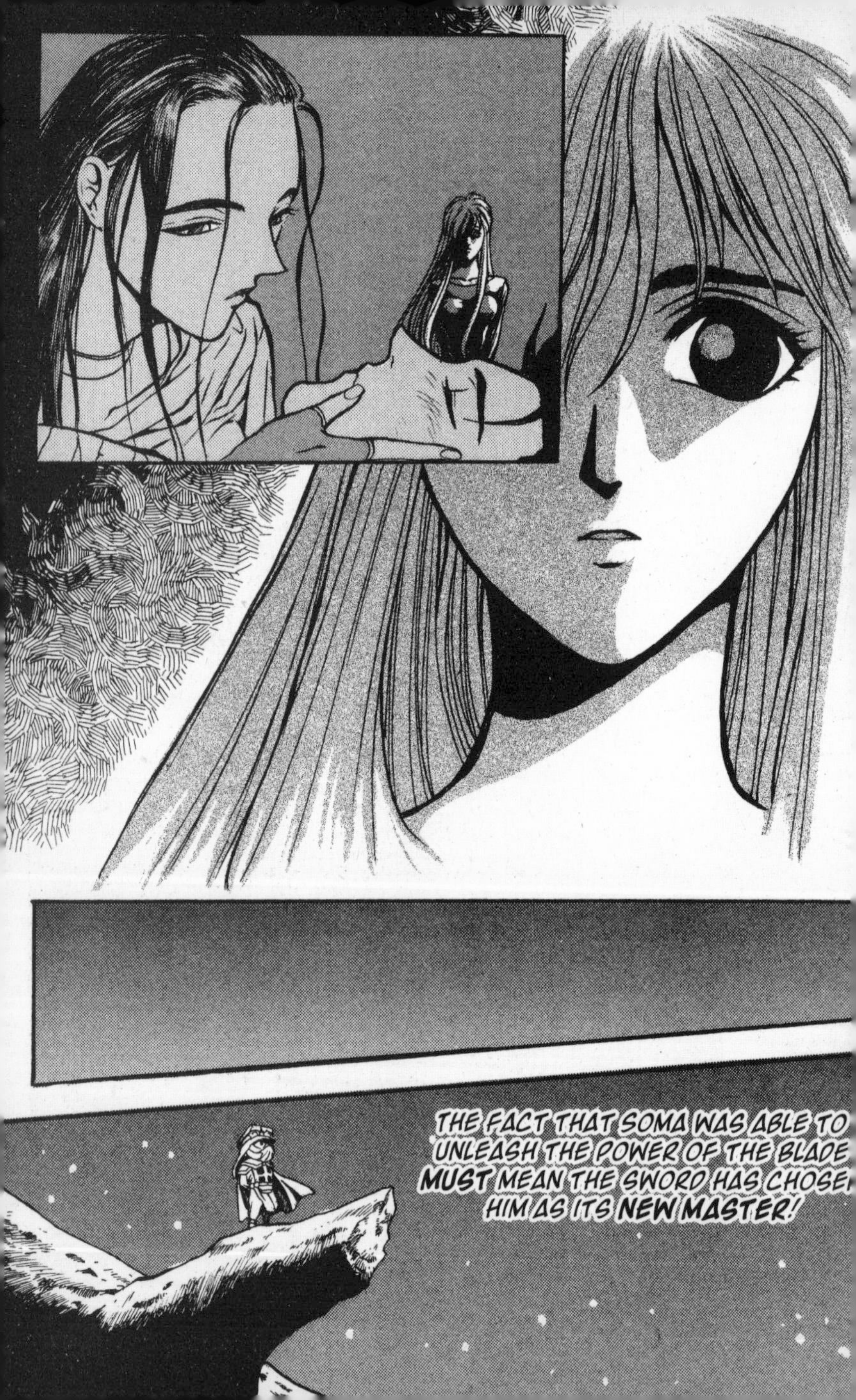
THE FACT THAT SOMA WAS ABLE TO UNLEASH THE POWER OF THE BLADE **MUST** MEAN THE SWORD HAS CHOSE HIM AS ITS **NEW MASTER**!

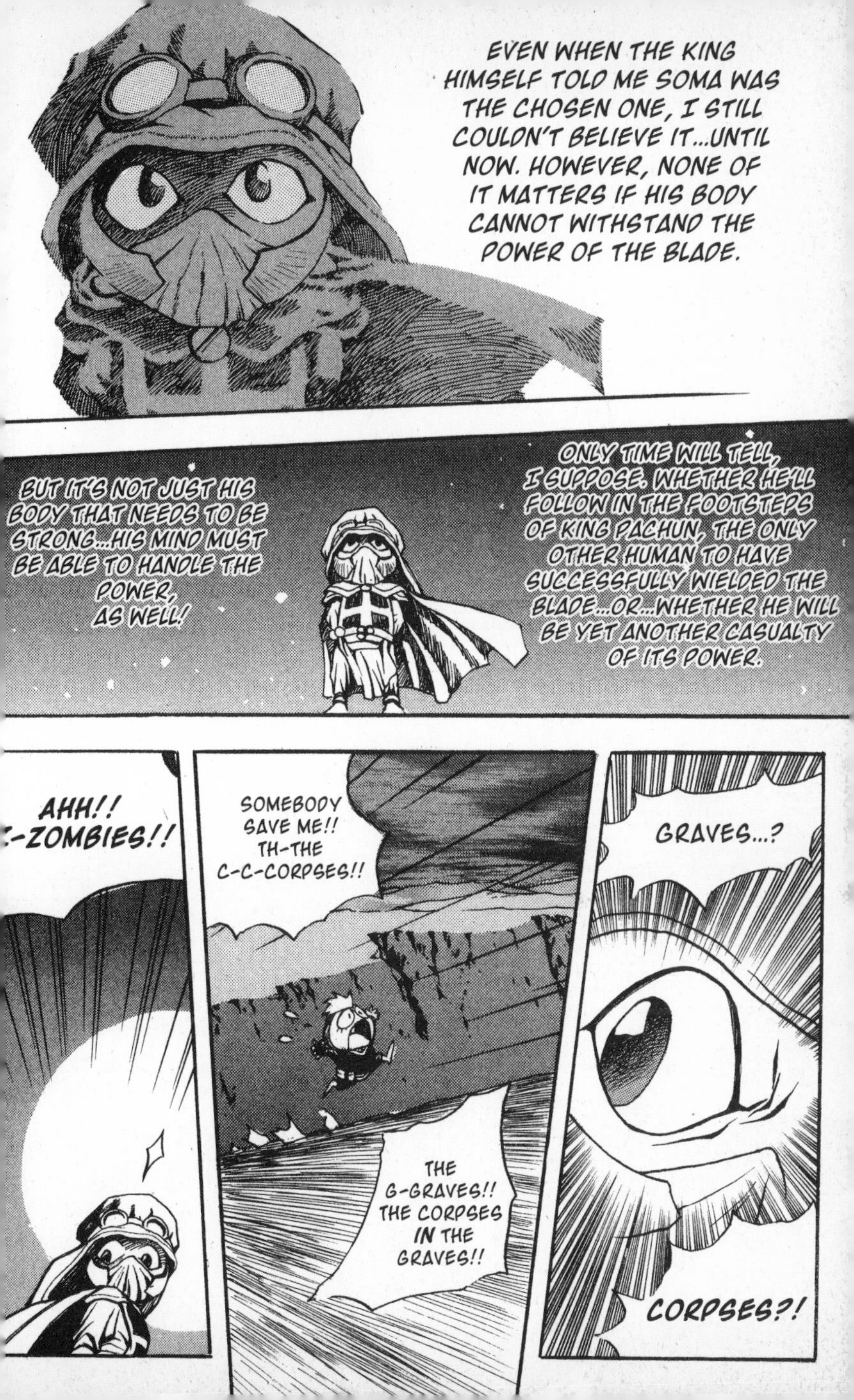
EVEN WHEN THE KING HIMSELF TOLD ME SOMA WAS THE CHOSEN ONE, I STILL COULDN'T BELIEVE IT...UNTIL NOW. HOWEVER, NONE OF IT MATTERS IF HIS BODY CANNOT WITHSTAND THE POWER OF THE BLADE.
BUT IT'S NOT JUST HIS BODY THAT NEEDS TO BE STRONG...HIS MIND MUST BE ABLE TO HANDLE THE POWER, AS WELL!
ONLY TIME WILL TELL, I SUPPOSE. WHETHER HE'LL FOLLOW IN THE FOOTSTEPS OF KING PACHUN, THE ONLY OTHER HUMAN TO HAVE SUCCESSFULLY WIELDED THE BLADE...OR...WHETHER HE WILL BE YET ANOTHER CASUALTY OF ITS POWER.
AHH!! -ZOMBIES!!
SOMEBODY SAVE ME!! TH-THE C-C-CORPSES!!
THE G-GRAVES!! THE CORPSES IN THE GRAVES!!
GRAVES...?
CORPSES?!

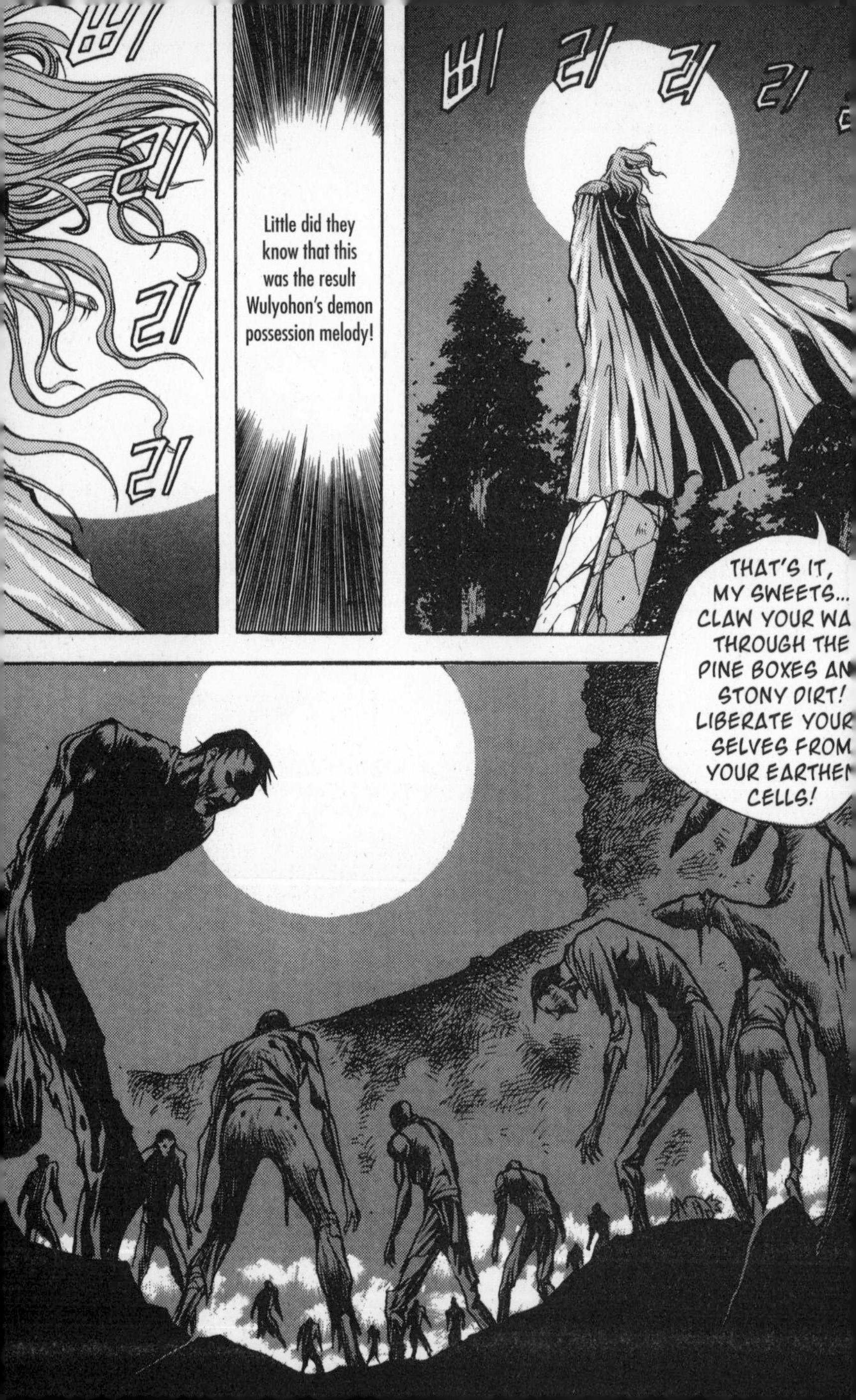

삐
리
리
리
Little did they know that this was the result Wulyohon's demon possession melody!
삐리리리
THAT'S IT, MY SWEETS... CLAW YOUR WA THROUGH THE PINE BOXES AN STONY DIRT! LIBERATE YOUR SELVES FROM YOUR EARTHEN CELLS!

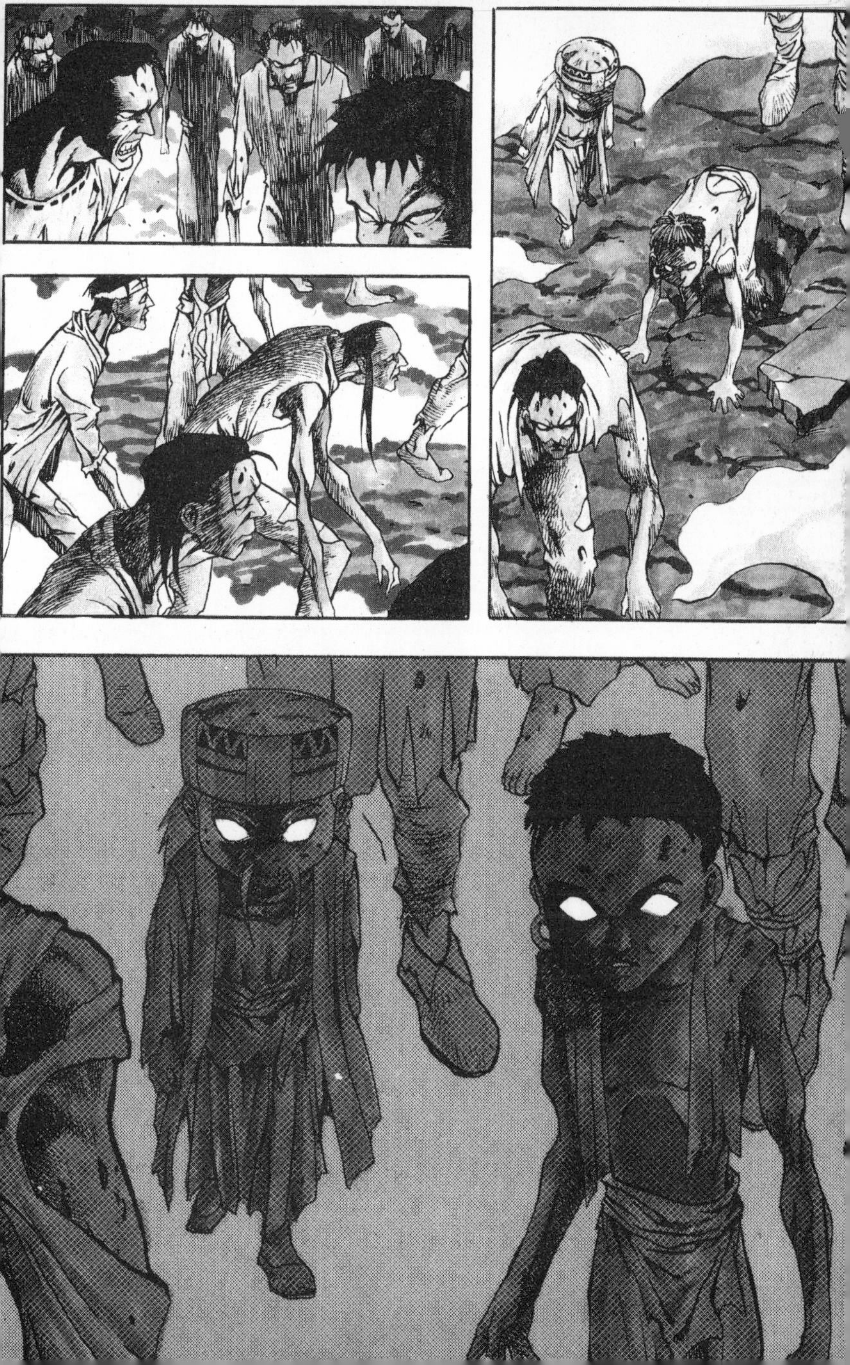

PLEEEASE!! I'M TOO YOUNG TO BE EATEN BY ZOMBIES!!

GET YOUR DIAPER OUTTA MY FACE!

IDIOT! YOUR MAN BOOBS ARE BLOCKING MY VIEW!!

HUH?!

CHUN GOONGGU-- EXTEND SHIELD!!

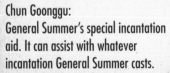

Chun Goonggu:
General Summer's special incantation aid. It can assist with whatever incantation General Summer casts.

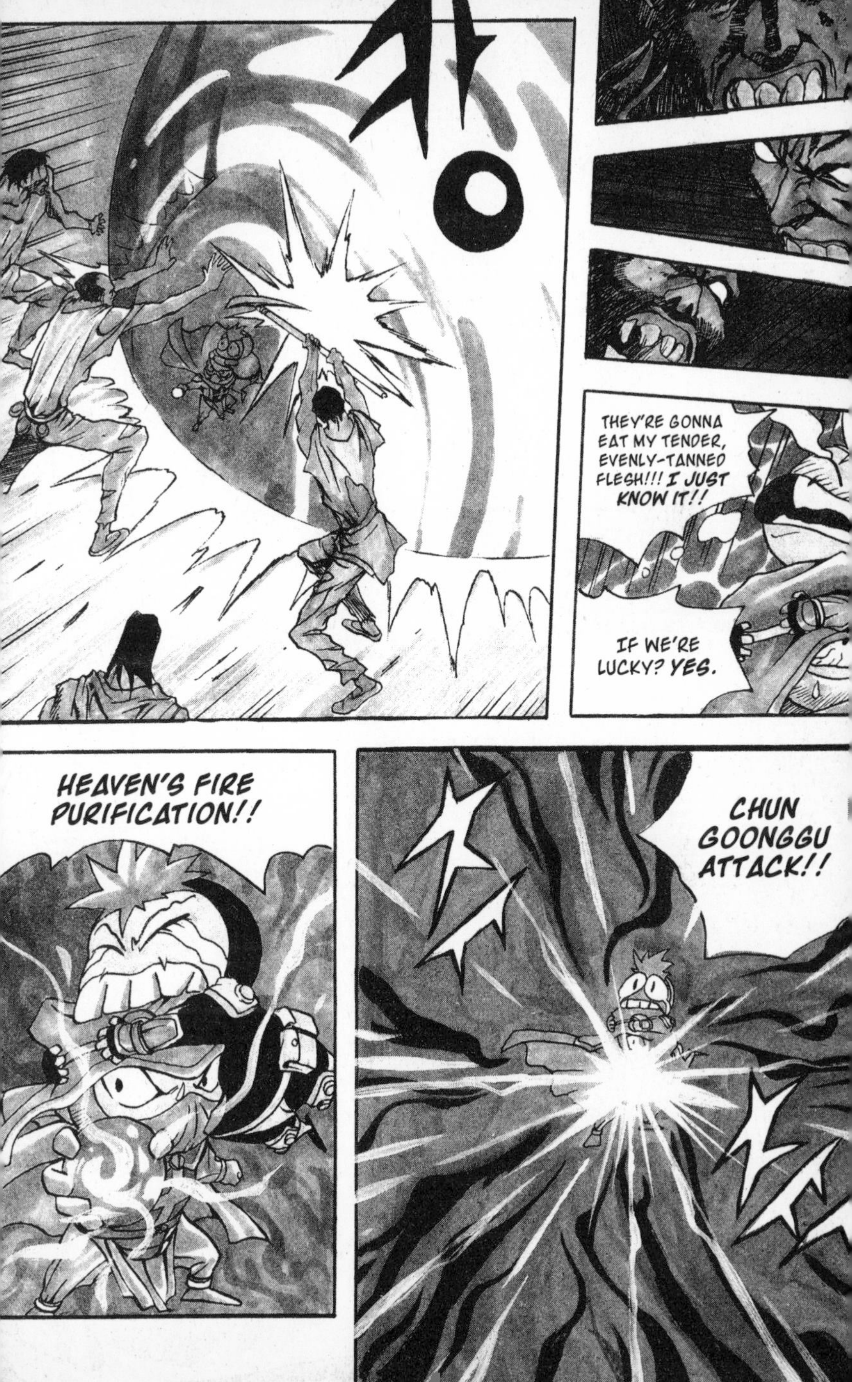
THEY'RE GONNA EAT MY TENDER, EVENLY-TANNED FLESH!!! I JUST KNOW IT!!
IF WE'RE LUCKY? YES.
HEAVEN'S FIRE PURIFICATION!!
CHUN GOONGGU ATTACK!!

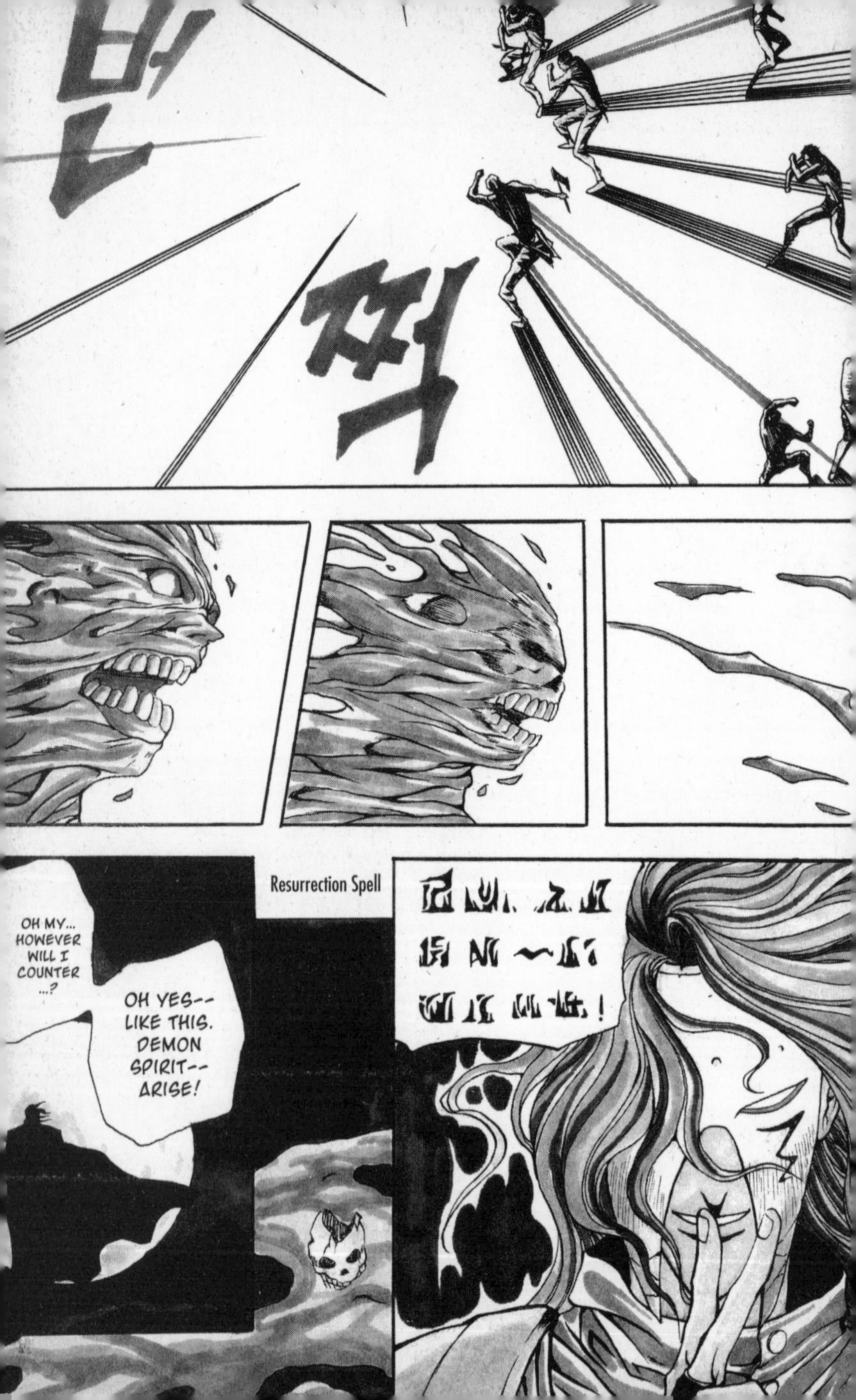
번쩍
OH MY... HOWEVER WILL I COUNTER ...?
OH YES-- LIKE THIS. DEMON SPIRIT-- ARISE!
Resurrection Spell

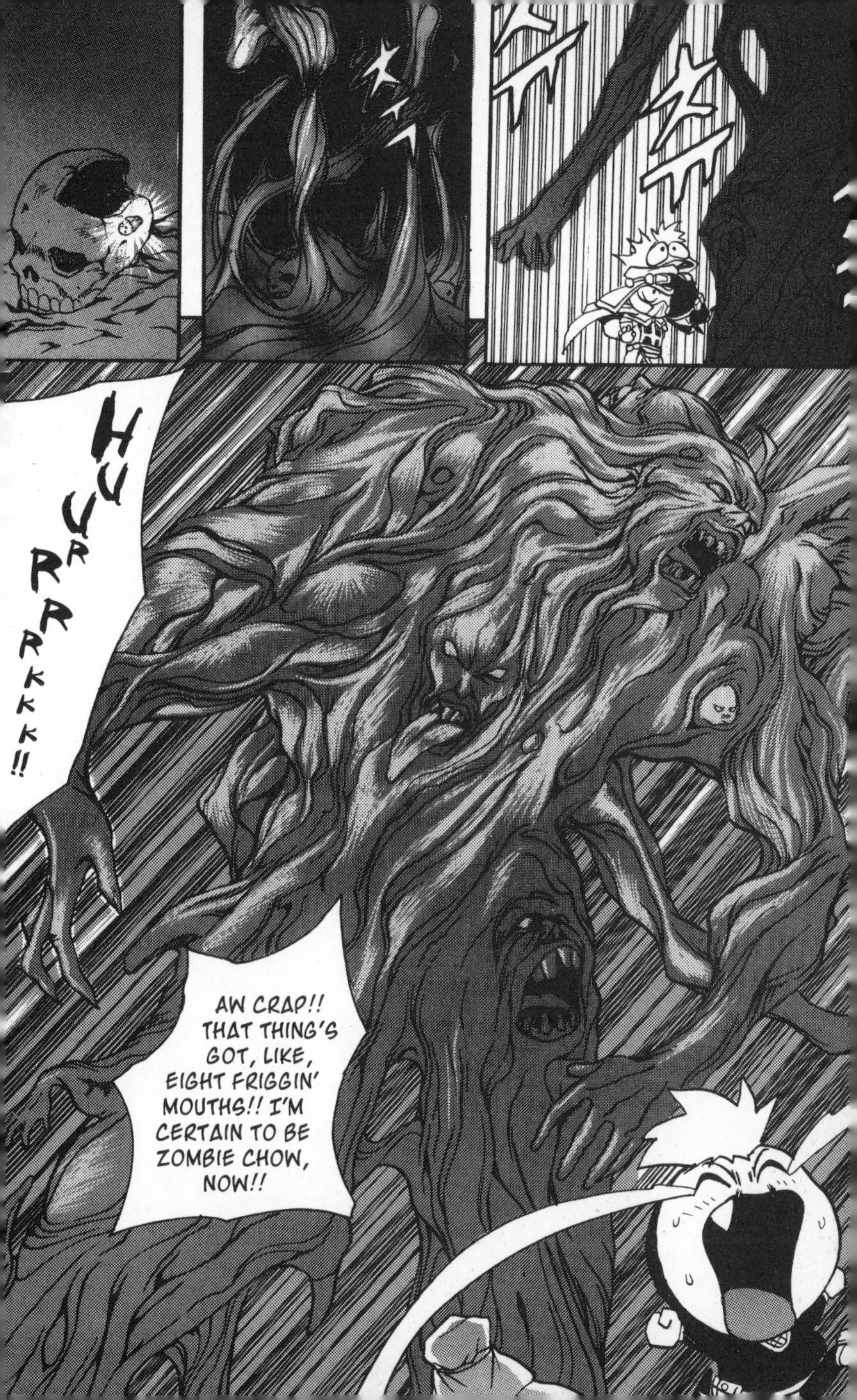
HUURRRRKKK!!
AW CRAP!! THAT THING'S GOT, LIKE, EIGHT FRIGGIN' MOUTHS!! I'M CERTAIN TO BE ZOMBIE CHOW, NOW!!

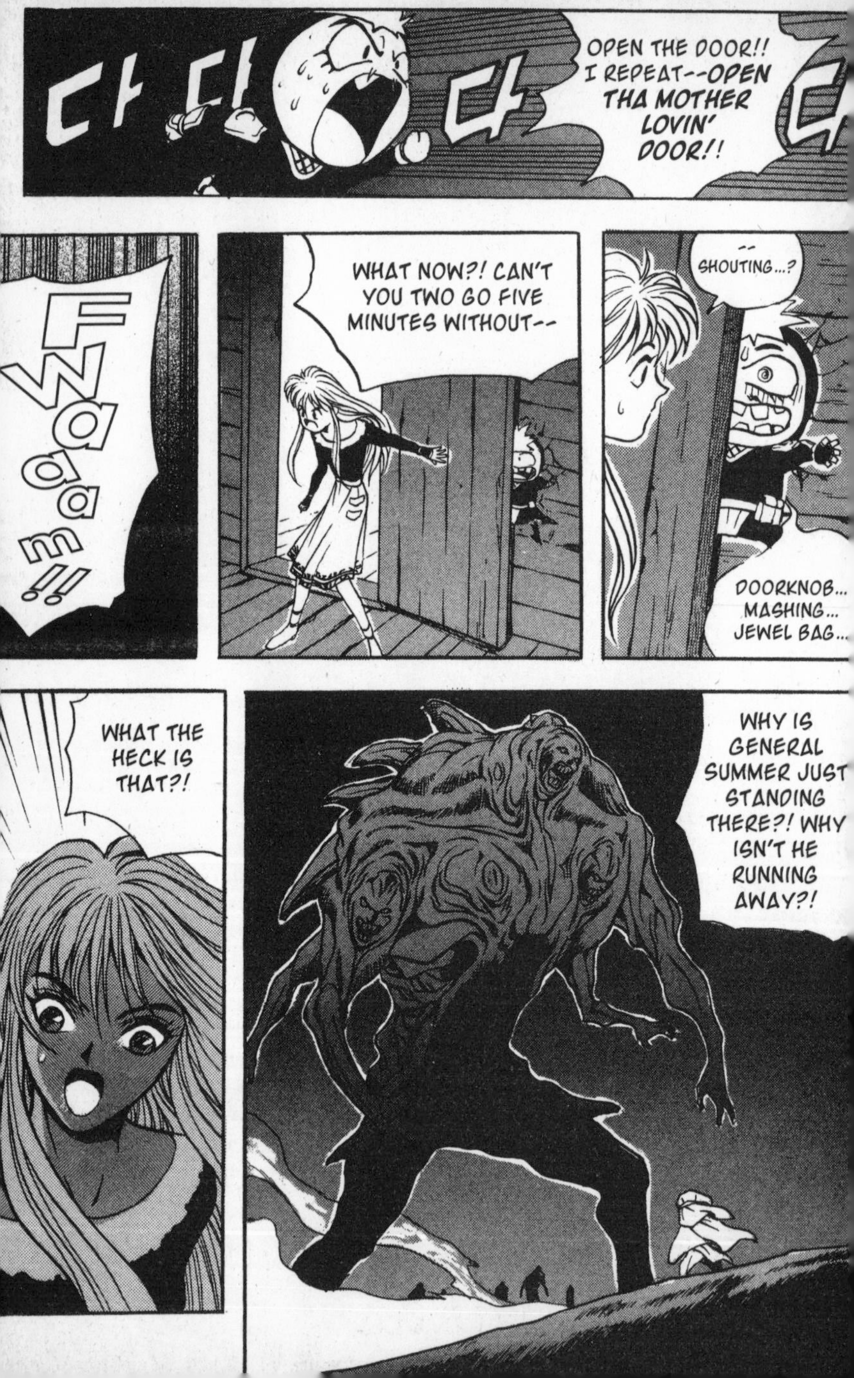
OPEN THE DOOR!! I REPEAT--OPEN THA MOTHER LOVIN' DOOR!!
FWaaam!!
WHAT NOW?! CAN'T YOU TWO GO FIVE MINUTES WITHOUT--
--SHOUTING...?
DOORKNOB... MASHING... JEWEL BAG...
WHAT THE HECK IS THAT?!
WHY IS GENERAL SUMMER JUST STANDING THERE?! WHY ISN'T HE RUNNING AWAY?!

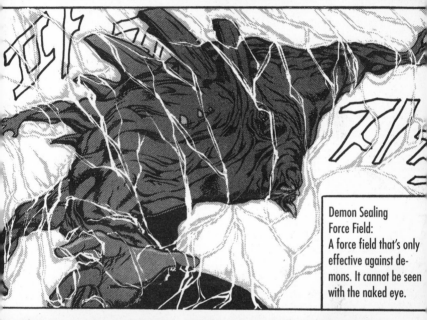

Demon Sealing
Force Field:
A force field that's only
effective against de-
mons. It cannot be seen
with the naked eye.

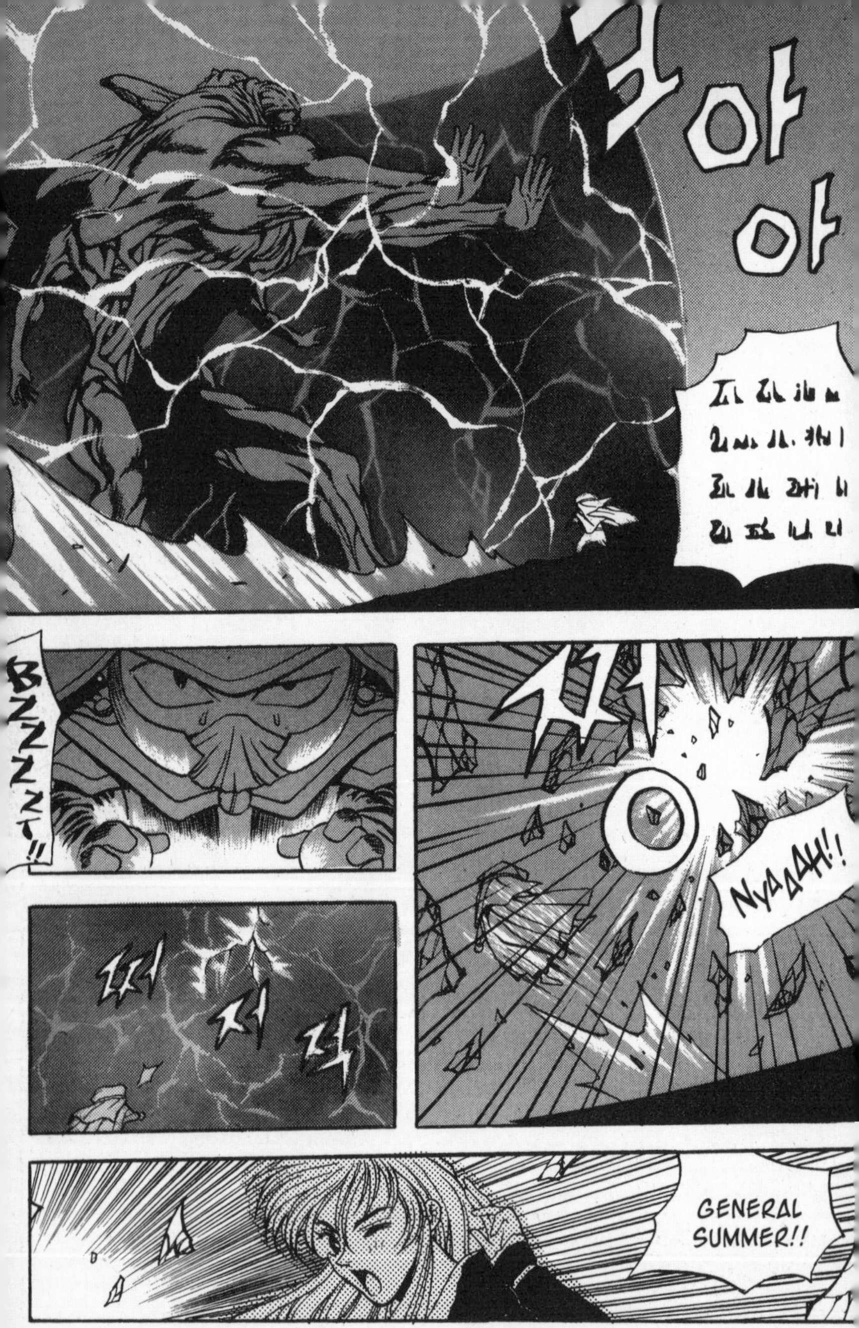
크아아
NYAAAH!!
BZZZZZT!!
지지직
GENERAL SUMMER!!

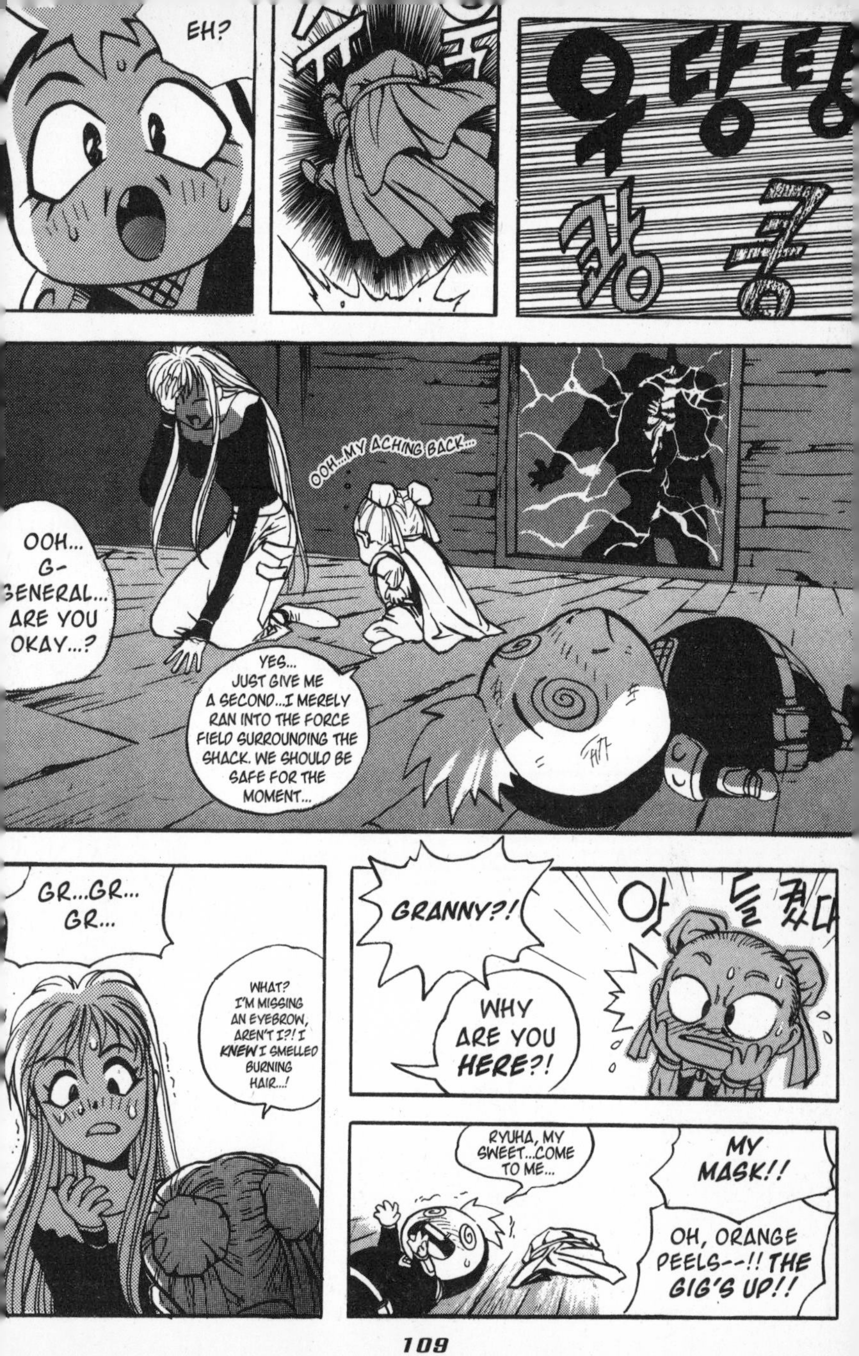
EH?
우당탕
쾅 쿵
OOH... G-GENERAL... ARE YOU OKAY...?
OOH...MY ACHING BACK...
YES... JUST GIVE ME A SECOND...I MERELY RAN INTO THE FORCE FIELD SURROUNDING THE SHACK. WE SHOULD BE SAFE FOR THE MOMENT...
GR...GR... GR...
WHAT? I'M MISSING AN EYEBROW, AREN'T I?! I KNEW I SMELLED BURNING HAIR...!
GRANNY?!
WHY ARE YOU HERE?!
앗 들켰다
RYUHA, MY SWEET...COME TO ME...
MY MASK!!
OH, ORANGE PEELS--!! THE GIG'S UP!!

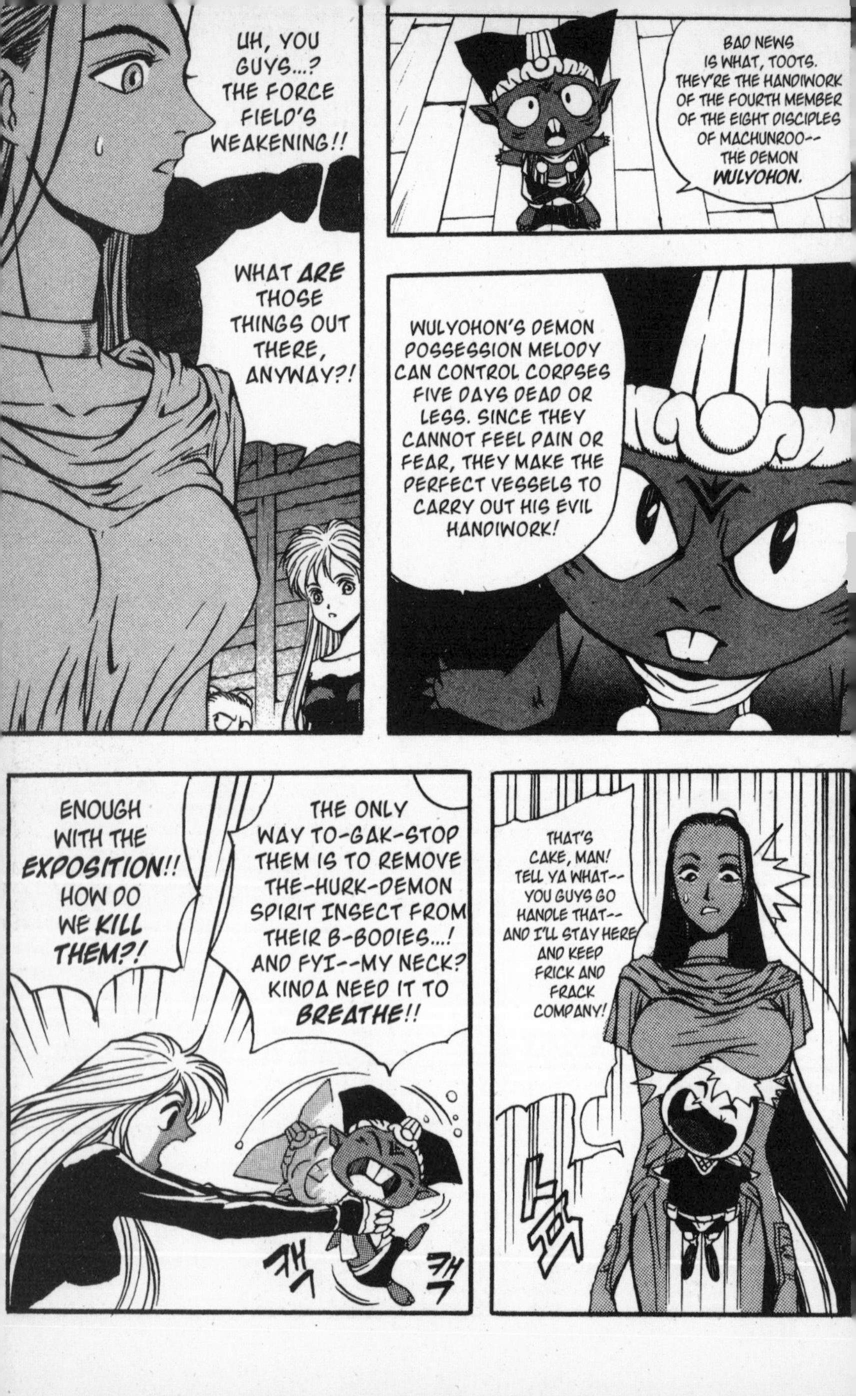
UH, YOU GUYS...? THE FORCE FIELD'S WEAKENING!!
WHAT ARE THOSE THINGS OUT THERE, ANYWAY?!
BAD NEWS IS WHAT, TOOTS. THEY'RE THE HANDIWORK OF THE FOURTH MEMBER OF THE EIGHT DISCIPLES OF MACHUNROO-- THE DEMON WULYOHON.
WULYOHON'S DEMON POSSESSION MELODY CAN CONTROL CORPSES FIVE DAYS DEAD OR LESS. SINCE THEY CANNOT FEEL PAIN OR FEAR, THEY MAKE THE PERFECT VESSELS TO CARRY OUT HIS EVIL HANDIWORK!
ENOUGH WITH THE EXPOSITION!! HOW DO WE KILL THEM?!
THE ONLY WAY TO-GAK-STOP THEM IS TO REMOVE THE-HURK-DEMON SPIRIT INSECT FROM THEIR B-BODIES...! AND FYI--MY NECK? KINDA NEED IT TO BREATHE!!
캑
캑
THAT'S CAKE, MAN! TELL YA WHAT-- YOU GUYS GO HANDLE THAT-- AND I'LL STAY HERE AND KEEP FRICK AND FRACK COMPANY!

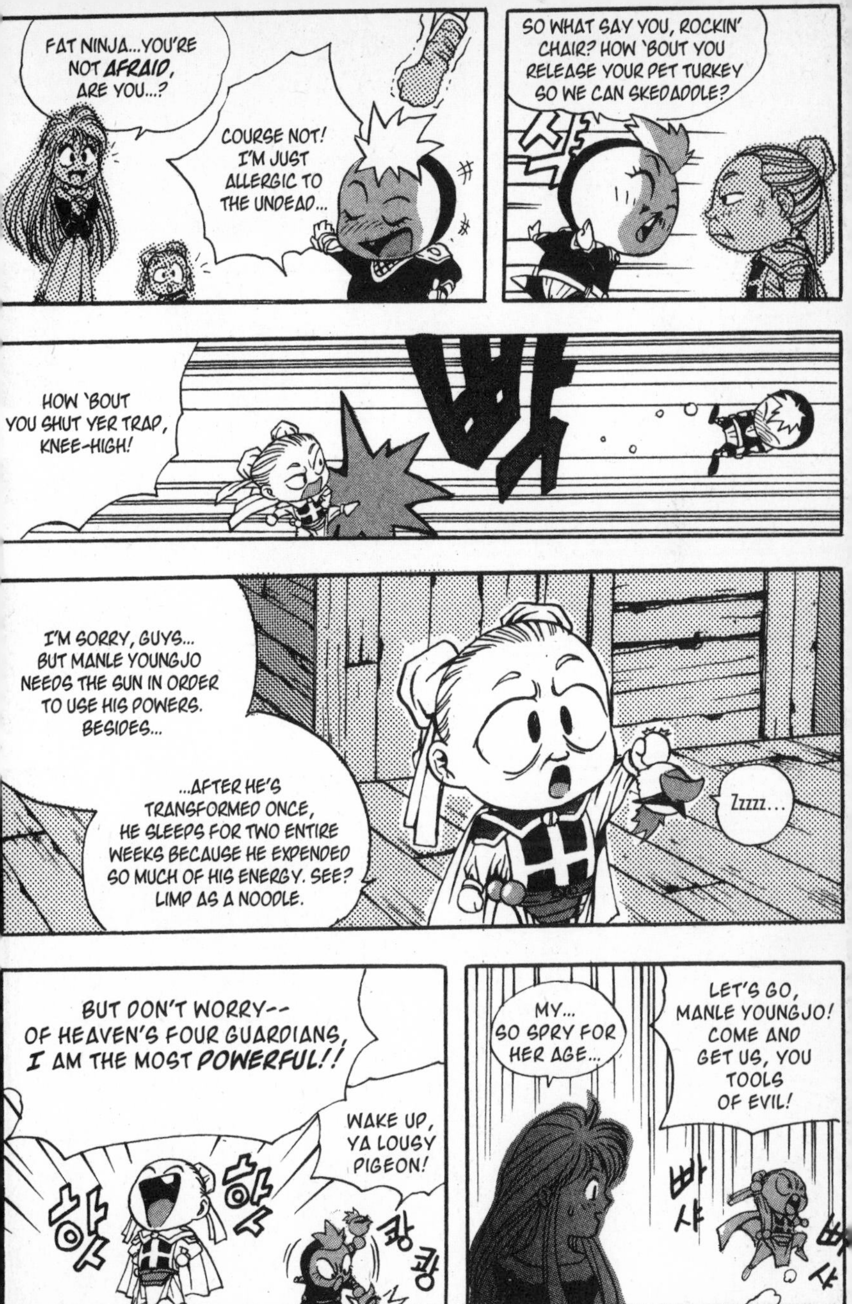
FAT NINJA...YOU'RE NOT AFRAID, ARE YOU...?
COURSE NOT! I'M JUST ALLERGIC TO THE UNDEAD...
SO WHAT SAY YOU, ROCKIN' CHAIR? HOW 'BOUT YOU RELEASE YOUR PET TURKEY SO WE CAN SKEDADDLE?
HOW 'BOUT YOU SHUT YER TRAP, KNEE-HIGH!
I'M SORRY, GUYS... BUT MANLE YOUNGJO NEEDS THE SUN IN ORDER TO USE HIS POWERS. BESIDES...
...AFTER HE'S TRANSFORMED ONCE, HE SLEEPS FOR TWO ENTIRE WEEKS BECAUSE HE EXPENDED SO MUCH OF HIS ENERGY. SEE? LIMP AS A NOODLE.
Zzzzz...
BUT DON'T WORRY--OF HEAVEN'S FOUR GUARDIANS, I AM THE MOST POWERFUL!!
WAKE UP, YA LOUSY PIGEON!
쾅 쾅
MY... SO SPRY FOR HER AGE...
LET'S GO, MANLE YOUNGJO! COME AND GET US, YOU TOOLS OF EVIL!
빠샤

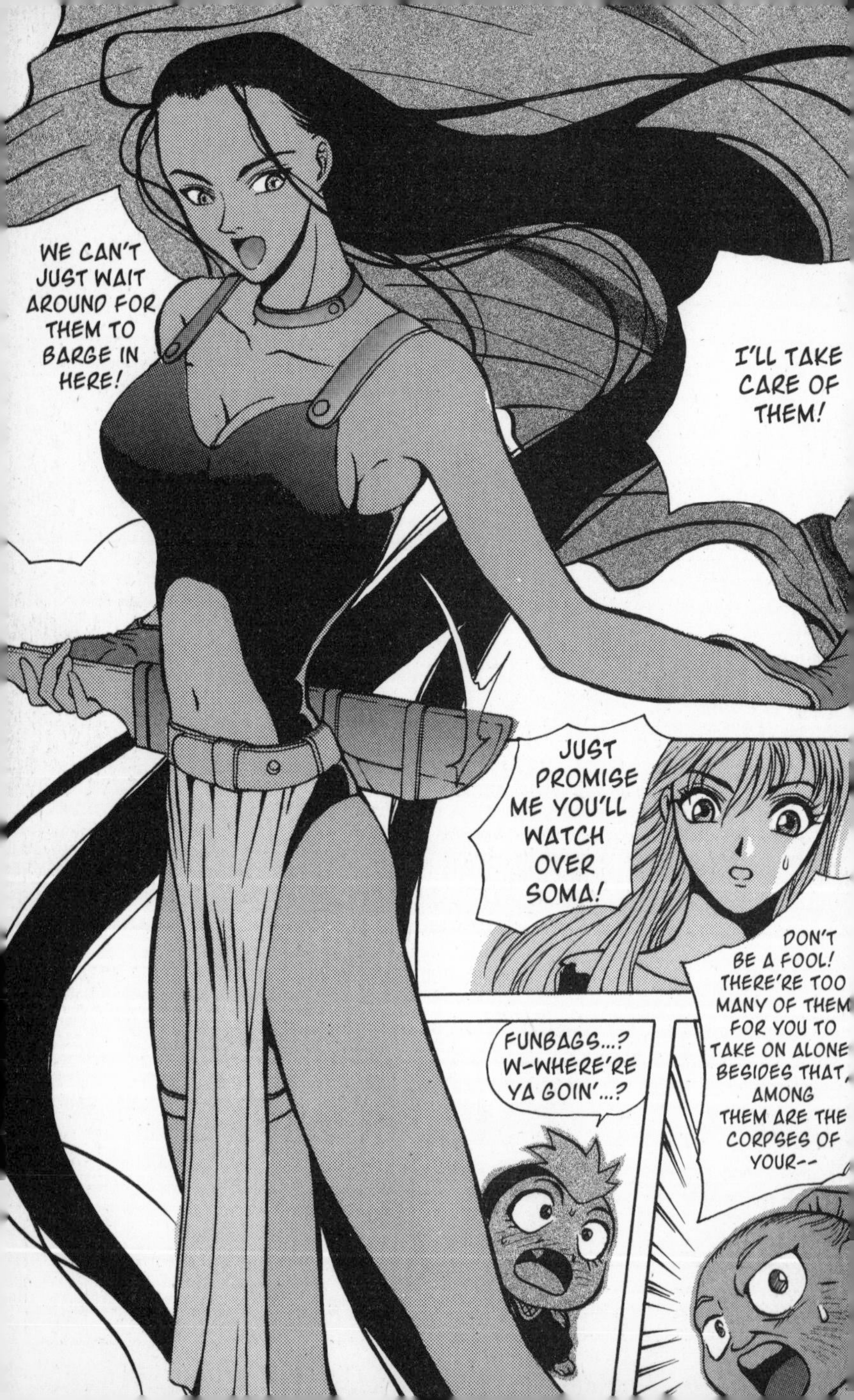
WE CAN'T JUST WAIT AROUND FOR THEM TO BARGE IN HERE!
I'LL TAKE CARE OF THEM!
JUST PROMISE ME YOU'LL WATCH OVER SOMA!
DON'T BE A FOOL! THERE'RE TOO MANY OF THEM FOR YOU TO TAKE ON ALONE BESIDES THAT, AMONG THEM ARE THE CORPSES OF YOUR--
FUNBAGS...? W-WHERE'RE YA GOIN'...?

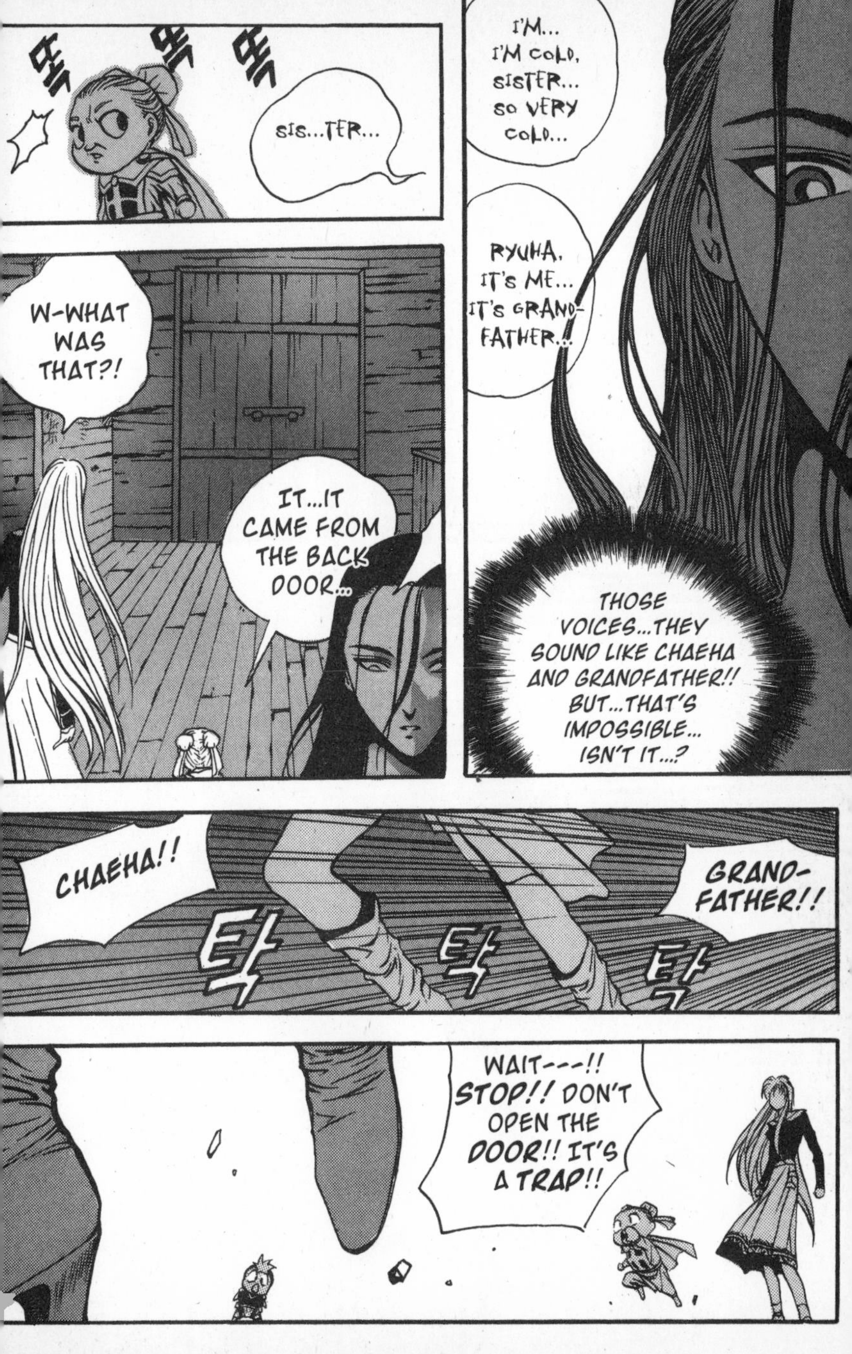

똑 똑 똑
SIS...TER...
W-WHAT WAS THAT?!
IT...IT CAME FROM THE BACK DOOR...
I'M... I'M COLD, SISTER... SO VERY COLD...
RYUHA, IT'S ME... IT'S GRANDFATHER...
THOSE VOICES...THEY SOUND LIKE CHAEHA AND GRANDFATHER!! BUT...THAT'S IMPOSSIBLE... ISN'T IT...?
CHAEHA!!
GRANDFATHER!!
탁 탁 탁
WAIT---!! STOP!! DON'T OPEN THE DOOR!! IT'S A TRAP!!

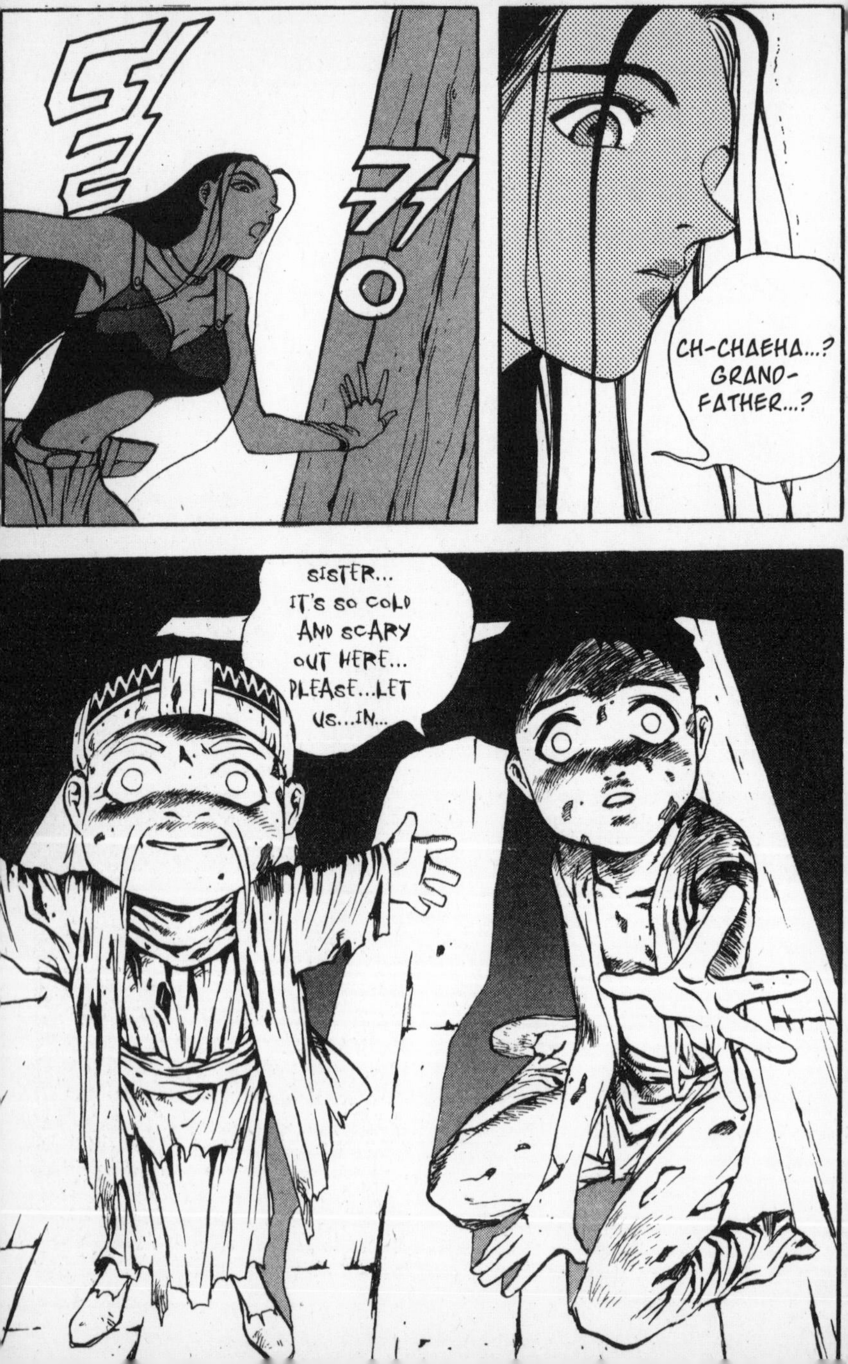
CH-CHAEHA...? GRAND-FATHER...?
SISTER... IT'S SO COLD AND SCARY OUT HERE... PLEASE...LET US...IN...

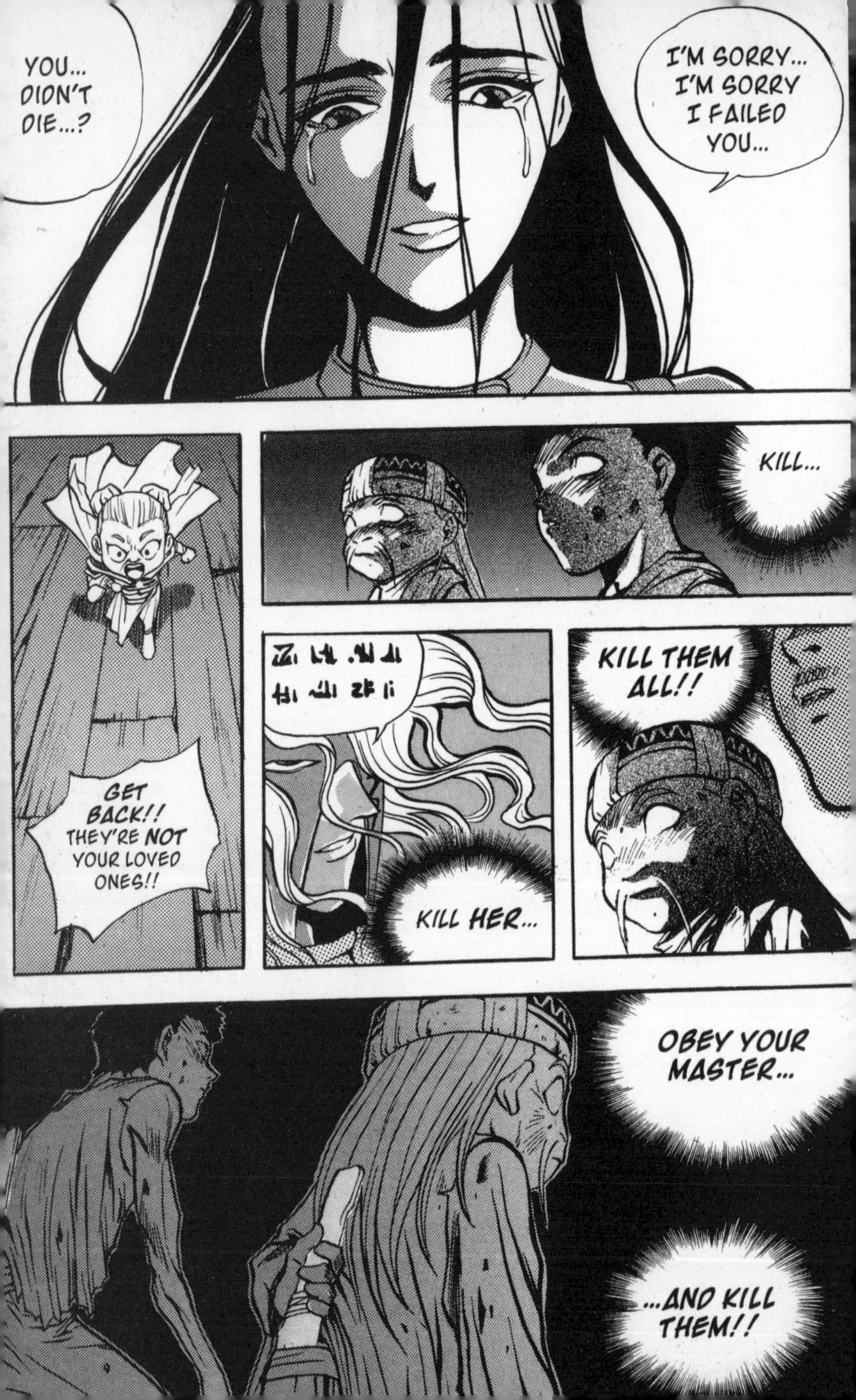
I'M SORRY... I'M SORRY I FAILED YOU...
YOU... DIDN'T DIE...?
KILL...
KILL THEM ALL!!
KILL HER...
GET BACK!! THEY'RE NOT YOUR LOVED ONES!!
OBEY YOUR MASTER...
...AND KILL THEM!!

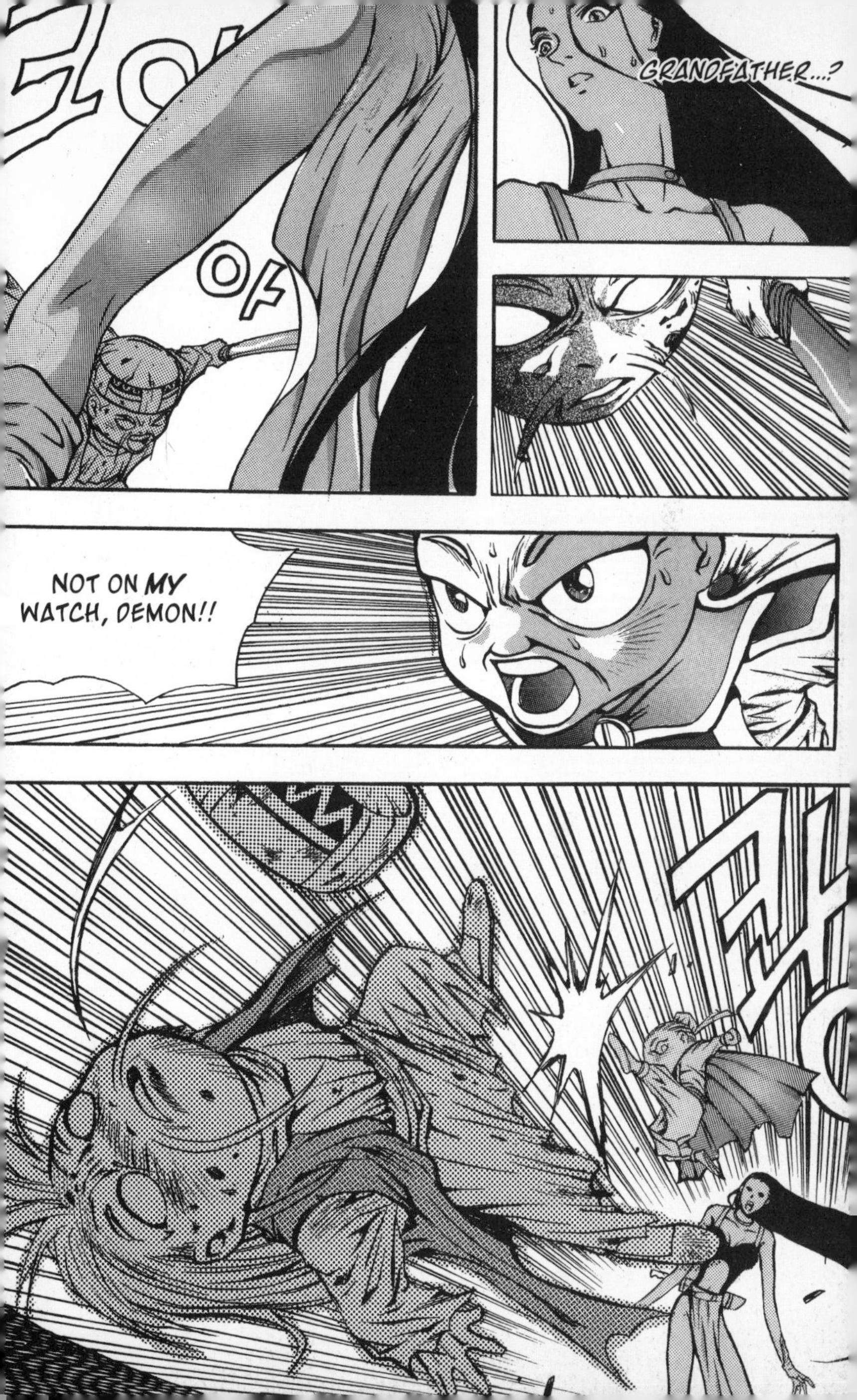
GRANDFATHER...?
NOT ON MY WATCH, DEMON!!

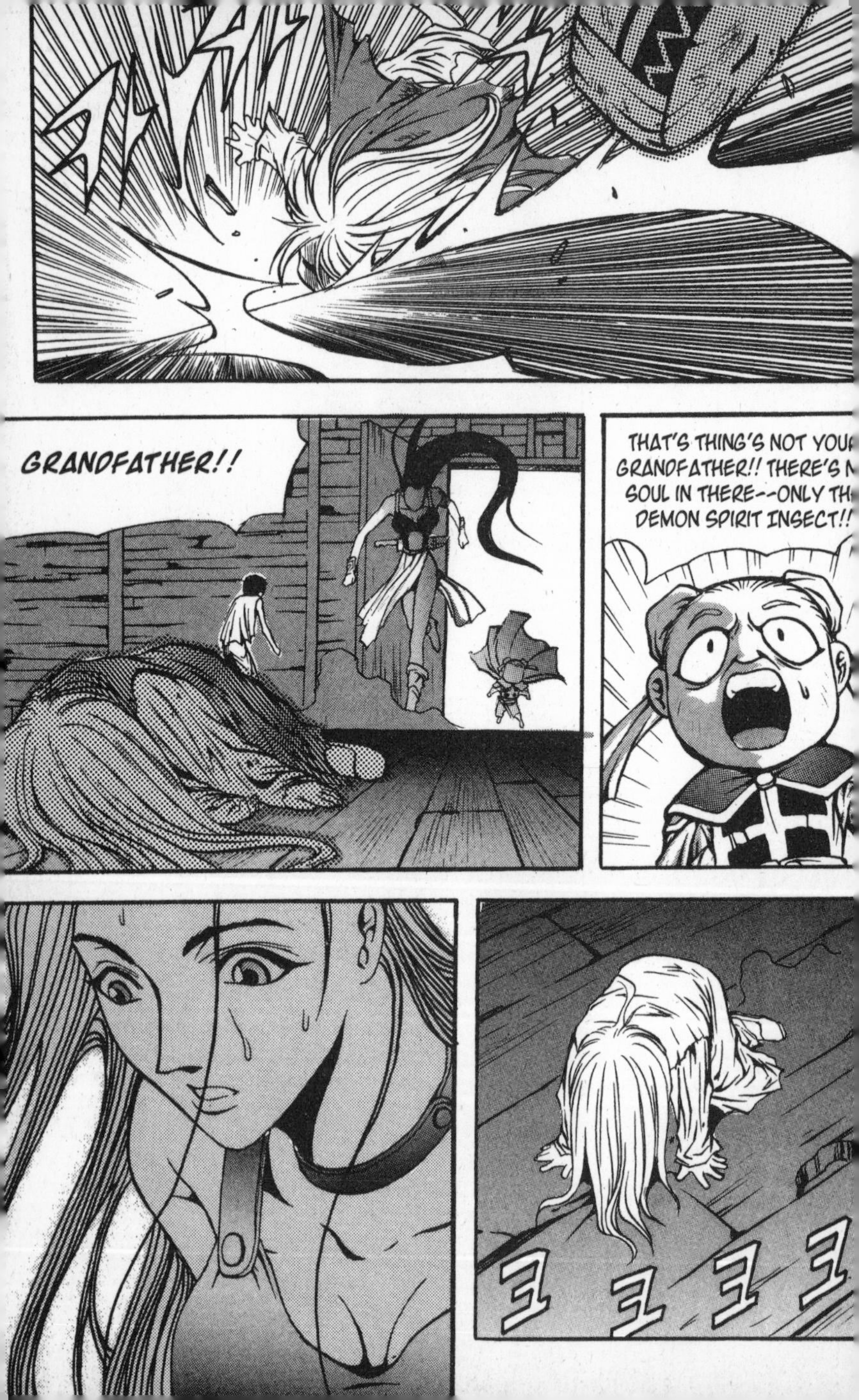
THAT'S THING'S NOT YOU
GRANDFATHER!! THERE'S
SOUL IN THERE--ONLY TH
DEMON SPIRIT INSECT!!
GRANDFATHER!!
ヨ ヨ ヨ ヨ

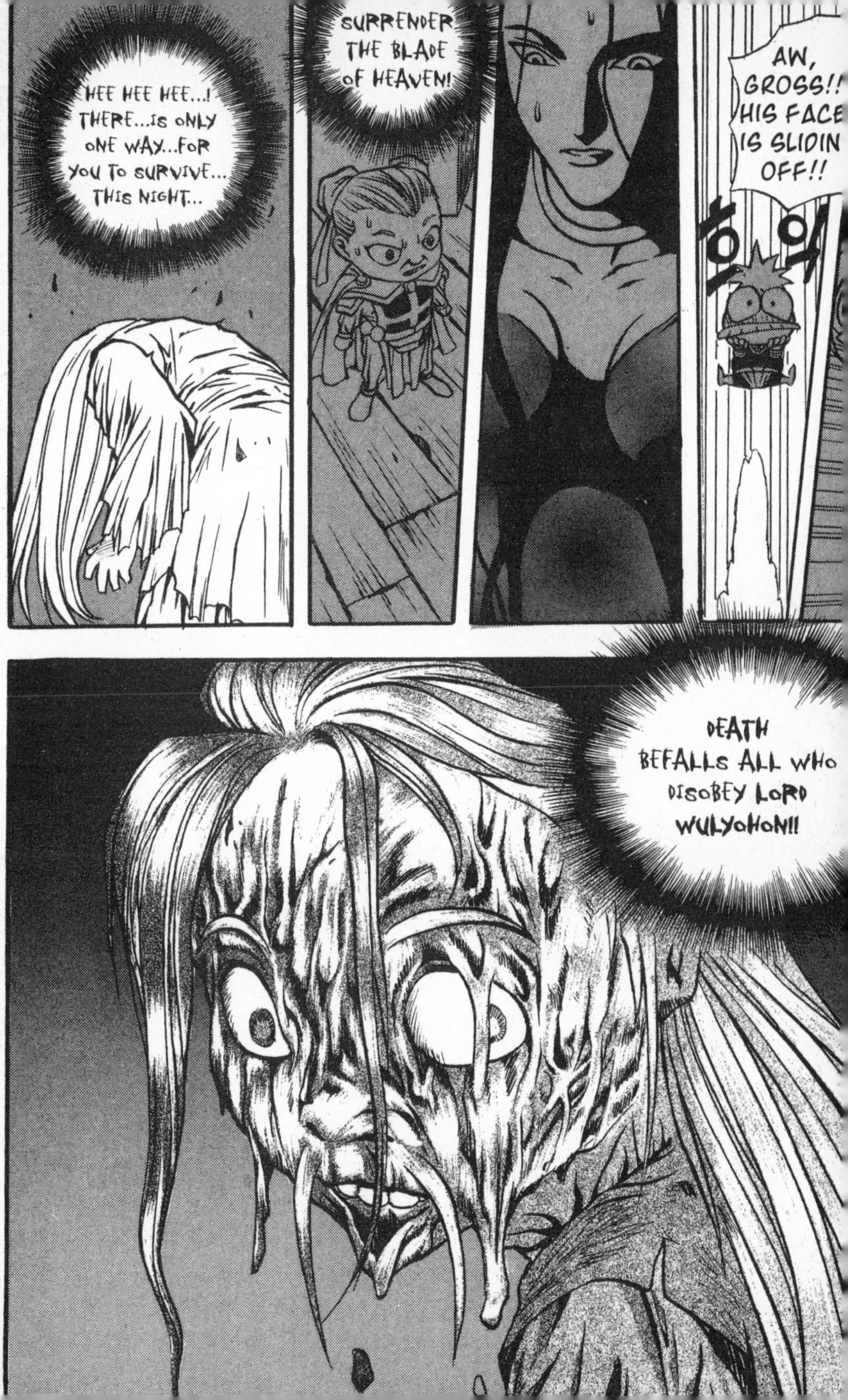
HEE HEE HEE...! THERE...IS ONLY ONE WAY...FOR YOU TO SURVIVE... THIS NIGHT...
SURRENDER THE BLADE OF HEAVEN!
AW, GROSS!! HIS FACE IS SLIDIN OFF!!
흐어
DEATH BEFALLS ALL WHO DISOBEY LORD WULYOHON!!

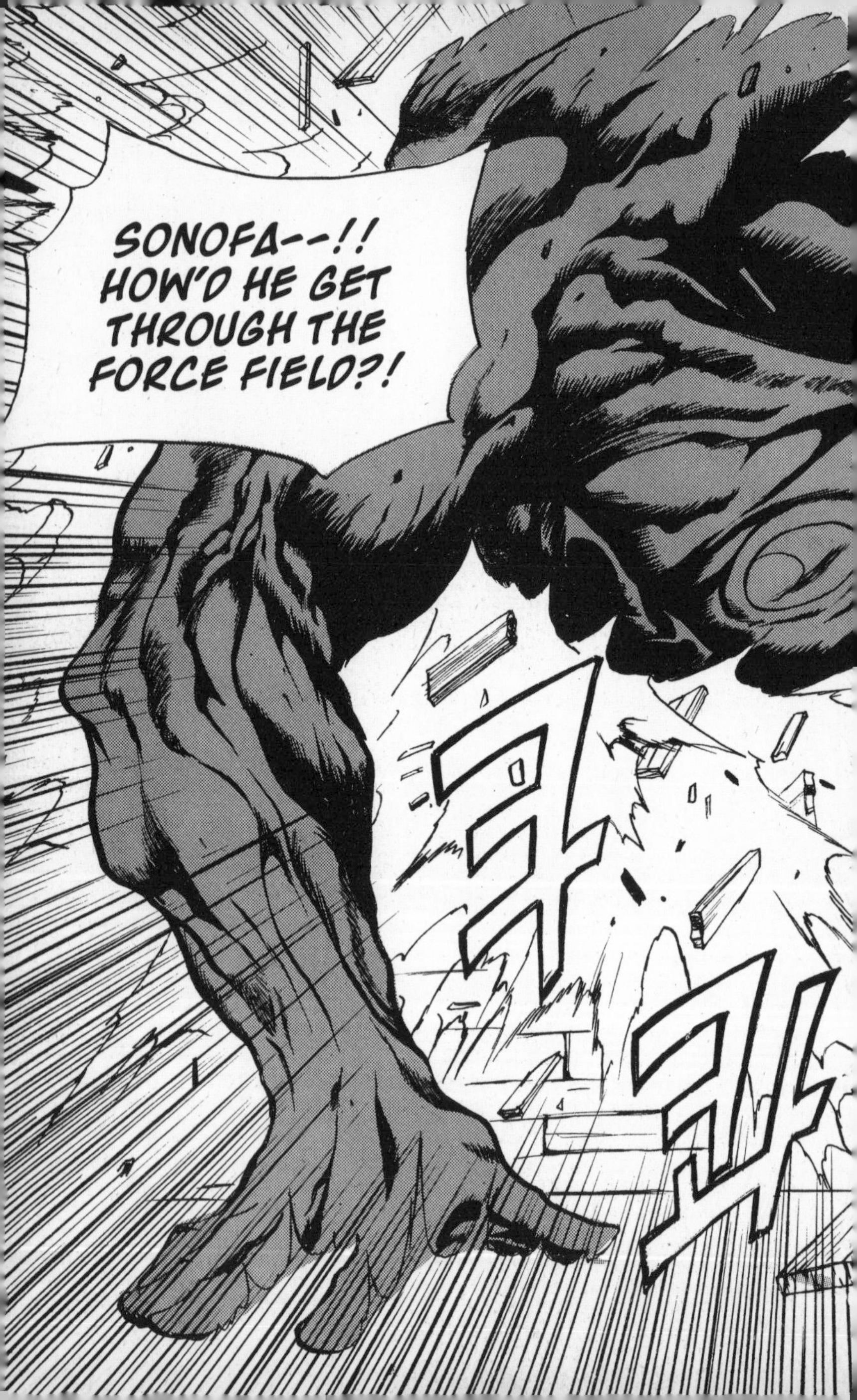
SONOFA--!! HOW'D HE GET THROUGH THE FORCE FIELD?!

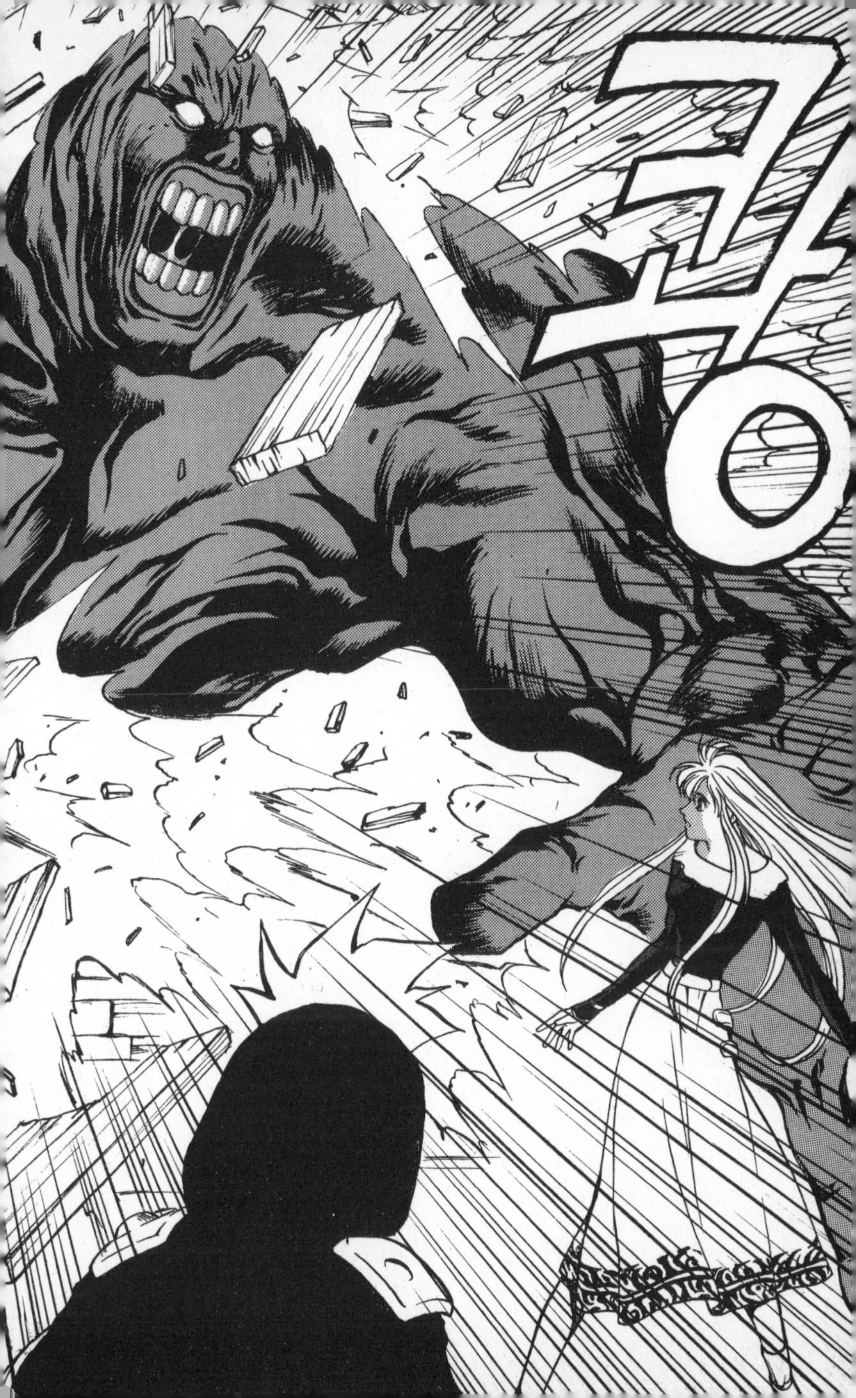

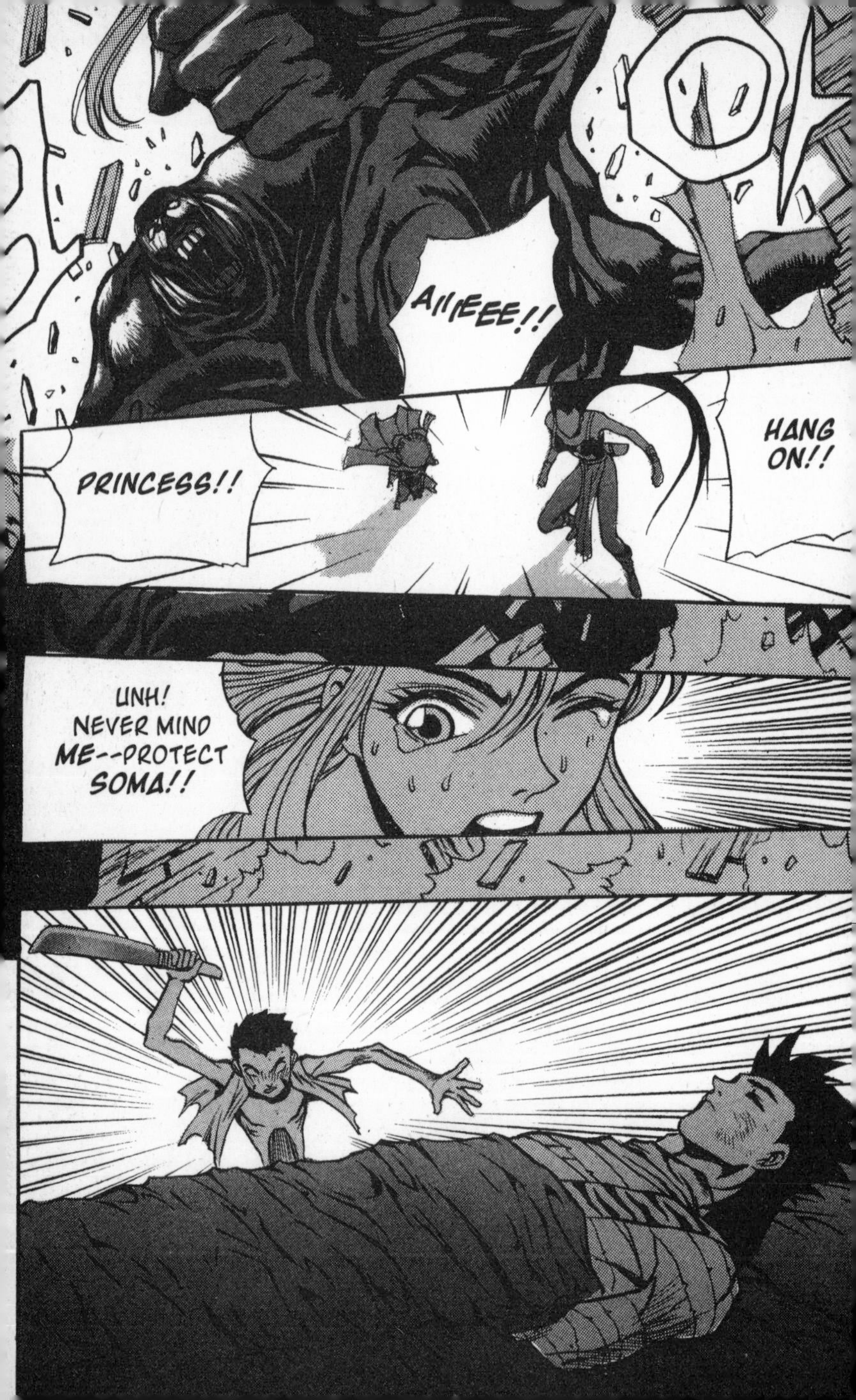
AIIIEEE!!
HANG ON!!
PRINCESS!!
UNH! NEVER MIND ME--PROTECT SOMA!!

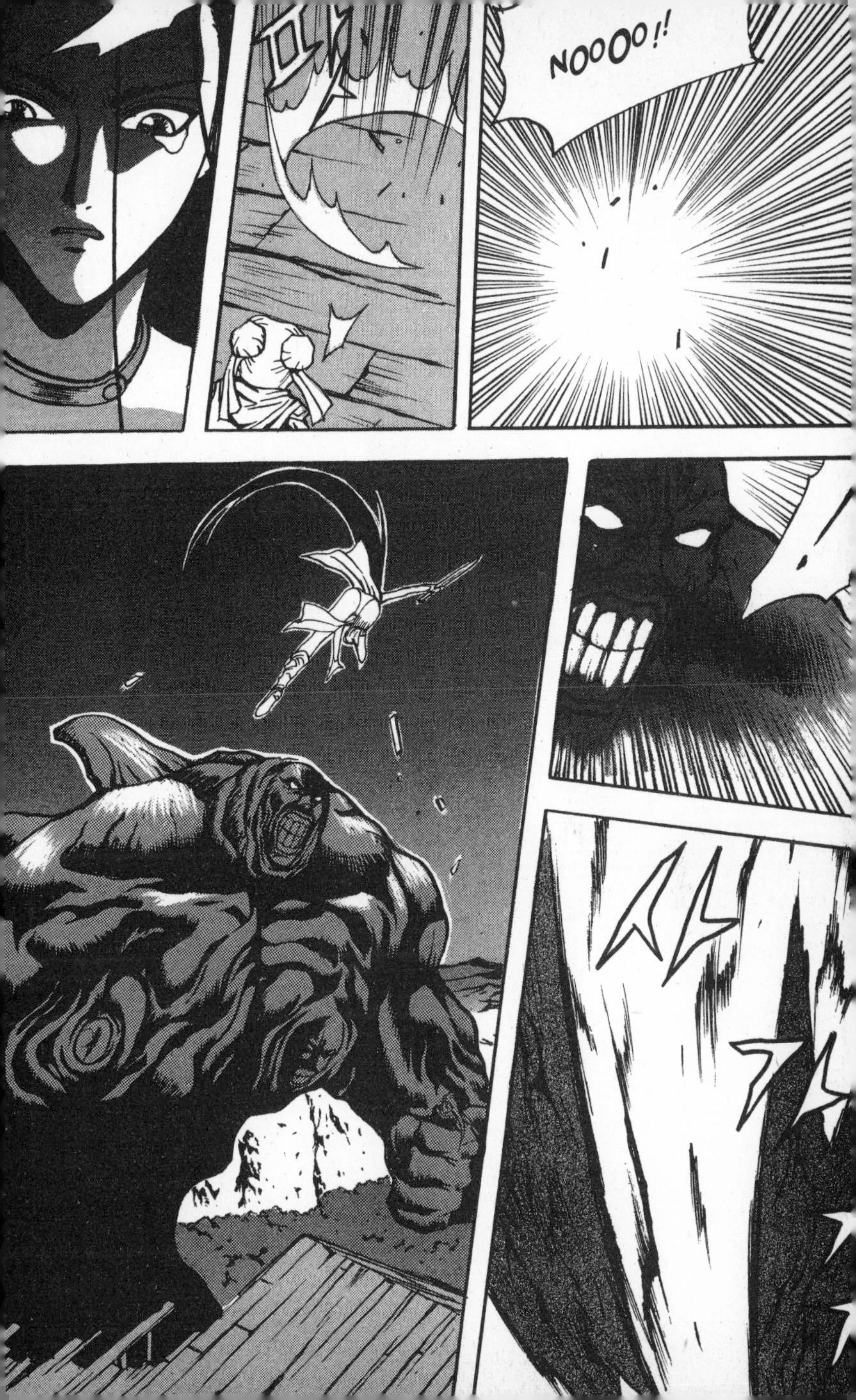
NOOOO!!

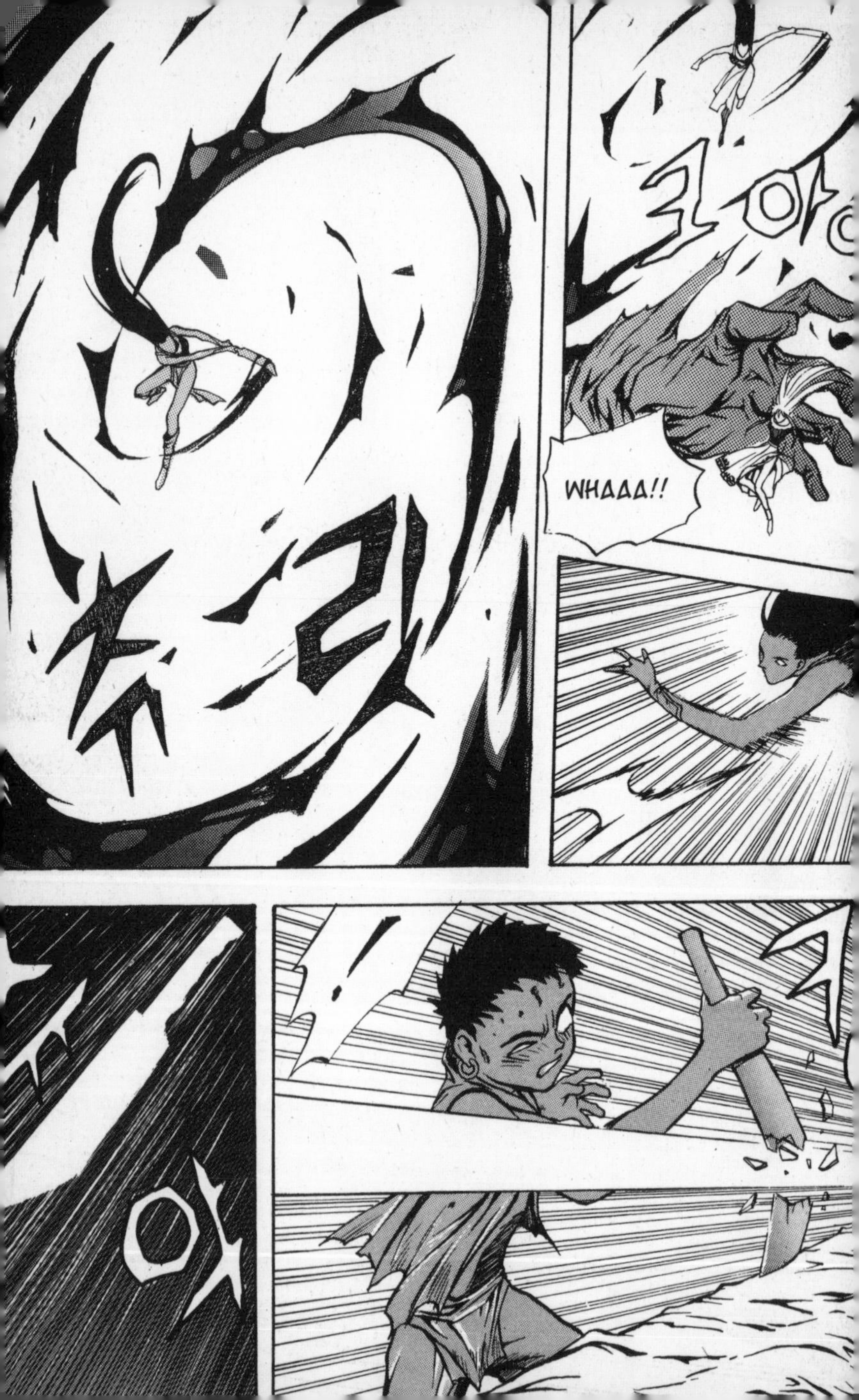
WHAAA!!

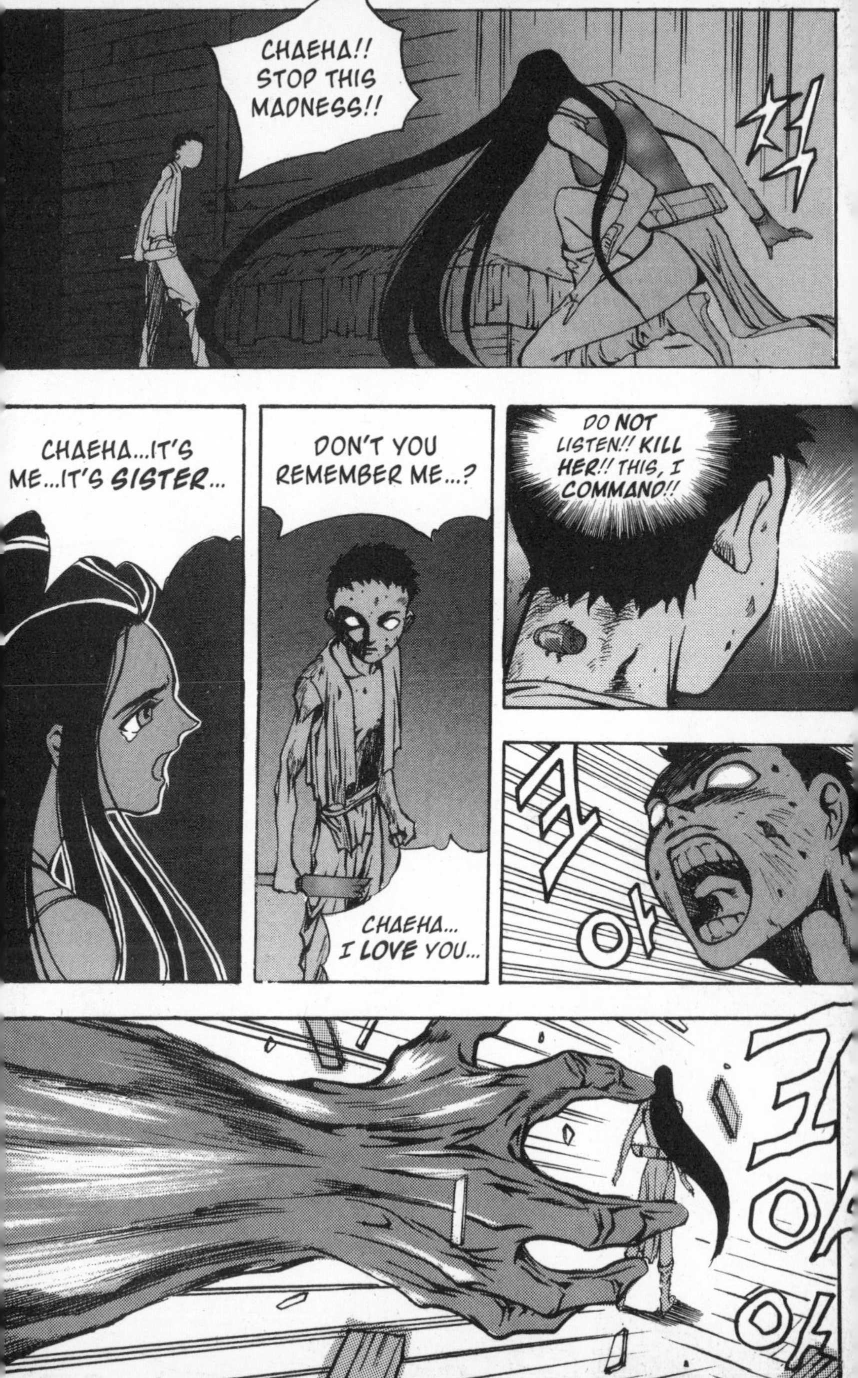
CHAEHA!! STOP THIS MADNESS!!
CHAEHA...IT'S ME...IT'S SISTER...
DON'T YOU REMEMBER ME...?
CHAEHA... I LOVE YOU...
DO NOT LISTEN!! KILL HER!! THIS, I COMMAND!!

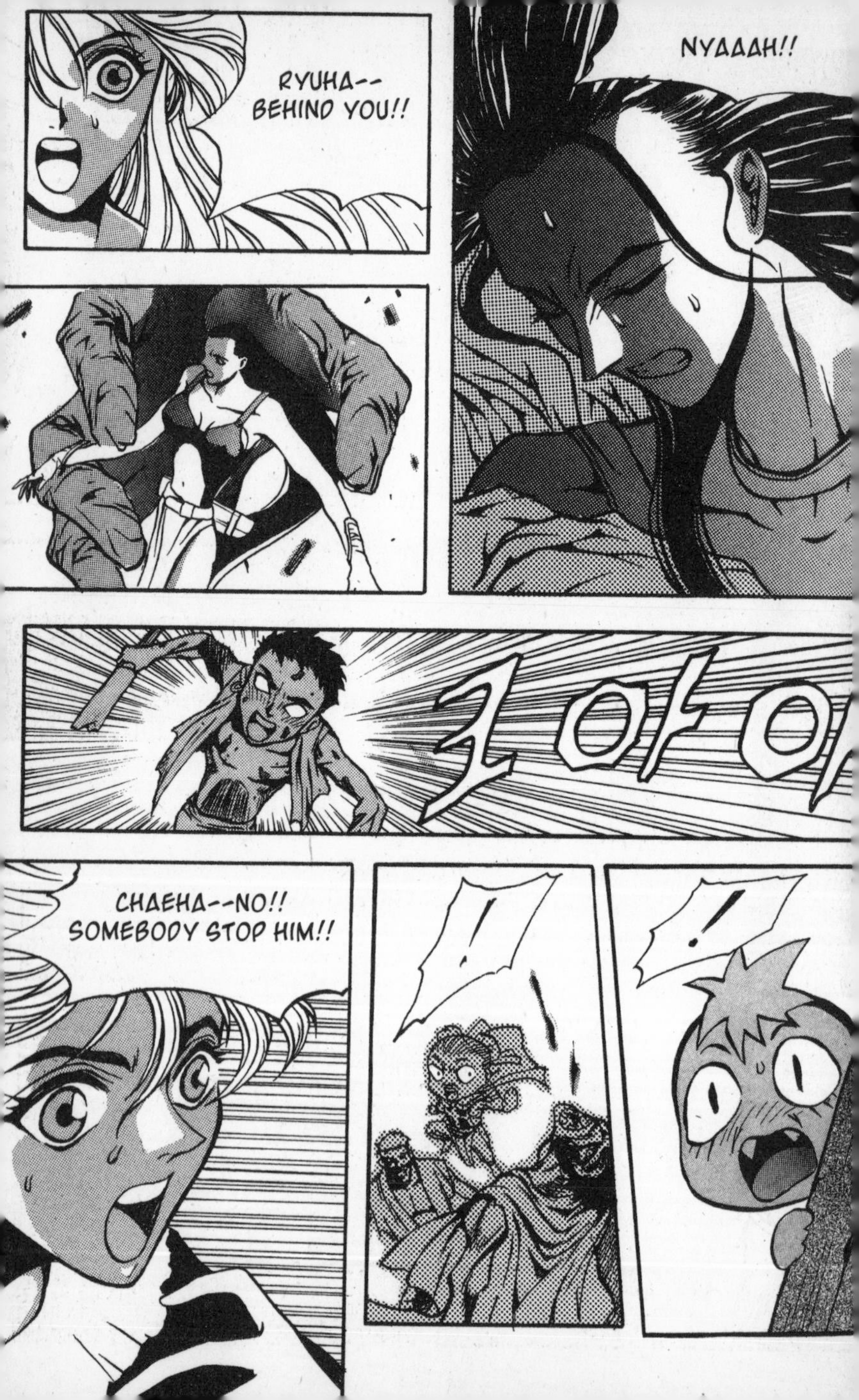
RYUHA--
BEHIND YOU!!
NYAAAH!!
CHAEHA--NO!!
SOMEBODY STOP HIM!!
!
!

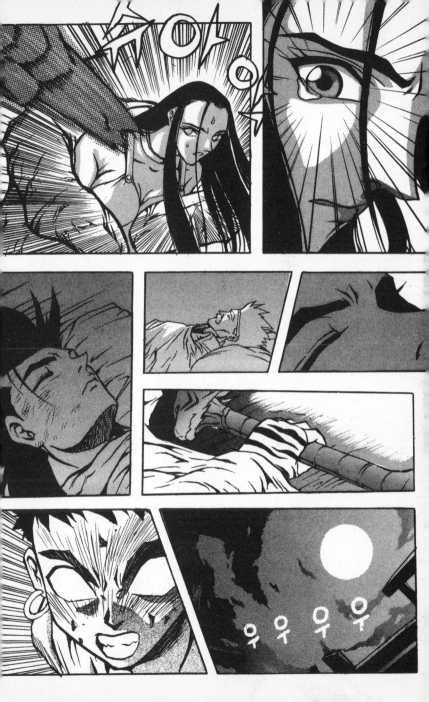

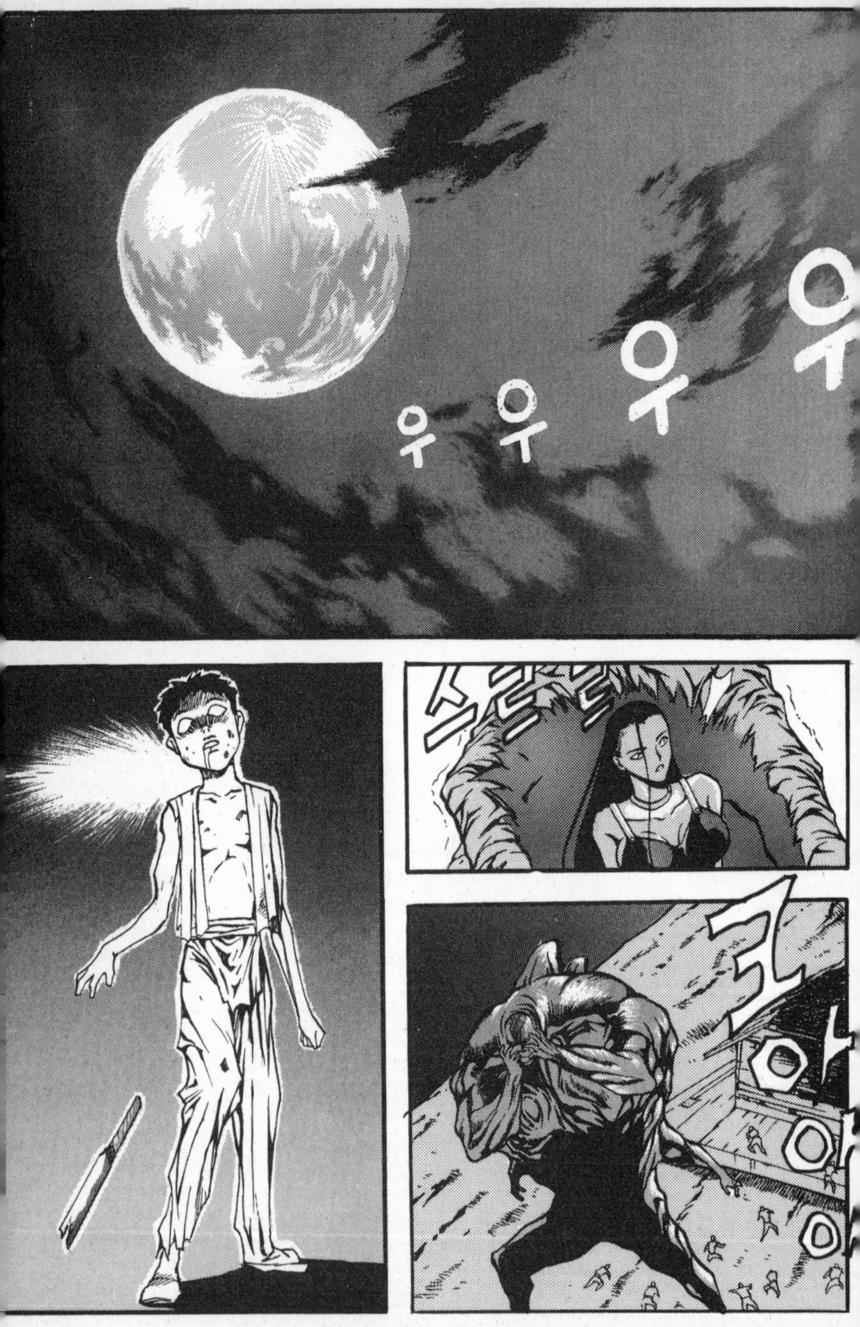
우우우우
스르르
크아아아

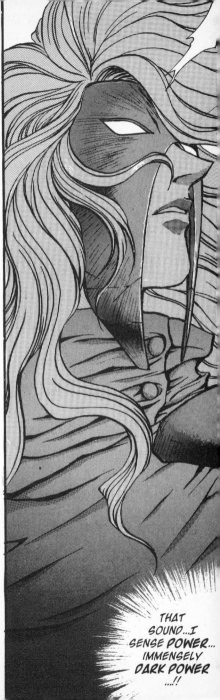

THAT SOUND...I SENSE *POWER*... IMMENSELY *DARK POWER* ...!!

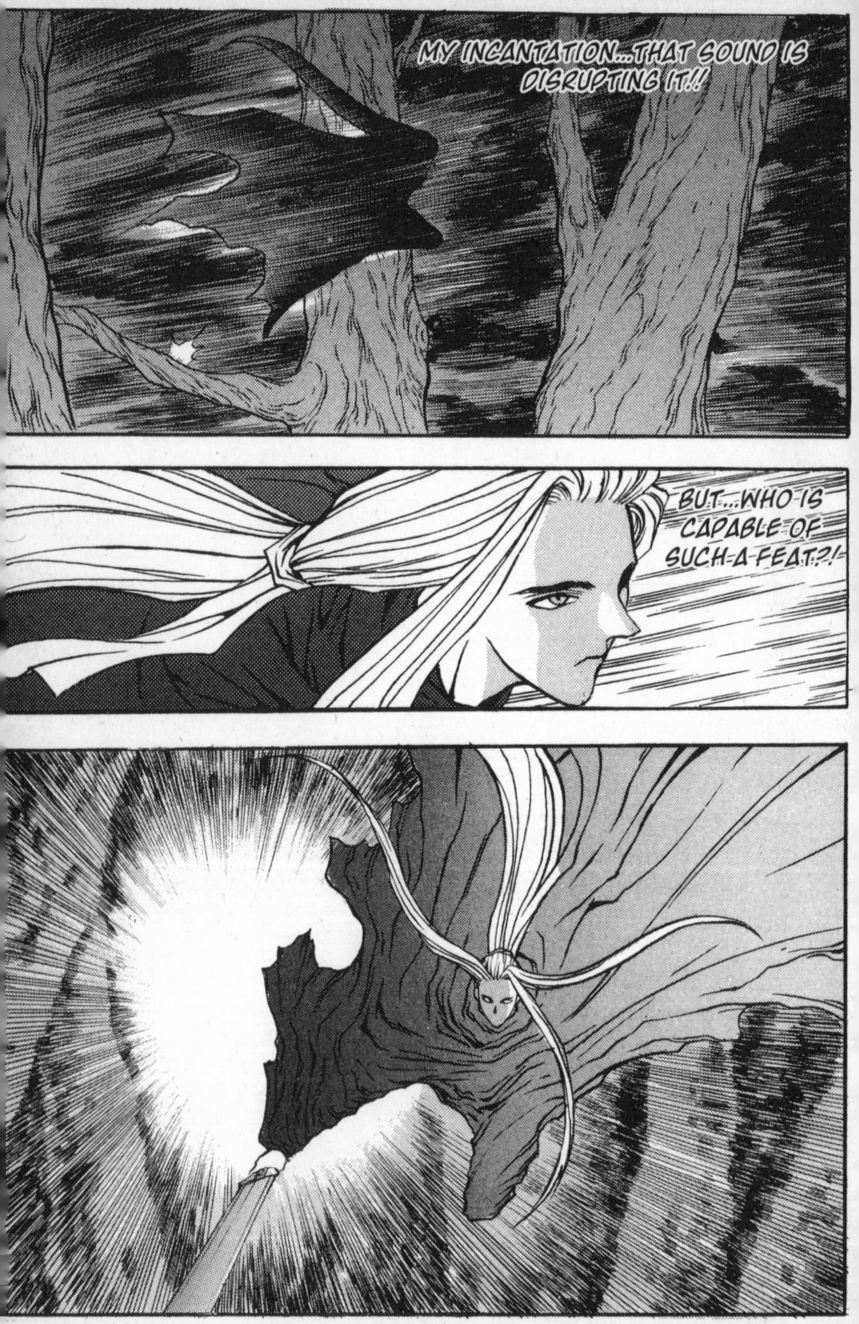
MY INCANTATION...THAT SOUND IS DISRUPTING IT!!
BUT...WHO IS CAPABLE OF SUCH A FEAT?!

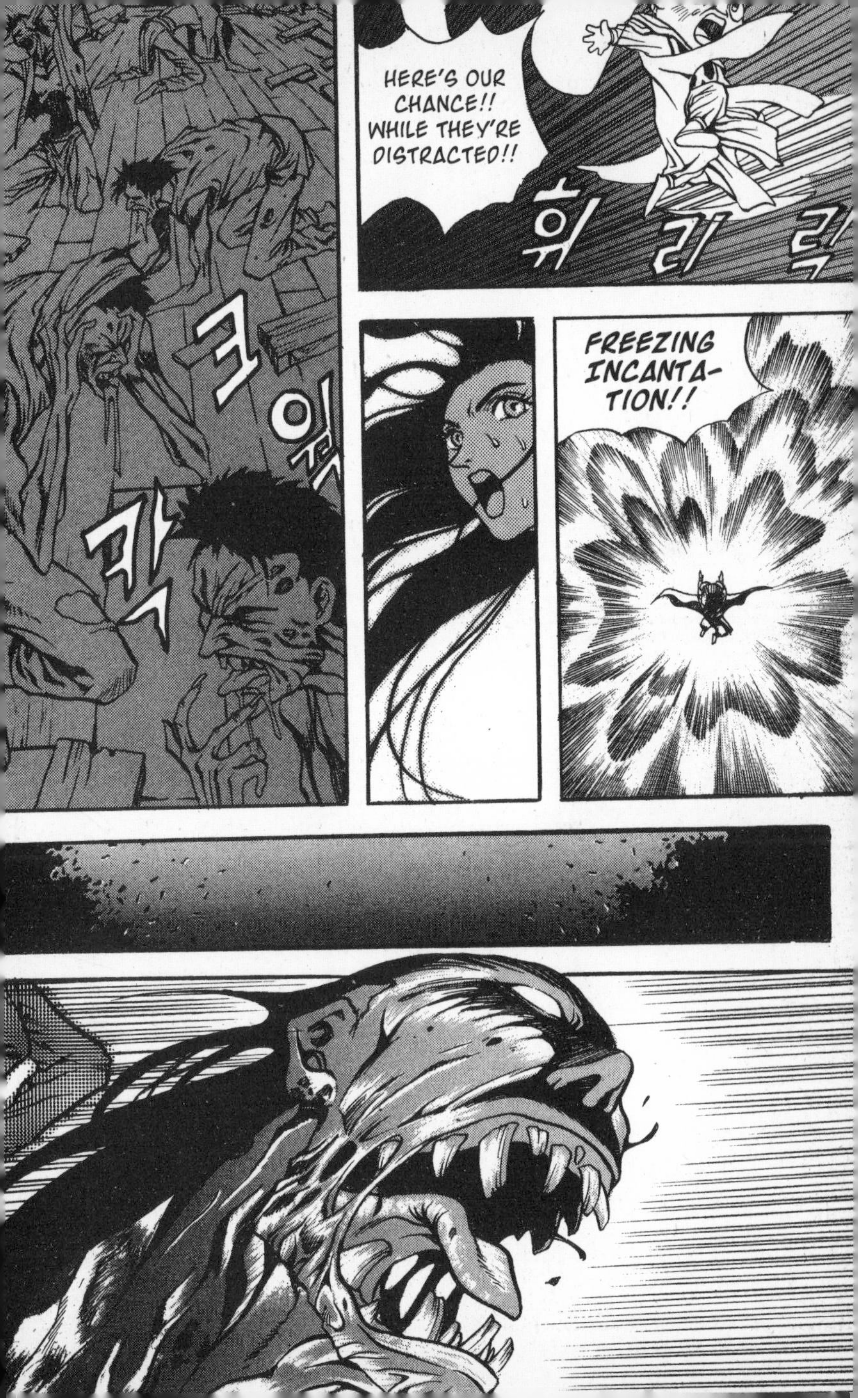
HERE'S OUR CHANCE!! WHILE THEY'RE DISTRACTED!!
휘리릭
FREEZING INCANTA-TION!!

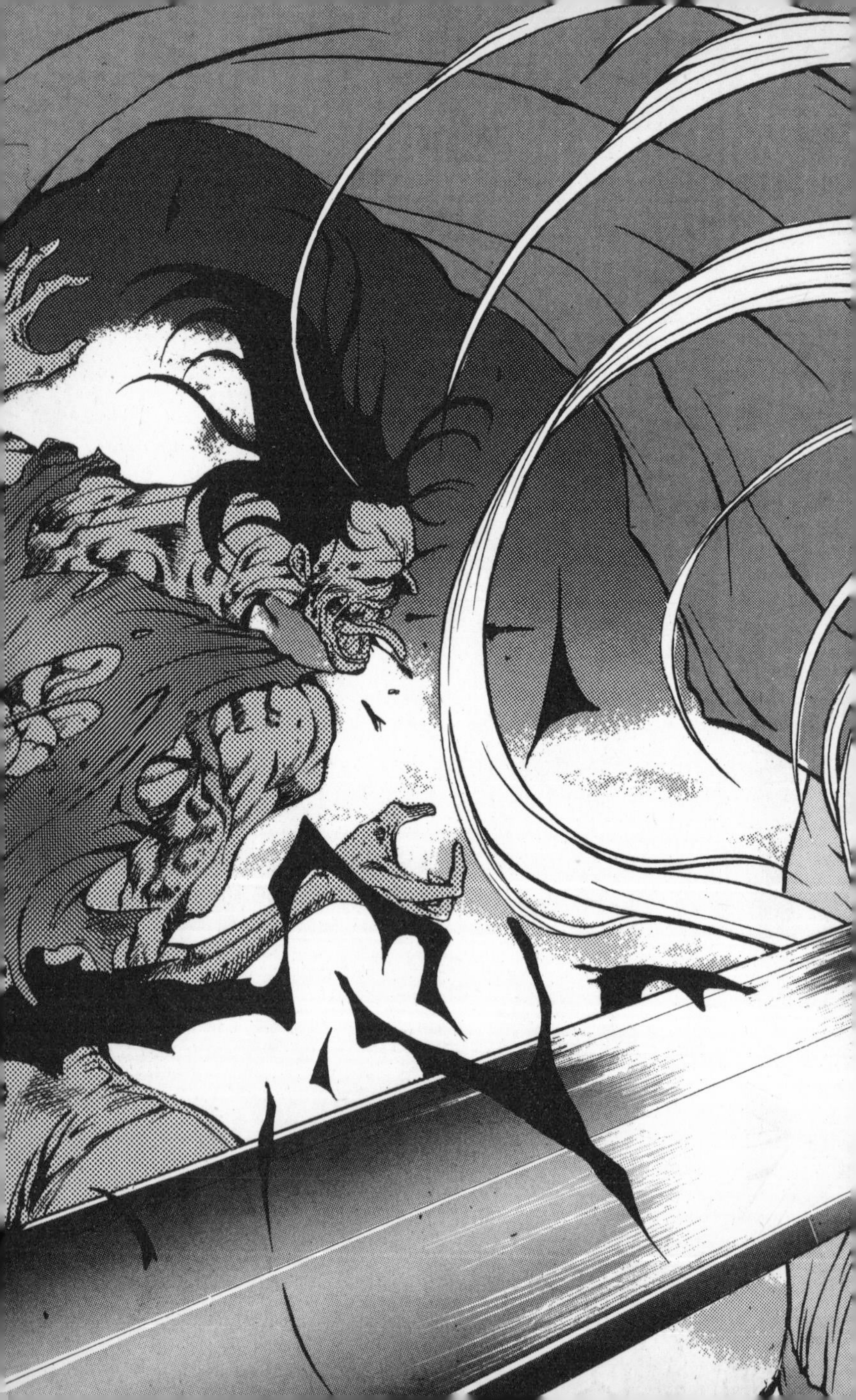

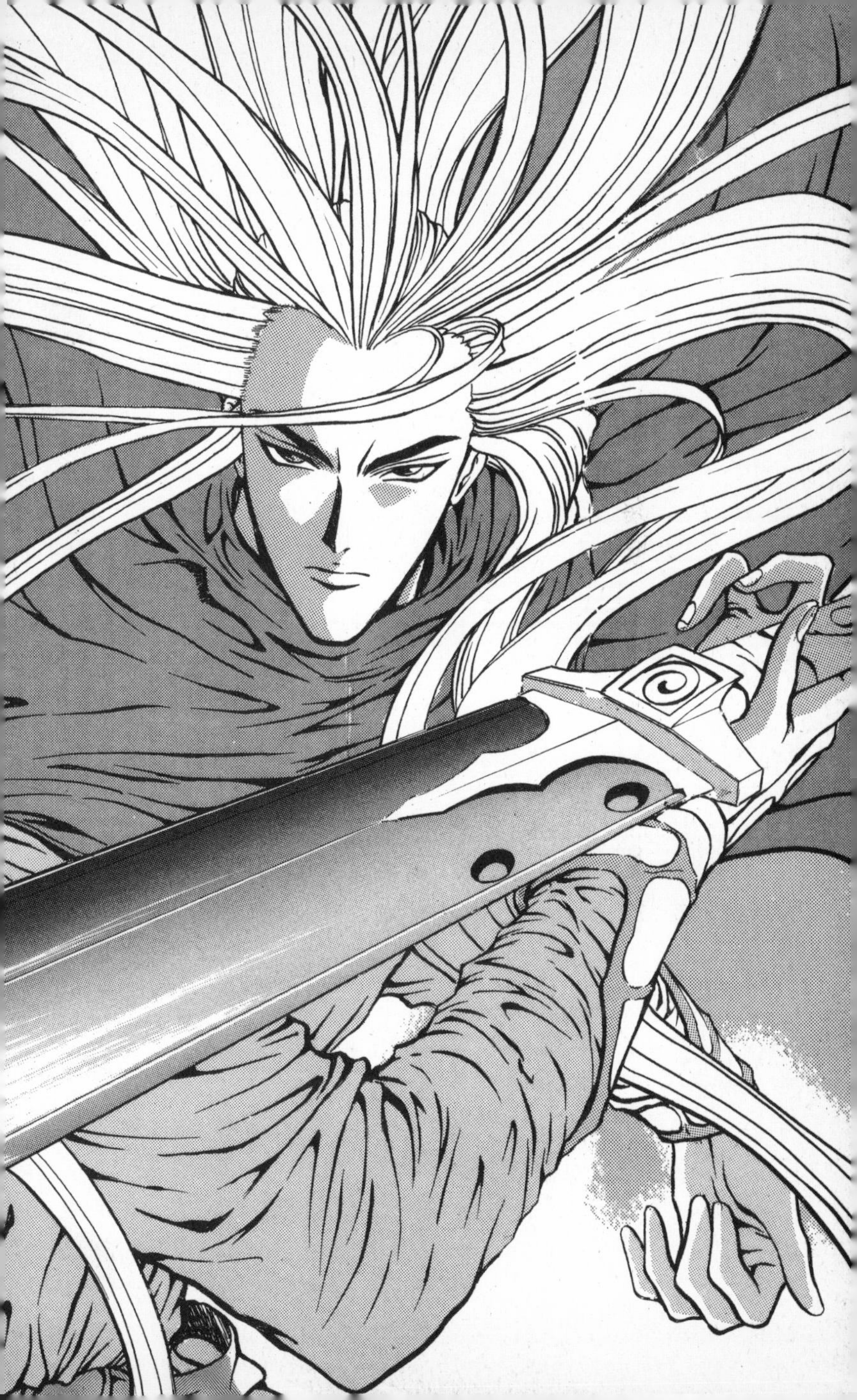

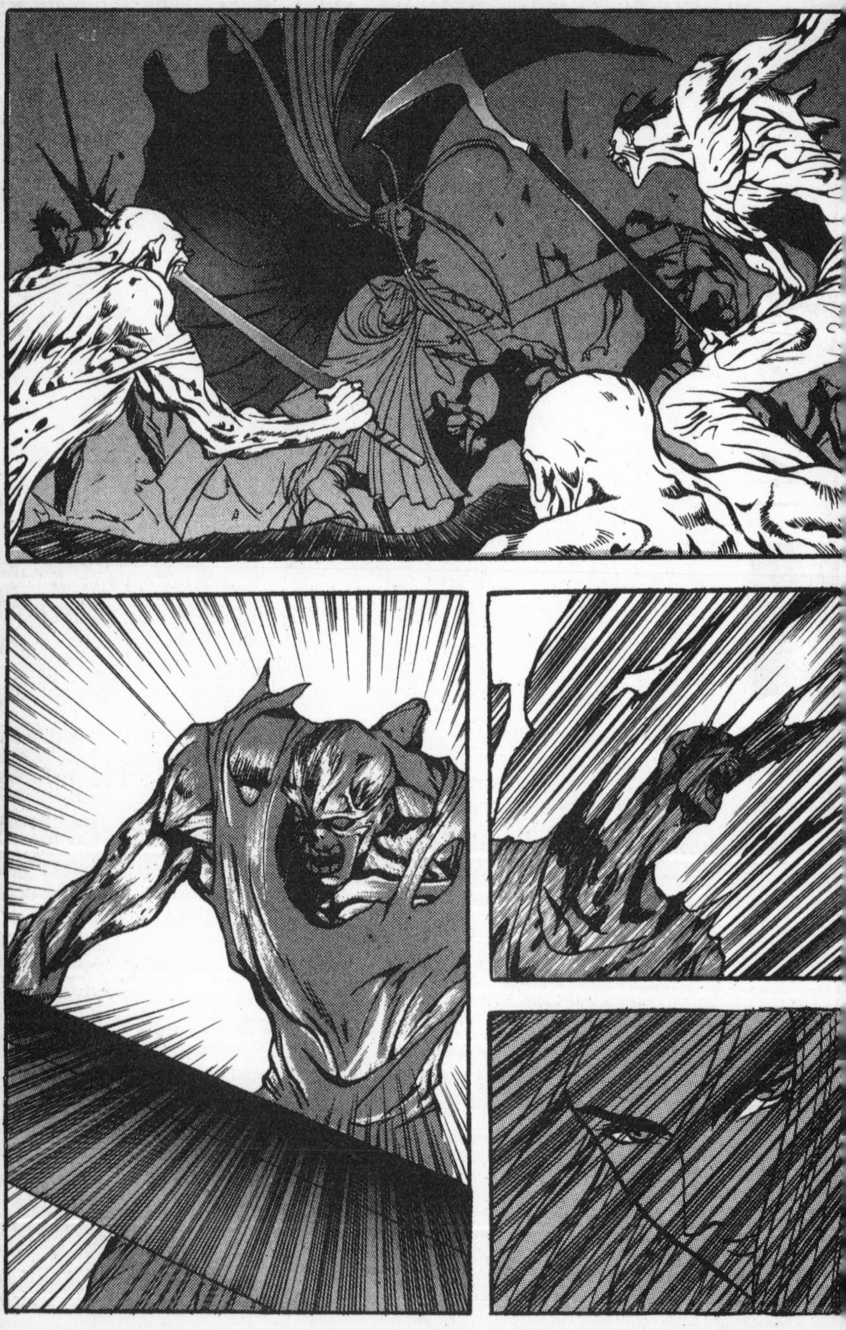

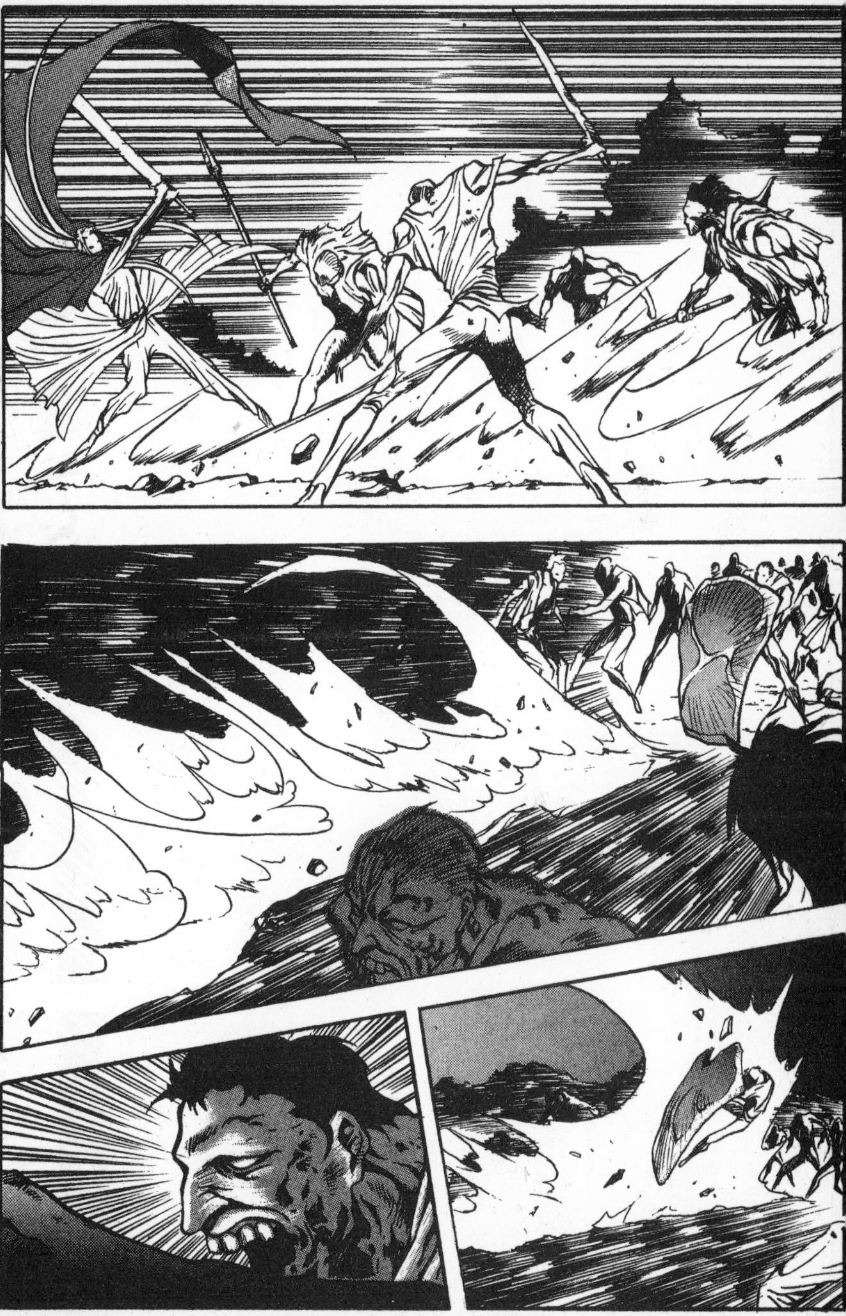

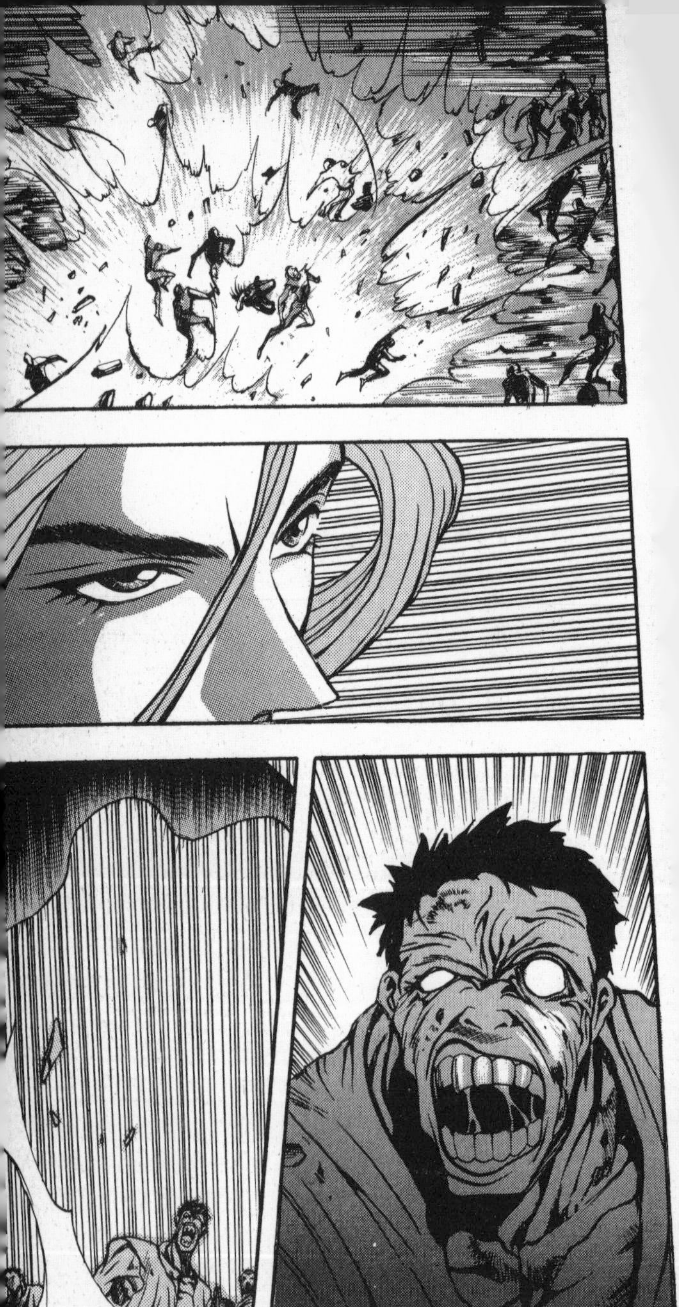

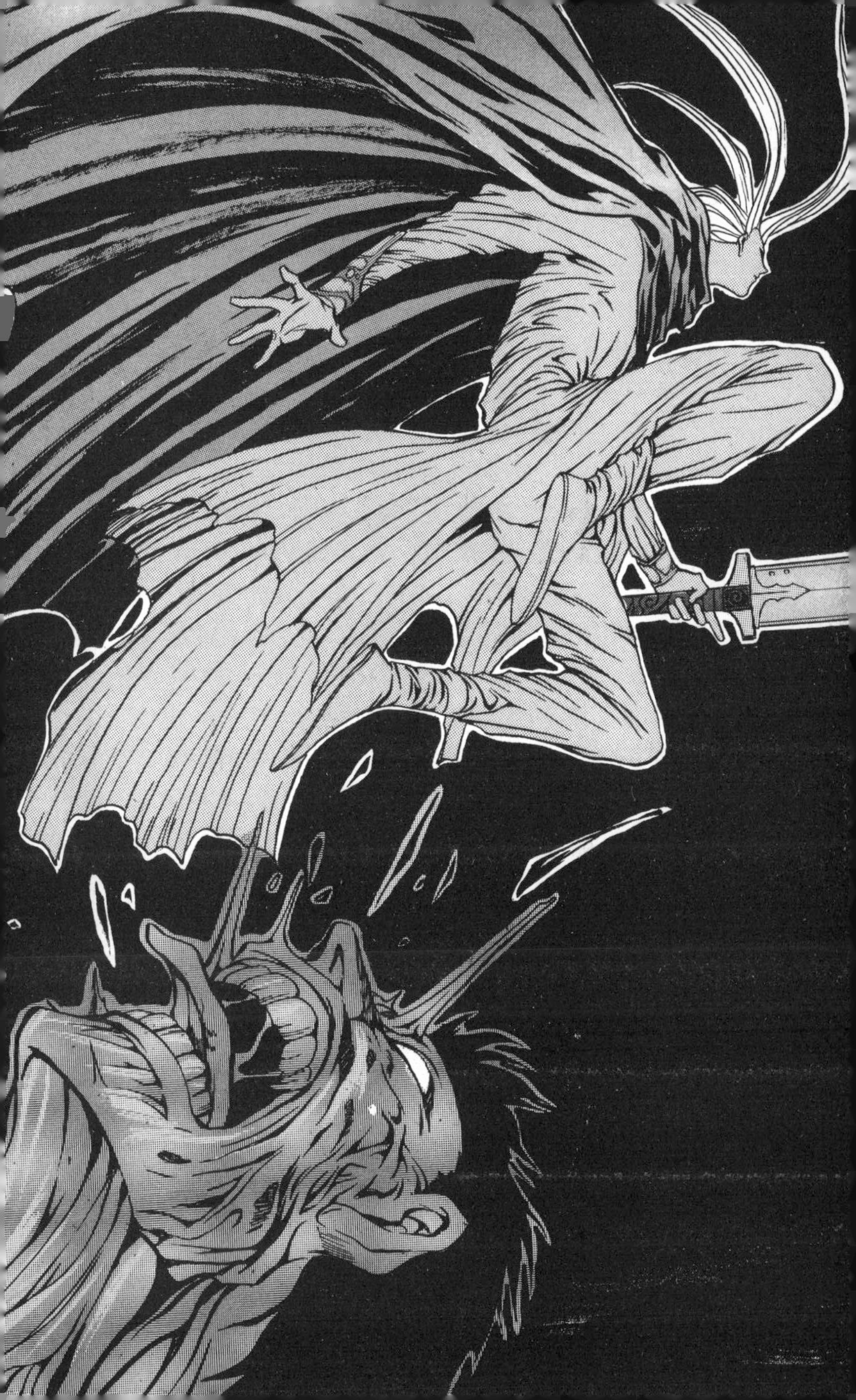

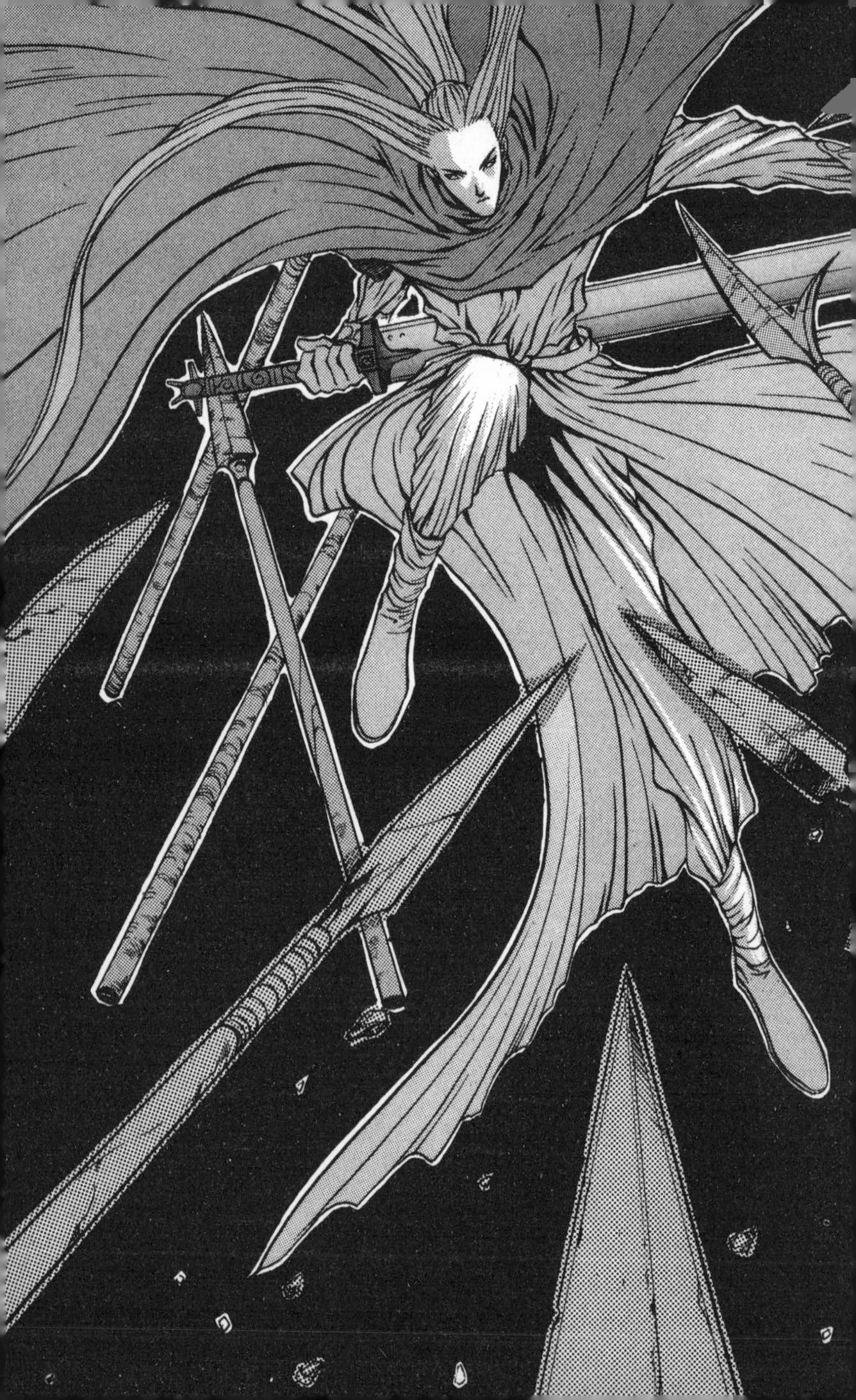

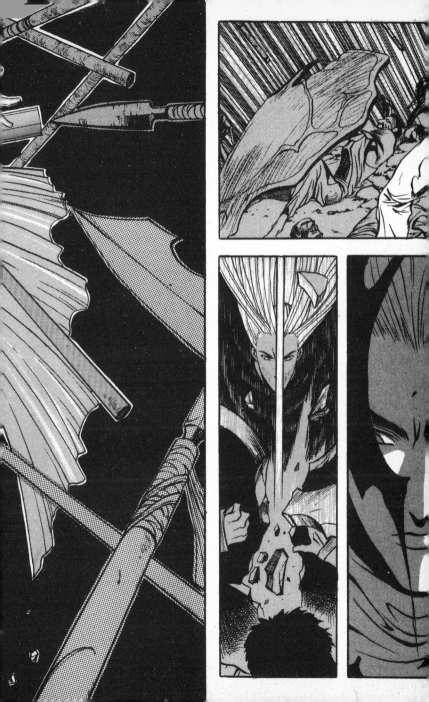

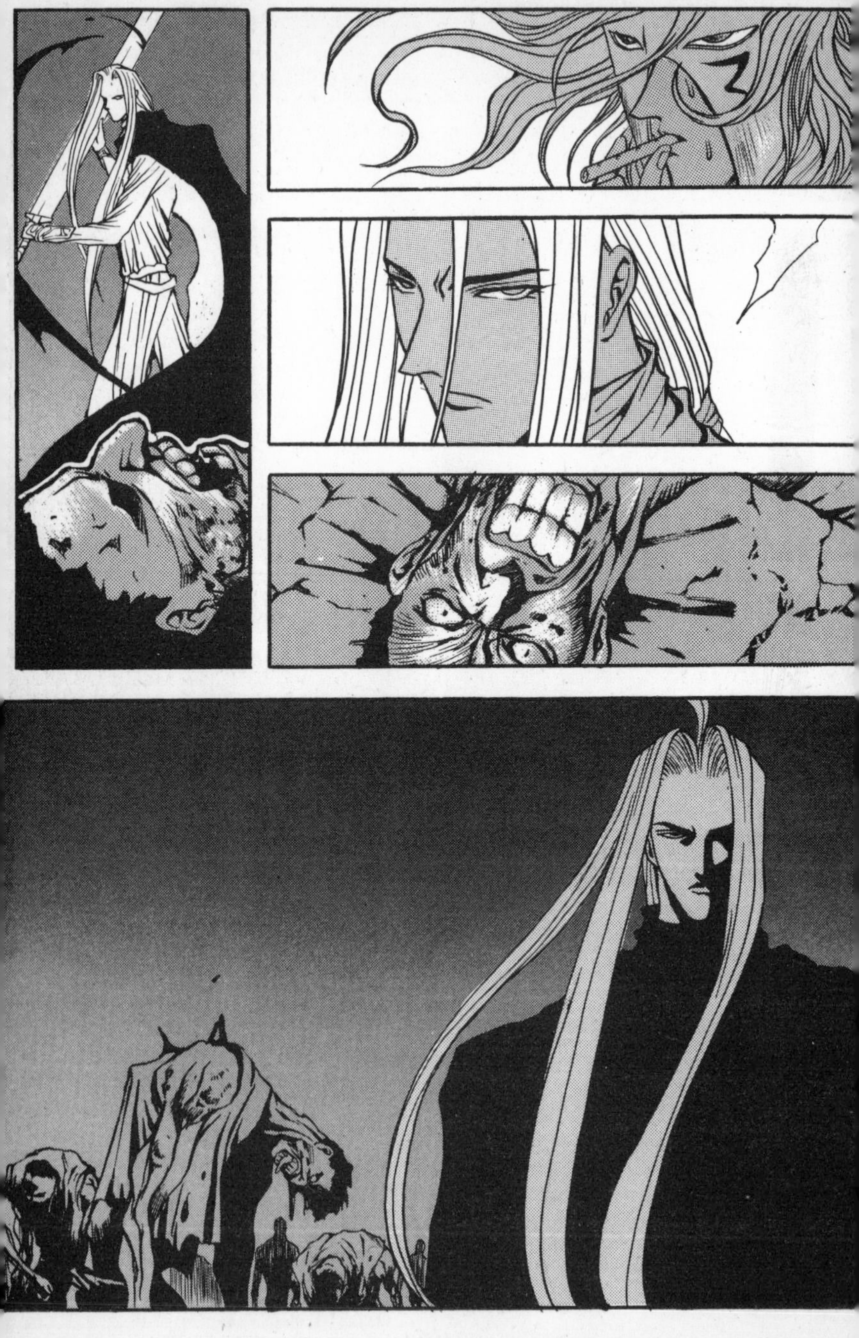

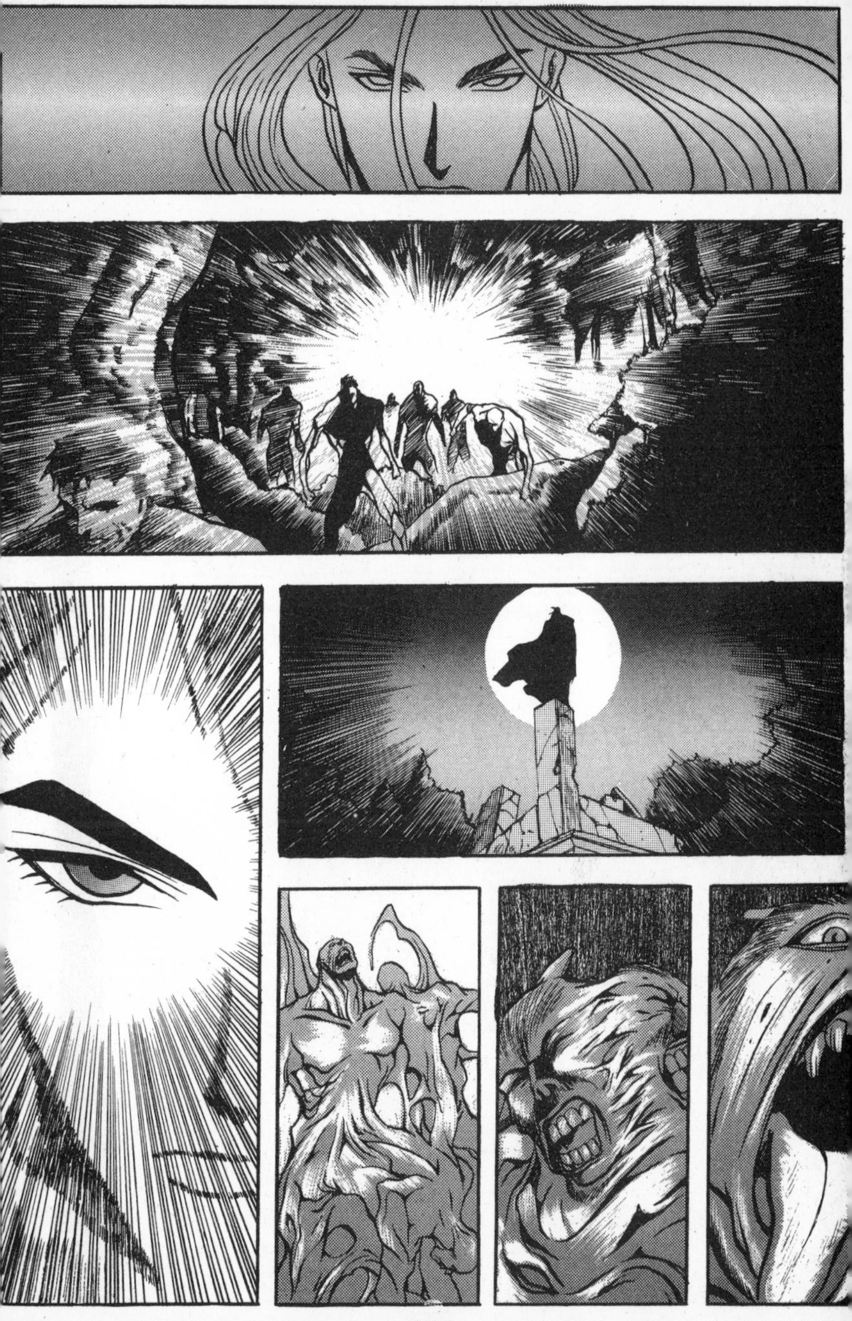

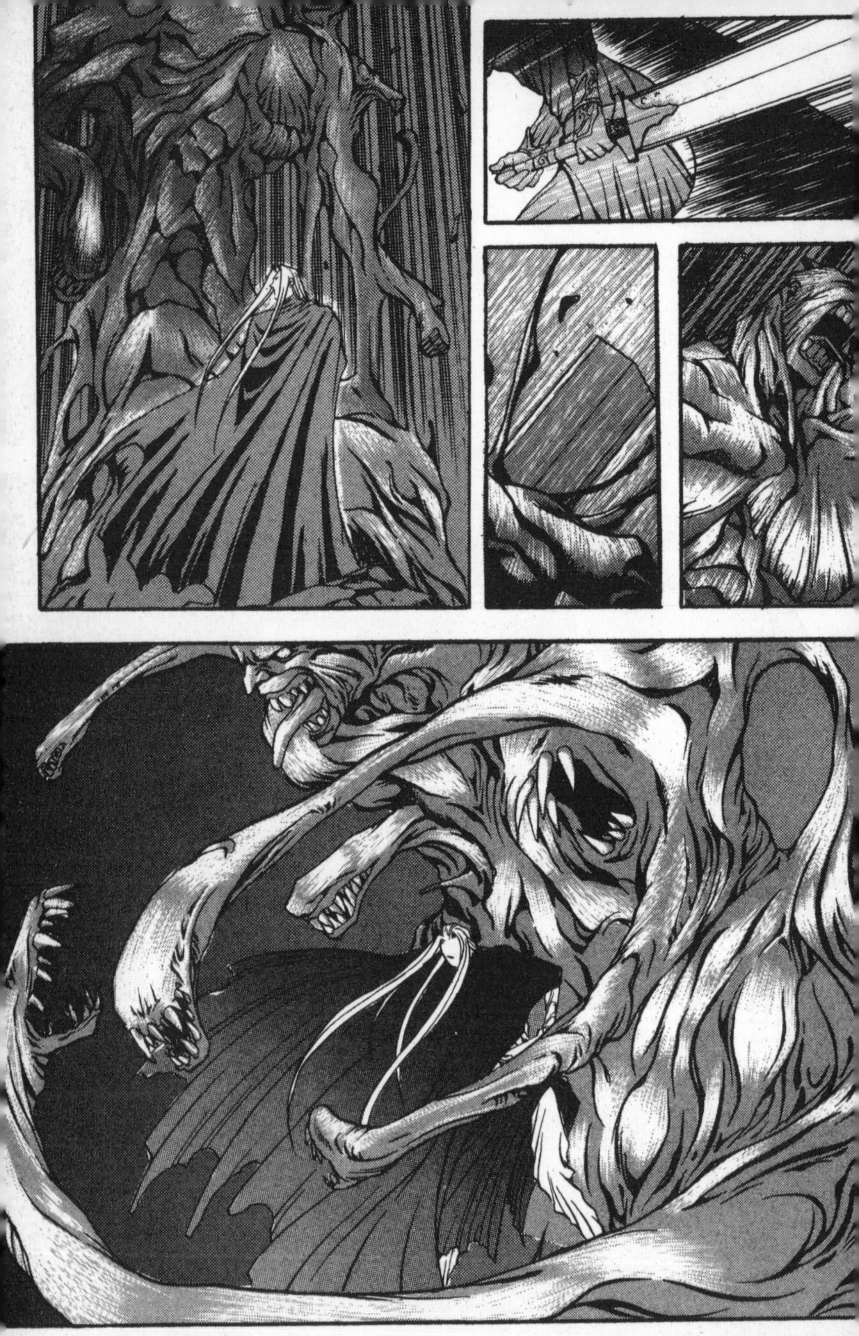

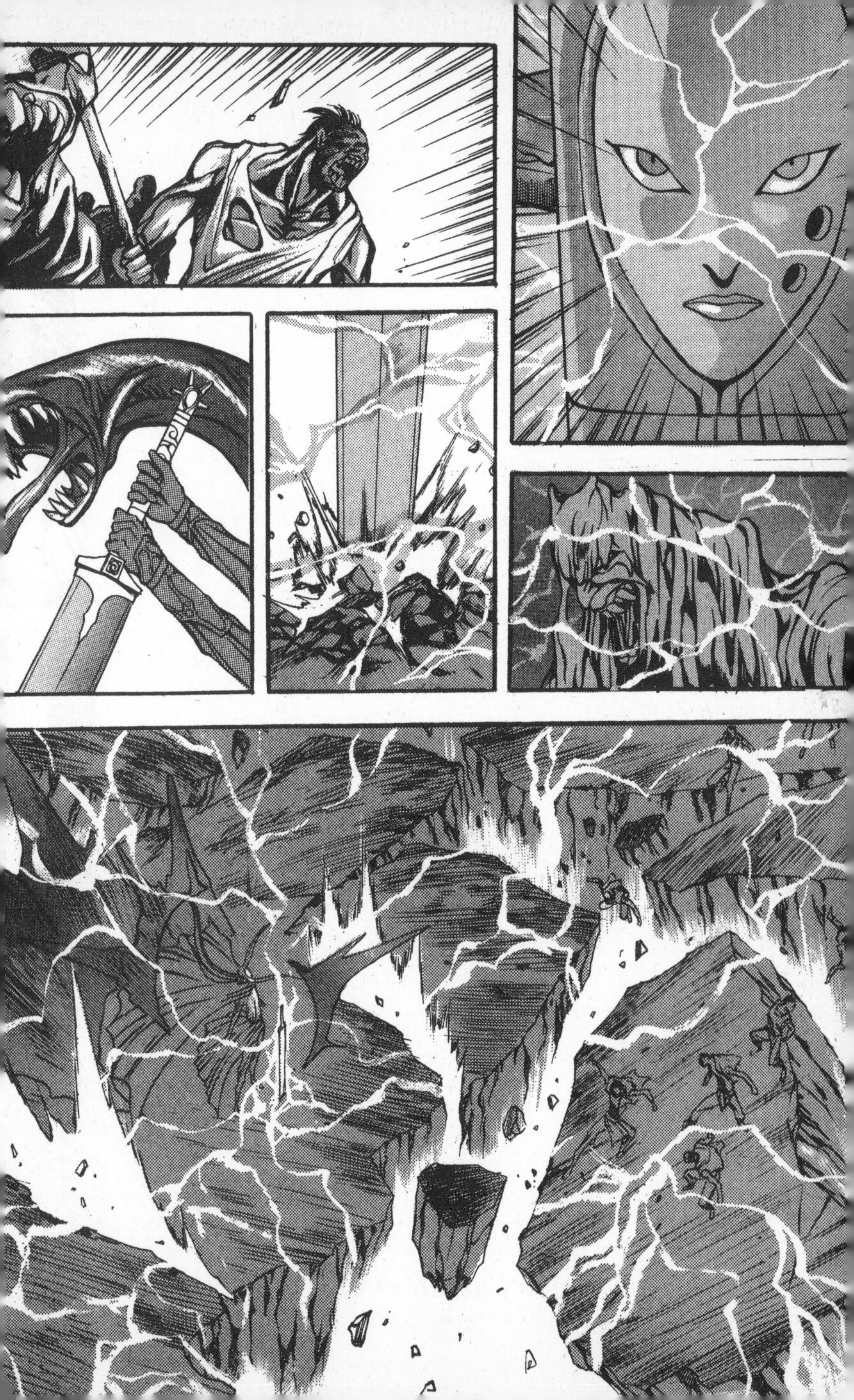

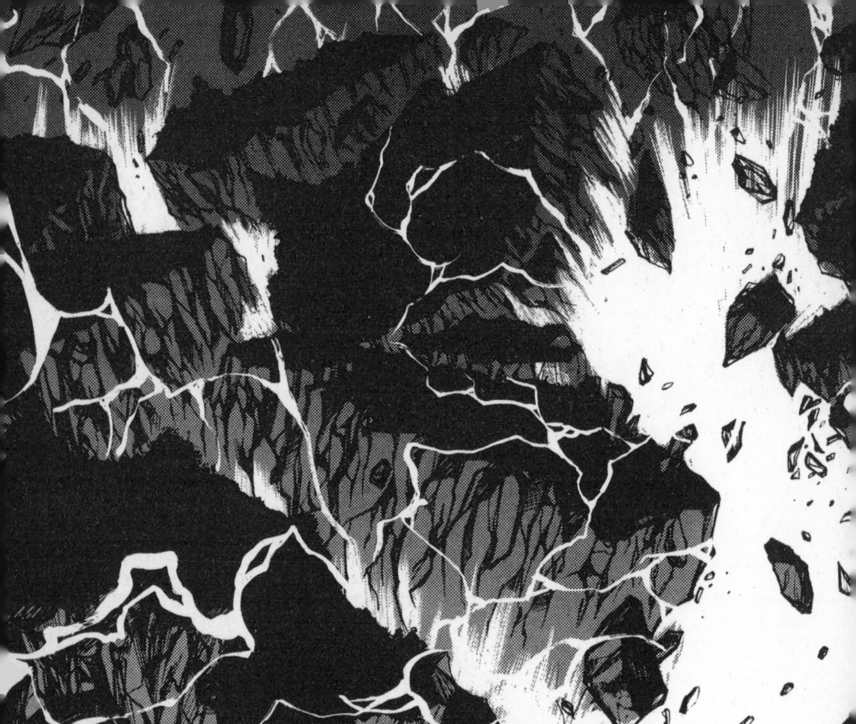
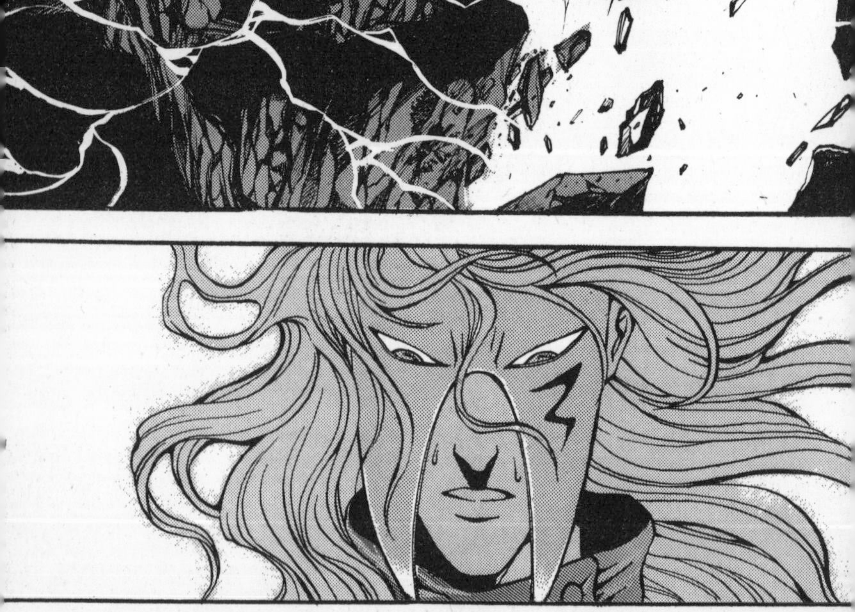

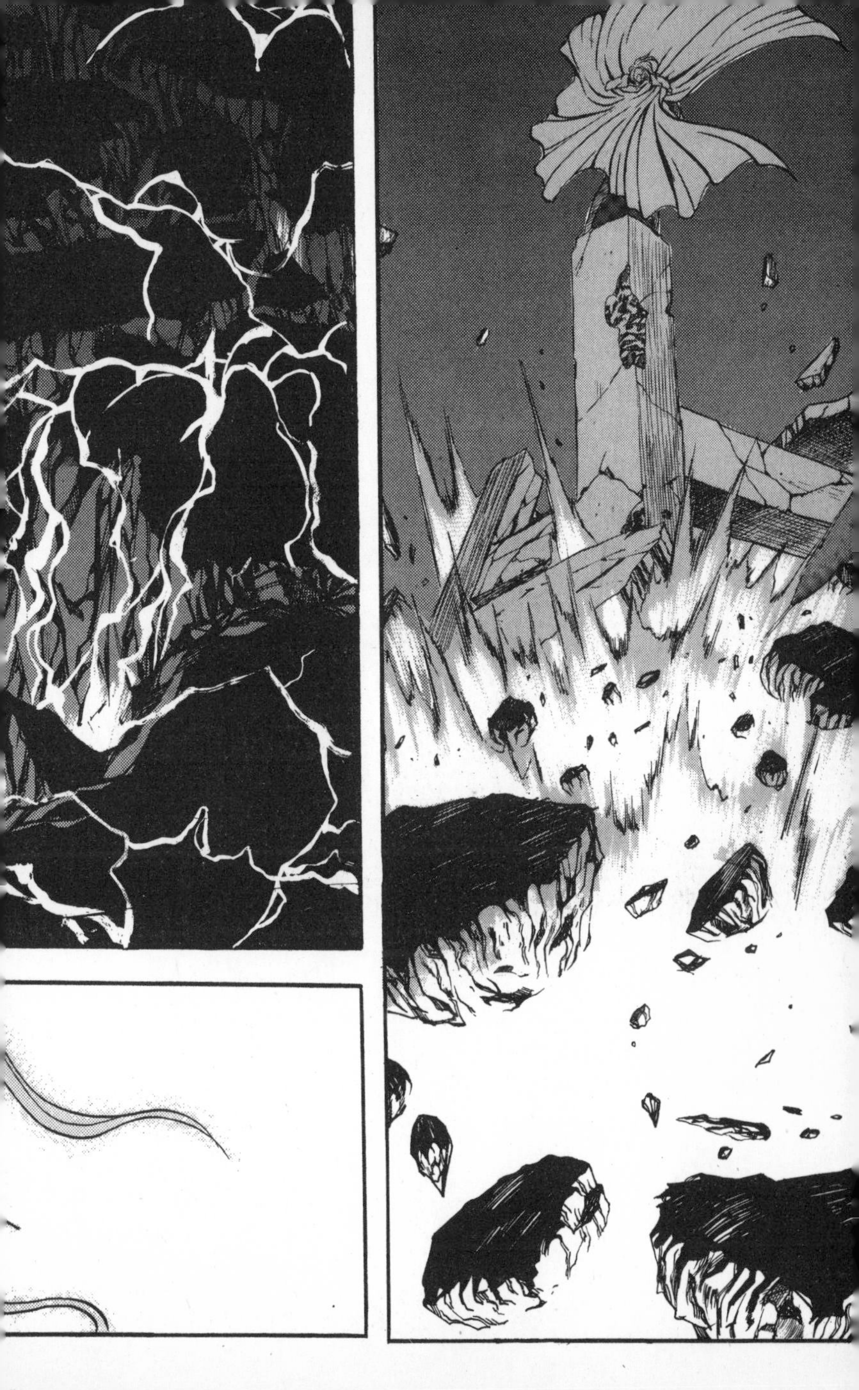

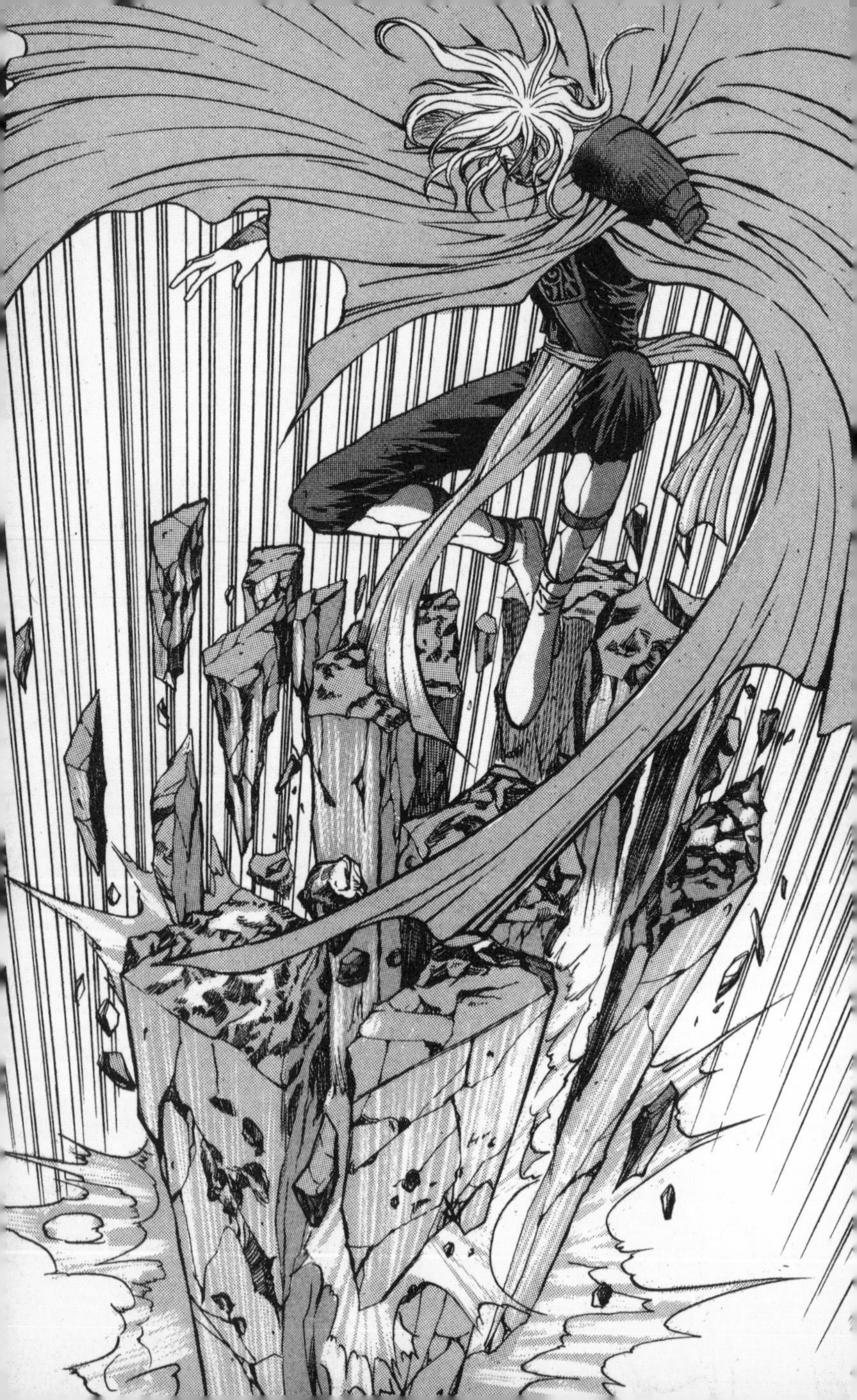

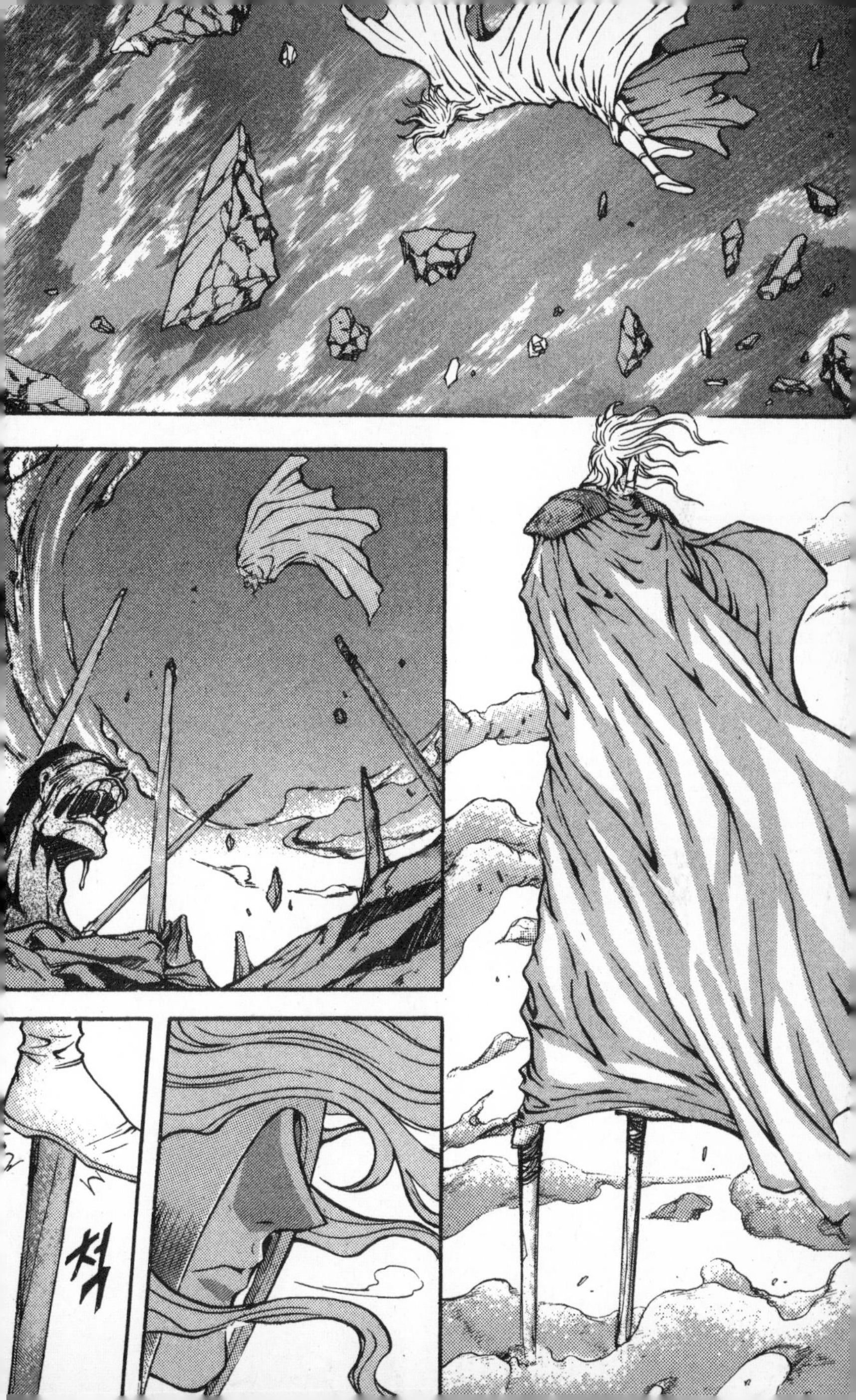
착

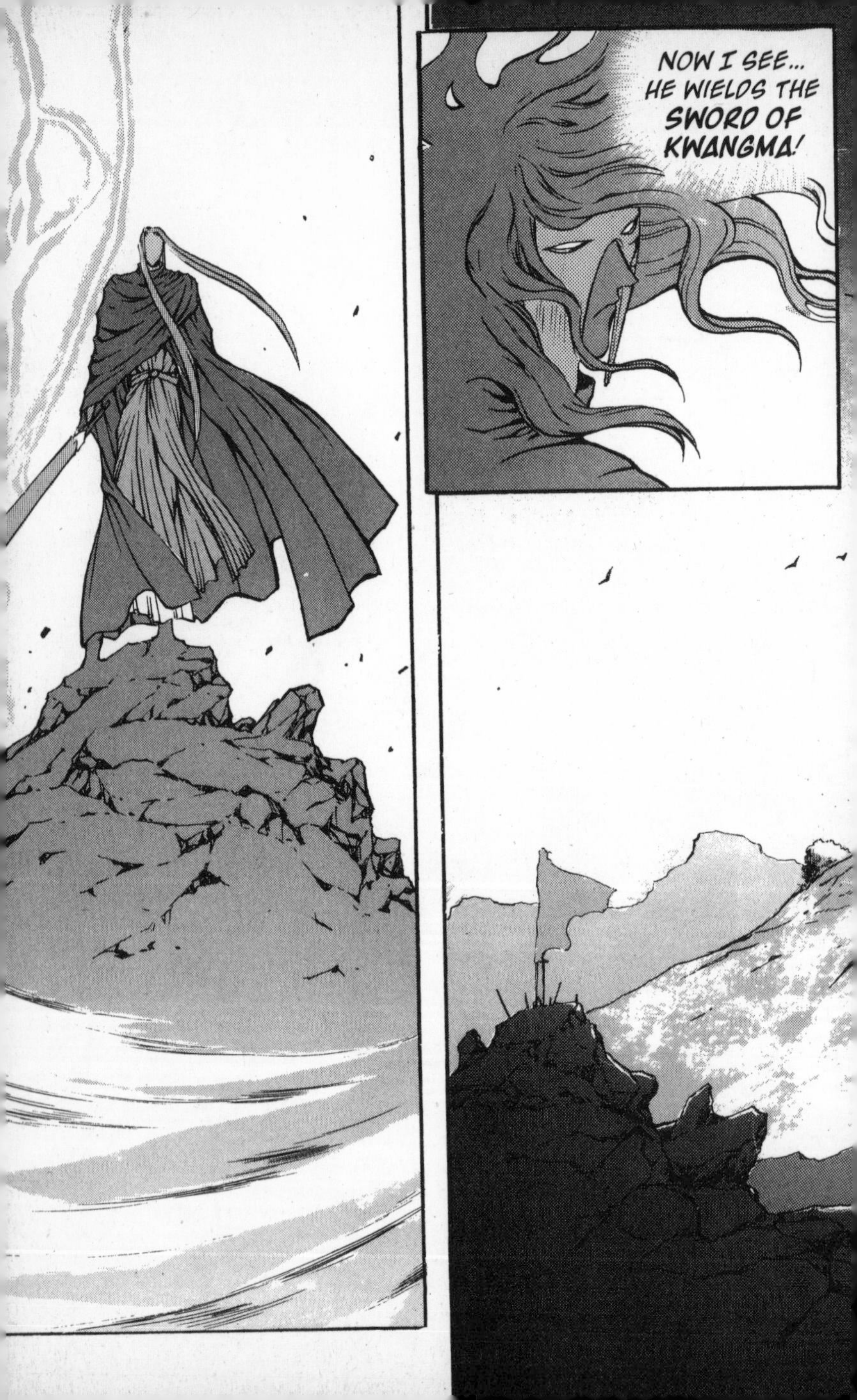
NOW I SEE... HE WIELDS THE SWORD OF KWANGMA!

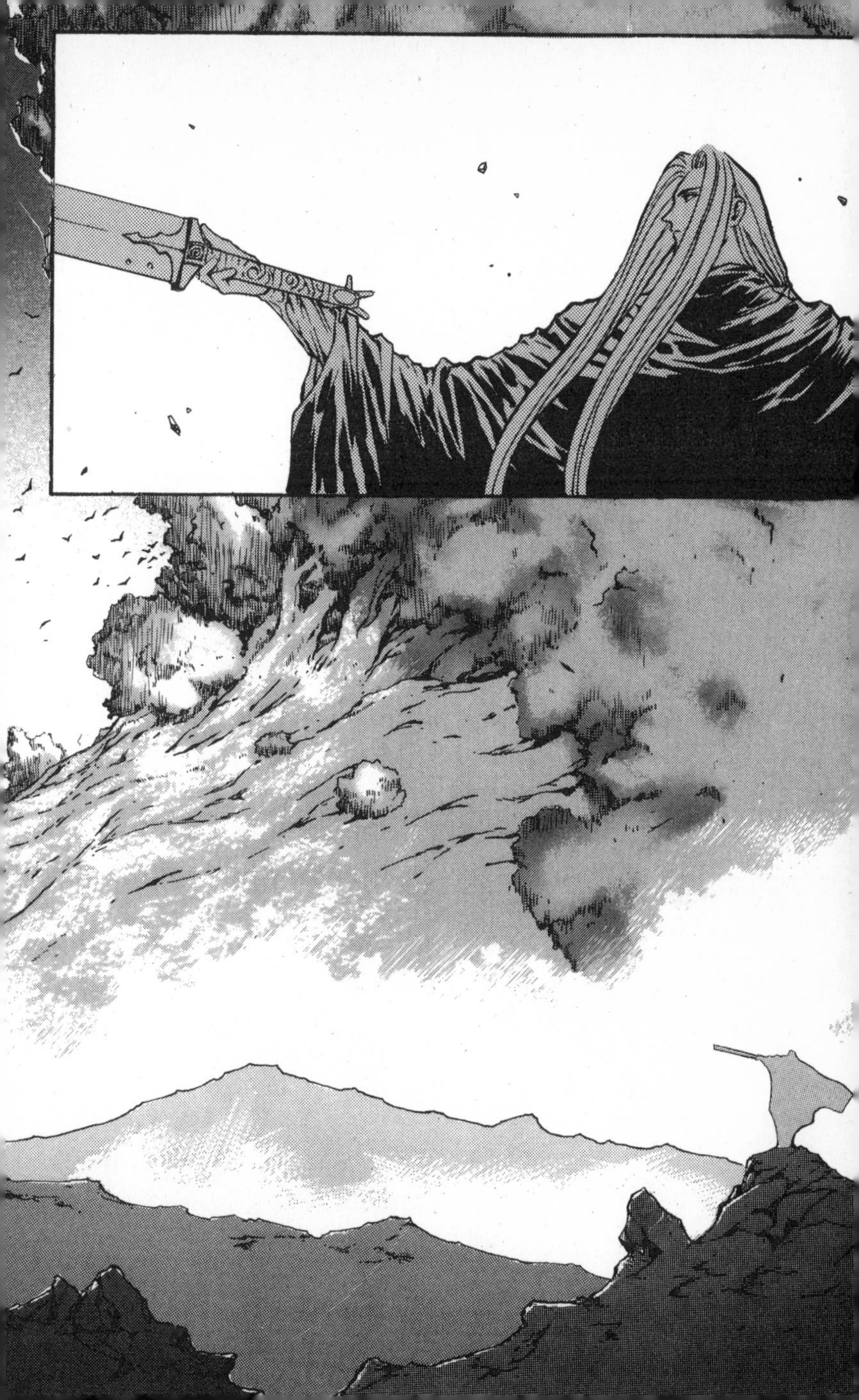

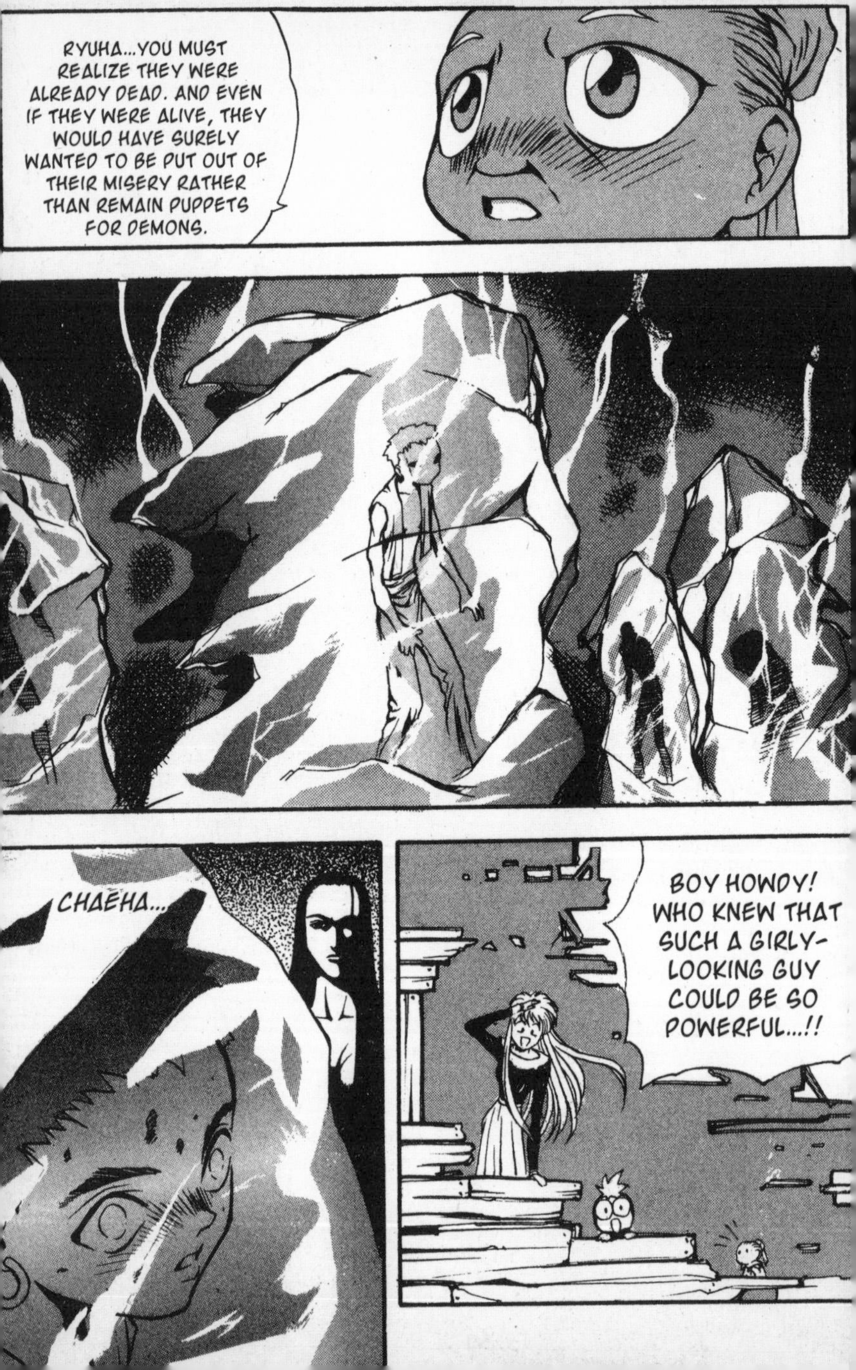
RYUHA...YOU MUST REALIZE THEY WERE ALREADY DEAD. AND EVEN IF THEY WERE ALIVE, THEY WOULD HAVE SURELY WANTED TO BE PUT OUT OF THEIR MISERY RATHER THAN REMAIN PUPPETS FOR DEMONS.
CHAEHA...
BOY HOWDY! WHO KNEW THAT SUCH A GIRLY-LOOKING GUY COULD BE SO POWERFUL...!!

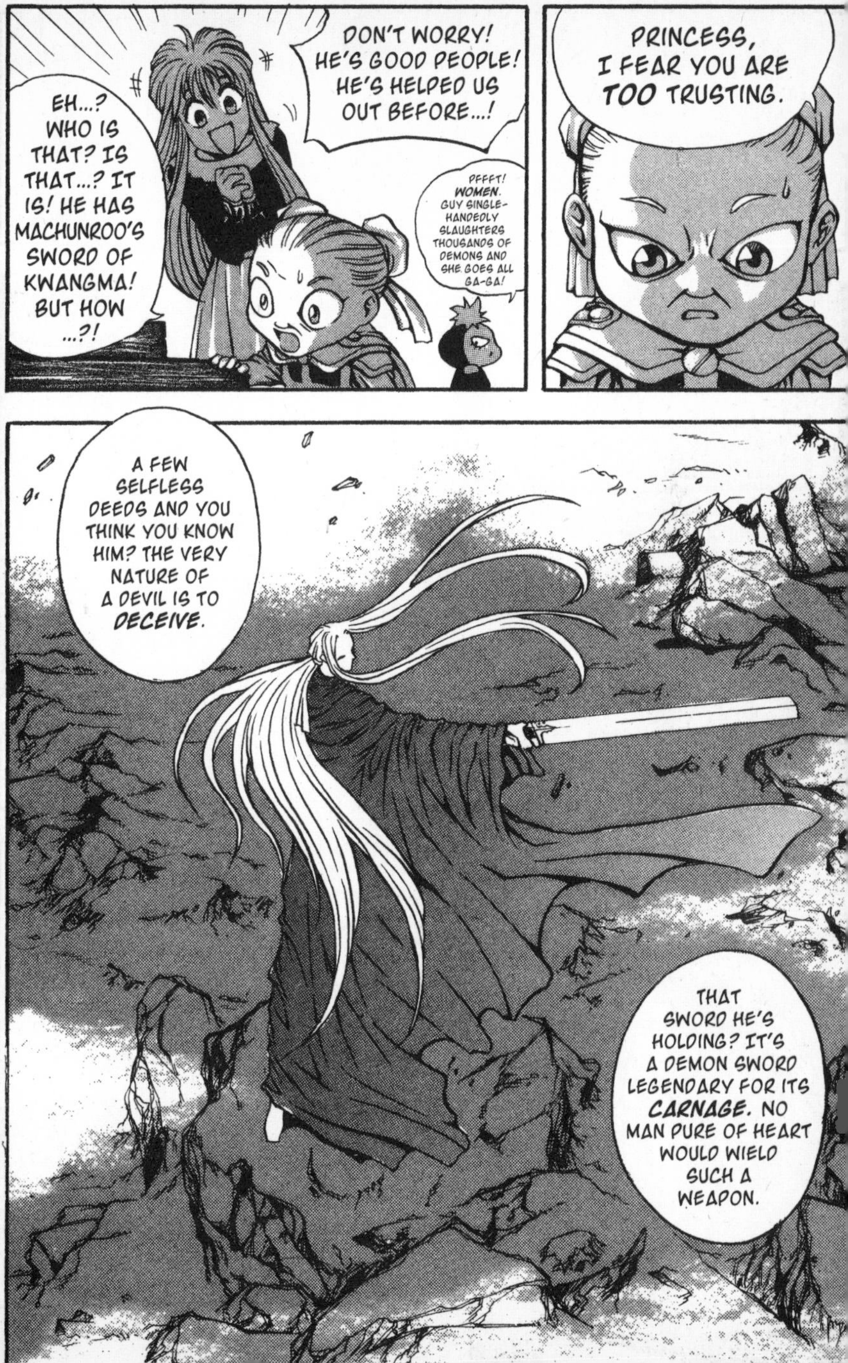
EH...? WHO IS THAT? IS THAT...? IT IS! HE HAS MACHUNROO'S SWORD OF KWANGMA! BUT HOW ...?!
DON'T WORRY! HE'S GOOD PEOPLE! HE'S HELPED US OUT BEFORE...!
PFFFT! WOMEN. GUY SINGLE-HANDEDLY SLAUGHTERS THOUSANDS OF DEMONS AND SHE GOES ALL GA-GA!
PRINCESS, I FEAR YOU ARE TOO TRUSTING.
A FEW SELFLESS DEEDS AND YOU THINK YOU KNOW HIM? THE VERY NATURE OF A DEVIL IS TO DECEIVE.
THAT SWORD HE'S HOLDING? IT'S A DEMON SWORD LEGENDARY FOR ITS CARNAGE. NO MAN PURE OF HEART WOULD WIELD SUCH A WEAPON.

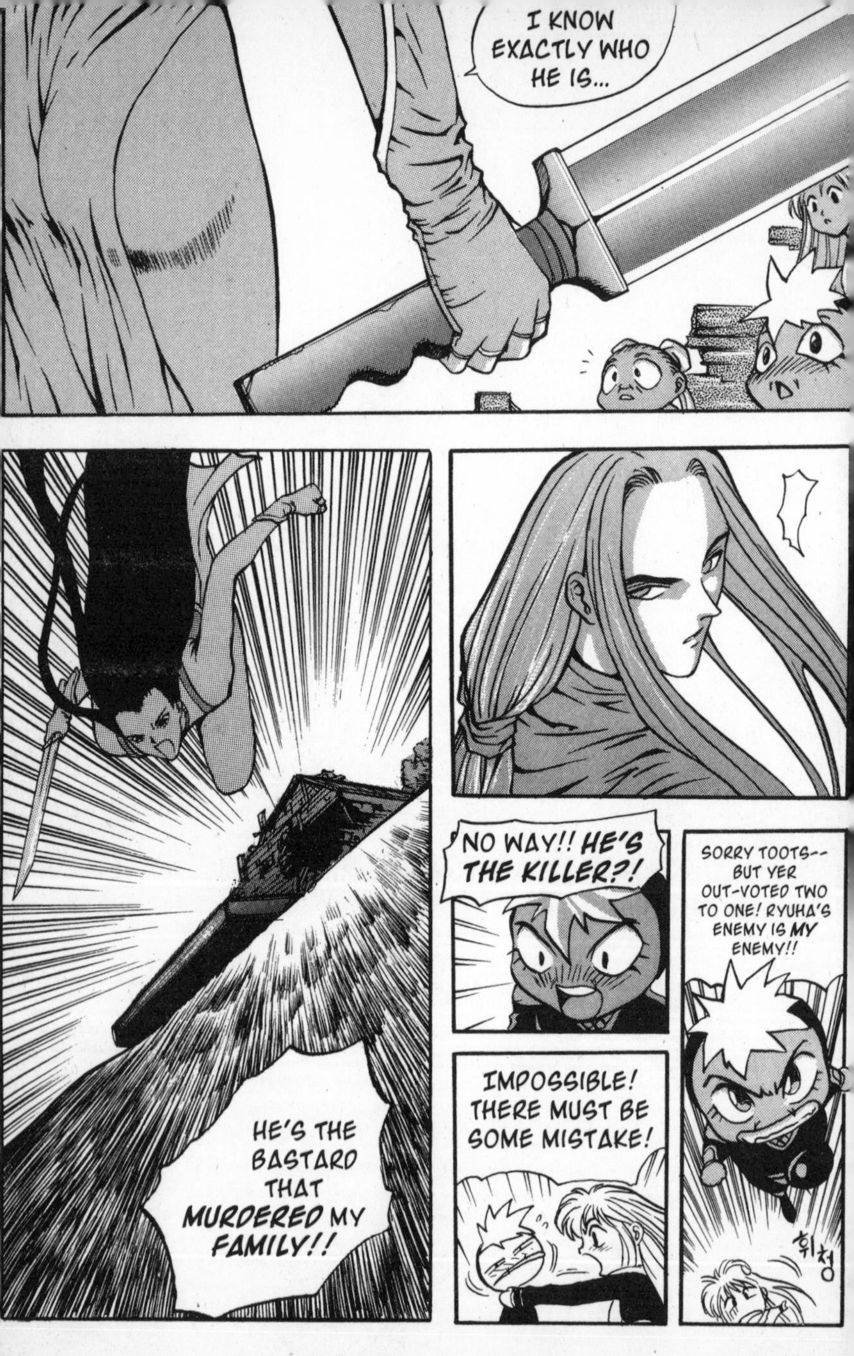
I KNOW EXACTLY WHO HE IS...
HE'S THE BASTARD THAT MURDERED MY FAMILY!!
!
NO WAY!! HE'S THE KILLER?!
IMPOSSIBLE! THERE MUST BE SOME MISTAKE!
SORRY TOOTS-- BUT YER OUT-VOTED TWO TO ONE! RYUHA'S ENEMY IS MY ENEMY!!
휘청

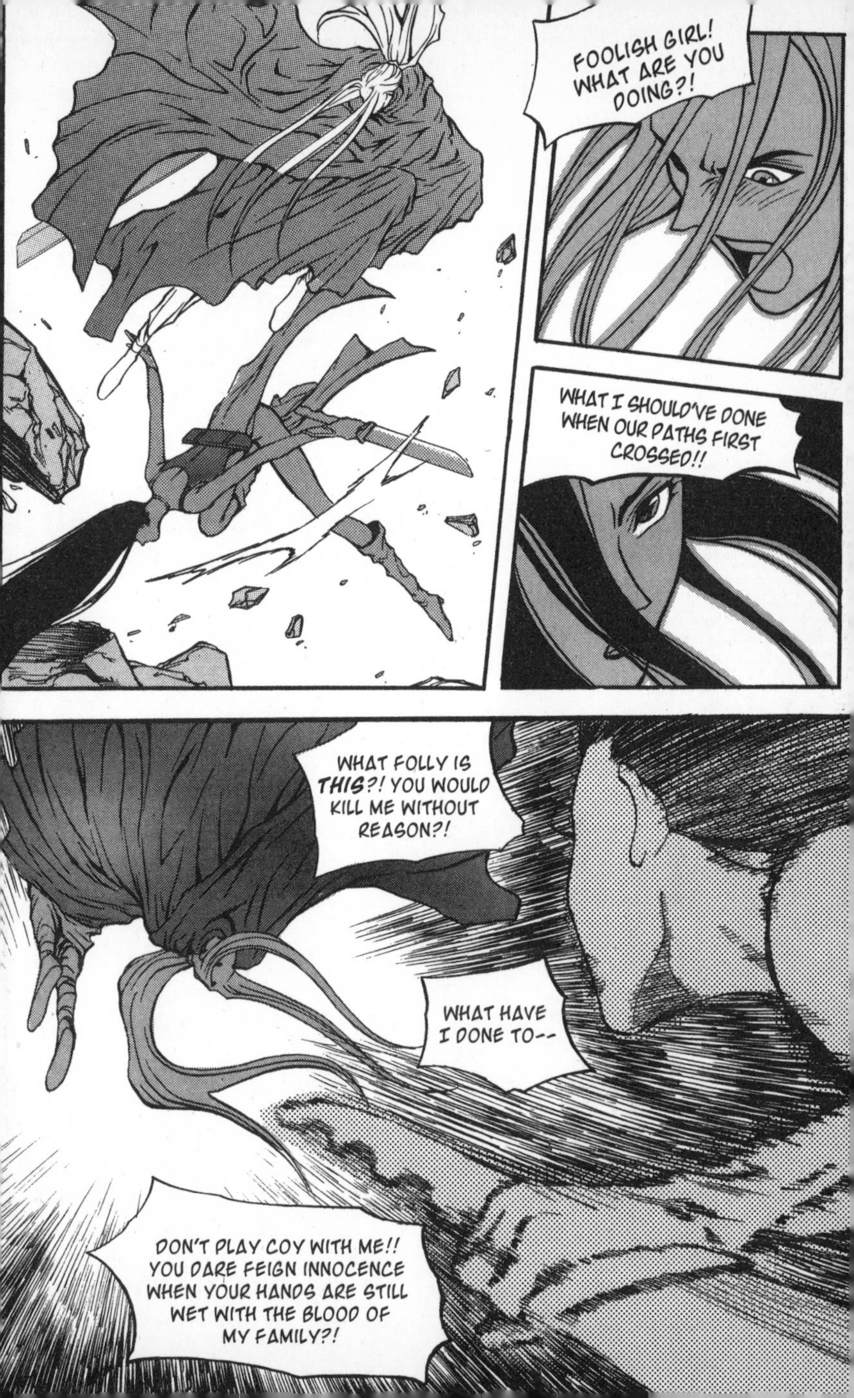
FOOLISH GIRL! WHAT ARE YOU DOING?!
WHAT I SHOULD'VE DONE WHEN OUR PATHS FIRST CROSSED!!
WHAT FOLLY IS *THIS*?! YOU WOULD KILL ME WITHOUT REASON?!
WHAT HAVE I DONE TO--
DON'T PLAY COY WITH ME!! YOU DARE FEIGN INNOCENCE WHEN YOUR HANDS ARE STILL WET WITH THE BLOOD OF MY FAMILY?!

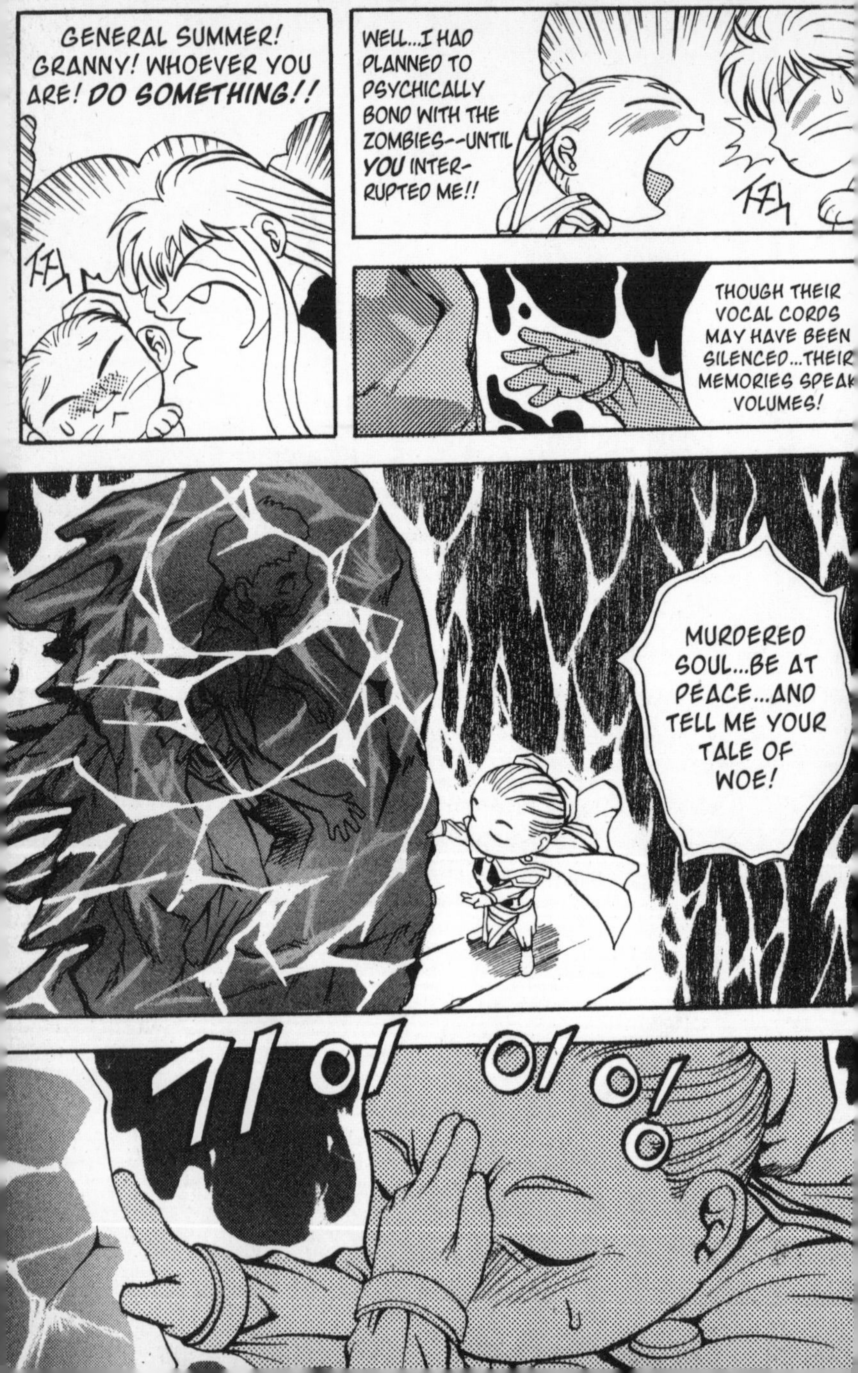
GENERAL SUMMER! GRANNY! WHOEVER YOU ARE! DO SOMETHING!!
WELL...I HAD PLANNED TO PSYCHICALLY BOND WITH THE ZOMBIES--UNTIL YOU INTER-RUPTED ME!!
THOUGH THEIR VOCAL CORDS MAY HAVE BEEN SILENCED...THEIR MEMORIES SPEAK VOLUMES!
MURDERED SOUL...BE AT PEACE...AND TELL ME YOUR TALE OF WOE!

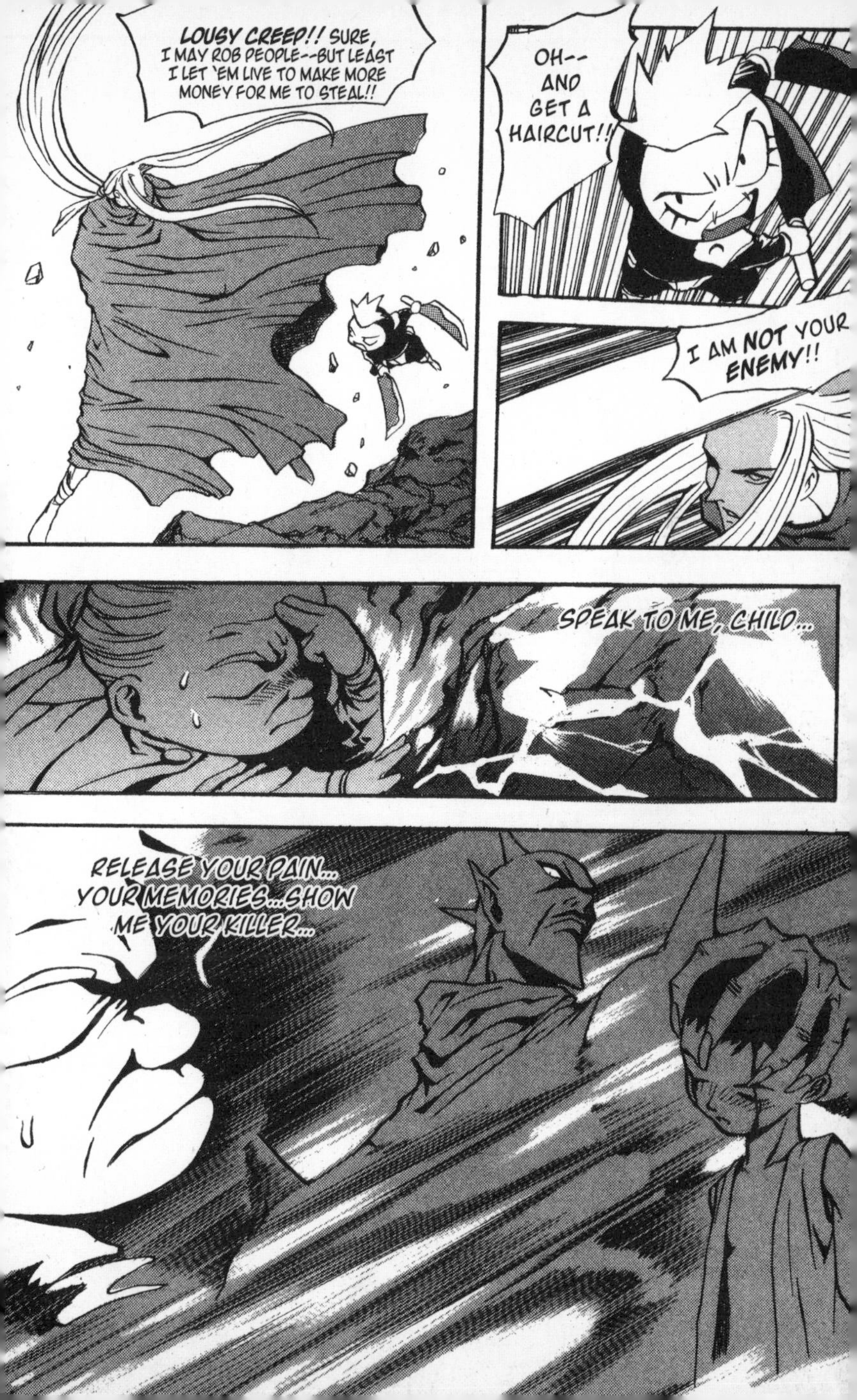
LOUSY CREEP!! SURE, I MAY ROB PEOPLE--BUT LEAST I LET 'EM LIVE TO MAKE MORE MONEY FOR ME TO STEAL!!
OH-- AND GET A HAIRCUT!!
I AM NOT YOUR ENEMY!!
SPEAK TO ME, CHILD...
RELEASE YOUR PAIN... YOUR MEMORIES...SHOW ME YOUR KILLER...

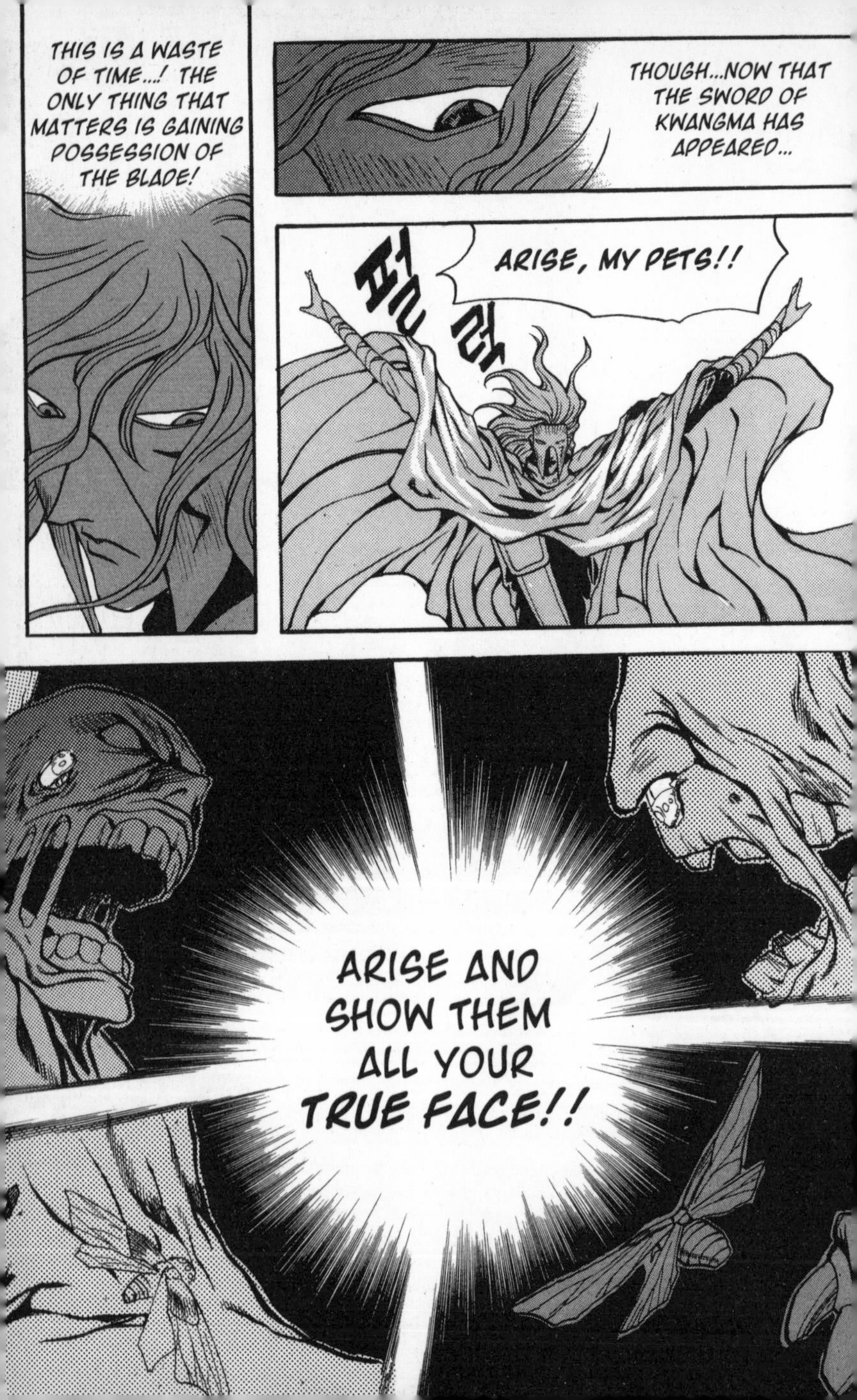
THIS IS A WASTE OF TIME...! THE ONLY THING THAT MATTERS IS GAINING POSSESSION OF THE BLADE!
THOUGH...NOW THAT THE SWORD OF KWANGMA HAS APPEARED...
ARISE, MY PETS!!
ARISE AND SHOW THEM ALL YOUR TRUE FACE!!

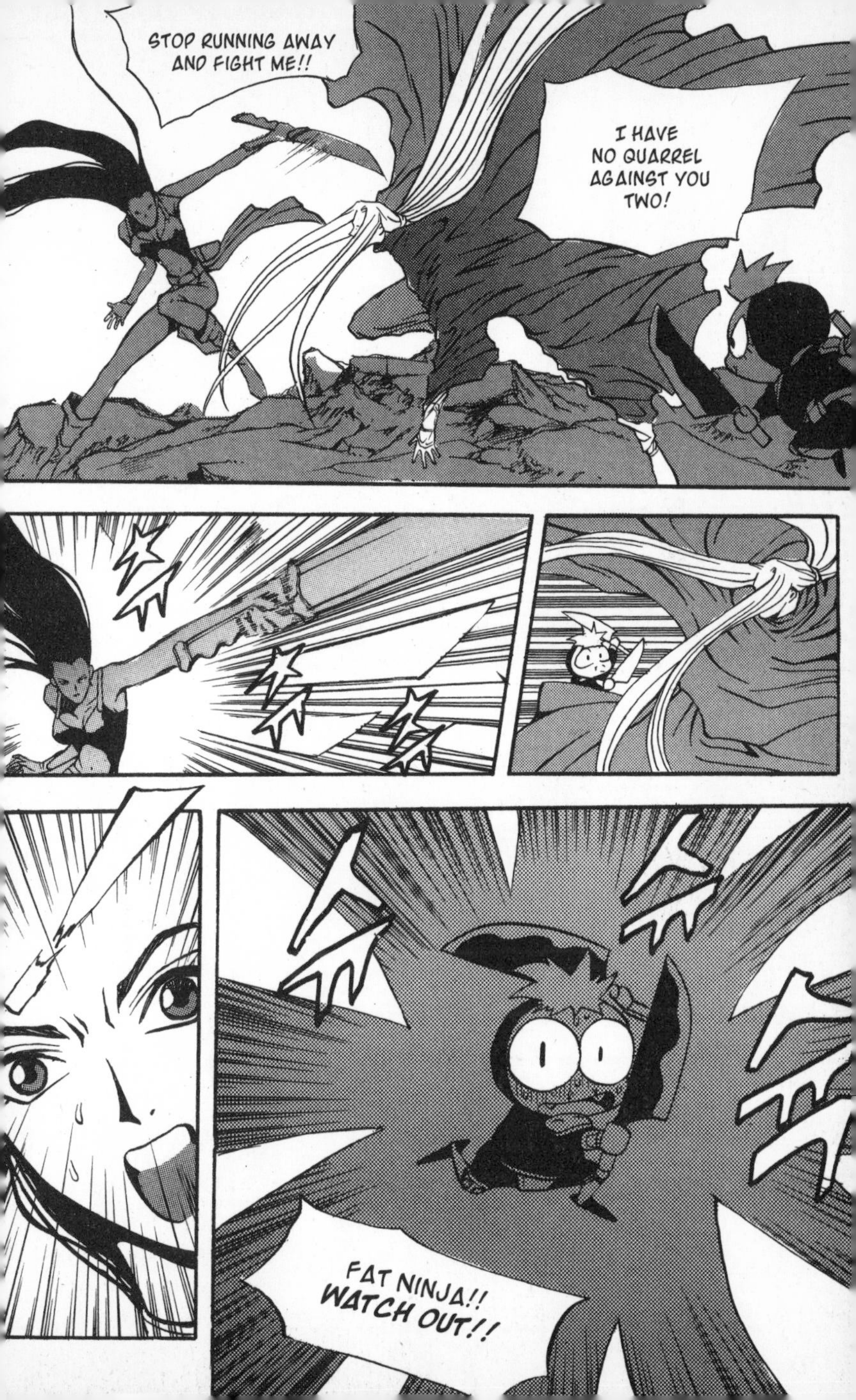
STOP RUNNING AWAY AND FIGHT ME!!
I HAVE NO QUARREL AGAINST YOU TWO!
FAT NINJA!! WATCH OUT!!

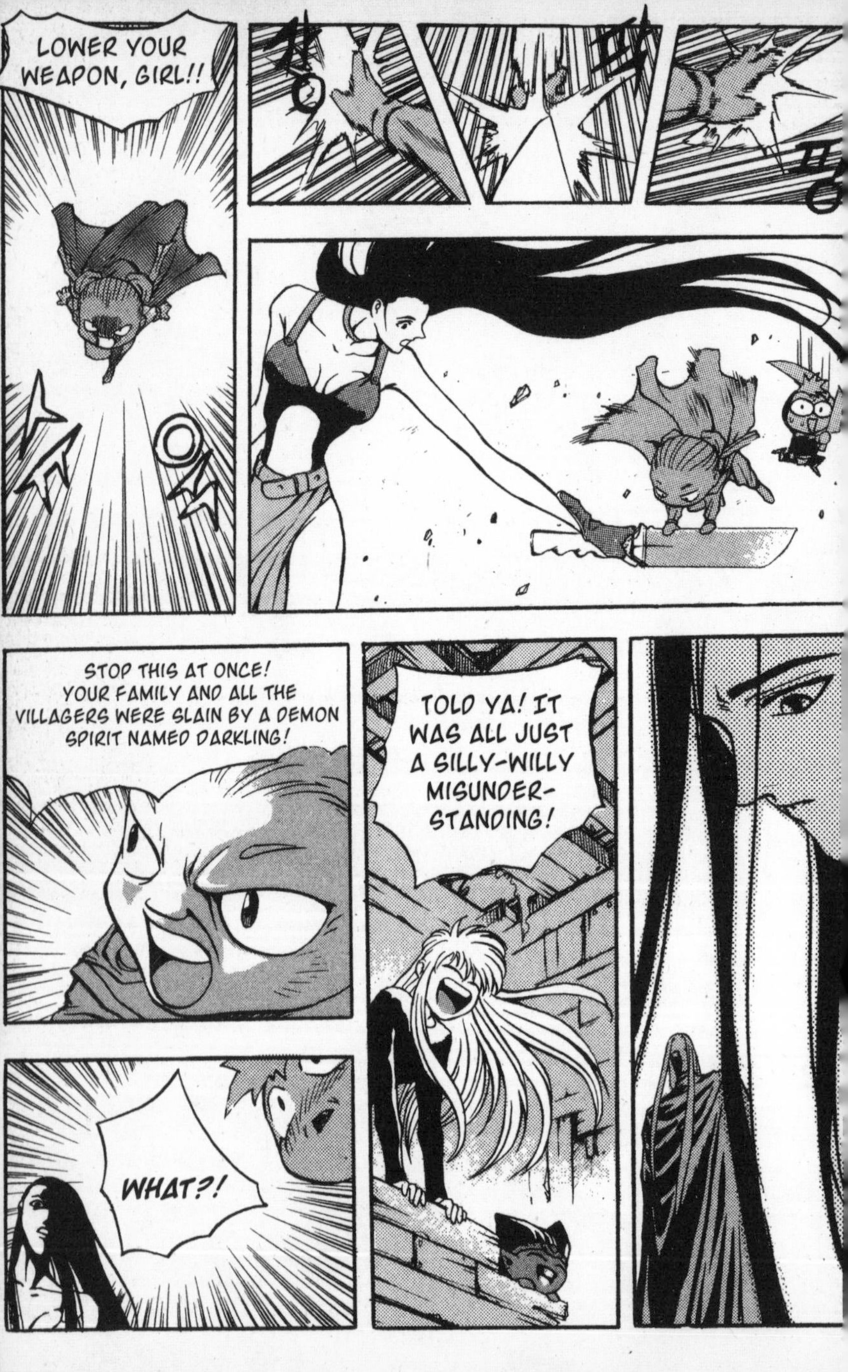
LOWER YOUR WEAPON, GIRL!!
STOP THIS AT ONCE! YOUR FAMILY AND ALL THE VILLAGERS WERE SLAIN BY A DEMON SPIRIT NAMED DARKLING!
WHAT?!
TOLD YA! IT WAS ALL JUST A SILLY-WILLY MISUNDER-STANDING!

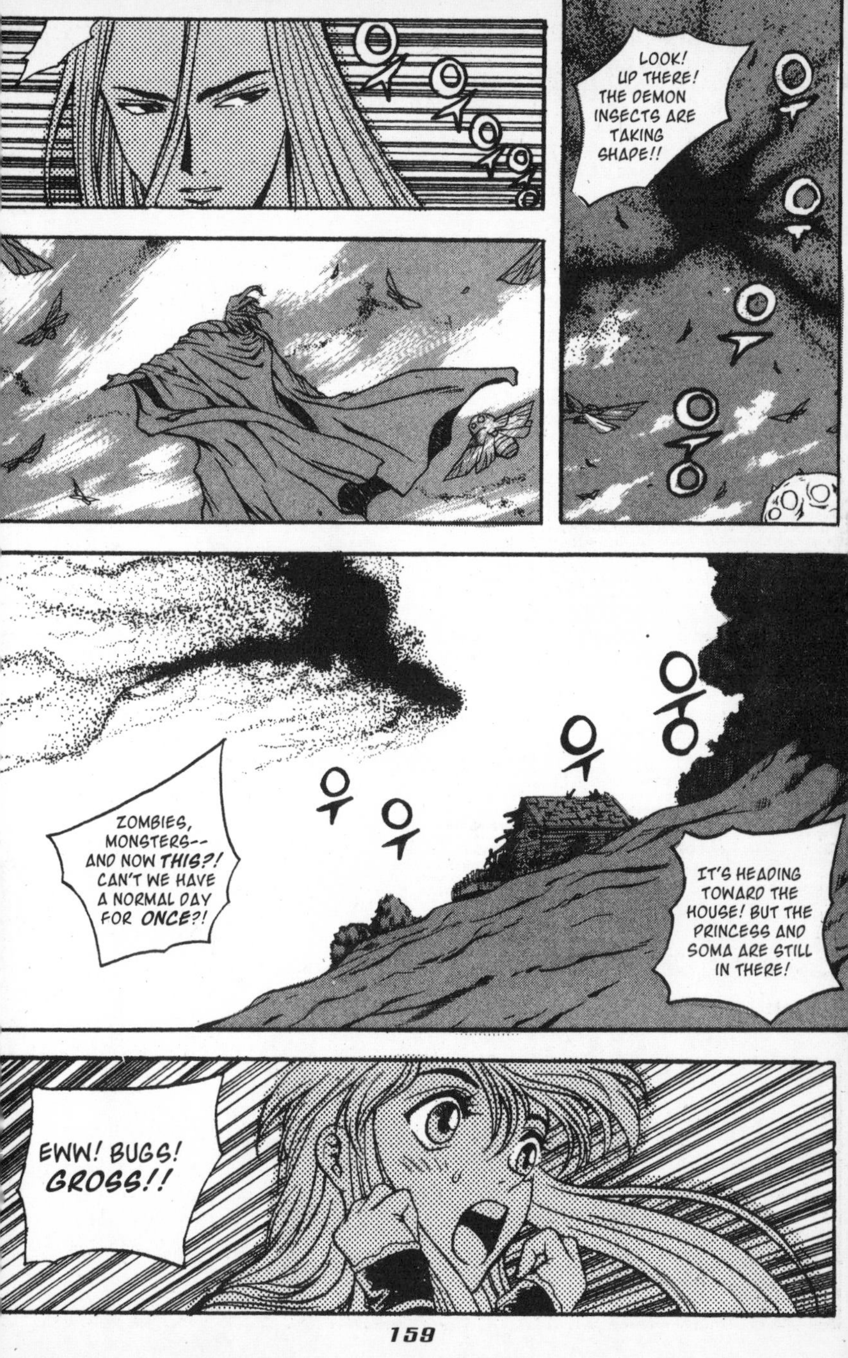
LOOK! UP THERE! THE DEMON INSECTS ARE TAKING SHAPE!!
IT'S HEADING TOWARD THE HOUSE! BUT THE PRINCESS AND SOMA ARE STILL IN THERE!
ZOMBIES, MONSTERS-- AND NOW THIS?! CAN'T WE HAVE A NORMAL DAY FOR ONCE?!
EWW! BUGS! GROSS!!

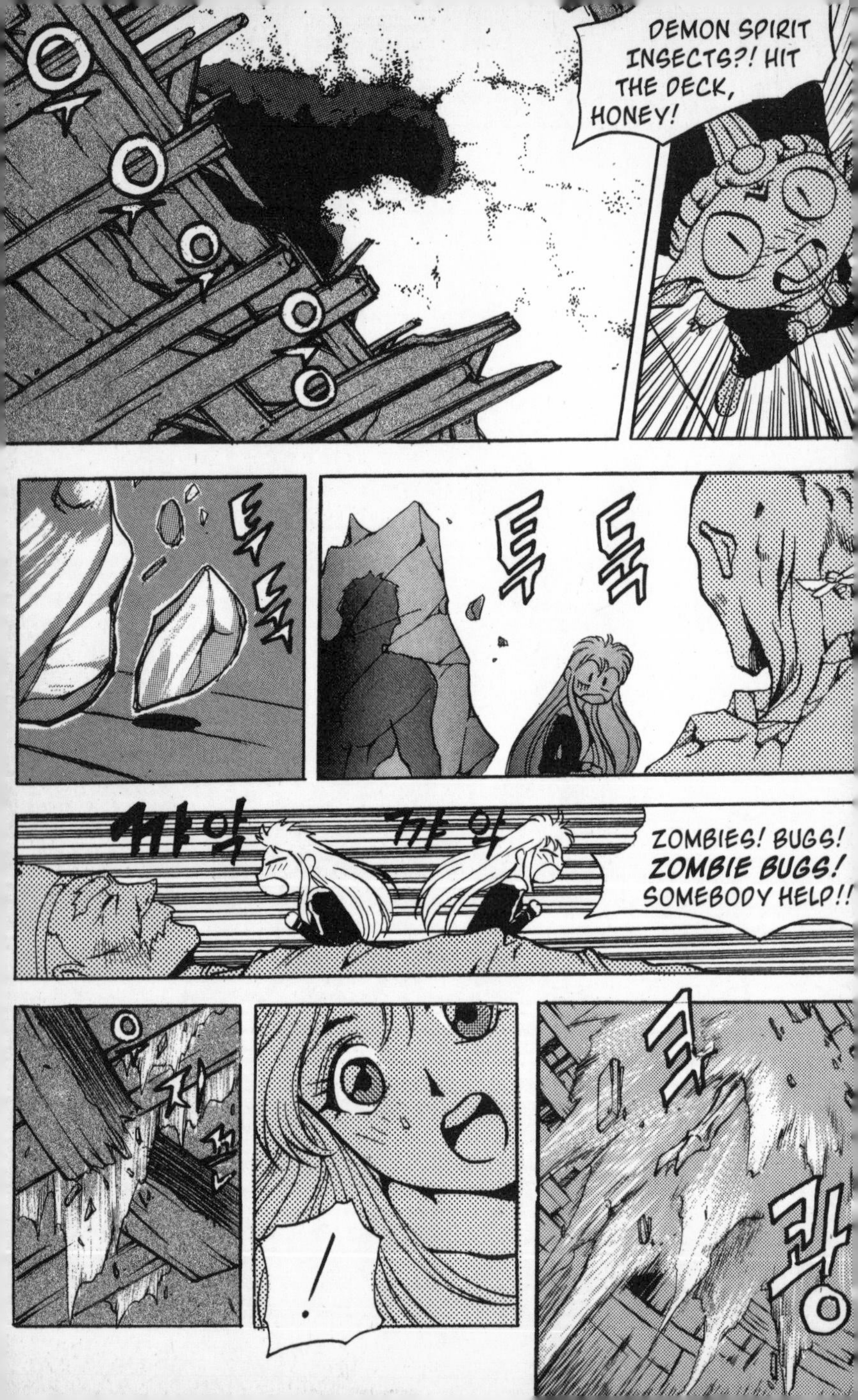
DEMON SPIRIT INSECTS?! HIT THE DECK, HONEY!
ZOMBIES! BUGS! ZOMBIE BUGS! SOMEBODY HELP!!

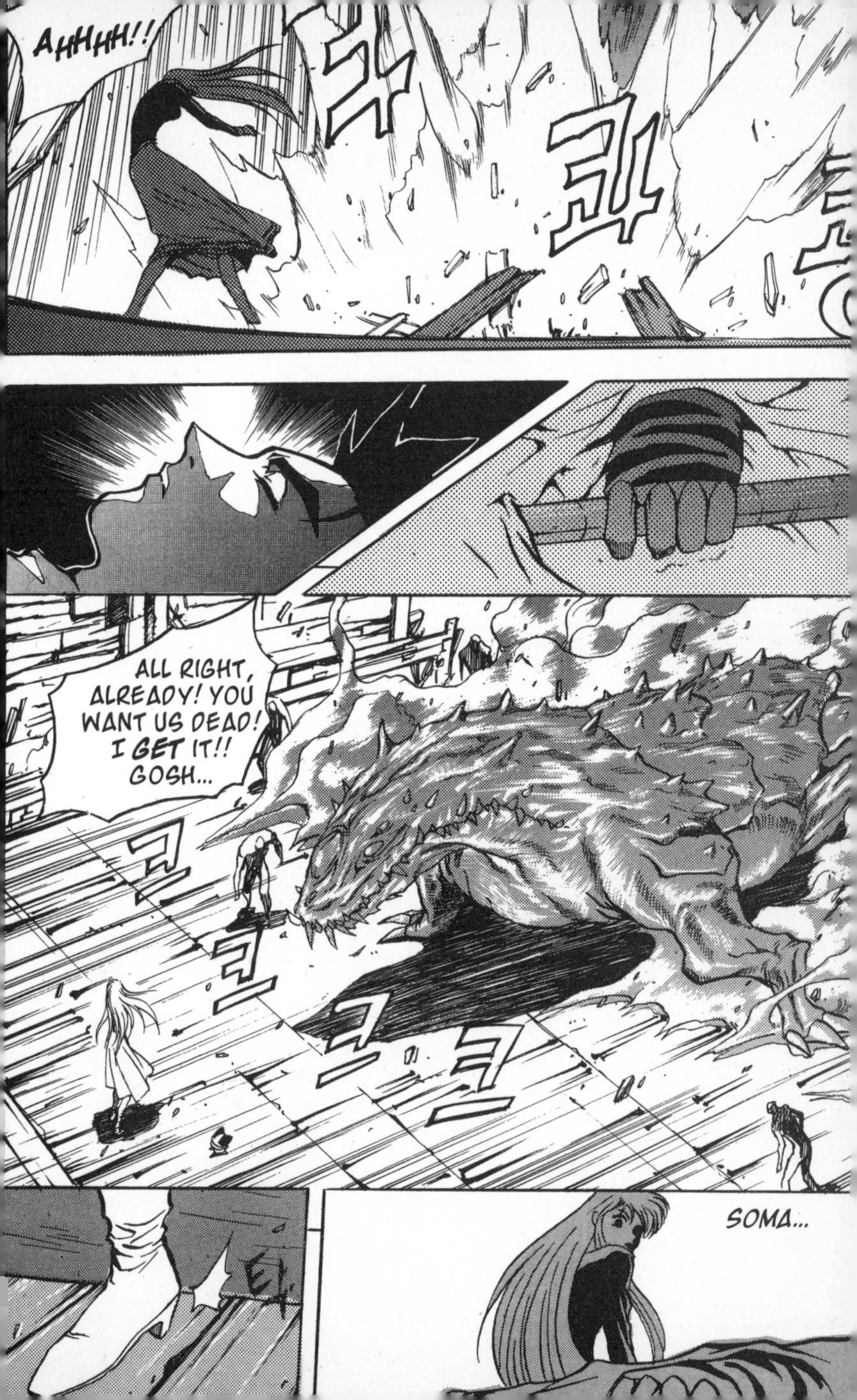
AHHHH!!
ALL RIGHT, ALREADY! YOU WANT US DEAD! I GET IT!! GOSH...
SOMA...

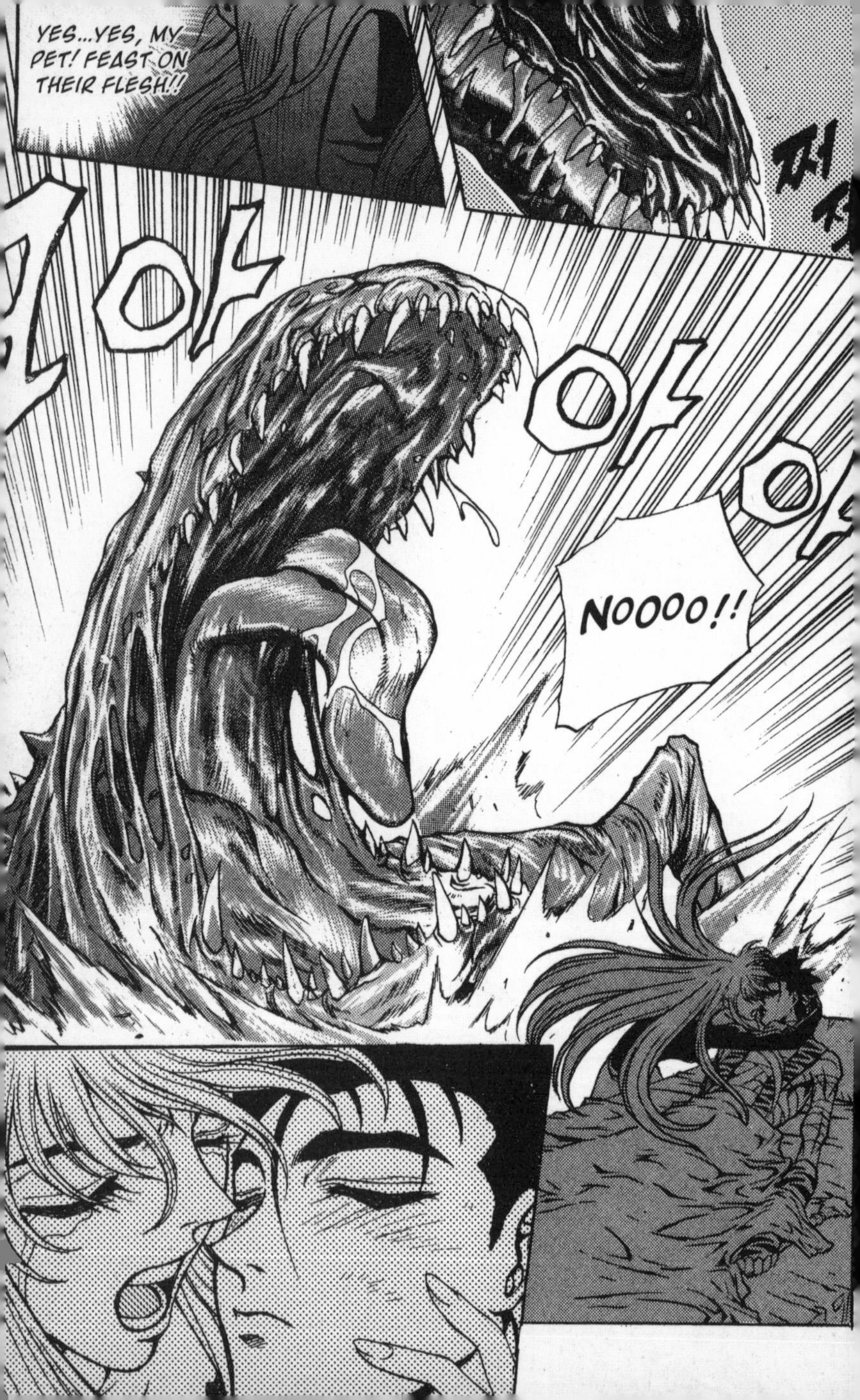
YES...YES, MY PET! FEAST ON THEIR FLESH!!
NOOOO!!

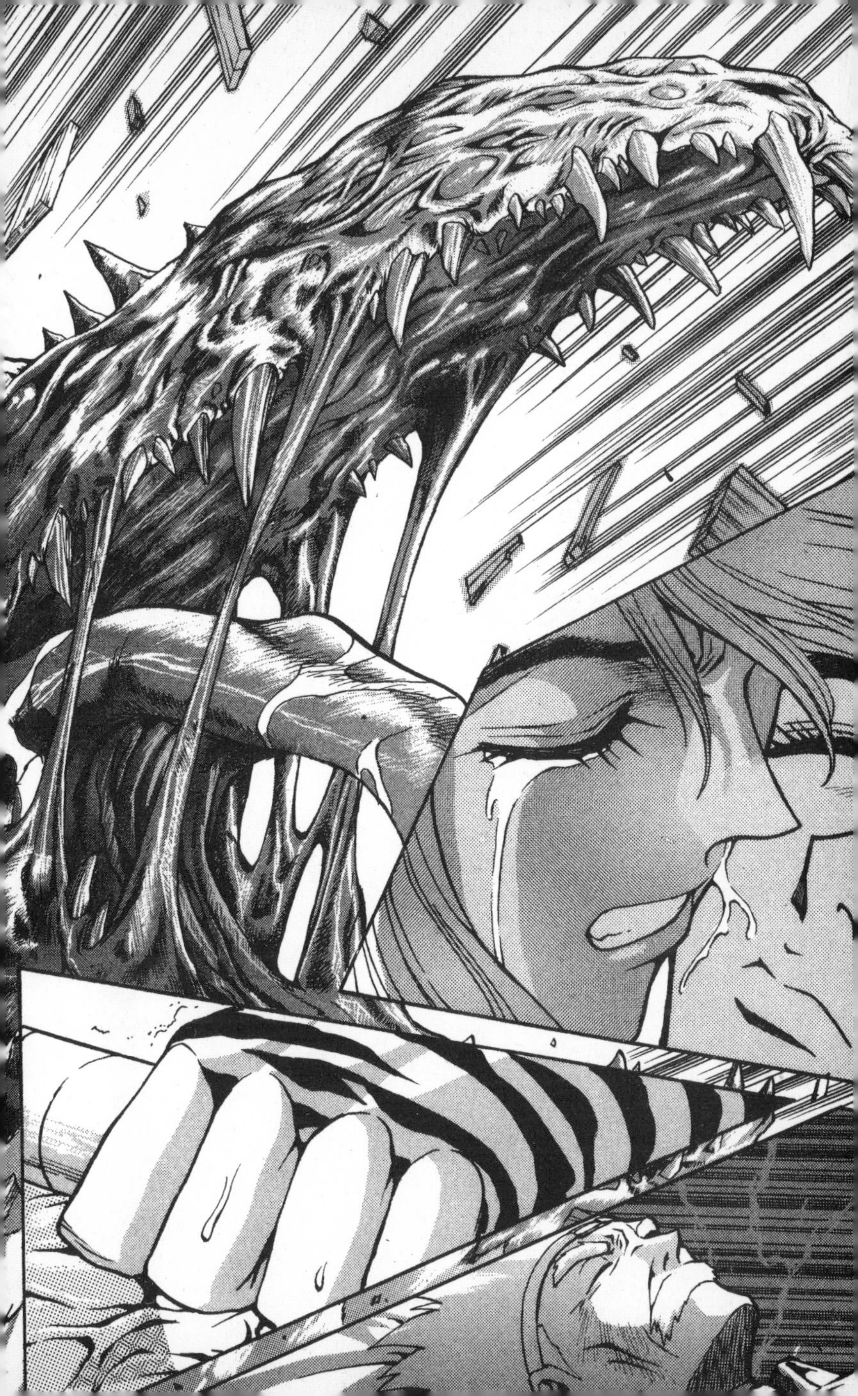

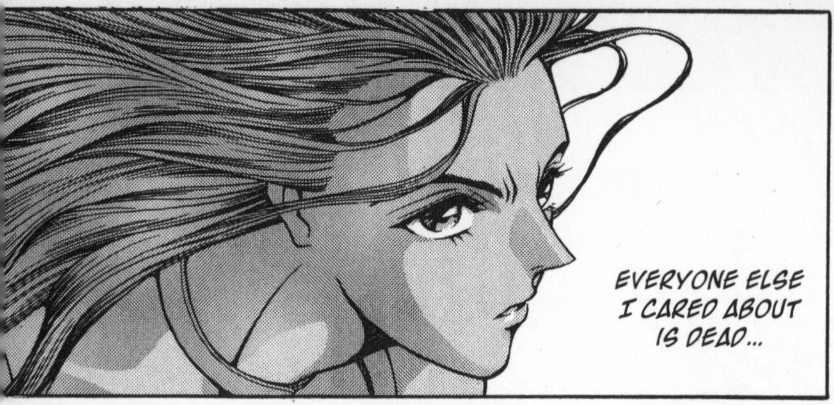
EVERYONE ELSE I CARED ABOUT IS DEAD...

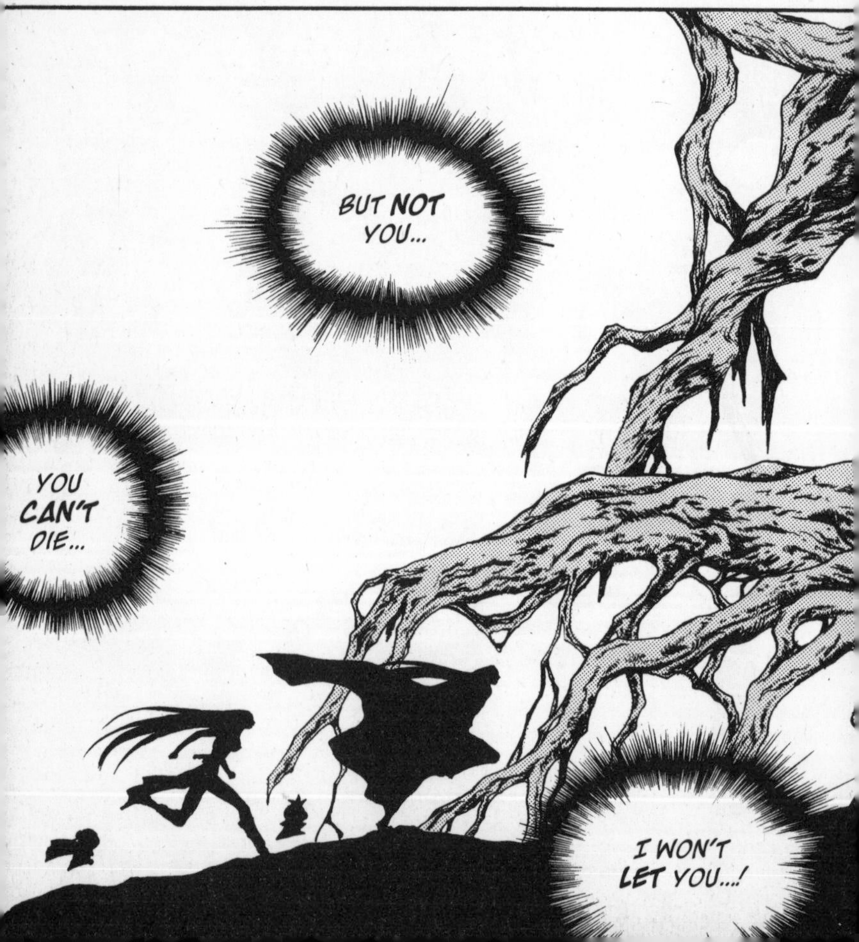
BUT NOT YOU...
YOU CAN'T DIE...
I WON'T LET YOU...!

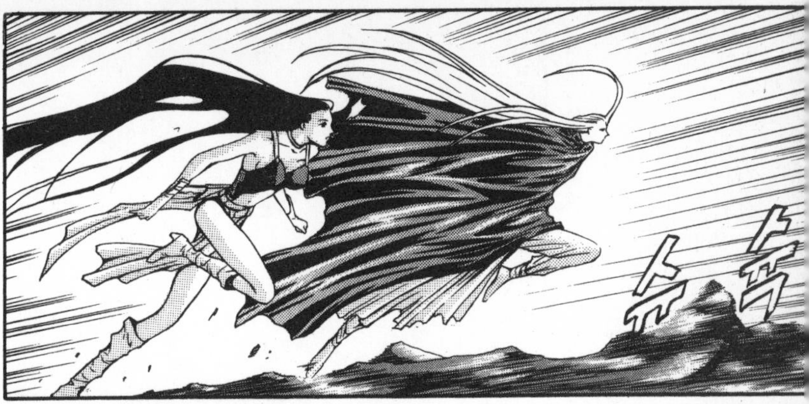
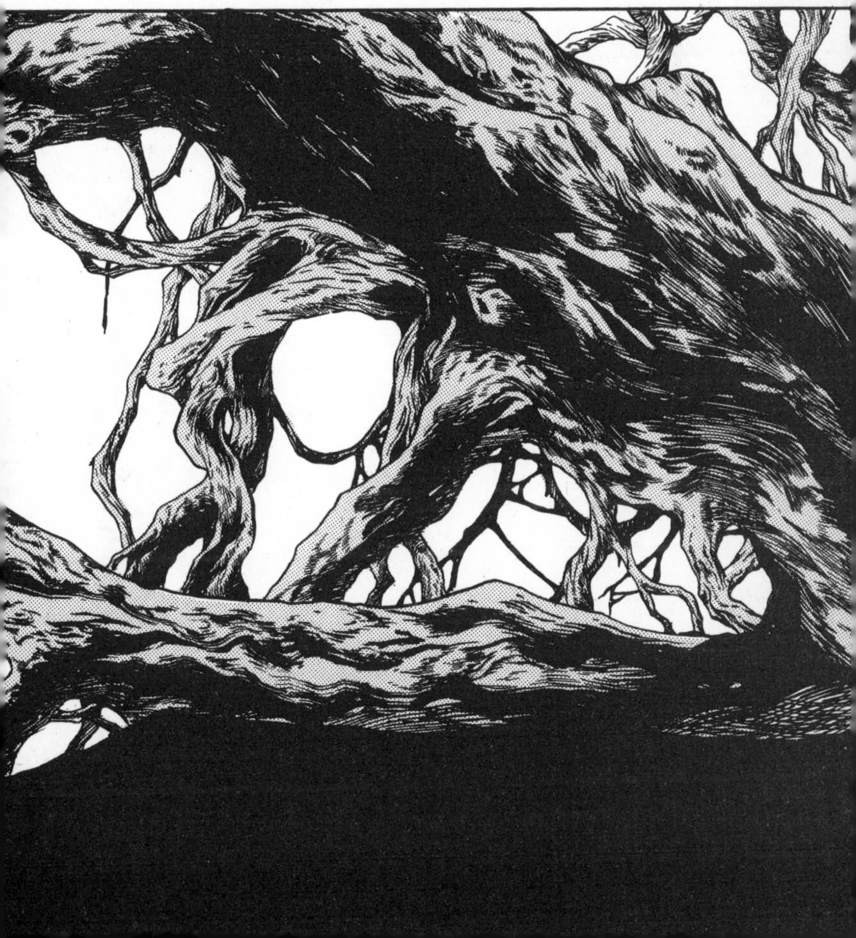

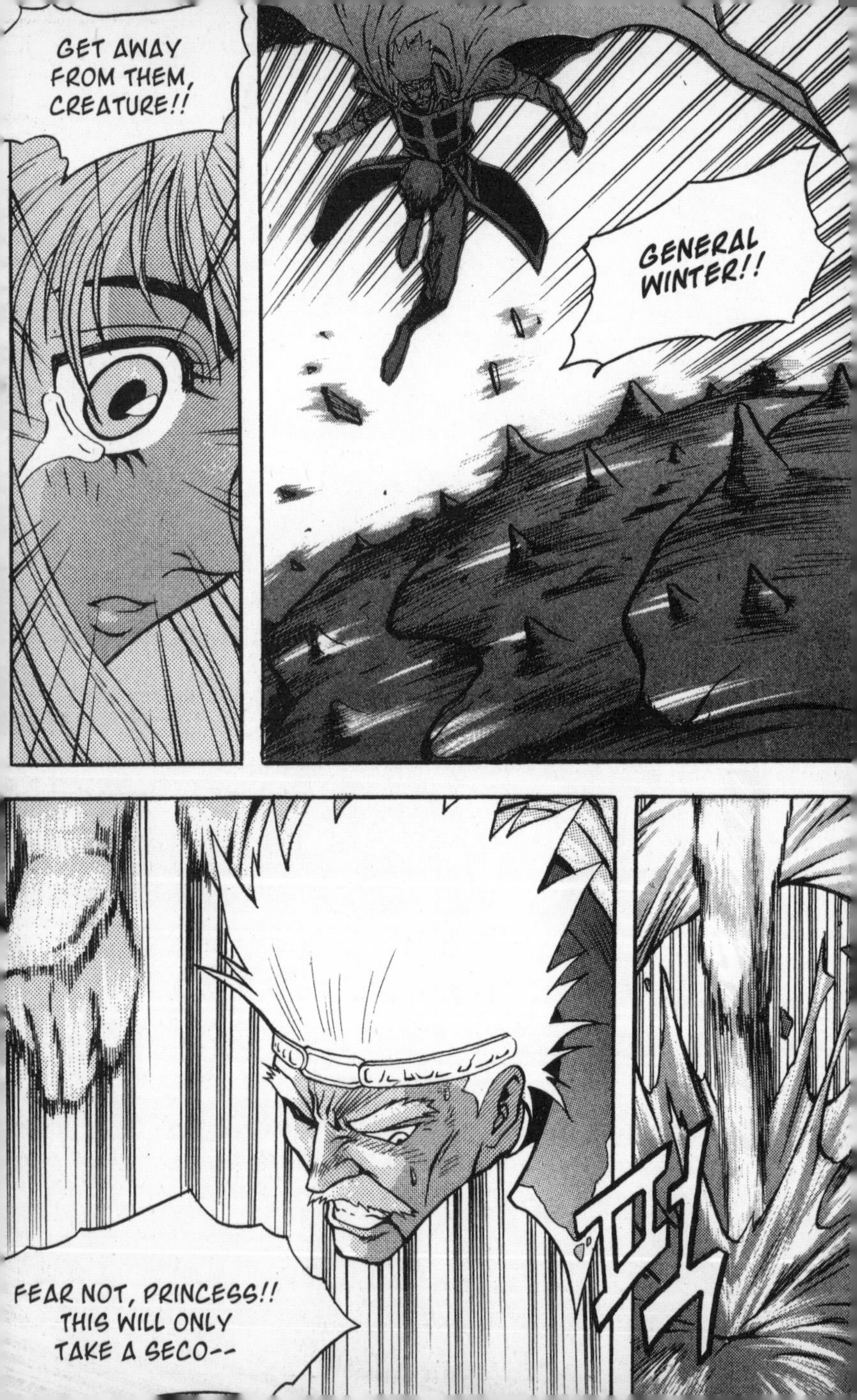
GENERAL WINTER!!
GET AWAY FROM THEM, CREATURE!!
FEAR NOT, PRINCESS!! THIS WILL ONLY TAKE A SECO--

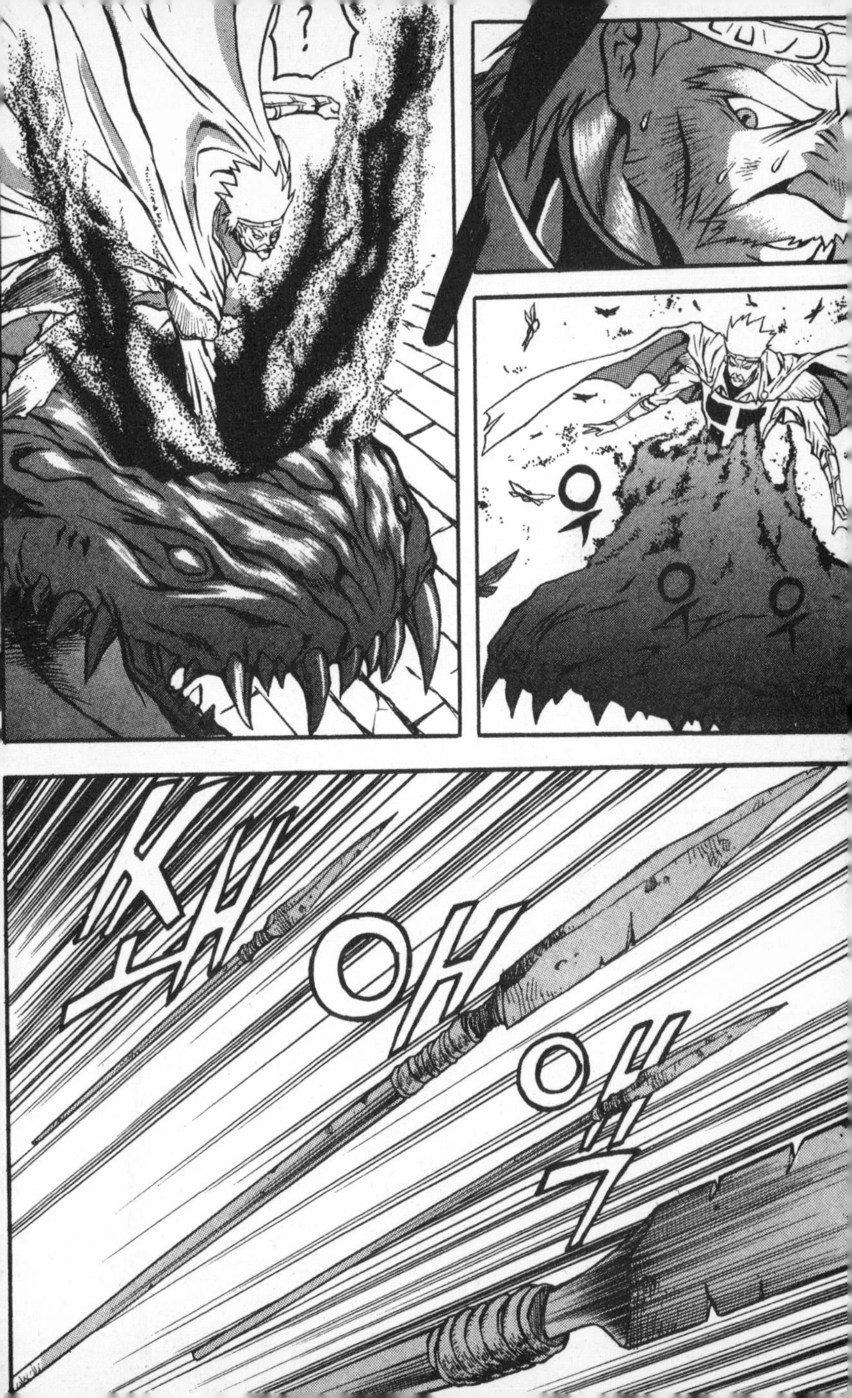
?

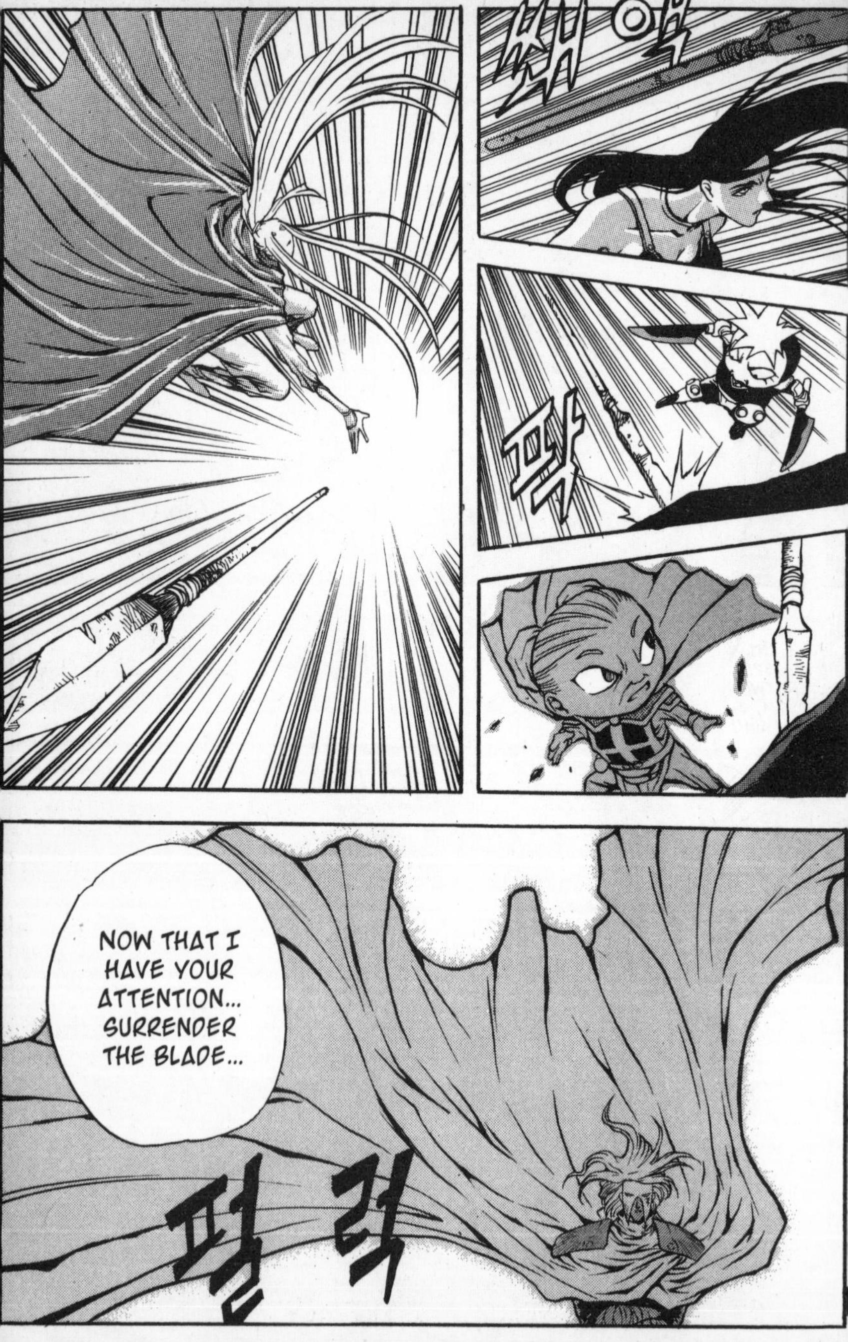
쌔액
팍
NOW THAT I HAVE YOUR ATTENTION... SURRENDER THE BLADE...
펄럭

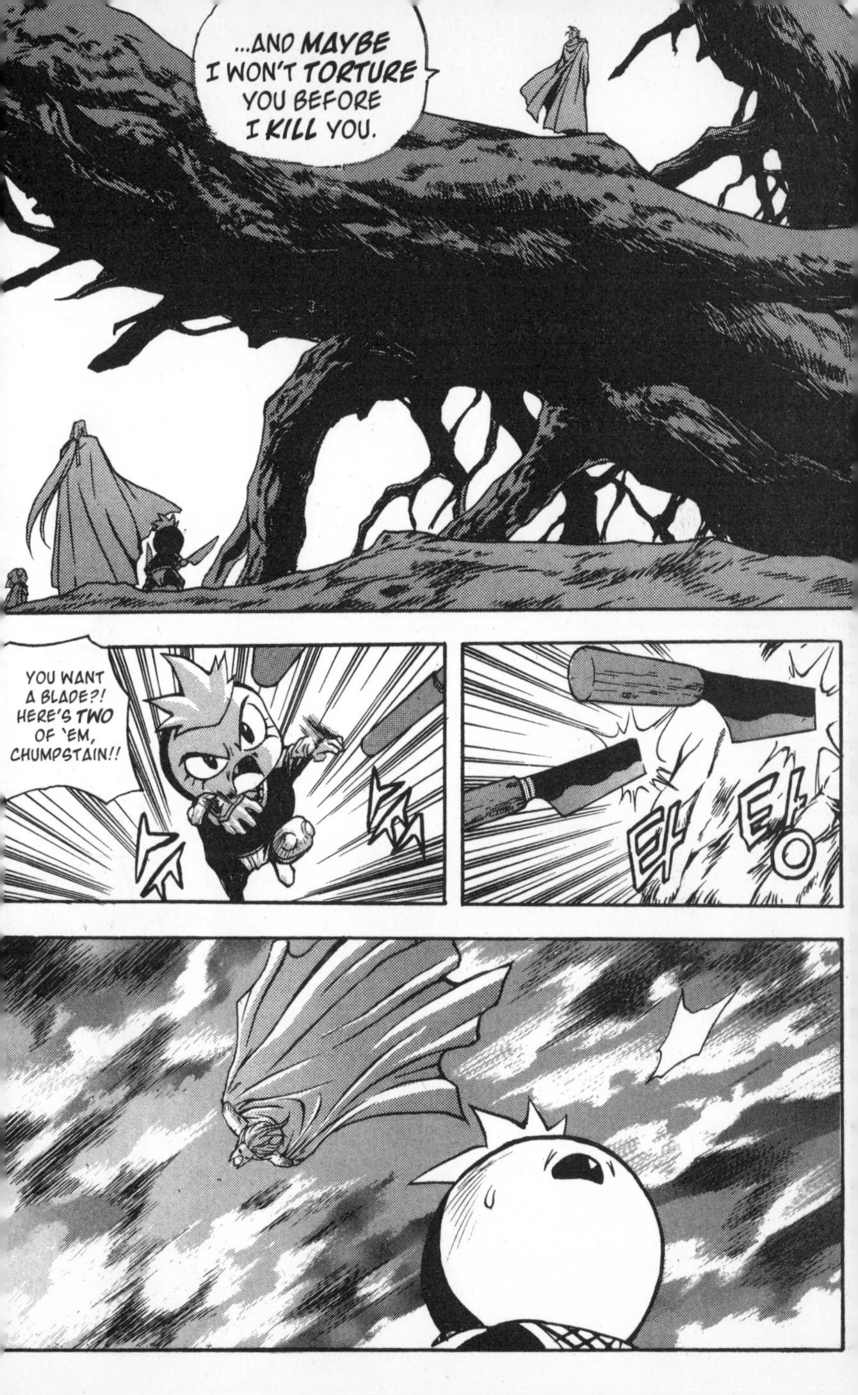
...AND MAYBE I WON'T TORTURE YOU BEFORE I KILL YOU.
YOU WANT A BLADE?! HERE'S TWO OF 'EM, CHUMPSTAIN!!
탁 탁

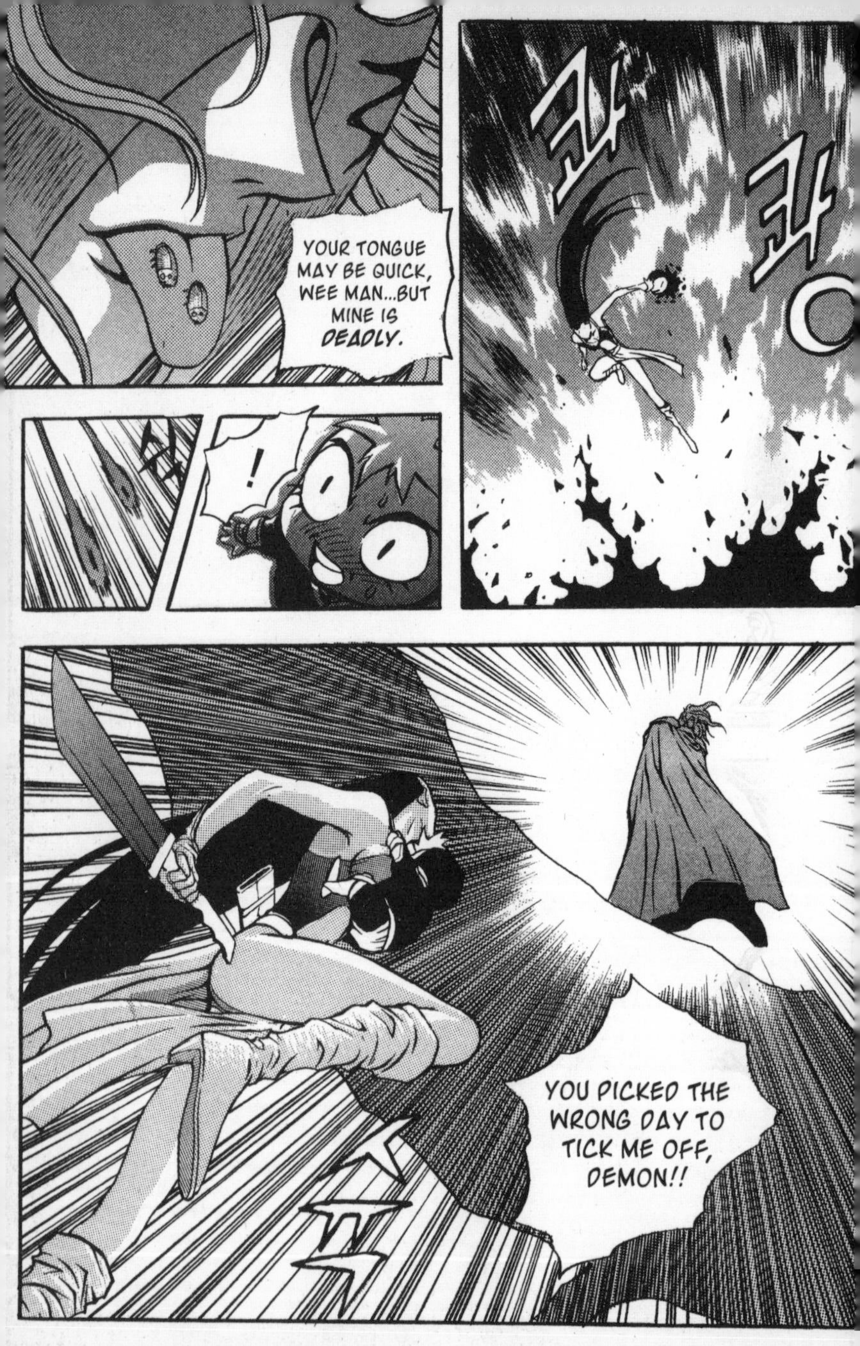
YOUR TONGUE MAY BE QUICK, WEE MAN...BUT MINE IS DEADLY.
!
YOU PICKED THE WRONG DAY TO TICK ME OFF, DEMON!!

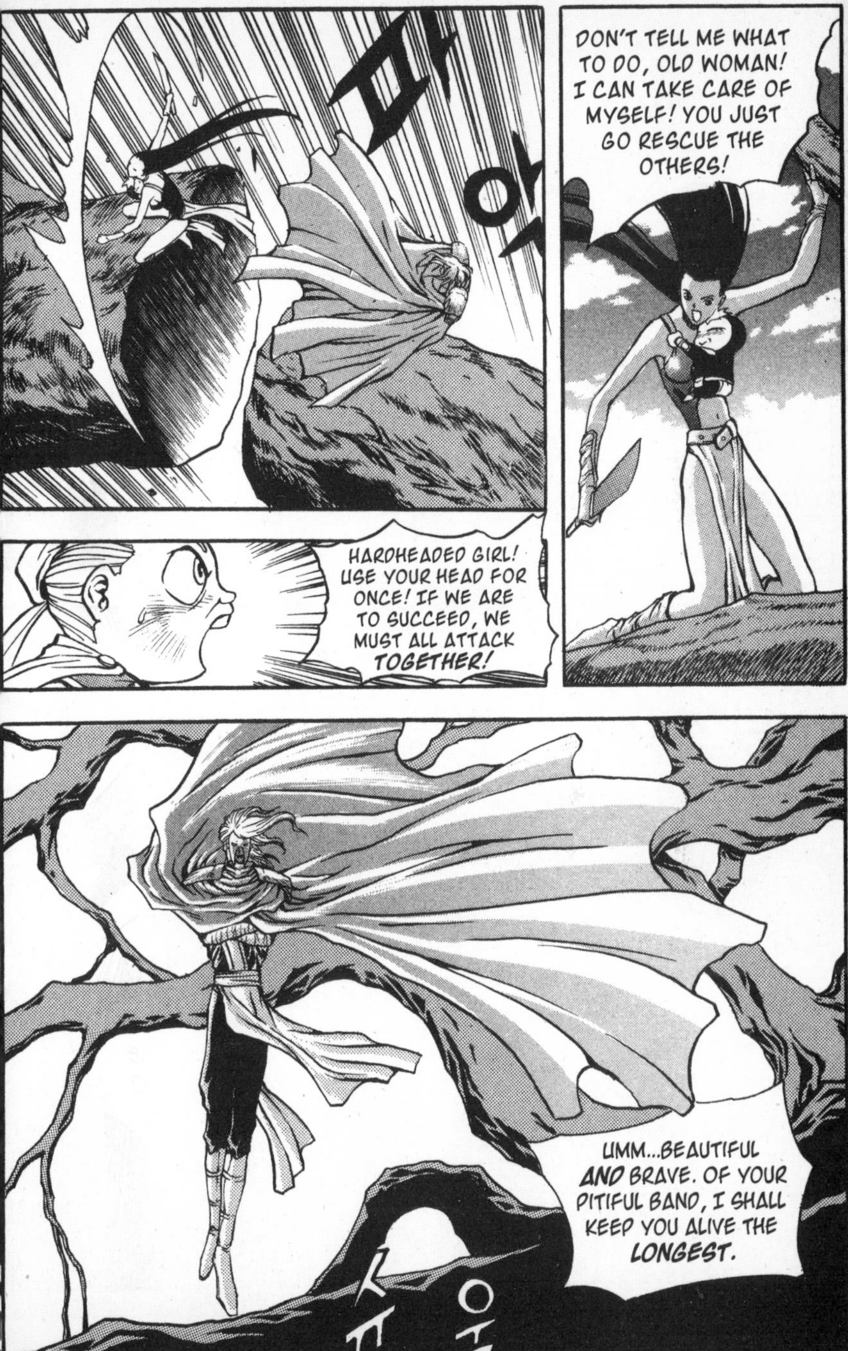
DON'T TELL ME WHAT TO DO, OLD WOMAN! I CAN TAKE CARE OF MYSELF! YOU JUST GO RESCUE THE OTHERS!
HARDHEADED GIRL! USE YOUR HEAD FOR ONCE! IF WE ARE TO SUCCEED, WE MUST ALL ATTACK TOGETHER!
UMM...BEAUTIFUL AND BRAVE. OF YOUR PITIFUL BAND, I SHALL KEEP YOU ALIVE THE LONGEST.

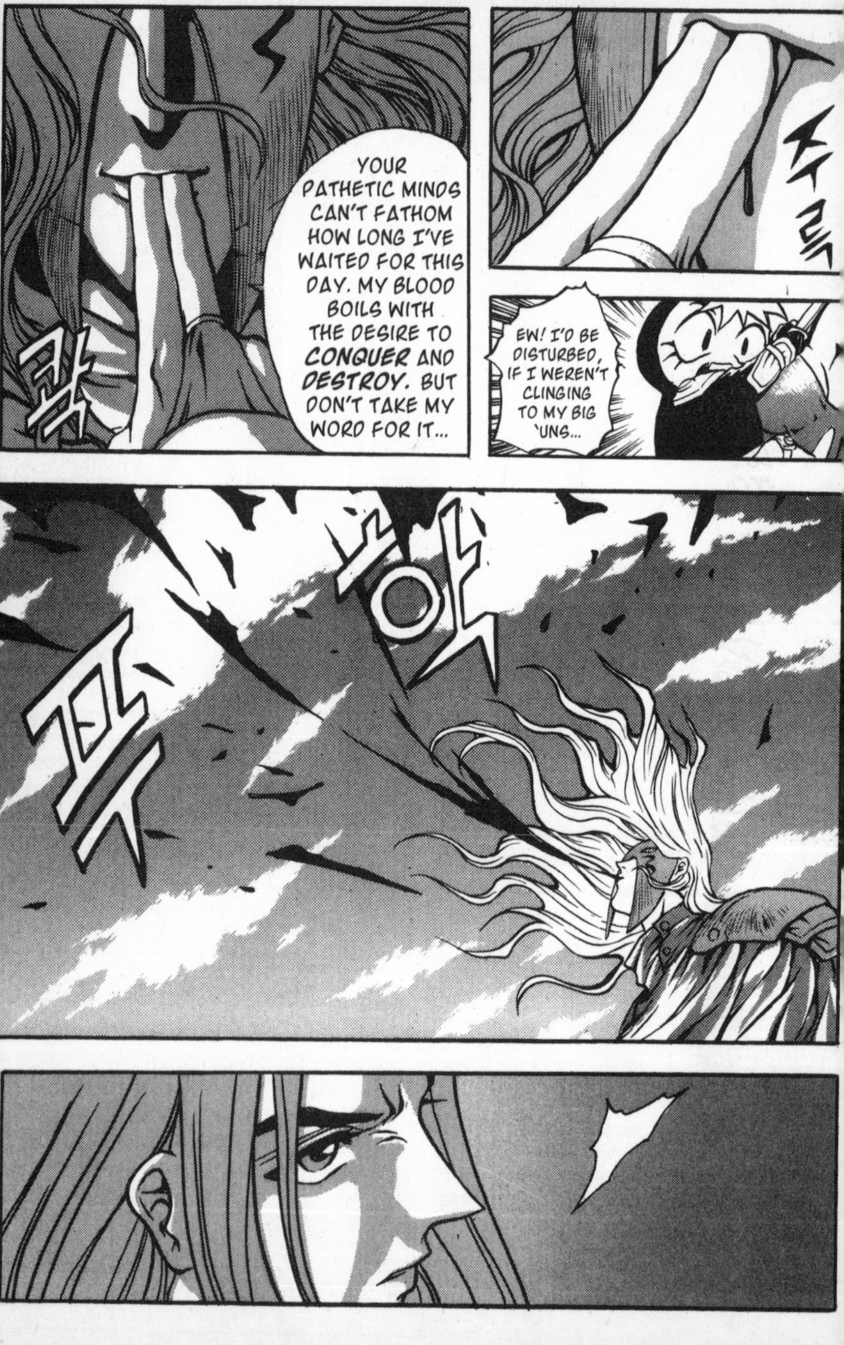
YOUR PATHETIC MINDS CAN'T FATHOM HOW LONG I'VE WAITED FOR THIS DAY. MY BLOOD BOILS WITH THE DESIRE TO **CONQUER** AND **DESTROY.** BUT DON'T TAKE MY WORD FOR IT...
EW! I'D BE DISTURBED, IF I WEREN'T CLINGING TO MY BIG 'UNS...

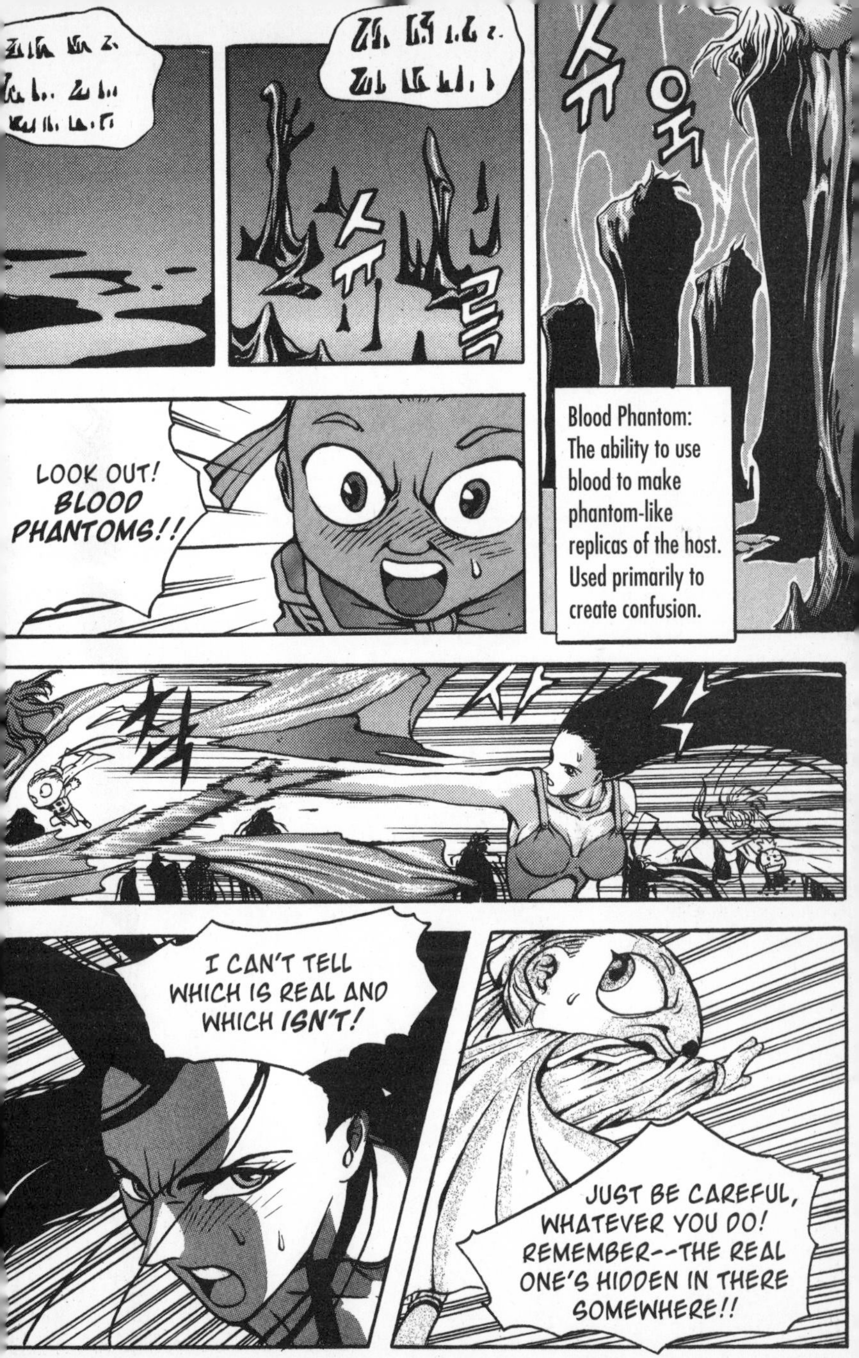
LOOK OUT! BLOOD PHANTOMS!!
Blood Phantom: The ability to use blood to make phantom-like replicas of the host. Used primarily to create confusion.
I CAN'T TELL WHICH IS REAL AND WHICH ISN'T!
JUST BE CAREFUL, WHATEVER YOU DO! REMEMBER--THE REAL ONE'S HIDDEN IN THERE SOMEWHERE!!

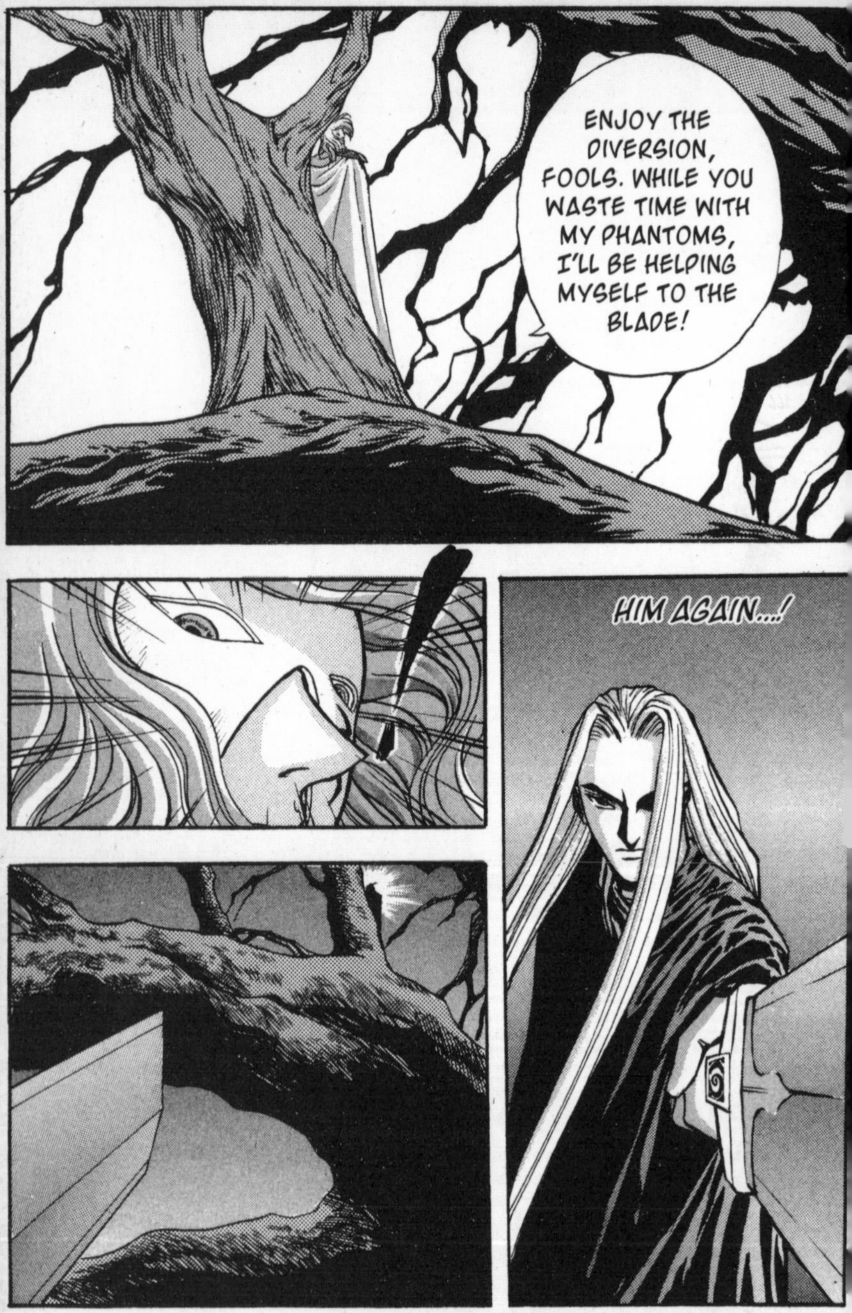
ENJOY THE DIVERSION, FOOLS. WHILE YOU WASTE TIME WITH MY PHANTOMS, I'LL BE HELPING MYSELF TO THE BLADE!
HIM AGAIN...!

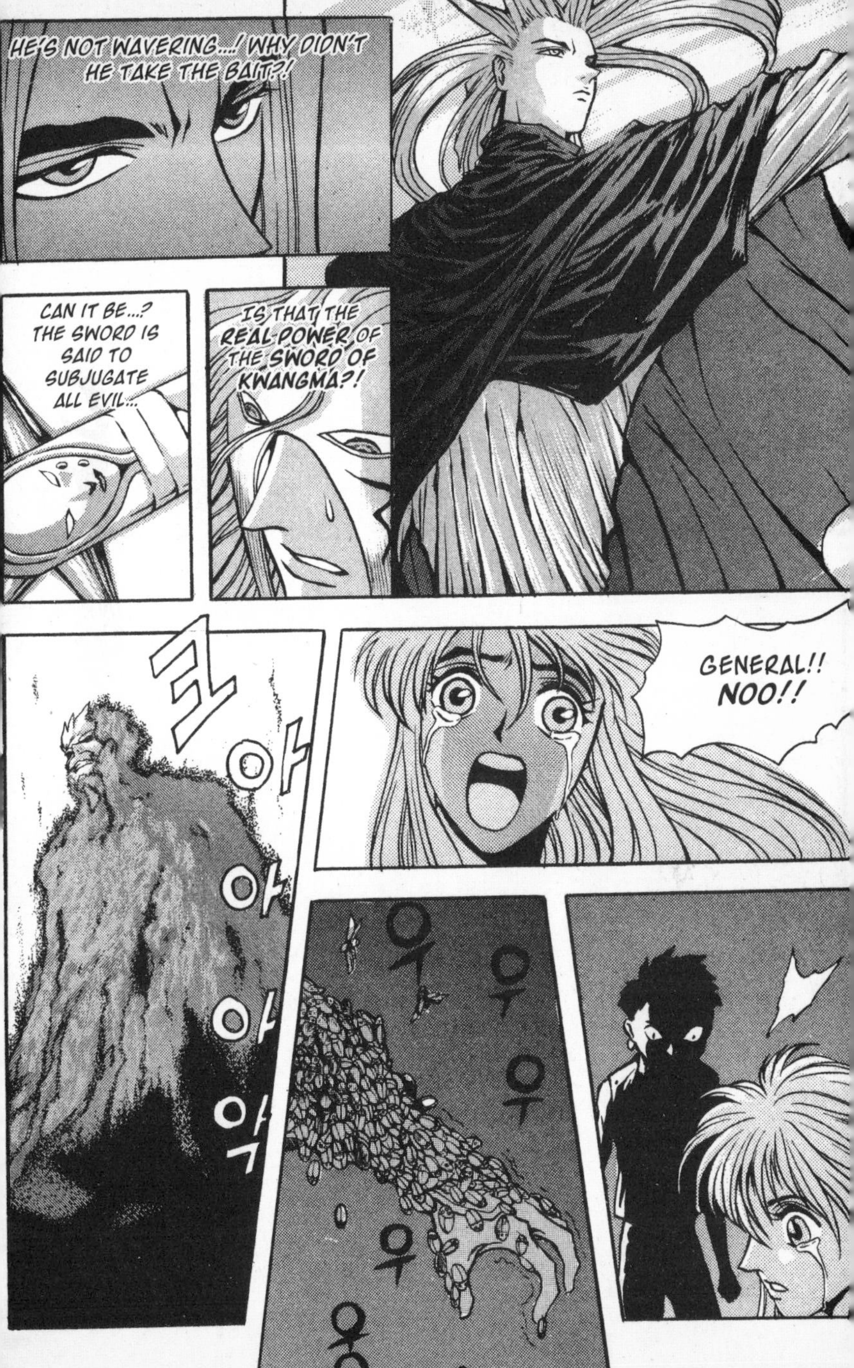
HE'S NOT WAVERING...! WHY DIDN'T HE TAKE THE BAIT?!
CAN IT BE...? THE SWORD IS SAID TO SUBJUGATE ALL EVIL...
IS THAT THE REAL POWER OF THE SWORD OF KWANGMA?!
크아아아악
GENERAL!! NOO!!

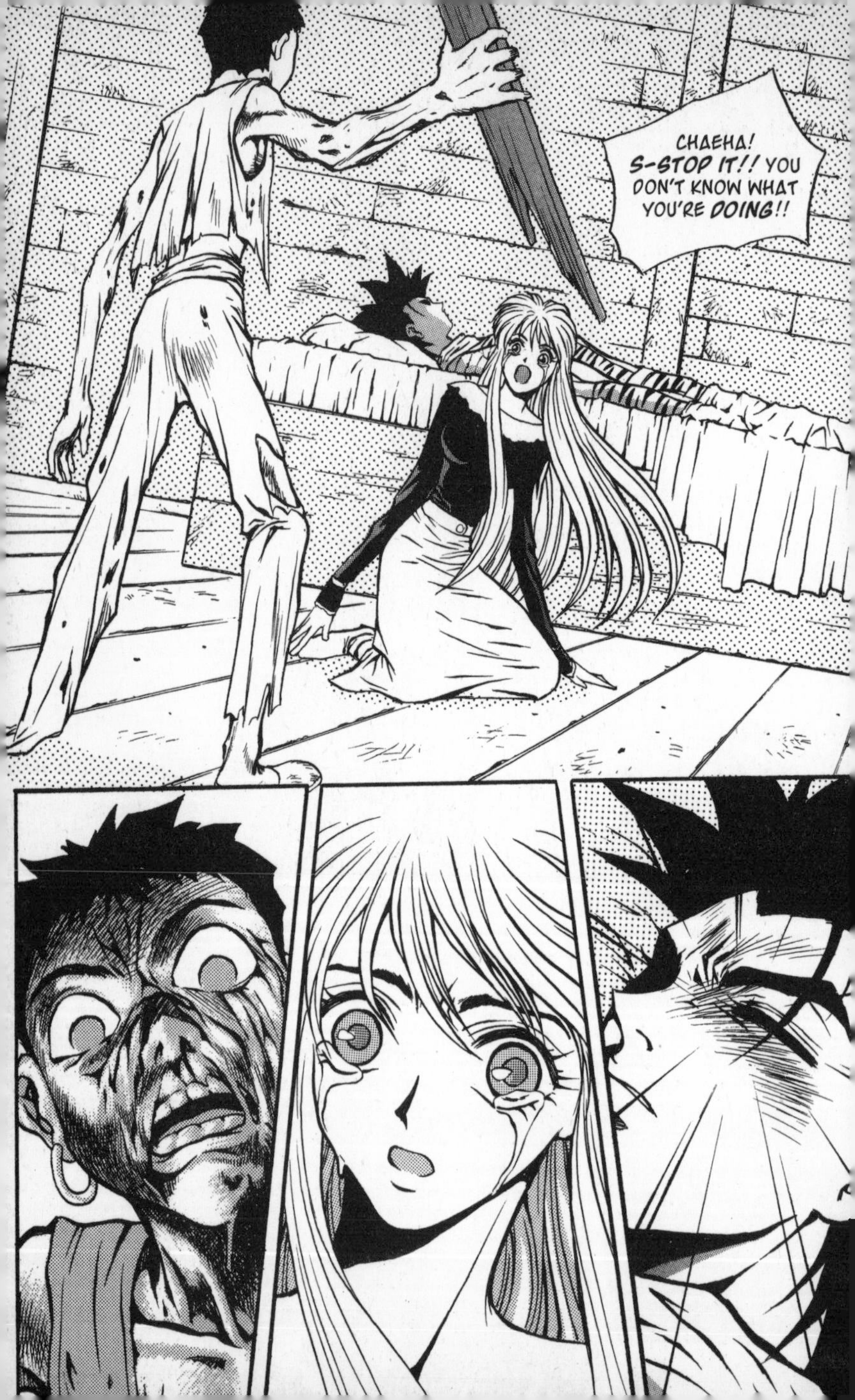
CHAEHA! S-STOP IT!! YOU DON'T KNOW WHAT YOU'RE DOING!!

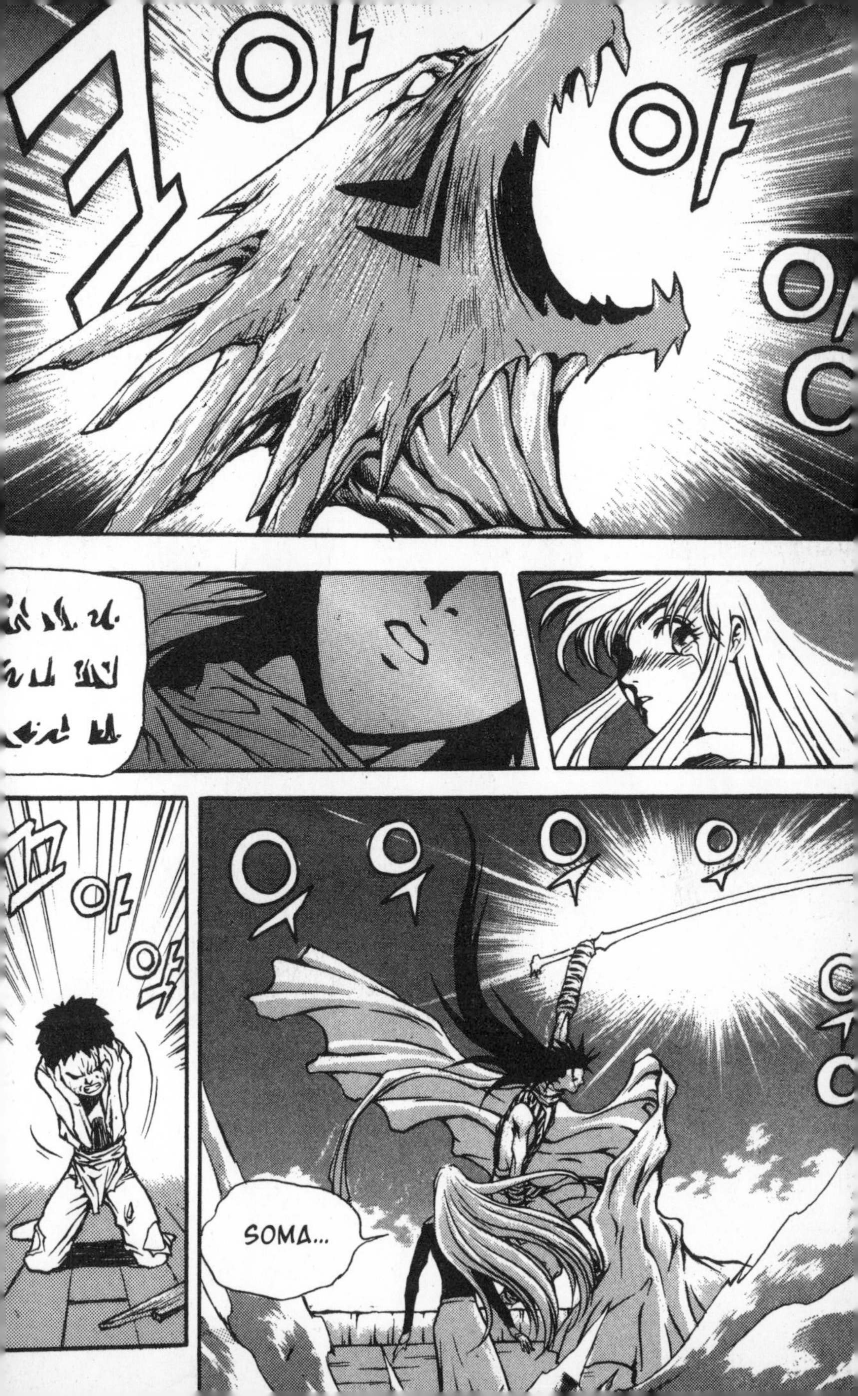
SOMA...

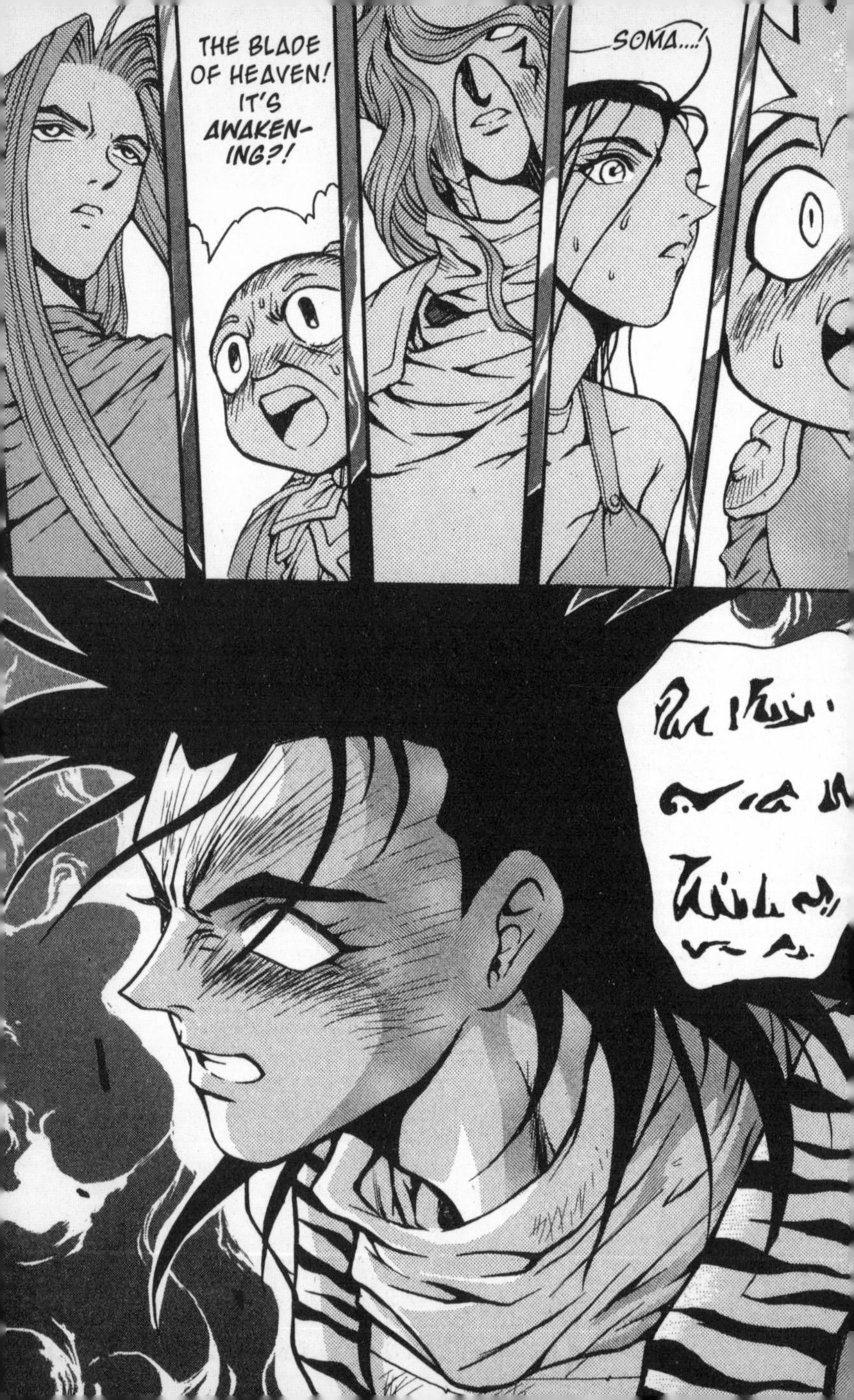
SOMA...!
THE BLADE OF HEAVEN! IT'S AWAKEN-ING?!

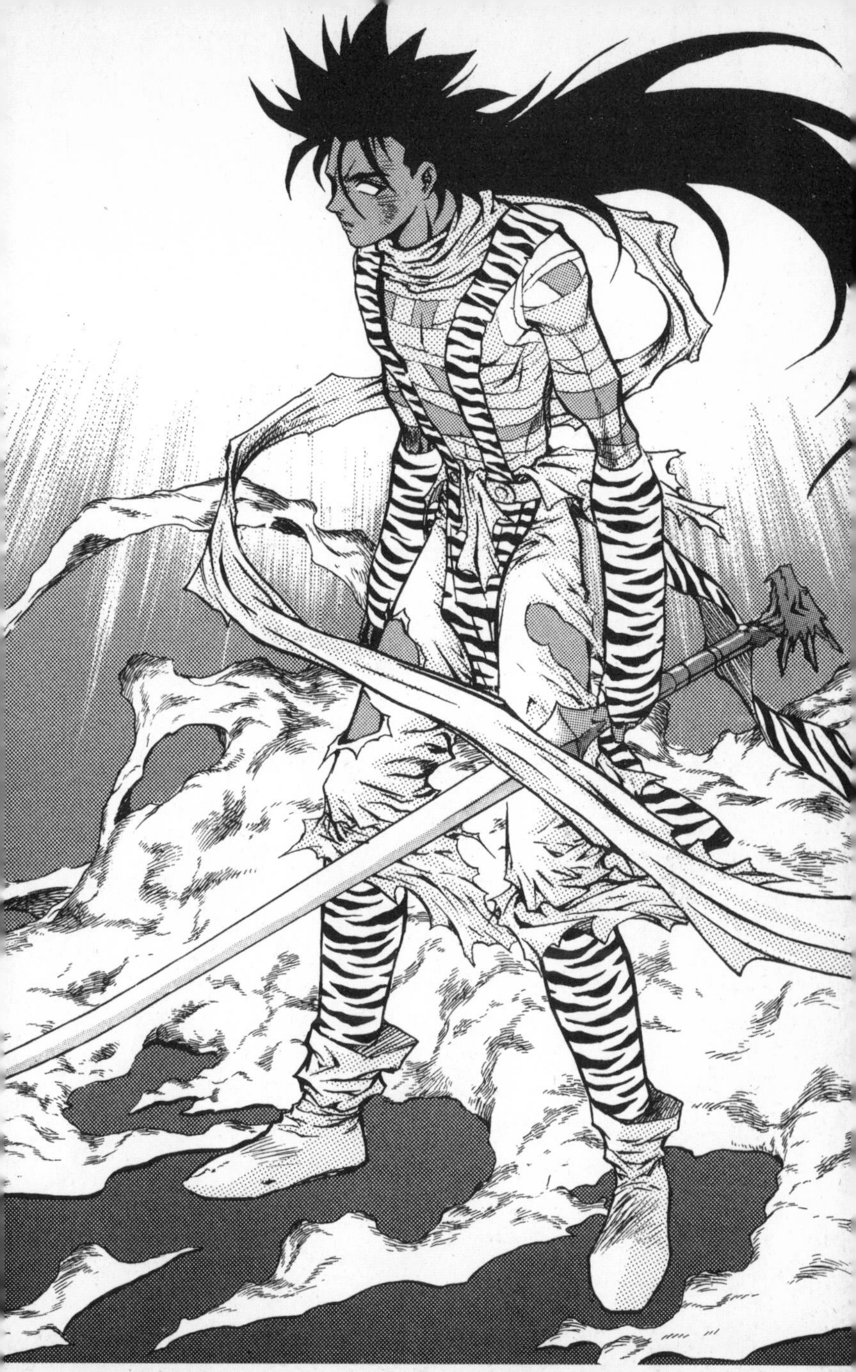

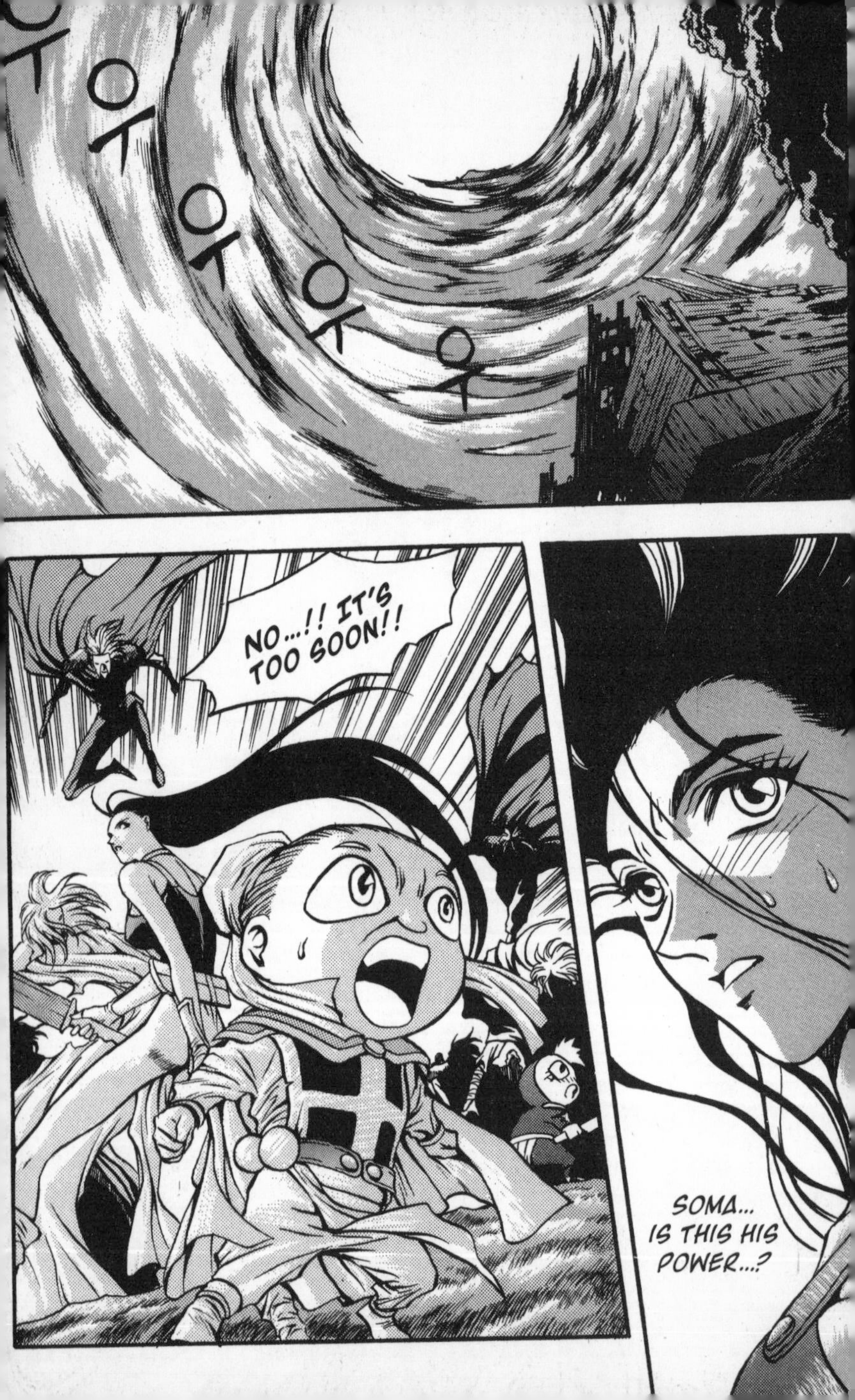
SOMA...
IS THIS HIS
POWER...?
NO...!! IT'S
TOO SOON!!

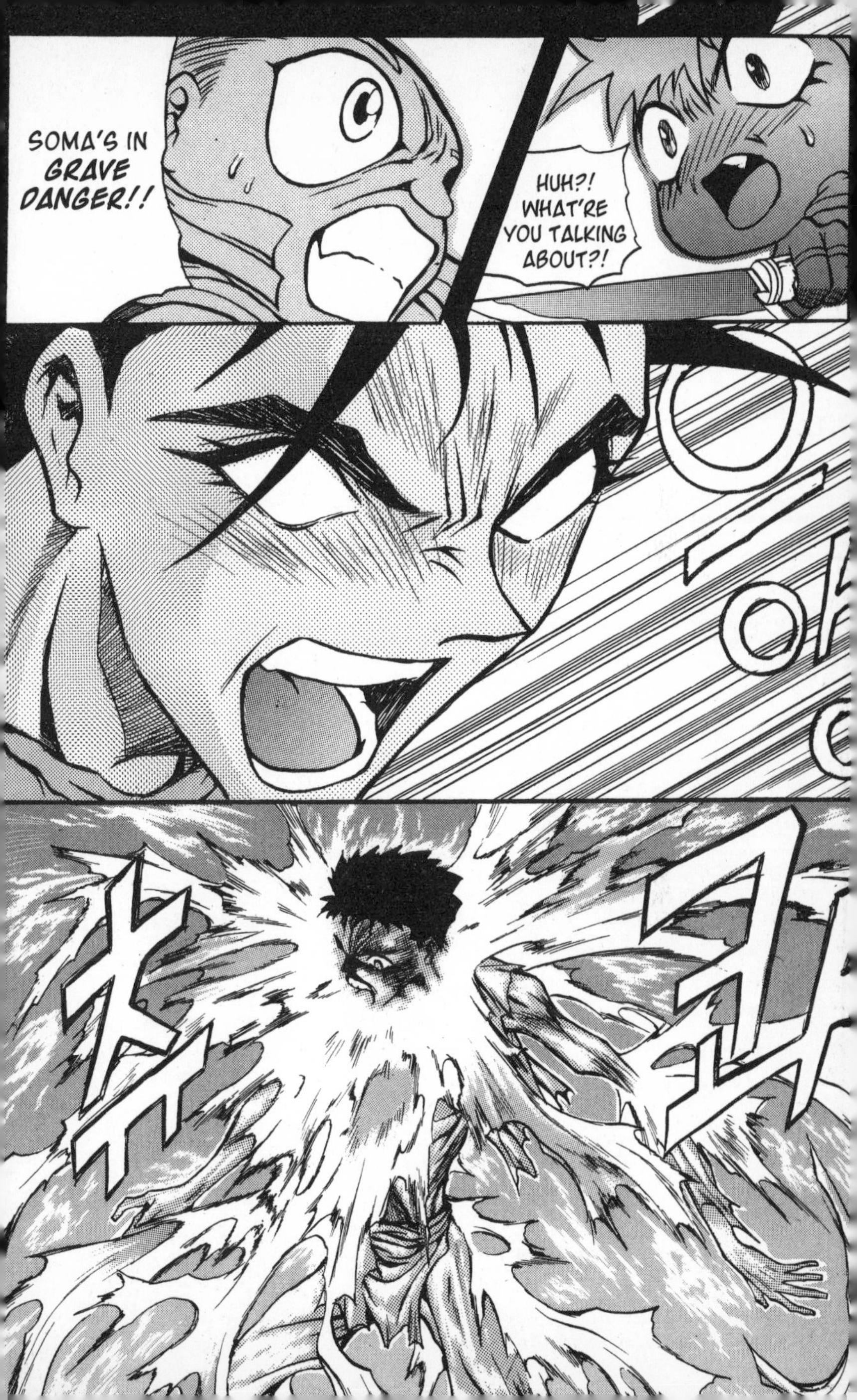
SOMA'S IN GRAVE DANGER!!
HUH?! WHAT'RE YOU TALKING ABOUT?!

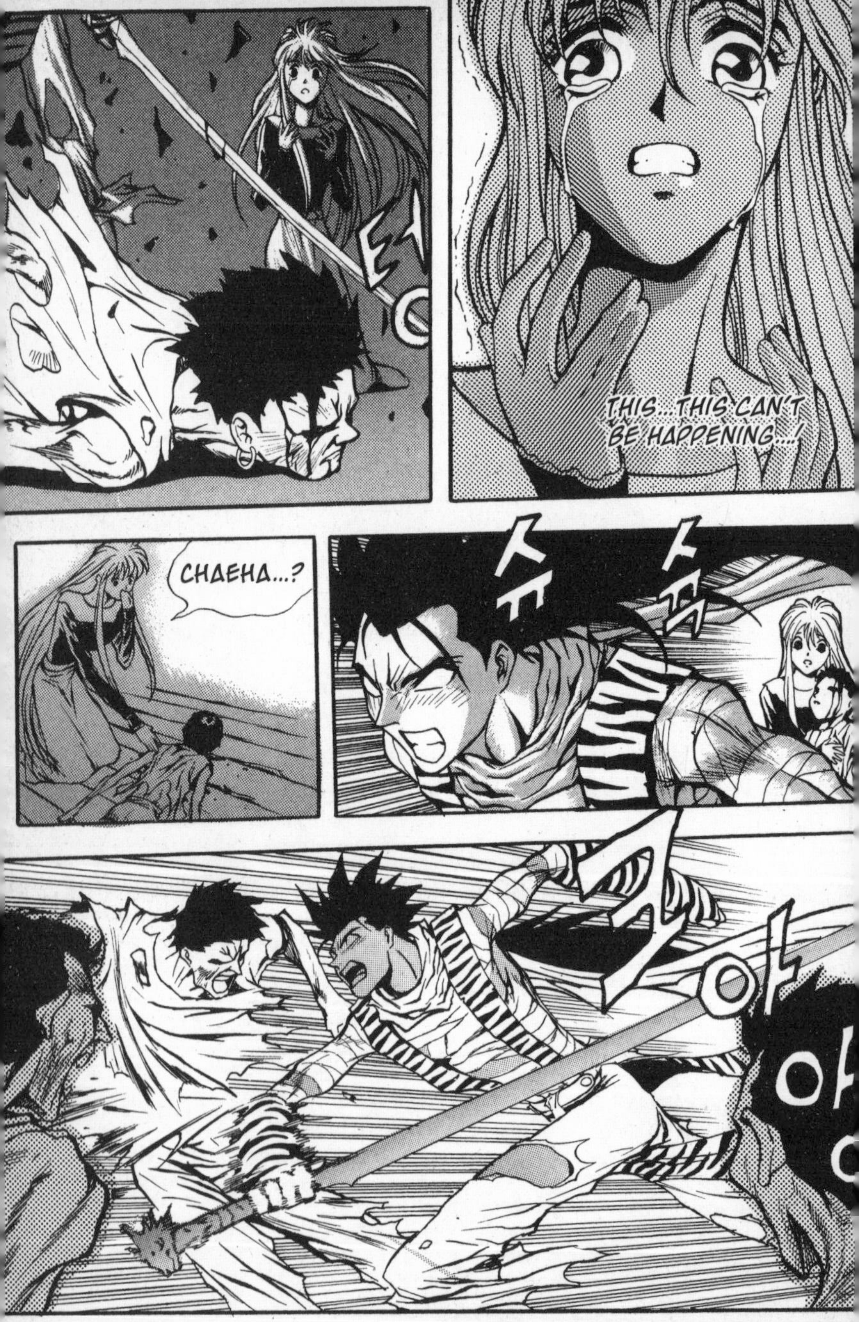
THIS... THIS CAN'T BE HAPPENING...!
CHAEHA...?

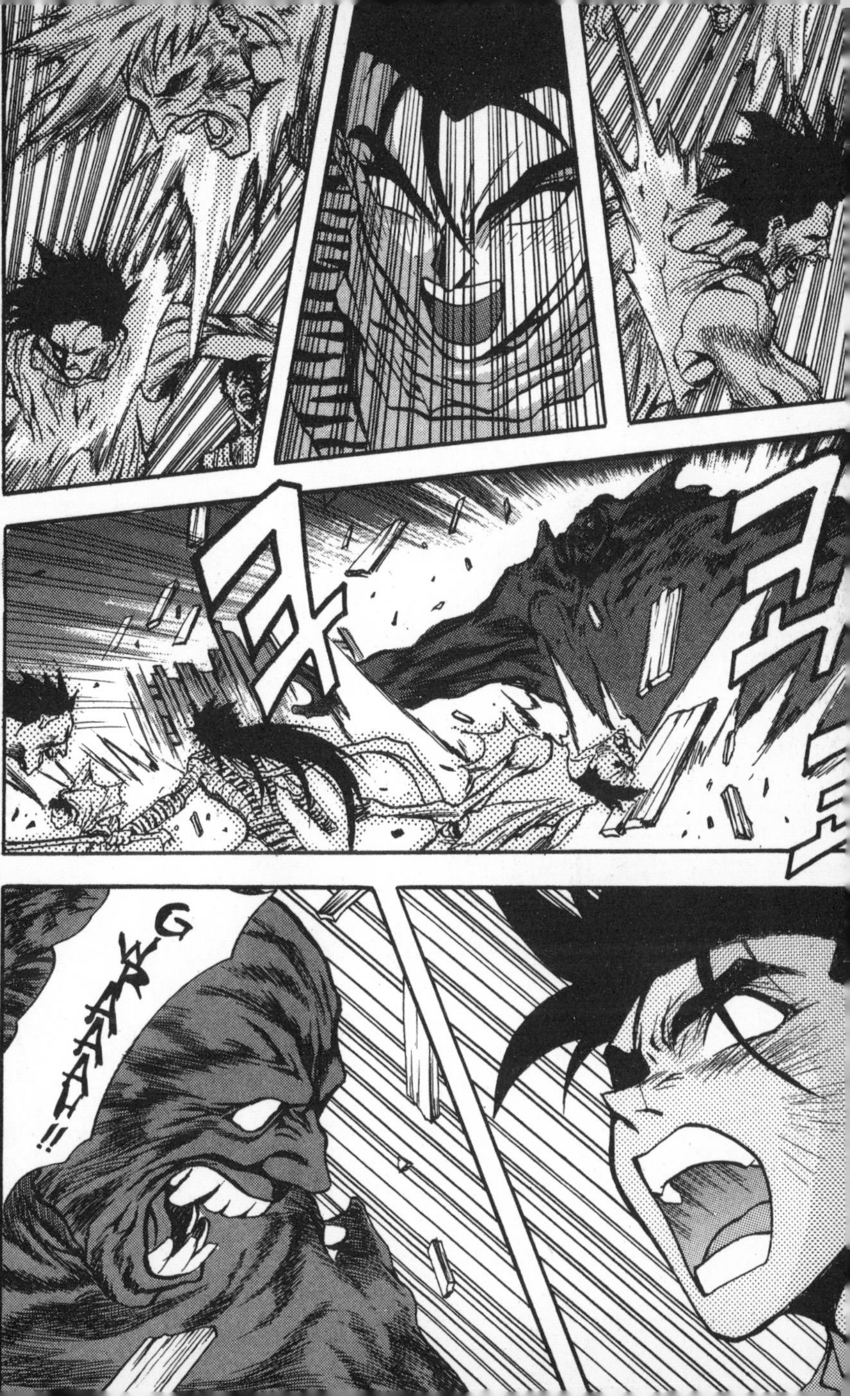
GWRAAAH!!

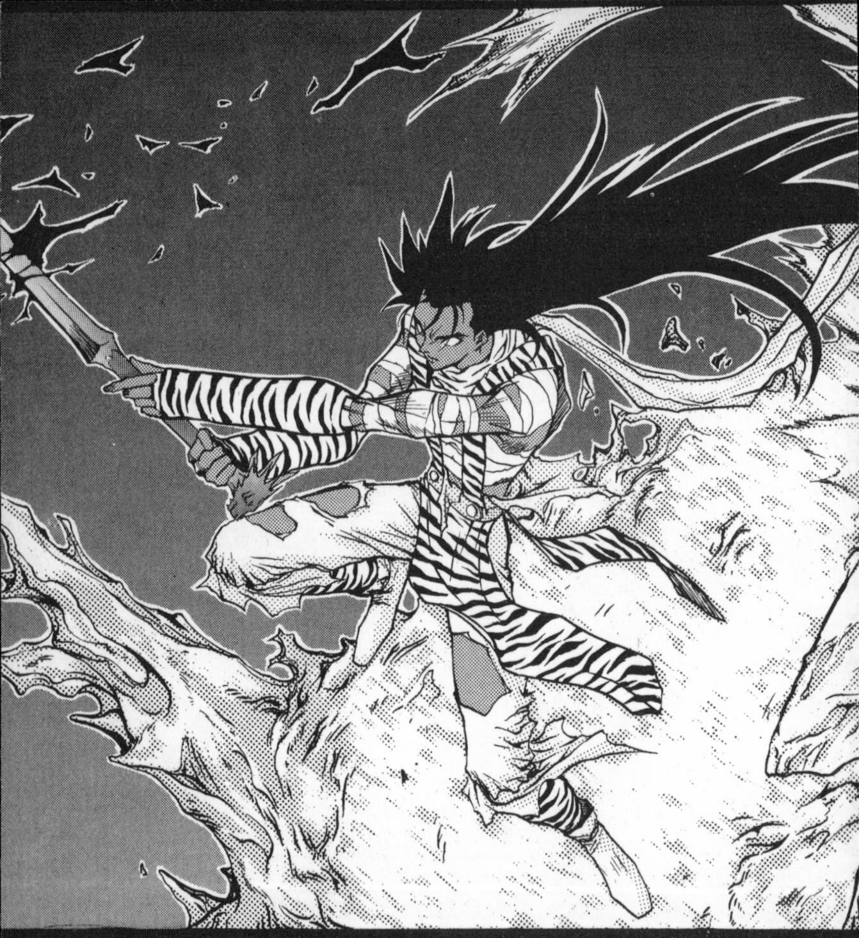
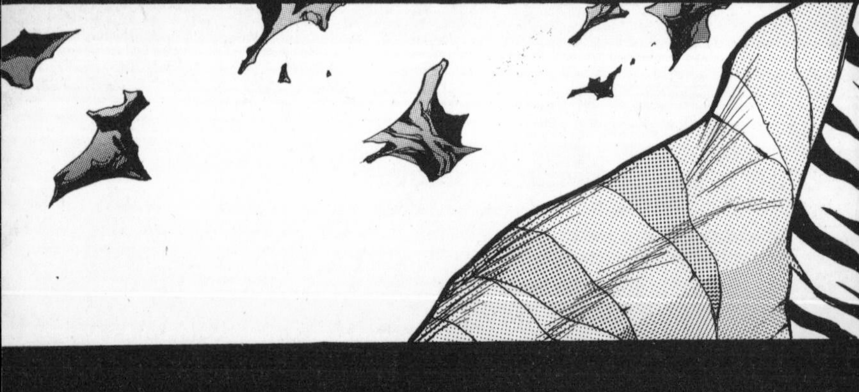

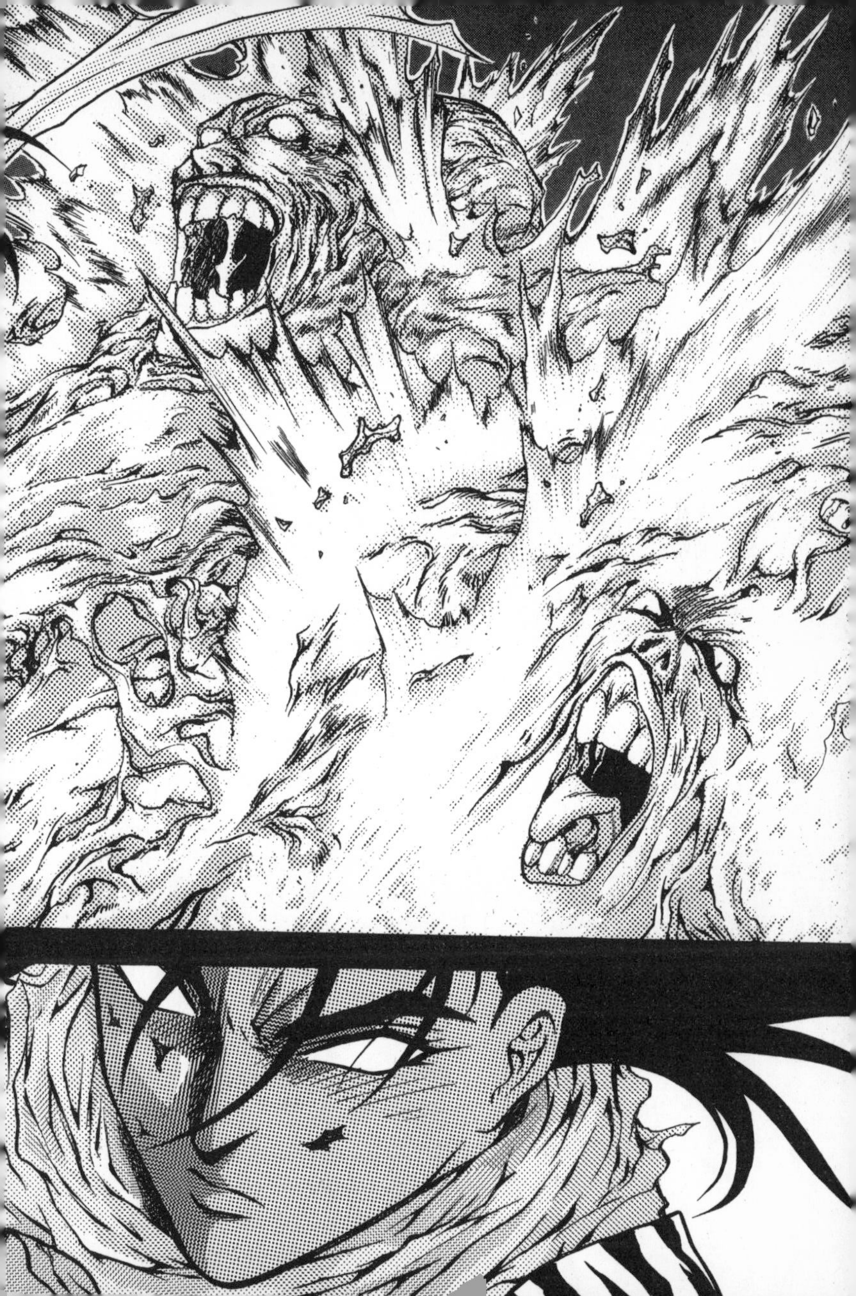

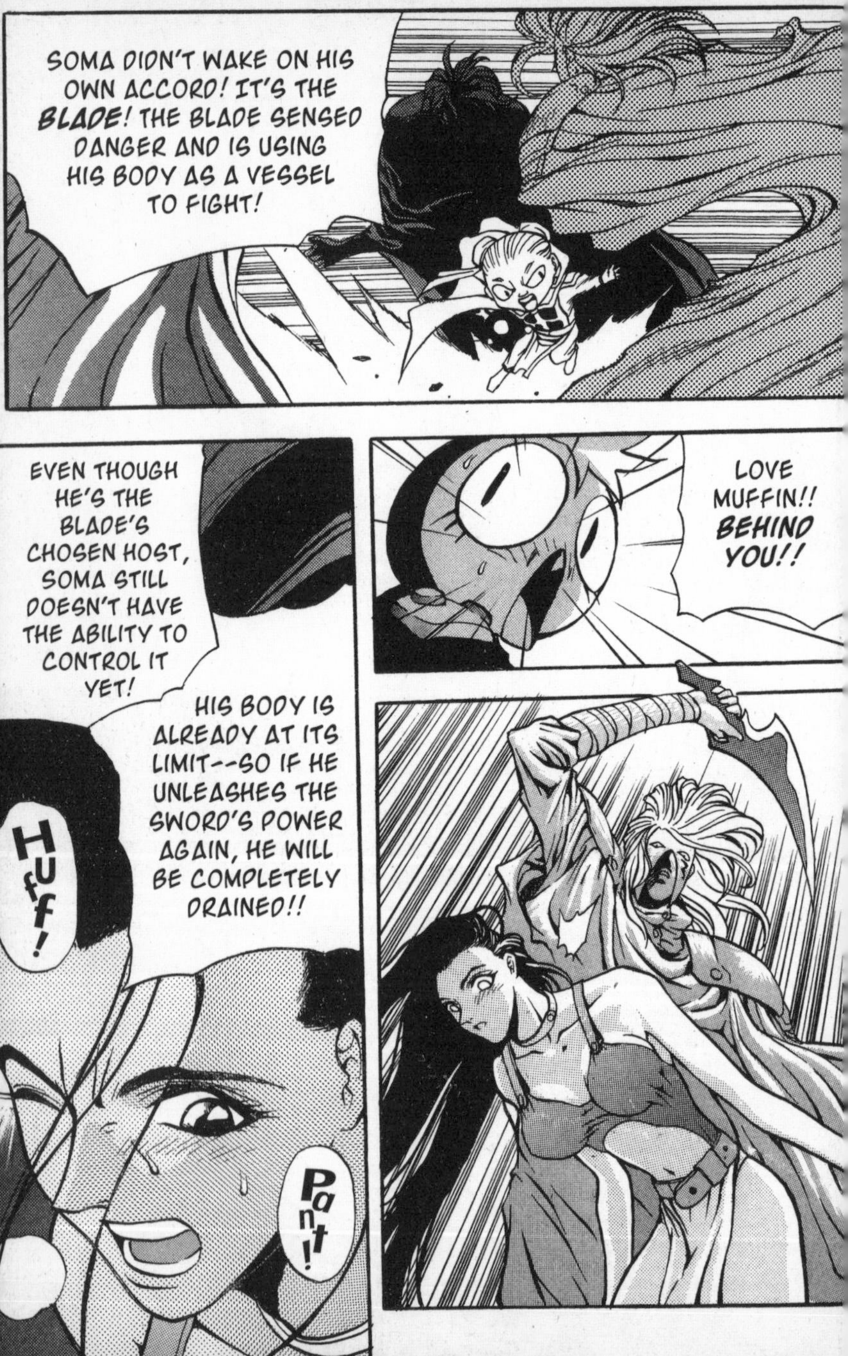
SOMA DIDN'T WAKE ON HIS OWN ACCORD! IT'S THE BLADE! THE BLADE SENSED DANGER AND IS USING HIS BODY AS A VESSEL TO FIGHT!
EVEN THOUGH HE'S THE BLADE'S CHOSEN HOST, SOMA STILL DOESN'T HAVE THE ABILITY TO CONTROL IT YET!
HIS BODY IS ALREADY AT ITS LIMIT--SO IF HE UNLEASHES THE SWORD'S POWER AGAIN, HE WILL BE COMPLETELY DRAINED!!
Huff!
Pant!
LOVE MUFFIN!! BEHIND YOU!!

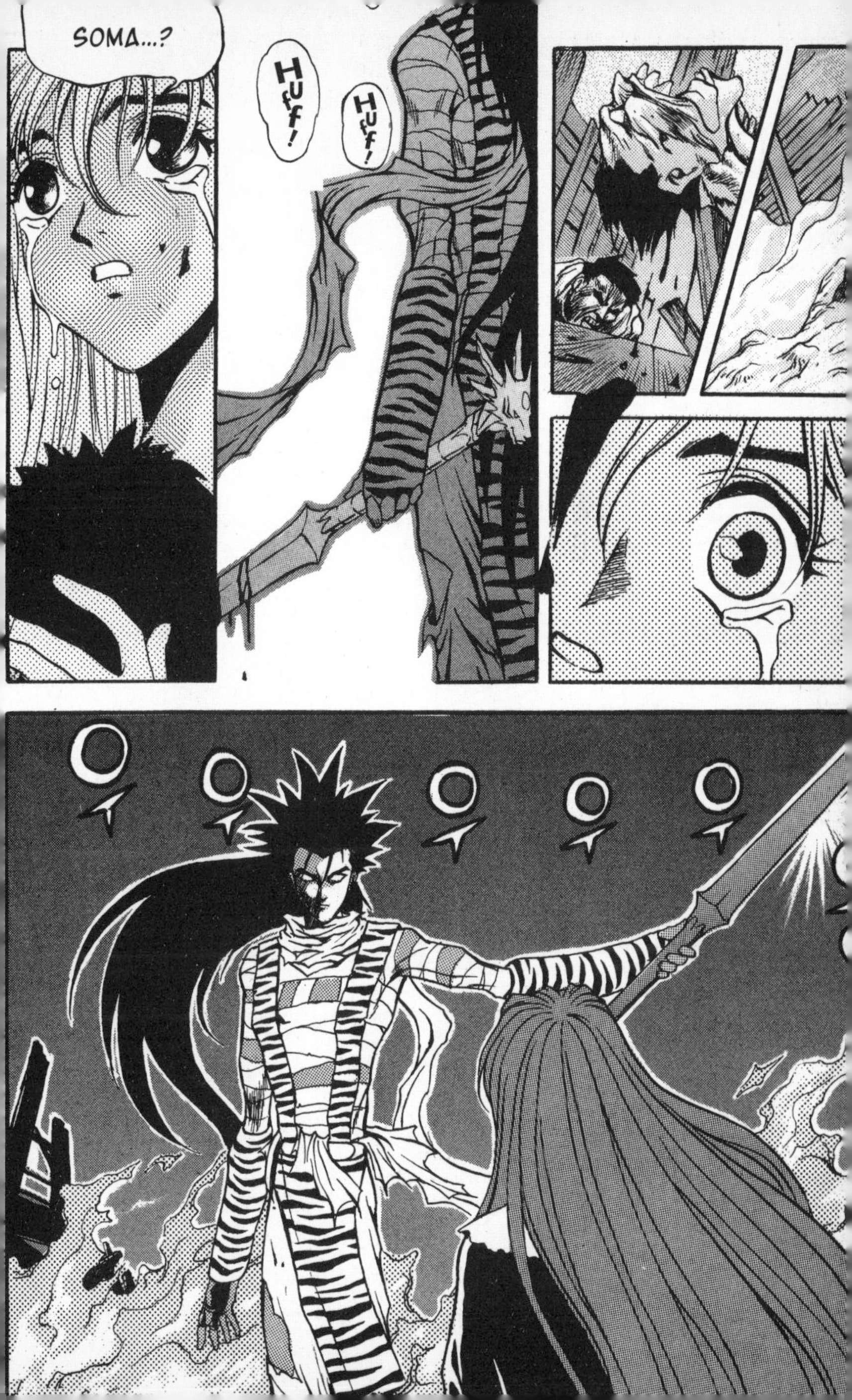
SOMA...?
Huf!
Huf!

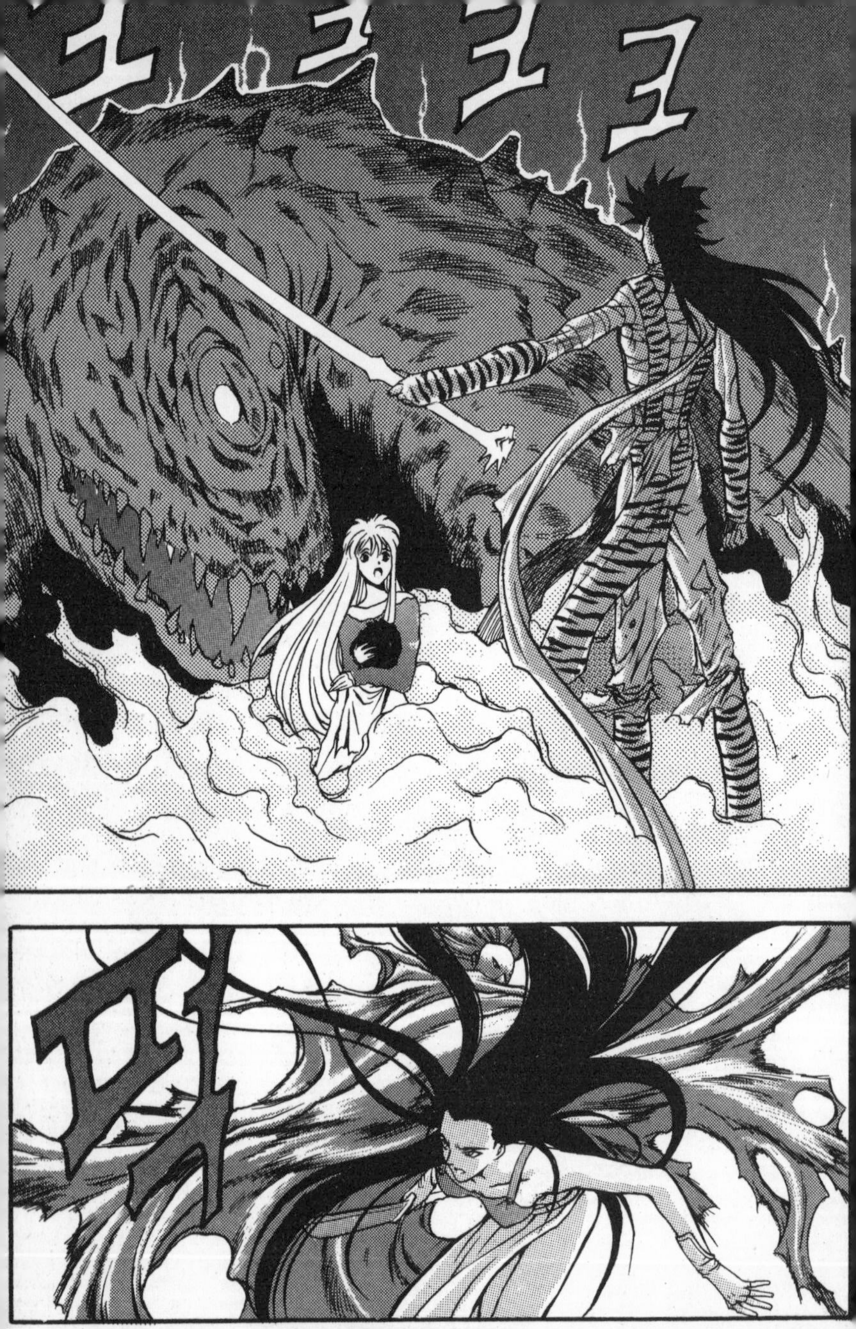

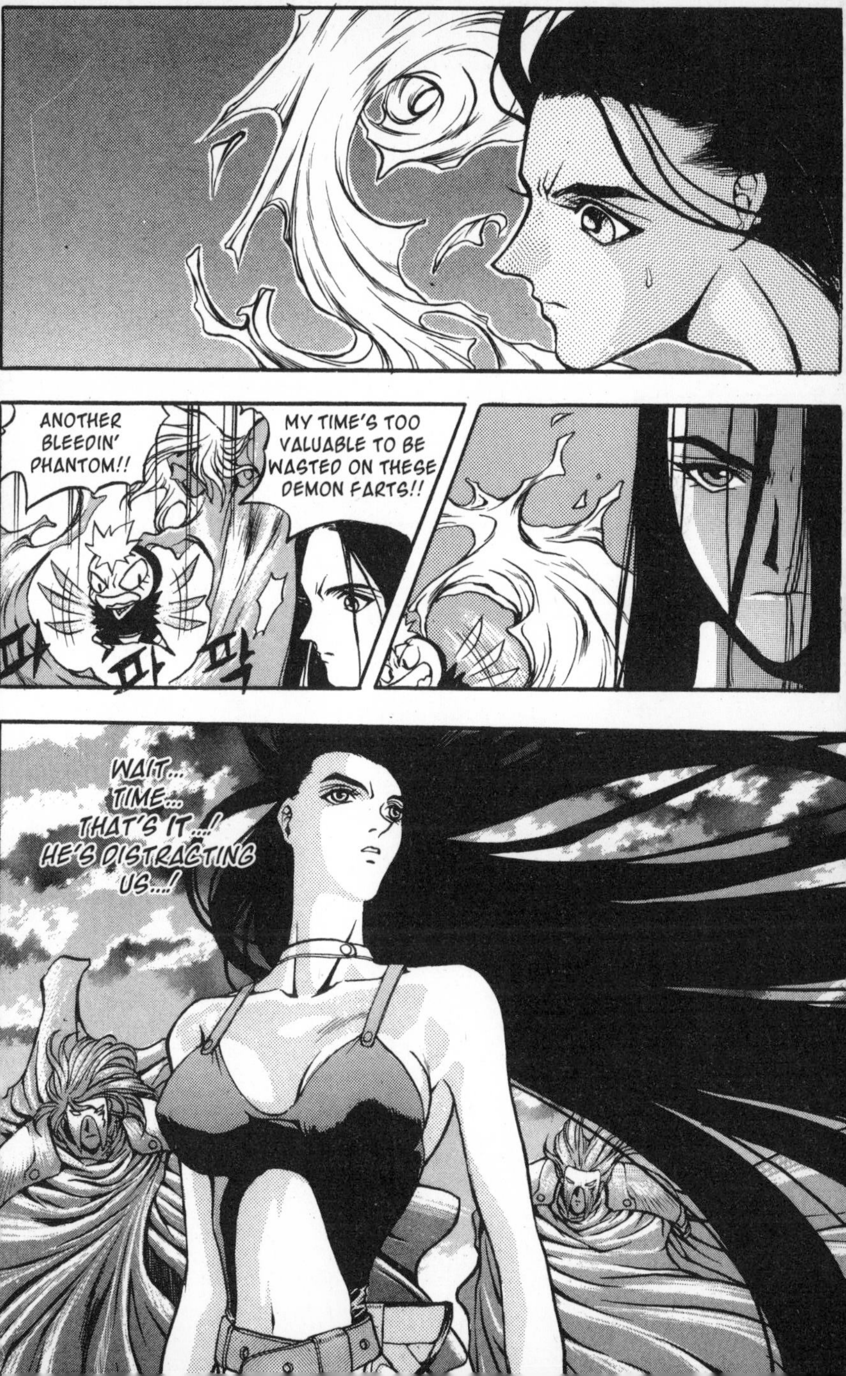
ANOTHER BLEEDIN' PHANTOM!!
MY TIME'S TOO VALUABLE TO BE WASTED ON THESE DEMON FARTS!!
WAIT... TIME... THAT'S IT...! HE'S DISTRACTING US...!

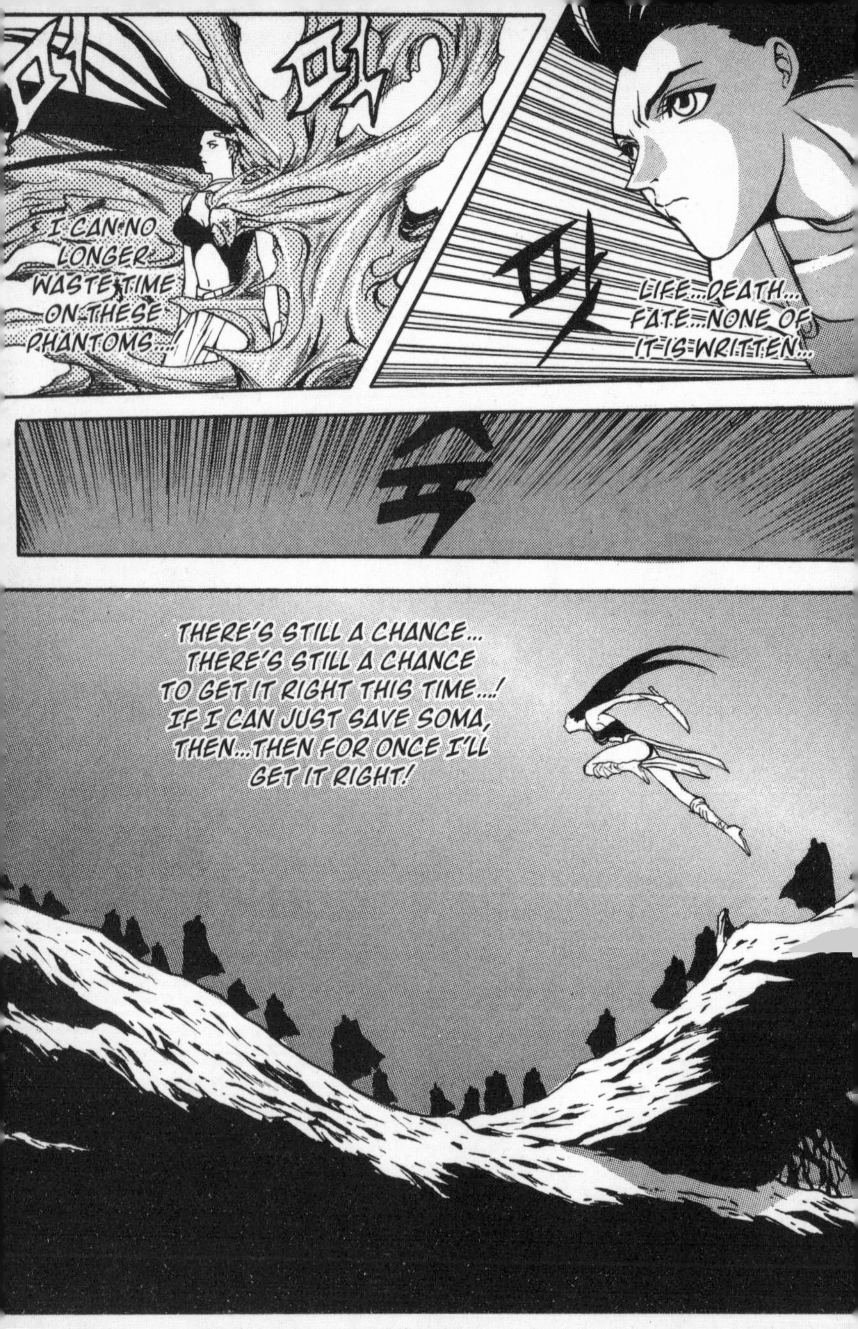
LIFE...DEATH...
FATE...NONE OF
IT IS WRITTEN...
I CAN NO
LONGER
WASTE TIME
ON THESE
PHANTOMS...!
THERE'S STILL A CHANCE...
THERE'S STILL A CHANCE
TO GET IT RIGHT THIS TIME...!
IF I CAN JUST SAVE SOMA,
THEN...THEN FOR ONCE I'LL
GET IT RIGHT!

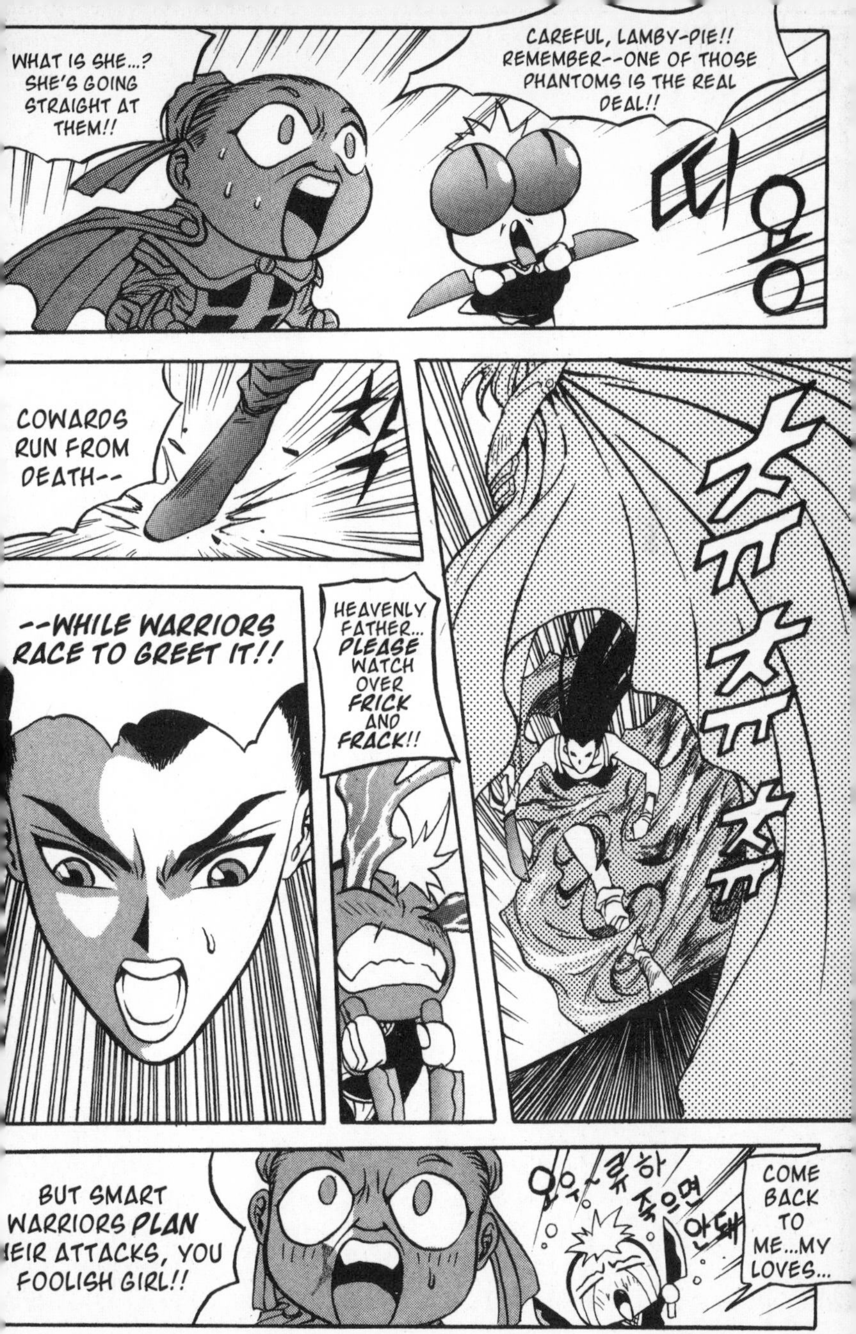
WHAT IS SHE...? SHE'S GOING STRAIGHT AT THEM!!
CAREFUL, LAMBY-PIE!! REMEMBER--ONE OF THOSE PHANTOMS IS THE REAL DEAL!!
띠옹
COWARDS RUN FROM DEATH--
--WHILE WARRIORS RACE TO GREET IT!!
HEAVENLY FATHER... PLEASE WATCH OVER FRICK AND FRACK!!
BUT SMART WARRIORS PLAN EIR ATTACKS, YOU FOOLISH GIRL!!
죽으면 안돼
COME BACK TO ME...MY LOVES...

He's fainting.

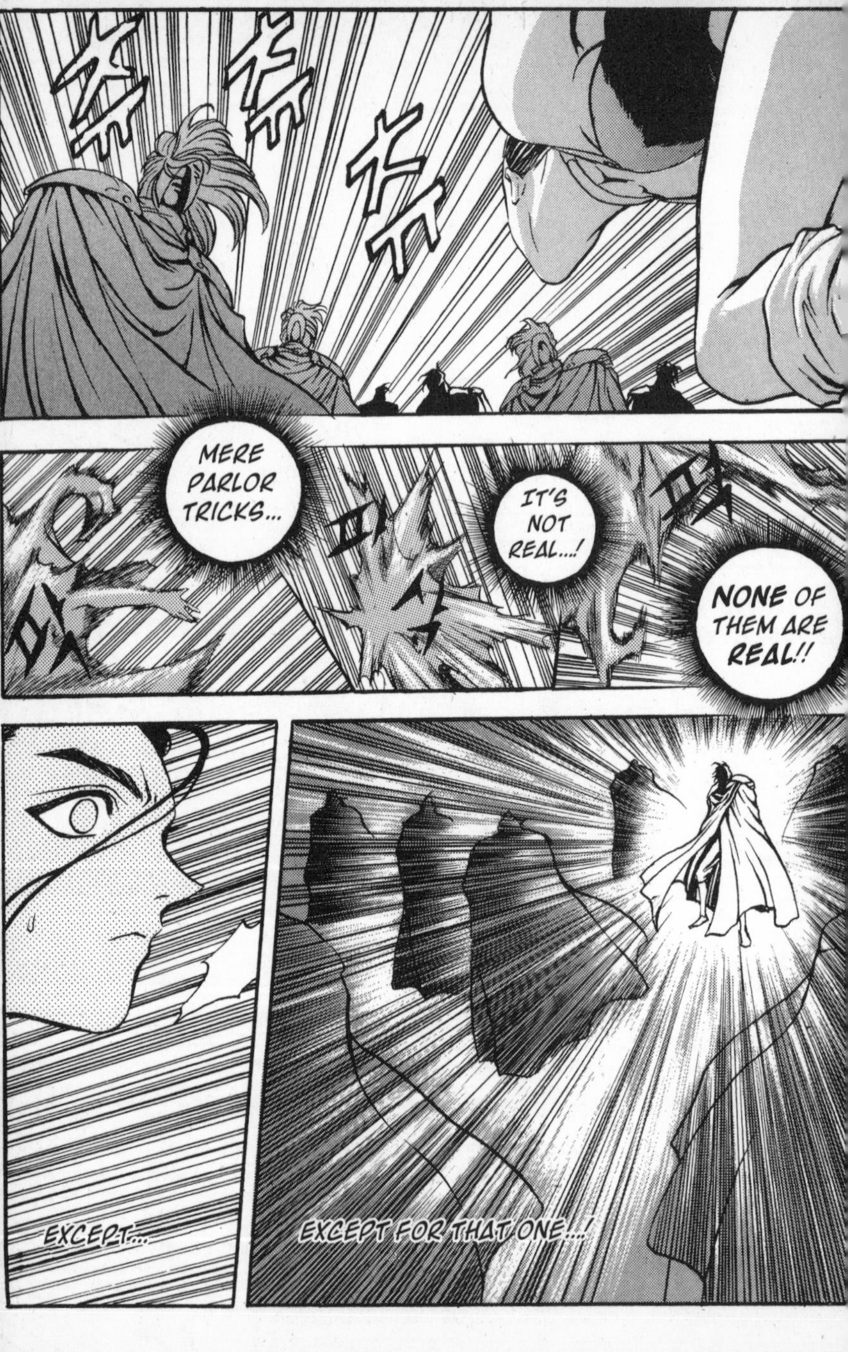
MERE PARLOR TRICKS...
IT'S NOT REAL...!
NONE OF THEM ARE REAL!!
EXCEPT...
EXCEPT FOR THAT ONE...!

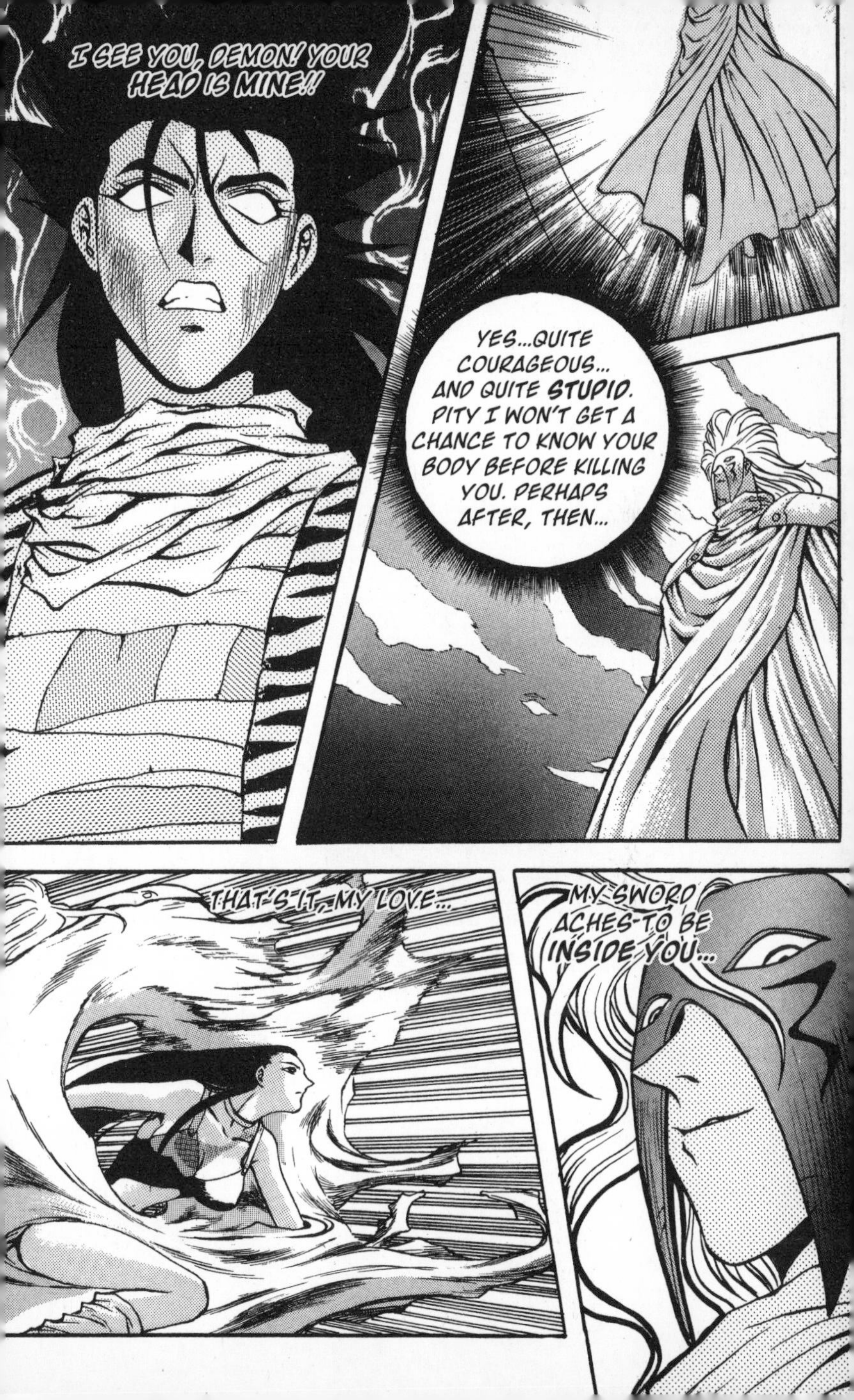
I SEE YOU, DEMON! YOUR HEAD IS MINE!!
YES...QUITE COURAGEOUS... AND QUITE **STUPID**. PITY I WON'T GET A CHANCE TO KNOW YOUR BODY BEFORE KILLING YOU. PERHAPS AFTER, THEN...
THAT'S IT, MY LOVE...
MY SWORD ACHES TO BE INSIDE YOU...

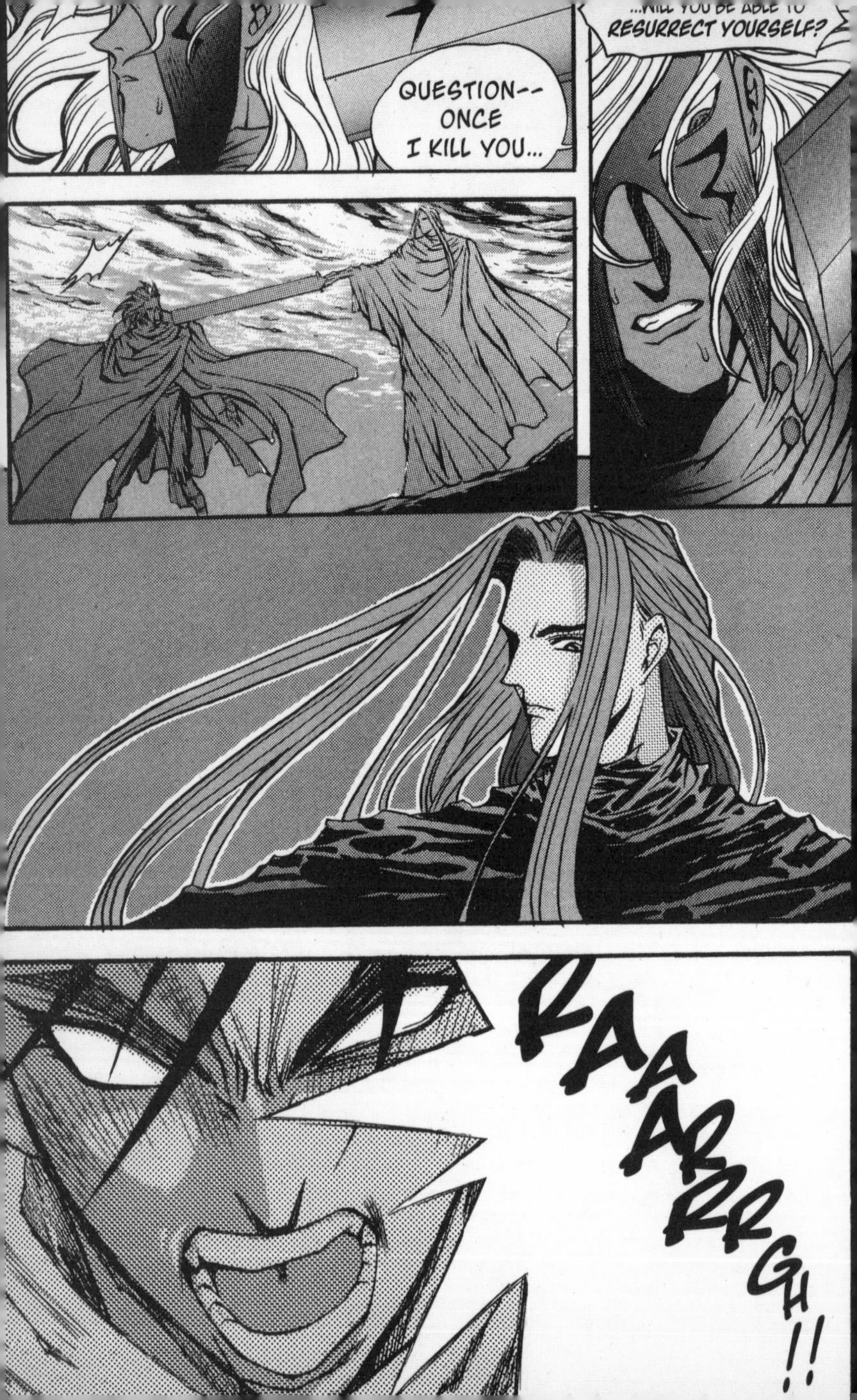
QUESTION-- ONCE I KILL YOU...
...WILL YOU BE ABLE TO RESURRECT YOURSELF?
RAAARRRGH!!

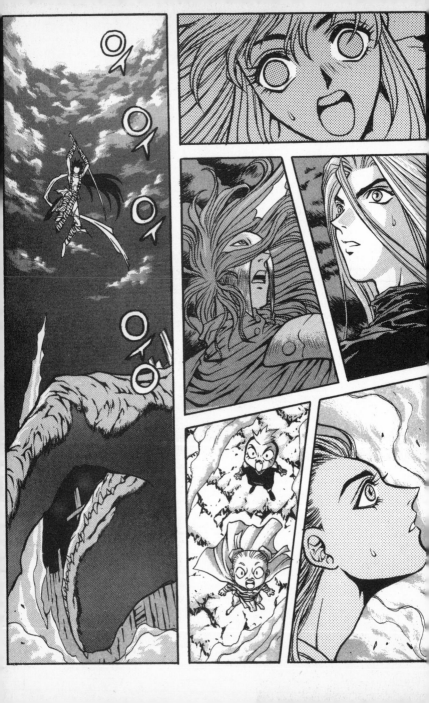

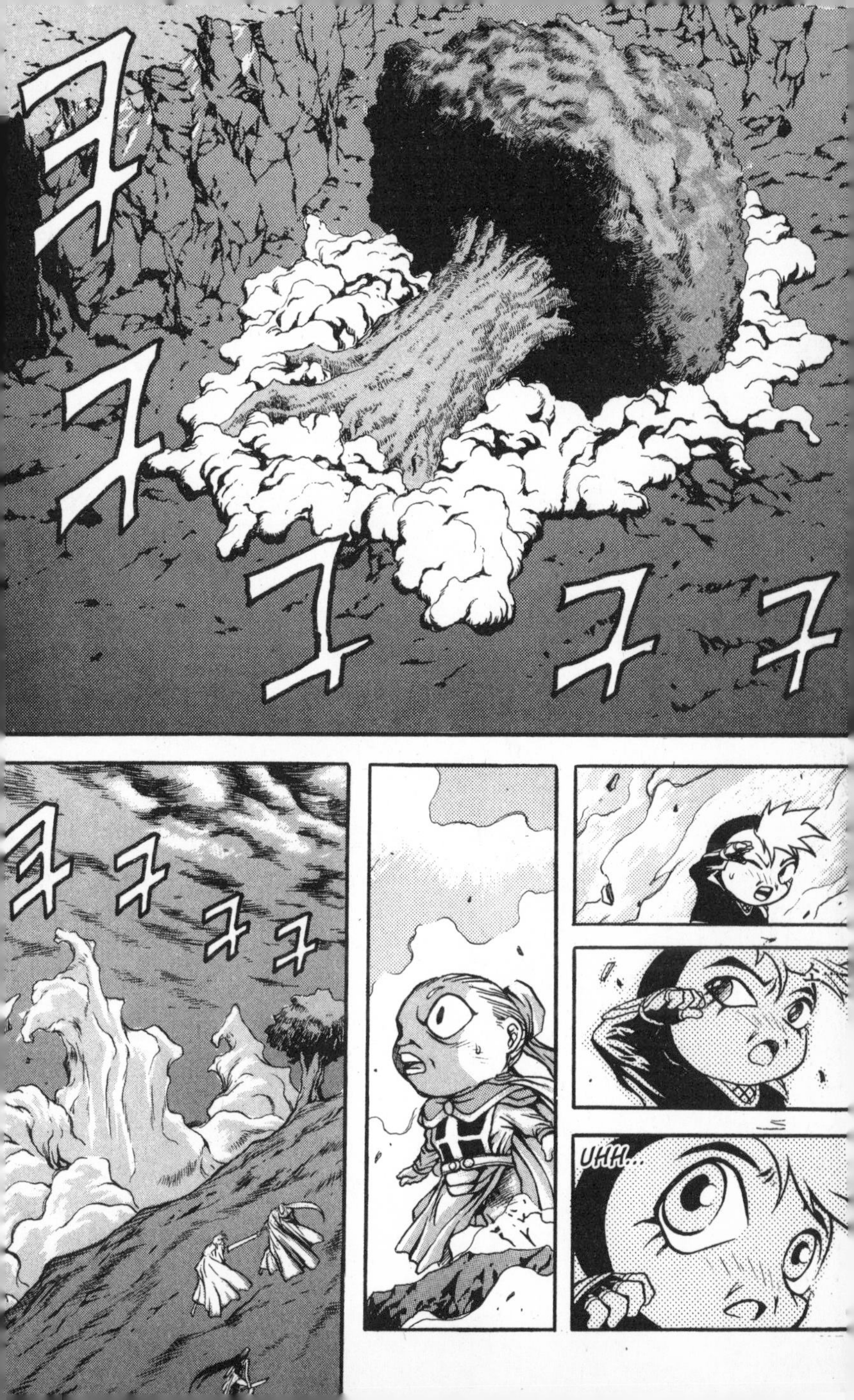
UHH...

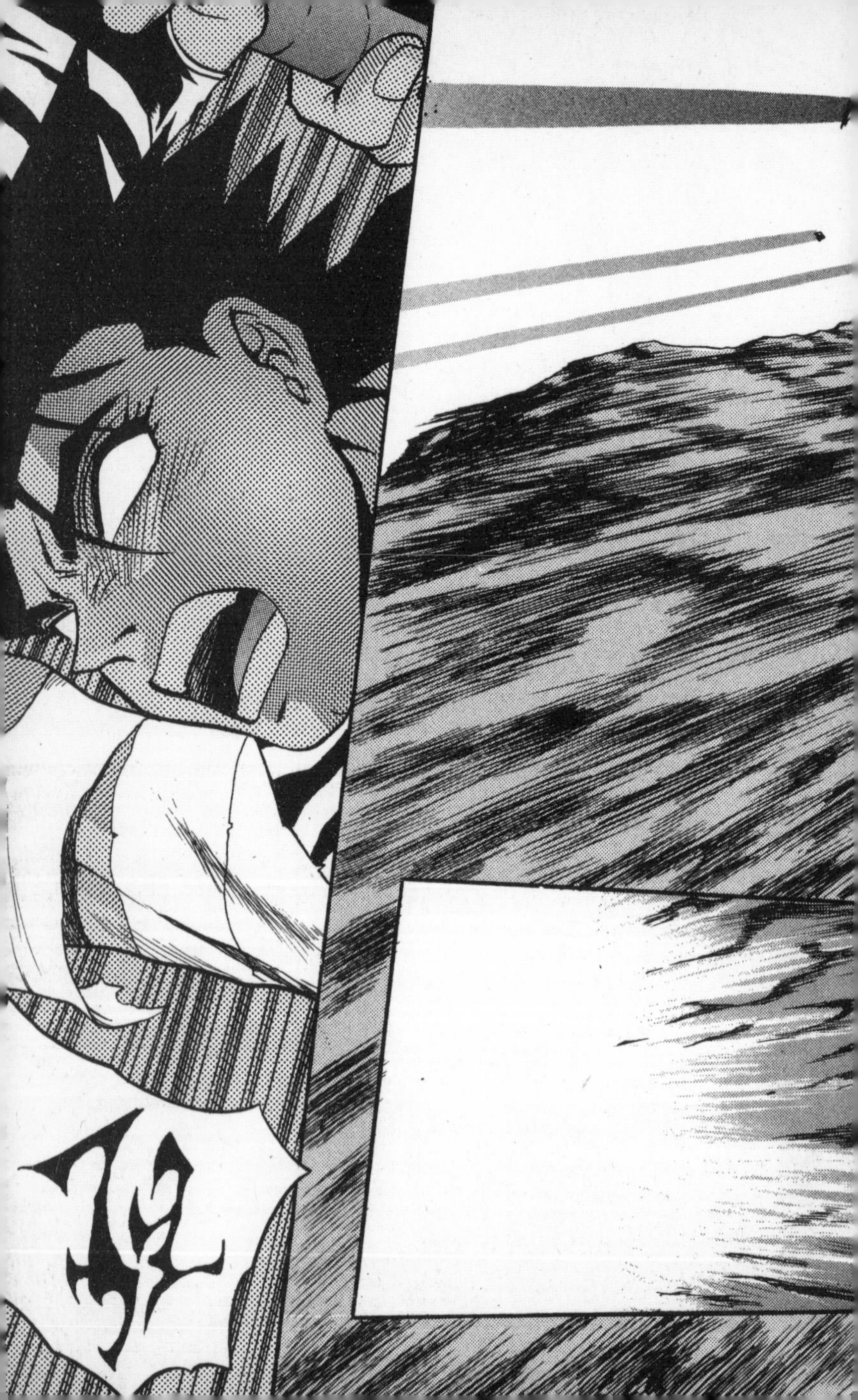

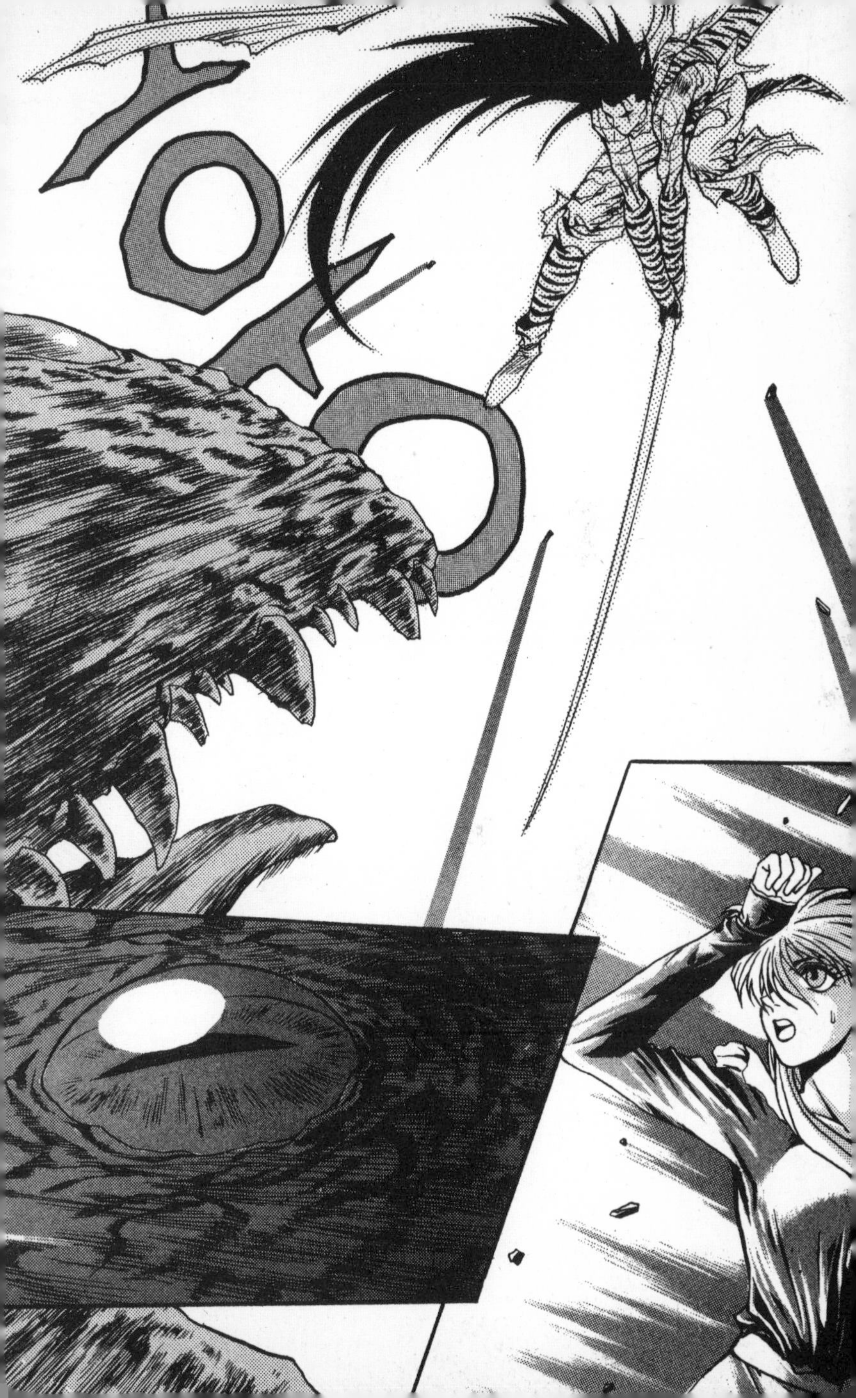

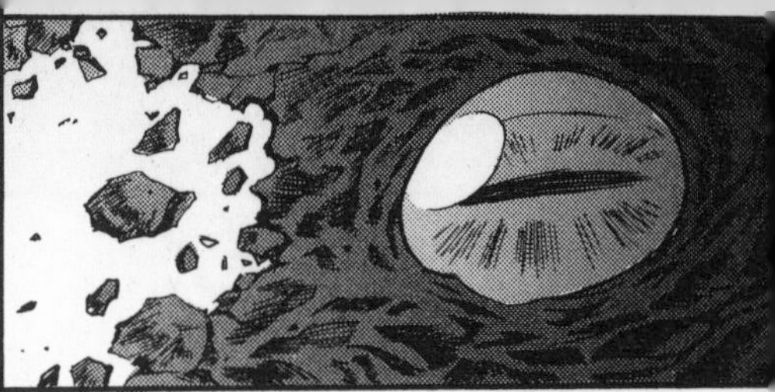
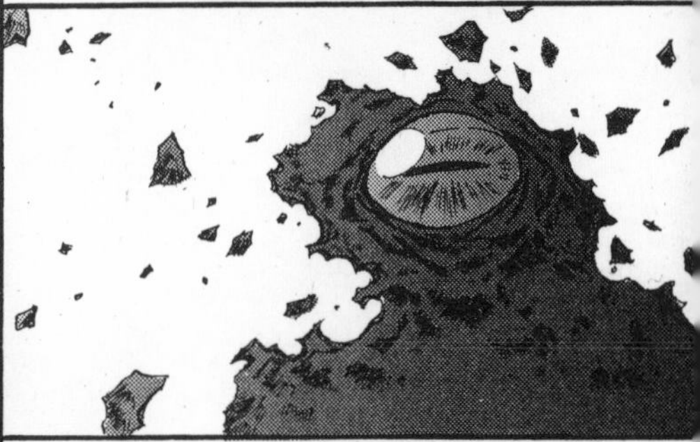
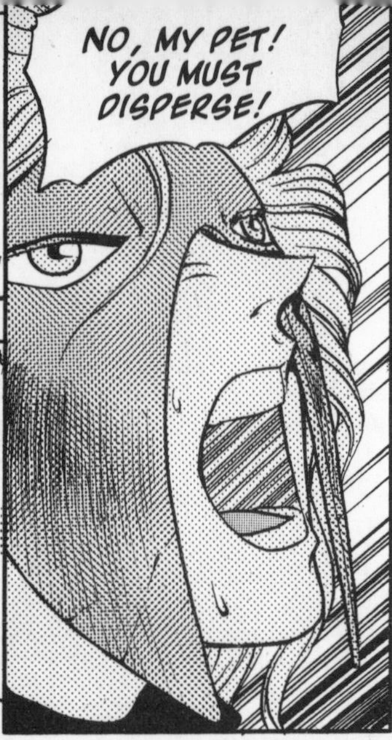
NO, MY PET! YOU MUST DISPERSE!
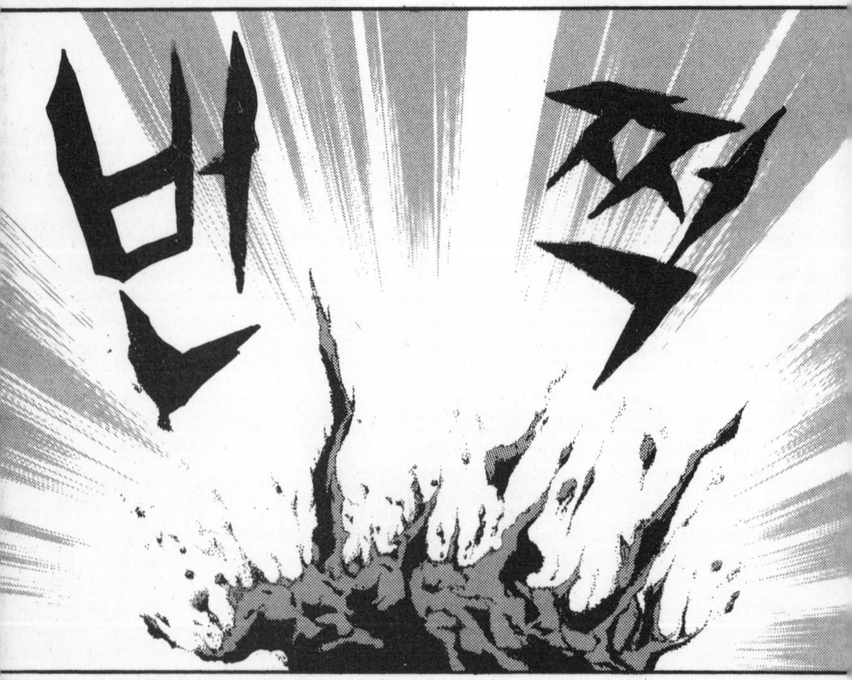

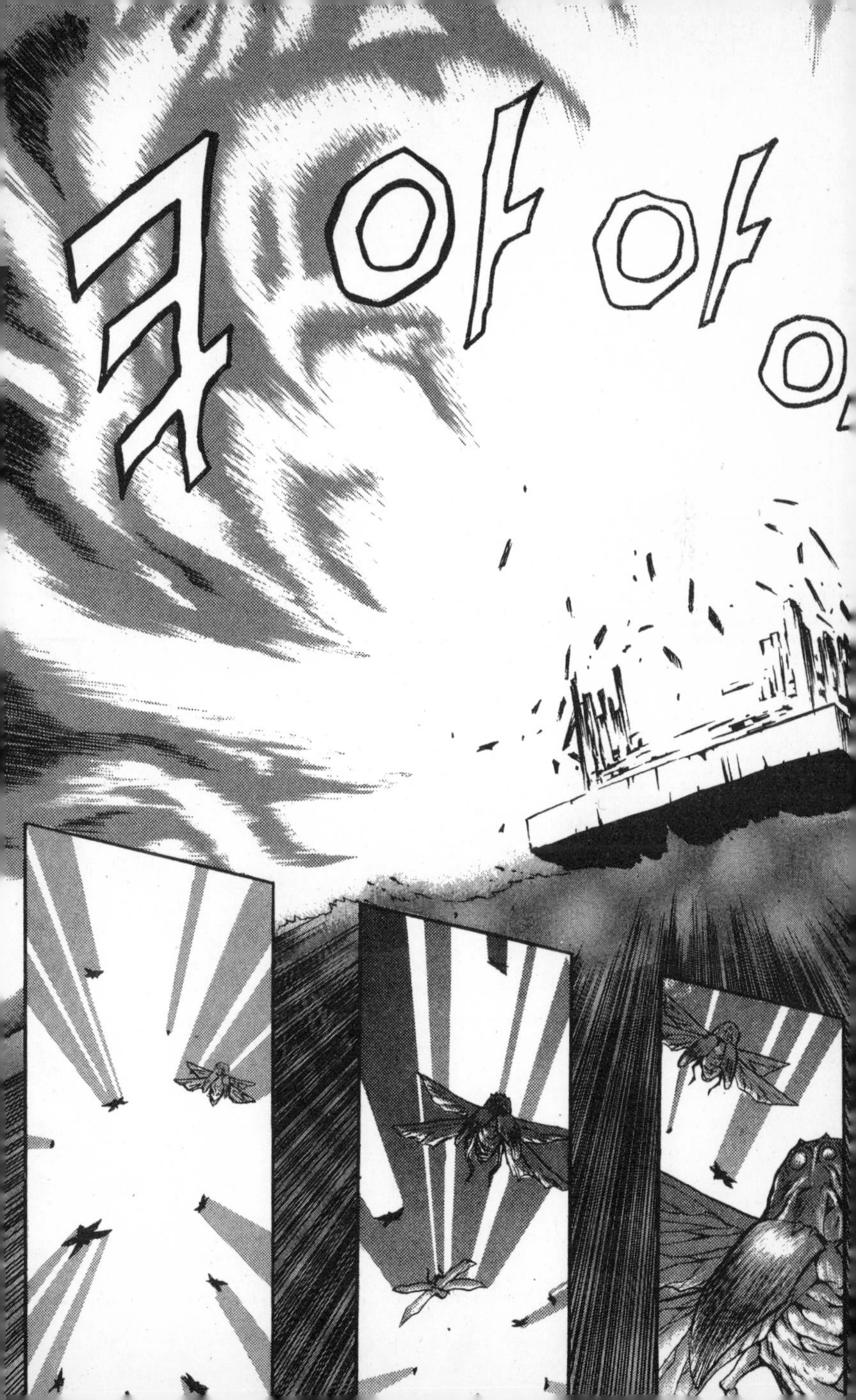
카아아아

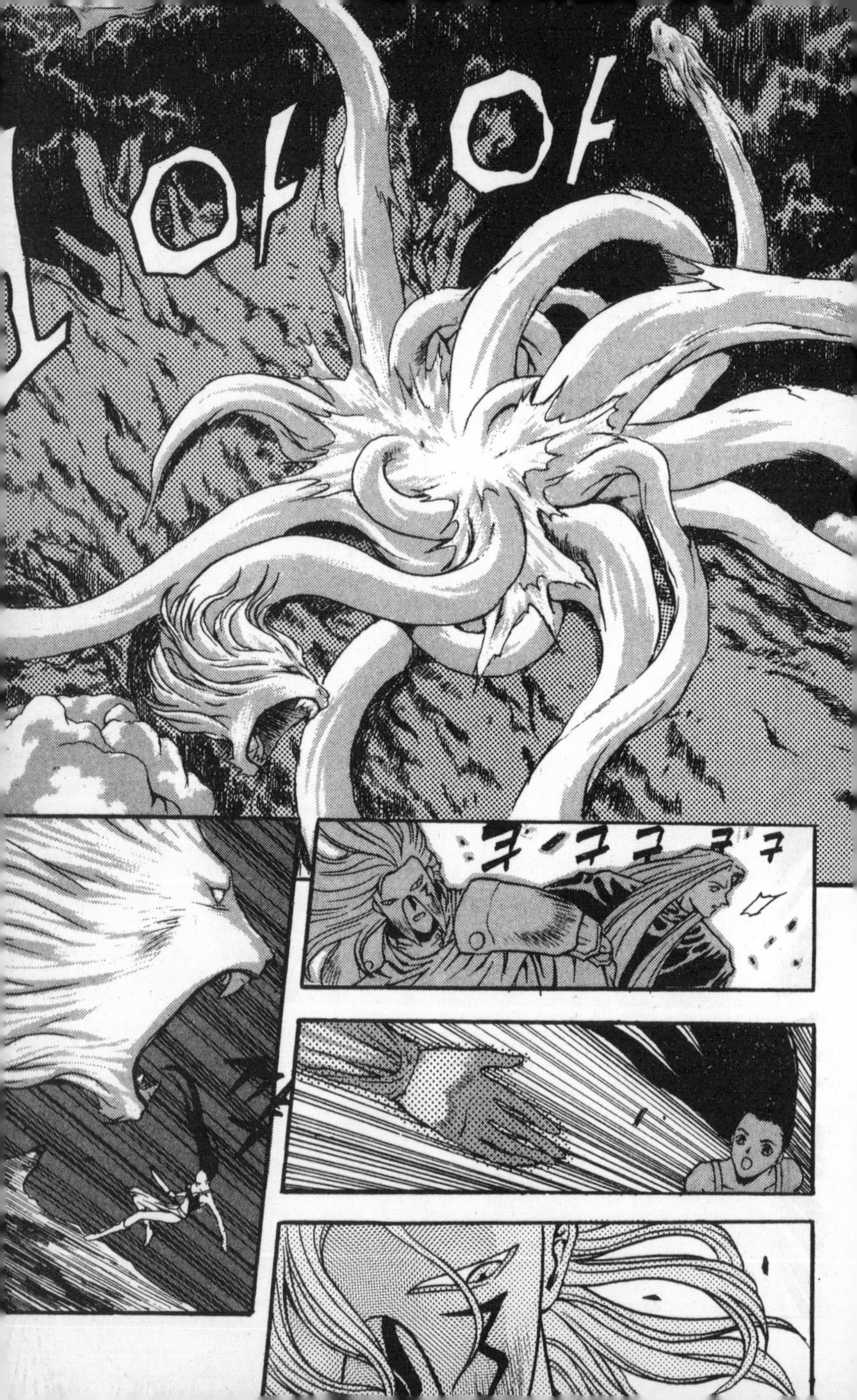

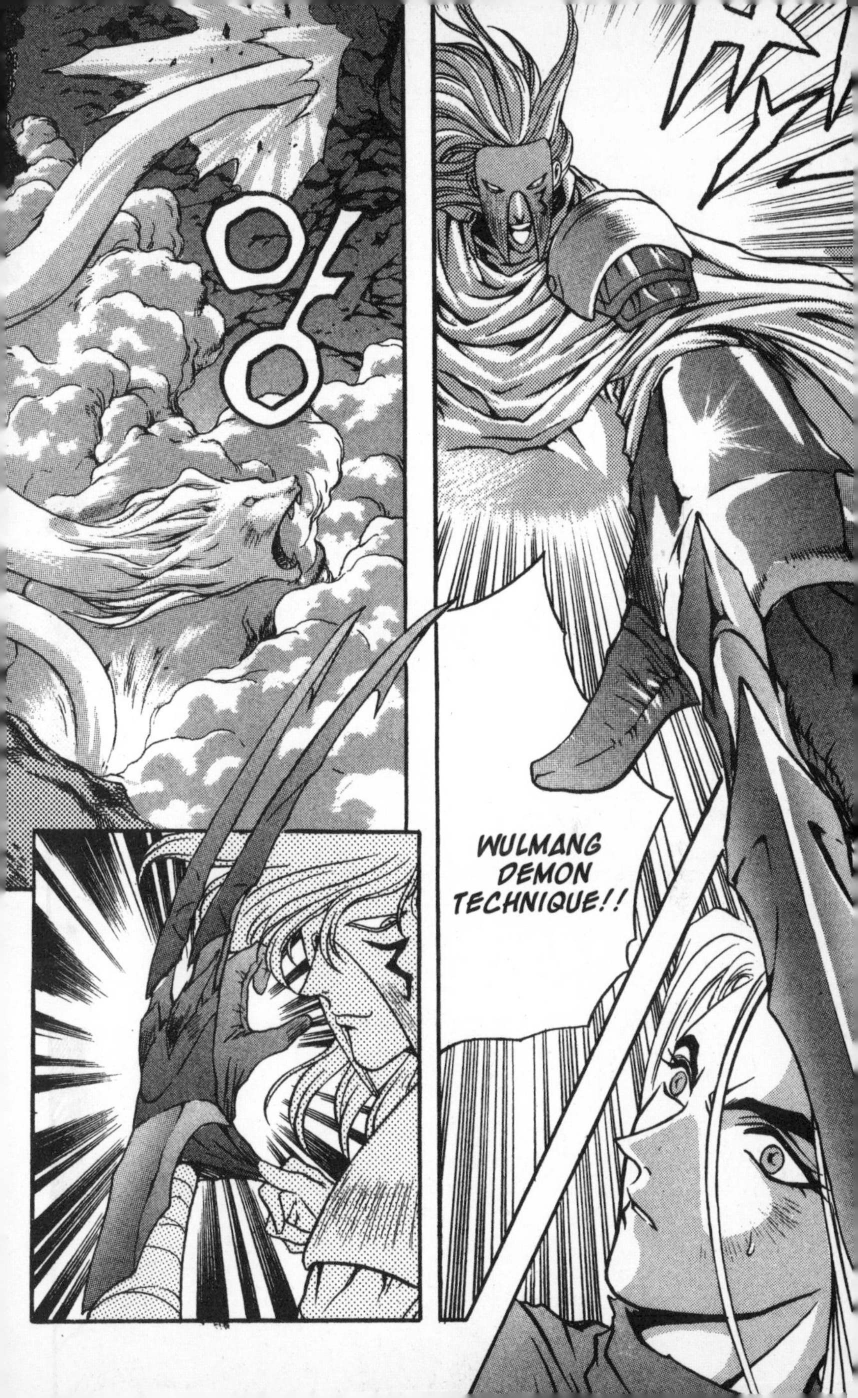
WULMANG DEMON TECHNIQUE!!

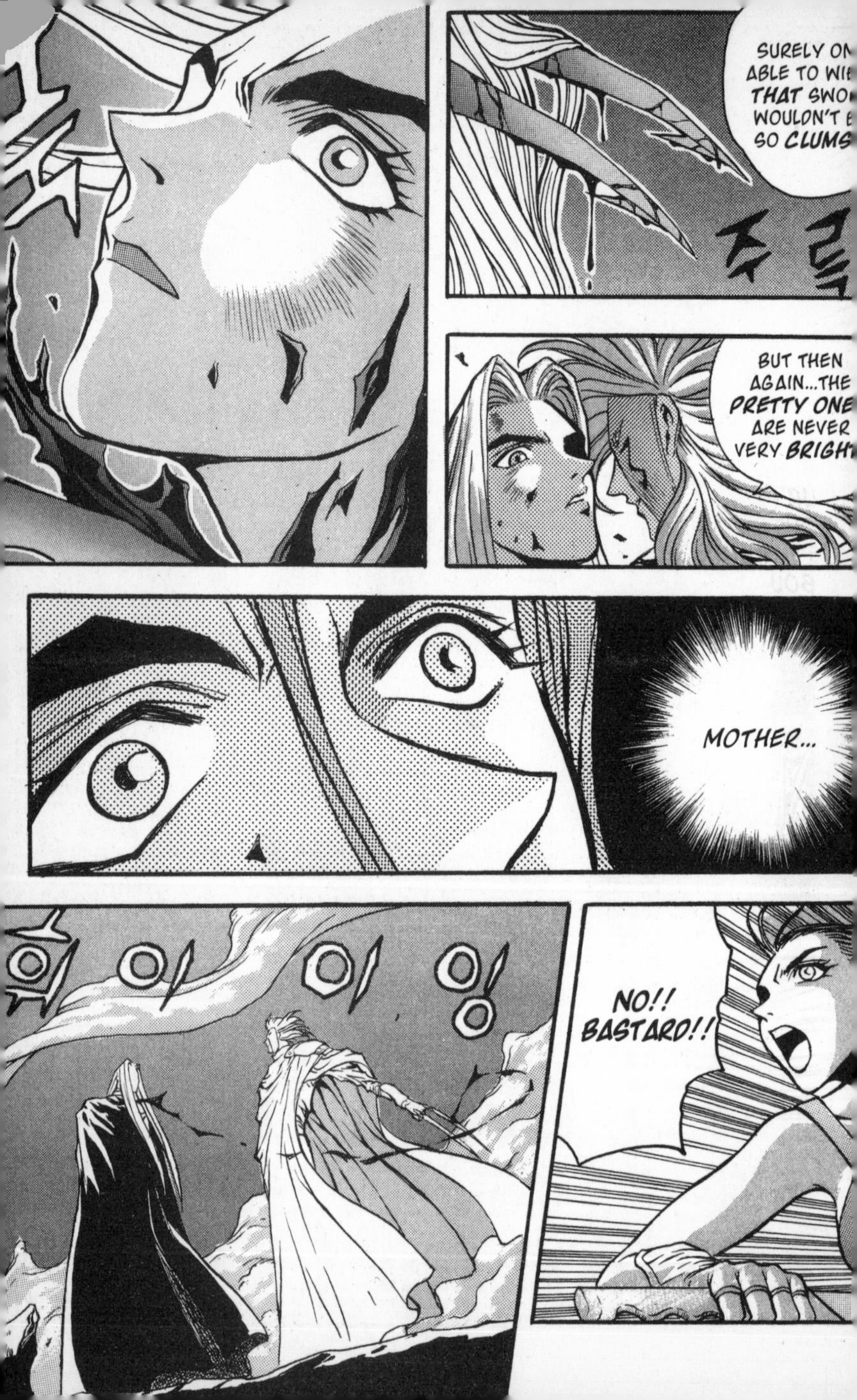
SURELY ON
ABLE TO WIE
THAT SWO
WOULDN'T B
SO CLUMS
BUT THEN
AGAIN...THE
PRETTY ONE
ARE NEVER
VERY BRIGH
MOTHER...
NO!!
BASTARD!!

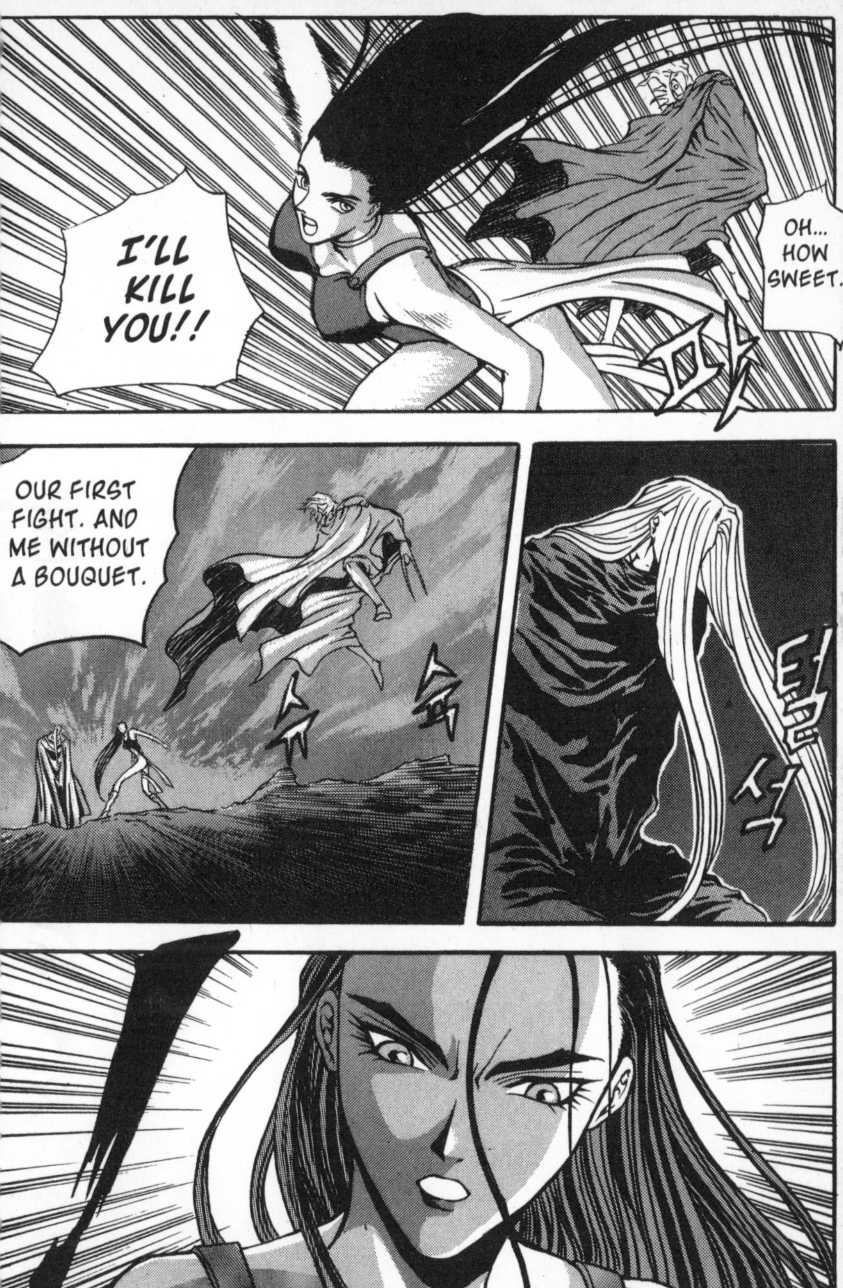
I'LL KILL YOU!!
OH... HOW SWEET.
OUR FIRST FIGHT. AND ME WITHOUT A BOUQUET.

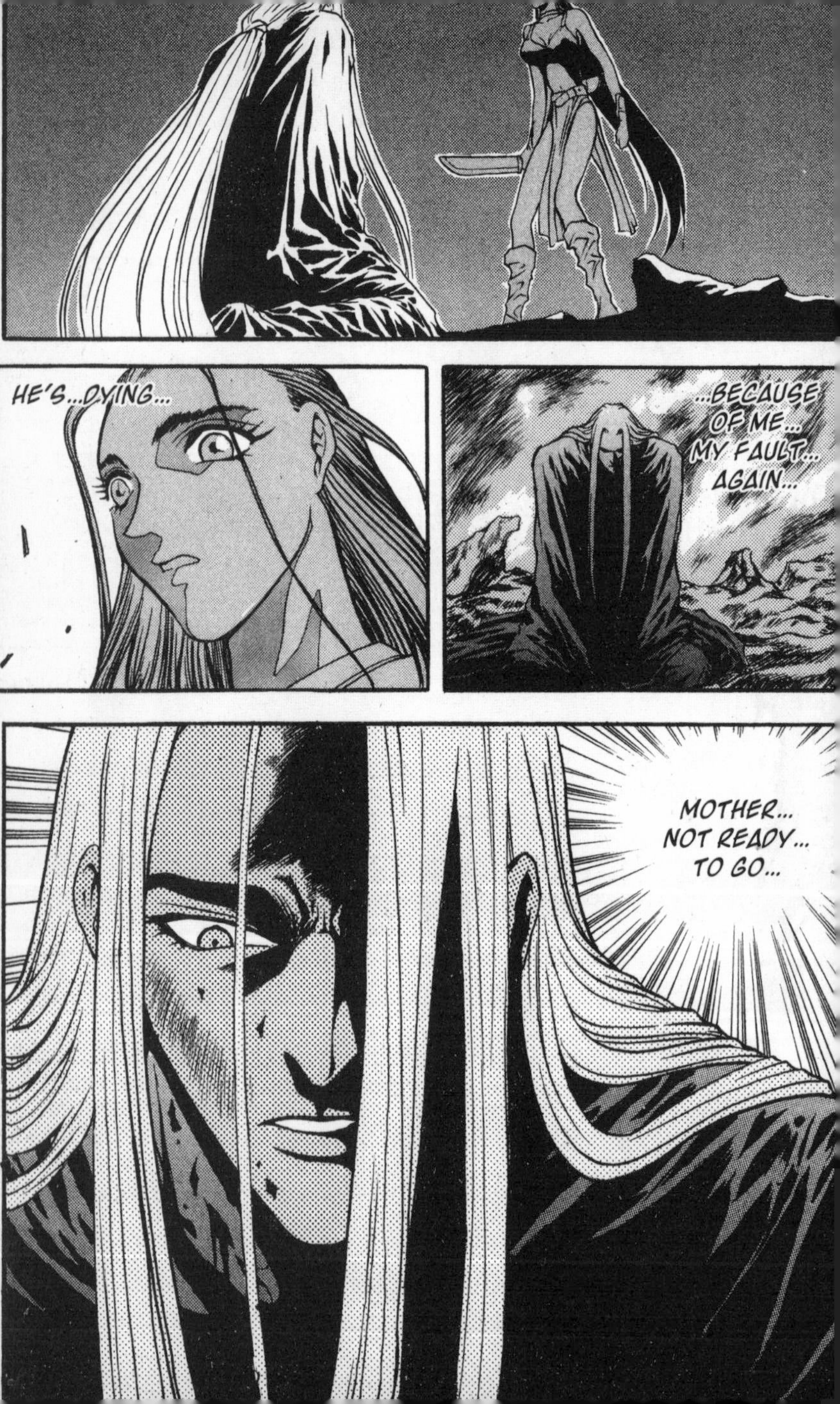
HE'S...DYING...
...BECAUSE OF ME... MY FAULT... AGAIN...
MOTHER... NOT READY... TO GO...

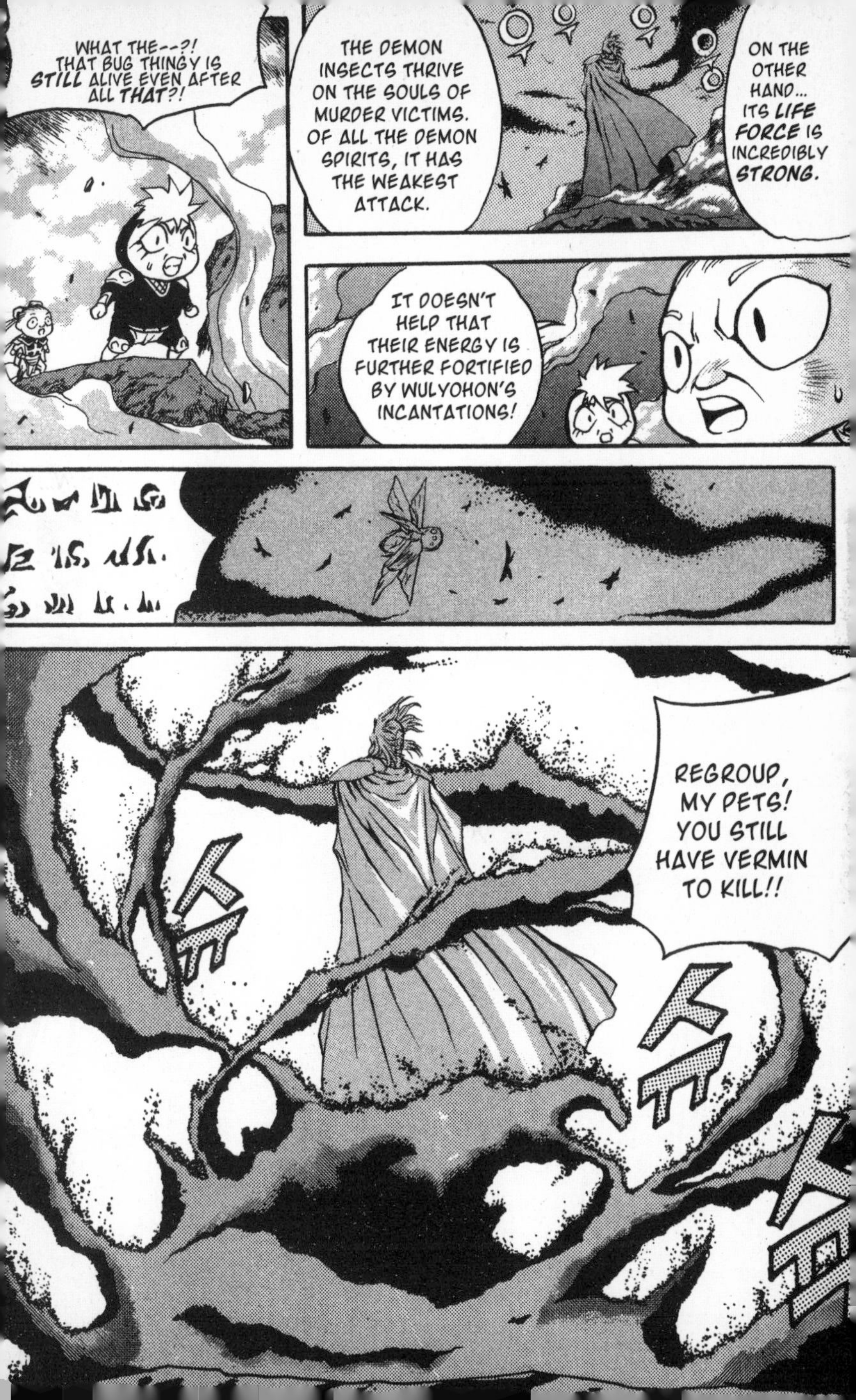

WHAT THE--?! THAT BUG THINGY IS STILL ALIVE EVEN AFTER ALL THAT?!
THE DEMON INSECTS THRIVE ON THE SOULS OF MURDER VICTIMS. OF ALL THE DEMON SPIRITS, IT HAS THE WEAKEST ATTACK.
ON THE OTHER HAND... ITS LIFE FORCE IS INCREDIBLY STRONG.
IT DOESN'T HELP THAT THEIR ENERGY IS FURTHER FORTIFIED BY WULYOHON'S INCANTATIONS!
REGROUP, MY PETS! YOU STILL HAVE VERMIN TO KILL!!

AS LONG AS I DRAW *BREATH*-- YOU SHALL **NOT** SUCCEED!!

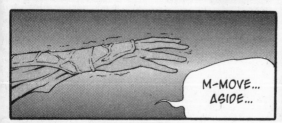

M-MOVE... ASIDE...

HUH?! NO!! YOU'RE TOO WEAK TO--

J-JUST DO IT!!
I CAN'T...UNH...
I C-CAN'T C-CONTAIN
IT MUCH L-LONGER...!!

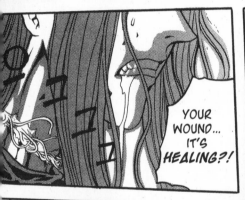

YOUR
WOUND...
IT'S
HEALING?!

HIS...HIS EYES...!

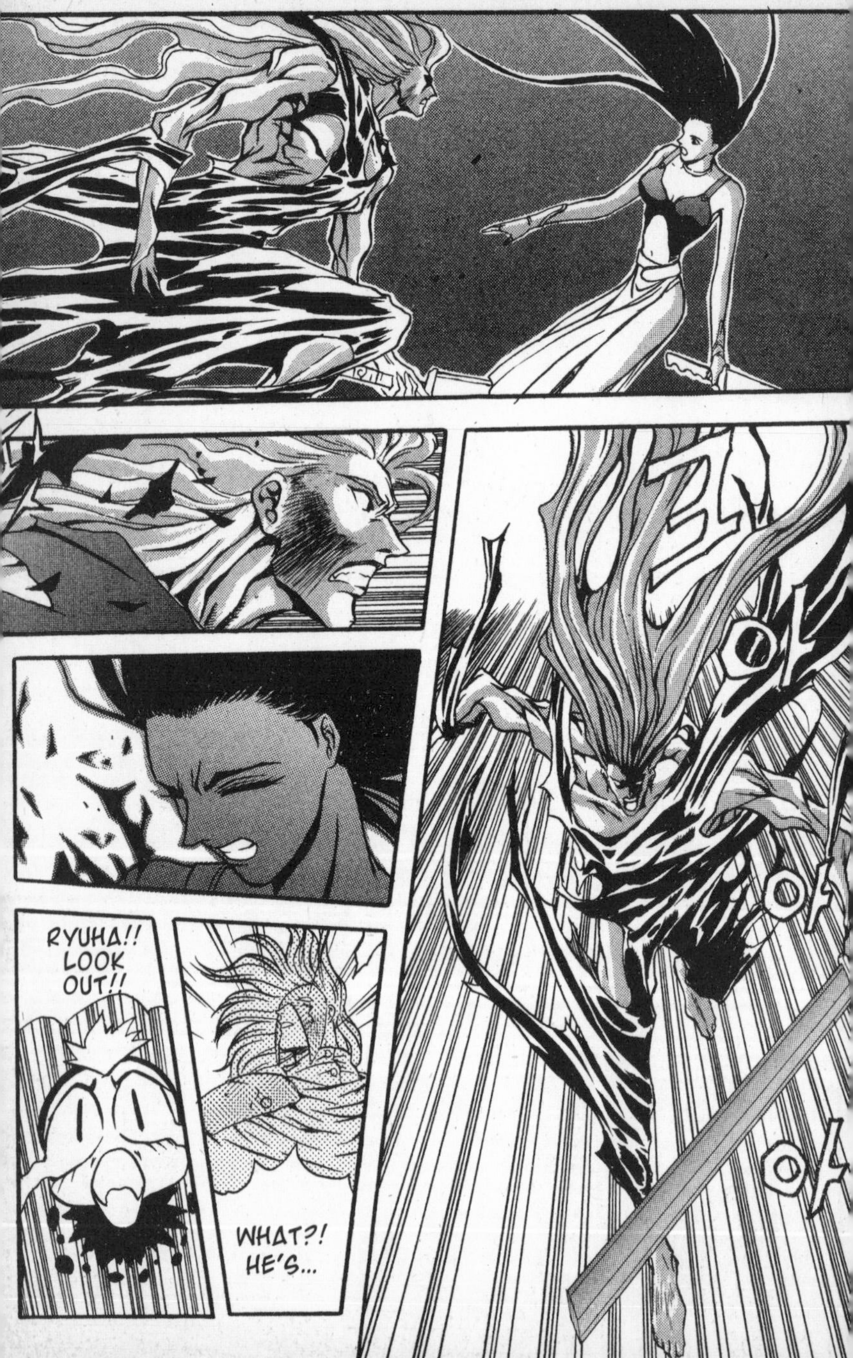
WHAT?! HE'S...
RYUHA!! LOOK OUT!!

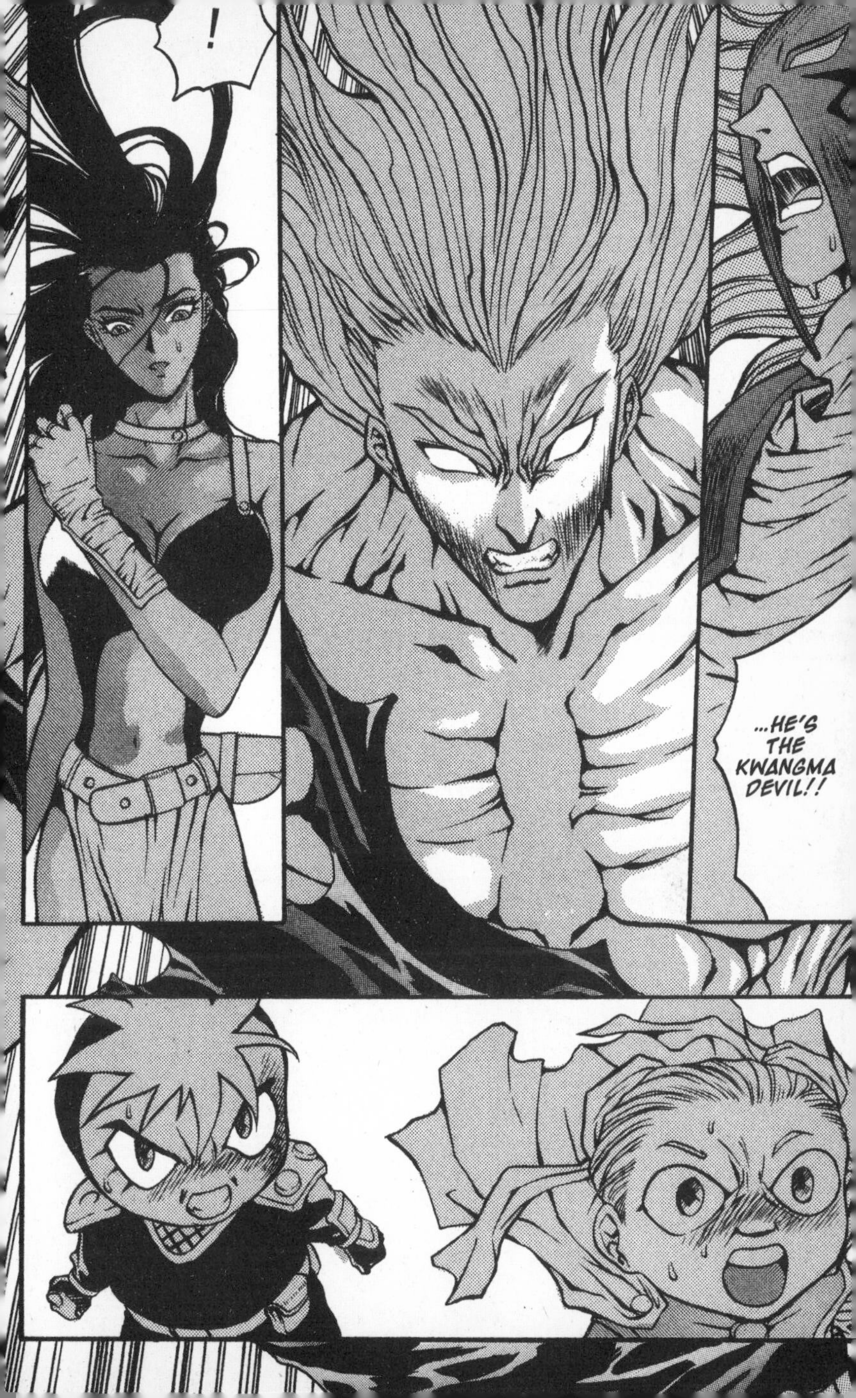
...HE'S THE KWANGMA DEVIL!!
!

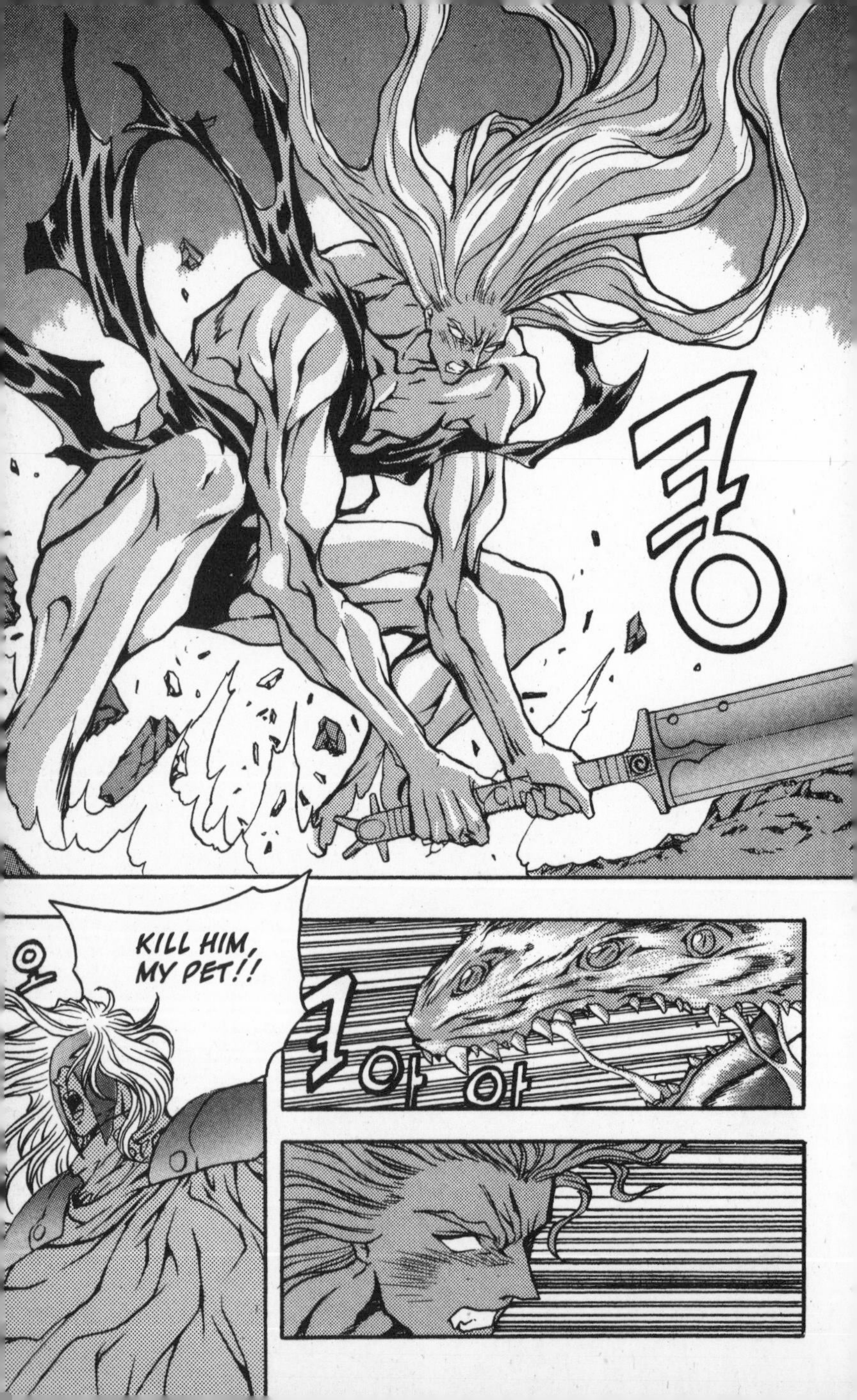
KILL HIM, MY PET!!

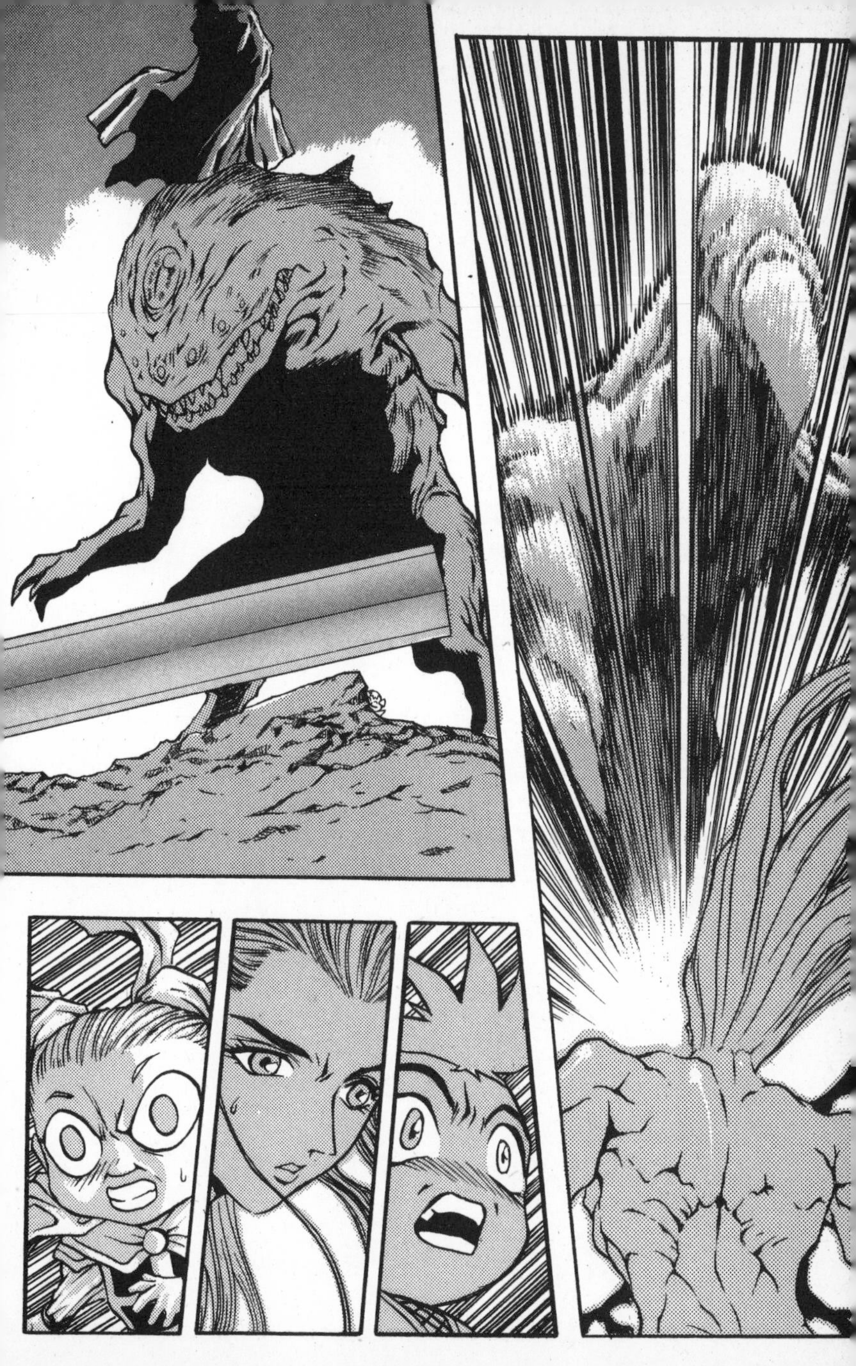

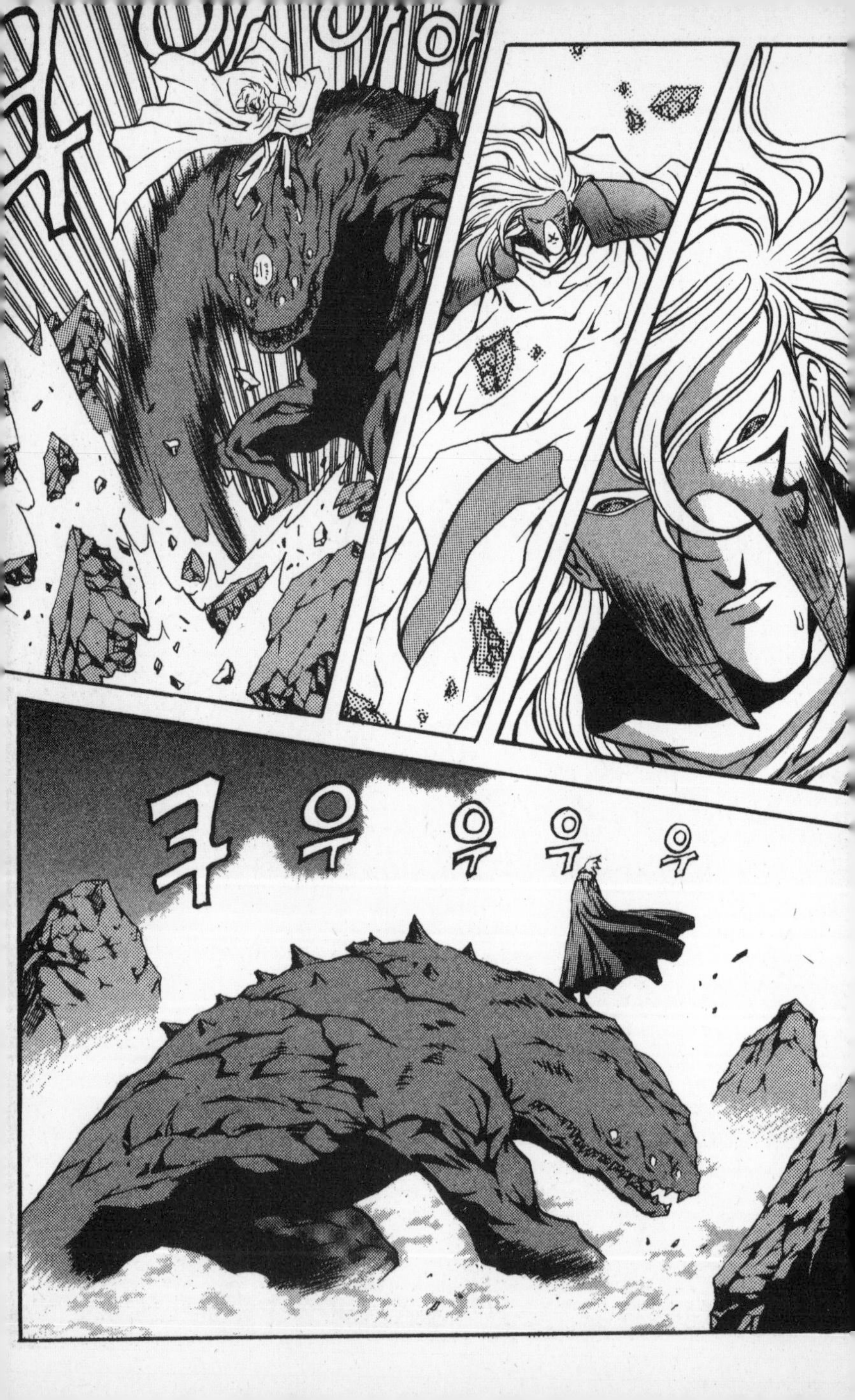
콰아아아!
쿠우우우우

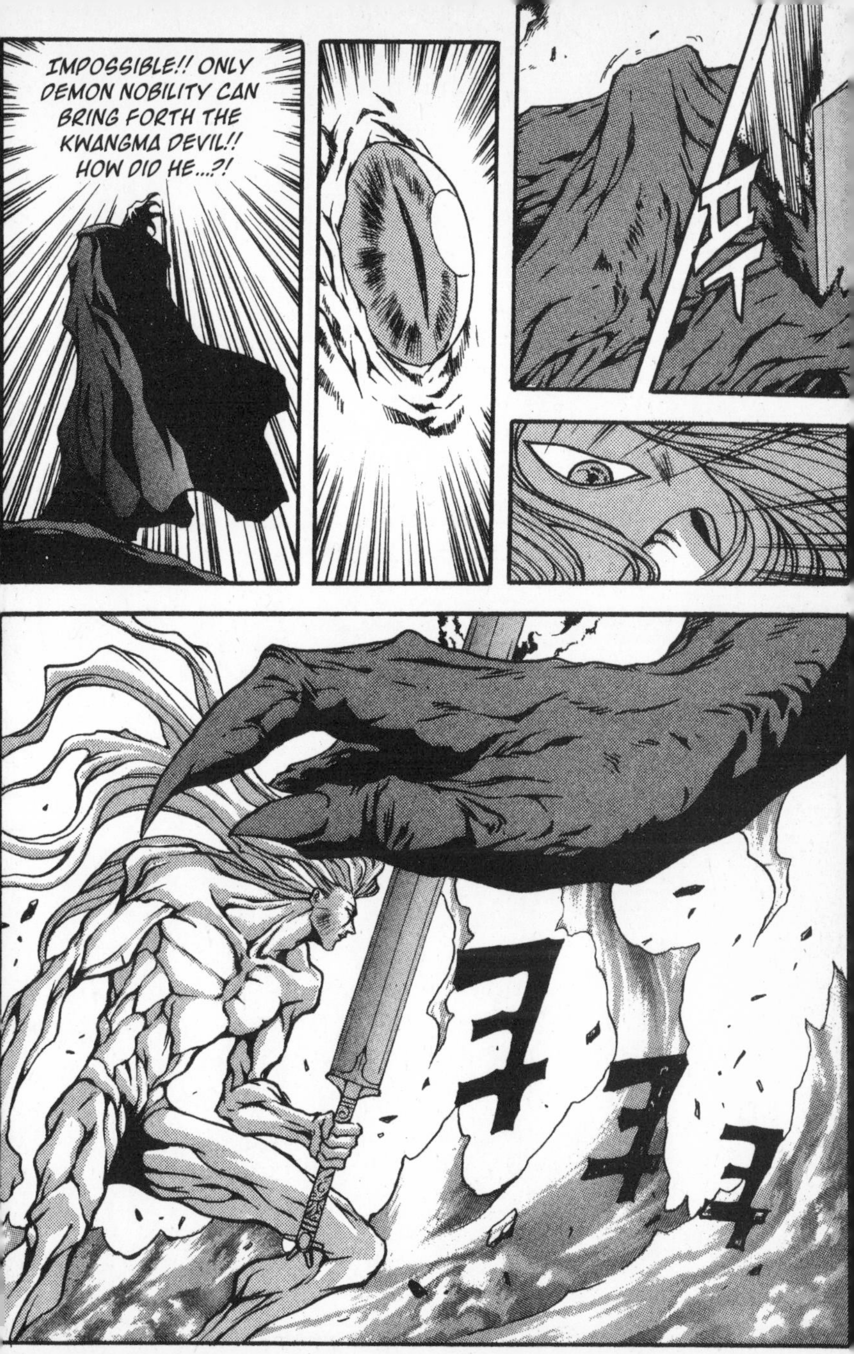
IMPOSSIBLE!! ONLY DEMON NOBILITY CAN BRING FORTH THE KWANGMA DEVIL!! HOW DID HE...?!

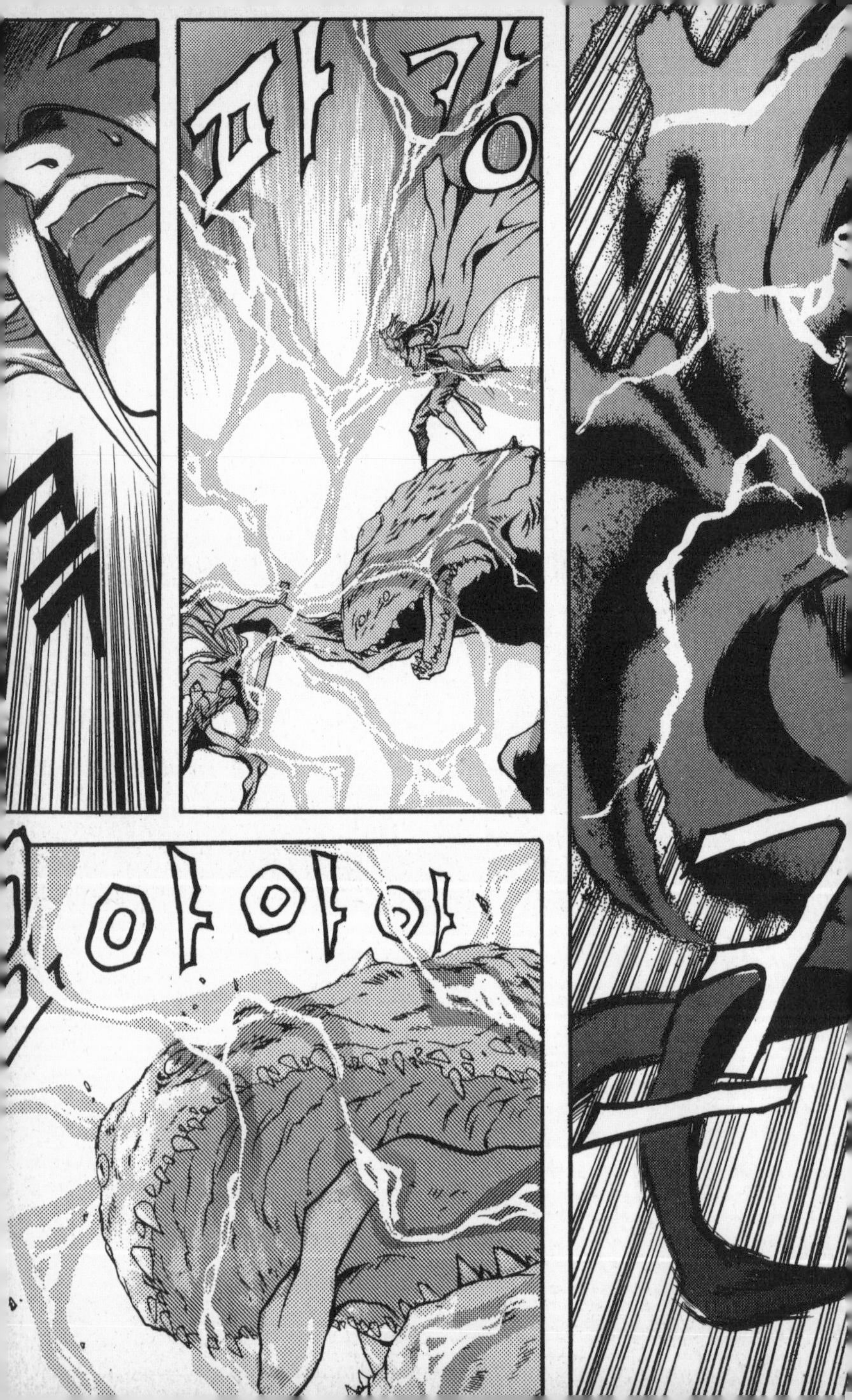

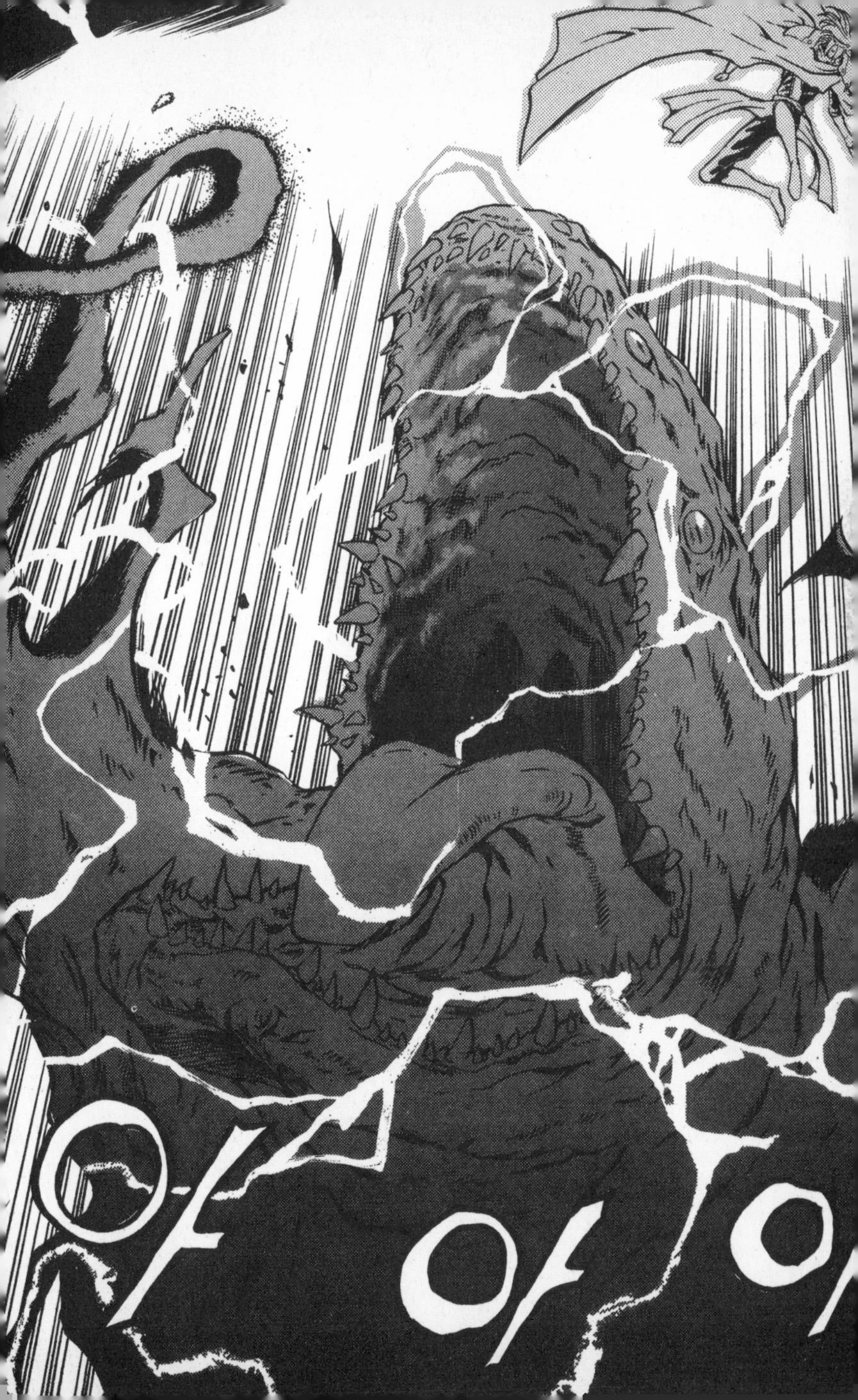

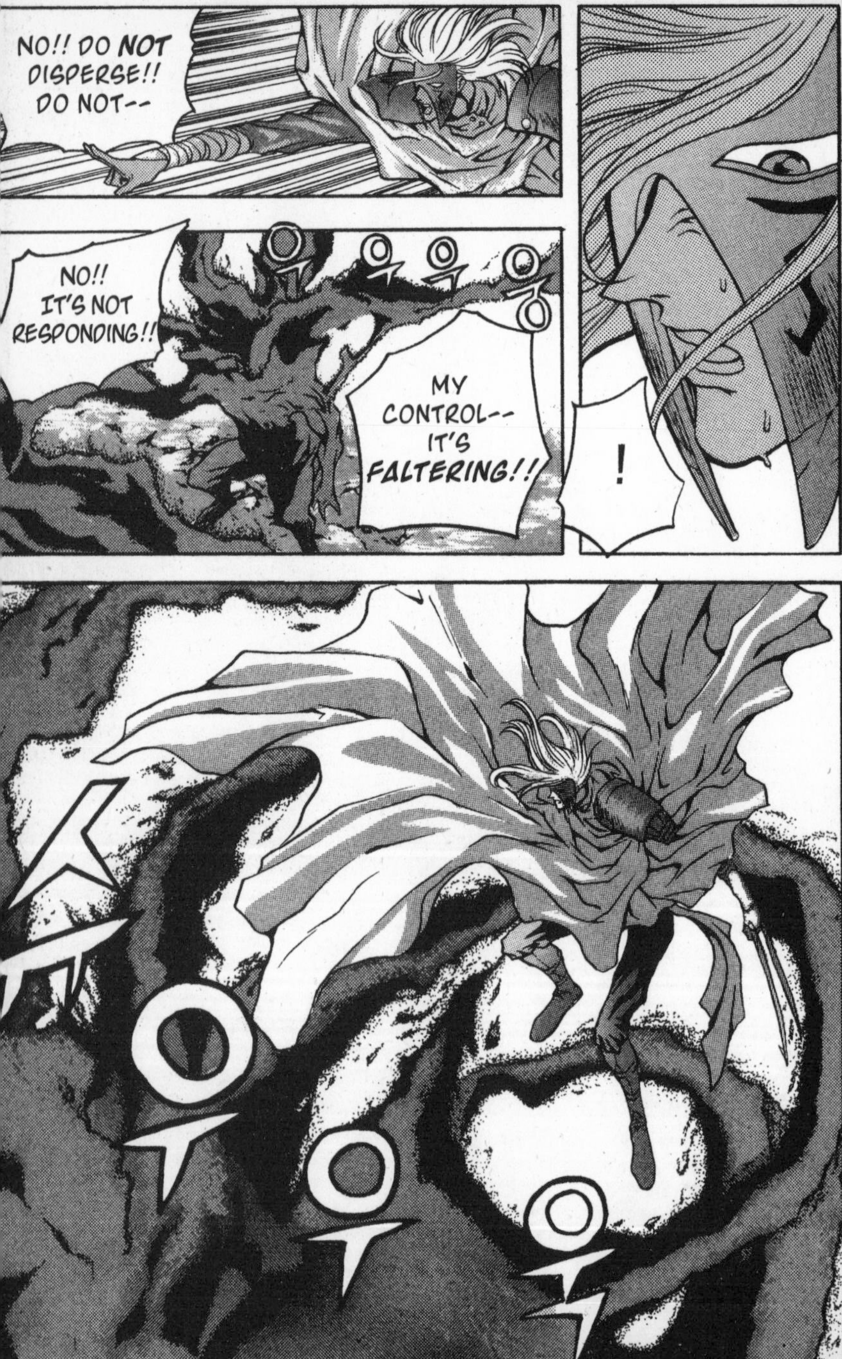
NO!! DO **NOT** DISPERSE!! DO NOT--
NO!! IT'S NOT RESPONDING!!
MY CONTROL-- IT'S **FALTERING!!**
!

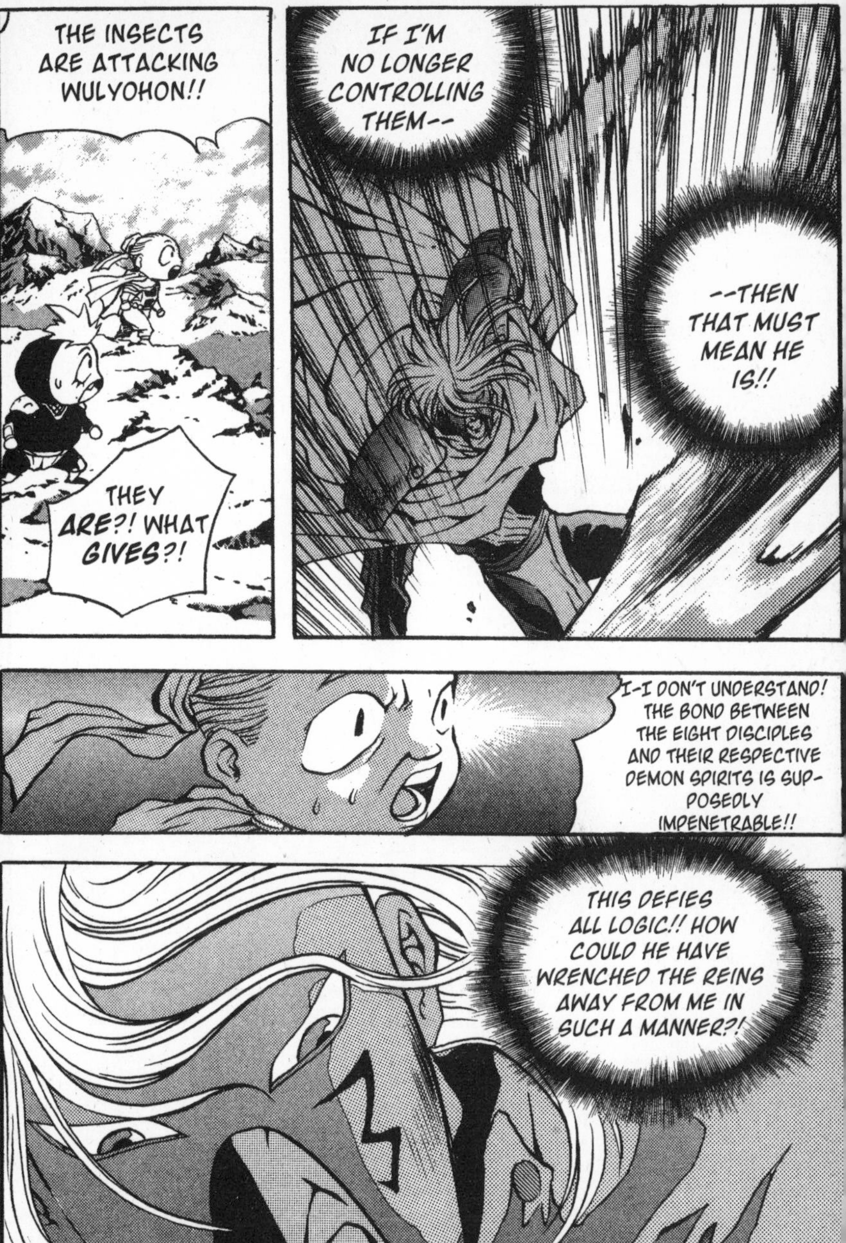
THE INSECTS ARE ATTACKING WULYOHON!!
THEY ARE?! WHAT GIVES?!
IF I'M NO LONGER CONTROLLING THEM--
--THEN THAT MUST MEAN HE IS!!
I-I DON'T UNDERSTAND! THE BOND BETWEEN THE EIGHT DISCIPLES AND THEIR RESPECTIVE DEMON SPIRITS IS SUPPOSEDLY IMPENETRABLE!!
THIS DEFIES ALL LOGIC!! HOW COULD HE HAVE WRENCHED THE REINS AWAY FROM ME IN SUCH A MANNER?!

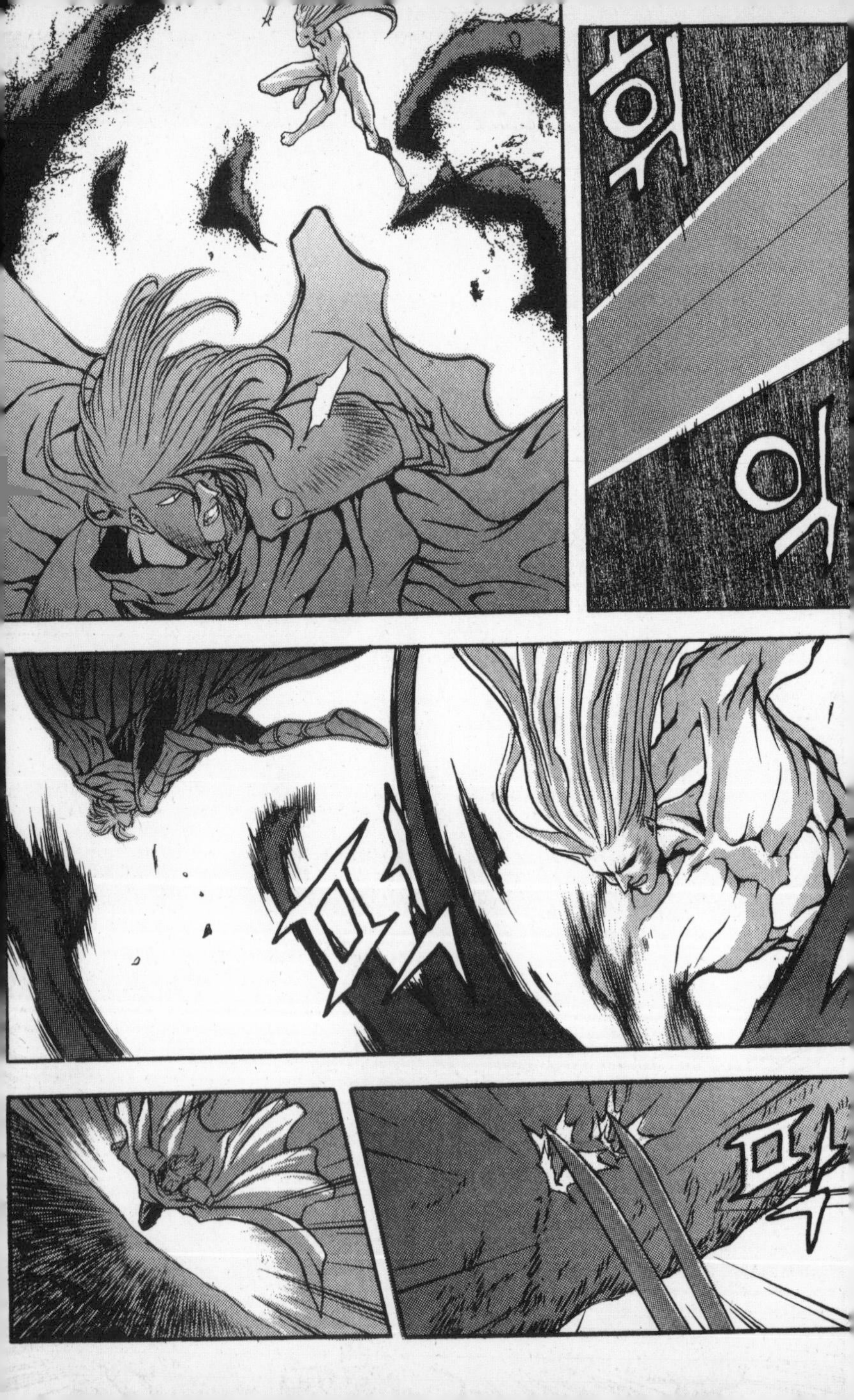

하
아
파
파

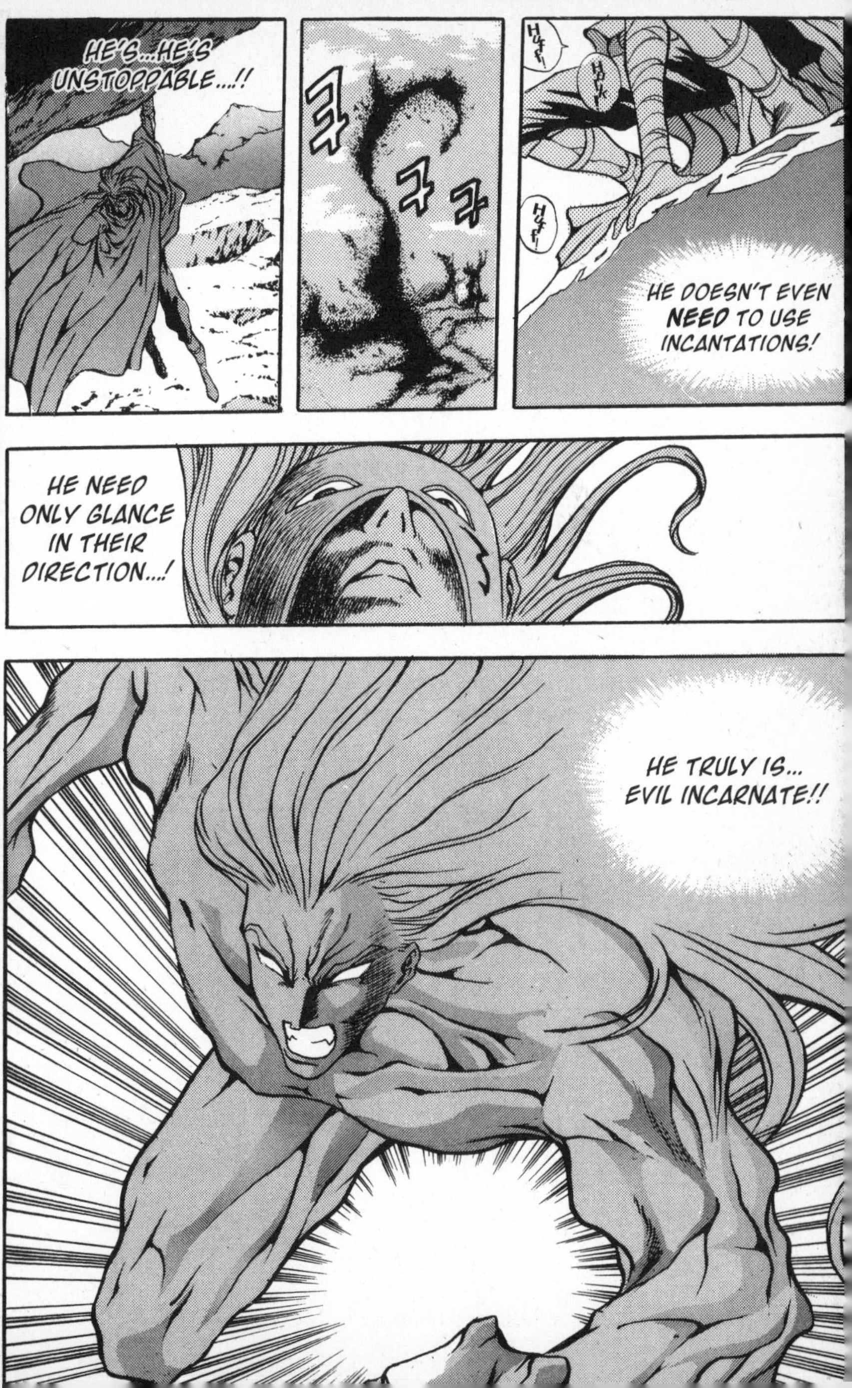
Huff!
Hack!
Huff!
HE DOESN'T EVEN NEED TO USE INCANTATIONS!
HE'S...HE'S UNSTOPPABLE...!!
HE NEED ONLY GLANCE IN THEIR DIRECTION...!
HE TRULY IS... EVIL INCARNATE!!

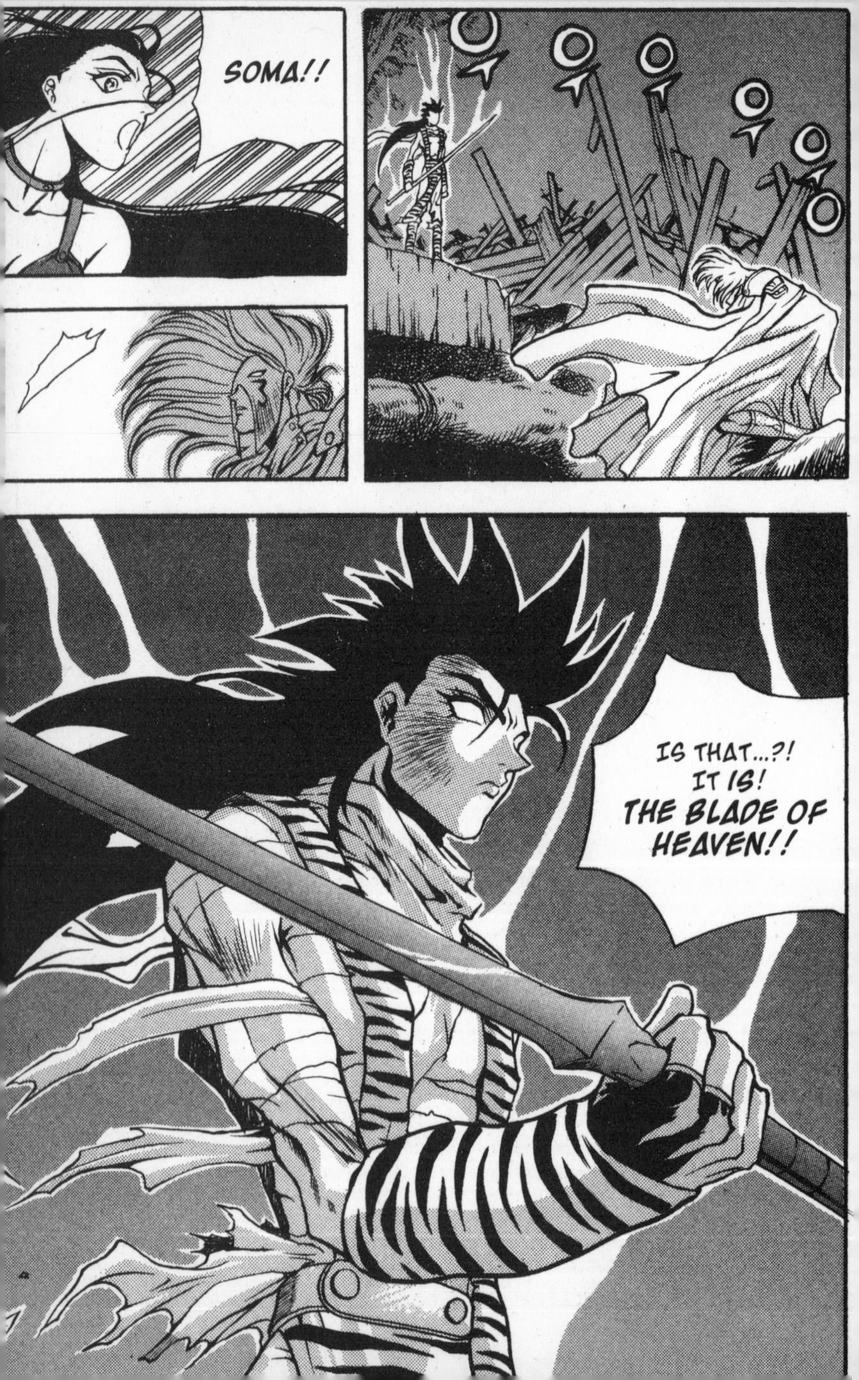
SOMA!!
IS THAT...?! IT IS! THE BLADE OF HEAVEN!!

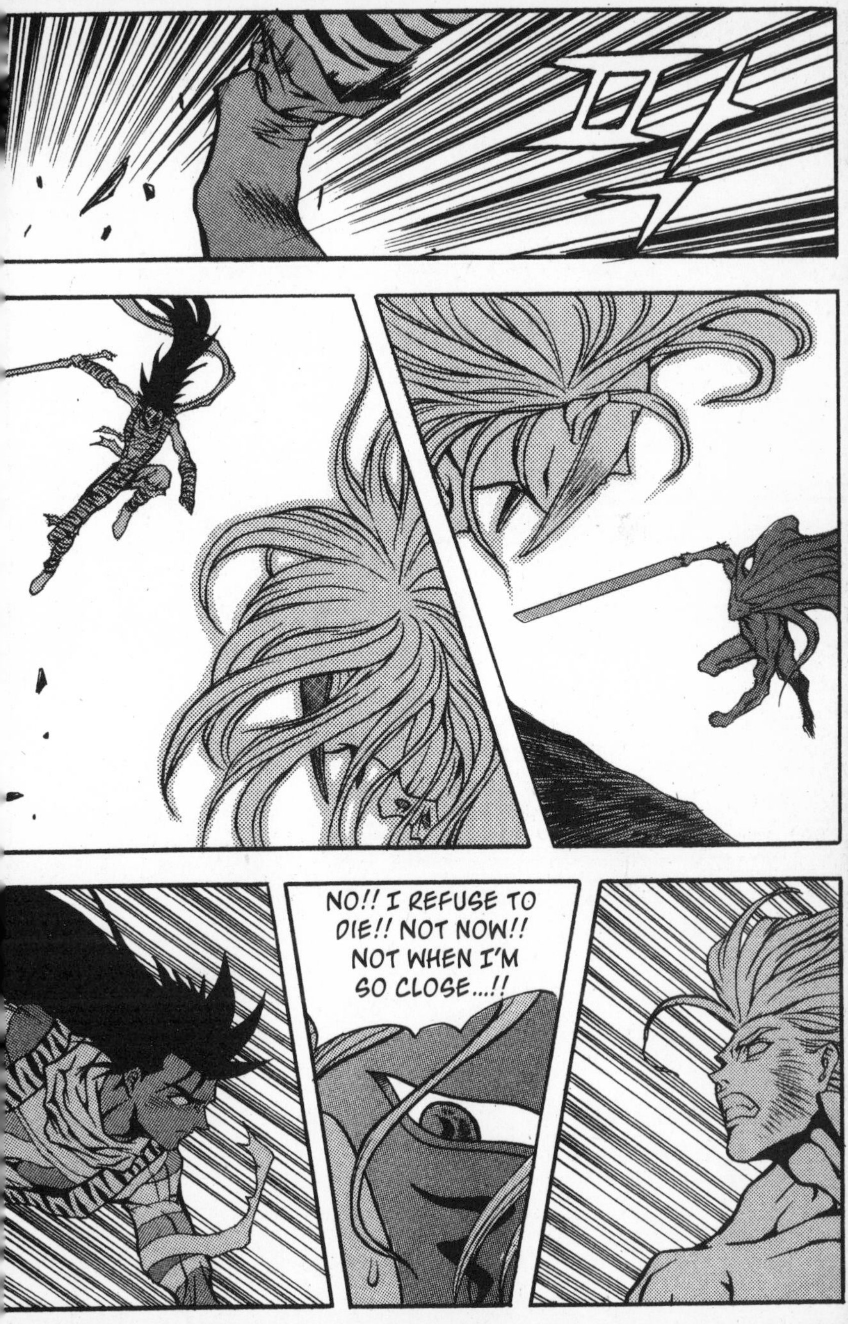
팍
NO!! I REFUSE TO DIE!! NOT NOW!! NOT WHEN I'M SO CLOSE...!!

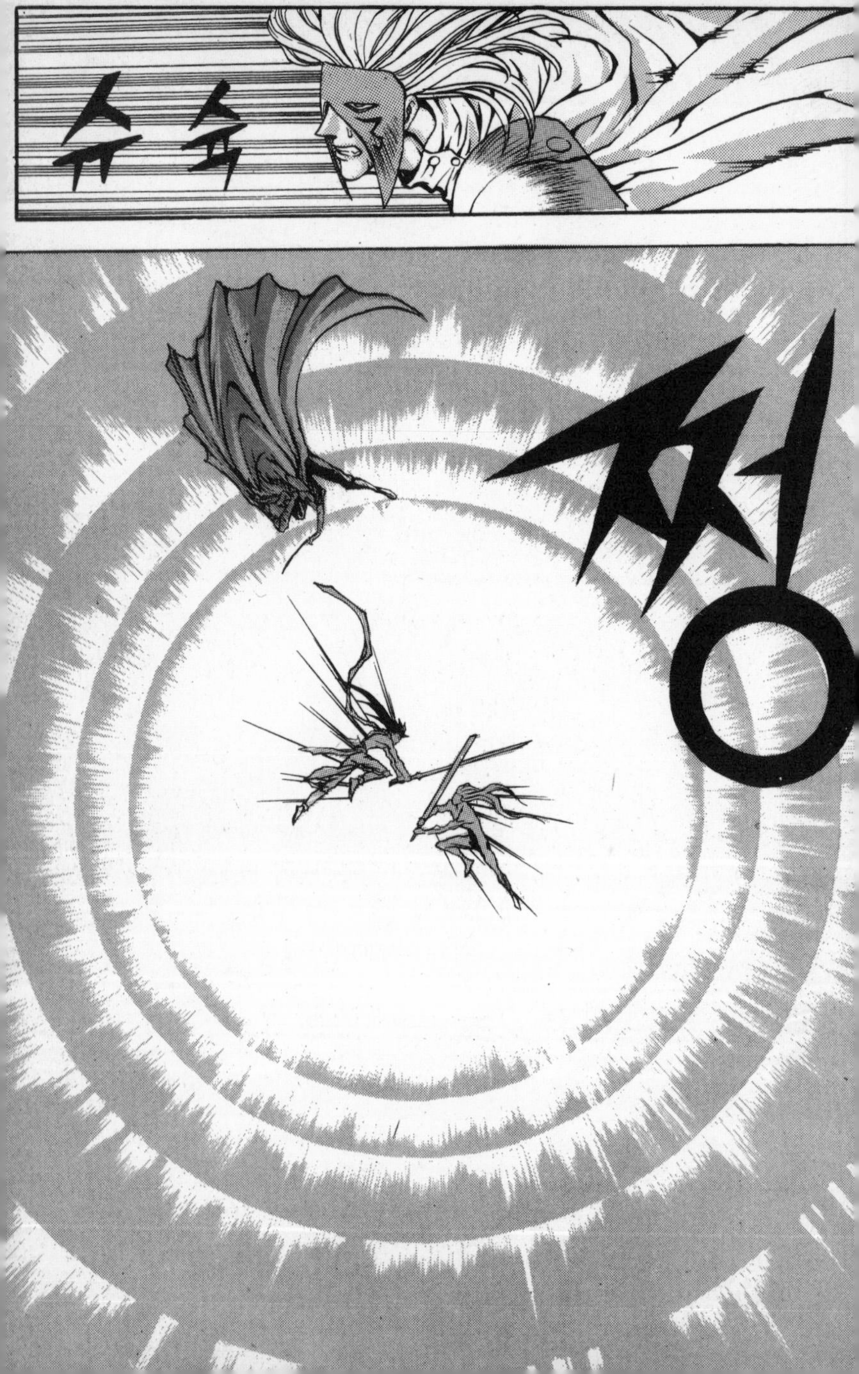
슈숙
쩡

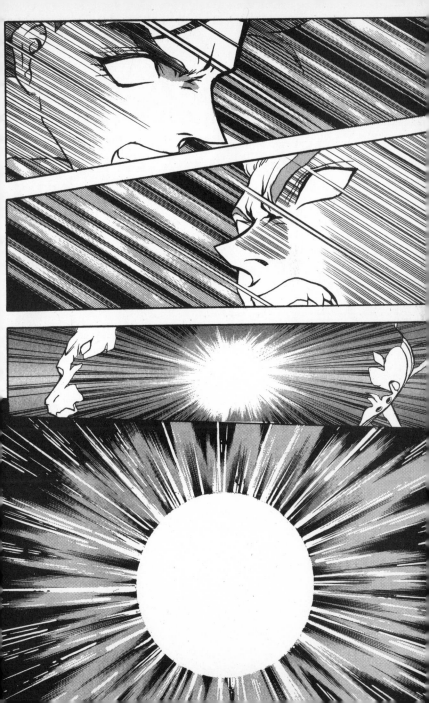

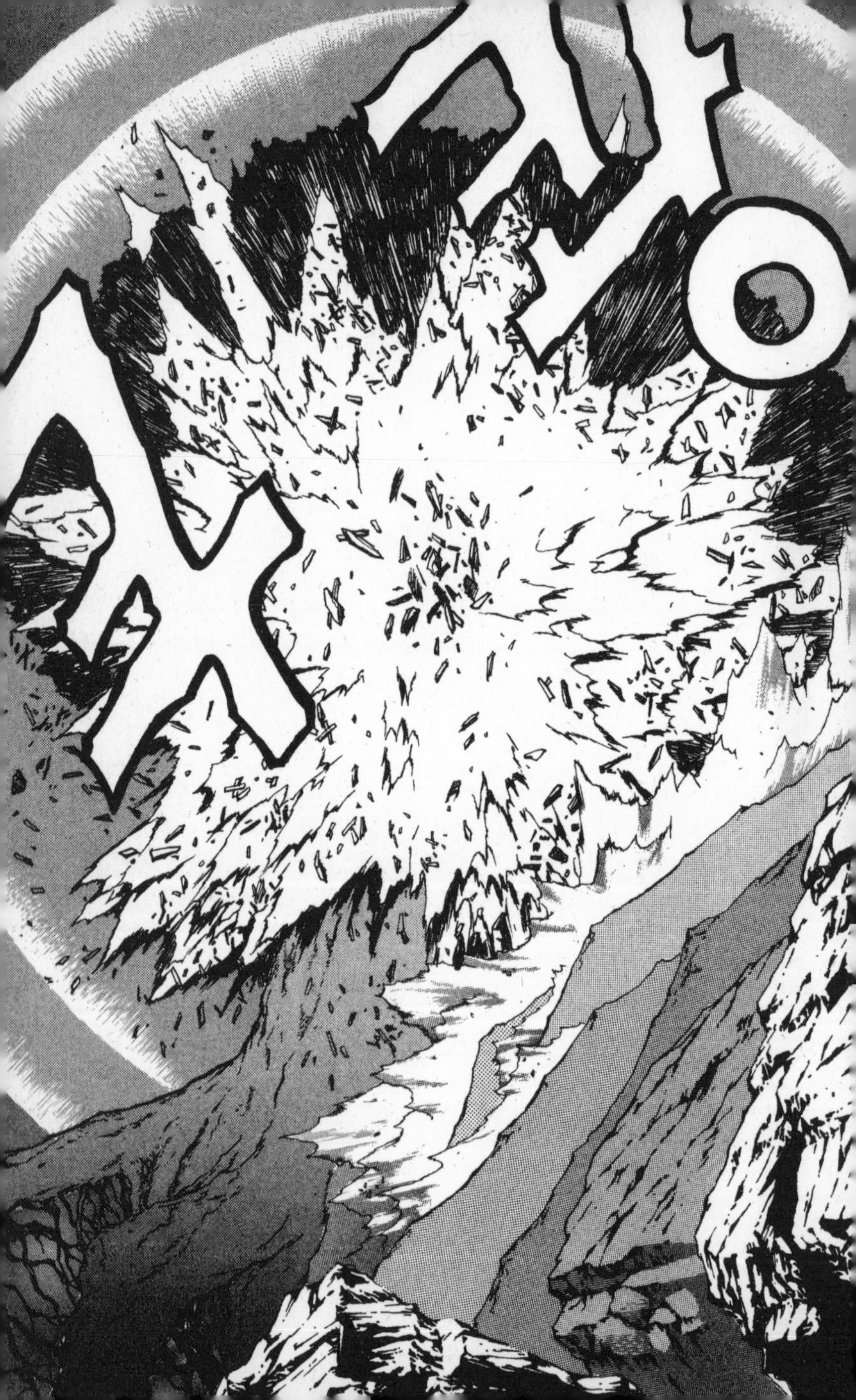

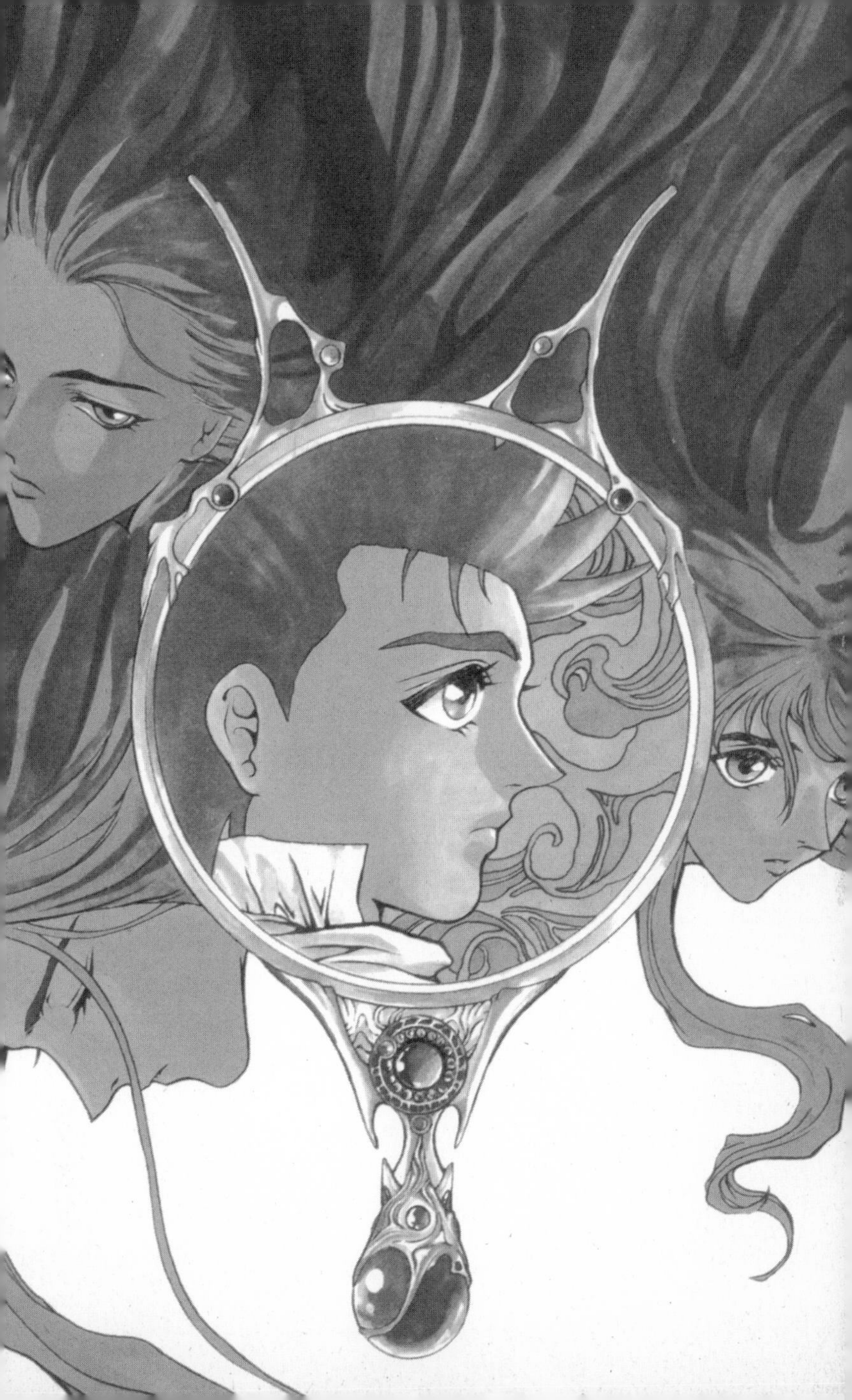

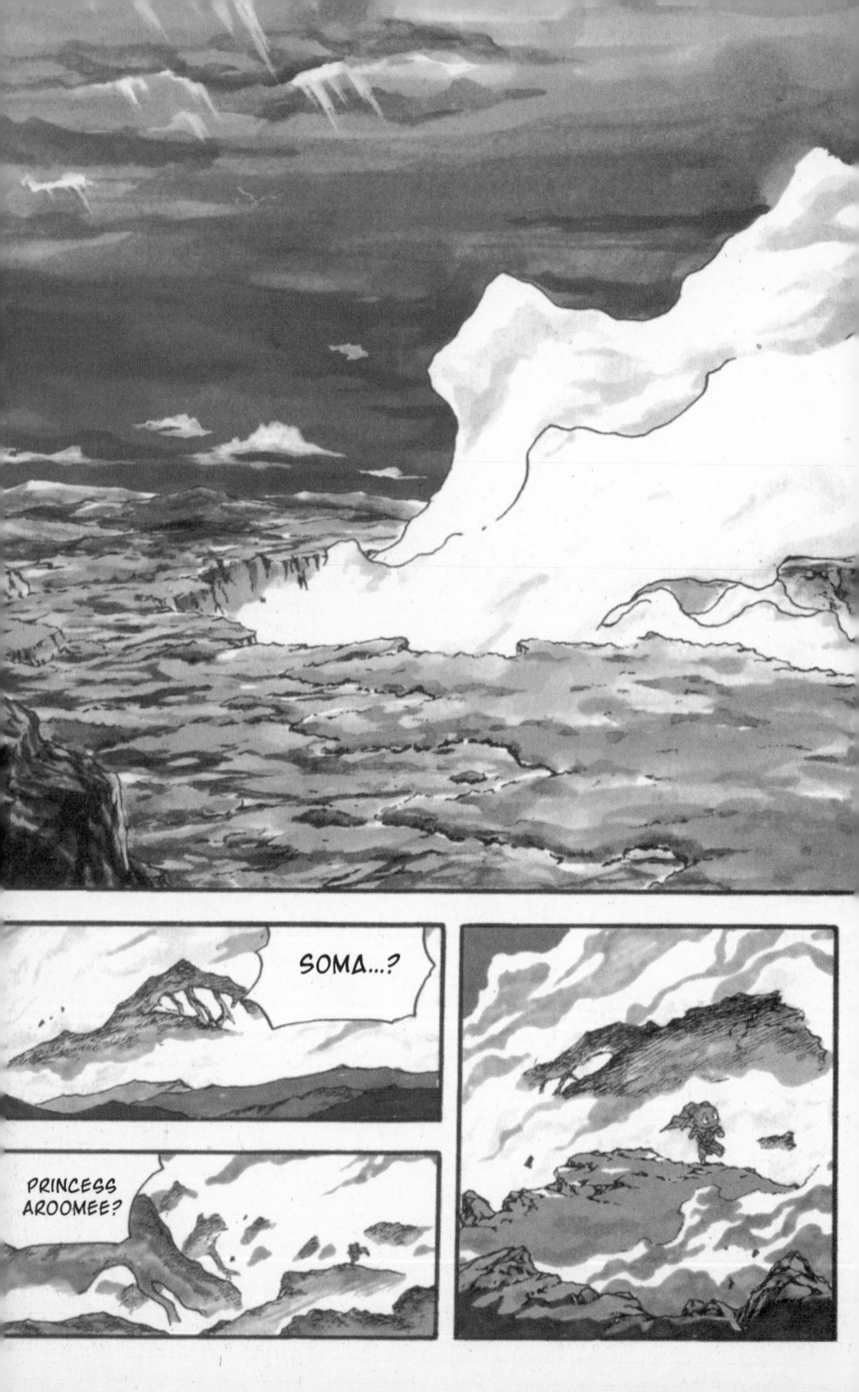
SOMA...?
PRINCESS AROOMEE?

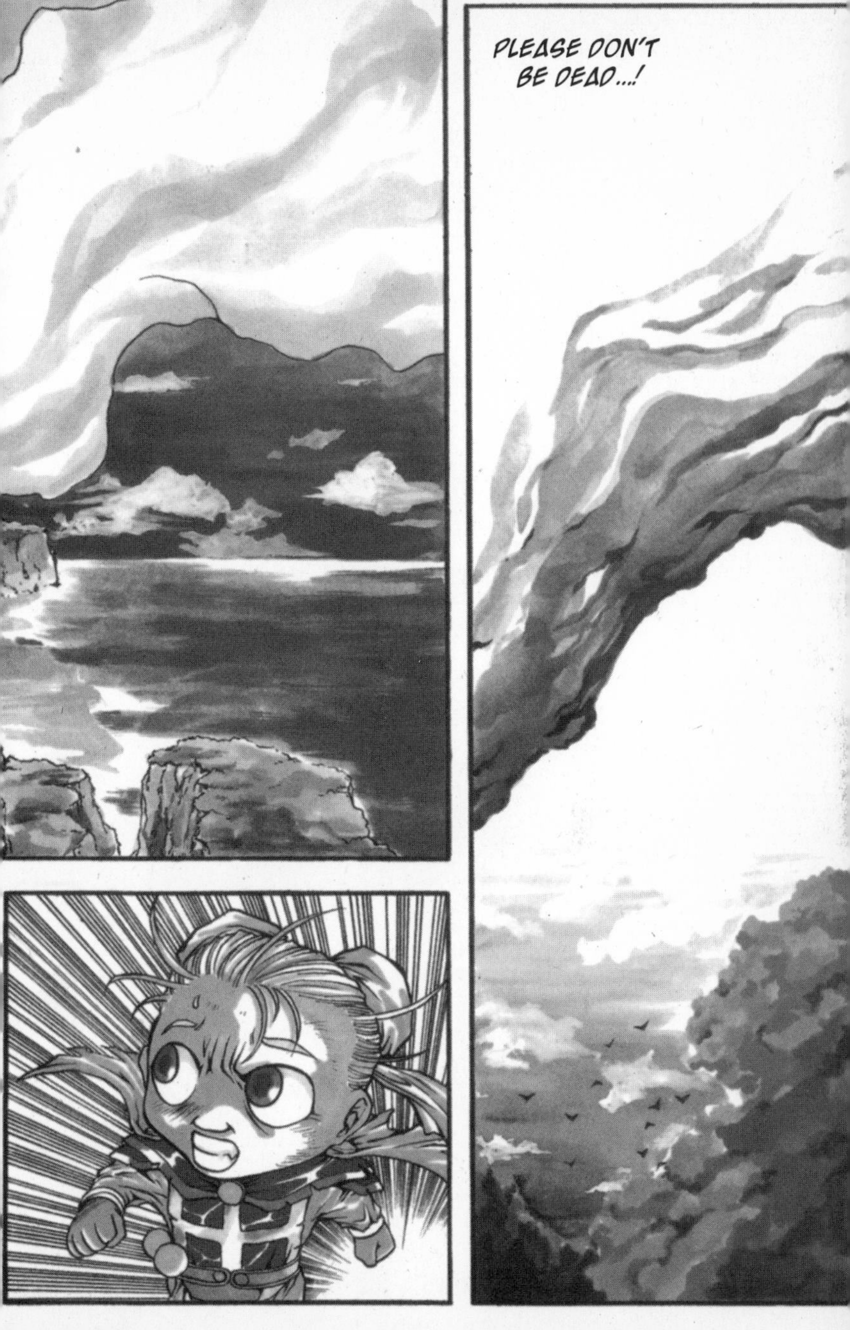
PLEASE DON'T BE DEAD...!

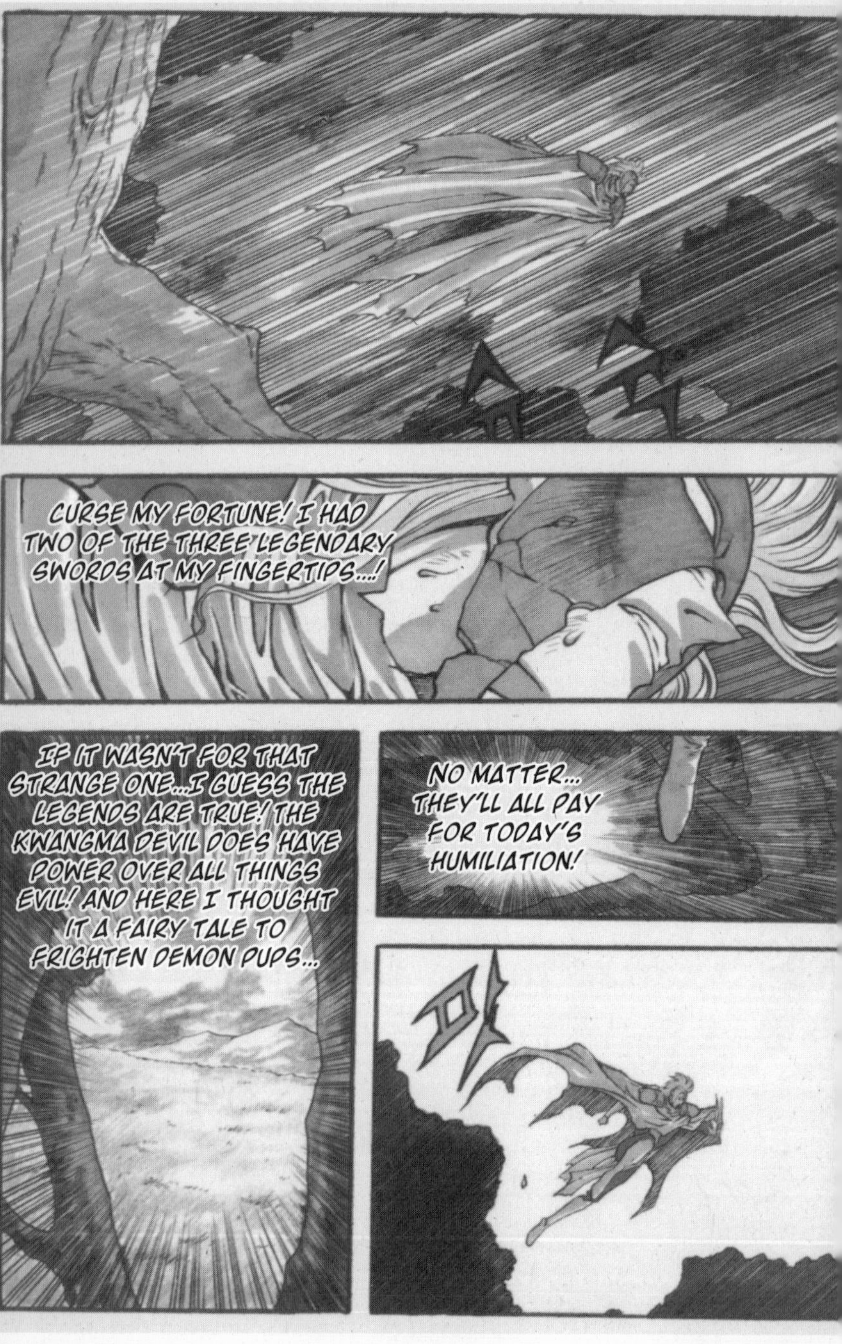
CURSE MY FORTUNE! I HAD TWO OF THE THREE LEGENDARY SWORDS AT MY FINGERTIPS...!
IF IT WASN'T FOR THAT STRANGE ONE...I GUESS THE LEGENDS ARE TRUE! THE KWANGMA DEVIL DOES HAVE POWER OVER ALL THINGS EVIL! AND HERE I THOUGHT IT A FAIRY TALE TO FRIGHTEN DEMON PUPS...
NO MATTER... THEY'LL ALL PAY FOR TODAY'S HUMILIATION!

!

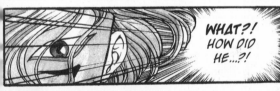

WHAT?!
HOW DID
HE....?!

FINE!! IF YOU INSIST
ON DYING TODAY,
THEN ALLOW ME TO
INDULGE YOU!!

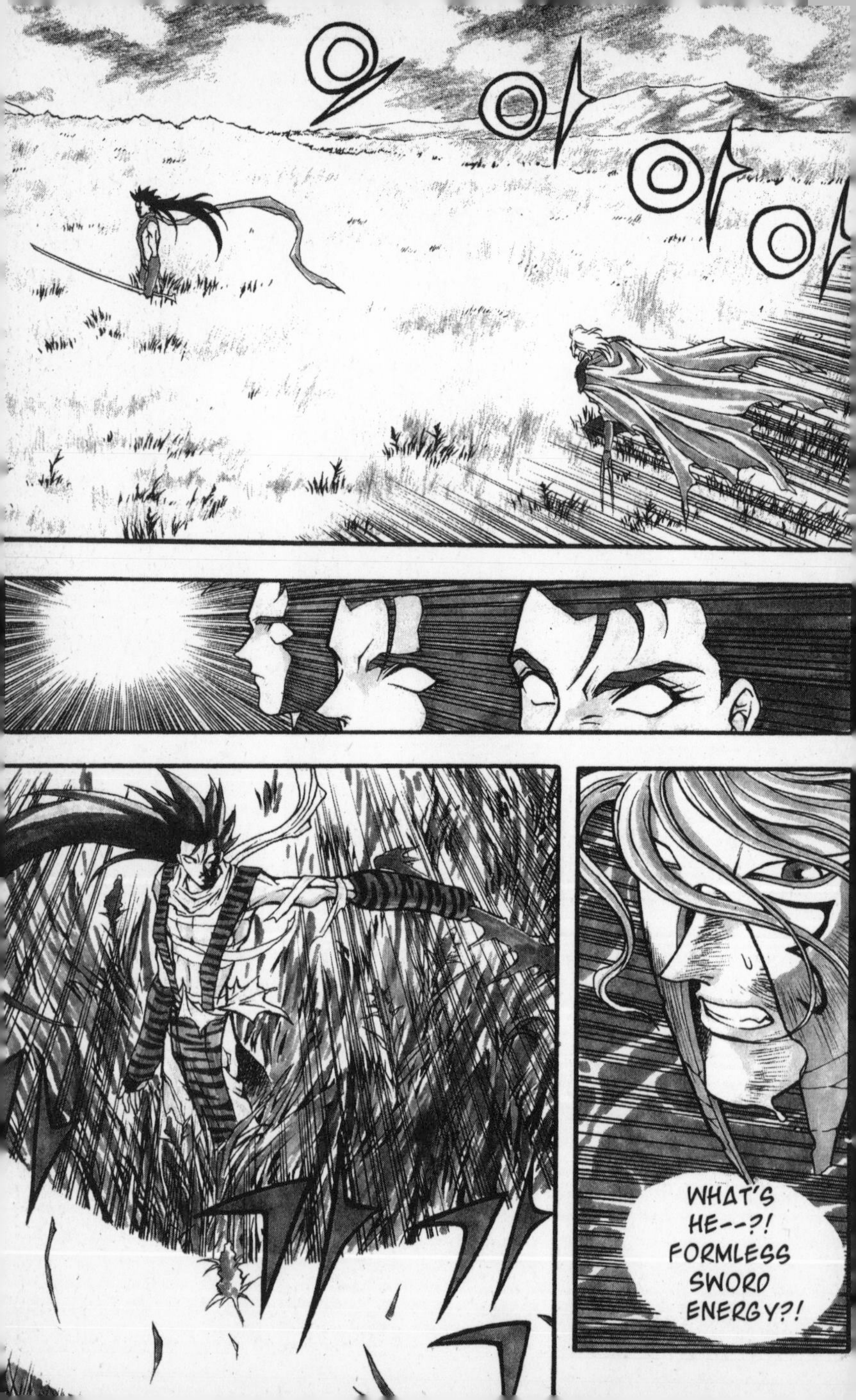

WHAT'S HE--?! FORMLESS SWORD ENERGY?!

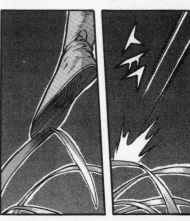

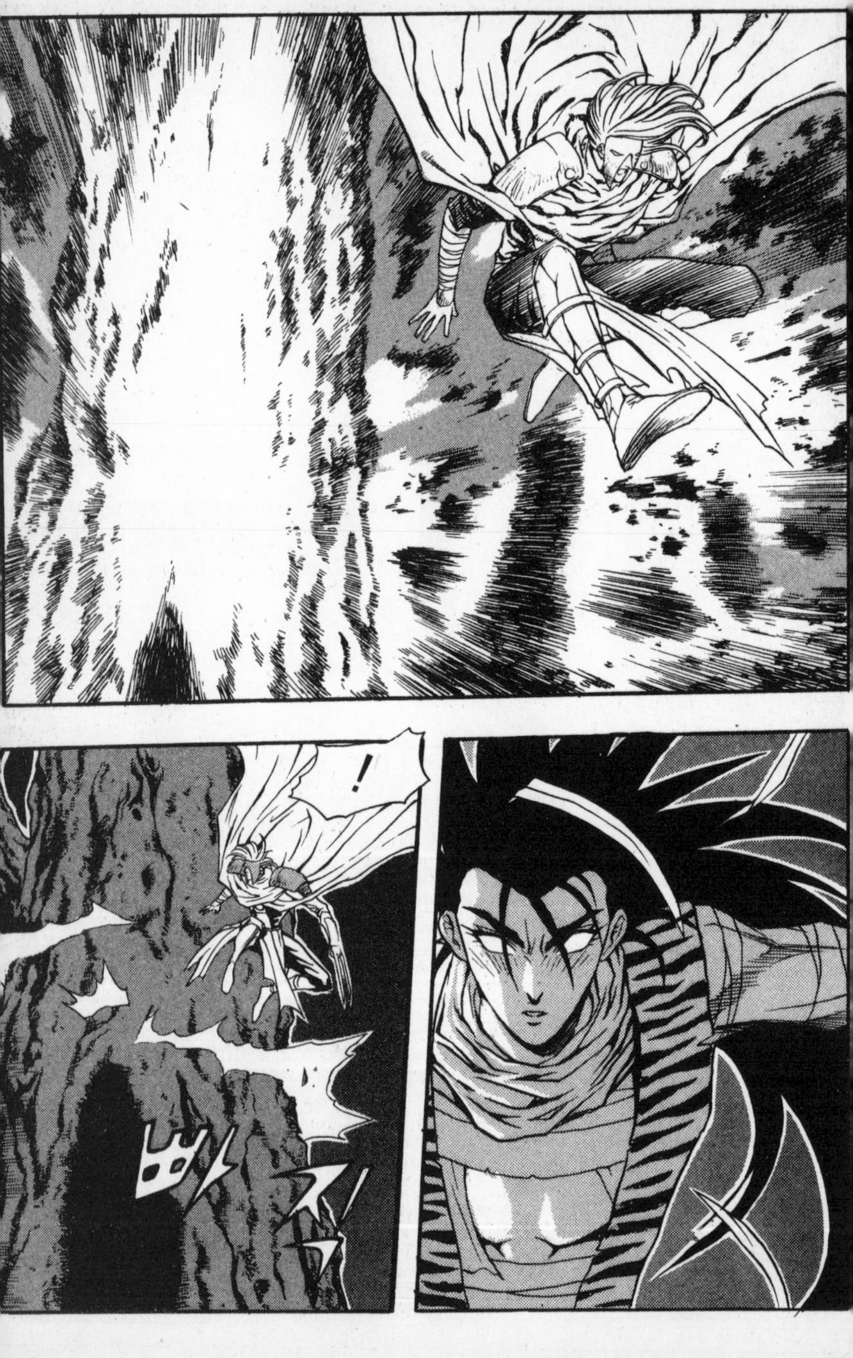
!

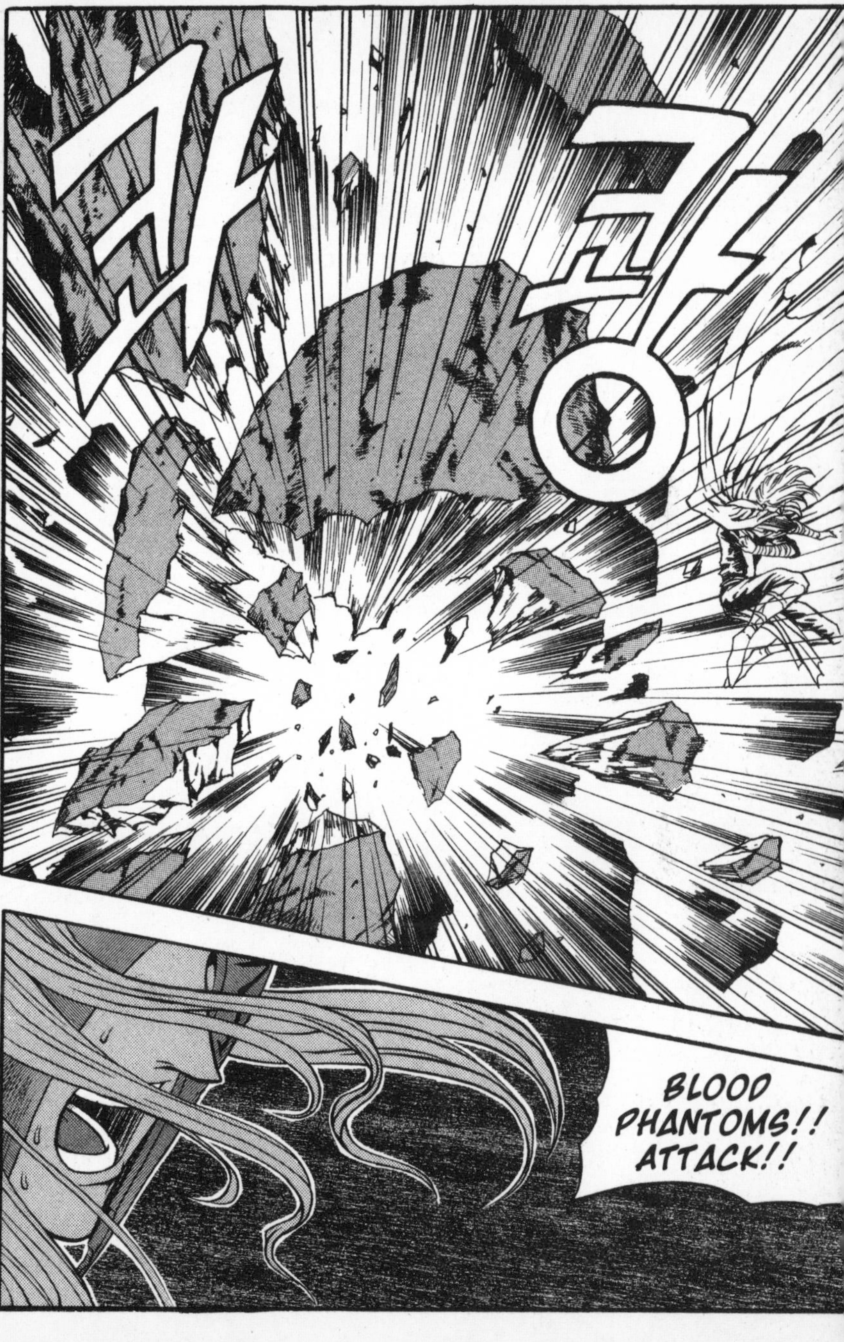
BLOOD PHANTOMS!! ATTACK!!

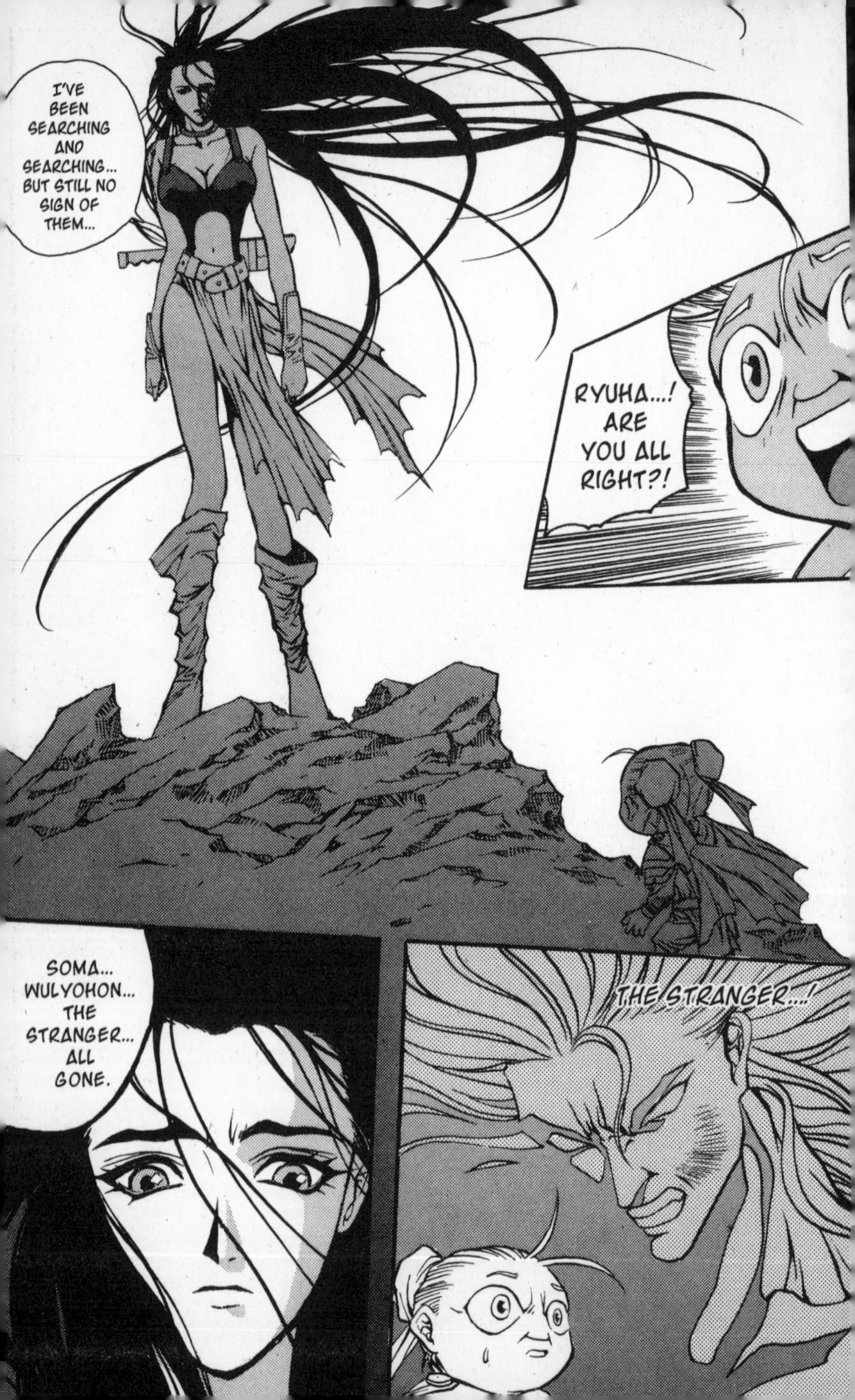
I'VE BEEN SEARCHING AND SEARCHING... BUT STILL NO SIGN OF THEM...
RYUHA...! ARE YOU ALL RIGHT?!
SOMA... WULYOHON... THE STRANGER... ALL GONE.
THE STRANGER...!

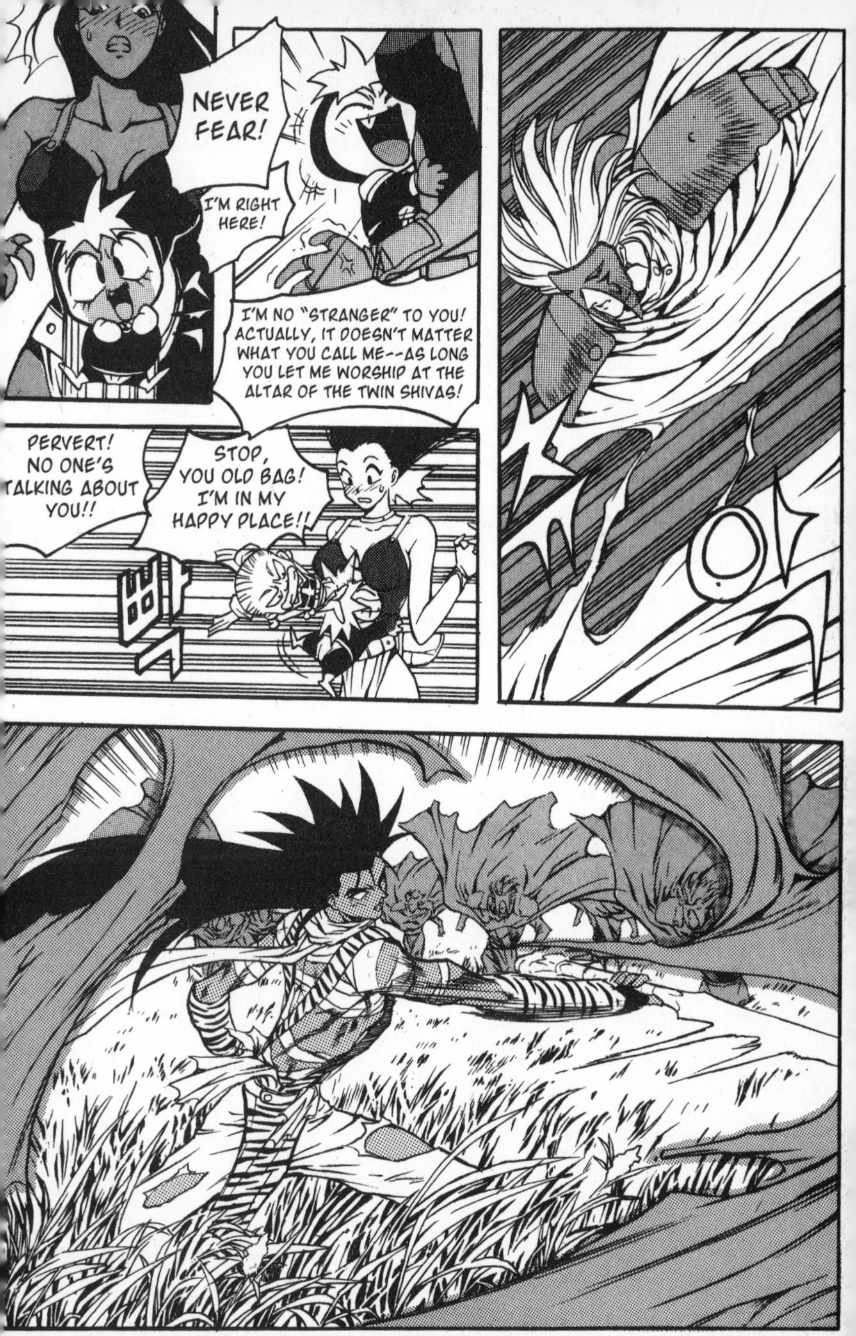
NEVER FEAR!
I'M RIGHT HERE!
I'M NO "STRANGER" TO YOU! ACTUALLY, IT DOESN'T MATTER WHAT YOU CALL ME--AS LONG YOU LET ME WORSHIP AT THE ALTAR OF THE TWIN SHIVAS!
PERVERT! NO ONE'S TALKING ABOUT YOU!!
STOP, YOU OLD BAG! I'M IN MY HAPPY PLACE!!
빡

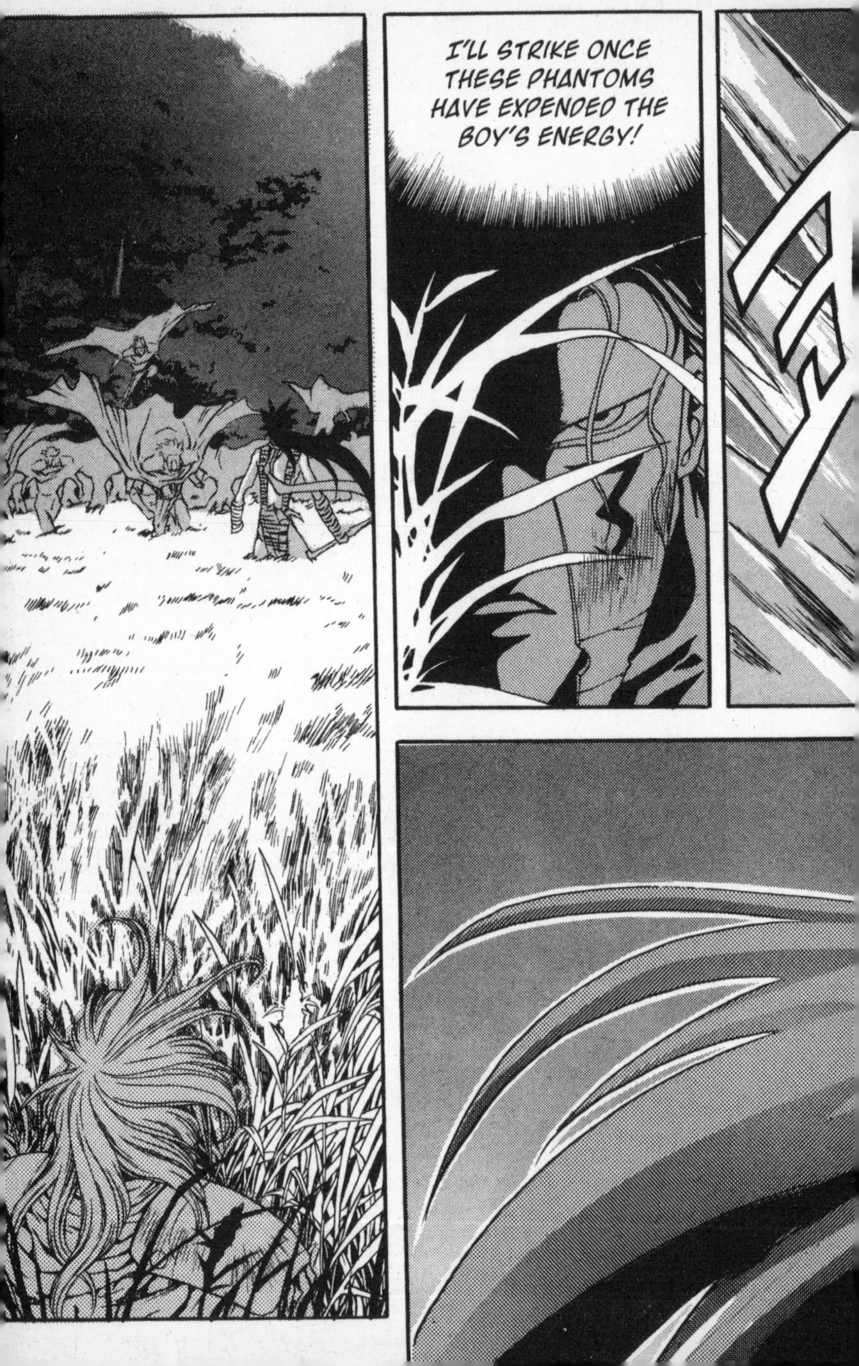
I'LL STRIKE ONCE THESE PHANTOMS HAVE EXPENDED THE BOY'S ENERGY!

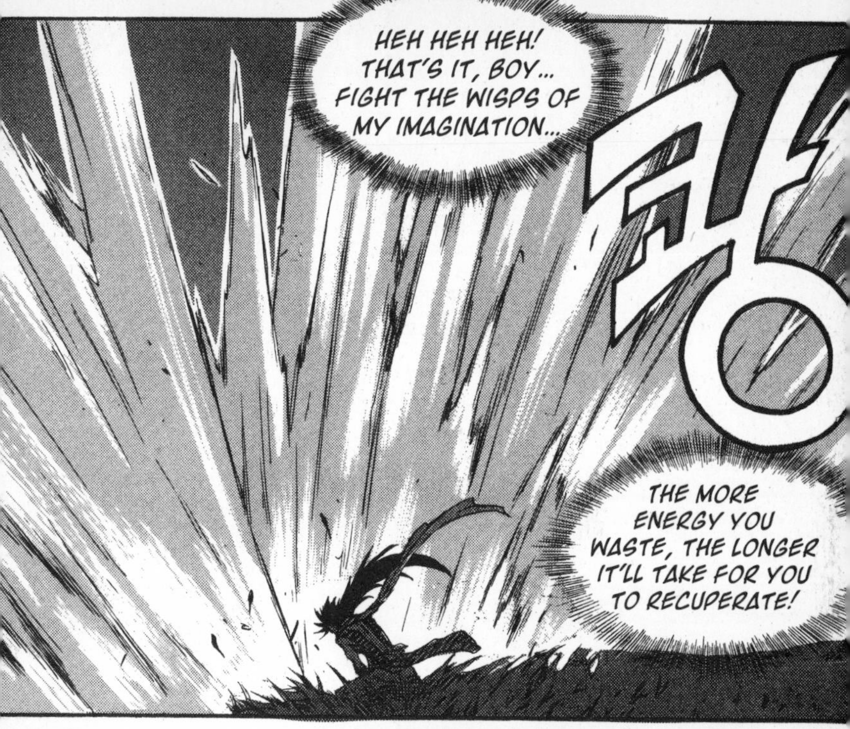
HEH HEH HEH! THAT'S IT, BOY... FIGHT THE WISPS OF MY IMAGINATION...
THE MORE ENERGY YOU WASTE, THE LONGER IT'LL TAKE FOR YOU TO RECUPERATE!
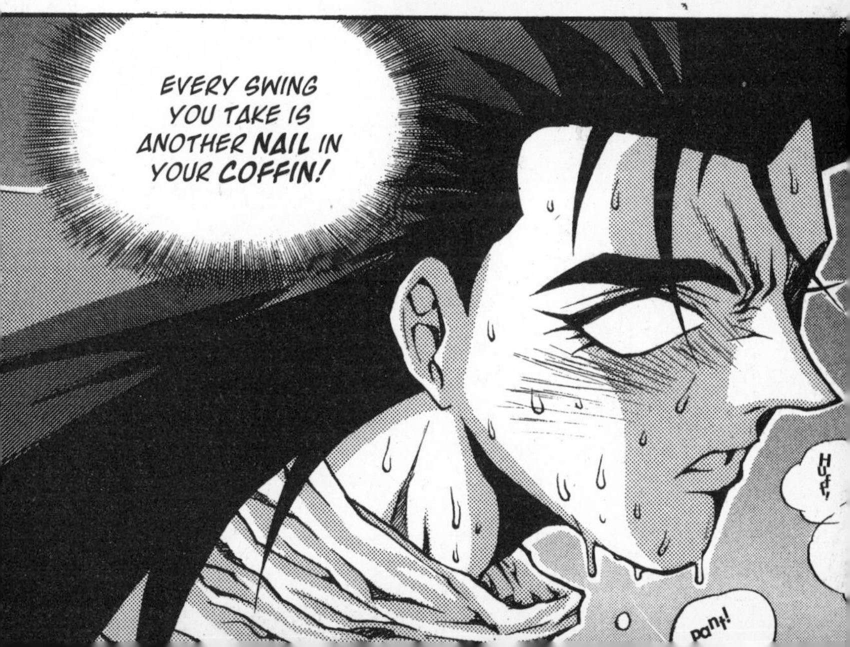
EVERY SWING YOU TAKE IS ANOTHER **NAIL** IN YOUR **COFFIN**!
Huff!
pant!

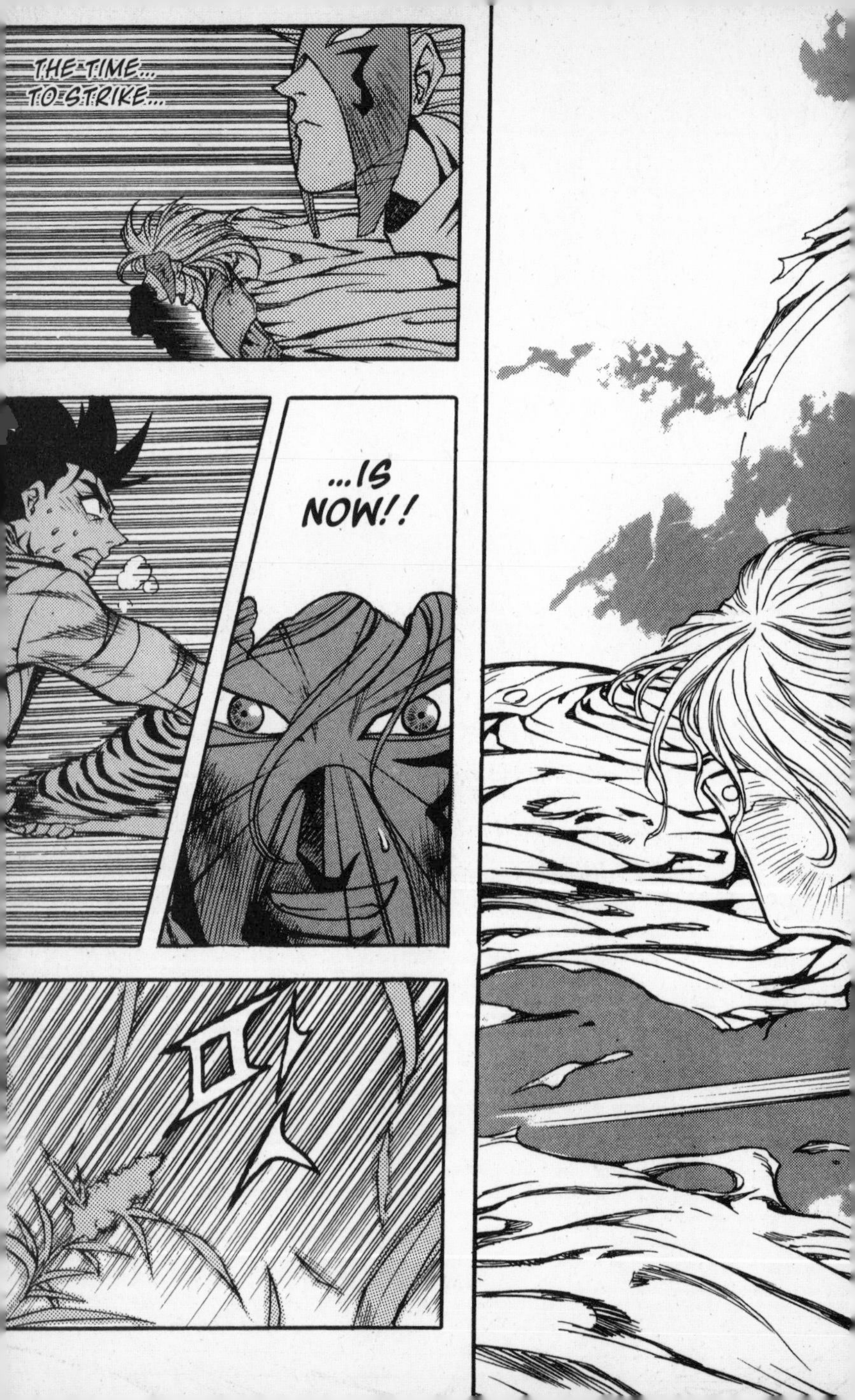
THE TIME... TO STRIKE...
...IS NOW!!

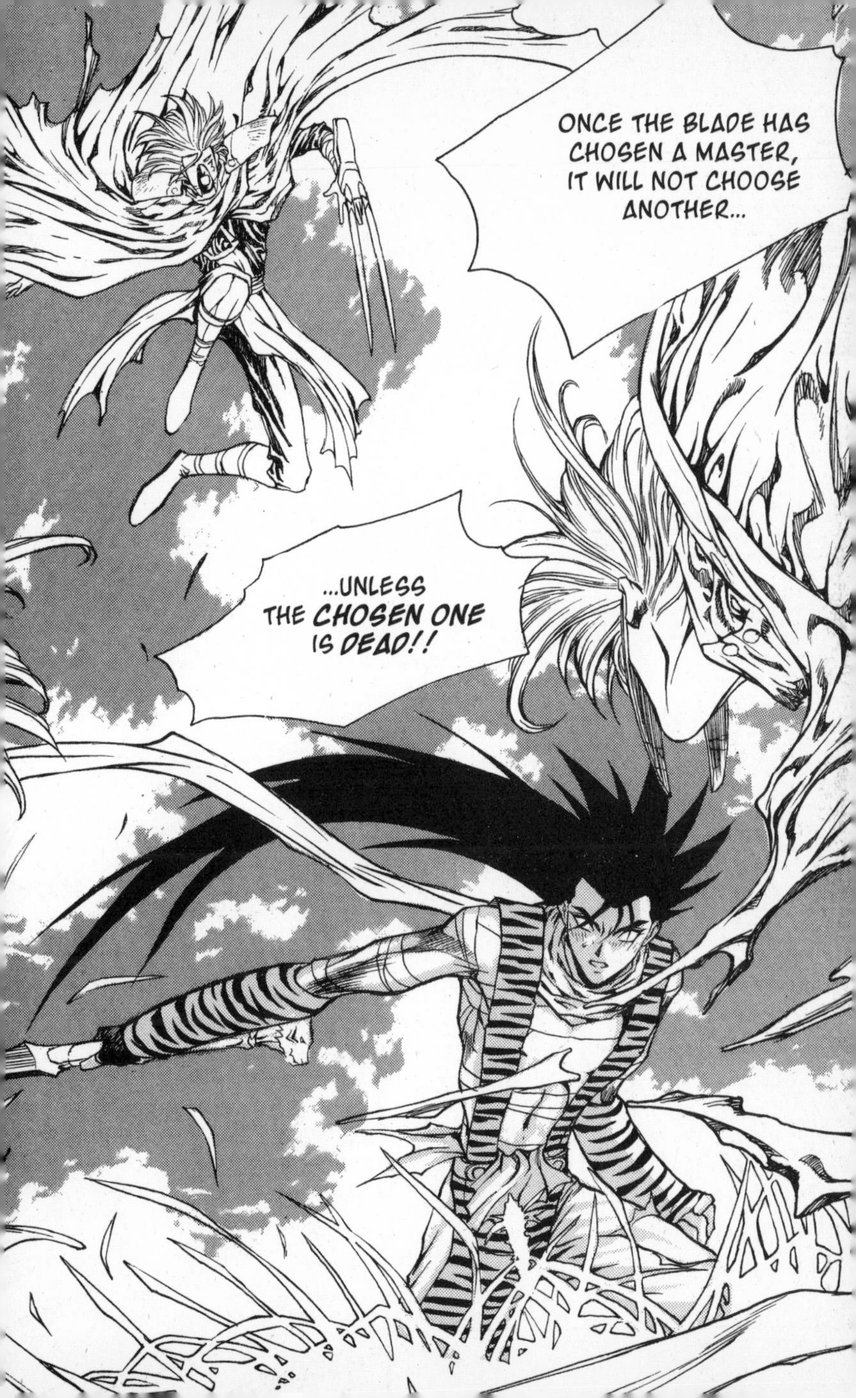
ONCE THE BLADE HAS CHOSEN A MASTER, IT WILL NOT CHOOSE ANOTHER...
...UNLESS THE CHOSEN ONE IS DEAD!!

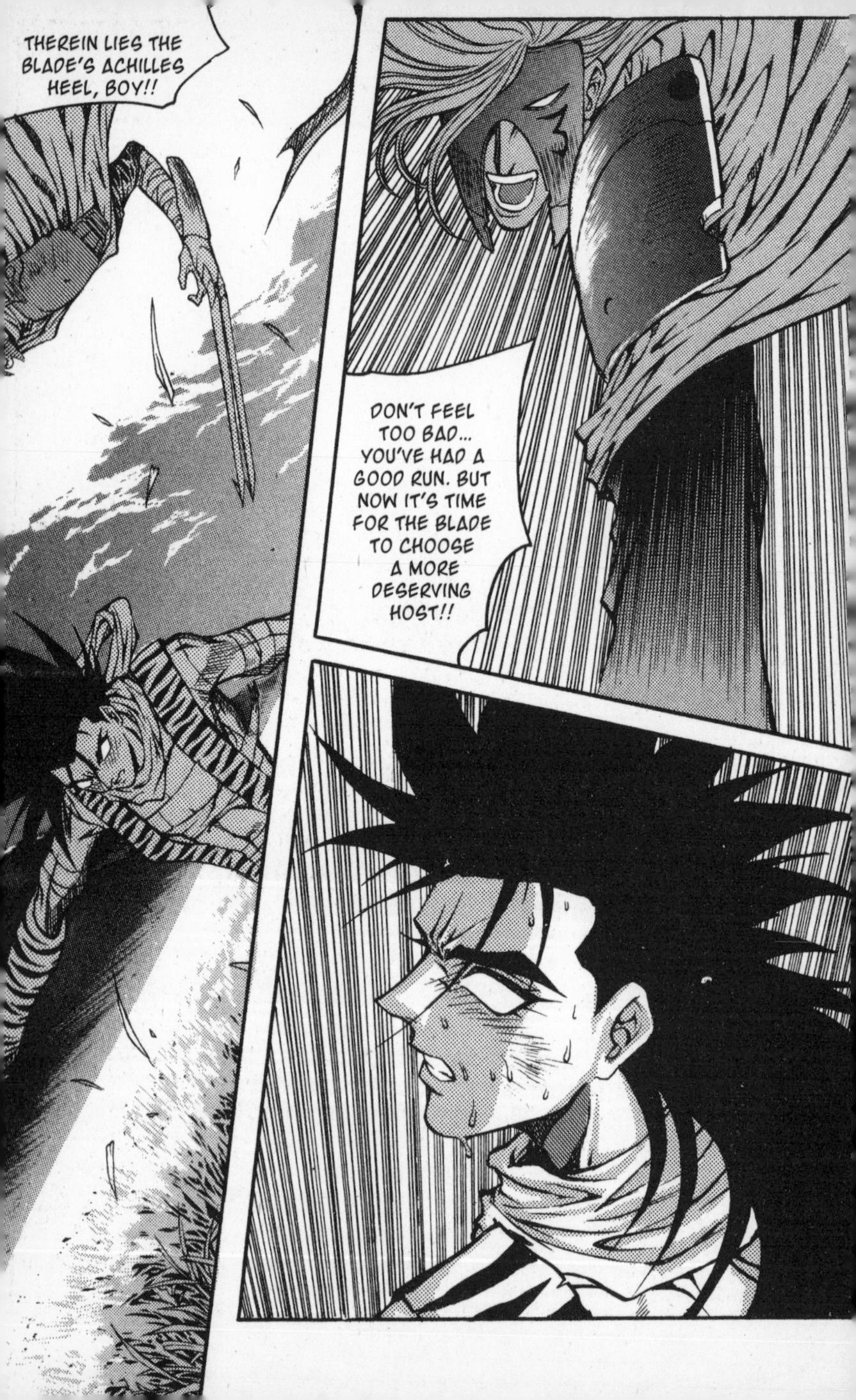
DON'T FEEL TOO BAD... YOU'VE HAD A GOOD RUN. BUT NOW IT'S TIME FOR THE BLADE TO CHOOSE A MORE DESERVING HOST!!
THEREIN LIES THE BLADE'S ACHILLES HEEL, BOY!!

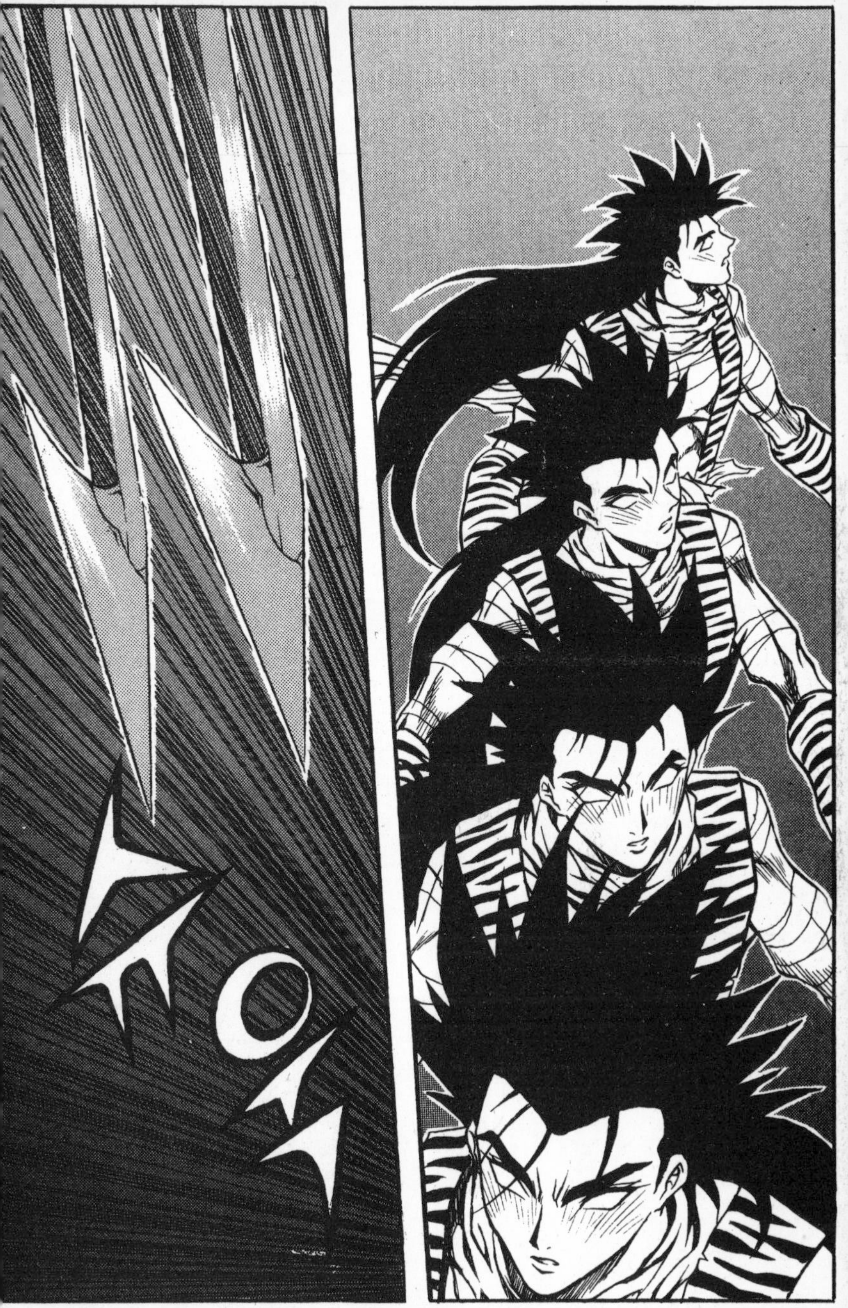

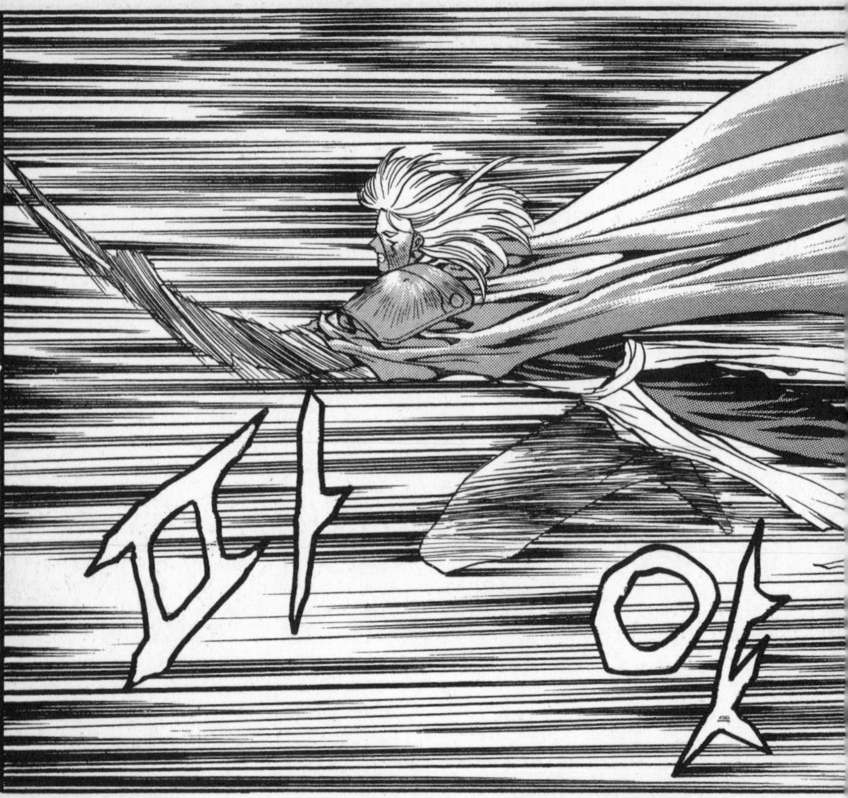
파야
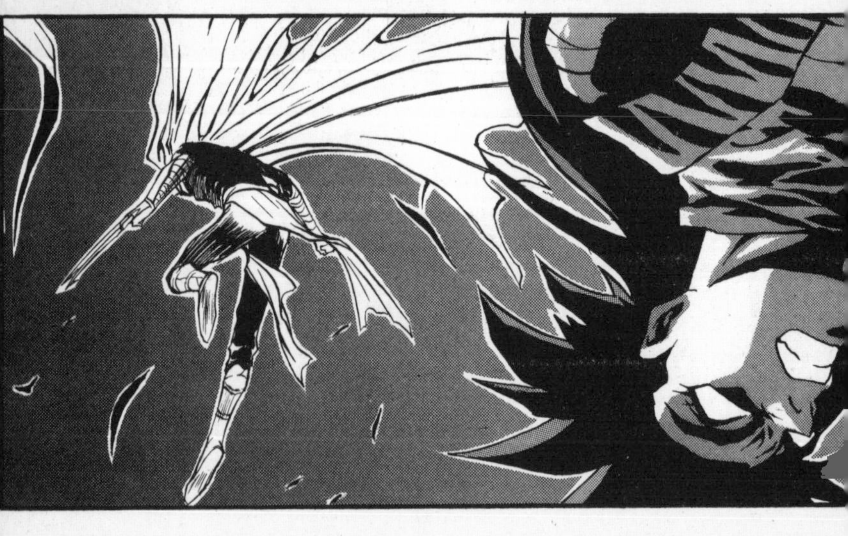

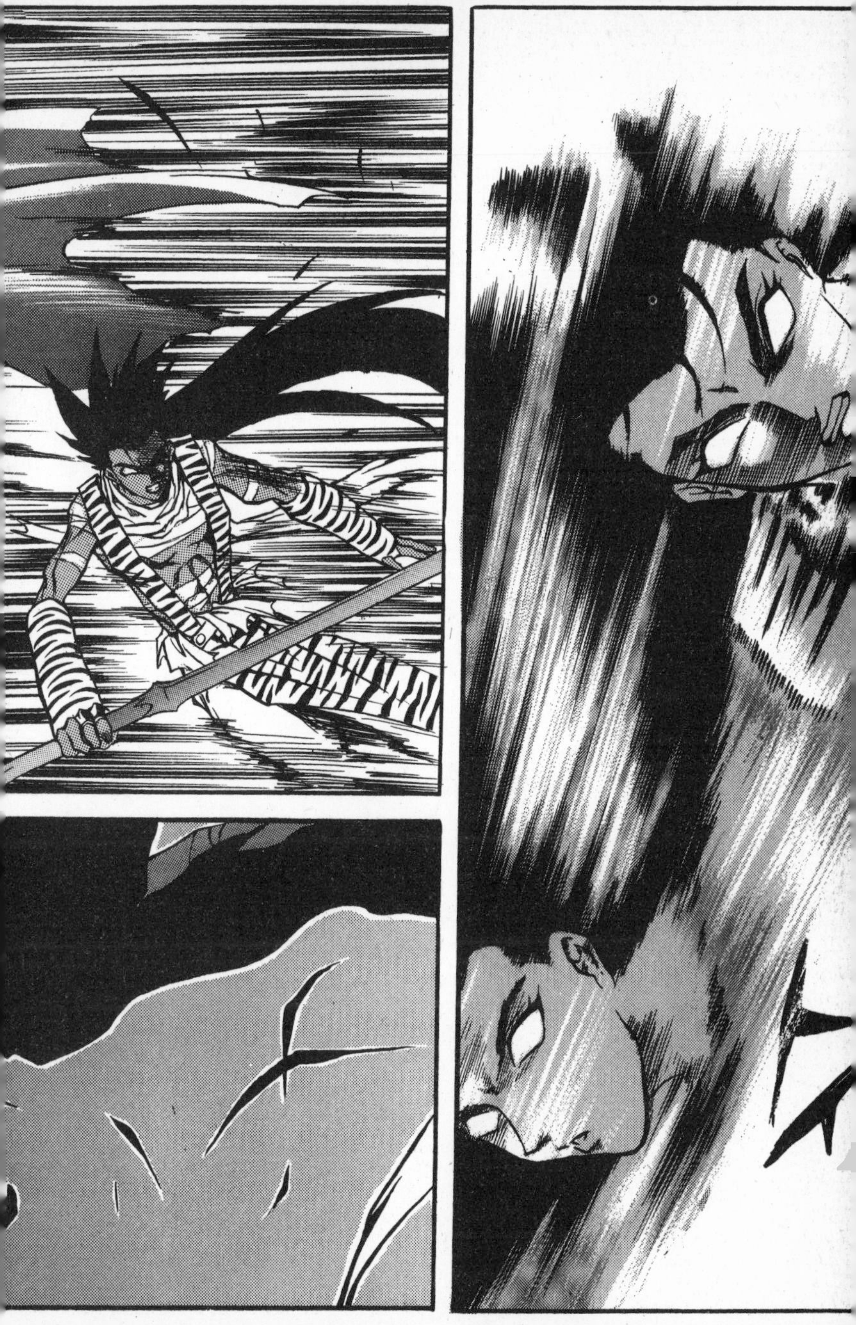

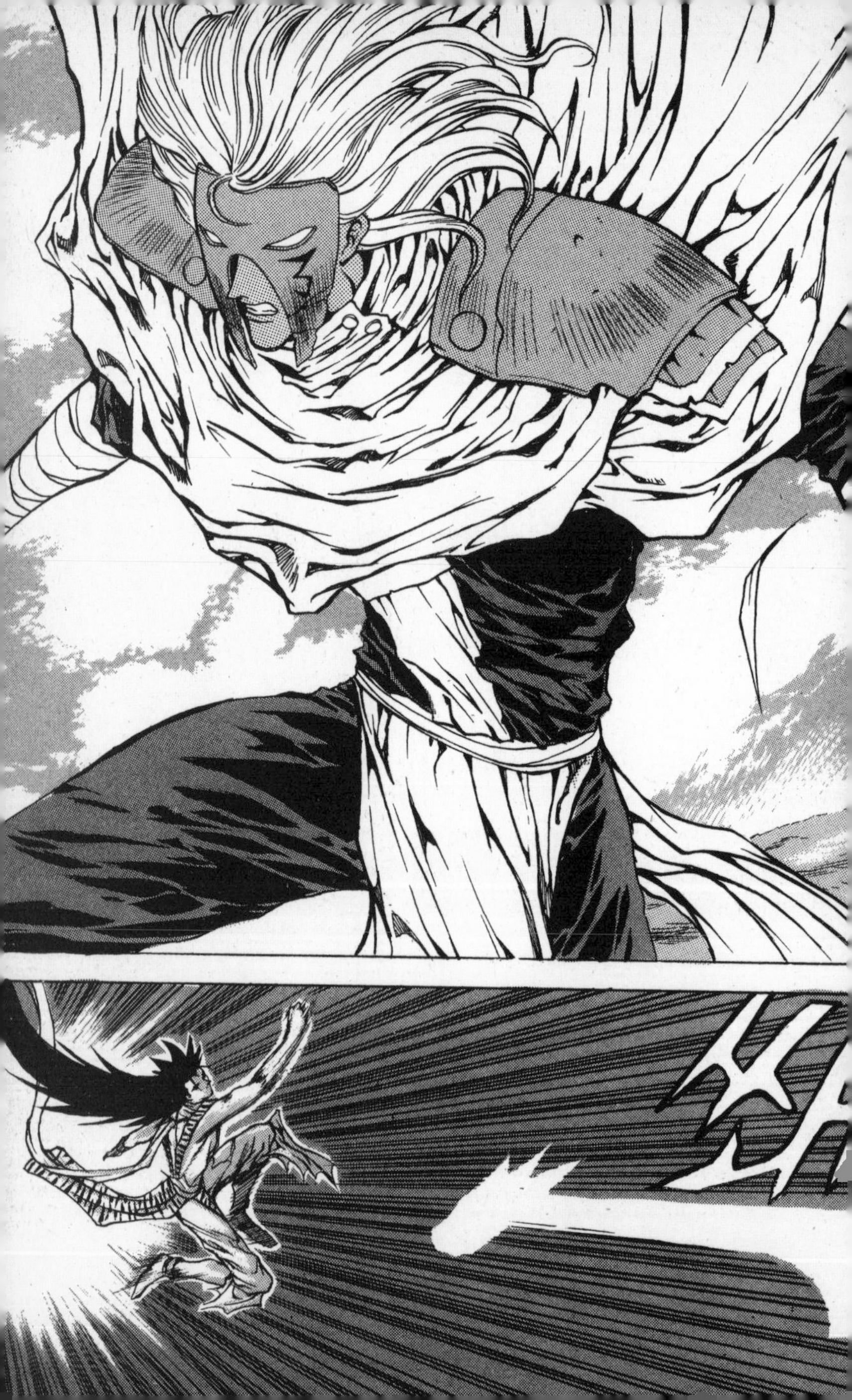

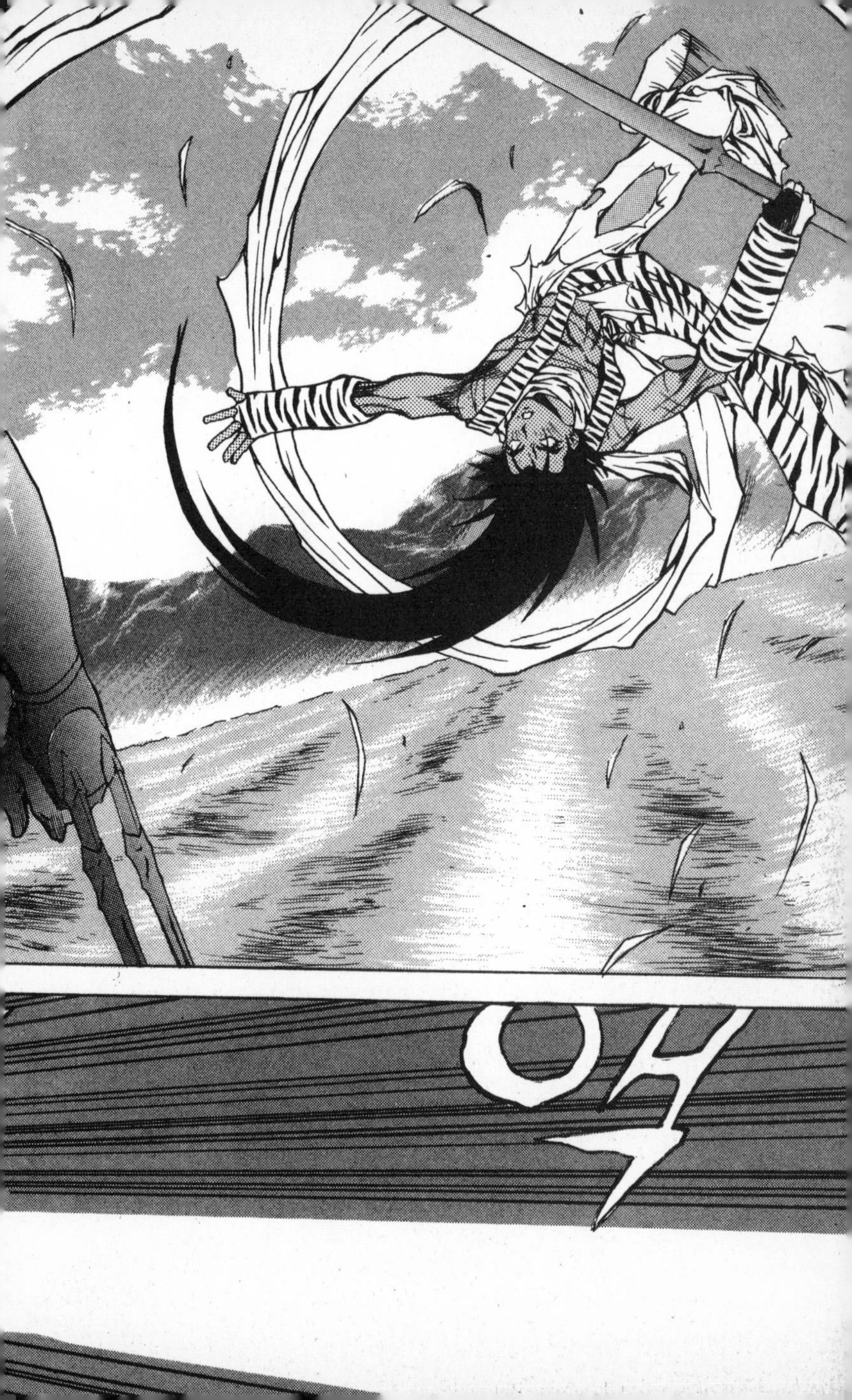

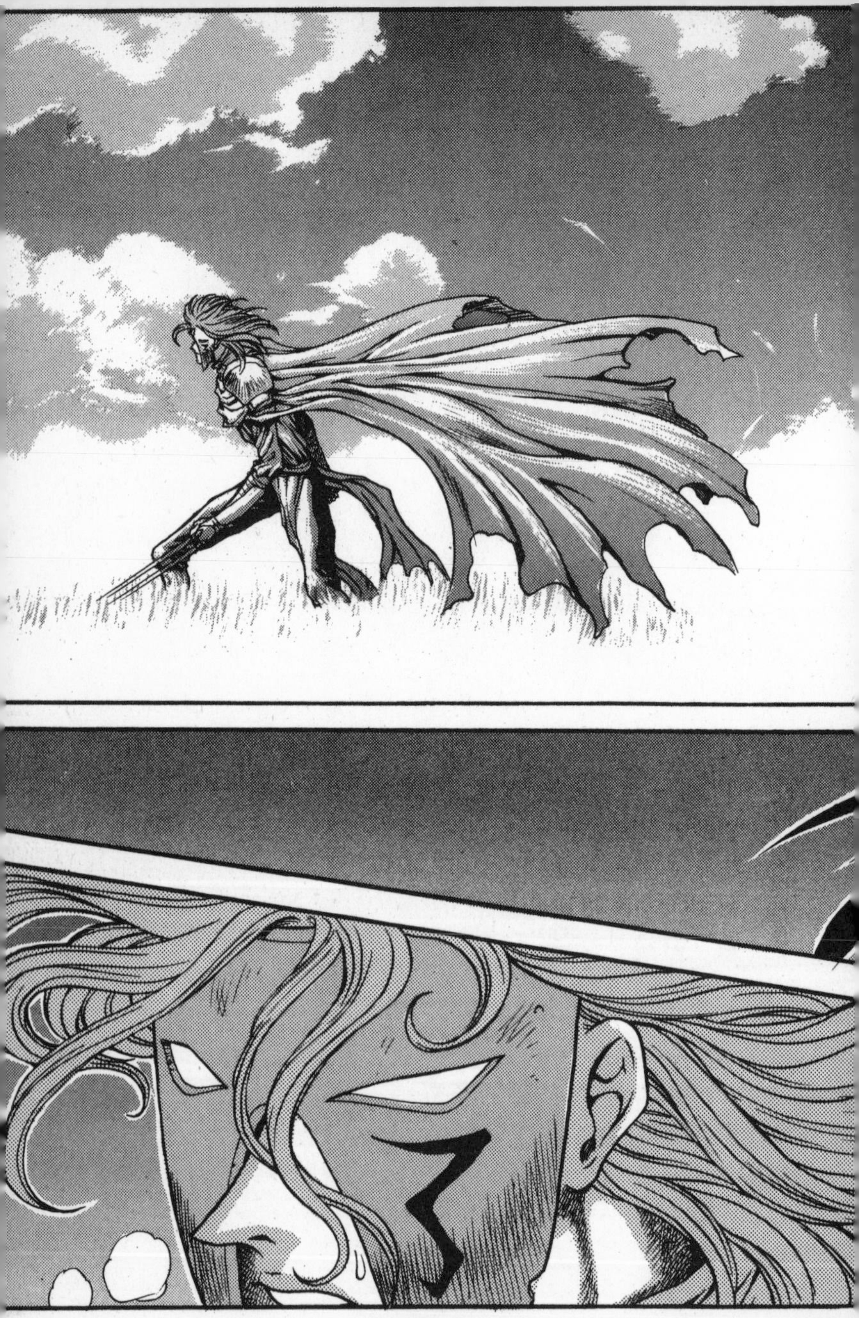

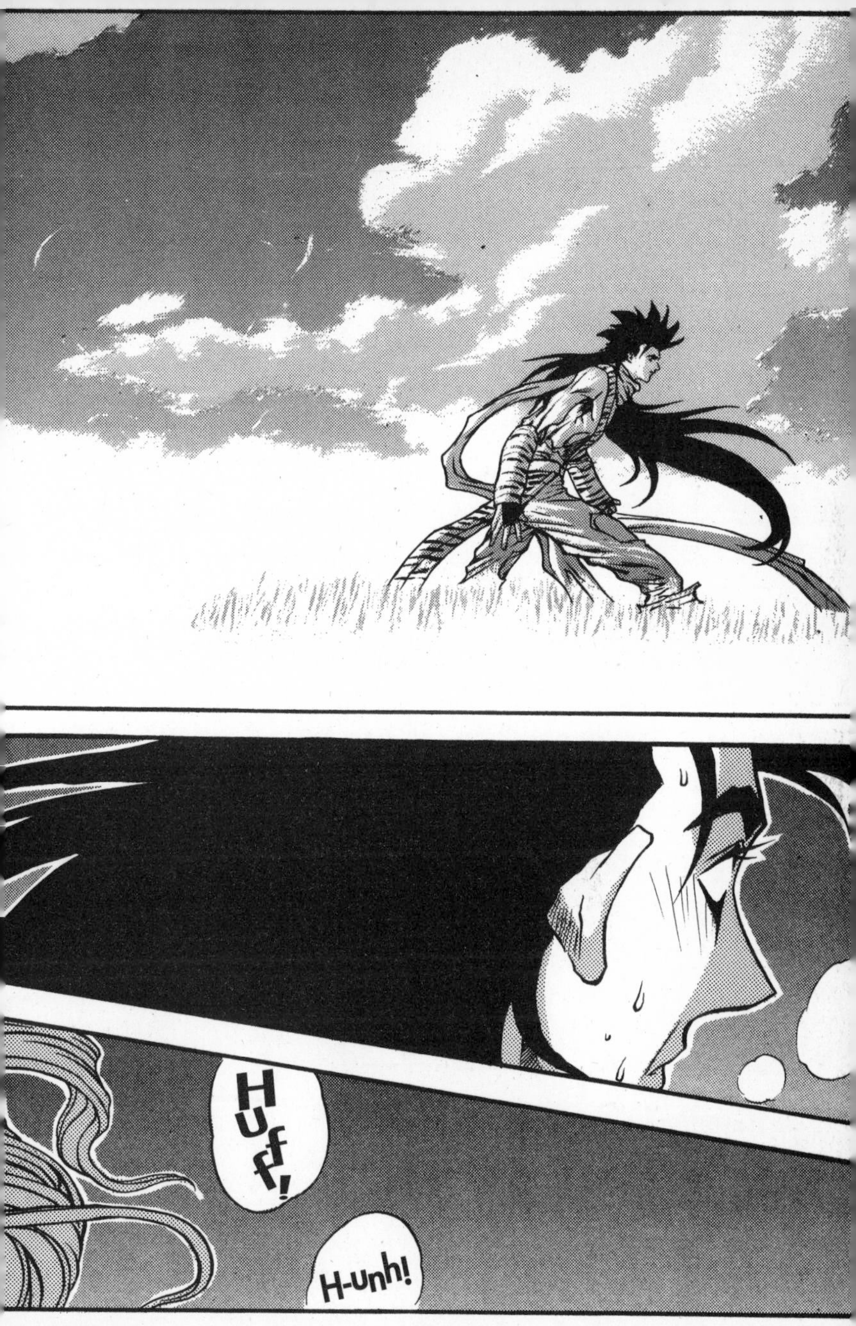
Huff!
H-unh!

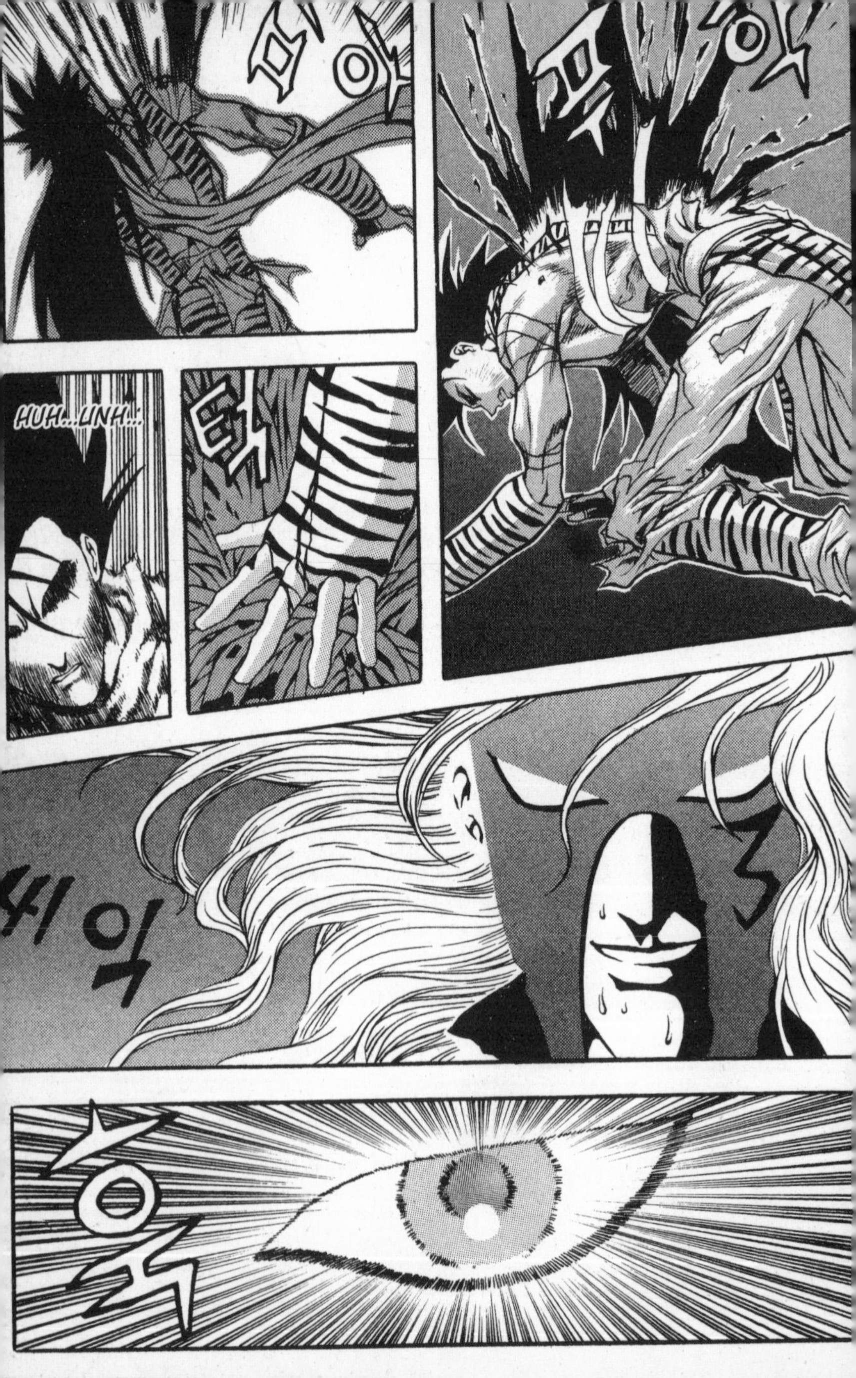
HUH...UNH...

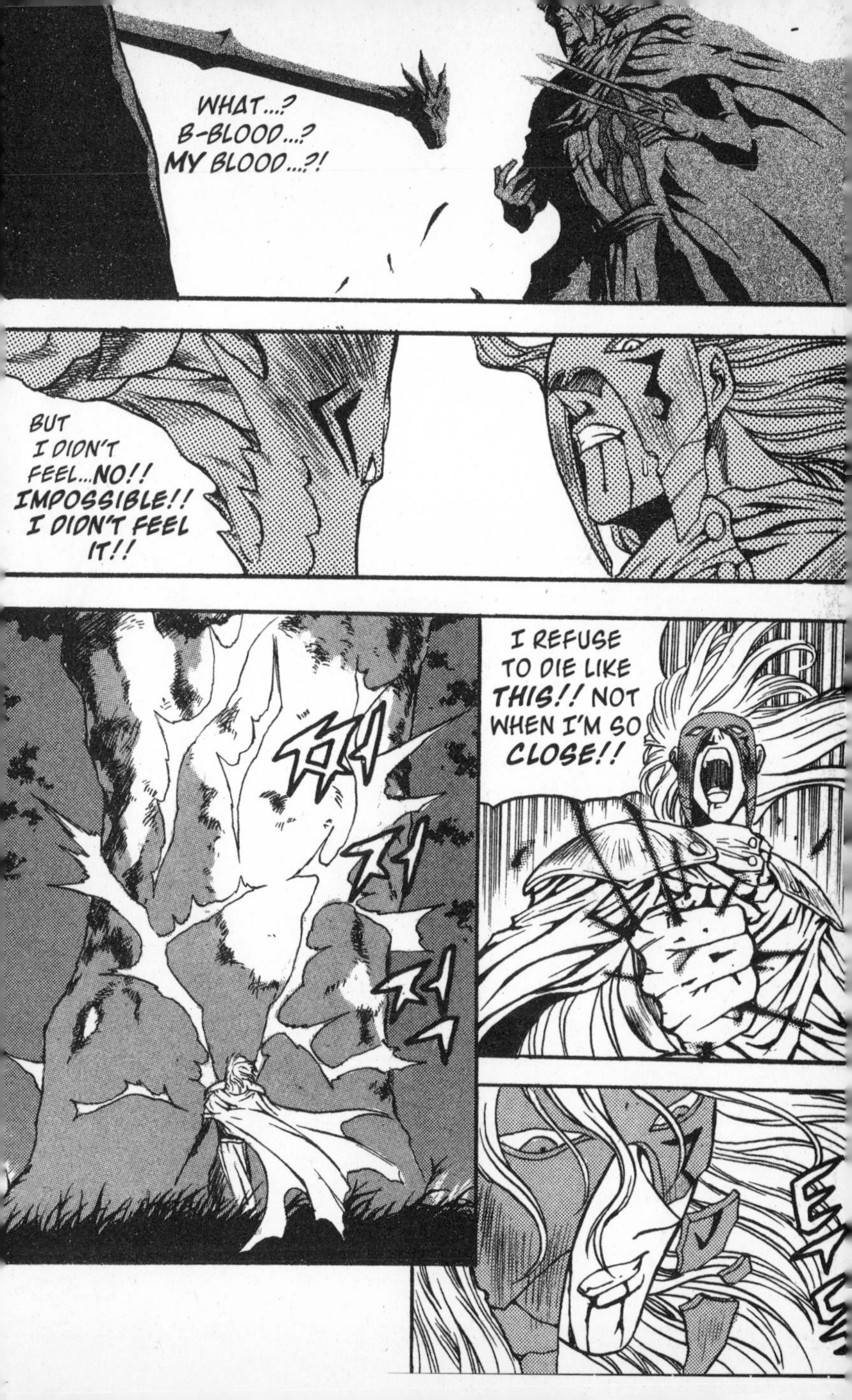
WHAT...? B-BLOOD...? MY BLOOD...?!
BUT I DIDN'T FEEL...NO!! IMPOSSIBLE!! I DIDN'T FEEL IT!!
I REFUSE TO DIE LIKE THIS!! NOT WHEN I'M SO CLOSE!!

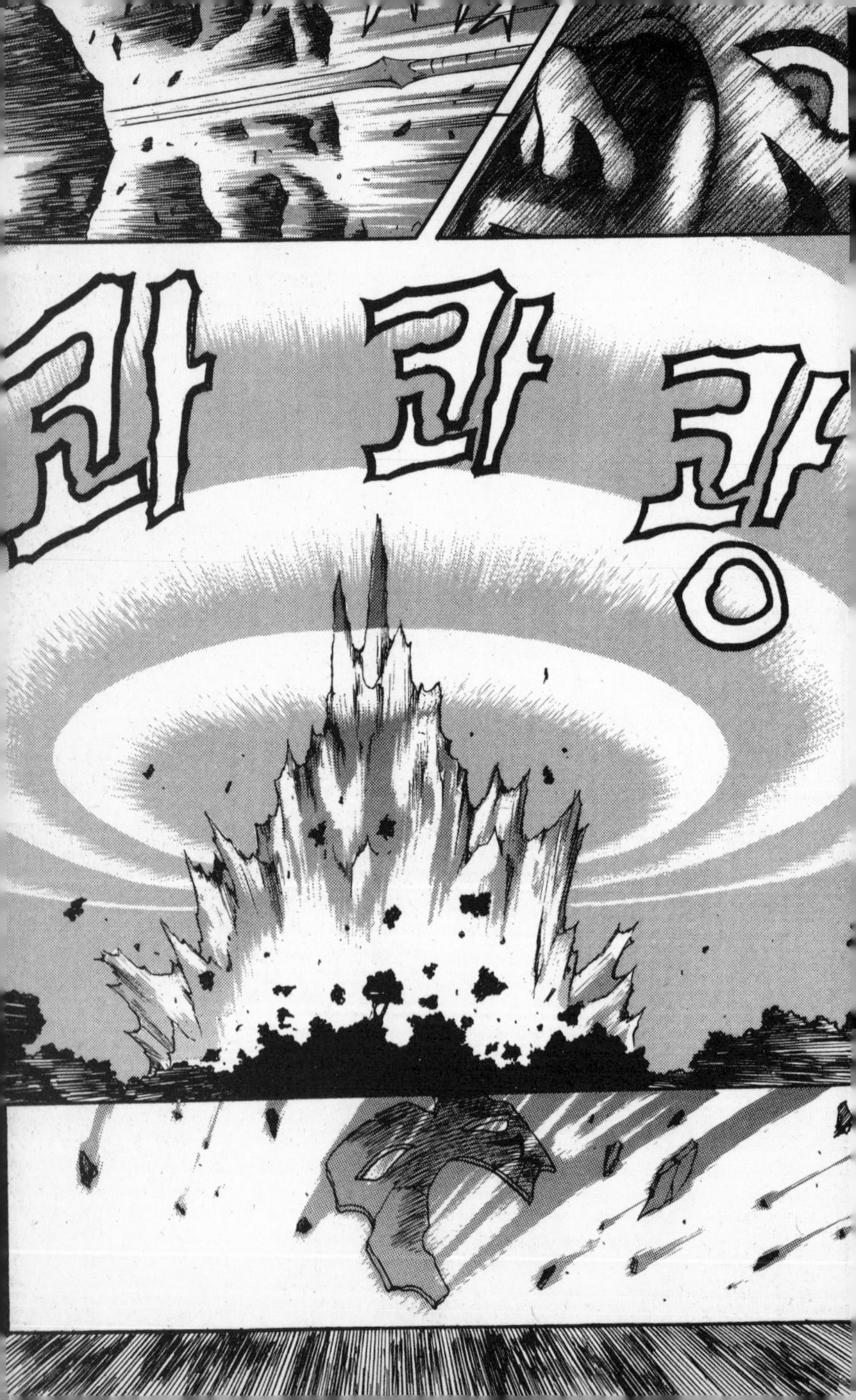
콰 콰 쾅

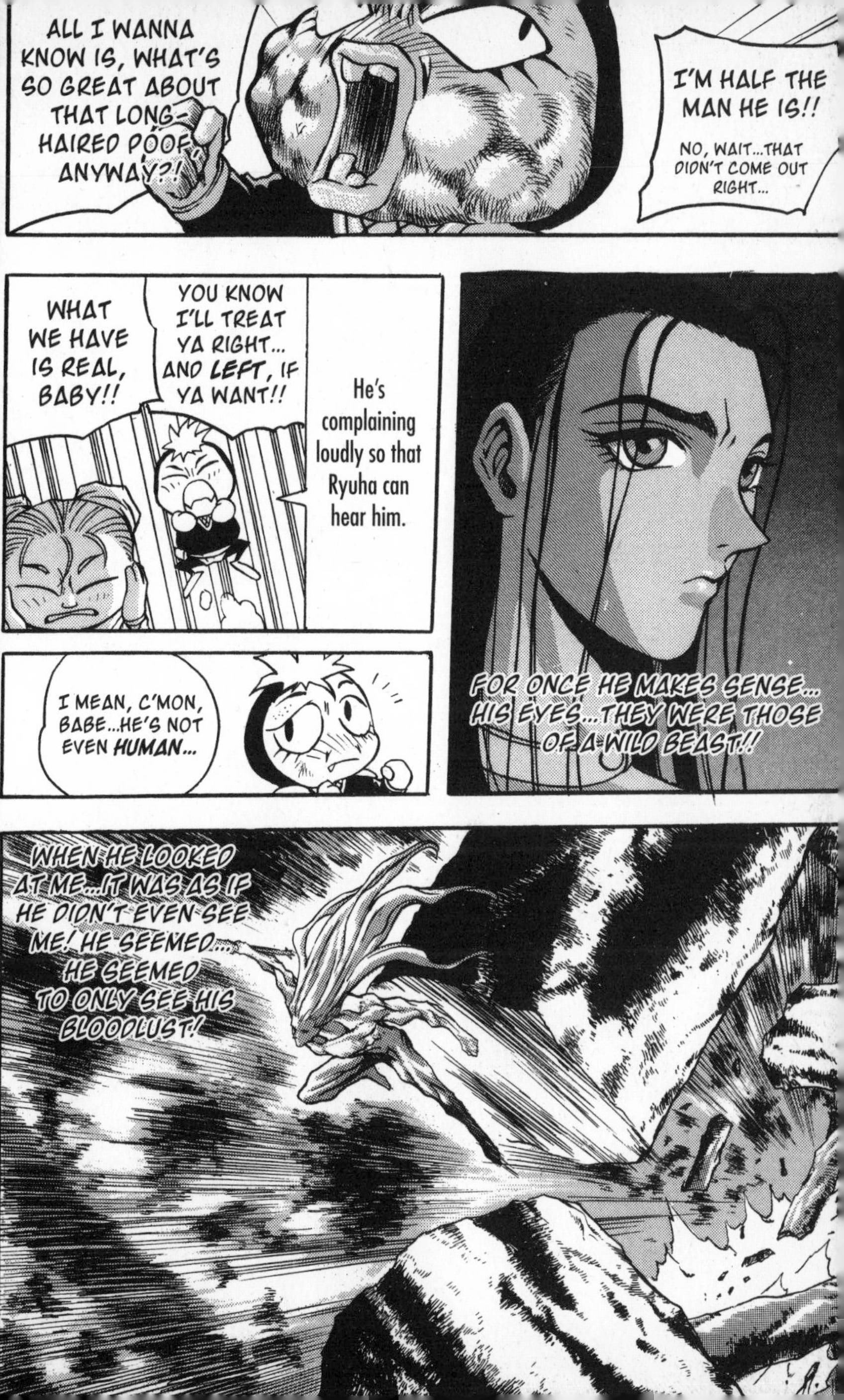
ALL I WANNA KNOW IS, WHAT'S SO GREAT ABOUT THAT LONG-HAIRED POOF, ANYWAY?!
I'M HALF THE MAN HE IS!!
NO, WAIT...THAT DIDN'T COME OUT RIGHT...
WHAT WE HAVE IS REAL, BABY!!
YOU KNOW I'LL TREAT YA RIGHT... AND LEFT, IF YA WANT!!
He's complaining loudly so that Ryuha can hear him.
I MEAN, C'MON, BABE...HE'S NOT EVEN HUMAN...
FOR ONCE HE MAKES SENSE... HIS EYES...THEY WERE THOSE OF A WILD BEAST!!
WHEN HE LOOKED AT ME...IT WAS AS IF HE DIDN'T EVEN SEE ME! HE SEEMED... HE SEEMED TO ONLY SEE HIS BLOODLUST!

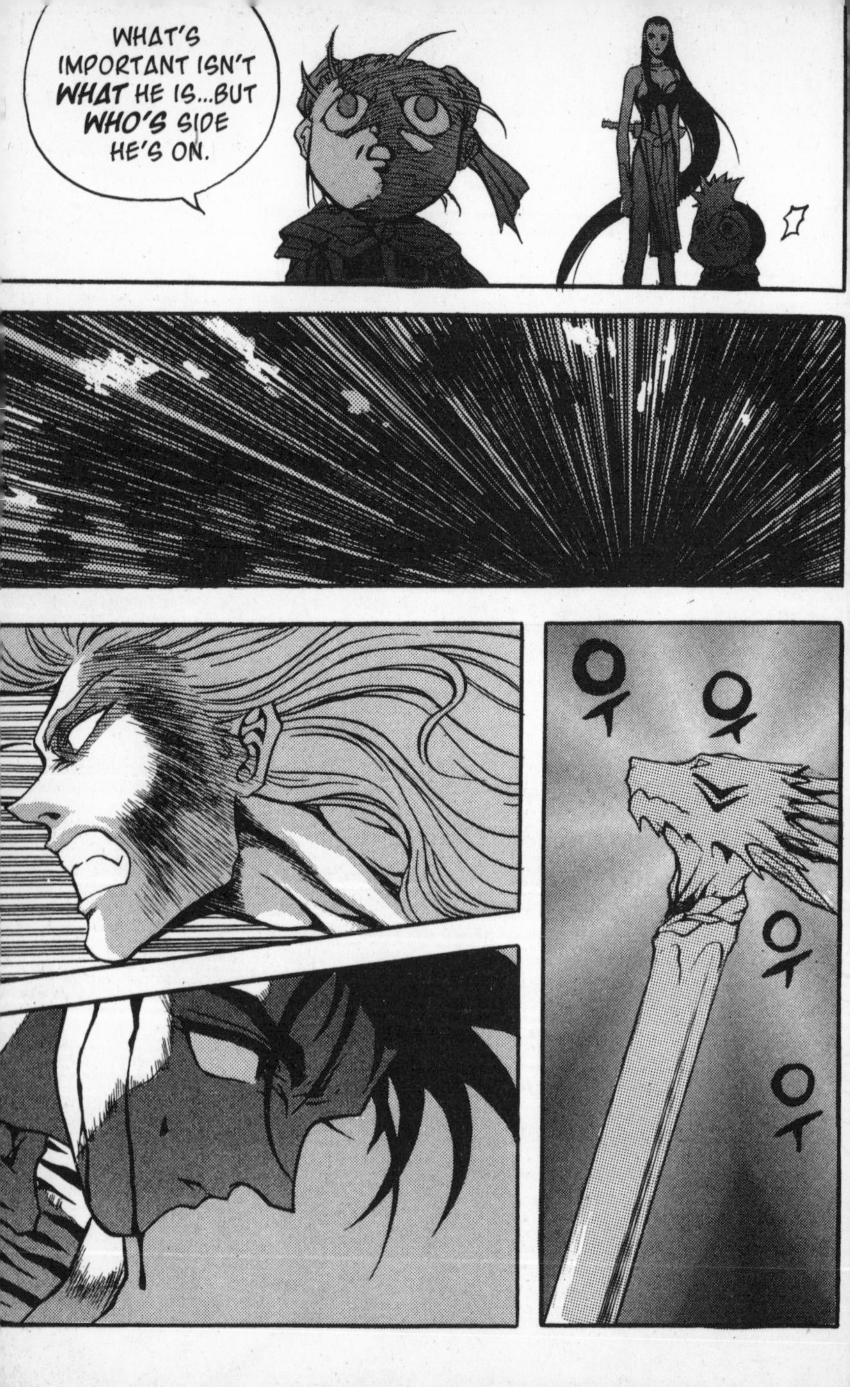
WHAT'S IMPORTANT ISN'T **WHAT** HE IS...BUT **WHO'S** SIDE HE'S ON.

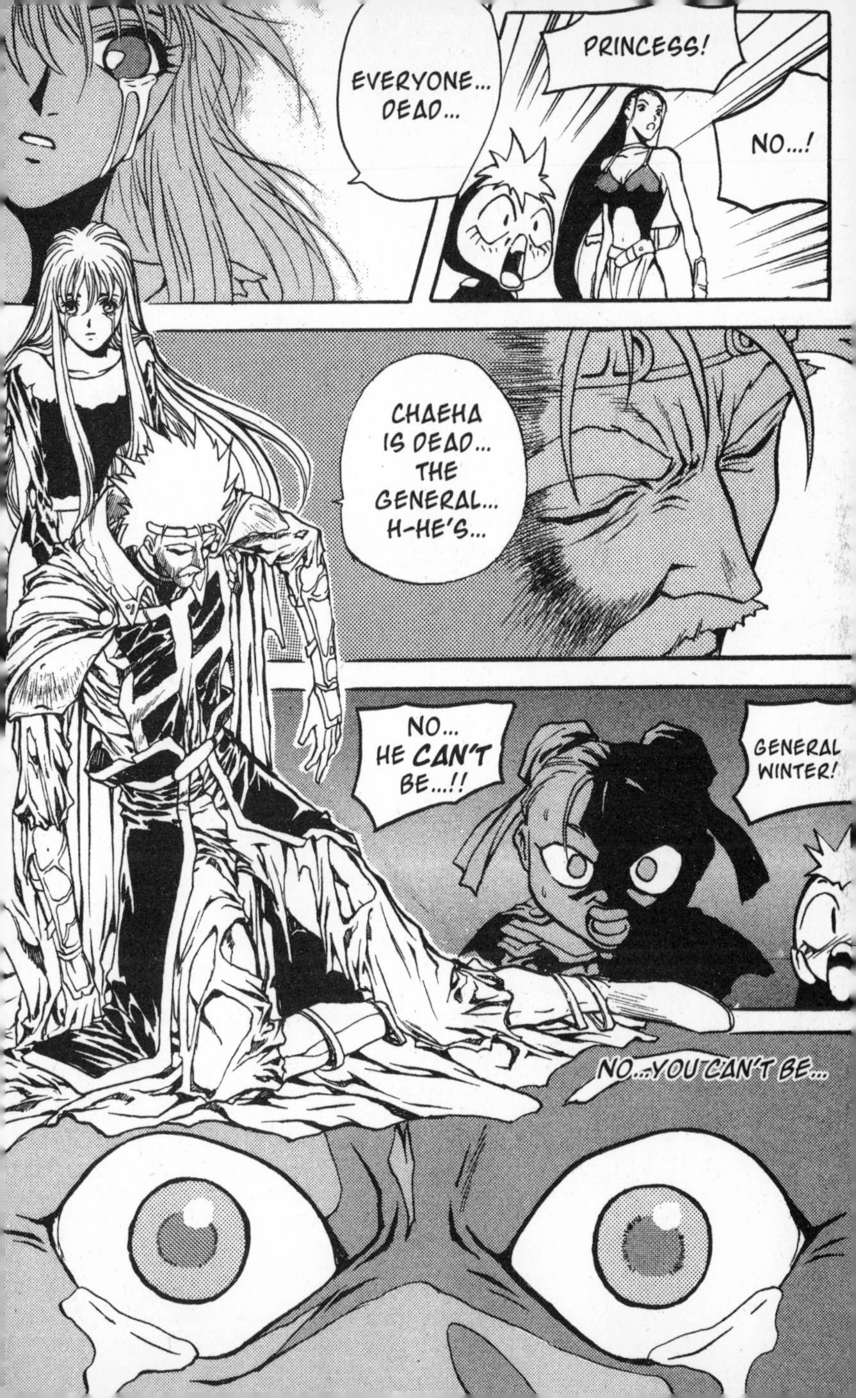
PRINCESS!
NO...!
EVERYONE... DEAD...
CHAEHA IS DEAD... THE GENERAL... H-HE'S...
GENERAL WINTER!
NO... HE **CAN'T** BE...!!
NO...YOU CAN'T BE...

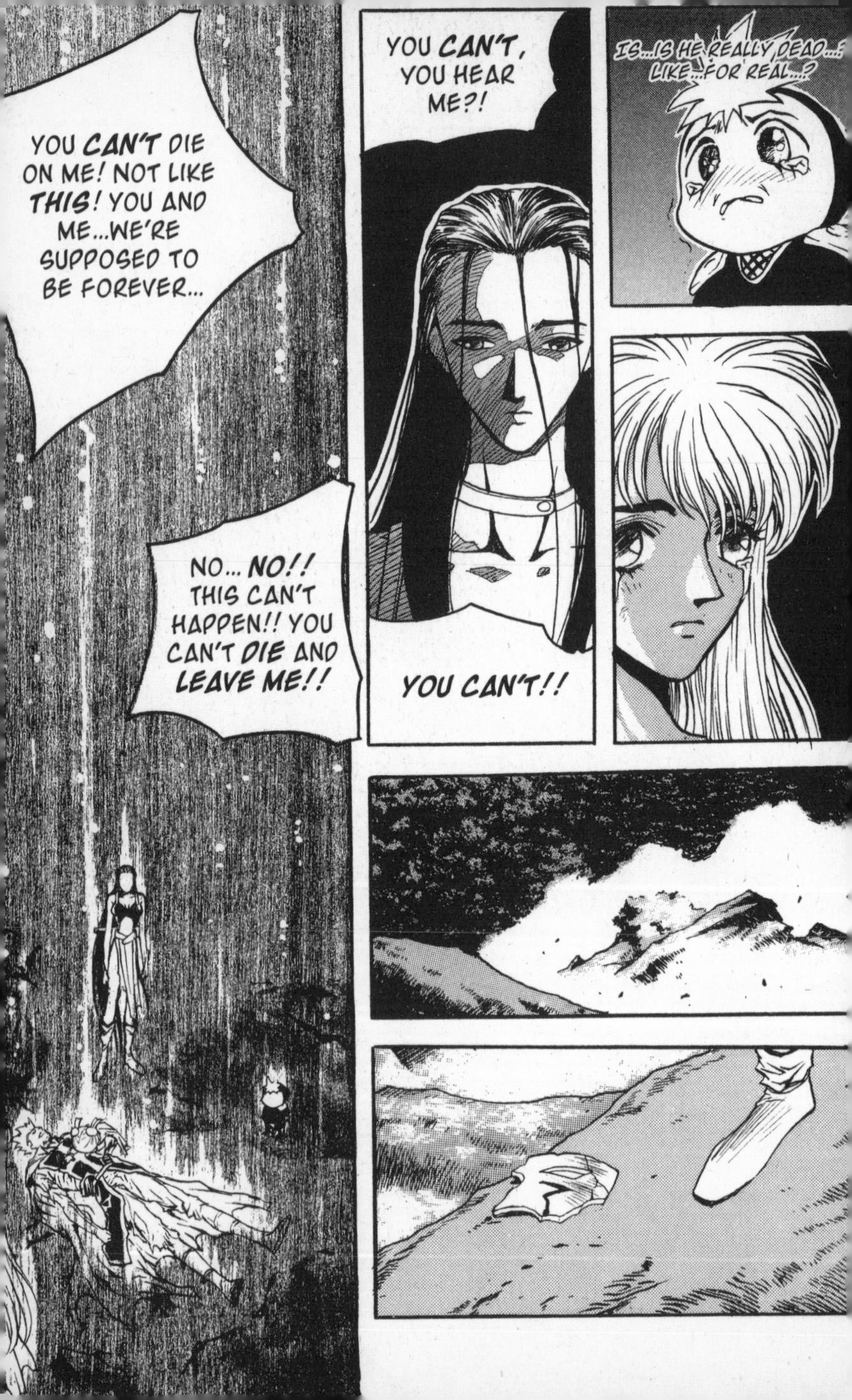
IS...IS HE REALLY DEAD...? LIKE...FOR REAL...?
YOU CAN'T, YOU HEAR ME?!
YOU CAN'T!!
YOU CAN'T DIE ON ME! NOT LIKE THIS! YOU AND ME...WE'RE SUPPOSED TO BE FOREVER...
NO... NO!! THIS CAN'T HAPPEN!! YOU CAN'T DIE AND LEAVE ME!!

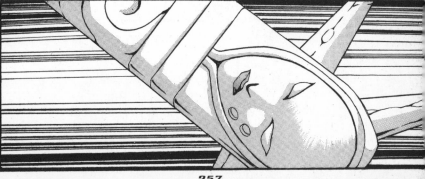

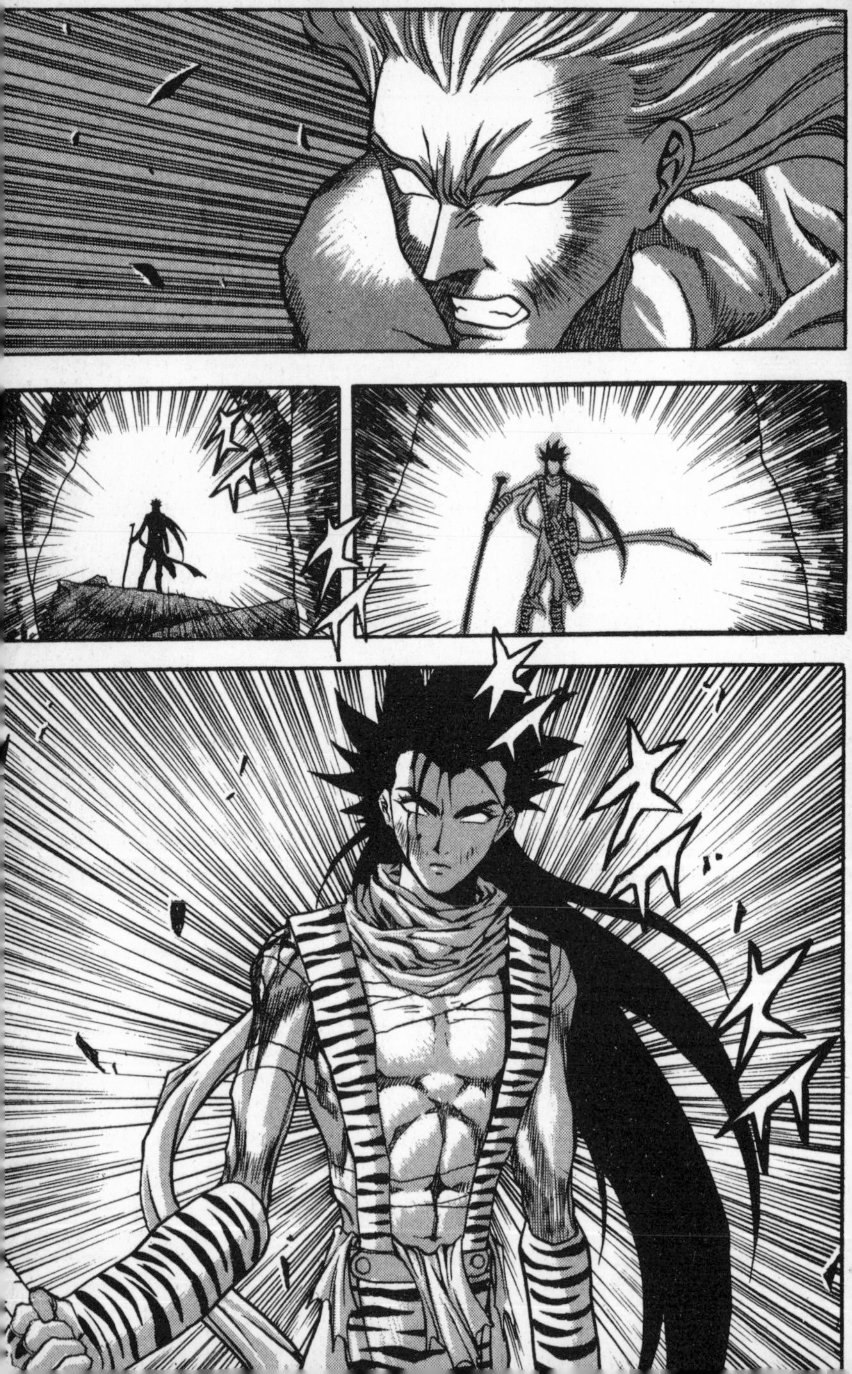

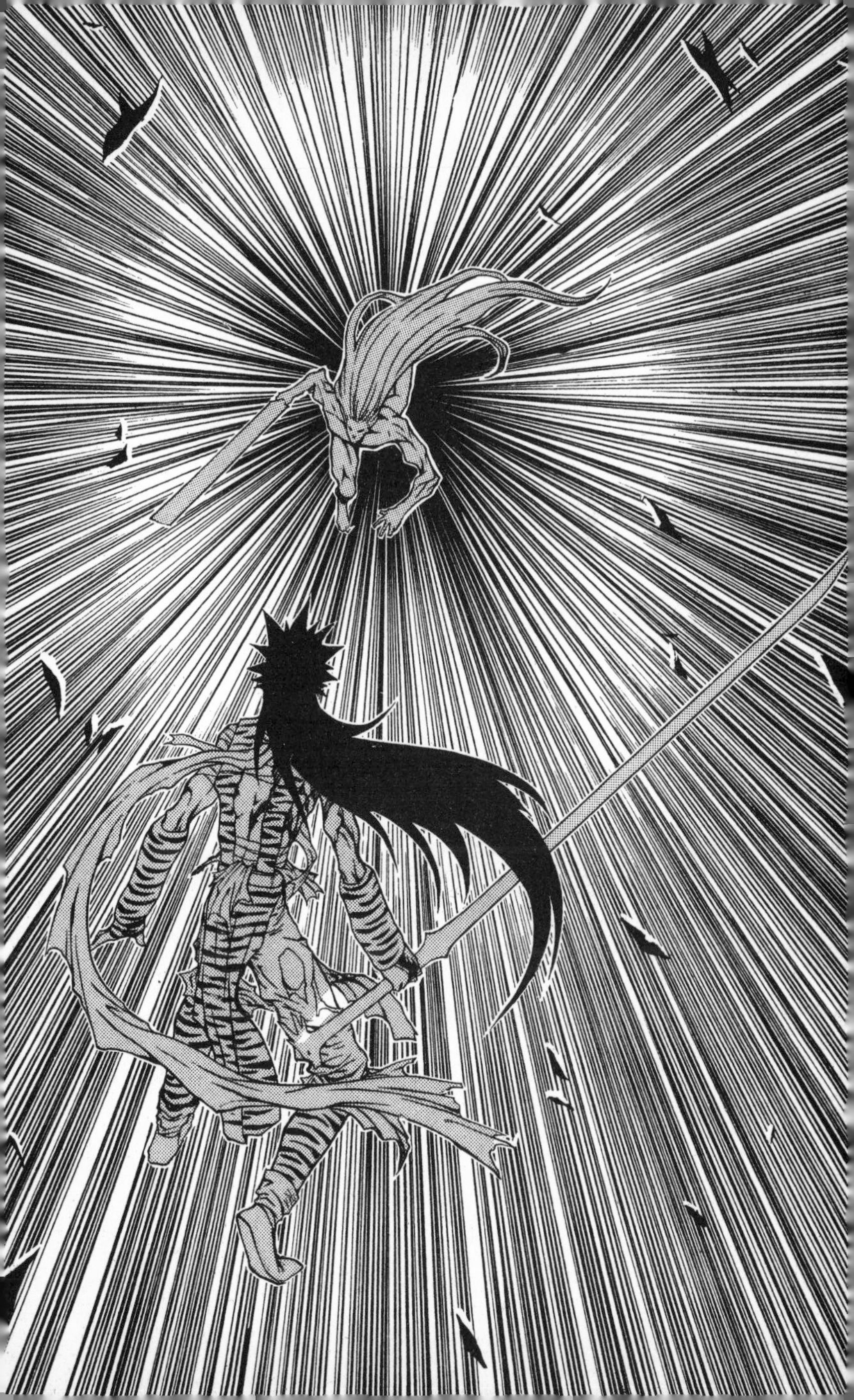

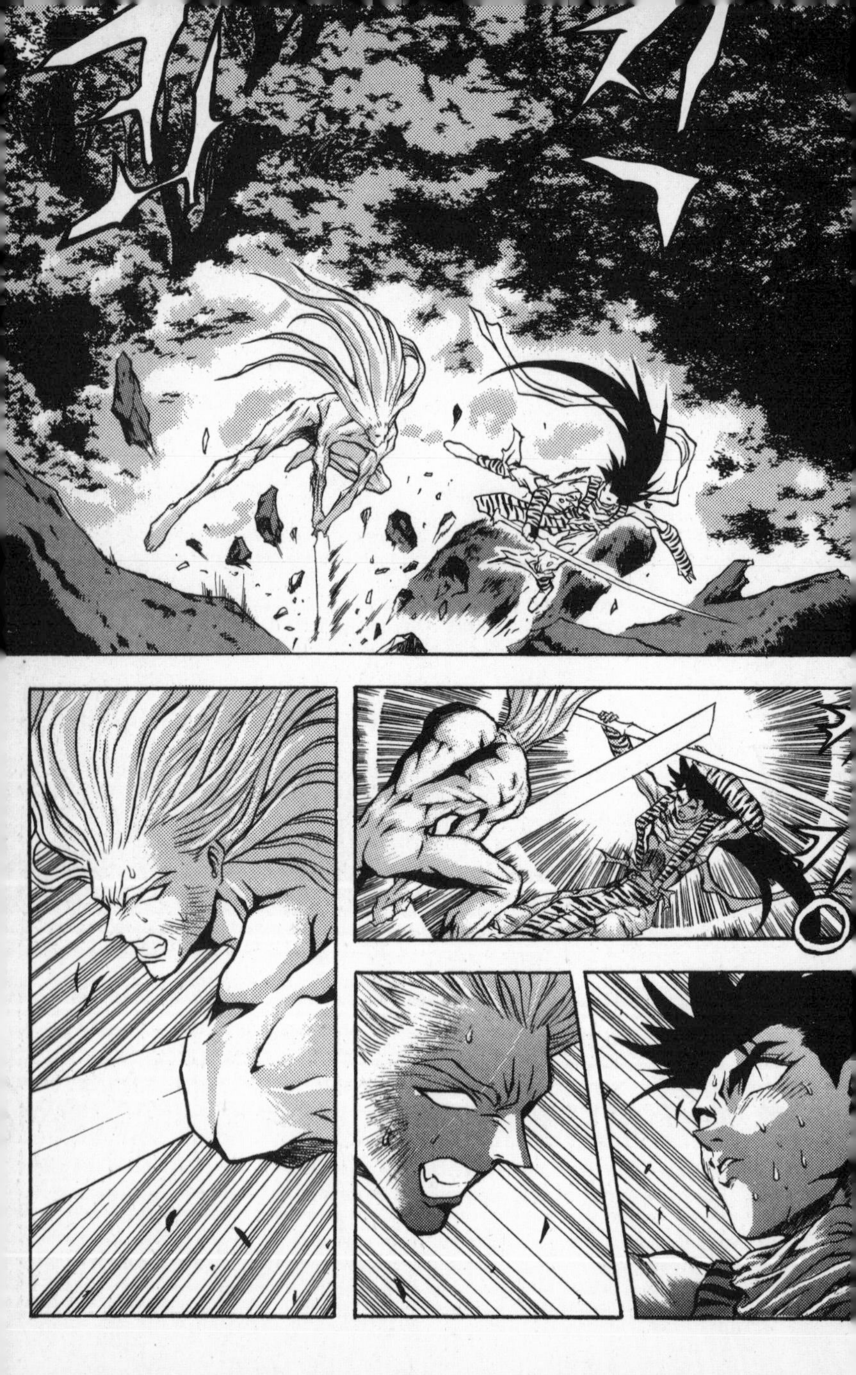

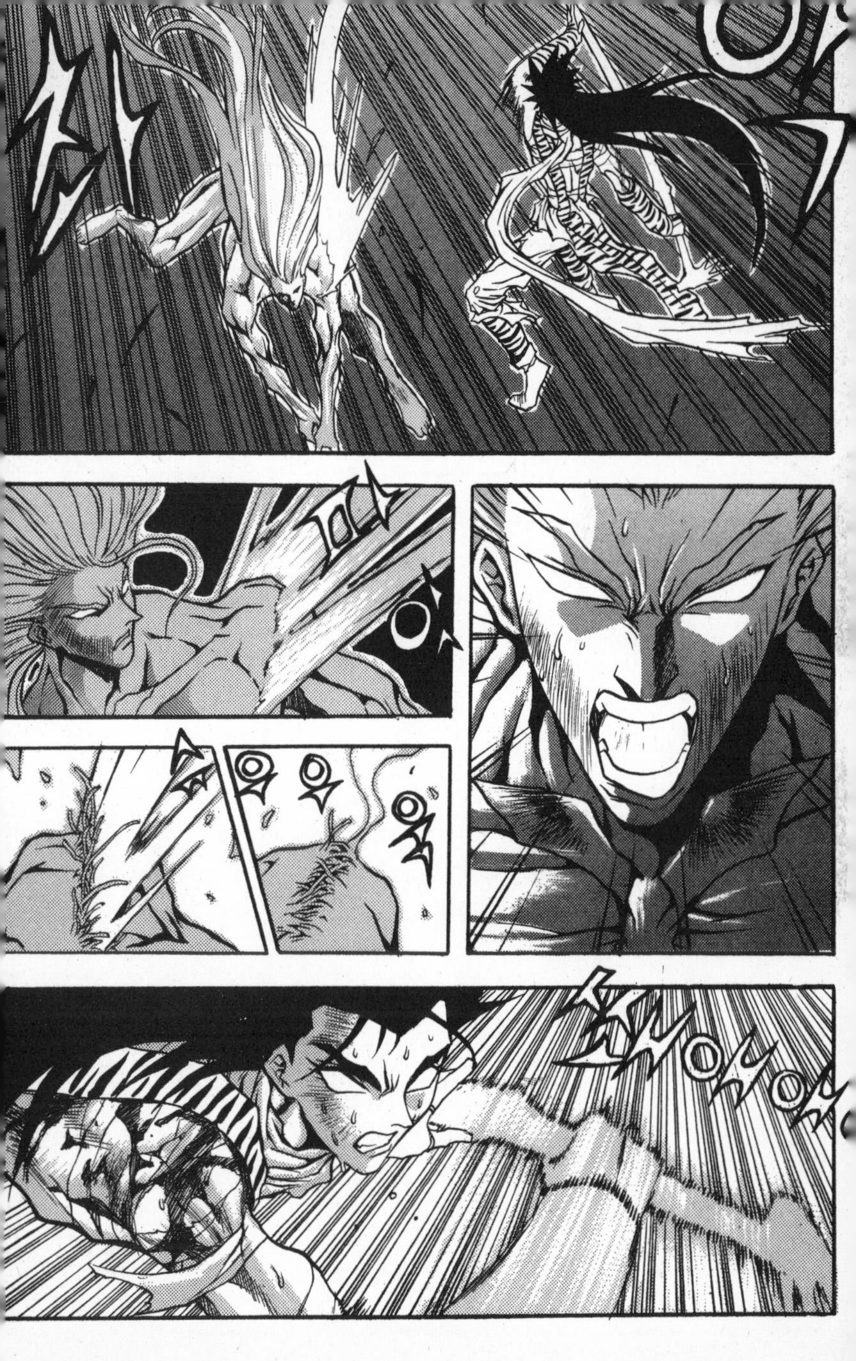

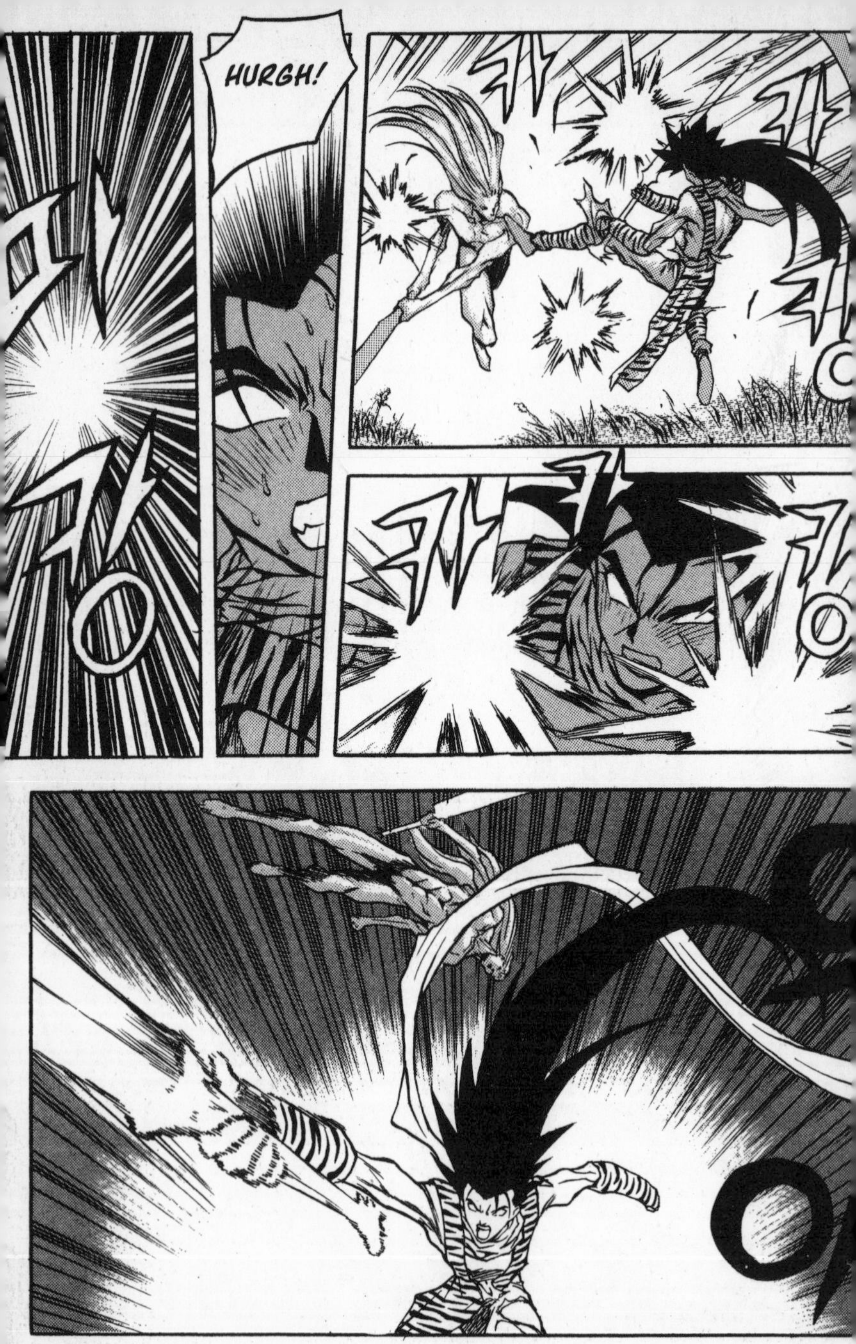
HURGH!

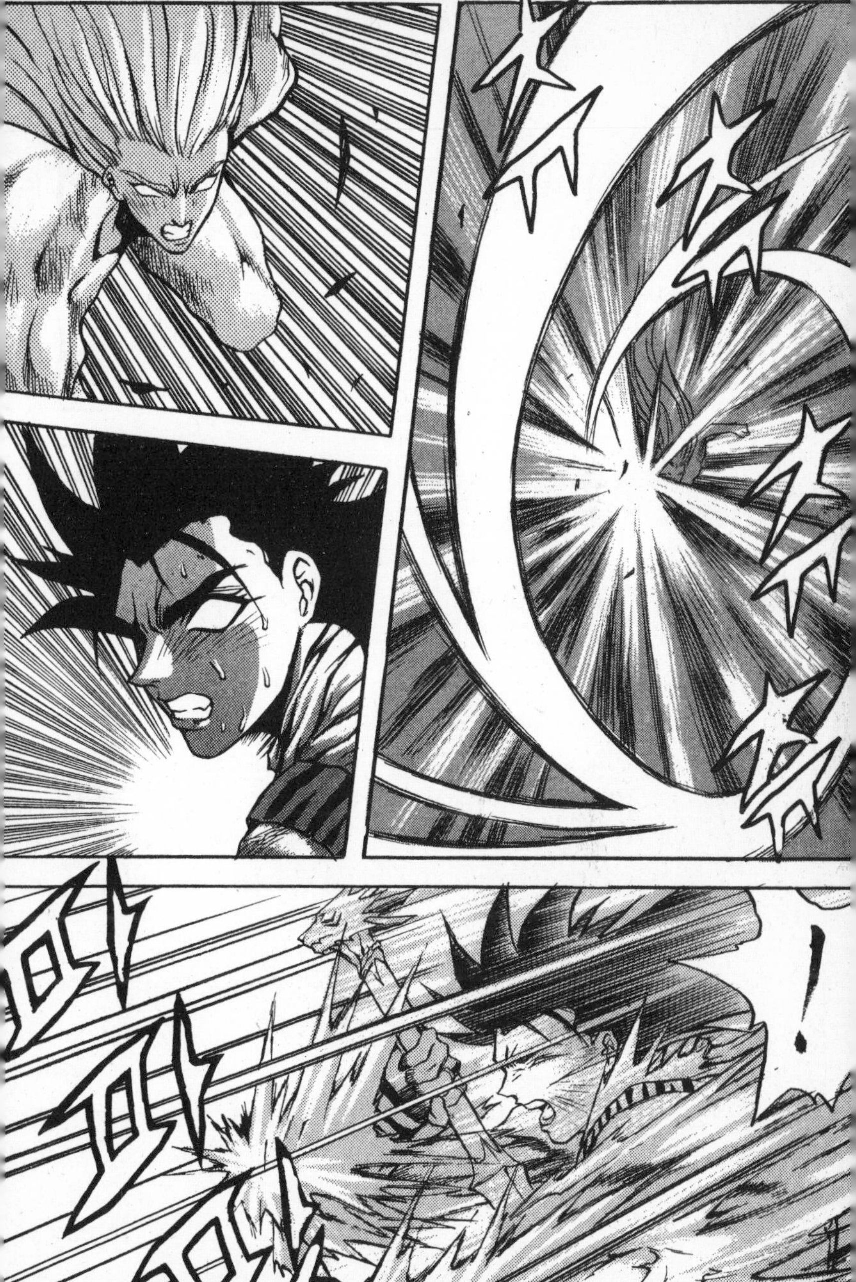
!

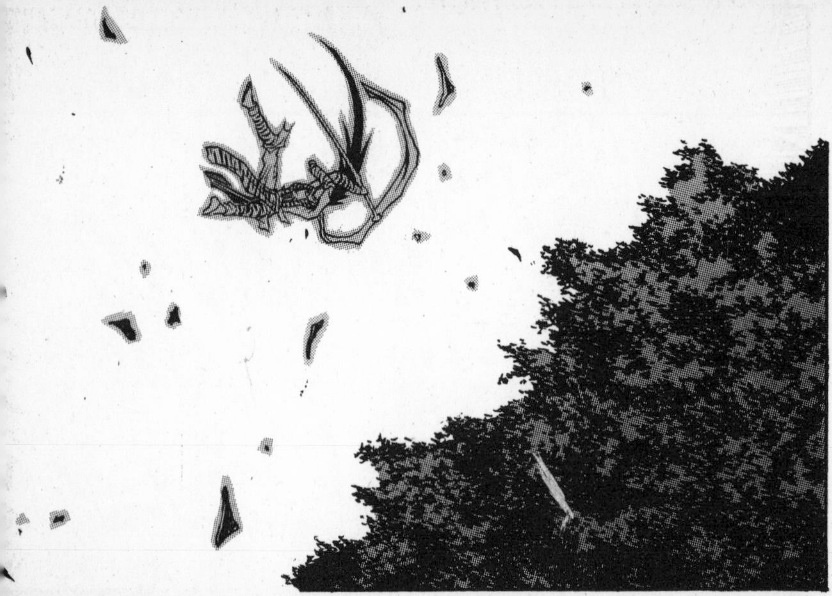
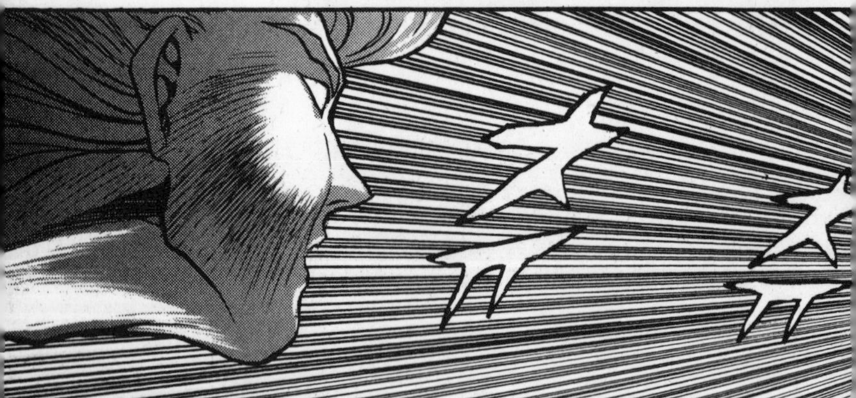
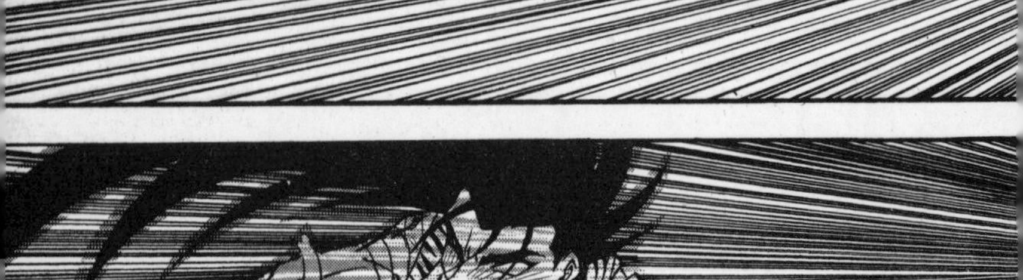

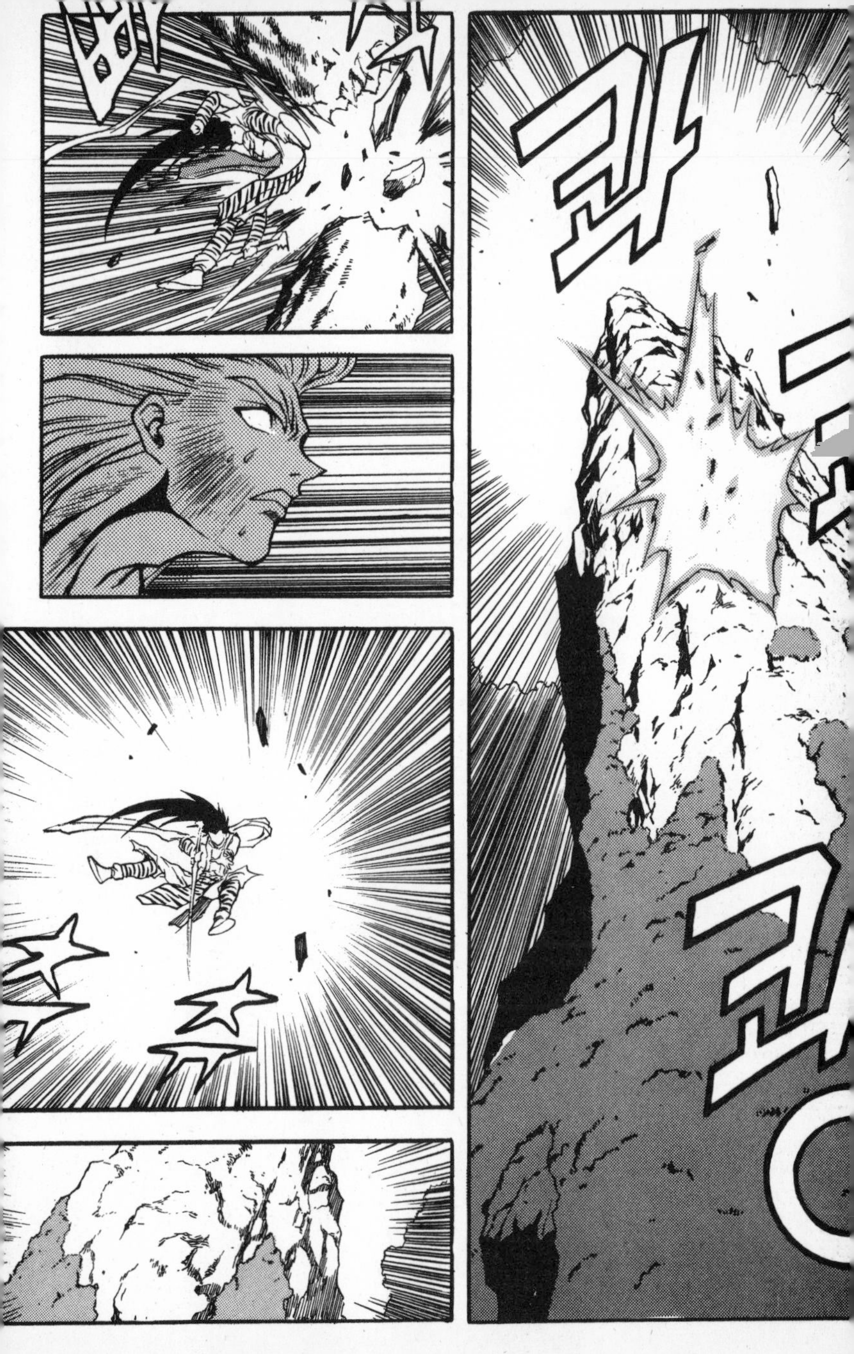

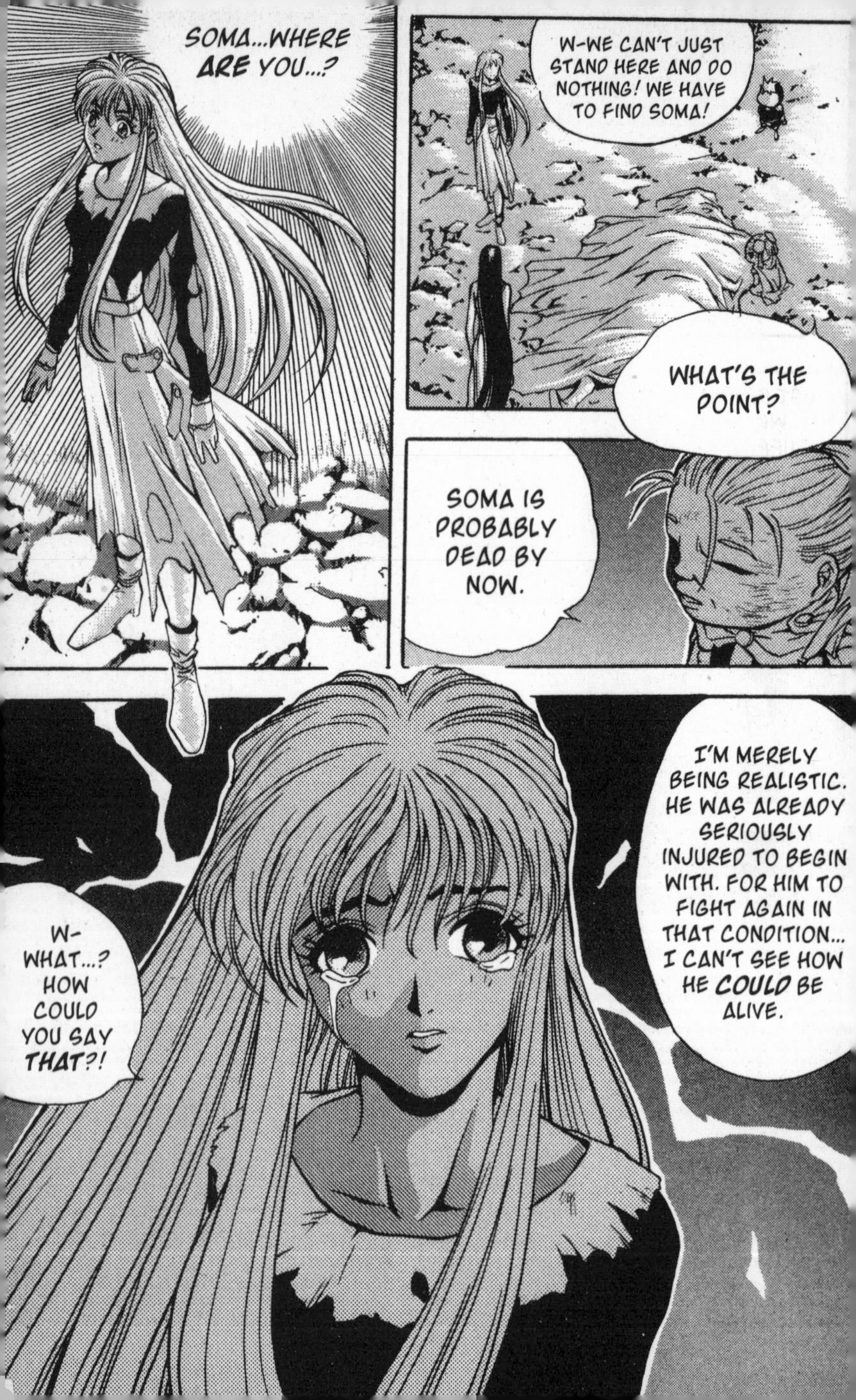
SOMA...WHERE ARE YOU...?
W-WE CAN'T JUST STAND HERE AND DO NOTHING! WE HAVE TO FIND SOMA!
WHAT'S THE POINT?
SOMA IS PROBABLY DEAD BY NOW.
W-WHAT...? HOW COULD YOU SAY THAT?!
I'M MERELY BEING REALISTIC. HE WAS ALREADY SERIOUSLY INJURED TO BEGIN WITH. FOR HIM TO FIGHT AGAIN IN THAT CONDITION... I CAN'T SEE HOW HE COULD BE ALIVE.

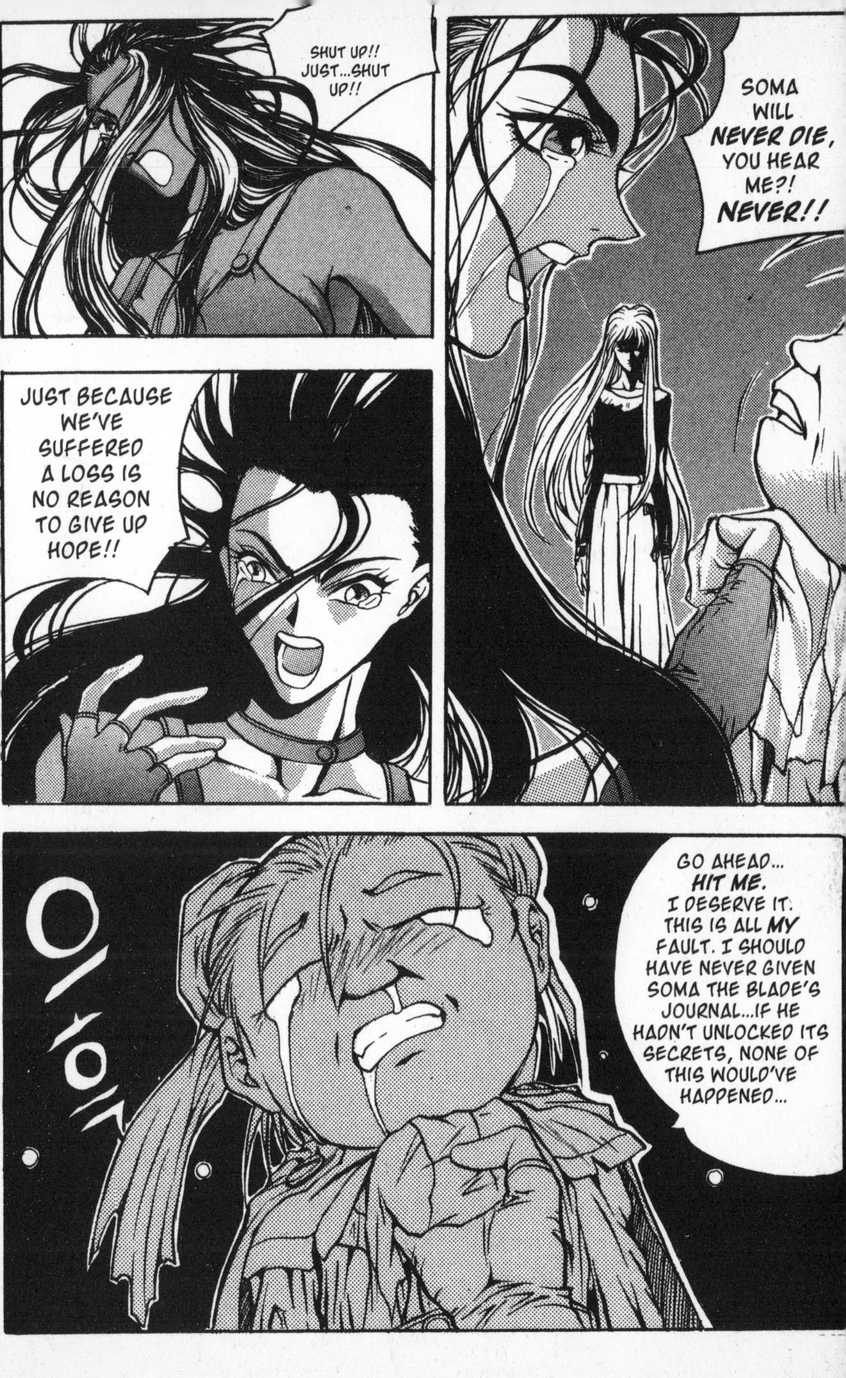
SOMA WILL NEVER DIE, YOU HEAR ME?! NEVER!!
SHUT UP!! JUST...SHUT UP!!
JUST BECAUSE WE'VE SUFFERED A LOSS IS NO REASON TO GIVE UP HOPE!!
GO AHEAD... HIT ME. I DESERVE IT. THIS IS ALL MY FAULT. I SHOULD HAVE NEVER GIVEN SOMA THE BLADE'S JOURNAL...IF HE HADN'T UNLOCKED ITS SECRETS, NONE OF THIS WOULD'VE HAPPENED...
OIOI

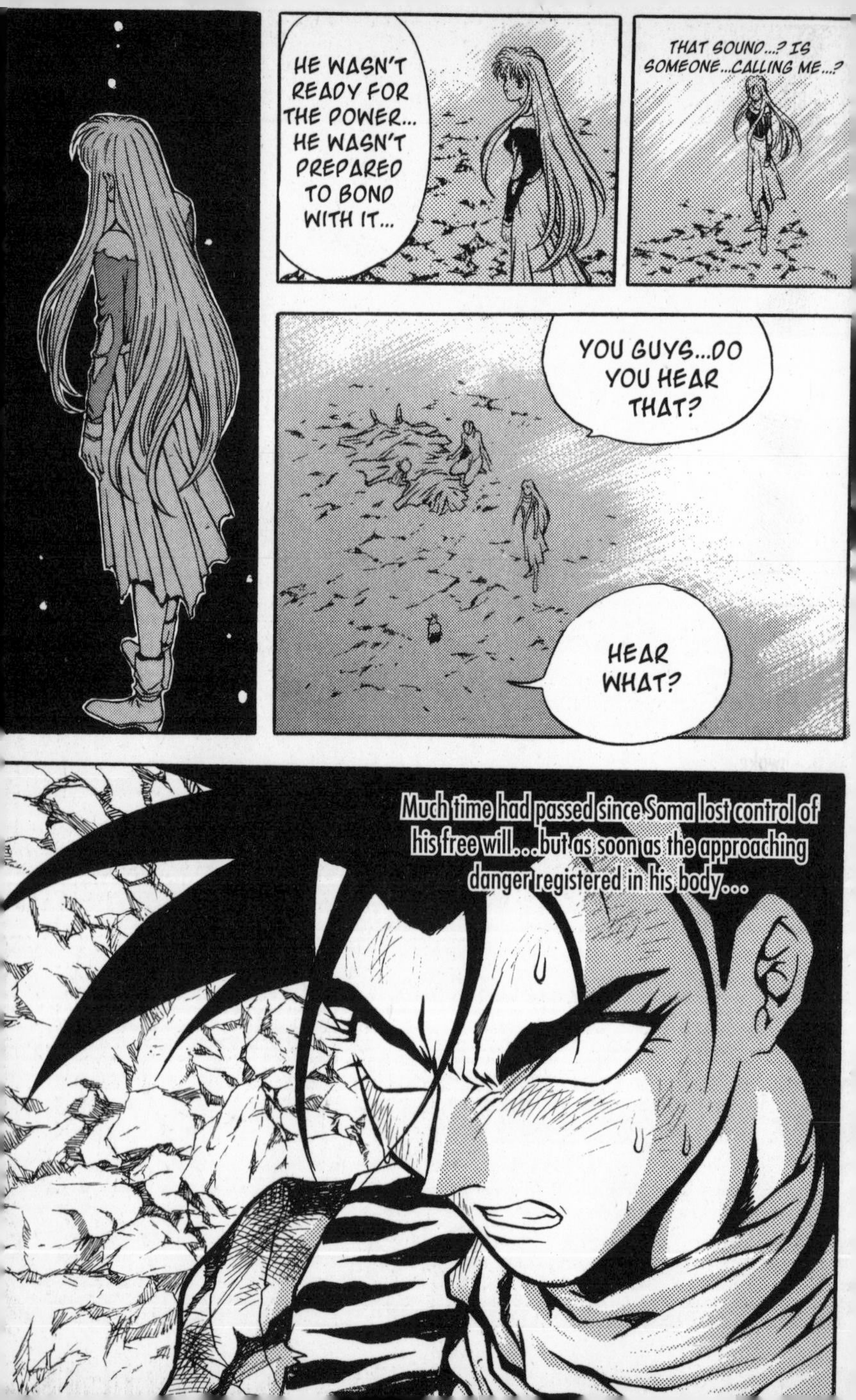
HE WASN'T READY FOR THE POWER... HE WASN'T PREPARED TO BOND WITH IT...
THAT SOUND...? IS SOMEONE...CALLING ME...?
YOU GUYS...DO YOU HEAR THAT?
HEAR WHAT?
Much time had passed since Soma lost control of his free will...but as soon as the approaching danger registered in his body...

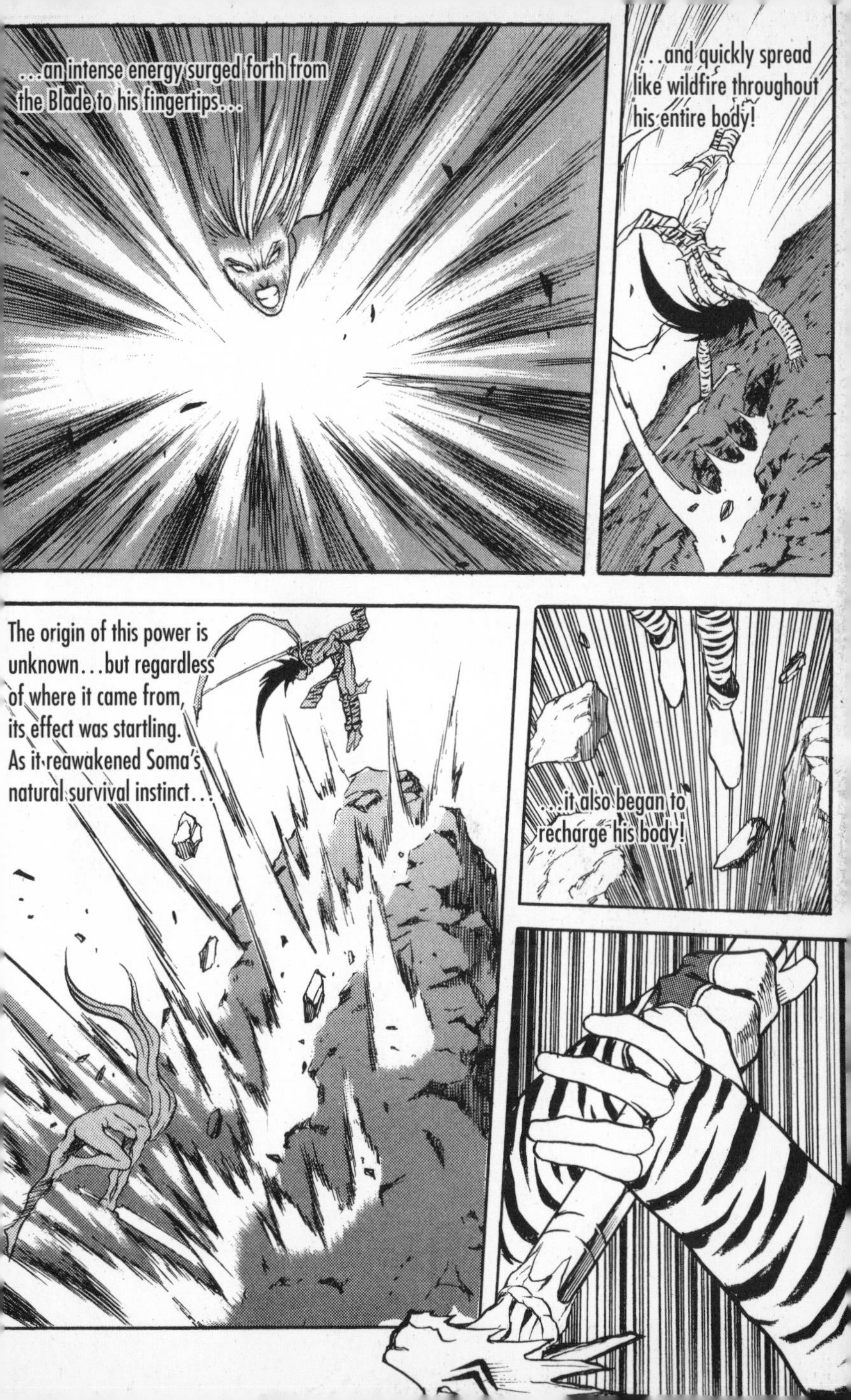
...an intense energy surged forth from the Blade to his fingertips...
...and quickly spread like wildfire throughout his entire body!
The origin of this power is unknown...but regardless of where it came from, its effect was startling. As it reawakened Soma's natural survival instinct...
...it also began to recharge his body!

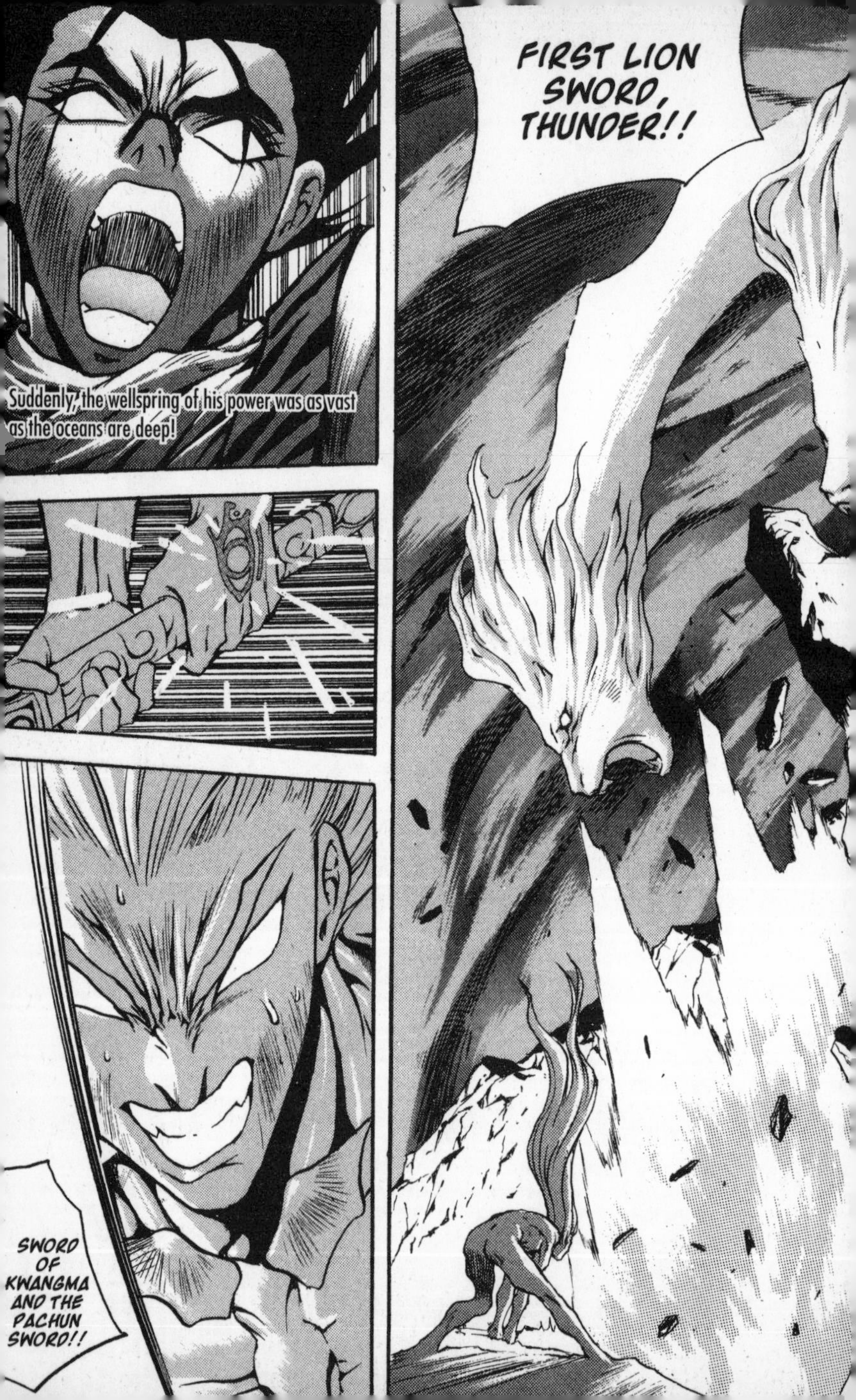
Suddenly, the wellspring of his power was as vast as the oceans are deep!
SWORD OF KWANGMA AND THE PACHUN SWORD!!
FIRST LION SWORD, THUNDER!!

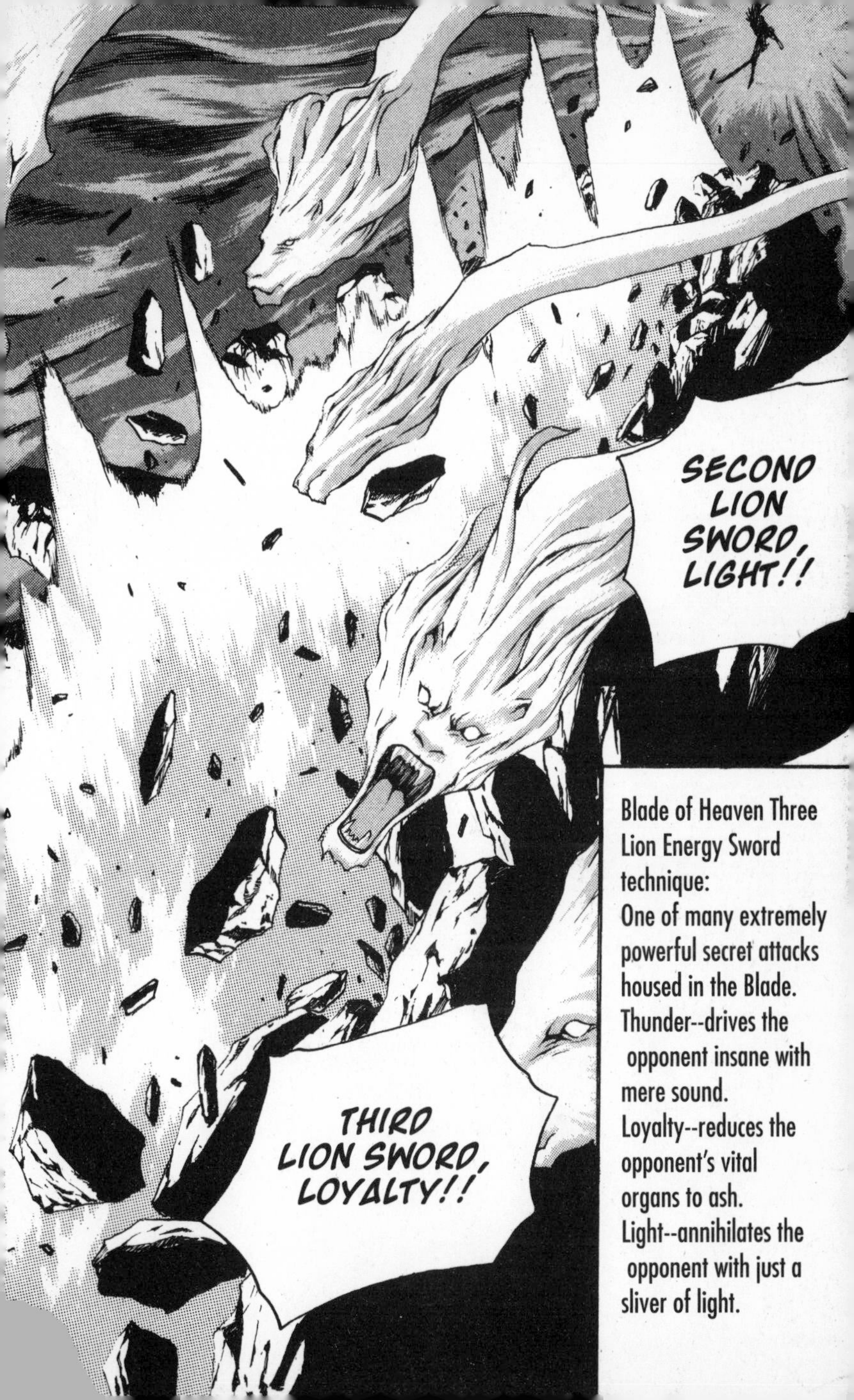
SECOND LION SWORD, LIGHT!!
Blade of Heaven Three Lion Energy Sword technique: One of many extremely powerful secret attacks housed in the Blade. Thunder--drives the opponent insane with mere sound. Loyalty--reduces the opponent's vital organs to ash. Light--annihilates the opponent with just a sliver of light.
THIRD LION SWORD, LOYALTY!!

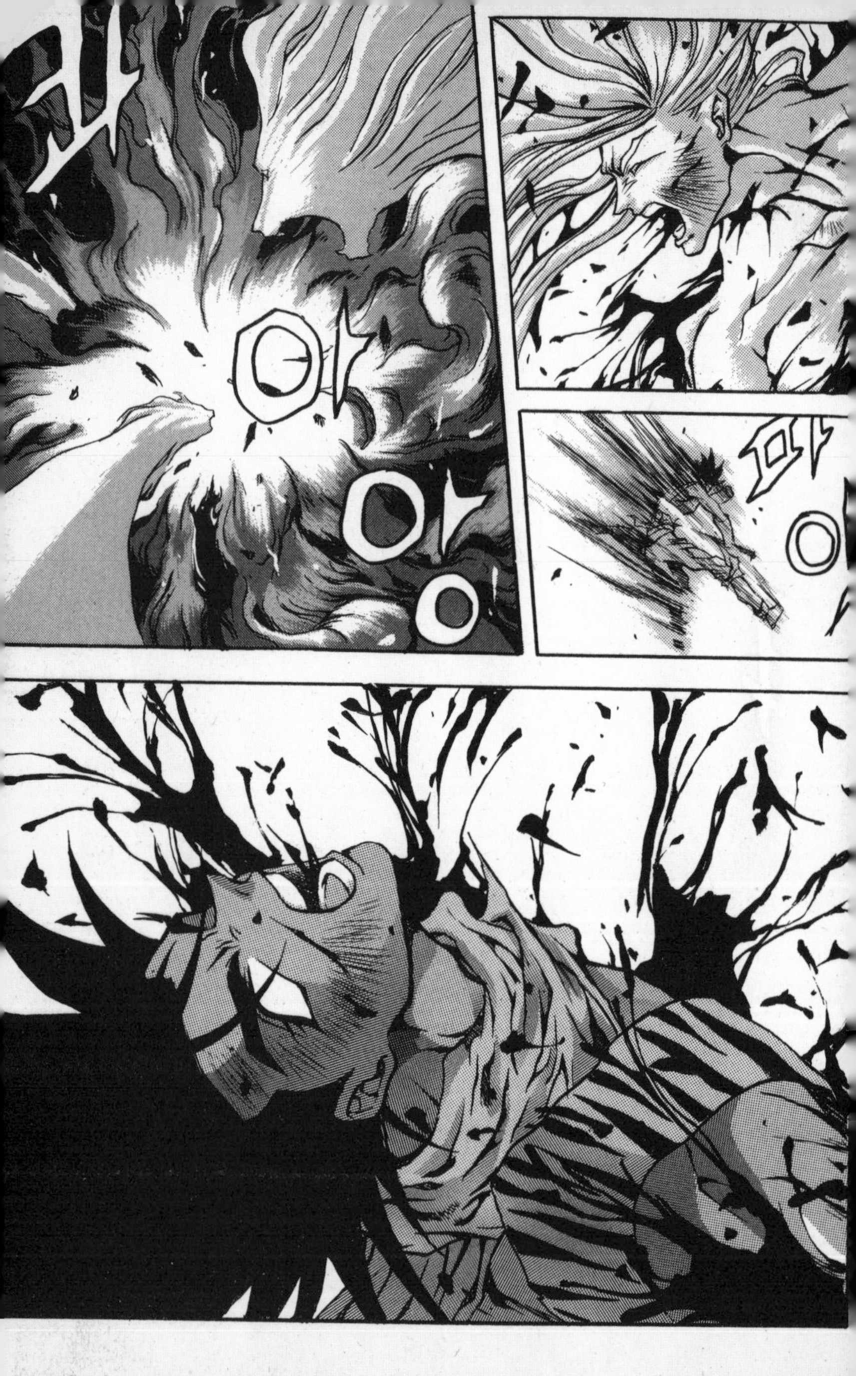
아아

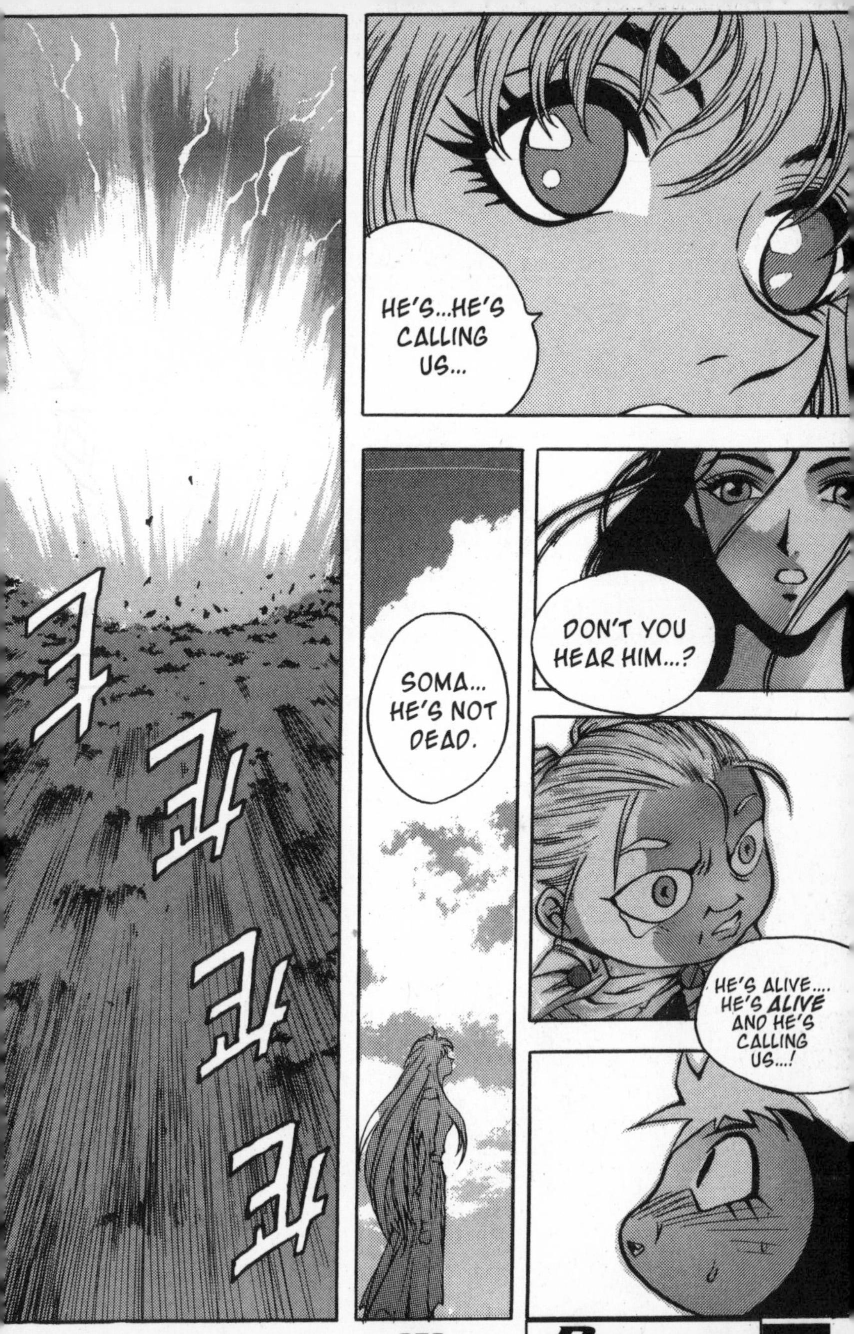
HE'S...HE'S CALLING US...
DON'T YOU HEAR HIM...?
HE'S ALIVE.... HE'S *ALIVE* AND HE'S CALLING US...!
SOMA... HE'S NOT DEAD.

END

IN THE NEXT BONE-CRUNCHING VOLUME OF

BLADE OF HEAVEN

IN THE AFTERMATH OF THE BATTLE, SOMA WAKES FROM HIS COMATOSE STATE, ONLY TO BE SHAKEN TO HIS CORE BY THE TERRIBLE LOSS OF LIFE AND UNBELIEVABLE DESTRUCTION THAT HAS OCCURRED SINCE HIS POSSESSION BY THE BLADE OF HEAVEN. SOMA'S GUILT PUSHES HIM INTO A NEARLY CATATONIC STATE, WHERE THE BLADE ONCE AGAIN GAINS CONTROL OVER HIM. INFLUENCED BY THE BLADE, THE GROUP NOW BEGINS SEARCHING FOR ITS SISTER PIECES. MEANWHILE, GRANNY STAYS BEHIND AND MAKES A SHOCKING DISCOVERY REGARDING THE LATE, GREAT GEN. WINTER...

GET READY TO RUMBLE IN

BLADE OF HEAVEN VOLUME 4!

BIZENGHAST

Dear Diary, I'm starting to feel

that I'm not like other people...

SPOTLIGHT TOKYOPOP MANGA SUPPLEMENT

SAKURA TAISEN

BY OHJI HIROI & IKKU MASA

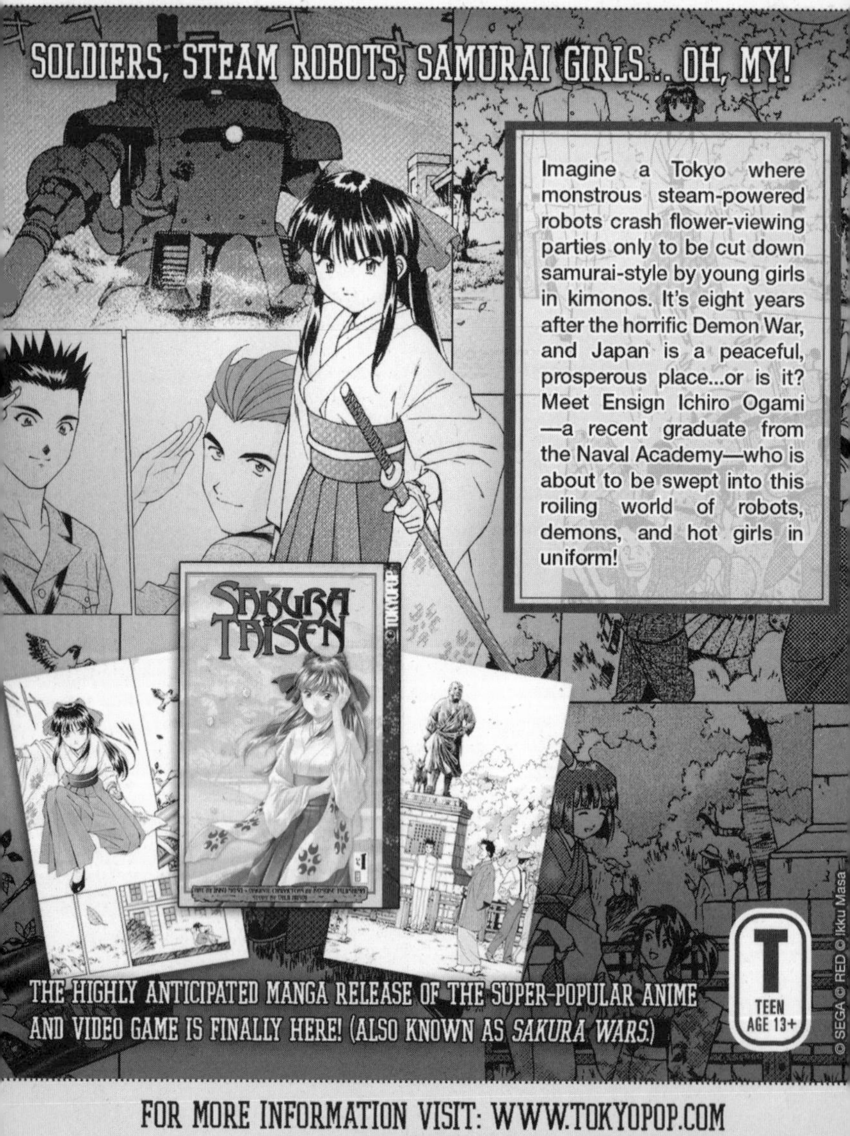
SOLDIERS, STEAM ROBOTS, SAMURAI GIRLS... OH, MY!
Imagine a Tokyo where monstrous steam-powered robots crash flower-viewing parties only to be cut down samurai-style by young girls in kimonos. It's eight years after the horrific Demon War, and Japan is a peaceful, prosperous place...or is it? Meet Ensign Ichiro Ogami—a recent graduate from the Naval Academy—who is about to be swept into this roiling world of robots, demons, and hot girls in uniform!
SAKURA TAISEN
TOKYOPOP
THE HIGHLY ANTICIPATED MANGA RELEASE OF THE SUPER-POPULAR ANIME AND VIDEO GAME IS FINALLY HERE! (ALSO KNOWN AS *SAKURA WARS*.)
T
TEEN
AGE 13+

FOR MORE INFORMATION VISIT: WWW.TOKYOPOP.COM